Major Problems in
American History
Volume II

KATHLEEN L. RILEY

MAJOR PROBLEMS IN AMERICAN HISTORY SERIES

GENERAL EDITOR

THOMAS G. PATERSON

Major Problems in American History

Volume II

Since 1865

DOCUMENTS AND ESSAYS

EDITED BY

ELIZABETH COBBS HOFFMAN

SAN DIEGO STATE UNIVERSITY

JON GJERDE

UNIVERSITY OF CALIFORNIA, BERKELEY

HOUGHTON MIFFLIN COMPANY
Boston   New York

Editor in Chief: Jean L. Woy
Sponsoring Editor: Colleen Shanley Kyle/Mary Dougherty
Senior Development Editor: Frances Gay
Senior Project Editor: Christina M. Horn
Associate Production/Design Coordinator: Christine Gervais
Manufacturing Manager: Florence Cadran
Senior Marketing Manager: Sandra McGuire

Cover image: *Lower East Side,* by Kindred McCleary. Smithsonian American Art
    Museum/Art Resource, NY.

Printed in the U.S.A.

Library of Congress Control Number: 2001131500

ISBN: 0-618-06134-7

123456789-CRS-05 04 03 02 01

For
Victoria and Gregory Shelby
and
Christine and Kari Gjerde

Contents

C H A P T E R   1 0
The Cold War and the Nuclear Age
Page 278

CHAPTER 15
Ronald Reagan and the Conservative Resurgence
Page 437

Preface

History is a matter of interpretation. Individual scholars rescue particular stories from the welter of human experience, organize them into a pattern, and offer arguments to suggest how these phenomena reflected or reshaped human society at a given moment. This means that yet other historians might select different stories, organize them into a pattern, and arrive at a contrasting interpretation of the same period of time or even the same event. All scholars use evidence, but the choice and interpretation of evidence is to some extent inevitably an expression of personal judgment. History is not separate from historians.

The goal of *Major Problems in American History* is to place meat on this bare-bones description of how the study of the past "works." Like most instructors, we want students to learn and remember the "important" facts, yet at the same time we want to make clear that historians often disagree on what is important. And, even when historians do agree on what is worthy of commentary, they often disagree on what a certain piece of evidence signifies. For example, scholars know that the Declaration of Independence was written in 1776 but may well debate why the colonists felt compelled to take this dramatic step.

The two volumes that make up this book bring together primary documents and secondary sources on the major debates in American history. The primary sources give students evidence to work with. They represent a mix of the familiar and unfamiliar. Certain pieces are a "must" in any compilation for a survey course because they had a powerful, widely noted impact on American history, such as Tom Paine's *Common Sense,* Lincoln's Second Inaugural, *Brown v. Board of Education,* or the manifesto of the National Organization for Women. We have also selected pieces that evoke the mood of the period and the personal experiences of individuals who reflected their times but may not have changed them. Included are statements by pioneer women on the frontier, immigrant workers, African American soldiers and educators, eyewitnesses to the terrors of World War II, children in rebellion against their parents during the 1960s, and so on. These documents often show conflicting points of view, from the "bottom up," as well as the "top down." We hope that they will give both students and professors a wide variety of reference points for classroom discussion, as well as help students become familiar with some principal facts of the topic under discussion.

The secondary sources in these volumes fulfill a somewhat different goal, which is to expose students to the elemental historical debates for each broad period. We have chosen, therefore, to focus on classic debates, often combining very recent essays with more seasoned pieces by eminent historians who set the terms of discussion for an entire generation or more. Our purpose is to make the interpretive contrasts as clear as possible for students who are just learning to distinguish interpretation from fact and to discern argument within description. This book seeks to stimulate classroom debate by providing clearly delineated, alternative approaches to historical problems. In addition, the essays often make direct reference to one of the primary documents, demonstrating to students how historians integrate evidence in an interpretation. Sometimes historians refer to one another, pointing to the process of revisionism.

Volume II, prepared by Elizabeth Cobbs Hoffman, begins with Reconstruction and ends at the beginning of the twenty-first century. It focuses on some of the enduring themes of American history, including the impact of changing technologies on the lives of workers and families, and the periodic waves of reform that have defined the nation since its inception. The transformation of gender expectations and race relations are also highlighted throughout the volume. Our goal is to strike a balance between social and cultural history (as indicated by chapters about Progressivism, the 1950s baby boom, the civil rights movement, and the sixties) and politics (emphasized, for example, in chapters on World Wars I and II, the New Deal, and Vietnam). The book incorporates the voices of everyday folk as well as the elite. It seeks to give students a fair representation of the different categories scholars today use to organize the historical story, including gender, class, race, and ethnicity.

This book follows the same general format as other volumes in the *Major Problems in American History* series. Each chapter begins with a short introduction that orients the student to the topic. In these volumes for the U.S. history survey course, we have included a new section called "Questions to Think About" after the chapter introduction, to help students focus their reading of the subsequent material. Next come eight to ten primary documents, followed by two essays that highlight contrasting interpretations. Headnotes at the start of the document and essay sections help readers know what to look for and identify key themes and debates. Each chapter concludes with a "Further Reading" section. This selected bibliography is intentionally brief, to tempt readers into further research without overwhelming them. In addition, we have included at the beginning of these two volumes an "Introduction to Students" that gives suggestions on how to read primary and secondary sources and critically analyze their content, point of view, and inferences. The introduction encourages students to draw their own conclusions and use evidence to back up their reasoning.

Many friends and colleagues have contributed to these volumes. We especially wish to thank Robin Einhorn, David Henkin, James Kettner, and Mary Ryan of the University of California, Berkeley; William Cheek, Sarah Elkind, John Putman, Harry McDean, and Andrew Wiese of San Diego State University; Brian Balogh of the University of Virginia; Drew Cayton of Miami University of Ohio; Eric Hinderaker of the University of Utah; Phil Morgan of Johns Hopkins; Bruce Schulman of Boston University; James Stewart of Macalaster College; and Louis Warren of the University of California at Davis.

We received detailed and extremely helpful reviews from Elizabeth Ansnes, San Jose State University; Robert Buzzanco, University of Houston; Brian Greenberg, Monmouth University; Steven Hahn, Northwestern University; Marianne Holdzkum, Ohio State University; Eugene E. Leach, Trinity College, Hartford;

Daniel J. McIrney, Utah State University; Thomas C. Rust, Montana State University—Billings; and Karin Wulf, American University. We are very grateful to them. We also received valuable assistance from our graduate students, Chris Agee, Dee Bielenberg, Walter Gustafson, David Johnson, Leland Smith, and Wendy Warren. Thomas G. Paterson, the editor of the *Major Problems* series, provided support and timely advice. The editors at Houghton Mifflin, Colleen Shanley Kyle, Frances Gay, Christina Horn, and Jean Woy, helped to keep us on track as we struggled to complete the manuscript amidst the many competing priorities within academia. We are grateful for their kind encouragement and helpful recommendations.

The life of the mind is exceptionally fulfilling, but it is happiest when set within the life of the family. We wish to express our deep gratitude to our spouses, Ruth Gjerde and Daniel Hoffman, for their love and patience. We dedicate the book to our four children and the young people of their generation, for whom it is written. To paraphrase the poet Emily Dickinson, this is our letter to their world.

E. C. H.
J. G.

Introduction to Students: How to Read Primary and Secondary Sources

College study encompasses a number of subjects. Some disciplines, such as mathematics, are aimed at problems and proofs. Students learn methods to discover the path to a correct answer. History is different. Unlike math, it is focused much more on interpretation and imagination. Historians study and analyze sources to construct arguments about the past. They generally understand that there is no "right" answer, even if there are some arguments that are more convincing than others. They search less for a proof than an interpretation, less for absolute truth than for understanding. A historical imagination is useful in creating these interpretations. People in the past thought and acted differently than we do today. Their views of science, of religion, of the place of women and men—to cite only a few examples—were not the same as our views. When we as historians create an argument about the past, we must imagine a world unlike the one we now inhabit.

The "problems" in U.S. history on which this text focuses, then, are different from math "problems." They are a series of issues in the American past that might be addressed, discussed, and debated, but not necessarily solved. The text provides readers with two types of tools to grapple with these problems. The first is the *primary source,* which is a piece of evidence that has survived from the period we are analyzing. Primary sources come in a variety of forms, including pictures, artifacts, and written texts. And they may have survived in a number of ways. Archaeologists might uncover pieces of evidence when they undertake digs of lost civilizations; ethnologists might transcribe stories told by people; economists might take bits of evidence to create numerical measures of past behavior; and historians might scrutinize surviving written sources. This volume by and large presents written texts, varying from political tracts to private letters. Some of the texts, however, are transcriptions, that is, texts written by someone who noted what another person said.

As historians, we must be critical of primary sources for a number of reasons. First of all, we must consider whether a source is really from the historical period we are studying. You might have occasionally read stories in the newspaper about paintings that had been attributed to famous artists but were discovered to be frauds painted by an unknown copyist. When the fraud is discovered, the painting's value plummets. The same can be said for a primary source. If it is not valid, it is not as valuable. A letter alleged to have been written by George Washington clearly is not of much use for revealing his innermost thoughts if we discover the document was written in 1910. But we should also be aware of the opposite: not all pieces of evidence have survived to the present. We might ask if there is a bias in the likelihood of one point of view surviving and another being lost. Or we might ask if some points of view were not given as much voice in the era we are studying. The experiences of slaveholders, for example, might have been more commonly written and published than those of slaves. Because they were rarely given the opportunity to publish their thoughts, slaves—in addition to others such as Native Americans and women—have bequeathed us some sources that have survived as transcriptions. As essential as these sources are in reconstructing the past, as historians we must be critical of them as well. Did the people writing down the spoken words accurately set them to paper or did they inject their own thoughts?

Once we consider the validity of sources and understand that some sources were more likely to survive than others, another reason to critique the sources is that they are not "objective" portrayals of the past. By nature, they are points of view. Like anyone in a society, the writer of each primary source provides us with his or her viewpoint and thus gives us a window through which to view his or her world, complete with its biases. When we read about the American Revolution, for example, we will see many different perspectives on the events leading up to the Declaration of Independence by the American colonies. Those who opposed independence saw the events in a very different light from those who led the independence movement. We have often read about the advocates of independence who saw the British as threats to American freedom. Theirs is a story of realizing that the American colonies would be better off as an independent nation and bringing this vision to fruition. Americans for generations have viewed this as a truly heroic episode in U.S. history. But many contemporaries were not as sure that independence was the correct course of action. Many British American colonists opposed independence because they felt they were more secure if they remained in the British Empire. Countless members of Indian nations were suspicious of the intentions of the American "patriots" and remained loyal to the king. African American slaves were often leery of the aims of their patriot owners. The fact that people had different viewpoints allows us to grapple with the multiple perspectives of the past. In the end, there is no single story that encompasses the American past, but rather a series of competing narratives.

When you are reading the documents in this volume, then, you are urged to criticize each document. We are certain that these are valid sources, and so you should be especially critical of the point of view contained in each document. Consider both the document and its author. Who wrote or spoke the words in the document? What was his or her reason for expressing the thoughts? Given the background and motivations of the authors, what are their perspectives and potential biases? How do they see the world differently from the way others do? And why do you think these different perspectives exist? Whose viewpoint do you agree with most? Why? It is not too much to say that the student of history is similar to a detective who seeks out sources and clues that illuminate the lives and events of the past.

In addition to primary sources, each chapter in this volume contains two essays that represent what we call a *secondary source*. Secondary sources are the written work of historians who have conducted painstaking research in primary sources. Historians work with an array of primary sources that they uncover and use as evidence to construct an argument that addresses one of the major problems in American history. A secondary source is so named because it is one step removed from the primary source. As you will notice, the writers of the essays in each chapter do not necessarily reach similar conclusions. On the contrary, they illustrate differing opinions about why events occurred and what they mean for us today.

Hence secondary sources, like primary sources, do not provide us with the "truth," even to the extent that they are based on verifiable facts. Rather, historians' conclusions vary just as your ideas about the documents might differ from those of someone else in your class. And they differ for a number of reasons. First, interpretations are influenced by the sources on which they depend. Occasionally, a historian might uncover a cache of primary sources heretofore unknown to other scholars, and these new sources might shed new light on a topic. Here again historians are like detectives.

Second and more important, however, historians carry their own perspectives to the research. As they read secondary sources, analyze primary texts, and imagine the past, historians usually develop arguments that differ in emphasis from those developed by others. As they combine their analyses with their own perspectives, they create an argument to explain the past. Historians' individual points of view and even society's dominant point of view influence their thinking. If analyzing sources resembles working as a detective, writing history is similar to being a judge who attempts to construct the most consistent argument from the sources and information at hand. And historians can be sure that those who oppose their viewpoints will analyze their use of sources and the logic of their argument. Those who might disagree with them—and that might include you—will criticize them if they make errors of fact or logic.

The essays were selected for this text in part because they reflect differing conclusions with which you may or may not agree. For example, what caused the Civil War? For decades, historians have given us a number of answers. Some have said the war could have been prevented if politicians had been more careful to avoid sectional divisions or if the U.S. political system had been suitable for compromise. Others have observed that the divisions that developed between North and South over time became so acute that they could not be compromised away. A civil war in their view was well nigh inevitable. Or what are we to make of the "Age of Jackson"? Some historians have celebrated this period as a flowering of American democracy. The increased voting rights for men fostered raucous political parades that celebrated the American freedoms. Others have noted that these rights were given only to white men and that the "freedoms" were in name only. Or how do we make sense of the Vietnam War nearly forty years after the first American troops landed? Was it a terrible mistake that undermined confidence in the United States both at home and abroad, or was it, in President Reagan's words, a "noble cause"?

An important question left unanswered in all of these chapters is what do *you* think is the correct interpretation? In the end, maybe you don't agree completely with any of the essayists. In fact, you might wish to create your own argument that uses primary sources found here and elsewhere and that accepts parts of one essay and parts of another. When you do this, you have become a historian, a person who attempts to analyze texts critically, someone who is actively engaged in the topic. If that occurs, this volume is a success.

When we discuss the discipline of history with people, we typically get one of two responses. One group of people says something like "I hated history in school."

The other group says something like "history was my favorite subject when I went to school." Invariably the people who hated history cite all the boring facts that they had to memorize. In contrast, those who loved history remember a teacher or professor who brought the subject alive by invoking the worlds of people in the past. As we have tried to indicate in this short overview, history is not about memorizing boring facts but rather an active enterprise of thought and interpretation. Historians are not rote learners; studying history does not entail simply memorization. Instead, historians are detectives and judges, people who interpret and imagine what happened in history and why, individuals who study the past in order to understand the world in which they live in the present. Facts are important, but they are only building blocks in a larger enterprise of interpretation. In sum, our intent with this text is to show how primary and secondary sources can be utilized to aid you in understanding and interpreting major problems in the American past. It is also aimed at keeping that group of people who hates studying history as small as possible and enlarging that second group who considers history their passion. Frankly, it's more fun to talk to the latter.

Major Problems in
American History
Volume II

CHAPTER

1

Reconstruction, 1865–1877

Even before the Civil War was over, President Lincoln and congressional leaders began to puzzle over how best to reintegrate the people of the South into the Union. Before he was assassinated, President Lincoln proposed the "10 percent plan," which would have allowed a state government to reestablish itself once one-tenth of those who had voted in 1860 took an oath of loyalty to the United States. Radicals in Congress were appalled by the leniency of Lincoln's plan and pushed through their own bill, which increased to one-half the proportion of the voters who were required to swear that they had never supported secession. Lincoln's assassination cut short this increasingly vituperative debate, but it did not end the controversy over Reconstruction, a controversy that would engross the nation for nearly fifteen years. Significantly, political disagreements over Reconstruction policy were vast, and the strategies advocated were so varied that Reconstruction took a crooked path. As approaches to rebuilding the South shifted, the hopes among some of transforming southern society grew and then were dashed. Ultimately, despite important legal precedents that were set in the era, many of the social, political, and economic conventions that had characterized antebellum society endured after Reconstruction ended.

Although people differed on what was the best policy for Reconstruction, everyone agreed that the Confederate states were in dire straits. The war had devastated the South: entire cities lay in ruins; two-thirds of the southern railroads had been destroyed; and at least one-third of the South's livestock had disappeared. Likewise, the abolition of slavery unalterably transformed southern society at the same time that it gave hope to people freed from their bondage (known as freedmen). Following Lincoln's death, many believed that Andrew Johnson, who succeeded Lincoln as president, would advocate a severe form of Reconstruction. Instead, Johnson engineered a plan that seemed to many northerners to be much too charitable. Although he distrusted the southern elite, Johnson nonetheless pardoned many of the Confederate leaders, who in turn were instrumental in creating new state legislatures that did not seem sufficiently contrite to many northerners. When some reconstructed legislatures passed "black codes" in 1865, which among other things forced freedmen to carry passes and prohibited them from owning land, Johnson did not oppose them. In the years that followed, Johnson's behavior became increasingly partisan. He opposed the Fourteenth Amendment (which gave freed slaves citizenship and guaranteed them due process of law), and he campaigned against the Republican Party in the election of 1866. Ironically, Johnson's course of action, combined with

the intransigence of unrepentant southern leaders, was a major factor in bringing
about the era of Radical Reconstruction beginning in 1866. Because he was so im-
politic, Johnson strengthened the resolve of Congress to enact a more radical policy.

The Republican Party won such a resounding victory in the elections of 1866
that it did not need to fear vetoes from Johnson. When Congress reconvened in 1867,
it set a much harsher and more radical plan of Reconstruction. It passed the Reconstruction Act of 1867, which created military districts in the South, guaranteed male
freedmen the right to vote in state elections, and disfranchised Confederate leaders.
Congress later passed and sent to the states the Fifteenth Amendment, which gave
black men the right to vote. As a consequence of its conflict with Johnson, Congress
impeached him and nearly removed him from office. As much of a departure as
Radical Reconstruction was from Johnson's plan, however, it was not as radical as
many political leaders would have liked. Freedmen received political rights, but
Congress did not radically expand public education or confiscate the land owned by
Confederate sympathizers, as some of its members had advocated. As a result, freedmen were denied the economic independence that a grant of "forty acres and a
mule" would have provided.

If Reconstruction was engineered in Washington, new social conventions were
forged in the South that would be extremely important in the future. The lives of
former slaves were dramatically changed, and freedmen expressed their understanding of freedom in a variety of ways. Most immediately, they hoped to be independent
of the control of white people, which was the most obvious expression of freedom.
Yet freedom was observed in a variety of ways. Many attempted to reunite families
that had been rent asunder by sale; others celebrated by conducting religious services
independent of white control; and still others fostered schools to educate their
children, an education they had been denied in slavery. For some time, these efforts
were advanced by governmental institutions. The Freedman's Bureau, for example,
was an agency established in 1865 that assisted freedmen in finding employment
and establishing schools. More importantly, many African Americans played important roles in the new Republican Party of the South, and by 1868 black men were
seated for the first time in southern state legislatures. African Americans' influence
grew to such an extent that between 1869 and 1877, more than 600 black men
served in state legislatures, six served as lieutenant governors, fourteen were members
of the U.S. House of Representatives, and two were U.S. senators.

These political gains, however, were short-lived. In spite of the electoral successes
of African Americans, the Democratic Party enjoyed increasing political success as
former Confederates eventually had their political rights restored. As early as 1870,
the governors of Alabama and Georgia were Democrats. These electoral victories
were complemented by extralegal violence. The Ku Klux Klan, a secretive terrorist
organization, successfully intimidated Republicans—and especially black Republicans—beginning in 1866. Of those black people who had been delegates to state
constitutional conventions in 1867, for example, at least one-tenth were attacked
and seven were killed. Changes in the electorate in conjunction with intimidation
shifted the trajectory of Reconstruction once again as radical transformation was
replaced with a movement toward "redemption," white southerners' term for
reclaiming the world they had known before the Civil War.

The end of Reconstruction was hastened by events in the North as well as the
South. Ulysses S. Grant, elected president in 1868, was a better general than politician, and his administration became mired in scandal shortly after he took office.
In 1873, the nation was rocked by a financial panic that led to a depression lasting
six years. The scandals and the economic depression weakened the Republican Party.

Meanwhile Congress, in part because of the resurgence of the Democratic Party, and the Supreme Court were weakening in their resolve to continue a strict policy of Reconstruction. The death knell for Reconstruction was the national election of 1876, when it became clear that the North was no longer willing to pursue its earlier goals. The election of the Democratic candidate for president was avoided only by a deal in 1877 wherein Rutherford B. Hayes would be declared president if he promised to withdraw federal troops from those states in the South where they still remained. The deal was made. Reconstruction was over.

Q U E S T I O N S   T O   T H I N K   A B O U T

What were the failures of Reconstruction and what were its successes? Why did it collapse? Did Reconstruction come to an end primarily because it was abandoned by the North, opposed by the white South, or undermined by a lack of unity within the Republican Party at the local level?

D O C U M E N T S

The South was in a state of astonishing flux after the collapse of the Confederacy. Document 1 consists of reminiscences of former slaves about the coming of freedom and the challenges they faced in the early years of Reconstruction. These hazards were heightened by the "black codes" enacted in many southern states, one of which is given in Document 2. This example from Louisiana in 1865 illustrates the many ways in which the rights of "freedom" were abridged. The next three documents illustrate the many viewpoints on how the federal government should reconstruct the South in the years immediately after the war. In Document 3, President Andrew Johnson argues against black suffrage because he fears that "the subjugation of the States to negro domination would be worse than the military despotism under which they are now suffering." In contrast, Thaddeus Stevens, a Radical representative in Congress, argues for passage of the Reconstruction Act of 1867 in Document 4 because he believes that only an unfaltering federal presence will prevent "traitors" from ruling the South. The radical implications of the debate on Reconstruction had an impact in other arenas of political debate, as Document 5 shows. Elizabeth Cady Stanton argues that the very radicals who are pushing for increased rights for freed slaves are deferring the issue of women's suffrage. Document 6 is the text of the Fourteenth Amendment, which among other things provides the due process of law for all citizens advocated by Stevens in Document 4. As radical as these measures were, their successful implication was made difficult by conditions in the United States, as the final three documents show. Document 7 is a recollection by a freedman in 1871 of a visit in the night by the Ku Klux Klan. Consider how difficult it would be to retain one's political leanings in the face of such threats. In Document 8, Carl Schurz, a senator from Missouri, concludes in 1872 that federal oversight of the South has been a failure. Schurz, who advocated suffrage for African American men in 1865, now believes that many of the Reconstruction policies—including black suffrage—were mistaken and he advocates a retreat in Reconstruction policy. Finally, in Document 9, L. Q. C. Lamar, a representative from Mississippi, denounces Reconstruction in the South. Lamar's speech, given in 1874, was a signal of the direction of Reconstruction. Within three years, the South would be "redeemed."

1. African Americans Talk About Their Personal Experiences of Newfound Freedom, c. 1865

FELIX HAYWOOD From San Antonio, Texas. Born in Raleigh, North Carolina. Age at Interview: 88

The end of the war, it come just like that—like you snap your fingers. . . . How did we know it! Hallelujah broke out—

> Abe Lincoln freed the nigger
>   With the gun and the trigger;
> And I ain't going to get whipped any more.
>   I got my ticket,
> Leaving the thicket,
>   And I'm a-heading for the Golden Shore!

Soldiers, all of a sudden, was everywhere—coming in bunches, crossing and walking and riding. Everyone was a-singing. We was all walking on golden clouds. Hallelujah!

> Union forever,
>   Hurrah, boys, hurrah!
> Although I may be poor,
>   I'll never be a slave—
> Shouting the battle cry of freedom.

Everybody went wild. We felt like heroes, and nobody had made us that way but ourselves. We was free. Just like that, we was free. It didn't seem to make the whites mad, either. They went right on giving us food just the same. Nobody took our homes away, but right off colored folks started on the move. They seemed to want to get closer to freedom, so they'd know what it was—like it was a place or a city. Me and my father stuck, stuck close as a lean tick to a sick kitten. The Gudlows started us out on a ranch. My father, he'd round up cattle—unbranded cattle—for the whites. They was cattle that they belonged to, all right; they had gone to find water 'long the San Antonio River and the Guadalupe. Then the whites gave me and my father some cattle for our own. My father had his own brand—7 B)—and we had a herd to start out with of seventy.

We knowed freedom was on us, but we didn't know what was to come with it. We thought we was going to get rich like the white folks. We thought we was going to be richer than the white folks, 'cause we was stronger and knowed how to work, and the whites didn't, and they didn't have us to work for them any more. But it didn't turn out that way. We soon found out that freedom could make folks proud, but it didn't make 'em rich.

B. A. Botkin, ed., *Lay My Burden Down: A Folk History of Slavery* (Chicago: University of Chicago Press, 1945), pp. 65–70, 223–224, 241–242, 246–247. Copyright 1945 by B. A. Botkin. Reprinted by permission of Curtis Brown, Ltd.

Did you ever stop to think that thinking don't do any good when you do it too late? Well, that's how it was with us. If every mother's son of a black had thrown 'way his hoe and took up a gun to fight for his own freedom along with the Yankees, the war'd been over before it began. But we didn't do it. We couldn't help stick to our masters. We couldn't no more shoot 'em than we could fly. My father and me used to talk 'bout it. We decided we was too soft and freedom wasn't going to be much to our good even if we had a education.

WARREN MCKINNEY, From Hazen, Arkansas. Born in South Carolina. Age at Interview: 85.

I was born in Edgefield County, South Carolina. I am eighty-five years old. I was born a slave of George Strauter. I remembers hearing them say, "Thank God, I's free as a jay bird." My ma was a slave in the field. I was eleven years old when freedom was declared. When I was little, Mr. Strauter whipped my ma. It hurt me bad as it did her. I hated him. She was crying. I chunked him with rocks. He run after me, but he didn't catch me. There was twenty-five or thirty hands that worked in the field. They raised wheat, corn, oats, barley, and cotton. All the children that couldn't work stayed at one house. Aunt Mat kept the babies and small children that couldn't go to the field. He had a gin and a shop. The shop was at the fork of the roads. When the war come on, my papa went to build forts. He quit Ma and took another woman. When the war close, Ma took her four children, bundled 'em up and went to Augusta. The government give out rations there. My ma washed and ironed. People died in piles. I don't know till yet what was the matter. They said it was the change of living. I seen five or six wooden, painted coffins piled up on wagons pass by our house. Loads passed every day like you see cotton pass here. Some said it was cholera and some took consumption. Lots of the colored people nearly starved. Not much to get to do and not much houseroom. Several families had to live in one house. Lots of the colored folks went up North and froze to death. They couldn't stand the cold. They wrote back about them dying. No, they never sent them back. I heard some sent for money to come back. I heard plenty 'bout the Ku Klux. They scared the folks to death. People left Augusta in droves. About a thousand would all meet and walk going to hunt work and new homes. Some of them died. I had a sister and brother lost that way. I had another sister come to Louisiana that way. She wrote back.

I don't think the colored folks looked for a share of land. They never got nothing 'cause the white folks didn't have nothing but barren hills left. About all the mules was wore out hauling provisions in the army. Some folks say they ought to done more for the colored folks when they left, but they say they was broke. Freeing all the slaves left 'em broke.

That reconstruction was a mighty hard pull. Me and Ma couldn't live. A man paid our ways to Carlisle, Arkansas, and we come. We started working for Mr. Emenson. He had a big store, teams, and land. We liked it fine, and I been here fifty-six years now. There was so much wild game, living was not so hard. If a fellow could get a little bread and a place to stay, he was all right. After I come to this state, I voted some. I have farmed and worked at odd jobs. I farmed mostly. Ma went back to her old master. He persuaded her to come back home. Me and her went back and run a farm four or five years before she died. Then I come back here.

LEE GUIDON, From South Carolina. Born in South Carolina.
Age at Interview: 89.

Yes, ma'am, I sure was in the Civil War. I plowed all day, and me and my sister helped take care of the baby at night. It would cry, and me bumping it [in a straight chair, rocking]. Time I git it to the bed where its mama was, it wake up and start crying all over again. I be so sleepy. It was a puny sort of baby. Its papa was off at war. . . .

After freedom a heap of people say they was going to name theirselves over. They named theirselves big names, then went roaming round like wild, hunting cities. They changed up so it was hard to tell who or where anybody was. Heap of 'em died, and you didn't know when you hear about it if he was your folks hardly. Some of the names was Abraham, and some called theirselves Lincum. Any big name 'cepting their master's name. It was the fashion. I heard 'em talking 'bout it one evening, and my pa say, "Fine folks raise us and we gonna hold to our own names." That settled it with all of us. . . .

I reckon I do know 'bout the Ku Kluck. I knowed a man named Alfred Owens. He seemed all right, but he was a Republican. He said he was not afraid. He run a tanyard and kept a heap of guns in a big room. They all loaded. He married a Southern woman. Her husband either died or was killed. She had a son living with them. The Ku Kluck was called Upper League. They get this boy to unload all the guns. Then the white men went there. The white man give up and said, "I ain't got no gun to defend myself with. The guns all unloaded, and I ain't got no powder and shot." But the Ku Kluck shot in the houses and shot him up like lacework. He sold fine harness, saddles, bridles—all sorts of leather things. The Ku Kluck sure run them outen their country. They say they not going to have them round, and they sure run them out, back where they came from. . . .

For them what stayed on like they were, Reconstruction times 'bout like times before that 'cepting the Yankee stole out and tore up a scandalous heap. They tell the black folks to do something, and then come white folks you live with and say Ku Kluck whup you. They say leave, and white folks say better not listen to them old Yankees. They'll git you too far off to come back, and you freeze. They done give you all the use they got for you. How they do? All sorts of ways. Some stayed at their cabins glad to have one to live in and farmed on. Some running round begging, some hunting work for money, and nobody had no money 'cepting the Yankees, and they had no homes or land and mighty little work for you to do. No work to live on. Some going every day to the city. That winter I heard 'bout them starving and freezing by the wagon loads.

I never heard nothing 'bout voting till freedom. I don't think I ever voted till I come to Mississippi. I votes Republican. That's the party of my color, and I stick to them as long as they do right. I don't dabble in white folks' business, and that white folks' voting is their business. If I vote, I go do it and go on home. . . .

When I owned most, I had six head mules and five head horses. I rented 140 acres of land. I bought this house and some other land about. The anthrax killed nearly all my horses and mules. I got one big fine mule yet. Its mate died. I lost my house. My son give me one room, and he paying the debt off now. It's hard for colored folks to keep anything. Somebody gets it from 'em if they don't mind.

The present times is hard. Timber is scarce. Game is about all gone. Prices higher. Old folks cannot work. Times is hard for younger folks too. They go to town too much and go to shows. They going to a tent show now. Circus coming, they say. They spending too much money for foolishness. It's a fast time. Folks too restless. Some of the colored folks work hard as folks ever did. They spends too much. Some folks is lazy. Always been that way.

I signed up to the government, but they ain't give me nothing 'cepting powdered milk and rice what wasn't fit to eat. It cracked up and had black something in it. A lady said she would give me some shirts that was her husband's. I went to get them, but she wasn't home. These heavy shirts give me heat. They won't give me the pension, and I don't know why. It would help me buy my salts and pills and the other medicines like Swamp Root. They won't give it to me.

TOBY JONES, From Madisonville, Texas. Born in South Carolina.
Age at Interview: 87.

I worked for Massa 'bout four years after freedom, 'cause he forced me to, said he couldn't 'ford to let me go. His place was near ruint, the fences burnt, and the house would have been, but it was rock. There was a battle fought near his place, and I taken Missy to a hideout in the mountains to where her father was, 'cause there was bullets flying everywhere. When the war was over, Massa come home and says, "You son of a gun, you's supposed to be free, but you ain't, 'cause I ain't gwine give you freedom." So I goes on working for him till I gits the chance to steal a hoss from him. The woman I wanted to marry, Govie, she 'cides to come to Texas with me. Me and Govie, we rides that hoss 'most a hundred miles, then we turned him a-loose and give him a scare back to his house, and come on foot the rest the way to Texas.

All we had to eat was what we could beg, and sometimes we went three days without a bite to eat. Sometimes we'd pick a few berries. When we got cold we'd crawl in a brushpile and hug up close together to keep warm. Once in awhile we'd come to a farmhouse, and the man let us sleep on cottonseed in his barn, but they was far and few between, 'cause they wasn't many houses in the country them days like now.

When we gits to Texas, we gits married, but all they was to our wedding am we just 'grees to live together as man and wife. I settled on some land, and we cut some trees and split them open and stood them on end with the tops together for our house. Then we deadened some trees, and the land was ready to farm. There was some wild cattle and hogs, and that's the way we got our start, caught some of them and tamed them.

I don't know as I'spected nothing from freedom, but they turned us out like a bunch of stray dogs, no homes, no clothing, no nothing, not 'nough food to last us one meal. After we settles on that place, I never seed man or woman, 'cept Govie, for six years, 'cause it was a long ways to anywhere. All we had to farm with was sharp sticks. We'd stick holes and plant corn, and when it come up we'd punch up the dirt round it. We didn't plant cotton, 'cause we couldn't eat that. I made bows and arrows to kill wild game with, and we never went to a store for nothing. We made our clothes out of animal skins.

2. Louisiana Black Codes Reinstate Provisions of the Slave Era, 1865

SECTION 1. *Be it therefore ordained by the board of police of the town of Opelousas,* That no negro or freedman shall be allowed to come within the limits of the town of Opelousas without special permission from his employers, specifying the object of his visit and the time necessary for the accomplishment of the same. . . .

SECTION 2. *Be it further ordained,* That every negro freedman who shall be found on the streets of Opelousas after 10 o'clock at night without a written pass or permit from his employer shall be imprisoned and compelled to work five days on the public streets, or pay a fine of five dollars.

SECTION 3. No negro or freedman shall be permitted to rent or keep a house within the limits of the town under any circumstances, and any one thus offending shall be ejected and compelled to find an employer or leave the town within twenty-four hours. . . .

SECTION 4. No negro or freedman shall reside within the limits of the town of Opelousas who is not in the regular service of some white person or former owner, who shall be held responsible for the conduct of said freedman. . . .

SECTION 5. No public meetings or congregations of negroes or freedmen shall be allowed within the limits of the town of Opelousas under any circumstances or for any purpose without the permission of the mayor or president of the board. . . .

SECTION 6. No negro or freedman shall be permitted to preach, exhort, or otherwise declaim to congregations of colored people without a special permission from the mayor or president of the board of police. . . .

SECTION 7. No freedman who is not in the military service shall be allowed to carry firearms, or any kind of weapons, within the limits of the town of Opelousas without the special permission of his employer, in writing, and approved by the mayor or president of the board of police. . . .

SECTION 8. No freedman shall sell, barter, or exchange any articles of merchandise or traffic within the limits of Opelousas without permission in writing from his employer or the mayor or president of the board. . . .

SECTION 9. Any freedman found drunk within the limits of the town shall be imprisoned and made to labor five days on the public streets, or pay five dollars in lieu of said labor.

Condition of the South, Senate Executive Document No. 2, 39 Cong., 1 Sess., pp. 92–93.

SECTION 10. Any freedman not residing in Opelousas who shall be found within the corporate limits after the hour of 3 p.m. on Sunday without a special permission from his employer or the mayor shall be arrested and imprisoned and made to work. . . .

SECTION 11. All the foregoing provisions apply to freedmen and freedwomen, or both sexes. . . .

E. D. ESTILLETTE,
President of the Board of Police.
JOS. D. RICHARDS, *Clerk.*

Official copy:

J. LOVELL,
Captain and Assistant Adjutant General.

3. President Andrew Johnson Denounces Changes in His Program of Reconstruction, 1868

It is manifestly and avowedly the object of these laws to confer upon negroes the privilege of voting and to disfranchise such a number of white citizens as will give the former a clear majority at all elections in the Southern States. This, to the minds of some persons, is so important that a violation of the Constitution is justified as a means of bringing it about. The morality is always false which excuses a wrong because it proposes to accomplish a desirable end. We are not permitted to do evil that good may come. But in this case the end itself is evil, as well as the means. The subjugation of the States to negro domination would be worse than the military despotism under which they are now suffering. It was believed beforehand that the people would endure any amount of military oppression for any length of time rather than degrade themselves by subjection to the negro race. Therefore they have been left without a choice. Negro suffrage was established by act of Congress, and the military officers were commanded to superintend the process of clothing the negro race with the political privileges torn from white men.

The blacks in the South are entitled to be well and humanely governed, and to have the protection of just laws for all their rights of person and property. If it were practicable at this time to give them a Government exclusively their own, under which they might manage their own affairs in their own way, it would become a grave question whether we ought to do so, or whether common humanity would not require us to save them from themselves. But under the circumstances this is only a speculative point. It is not proposed merely that they shall govern themselves, but that they shall rule the white race, make and administer State laws, elect Presidents and members of Congress, and shape to a greater or less extent the future destiny of the whole country. Would such a trust and power be safe in such hands?

Andrew Johnson, "Third Annual Message," December 3, 1867, in *A Compilation of Messages and Papers of the Presidents, 1789–1897*, ed. James D. Richardson (Washington, D.C.: Bureau of National Literature and Art, 1899), Vol. VI, pp. 564–565.

The peculiar qualities which should characterize any people who are fit to decide upon the management of public affairs for a great state have seldom been combined. It is the glory of white men to know that they have had these qualities in sufficient measure to build upon this continent a great political fabric and to preserve its stability for more than ninety years, while in every other part of the world all similar experiments have failed. But if anything can be proved by known facts, if all reasoning upon evidence is not abandoned, it must be acknowledged that in the progress of nations negroes have shown less capacity for government than any other race of people. No independent government of any form has ever been successful in their hands. On the contrary, wherever they have been left to their own devices they have shown a constant tendency to relapse into barbarism. In the Southern States, however, Congress has undertaken to confer upon them the privilege of the ballot. Just released from slavery, it may be doubted whether as a class they know more than their ancestors how to organize and regulate civil society.

4. Congressman Thaddeus Stevens Demands a Radical Reconstruction, 1867

. . . It is to be regretted that inconsiderate and incautious Republicans should ever have supposed that the slight amendments [embodied in the pending Fourteenth Amendment] already proposed to the Constitution, even when incorporated into that instrument, would satisfy the reforms necessary for the security of the Government. Unless the rebel States, before admission, should be made republican in spirit, and placed under the guardianship of loyal men, all our blood and treasure will have been spent in vain. I waive now the question of punishment which, if we are wise, will still be inflicted by moderate confiscations, both as a reproof and example. Having these States, as we all agree, entirely within the power of Congress, it is our duty to take care that no injustice shall remain in their organic laws. Holding them "like clay in the hands of the potter," we must see that no vessel is made for destruction. Having now no governments, they must have enabling acts. The law of last session with regard to Territories settled the principles of such acts. Impartial suffrage, both in electing the delegates and ratifying their proceedings, is now the fixed rule. There is more reason why colored voters should be admitted in the rebel States than in the Territories. In the States they form the great mass of the loyal men. Possibly with their aid loyal governments may be established in most of those States. Without it all are sure to be ruled by traitors; and loyal men, black and white, will be oppressed, exiled, or murdered. There are several good reasons for the passage of this bill. In the first place, it is just. I am now confining my argument to negro suffrage in the rebel States. Have not loyal blacks quite as good a right to choose rulers and make laws as rebel whites? In the second place, it is a necessity in order to protect the loyal white men in the seceded States. The white Union men are in a great minority in each of those States. With them the blacks would act in a body; and it is believed that in each of said States, except one, the two united

Thaddeus Stevens, Speech in the House, January 3, 1867, *Congressional Globe,* 39 Cong., 2 Sess., Vol. 37, pt. 1, pp. 251–253. This document can also be found in Harold M. Hyman, ed., *Radical Republicans and Reconstruction* (Bobbs-Merrill, 1967), pp. 373–375.

would form a majority, control the States, and protect themselves. Now they are the victims of daily murder. They must suffer constant persecution or be exiled. The convention of southern loyalists, lately held in Philadelphia, almost unanimously agreed to such a bill as an absolute necessity.

Another good reason is, it would insure the ascendancy of the Union party. Do you avow the party purpose? exclaims some horror-stricken demagogue. I do. For I believe, on my conscience, that on the continued ascendancy of that party depends the safety of this great nation. If impartial suffrage is excluded in rebel States then every one of them is sure to send a solid rebel representative delegation to Congress, and cast a solid rebel electoral vote. They, with their kindred Copperheads of the North, would always elect the President and control Congress. While slavery sat upon her defiant throne, and insulted and intimidated the trembling North, the South frequently divided on questions of policy between Whigs and Democrats, and gave victory alternately to the sections. Now, you must divide them between loyalists, without regard to color, and disloyalists, or you will be the perpetual vassals of the free-trade, irritated, revengeful South. For these, among other reasons, I am for negro suffrage in every rebel State. If it be just, it should not be denied; if it be necessary, it should be adopted; if it be a punishment to traitors, they deserve it.

But it will be said, as it has been said, "This is negro equality!" What is negro equality, about which so much is said by knaves, and some of which is believed by men who are not fools? It means, as understood by honest Republicans, just this much, and no more: every man, no matter what his race or color; every earthly being who has an immortal soul, has an equal right to justice, honesty, and fair play with every other man; and the law should secure him those rights. The same law which condemns or acquits an African should condemn or acquit a white man. The same law which gives a verdict in a white man's favor should give a verdict in a black man's favor on the same state of facts. Such is the law of God and such ought to be the law of man. This doctrine does not mean that a negro shall sit on the same seat or eat at the same table with a white man. That is a matter of taste which every man must decide for himself. The law has nothing to do with it.

5. Elizabeth Cady Stanton Questions Abolitionist Support for Female Enfranchisement, 1868

To what a depth of degradation must the women of this nation have fallen to be willing to stand aside, silent and indifferent spectators in the reconstruction of the nation, while all the lower stratas of manhood are to legislate in their interests, political, religious, educational, social and sanitary, moulding to their untutored will the institutions of a mighty continent. . . .

While leading Democrats have been thus favorably disposed, what have our best friends said when, for the first time since the agitation of the question [the enfranchisement of women], they have had an opportunity to frame their ideas into statutes to amend the constitutions of two States in the Union.

Elizabeth Cady Stanton, "Who Are Our Friends?" *The Revolution,* 15 (January 1868).

Charles Sumner, Horace Greeley, Gerrit Smith and Wendell Phillips, with one consent, bid the women of the nation stand aside and behold the salvation of the negro. Wendell Phillips says, "one idea for a generation," to come up in the order of their importance. First negro suffrage, then temperance, then the eight hour movement, then woman's suffrage. In 1958, three generations hence, thirty years to a generation, Phillips and Providence permitting, woman's suffrage will be in order. What an insult to the women who have labored thirty years for the emancipation of the slave, now when he is their political equal, to propose to lift him above their heads. Gerrit Smith, forgetting that our great American idea is "individual rights," in which abolitionists have ever based their strongest arguments for emancipation, says, this is the time to settle the rights of races; unless we do justice to the negro we shall bring down on ourselves another bloody revolution, another four years' war, but we have nothing to fear from woman, she will not revenge herself! . . .

Horace Greeley has advocated this cause for the last twenty years, but to-day it is too new, revolutionary for practical consideration. The enfranchisement of woman, revolutionizing, as it will, our political, religious and social condition, is not a measure too radical and all-pervading to meet the moral necessities of this day and generation.

Why fear new things; all old things were once new. . . . We live to do new things! When Abraham Lincoln issued the proclamation of emancipation, it was a new thing. When the Republican party gave the ballot to the negro, it was a new thing, startling too, to the people of the South, very revolutionary to their institutions, but Mr. Greeley did not object to all this because it was new. . . .

And now, while men like these have used all their influence for the last four years, to paralyze every effort we have put forth to rouse the women of the nation, to demand their true position in the reconstruction, they triumphantly turn to us, and say the greatest barrier in the way of your demand is that "the women themselves do not wish to vote." What a libel on the intelligence of the women of the nineteenth century. What means the 12,000 petitions presented by John Stuart Mill in the British Parliament from the first women in England, demanding household suffrage? What means the late action in Kansas, 10,000 women petitioned there for the right of suffrage, and 9,000 votes at the last election was the answer. What means the agitation in every State in the Union? In the very hour when Horace Greeley brought in his adverse report in the Constitutional Convention of New York, at least twenty members rose in their places and presented petitions from every part of the State, demanding woman's suffrage. What means that eloquent speech of George W. Curtis in the Convention, but to show that the ablest minds in the State are ready for this onward step?

6. The Fourteenth Amendment Grants Citizenship and Due Process of Law to African Americans, 1868

Section 1. All persons born or naturalized in the United States, and subject to the jurisdiction thereof, are citizens of the United States and of the State wherein they reside. No State shall make or enforce any law which shall abridge the privileges or

U.S. Constitution, amend. 14.

immunities of citizens of the United States; nor shall any State deprive any person of life, liberty, or property, without due process of law; nor deny to any person within its jurisdiction the equal protection of the laws.

Section 2. Representatives shall be apportioned among the several States according to their respective numbers, counting the whole number of persons in each State, excluding Indians not taxed. But when the right to vote at any election for the choice of electors for President and Vice-President of the United States, Representatives in Congress, the executive and judicial officers of a State, or the members of the legislature thereof, is denied to any of the male inhabitants of such State, being twenty-one years of age, and citizens of the United States, or in any way abridged, except for participation in rebellion, or other crime, the basis of representation therein shall be reduced in the proportion which the number of such male citizens shall bear to the whole number of male citizens twenty-one years of age in such State.

Section 3. No person shall be a Senator or Representative in Congress, or elector of President and Vice-President, or hold any office, civil or military, under the United States or under any State, who, having previously taken an oath as a member of Congress, or as an officer of the United States, or as a member of any State legislature, or as an executive or judicial officer of any State, to support the Constitution of the United States, shall have engaged in insurrection or rebellion against the same, or given aid or comfort to the enemies thereof. But Congress may, by a vote of two-thirds of each house, remove such disability.

Section 4. The validity of the public debt of the United States, authorized by law, including debts incurred for payment of pensions and bounties for services in suppressing insurrection or rebellion, shall not be questioned. But neither the United States nor any State shall assume or pay any debt or obligation incurred in aid of insurrection or rebellion against the United States, or any claim for the loss or emancipation of any slave; but all such debts, obligations, and claims shall be held illegal and void.

Section 5. The Congress shall have power to enforce, by appropriate legislation, the provisions of this article.

7. Elias Hill, an African American Man, Recounts a Nighttime Visit from the Ku Klux Klan, 1871

On the night of the 5th of last May, after I had heard a great deal of what they had done in that neighborhood, they came. It was between 12 and 1 o'clock at night when I was awakened and heard the dogs barking, and something walking, very much like horses. As I had often laid awake listening for such persons, for they had been all through the neighborhood, and disturbed all men and many women, I supposed that it was them. . . . Some one then hit my door. It flew open. One ran in the house, and stopping about the middle of the house, which is a small cabin, he turned around, as it seemed to me as I lay there awake, and said, "Who's here?" Then I knew they would take me, and I answered, "I am here." He shouted for joy, as it seemed, "Here

Report to the Joint Select Committee to Inquire into the Condition of Affairs in the Late Insurrectionary States, 42 Cong., 2 Sess., December 4, 1871–June 10, 1872, Vol. I, Serial 1483, pp. 44–46.

he is! Here he is! We have found him!" and he threw the bedclothes off of me and caught me by one arm, while another man took me by the other and they carried me into the yard between the houses, my brother's and mine, and put me on the ground beside a boy. The first thing they asked me was, "Who did that burning? Who burned our houses?"—gin-houses, dwelling-houses and such. Some had been burned in the neighborhood. I told them it was not me; I could not burn houses; it was unreasonable to ask me. Then they hit me with their fists, and said I did it, I ordered it. They went on asking me didn't I tell the black men to ravish all the white women. No, I answered them. They struck me again with their fists on my breast, and then they went on, "When did you hold a night-meeting of the Union League, and who were the officers? Who was the president?" I told them I had been the president, but that there had been no Union League meeting held at that place where they were formerly held since away in the fall. This was the 5th of May. They said that Jim Raney, that was hung, had been at my house since the time I had said the League was last held, and that he had made a speech. I told them he had not, because I did not know the man. I said, "Upon honor." They said I had no honor, and hit me again. They went on asking me hadn't I been writing to Mr. A. S. Wallace, in Congress, to get letters from him. I told them I had. They asked what I had been writing about? I told them, "Only tidings." They said, with an oath, "I know the tidings were d—d good, and you were writing something about the Ku-Klux, and haven't you been preaching and praying about the Ku-Klux?" One asked, "Haven't you been preaching political sermons?" Generally, one asked me all the questions, but the rest were squatting over me—some six men I counted as I lay there. Said one, "Didn't you preach against the Ku-Klux," and wasn't that what Mr. Wallace was writing to me about. "Not at all," I said. "Let me see the letter," said he; "what was it about?" I said it was on the times. They wanted the letter. I told them if they would take me back into the house, and lay me in the bed, which was close adjoining my books and papers, I would try and get it. They said I would never go back to that bed, for they were going to kill me—"Never expect to go back; tell us where the letters are." I told them they were on the shelf somewhere, and I hoped they would not kill me. Two of them went into the house. My sister says that as quick as they went into the house they struck the clock at the foot of the bed. I heard it shatter. One of the four around me called out, "Don't break any private property, gentlemen, if you please; we have got him we came for, and that's all we want." I did not hear them break anything else. They staid in there a good while hunting about and then came out and asked me for a lamp. I told them there was a lamp somewhere. They said "Where?" I was so confused I said I could not tell exactly. They caught my leg—you see what it is—and pulled me over the yard, and then left me there, knowing I could not walk nor crawl, and all six went into the house. I was chilled with the cold lying in the yard at that time of night, for it was near 1 o'clock, and they had talked and beat me and so on until half an hour had passed since they first approached. After they had staid in the house for a considerable time, they came back to where I lay and asked if I wasn't afraid at all. They pointed pistols at me all around my head once or twice, as if they were going to shoot me, telling me they were going to kill me; wasn't I ready to die, and willing to die? Didn't I preach? That they came to kill me—all the time pointing pistols at me. This second time they came out of the house, after plundering the house, searching for letters, they came at me with these pistols, and asked if I was ready to die. I told them that I was not exactly ready; that I would rather live; that I hoped they would not kill me that time. They said they would; I had better prepare. One caught me by the leg and hurt me, for my leg for forty years has been drawn each year, more and more year by year, and I made moan when it hurt so. One said "G-d d——n it, hush!" He had a horsewhip, and he told me to pull up my shirt, and he hit me. He told me at evey lick, "Hold up your shirt." I made a moan every time he cut with the horsewhip. I reckon he struck me eight cuts right on the hip bone; it was almost the only place he could hit my body, my legs are so short—all my limbs drawn up and withered away with pain. I saw one of them standing over me or by me motion to them to quit. They all had disguises on. I then thought they would not kill me. One of them then took a strap, and buckled it around my neck and said, "Let's take him to the river and drown him." "What course is the river?" they asked me. I told them east. Then one of them went feeling about, as if he was looking for something, and said, "I don't see no east! Where is the d——d thing?" as if he did not understand what I meant. After pulling the strap around my neck, he took it off and gave me a lick on my hip where he had struck me with the horsewhip. One of them said, "Now, you see, I've burned up the d——d letter of Wallace's and all," and he brought out a little book and says, "What's this for?" I told him I did not know; to let me see with a light and I could read it. They brought a lamp and I read it. It was a book in which I had keep an account of the school. I had been licensed to keep a school. I read them some of the names. He said that would do, and asked if I had been paid for those scholars I had put down. I said no. He said I would now have to die. I was somewhat afraid, but one said not to kill me. They said "Look here! Will you put a card in the paper next week like June Moore and Sol Hill?" They had been prevailed on to put a card in the paper to renounce all republicanism and never vote. I said, "If I had the money to pay the expense, I could." They said I could borrow, and gave me another lick. They asked me, "Will you quit preaching?" I told them I did not know. I said that to save my life. They said I must stop that republican paper that was coming to Clay Hill. It has been only a few weeks since it stopped. The republican weekly paper was then coming to me from Charleston. It came to my name. They said I must stop it, quit preaching, and put a card in the newspaper renouncing republicanism, and they would not kill me; but if I did not they would come back the next week and kill me. . . .

[Satisfied that he could no longer live in that community, he had written to make inquiry about the means of going himself to Liberia.]

8. Missouri Senator Carl Schurz Admits the Failures of Reconstruction, 1872

. . . But the stubborn fact remains that they [Southern black voters and officeholders] *were* ignorant and inexperienced; that the public business *was* an unknown world to them, and that in spite of the best intentions they *were* easily misled, not infrequently by the most reckless rascality which had found a way to their confidence. Thus their political rights and privileges were undoubtedly well calculated, and even

---

Carl Schurz, Speech in the Senate, January 30, 1872, in *Speeches, Correspondence, and Political Papers of Carl Schurz,* ed. Frederic Bancroft (New York: G. P. Putnam's & Co., 1913), pp. 326–327.

necessary, to protect their rights as free laborers and citizens; but they were not well calculated to secure a successful administration of other public interests.

I do not blame the colored people for it; still less do I say that for this reason their political rights and privileges should have been denied them. Nay, sir, I deemed it necessary then, and I now reaffirm that opinion, that they should possess those rights and privileges for the permanent establishment of the logical and legitimate results of the war and the protection of their new position in society. But, while never losing sight of this necessity, I do say that the inevitable consequence of the admission of so large an uneducated and inexperienced class to political power, as to the probable mismanagement of the material interests of the social body, should at least have been mitigated by a counterbalancing policy. When ignorance and inexperience were admitted to so large an influence upon public affairs, intelligence ought no longer to so large an extent have been excluded. In other words, when universal suffrage was granted to secure the equal rights of all, universal amnesty ought to have been granted to make all the resources of political intelligence and experience available for the promotion of the welfare of all.

But what did we do? To the uneducated and inexperienced classes—uneducated and inexperienced, I repeat, entirely without their fault—we opened the road to power; and, at the same time, we condemned a large proportion of the intelligence of those States, of the property-holding, the industrial, the professional, the tax-paying interest, to a worse than passive attitude. We made it, as it were, easy for rascals who had gone South in quest of profitable adventure to gain the control of masses so easily misled, by permitting them to appear as the exponents and representatives of the National power and of our policy; and at the same time we branded a large number of men of intelligence, and many of them of personal integrity, whose material interests were so largely involved in honest government, and many of whom would have cooperated in managing the public business with care and foresight—we branded them, I say, as outcasts, telling them that they ought not to be suffered to exercise any influence upon the management of the public business, and that it would be unwarrantable presumption in them to attempt it.

I ask you, sir, could such things fail to contribute to the results we read to-day in the political corruption and demoralization, and in the financial ruin of some of the Southern States? These results are now before us. The mistaken policy may have been pardonable when these consequences were still a matter of conjecture and speculation; but what excuse have we now for continuing it when those results are clear before our eyes, beyond the reach of contradiction?

9. Mississippi Congressman L. Q. C. Lamar Denounces Reconstruction, 1874

When, in order to consummate your policy, you divided the southern country into military districts, your military commanders, distrusting the purposes of the southern people and knowing the negroes were incompetent to manage the affairs of government, called to their aid and installed into all the offices of the States, from the

From L. Q. C. Lamar, Speech in the House, June 8, 1874, *Congressional Record,* 43 Cong., 1 Sess., Vol. 2, pt. 6, p. 429.

highest to the lowest, a set of men from the North who were strangers to our people, not possessing their confidence, not elected by them, not responsible to them, having no interest in common with them, and hostile to them to a certain extent in sentiment.

I am not going to characterize these men by any harshness of language. I am speaking of a state of things more controlling than ordinary personal characteristics. Even if it were true that they came to the South for no bad purposes, they were put in a position which has always engendered rapacity, cupidity corruption, grinding oppression, and taxation in its most devouring form. They were rulers without responsibility, in unchecked control of the material resources of a people with whom they had not a sentiment in sympathy or an interest in common, and whom they habitually regarded and treated as rebels who had forfeited their right to protection. These men, thus situated and thus animated, were the fisc of the South. They were the recipients of all the revenues, State and local. Not a dollar of taxes, State or local, but what went into their pockets. The suffering people on whom the taxes were laid could not exercise the slightest control, either as to the amount imposed or the basis upon which they were laid. The consequence was that in a few short years eight magnificent Commonwealths were laid in ruins. This condition of things still exists with unabated rigor in those Southern States. For when, by your reconstruction measures, you determined to provide civil governments for these States, the machinery by which these men carried their power over into those civil governments was simple and effectual. Under your policy generally—I repeat, my purpose to-day is not arraignment—under that policy you disfranchised a large portion of the white people of the Southern States. The registration laws and the education laws in the hands of these men kept a still larger proportion away.

But there was an agency more potent still.

By persistent misrepresentation a majority in Congress was made to believe that the presence of the United States Army would be necessary not merely to put these governments in force, but to keep them in operation and to keep them from being snatched away and worked to the oppression and ruin of the black race and the few loyal men who were there attempting to protect their rights. Thus was introduced into those so-called reconstructed civil governments the Federal military as an operative and predominant principle. Thus, with a quick, sudden, and violent hand, these men tore the two races asunder and hurled one in violent antagonism upon the other, and to this day the negro vote massed into an organization hostile to the whites is an instrument of absolute power in the hands of these men. These governments are in external form civil, but they are in their essential principle military. They are called local governments, but in reality they are Federal executive agencies. Not one of them emanates from the uncontrolled will of the people, white or black; not one which rests upon the elective principle in its purity. They have been aptly styled by a distinguished statesman and jurist in Mississippi, (Hon. W. P. Harris,) State governments without States, without popular constituencies. For they are as completely insulated from the traditions, the feelings, the interests, and the free suffrages of the people, white and black, as if they were outside the limits of those States. Where is the public sentiment which guides and enlightens those to whom is confided the conduct of public affairs? Where is the moral judgment of a virtuous people to which they are amenable? Where is the moral indignation which falls like the scathing lightning upon the delinquent or guilty public officer? Sir, that class and race in which reside these great moral agencies are prostrated, their interests, their prosperity jeopardized, their protests unheeded, and every murmur of discontent and every effort to throw off their oppression misrepresented here as originating in the spirit which inaugurated the rebellion. Sir, the statement that these southern governments have no popular constituencies is true, but they nevertheless have a constituency to whom they bear a responsibility inexorable as death. It is limited to the one point of keeping the State true and faithful to the Administration; all else is boundless license. That constituency is here in Washington; its heart pulsates in the White House. There is its intelligence and there is its iron will. I do not exaggerate when I say that every one of these governments depends, every moment of their existence, upon the will of the President. That will makes and unmakes them. A short proclamation backed by one company determines who is to be governor of Arkansas. A telegram settles the civil magistracy of Texas. A brief order to a general in New Orleans wrests a State government from the people of Louisiana and vests its control in the creatures of the Administration.

E S S A Y S

The collapse of Reconstruction had enormous costs for the African American populations of the South. Arguably, its failure also postponed the economic and social recovery of the entire region until well into the twentieth century. Historians have long debated the meaning of Reconstruction and particularly the reasons for its abandonment. In the first essay, Thomas Holt of the University of Chicago argues that in spite of many obstacles, advocates of Reconstruction had a fighting chance. It was lost to them partly because of their own political miscalculations, and especially because of the enormous difficulty in achieving Republican Party unity in the South. Not only did race divide white and black Republicans, but class differences divided "freemen" and "freedmen" as well. Eric Foner of Columbia University takes a somewhat different tack, emphasizing the tremendous odds against success. White southerners violently opposed reform, and over time northerners became fatigued by the struggle. Political expediency (and anger at President Andrew Johnson) drove Reconstruction at the federal level from the first, and when the reforms became inexpedient, the policy died out.

Social Class Divides Negro State Legislators in South Carolina, Impeding Reconstruction

THOMAS HOLT

Reconstruction was "a frightful experiment which never could have given a real statesman who learned or knew the facts the smallest hope of success." Daniel H. Chamberlain, the last Republican governor of South Carolina, wrote this postmortem a quarter of a century after he had been driven from office by a violent and fraudulent campaign to restore native whites to power in the fall and winter of 1876–77. Undoubtedly his view was colored by the social milieu of America at the

Thomas C. Holt, "Negro State Legislators in South Carolina During Reconstruction," in *Southern Black Leaders of the Reconstruction Era,* ed. Howard N. Rabinowitz (Urbana: University of Illinois Press), pp. 223–226, 229–230, 233–234, 236–244. Copyright 1982, Board of Trustees of the University of Illinois. Used by permission of the University of Illinois Press.

turn of the century, when racism of the most virulent type had become the intellectual orthodoxy. On the other hand, these later reflections do not differ much from his assessment just two months after he had been forced to relinquish his office. In June 1877 he explained to William Lloyd Garrison that "defeat was inevitable under the circumstances of time and place which surrounded me. I mean here exactly that the uneducated negro was too weak, no matter what his numbers, to cope with the whites." In later years he described that weakness more explicitly: blacks were "an aggregation of ignorance and inexperience and incapacity."

The story of Reconstruction in South Carolina and elsewhere has been considerably revised since Chamberlain presented his analysis of its failure; yet, his basic premise is still shared by many revisionists. "The failure of the Radical government . . . was due not so much to its organization as to its personnel," Francis B. Simkins and Robert H. Woody wrote in 1932. Given the armed support of the federal establishment and the overwhelming black majority in South Carolina, the failure of the Republican regime could only have been caused by the venality, ignorance, and corruption of the leadership. Northern adventurers, mediocre scalawags, and uneducated, "excitable" freedmen constituted a legislature so guilty of mismanagement and fraud that the white minority rose up in justifiable wrath to put it down. Simkins and Woody were more charitable to the achievements of the Reconstruction regime than Chamberlain, but they leave little doubt that the inexperienced, undisciplined ex-slaves were the weak link in the Republican coalition.

While Simkins and Woody read the supposed incapacities of the slave into the failures of Reconstruction, a recent revisionist history of slavery reverses the process: the failures of the postemancipation political order help confirm a controversial description of the slave regime. Eugene Genovese, in *Roll, Jordan, Roll,* evokes a seminal, sometimes brilliant picture of the slave's worldview; but the essence of his argument is that that worldview was conditioned by a basically paternalistic master-slave relationship. Furthermore, the long-term consequence of that paternalism on blacks was to transform "elements of personal dependency into a sense of collective weakness." Although the slaves were able to manipulate the masters' paternalism in ways that reaffirmed their individual manhood, "they could not grasp their collective strength as a people and act like political men." This "political paralysis," this absence of "a stern collective discipline," not only accounts for their failure to mount significant slave revolts or to take advantage of their masters' strategic weakness to strike for freedom during the Civil War, but also explains their failure to "organize themselves more effectively in politics" after the war. In short, the behavior of the freedman confirms the conditioning of the slave.

But it is difficult to reconcile any of these views with events in South Carolina during Reconstruction. Certainly the cause of its failure cannot be laid to the political incapacity and inexperience of the black masses. They were uneducated. They were inexperienced. But they overcame these obstacles to forge a formidable political majority in the state that had led the South into secession. During the Reconstruction era 60 percent of South Carolina's population was black. This popular majority was turned into a functioning political majority as soon as Reconstruction legislation was put into effect with the registration for the constitutional convention in 1867. Despite violence and economic intimidation, the black electorate grew rather than declined between 1868 and 1876. The only effective political opposition before the election of 1876 came from so-called reform tickets, especially in 1870 and 1874. On these occasions, black and white Republican dissidents fused with Democrats to challenge the regular Republican party. But the strength of these challenges was generally confined to the predominantly white up-country counties and Charleston with its large white plurality and freeborn Negro bourgeoisie. Indeed, many observers condemned the unflinching, "blind" allegiance of black Republicans as evidence of their lack of political sophistication. But given the political alternatives and the records of so-called reform and fusion candidates, the black electorate could just as easily be credited with a high degree of political savvy. For South Carolina certainly, Frederick Douglass was right: the Republican party—despite its weaknesses and inadequacies—was the deck, all else the sea. . . .

Activities other than partisan politics also demonstrate the freedmen's capacity for collective political action. For example, in the lowland rice-growing areas, cash-poor planters instituted a system wherein their workers were paid in scrip rather than currency. The scrip or "checks" could be redeemed only at designated stores in exchange for goods priced significantly above normal retail items. Although the legislature made some attempts in 1872 and again in 1875 to reform and control the system, its essential features remained unchanged: the workers exchanged low-paid labor for high-priced goods. Since their political representatives appeared to be unable to correct this problem, in July 1876 the workers took matters into their own hands. They struck. The strike was widespread and involved considerable violence against nonstrikers. Governor Chamberlain sent in the militia and had the strike leaders jailed. He also sent Negro Congressman Robert Smalls to convince the strikers to renounce violence and concede scabs their right to work. Smalls reported to the governor that he had succeeded in his mission, but subsequent reports of continued violence suggest that the right-to-work principle was attended more in the breach than in the observance. Eventually the planters capitulated and abolished the scrips system. . . .

Ultimately the failures of South Carolina Republicans must be laid not to their black ex-slave constituents but to the party leadership. Thus Simkins and Woody are partly right when they blame the personnel of the South Carolina government, but they are wrong to the extent that they find venality, corruption, ignorance, and inexperience as the primary causal factors. Surely there were venal men. Clearly corruption was rife. But there were corrupt Democrats before, during, and after Reconstruction, including the architects of the Democratic campaign of 1876, Martin W. Gary and M. C. Butler. Republican corruption merely offered a propagandistic advantage in the Democratic efforts to discredit the Radical regime. With the possible exception of the land-commission frauds, corruption was secondary to the major failures of that regime while in office and to its ability to sustain office. Very likely native whites viewed the fact that blacks wielded political power as itself a form of corruption of governmental process.

South Carolina was unique among American state governments in that blacks enjoyed control over the legislature and many other political entities. Of the 487 men elected to various state and federal offices between 1867 and 1876, 255 were black. While it is true that they never succeeded in elevating any of their number to the U.S. Senate, they did fill nine of the state's fifteen congressional terms between 1870 and 1876, including four of the five seats available from 1870 to 1874. J. J. Wright was elected to one of the three positions on the state supreme court in 1870, which he held until 1877. However, no black was ever even nominated for the governorship, and all of the circuit judges, comptrollers general, attorneys general, and superintendents of education during this period were white. Only a handful of blacks served in the important county offices of sheriff, auditor, treasurer, probate judge, and clerk of court. More commonly blacks were elected to such local offices as school commissioner and trial justice; but even among these they were not a majority.

Clearly blacks enjoyed their greatest power in the General Assembly. Their membership averaged from just over one-third during the first five sessions of the Senate to about one-half during the last five; but in the House of Representatives they were never less than 56 percent of the membership. . . . More important than their membership was their growing control of key committees and leadership posts in both branches of the General Assembly. Samuel J. Lee became the first black Speaker of the House in 1872; he was succeeded by Robert B. Elliott from 1874 to 1876. The president pro tem of the Senate was a black after 1872, as was the lieutenant governor, who presided over that body. Better than two-thirds of the respective committee chairmanships were held by blacks in the House after 1870 and in the Senate after 1872. Furthermore, in both houses the key committees—those controlling money bills or the flow of major legislation—generally had black chairmen.

Little wonder then that former slaveholders viewed the new order with alarm. Indeed, the displaced local whites often became hysterical in their denunciations of the new order. For example, when William J. Whipper was elected to a judgeship in the important Charleston circuit, the *News and Courier* ran a banner headline declaring its "Civilization In Peril." As a deliberate Republican policy, the judicial system had been kept inviolately white and conservative. The election of a black radical to fill one of the most important of these posts was the first step toward the creation of "an African dominion," indeed "a new Liberia." Here, as elsewhere in the South, to involve blacks in the political process was "to Africanize" the social system.

The biographical profile of the Negro leadership justifies neither the fears of white contemporaries nor the charges of many historians of that era. While the overwhelming majority of their constituents were black, illiterate, and propertyless ex-slave farmworkers, most of the political leadership was literate, a significant number had been free before the Civil War, many were owners of property, and most were employed in skilled or professional occupations after the war. At least one in four of the 255 Negroes elected to state and federal offices between 1868 and 1876 were of free origins. Indeed, counting only those for whom information is available, one finds that almost 40 percent had been free before the Civil War. Of those whose educational attainments are known, 87 percent were literate, and the 25 identifiable illiterates approximately matched the number who had college or professional training. Information on property ownership is available for little more than half the legislators. Seventy-six percent of these men possessed either real or taxable personal property, and 27 percent of them were worth $1,000 or more. Indeed, one in four held over $1,000 in real property alone. . . .

Thus, while there were differences in their respective social and economic backgrounds, neither the freeborn nor ex-slave legislators conform to the traditional stereotype of ignorant, pennyless sharecroppers rising from cotton fields to despoil the legislature and plunder the state. In truth, most of the freeborn and many of the slaveborn were a "middle" class of artisans, small farmers, and shopkeepers located on the social spectrum somewhere between the vast majority of Negro sharecroppers and the white middle and upper classes. Indeed, because of their education, class position, and general aspirations, they were more likely to embrace than reject the petty bourgeois values of their society.

But while their political opponents have distorted the social and economic backgrounds of the Negro leadership, charges that they were politically inexperienced can scarcely be denied. Northern as well as southern blacks had few if any opportunities to gain experience in partisan politics during the antebellum period. Most could not vote in the state in which they resided, and they were unlikely to hold office in any state. In various ways, employees of the missionary societies and churches, the army, and the Freedmen's Bureau gained experience in public life and in serving and mobilizing constituents. Between 1865 and 1868 about one-fourth of the black elected officials had been affiliated with one or more of these institutions, as also had more than 37 percent of those who served in the first Republican government in 1868. But, of course, while these affiliations could help prepare men for public service, they were no substitute for direct legislative and partisan political experience.

The black legislator's lack of prior political experience was further exacerbated by the likelihood of an abbreviated service for most of their number. The high turnover in the House of Representatives suggests the volatility of that body. Only two black members, William M. Thomas of Colleton and Joseph D. Boston of Newberry, served the entire four terms of the Reconstruction period. Eight other men served three terms; but 61 percent of the 212 blacks elected to the House between 1868 and 1876 were one-term members. Only 15 of these advanced to higher elective offices in the state senate or executive branch or at the federal level. Clearly, for the most of its sessions, the House of Representatives was composed of a disproportionate number of freshmen legislators.

It is difficult to evaluate the political impact of this rather high turnover in membership. Generally, a low turnover rate is evidence of significant institutionalization in a legislature that is reflected in strong party leadership and discipline. Conversely the relatively weak party discipline of the South Carolina Republican party would appear to be congruent with the high turnover of its members. Certainly the evidence of intraparty dissension and weak leadership among Republican legislators is formidable by almost any standard. The index of relative cohesion developed by sociologist Stuart Rice in the 1920s provides one way of measuring unity or conflict within a party or subgroup. On the Rice scale a score of 100 indicates unanimity of the group, while a score of 0 indicates a perfect split, half of the members voting for a measure and half against it. Throughout the Reconstruction era, Democrats voted together more consistently than did Republicans. While the Democrats' average score was never less than 68, the Republicans never exceeded 50. . . .

Although no single bloc or segment of the Republican party was solely responsible for its weakness, there were political differences within the party that diminished its strength. Evidence suggests that the lack of party solidarity revealed on legislative roll calls reflected differences in aspirations and ideological orientations of various subgroups within the party. From the beginning of Reconstruction there had been conflict between white and Negro Republicans and between Negroes with roots in the freeborn mulatto bourgeoisie and the black ex-slaves. During the early meetings between 1865 and 1868, Negro aspirations for greater representation and power clashed with white efforts to maintain political control, and the demands for universal manhood suffrage and land reform articulated by black ex-slaves did not always resonate with the policy objectives and ideological orientation of their freeborn colleagues. At the end of the Reconstruction era, such differences in interests, perceptions, and orientation still undermined party unity. The cohesion indices for all ten legislative sessions and the agreement scores for the 1876 session generally reflect these conflicts. For instance, by calculating the average number of times a given subgroup voted with other Republicans, one can uncover the breaks in the party's ranks. In 1876 the average agreement score for white Republicans was 37.3 as compared with 44.6 for Negroes. Similarly, black former slaves scored 46.9 as compared with 38.7 for mulattoes of free origin. Clearly, what little political stability Republicans could lay claim to was provided not by the better educated and more experienced whites or by the brown bourgeoisie, but by the blacks of slave origin. . . .

It is not surprising that white Republican legislators did not see eye to eye with their black colleagues; there was ample evidence of distrust and animosity between these segments of the party. During the early years of Reconstruction, whites actively discouraged blacks from seeking their appropriate share of offices and power. On several occasions during the first two years of Republican rule, whites tried to exclude blacks from major state executive offices, congressional seats, judgeships, and even key party leadership posts. During the 1870 campaign Negroes rebelled against this policy and demanded their fair share of state and party offices. Nevertheless, during the final year of Republican rule, the party again would be split badly by the governor's effort to deny an important judicial post to William J. Whipper, a northern black lawyer.

Such conflicts cannot be traced solely to racial animosities, but there is evidence that racism was a contributing factor. For example, in 1868 Franklin J. Moses, Jr., Speaker of the House and governor of the state from 1872 to 1874, advised Governor Robert K. Scott to appoint only native whites to state judicial posts. In 1871 State Representative T. N. Talbert was even more explicit. "My policy," he wrote the governor, "is to get as many of the native whites of the state to unite with us as we can and try and induce Northern men to come and settle among us. There is not enough virtue and intelligence among the Blacks to conduct the government in such a way as will promote peace and prosperity."

Given the nation's racial climate it is not surprising, perhaps, that tensions would develop between Negro and white Republicans or that they would often perceive policy issues differently; but there was no reason to expect that Negro legislators would be so much less cohesive among themselves than their Democratic rivals. For much of the Reconstruction period a unified Negro leadership could have dominated the legislature. Their overwhelming majority in the House together with a consistently large plurality in the Senate should have enabled Negroes, given inevitable absenteeism and defections among white Republicans and Democrats, to attain most of their major legislative objectives. But in fact Negro leaders were often at odds on legislative objectives, political policies, and ideology. Furthermore, the nature of their disunity followed a consistent pattern from the earliest political meetings and is best explained by reference to differences in their socioeconomic status and antebellum experience.

The most visible, though not necessarily most significant, divisions were between the black ex-slaves and those mulattoes who had been free before the war. The number of freeborn brown officeholders was far out of proportion to their share of the state's population, especially in the early conventions and legislative sessions, and their control of leadership positions was even more striking. In the 1868–70 House of Representatives, for example, half the committee chairmanships held by Negroes were filled by freeborn mulattoes. Between 1868 and 1876, over half the Negro state senators were drawn from this class and their average term of service was longer than that of black freedmen. Five of the seven Negroes elected to the state executive branch were freeborn brown men as well as four of the state's seven Negro congressmen.

Obviously, free brown men successfully offered themselves as prominent leaders of a predominantly black ex-slave electorate, but their very success aroused jealousy and political divisiveness within the party. In 1871 black leader Martin R. Delany complained to Frederick Douglass about mulatto dominance of patronage positions. In 1870 William H. Jones, Jr., black representative from Georgetown, publicly ridiculed Joseph H. Rainey, his mulatto rival for the state Senate, because of his extremely light complexion. State Senator William B. Nash, a black ex-slave, once referred to his mulatto colleagues as "simply mongrels."

It is misleading, however, to consider these intraracial tensions as merely a consequence of differences in skin color and antebellum origins. The fact is that among South Carolina Negroes a light complexion and free origins correlated very strongly with other indicators of bourgeois class status; mulattoes and those who had been free before the war were more likely to own property and thus to enjoy higher status than black ex-slaves, who were more likely to be propertyless. These general patterns were reflected in the General Assembly, where legislators of free origins were generally better educated than the freedmen, more likely to own property, and more likely to be employed as artisans or in a profession rather than as farmworkers. These objective differences, as minor as they might have appeared to whites, generated not only consciousness of class differences but social institutions that confirmed and reinforced those differences. The Brown Fellowship Society was one such institution. Founded in 1790, the society limited its members to free brown men, providing them with a variety of financial services as well as social connections. At least three legislators belonged to the Brown Fellowship Society, and several others were members of social clubs with a similar orientation though less prestige. Church affiliation was another indicator of status aspirations if not class position. Thomas W. Cardozo, brother of Francis L. Cardozo and a representative of the American Missionary Association in 1865, complained to his superiors that he could not "worship intelligently with the colored people [meaning black freedmen]" and urged the formation of a separate missionary church for himself and his teachers. The pattern of religious affiliation among Negro legislators suggests that Cardozo's prejudices were not uncommon. Of the legislators whose religious affiliations can be identified, all but one of the freeborn were Catholic, Presbyterian, or Episcopalian, while 70 percent of the former slaves were either Methodist or Baptist.

It appears that these differences in social background and status produced differing perspectives on public policy. During the 1868 Constitutional Convention, for example, black ex-slave delegates voted with other Negro delegates an average of 72 percent of the time, while freeborn mulatto delegates averaged 67.9 percent. The differences in voting behavior were more dramatic when sensitive issues of land reform and confiscation were debated. Robert C. De Large's resolution to halt the disfranchisement of ex-Confederates and the confiscation of their property was one early test of radical and conservative tendencies in the convention. Although De Large's motion was opposed by a majority of the Negro delegates, it drew its heaviest support from mulatto delegates who had been free before the war, about 40 percent of whom supported the resolution, and its heaviest opposition from those blacks who had been slaves, about 75 percent of whom opposed it. Debates on whether to impose literacy and poll-tax requirements for voting reveal similar divisions. Delegates from the antebellum free class argued strenuously, though unsuccessfully, that illiterates and persons failing to pay a poll tax should not be allowed to vote. . . .

A closer examination of two issues, education and labor legislation, suggests the political difference that social class differences made in South Carolina. The establishment of an educational system was one of the most striking successes of the Republican regime. The system did not function as well as its founders had hoped, but its creation firmly established the principle of free public education in a state that had not had such a system before the war. It also provided the infrastructure on which later systems could be based. The freedmen enthusiastically took advantage of the new opportunity, and their leaders endorsed public schooling as a major goal of the postwar period. A resolution passed at one of the early conventions declared, "Knowledge is power." Curiously, in the view of some leaders, the endorsement of education as a major objective for the new black citizens served also to set off the uneducated as degraded and unfit to participate in public life. Thus convention delegates who advocated literacy and poll-tax qualifications for suffrage, all of whom were freeborn brown men of well-to-do backgrounds, were motivated by a desire to encourage education among the masses. According to this view, uneducated adults would be encouraged to go to school to avoid disfranchisement and the poll taxes levied on registered voters would pay the costs of maintaining the school system. As we have seen, the black freedmen in the convention as well as those in Chaplain Noble's class perceived the issue differently. A literacy requirement would be political suicide for a largely illiterate black electorate, so they decided they "had better not wait for eddication."

Despite their differences, legislators were successful in passing laws establishing schools for all. But their efforts to regulate the evolving free-labor market were much less productive. Two of the scores of bills introduced on labor subjects serve to illustrate the differing perceptions among Republicans. One, introduced by James Henderson, a Negro farmer from Newberry County, on January 8, 1870, would have established labor-contract agents to directly supervise and monitor relations between planters and workers. Several days later a substitute bill was introduced by George Lee, a Negro lawyer from Charleston. Lee's bill relied on the regular court system to settle contract disputes and gave the laborer a ninety-day lien on the crop at harvest. Thus, rather than direct state intervention to resolve labor disputes, the disputants had to assume the initiative and expense of litigation themselves. Normally the planter was better situated to undertake such risks than was the worker.

Clearly, many of the legislators preferred a laissez-faire approach to regulating the labor market. John Feriter, a white native Republican, declared that the "law of supply and demand must regulate the matter"; and Reuben Tomlinson, a white northern Republican and former abolitionist, insisted, "I don't believe it is in the power of the General Assembly to do anything except to give them [farmworkers] equal rights before the law." Apparently a majority of both white and black legislators agreed with Feriter and Tomlinson; they voted for Lee's bill, which approached this laissez-faire ideal, and against Henderson's bill, which advocated state regulation. However, the minority voting for Henderson's bill included 48 percent of the ex-slaves as compared with only 11 percent of the freeborn, and 35 percent of the blacks in contrast with only 18 percent of the mulattoes. It would appear then that those whose origins were closer to the masses of the electorate saw labor problems differently than their colleagues from more privileged backgrounds.

The 1876 legislative session was the last opportunity Republicans had to ensure economic justice for their constituents. Elected by a very close margin in 1874, Governor Daniel Chamberlain moved openly to build a political coalition of conservative Republicans and Democrats. His "reform" policies won general approval among Democrats. Chamberlain sought to cut government spending by reducing social services and education programs. He removed Republicans from important local offices and replaced them with Democrats. These policies won Democratic support but alienated and demoralized Republicans. J. W. Rice's despondent letter to Chamberlain protesting the appointment of several Democrats to Laurens County offices formerly held by Republicans was typical of the governor's correspondence during this period: "I am at last discouraged and thinking about resigning." Generally, the party morale declined and dissension increased. During the spring of 1876, Democrats watched gleefully as Republican conventions often tottered on the brink of physical violence. As A. P. Aldrich told a cheering audience, the Democrats planned "to keep Chamberlain and some of the carpetbaggers fighting, till they eat each other up all but the tails, and that he would keep the tails jumping at each other, until Southern raised gentlemen slide into office and take the reins of government."

Aldrich proved a true prophet. Both Wade Hampton, the Democratic gubernatorial candidate, and Daniel Chamberlain, the Republican, claimed victory after the November election that year, but only the Democrats possessed the unity and strength to enforce their claim. For five months there were two governments in South Carolina competing for control of the state and recognition by federal authorities. Although Republicans controlled the state house and the machinery of government, years of intraparty strife and rivalry had finally taken their toll. Unfavorable decisions by Republican-elected judges and defections and resignations of Republican officeholders weakened Chamberlain's authority, while Hampton grew more formidable as the crisis stretched from weeks into months. Hampton's unofficial militia of red-shirted gunmen imposed bloody curfews on blacks in much of the countryside, while Chamberlain's militia was disarmed and ineffective. Hampton collected $100,000 in state taxes, while Chamberlain was unable to command the allegiance of taxpayers or tax collectors. By March newly elected Republican President Rutherford B. Hayes had decided already to concede the disputed elections in the

South in exchange for the presidency, but it is doubtful that he could have decided otherwise in South Carolina even had he wanted to. By that time only a massive show of federal force could have saved the Republican regime; probably, such action was not politically feasible in 1877, nor is it clear that it could have been more than a temporary expedient.

The failure of South Carolina's Reconstruction then was not caused by a weak and ignorant electorate. Despite the economic threats and physical terrors of the 1876 campaign, black freedmen turned out in force and delivered a record vote to Republican candidates. True, there was "political paralysis," an absence of "stern collective discipline," and a failure of will; but these were shortcomings of the Republican leadership, not of the masses of black voters. Divisions among the leaders—between white and black and among Negroes themselves—diminished the power these voters had entrusted to them and betrayed the aspirations they had clearly articulated. The freedmen made an amazing transformation after the Civil War; slaves became political men acting forcefully to crush the most cherished illusions of their former masters. The tragedy of Reconstruction is that they received so much less than they gave.

The Odds Against the Success of Reconstruction Were Great

ERIC FONER

At first glance, the man who succeeded Abraham Lincoln seemed remarkably similar to his martyred predecessor. Both knew poverty in early life, neither enjoyed much formal schooling, and in both deprivation sparked a powerful desire for fame and worldly success. During the prewar decades, both achieved material comfort, Lincoln as an Illinois corporation lawyer, Andrew Johnson rising from tailor's apprentice to become a prosperous landowner. And for both, antebellum politics became a path to power and respect.

In terms of sheer political experience, few men have seemed more qualified for the Presidency than Andrew Johnson. Beginning as a Greenville, Tennessee, alderman in 1829, he rose to the state legislature and then to Congress. He served two terms as governor, and in 1857 entered the Senate. Even more than Lincoln, Johnson gloried in the role of tribune of the common man. His speeches lauded "honest yeomen" and thundered against the "slaveocracy"—a "pampered, bloated, corrupted aristocracy." The issues most closely identified with Johnson's prewar career were tax-supported public education, a reform enacted into law during his term as governor, and homestead legislation, which he promoted tirelessly in the Senate. . . .

In the weeks following Lincoln's assassination, leading Radicals met frequently with the new President to press the issue of black suffrage. Yet Johnson shared neither the Radicals' expansive conception of federal power nor their commitment to political equality for blacks. Despite his own vigorous exercise of authority as

Eric Foner, *A Short History of Reconstruction, 1863–1877* (New York: Harper & Row, 1990), pp. 82–83, 85, 89, 91–94, 101, 103, 114–116, 119–123, 184–185, 233–237, 240–242, 245. Copyright © Eric Foner. Reprinted by permission of HarperCollins Publishers, Inc.

military governor, Johnson had always believed in limited government and a strict construction of the Constitution. In Congress, he even opposed appropriations to pave Washington's muddy streets. His fervent nationalism in no way contradicted his respect for the rights of the states. Individual "traitors" should be punished, but the states had never, legally, seceded, or surrendered their right to govern their own affairs. . . .

The definitive announcement of Johnson's plan of Reconstruction came in two proclamations issued on May 29, 1865. The first conferred amnesty and pardon, including restoration of all property rights except for slaves, upon former Confederates who pledged loyalty to the Union and support for emancipation. Fourteen classes of Southerners, however, most notably major Confederate officials and owners of taxable property valued at more than $20,000, were required to apply individually for Presidential pardons. Simultaneously, Johnson appointed William W. Holden provisional governor of North Carolina, instructing him to call a convention to amend the state's prewar constitution so as to create a "republican form of government." Persons who had not been pardoned under the terms of the first proclamation were excluded from voting for delegates, but otherwise, voter qualifications in effect immediately before secession (when the franchise, of course, was limited to whites) would apply. Similar proclamations for other Southern states soon followed. . . .

Johnson's pardon policy reinforced his emerging image as the white South's champion. Despite talk of punishing traitors, the President proved amazingly lenient. No mass arrests followed the collapse of the Confederacy. Jefferson Davis spent two years in federal prison but was never put on trial; his Vice President, Alexander H. Stephens, served a brief imprisonment, returned to Congress in 1873, and ended his days as governor of Georgia. Some 15,000 Southerners, a majority barred from the general amnesty because of their wealth, filed applications for individual pardons. Soon they were being issued wholesale, sometimes hundreds in a single day. By 1866, over 7,000 had been granted. . . .

With Johnson's requirements fulfilled, the South in the fall of 1865 proceeded to elect legislators, governors, and members of Congress. In a majority of the states, former Whigs who had opposed secession swept to victory. . . . The vast majority of the new Senators and Congressmen had opposed secession, yet nearly all had followed their states into the rebellion. Active Unionists were resoundingly defeated. Probably the most closely watched contest occurred in North Carolina, where Jonathan Worth, a Unionist Whig and Confederate state treasurer, defeated Governor Holden. Once in office, Worth quickly restored the old elite, whose power Holden had to some extent challenged, to control of local affairs. The result confirmed the power of wartime political leadership in a state with a large population of non-slaveholding yeomen.

All in all, the 1865 elections threw into question the future of Presidential Reconstruction. Johnson himself sensed that something had gone awry: "There seems, in many of the elections," he wrote at the end of November, "something like defiance, which is all out of place at this time." The stark truth was that outside the Unionist mountains, Johnson's policies had failed to create a new political leadership to replace the prewar slaveocracy. If the architects of secession had been repudiated, the South's affairs would still be directed by men who, while Unionist in 1860, formed part of the antebellum political establishment. Their actions would do much to determine the fate of Johnson's Reconstruction experiment. . . .

As the new legislatures prepared to convene, the Southern press and the private correspondence of planters resounded with calls for what a New Orleans newspaper called "a new labor system . . . prescribed and enforced by the State." The initial response to these demands was embodied in the Black Codes, a series of state laws crucial to the undoing of Presidential Reconstruction. Intended to define the freedmen's new rights and responsibilities, the codes authorized blacks to acquire and own property, marry, make contracts, sue and be sued, and testify in court in cases involving persons of their own color. But these provisions were secondary to the attempt to stabilize the black work force and limit its economic options. Henceforth, the state would enforce labor agreements and plantation discipline, punish those who refused to contract, and prevent whites from competing for black workers.

Mississippi and South Carolina enacted the first and most severe Black Codes toward the end of 1865. Mississippi required all blacks to possess, each January, written evidence of employment for the coming year. Laborers leaving their jobs before the contract expired would forfeit wages already earned, and, as under slavery, be subject to arrest by any white citizen. A person offering work to a laborer under contract risked imprisonment or a fine of $500. To limit the freedmen's economic opportunities, they were forbidden to rent land in urban areas. Vagrancy—a crime whose definition included the idle, disorderly, and those who "misspend what they earn"—could be punished by fines or involuntary plantation labor; other criminal offenses included "insulting" gestures or language, "malicious mischief," and preaching the Gospel without a license. South Carolina's Code required blacks to pay an annual tax from $10 to $100 if they wished to follow any occupation other than farmer or servant (a severe blow to the free black community of Charleston and to former slave artisans). . . .

Although blacks protested all these measures, their most bitter complaints centered on apprenticeship laws that obliged black minors to work without pay for planters. These laws allowed judges to bind to white employers black orphans and those whose parents were deemed unable to support them. The former owner usually had preference, and the consent of the parents was not required. Blacks pleaded with the Freedmen's Bureau for help in releasing their own children or those of deceased relatives. "I think very hard of the former oners," declared one freedman, "for Trying to keep My blood when I kno that Slavery is dead." As late as the end of 1867, Bureau agents and local justices of the peace were still releasing black children from court-ordered apprenticeships. . . .

Throughout these months [summer and fall of 1865] letters passed back and forth among leading Radicals, lamenting Johnson's policies and promising to organize against them. But an unmistakable note of gloom pervaded this correspondence. "I hope you will do all that can be done for the protection of the poor negroes," Sen. Henry Wilson wrote Freedmen's Bureau Commissioner Howard, since "this nation seems about to abandon them to their disloyal masters." . . .

When the Thirty-Ninth Congress convened early in December, Johnson's position remained impressive. The President sincerely claimed to have created a new political order in the South, controlled by men loyal to the Union. He simply could

Abandonment, betrayal, neglect of the NEGRO

not believe, one suspects, that Northern Republicans would jettison his program over so quixotic an issue as the freedmen's rights. The door stood open for Johnson to embrace the emerging Republican consensus that the freedmen were entitled to civil equality short of the suffrage and that wartime Unionists deserved a more prominent role in Southern politics.

Those close to Johnson, however, knew he was not prone to compromise. Indeed, they relished the prospect of a political battle over Reconstruction. "A fight between the Radicals and the Executive is inevitable," declared Harvey Watterson. "Let it come. The sooner the better for the whole country." . . .

As the split with the President deepened, Republicans grappled with the task of embedding in the Constitution, beyond the reach of Presidential vetoes and shifting political majorities, the results of the Civil War. At one point in January, no fewer than seventy constitutional amendments had been introduced. Not until June, after seemingly endless debate and maneuvering, did the Fourteenth Amendment, the most important ever added to the Constitution, receive the approval of Congress. Its first clause prohibited the states from abridging equality before the law. The second provided for a reduction in a state's representation proportional to the number of male citizens denied suffrage. This aimed to prevent the South from benefiting politically from emancipation. Before the war, three-fifths of the slaves had been included in calculating Congressional representations; now, as free persons, all would be counted. Since Republicans were not prepared to force black suffrage upon the South, they offered white Southerners a choice—enfranchise the freedmen or sacrifice representation in Congress. The third clause barred from national and state office men who had sworn allegiance to the Constitution and subsequently aided the Confederacy. While not depriving "rebels" of the vote, this excluded from office most of the South's prewar political leadership, opening the door to power, Republicans hoped, for true Unionists. The Amendment also prohibited payment of the Confederate debt and empowered Congress to enforce its provisions through "appropriate" legislation.

Because it implicitly acknowledged the right of states to limit voting because of race, Wendell Phillips denounced the amendment as a "fatal and total surrender." Susan B. Anthony, Elizabeth Cady Stanton, and others in the women's suffrage movement also felt betrayed, because the second clause introduced the word "male" into the Constitution. Alone among suffrage limitations, those founded on sex would not reduce a state's representation.

Ideologically and politically, nineteenth-century feminism had been tied to abolition. Feminists now turned Radical ideology back upon Congress. If "special claims for special classes" were illegitimate and unrepublican, how could the denial of women's rights be justified? Should not sex, like race, be rejected as an unacceptable basis for legal distinctions among citizens? Rather than defining Reconstruction as "the negro's hour," they called it, instead, the hour for change: Another generation might pass "ere the constitutional door will again be opened." The dispute over the Fourteenth Amendment marked a turning point in nineteenth-century reform. Leaving feminist leaders with a deep sense of betrayal, it convinced them, as Stanton put it, that woman "must not put her trust in man" in seeking her rights. Women's leaders now embarked on a course that severed their historic alliance with abolitionism and created a truly independent feminist movement.)

The Fourteenth Amendment, one Republican newspaper observed, repudiated the two axioms on which the Radicals "started to make their fight last December: dead States and equal suffrage." Yet it clothed with constitutional authority the principle Radicals had fought to vindicate: equality before the law, overseen by the national government. For its heart was the first section, which declared all persons born or naturalized in the United States both national and state citizens and prohibited the states from abridging their "privileges and immunities," depriving any person of life, liberty, or property without "due process of law," or denying them "equal protection of the laws."

For more than a century, politicians, judges, lawyers, and scholars have debated the meaning of this elusive language. But the aims of the Fourteenth Amendment can be understood only within the political and ideological context of 1866: the break with the President, the need to find a measure able to unify all Republicans, and the growing party consensus in favor of strong federal action to protect the freedmen's rights, short of the suffrage. During many drafts, changes, and deletions, the Amendment's central principle remained constant: a national guarantee of equality before the law. This was "so just," a moderate Congressman declared, "that no member of this House can seriously object to it." In language that transcended race and region, the Amendment challenged legal discrimination throughout the nation and changed and broadened the meaning of freedom for all Americans. . . .

The Republicans who gathered in December 1866 for the second session of the Thirty-Ninth Congress considered themselves "masters of the situation." Johnson's annual message, pleading for the immediate restoration of the "now unrepresented States," was ignored. The President, declared the New York *Herald,* his erstwhile supporter, "forgets that we have passed through the fiery ordeal of a mighty revolution, and that the pre-existing order of things is gone and can return no more—that a great work of reconstruction is before us, and that we cannot escape it."

Black suffrage, it soon became clear, was on the horizon. In mid-December, Trumbull told the Senate that Congress possessed the authority to "enter these States and hurl from power the disloyal element which controls and governs them," an important announcement that moderates intended to overturn the Johnson governments. In January 1867, a bill enfranchising blacks in the District of Columbia became law over the President's veto. Then, Congress extended manhood suffrage to the territories. Even more radical proposals were in the air, including widespread disenfranchisement, martial law for the South, confiscation, the impeachment of the President. A *Herald* editorial writer apologized to Johnson for the paper's advocacy of his removal: Its editor always went with the political tide, and the tide now flowed toward the Radicals. . . .

Throughout these deliberations, Johnson remained silent. Toward the end of February, New York *Evening Post* editor Charles Nordhoff visited the White House. He found the President "much excited," certain "the people of the South . . . were to be trodden under foot 'to protect niggers.'" Nordhoff had once admired the President; now he judged him a "pig-headed man" governed by one idea: "bitter opposition to universal suffrage." Gone was the vision of a reconstructed South controlled by loyal yeomen. "The old Southern leaders . . . ," declared the man who had once railed against the Slave Power, "must rule the South." When the Reconstruction bill reached his desk on March 2, Johnson returned it with a veto, which Congress promptly overrode. Maryland Sen. Reverdy Johnson was the only member to break party ranks. Whatever its flaws, he declared, the bill offered the South a path back into the Union, and the President should abandon his intransigence and accede to the plainly expressed will of the people. Reverdy Johnson's was the only Democratic vote in favor of any of the Reconstruction measures of 1866–67.

In its final form, the Reconstruction Act of 1867 divided the Confederate states, except Tennessee, into five military districts under commanders empowered to employ the army to protect life and property. And without immediately replacing the Johnson regimes, it laid out the steps by which new state governments could be created and recognized by Congress—the writing of new constitutions providing for manhood suffrage, their approval by a majority of registered voters, and ratification of the Fourteenth Amendment. Simultaneously, Congress passed the Habeas Corpus Act, which greatly expanded citizens' ability to remove cases to federal courts.

Like all the decisions of the Thirty-Ninth Congress, the Reconstruction Act contained a somewhat incongruous mixture of idealism and political expediency. The bill established military rule, but only as a temporary measure to keep the peace, with the states assured a relatively quick return to the Union. It looked to a new political order for the South, but failed to place Southern Unionists in immediate control. It made no economic provision for the freedmen. Even black suffrage derived from a variety of motives and calculations. For Radicals, it represented the culmination of a lifetime of reform. For others, it seemed less the fulfillment of an idealistic creed than an alternative to prolonged federal intervention in the South, a means of enabling blacks to defend themselves against abuse, while relieving the nation of that responsibility.

Despite all its limitations, Congressional Reconstruction was indeed a radical departure, a stunning and unprecedented experiment in interracial democracy. In America, the ballot not only identified who could vote, it defined a collective national identity. Democrats had fought black suffrage on precisely these grounds. "Without reference to the question of equality," declared Indiana Sen. Thomas Hendricks, "I say we are not of the same race; we are so different that we ought not to compose one political community." Enfranchising blacks marked a powerful repudiation of such thinking. In some ways it was an astonishing leap of faith. Were the mass of freedmen truly prepared for political rights? Gen. E. O. C. Ord, federal commander in Arkansas, believed them "so servile and accustomed to submit" to white dictation that they would "not dare to present themselves at the polls." Even some Radicals harbored inner doubts, fearing that "demagogues" or their former masters would control the black vote, or that political rights would prove meaningless without economic independence.

In the course of Reconstruction, the freedmen disproved these somber forecasts. They demonstrated political shrewdness and independence in using the ballot to affect the conditions of their freedom. However inadequate as a response to the legacy of slavery, it remains a tragedy that the lofty goals of civil and political equality were not permanently achieved. And the end of Reconstruction came not because propertyless blacks succumbed to economic coercion, but because a tenacious black community, abandoned by the nation, fell victim to violence and fraud.

"We have cut loose from the whole dead past," wrote Wisconsin Sen. Timothy Howe, "and have cast our anchor out a hundred years." His colleague, Waitman T. Willey of West Virginia, adopted a more cautious tone: "The legislation of the last two years will mark a great page of history for good or evil—I hope the former. The crisis, however, is not yet past." . . .

Violence had been endemic in large parts of the South since 1865. But the advent of Radical Reconstruction stimulated its expansion. By 1870 the Ku Klux Klan and kindred organizations like the Knights of the White Camelia and the White Brotherhood were deeply entrenched in nearly every Southern state. The Klan, even in its heyday, did not possess a well-organized structure or clearly defined regional leadership. But the unity of purpose and common tactics of these local organizations make it possible to generalize about their goals and impact and the challenge they posed to the survival of Reconstruction. In effect, the Klan was a military force serving the interests of the Democratic party, the planter class, and all those who desired the restoration of white supremacy. Its purposes were political in the broadest sense, for it sought to affect power relations, both public and private, throughout Southern society. It aimed to destroy the Republican party's infrastructure, undermined the Reconstruction state, reestablish control of the black labor force, and restore racial subordination in every aspect of Southern life.

Violence was typically directed at Reconstruction's local leaders. As Emanuel Fortune, driven from Jackson County, Florida, by the Klan, explained: "The object of it is to kill out the leading men of the republican party . . . men who have taken a prominent stand." Jack Dupree, victim of a particularly brutal murder in Monroe County, Mississippi—assailants cut his throat and disemboweled him, all within sight of his wife, who had just given birth to twins—was "president of a republican club" and known as a man who "would speak his mind." Countless other local leaders fled their homes after brutal whippings. And many blacks suffered merely for exercising their rights as citizens. Alabama freedman George Moore reported how, in 1869, Klansmen came to his home, administered a beating, "ravished a young girl who was visiting my wife," and wounded a neighbor. "The cause of this treatment, they said, was that we voted the radical ticket." Nor did white Republicans escape the violence. Klansmen murdered three scalawag members of the Georgia legislature and drove ten others from their homes. The Klan in western North Carolina settled old scores with wartime Unionists, burned the offices of the Rutherford *Star,* and brutally whipped Aaron Biggerstaff, a Hero of America and Republican organizer. . . .

The issues of white supremacy, low taxes, and control of the black labor force dominated the Democratic campaigns of the mid-1870s. And their appeal became evident in 1873 and 1874 as Democrats solidified their hold on states already under their control and "redeemed" new ones. Texas Democrat Richard Coke defeated Gov. Edmund J. Davis in 1873 by a margin of better than two to one. Meanwhile, Virginia Democrats jettisoned the moderate Republicans with whom they had cooperated in 1869 and carried the state with a "straight-out" ticket and a platform of "race against race." The 1874 Southern elections proved as disastrous for Republicans as those in the North. Democrats won over two-thirds of the region's House seats, redeemed Arkansas, and gained control of Florida's legislature.

In these campaigns, which mostly took place in states where blacks comprised a minority of the population, Democratic victories depended mainly on the party's success at drawing the political color line. In Louisiana and Alabama, however, the brutality of white-line politics came to the fore. Louisiana's White League, organized in 1874, was openly dedicated to the violent restoration of white supremacy. It targeted local Republican officeholders for assassination, disrupted court sessions, and drove black laborers from their homes. In Red River Parish, the campaign degenerated into a violent reign of terror, which culminated in August in the cold-blooded murder of six Republican officials. In September 1874 3,500 leaguers, mostly Civil War veterans, overwhelmed an equal number of black militiamen and Metropolitan Police under the command of Confederate Gen. James Longstreet and occupied the city hall, statehouse, and arsenal. They withdrew only upon the arrival of federal troops, ordered to the scene by the President. A similar campaign of violence helped "redeem" Alabama for the Democrats in the elections of 1874.

The Crisis of 1875

By the time the Forty-Third Congress reassembled in December, the political landscape had been transformed. As a result of the Democratic landslide, this session would be the last time for over a decade that Republicans controlled both the White House and Congress. With political violence erupting in many parts of the South, and their party's hegemony in Washington about to expire, Benjamin Butler and other Stalwarts devised a program to safeguard what remained of Reconstruction. Their proposals included the Civil Rights Bill, a new Enforcement Act expanding the President's power to suppress conspiracies aimed at intimidating voters, a two-year army appropriation (to prevent the incoming Democratic House from limiting the military's role in the South), a bill expanding the jurisdiction of the federal courts, and a subsidy for the Texas & Pacific Railroad. The package embodied the idealism, partisanship, and crass economic advantage typical of Republican politics. Civil rights was the program's spearhead, and to make it more palatable, Butler dropped the bill's controversial clause requiring integrated schools.

Events in Louisiana disrupted the already tenuous party unity necessary to enact such a program. Having suppressed the New Orleans insurrection of September 1874, Grant, newly determined to "protect the colored voter in his rights," ordered Gen. Philip H. Sheridan to use federal troops to counteract violence and sustain the administration of Gov. William P. Kellogg. On January 4, 1875, when Democrats attempted to seize control of the state assembly by forcibly installing party members in five disputed seats, a detachment of troops entered the legislative chambers and escorted out the five claimants.

If, for Reconstruction's critics, South Carolina epitomized the evils of corruption and "black rule," Louisiana now came to represent the danger posed by excessive federal interference in local affairs. The spectacle of soldiers "marching into the Hall . . . and expelling members at the point of the bayonet" aroused more Northern opposition than any previous federal action in the South. In Boston a large body of "highly respectable citizens" gathered at Faneuil Hall to demand Sheridan's removal and compare the White League with the founding fathers as defenders of republican freedom. Wendell Phillips was among those present. Four decades earlier, Phillips had launched his abolitionist career in this very hall, when he reprimanded a speaker who praised the murderers of antislavery editor Elijah P. Lovejoy. Then, his eloquence converted the audience. Now, as he rebuked those who would "take from the President . . . the power to protect the millions" the nation had liberated from bondage, he heard only hisses, laughter, and cries of "played out, sit down." "Wendell Phillips and William Lloyd Garrison," commented the *New York Times,* "are not exactly extinct from American politics, but they represent ideas in regard to the South which the majority of the Republican party have outgrown." The uproar over Louisiana made Republicans extremely wary of further military intervention in the South. . . .

The full implications of the "let alone policy" became clear in the 1875 political campaign in Mississippi. White Mississippians interpreted the 1874 elections as a national repudiation of Reconstruction. Although the Democratic state convention adopted a platform recognizing the civil and political rights of blacks, the campaign quickly became a violent crusade to destroy the Republican organization and prevent blacks from voting. Democratic rifle clubs paraded through the black belt, disrupting Republican meetings and assaulting local party leaders. Unlike crimes by the Ku Klux Klan's hooded riders, those of 1875 were committed in broad daylight by undisguised men, as if to underscore the impotence of local authorities and Democrats' lack of concern about federal intervention. . . .

Appeals for protection poured into the offices of Governor Ames. "They are going around the streets at night dressed in soldiers clothes and making colored people run for their lives . . . ," declared a petition by black residents of Vicksburg. "We are intimidated by the whites. . . . We will not vote at all, unless there are troops to protect us." Convinced "the power of the U.S. alone can give the security our citizens are entitled to," Ames early in September requested Grant to send troops to the state. From his summer home on the New Jersey shore, the President dispatched instructions to Attorney General Edwards Pierrepont. One widely quoted sentence came to epitomize the North's retreat from Reconstruction: "The whole public are tired out with these annual autumnal outbreaks in the South . . . [and] are ready now to condemn any interference on the part of the Government." Pierrepont sent an aide to the state, who in October arranged a "peace agreement" whereby the only two active militia companies were disbanded and whites promised to disarm. But Democrats, as black state senator Charles Caldwell reported, held the agreement "in utter contempt." On election eve, armed riders drove freedmen from their homes and threatened to kill them if they tried to vote. The next day, Democrats destroyed the ballot boxes or replaced Republican votes with their own. "The reports which come to me almost hourly are truly sickening . . . ," Ames reported to his wife. "The government of the U.S. does not interfere." The result was a Democratic landslide. Nor did this conclude Mississippi's "Redemption." In plantation counties where Republicans still held local positions, violence continued after the election, with officials forced to resign under threat of assassination and vigilante groups meting out punishment to blacks accused of theft and other violations of plantation discipline. On Christmas Day, Charles Caldwell, "as brave a man as I ever knew," according to one associate, was shot in the back in Clinton after being lured to take a drink with a white "friend." When the legislature assembled, it impeached and removed from office black Lieut. Gov. Alexander K. Davis and then compelled Gov. Ames to resign and leave the state rather than face impeachment charges himself. . . .

All in all, from the inability of the Forty-Third Congress in its waning days to agree on a policy toward the South to Grant's failure to intervene in Mississippi, 1875 marked a milestone in the retreat from Reconstruction. As another Presidential election approached, it seemed certain that whoever emerged victorious, Reconstruction itself was doomed. . . .

More than any other state, national attention in 1876 focused on South Carolina, whose political climate was transformed by an event in the tiny town of Hamburg. What came to be known as the Hamburg Massacre began with the black militia's celebration of the July 4th centennial. When the son and son-in-law of a local white farmer arrived on the scene and ordered the militiamen to move aside for their carriage, harsh words were exchanged, although militia commander Dock Adams eventually opened his company's ranks and the pair proceeded on their way. Four days later, the black militia again gathered in Hamburg, as did a large number of armed whites. After Adams refused a demand by Gen. Matthew C. Butler, the area's most prominent Democratic politician, to disarm his company, fighting broke out, about forty militiamen retreated to their armory, and Butler made for Augusta, returning with a cannon and hundreds of white reinforcements. As darkness fell, the outnumbered militiamen attempted to flee the scene. Hamburg's black marshal fell mortally wounded and twenty-five men were captured; of these, five were murdered in cold blood. After the killings, the mob ransacked the homes and shops of the town's blacks.

Among the affair's most appalling features was the conduct of Gen. Butler, who either selected the prisoners to be executed (according to black eyewitnesses) or left the scene when the crowd began "committing depredations" (his own, hardly more flattering, account). In either case, Butler's conduct underscored the utter collapse of a sense of paternalist obligation, not to mention common decency, among those who called themselves the region's "natural leaders." Certainly, no one could again claim that the South's "respectable" elite disdained such violence, for in one of its first actions, South Carolina's Redeemer legislature in 1877 elected Butler to the U.S. Senate. . . .

With so much at stake, the 1876 campaign became the most tumultuous in South Carolina's history and the one significant exception to the Reconstruction pattern that cast blacks as the victims of political violence and whites as the sole aggressors. In September, black Republicans assaulted Democrats of both races leaving a Charleston meeting; several were wounded and one white lost his life. A month later a group of blacks began firing at a "joint discussion" at Cainhoy, a village near the city, resulting in the deaths of five whites and one black.

But the campaign of intimidation launched by [Democratic candidate Gen. Wade] Hampton's supporters far overshadowed such incidents. Rifle clubs disrupted Republican rallies with "violent and abusive tirades." A reign of terror reminiscent of Ku Klux Klan days swept over Edgefield, Aiken, Barnwell, and other Piedmont counties, with freedmen driven from their homes and brutally whipped, and "leading men" murdered. The belief that they need not fear federal intervention gave Democrats a free hand. Former slave Jerry Thornton Moore, president of an Aiken County Republican club, was told by his white landlord that opponents of Reconstruction planned to carry the election "if we have to wade in blood knee-deep." "Mind what you are doing," Moore responded, "the United States is mighty strong." Replied the landlord: "but, Thornton, . . . the northern people is on our side."

South Carolina's election, a Democratic observer acknowledged, "was one of the grandest farces ever seen." Despite the campaign of intimidation, [the incumbent Republican governor Daniel H.] Chamberlain polled the largest Republican vote in the state's history. But Edgefield and Laurens County Democrats carried out instructions to vote "early and often" and prevent blacks from reaching the polls, thereby producing massive majorities that enabled their party to claim a narrow statewide victory.

Early returns on election night appeared to foretell a national Democratic victory. [New York governor Samuel J.] Tilden carried New York, New Jersey, Connecticut, and Indiana, more than enough, together with a solid South, to give him the Presidency. *New York Times* editor George F. Jones even wired Hayes announcing his defeat. But in the early hours of the morning, someone at Republican headquarters noticed that if Hayes carried South Carolina, Florida, and Louisiana, where the party controlled the voting machinery, he would have a one-vote Electoral College majority. Both Gen. Daniel E. Sickles and William E. Chandler later claimed to have made this discovery and to have sent telegrams, over the signature of the sleeping party chairman, Zachariah Chandler, urging Republican officials to hold their states for Hayes. Soon after he awakened, Chandler announced: "Hayes has 185 electoral votes and is elected." . . .

Among other things, 1877 marked a decisive retreat from the idea, born during the Civil War, of a powerful national state protecting the fundamental rights of all American citizens.

FURTHER READING

Eric Anderson and Alfred Moss, eds., *The Facts of Reconstruction* (1991).
Michael Les Benedict, *A Compromise of Principle: Congressional Republicans and Reconstruction* (1974).
Laura Edwards, *Gendered Strife and Confusion: The Political Culture of Reconstruction* (1997).
Eric Foner, *Nothing but Freedom: Emancipation and Its Legacy* (1983).
Leon Litwack, *Been in the Storm So Long: The Aftermath of Slavery* (1979).
Nell Irvin Painter, *Exodusters: Black Migration to Kansas After Reconstruction* (1977).
Michael Perman, *The Road to Redemption* (1984).
Jonathan Wiener, *Social Origins of the New South* (1978).

CHAPTER
2

Western Settlement and the Frontier in American History

The nineteenth-century historian Frederick Jackson Turner described the frontier as "an area of free land" that was continually receding as American settlers moved westward. The frontier closed, he said, when settlers reached the outer limit of the western wilds, which had "constituted the richest free gift that was ever spread out before civilized man." In Turner's portrayal, the West was an empty landscape that was gradually peopled. It was also the place where a uniquely American identity was forged: individualistic but cooperative, and deeply egalitarian. Today, historians view the frontier very differently. To them, a frontier is not a line marking the start of an empty place but a zone of interaction where two or more societies vie for the use of land. A frontier "opens" when one human group intrudes upon another, and "closes" when one of them establishes dominance. The process is often a brutal one.

The Civil War spurred the opening of the Far West by removing southern resistance to settlement of the territories by "free labor." In 1862, in the midst of the war, the Republican-dominated Congress passed the Homestead Act. This legislation offered 160 acres of western public land free of charge to any citizen who was over the age of twenty-one or who headed a family, so long as he or she stayed on the land for five continuous years. Congress also funded the first transcontinental railroad in 1862, the Union Pacific. These two events placed Indians, soldiers, freed slaves, migrants from the East, and immigrants from Europe and Asia in conflict for the following four decades.

The clash between these competing peoples led to murder and massacre during the last quarter of the nineteenth century. Military spending on the Indian wars amounted to 60 percent of the federal budget in 1880. The U.S.-Indian wars reached their climax and ended with the defeat of the Sioux under Sitting Bull in 1881 and the Apaches under Geronimo in 1886, at a cost of twenty-five white soldiers for every Indian warrior killed. But the frontier still remained open. "Whites" battled the Chinese, non-Mormons attacked Mormons, and European immigrants clung together to maintain their separate identities. Indian reservations and the surrounding countryside were contested territory well into the twentieth century. Not only Indians, but Norwegians, Germans, Czechs, Mexicans, Chinese, *and African Americans as well struggled to sustain their cultures and establish safe homesteads. All vied for the land "pacified" by the U.S. cavalry.*

QUESTIONS TO THINK ABOUT

"Westerns" (both movies and novels) told generations of Americans "how the West was won." Is frontier settlement best understood as a saga of English-speaking pioneers, or as the story of competing ethnic and racial groups? Was the West truly the place where Americans were most free and most "American," or was it a place riddled with inequalities?

DOCUMENTS

The following documents reveal a variety of perspectives on the western migration. Document 1 is the Homestead Act of 1862, passed by the Civil War Congress. This act effected a massive public land transfer, fulfilling the promise of "free soil, free labor." Mary Barnard Aguirre, the author of Document 2, was one of the individuals whom the "cruel war" encouraged to move west. Raised in Maryland, Aguirre married a wealthy Mexican trader at age eighteen. The document recounts her favorable impressions of the vibrant Hispanic southwest, soon to be opened to Anglo homesteaders. Some Indian tribes, in their ongoing resistance to the United States, elected to join the Confederacy. Document 3 shows how the United States used their "disloyalty" to consolidate control over the Indian nations after the war. Documents 4 and 5 give Indian perspectives on the United States's wars of conquest. In Document 4, Katie Bighead, a Cheyenne eyewitness to the massacre of U.S. troops under General George Armstrong Custer, notes the superiority of arrows over guns in an ambush. Chief Joseph of the Nez Percé, the tribe that had come to the aid of the Lewis and Clark expedition seventy years earlier and that had welcomed teachers and missionaries, evokes the tragedy of American expansionism in his famous surrender speech of 1877, Document 5. Ten years later, the Dawes Act (Document 6) attempted to force Indians to hold land individually, rather than collectively, by dividing reservations with good, arable soil into homesteads of 160 acres. This act dispossessed many Indian nations of much of their remaining land and turned it over to homesteaders. Document 7 shows that the frontier attracted immigrants from all over the world, prompting ongoing clashes between people of different cultures. Miners in Wyoming responded violently in 1885 to the perceived threat of Chinese laborers, who were struggling to make new lives on the frontier. Document 8 shows that the struggle for land was not just between Indians and whites. African Americans also sought a piece of earth they could call their own, where they could live separately and without fear. In May 1879, a convention of 189 representatives from 19 states met in Nashville, Tennessee, to organize the "colored" western migration movement. Document 9 shows the efforts of Danish immigrants to form an ethnic enclave of their own within the diversity of the frontier. Finally, historian Frederick Jackson Turner helped to create for the American public the image of the romantic West, where (white) men were strong, women virtuous, and democracy triumphant. In his 1893 statement (Document 10), Turner described the effects of the frontier both on democracy and on the American personality. He also pronounced the frontier "closed."

1. The Homestead Act Provides
Free Land to Settlers, 1862

May 20, 1862.

Be it enacted by the Senate and House of Representatives of the United States of America in Congress assembled, That any person who is the head of a family, or who has arrived at the age of twenty-one years, and is a citizen of the United States, or who shall have filed his declaration of intention to become such, as required by the naturalization laws of the United States, and who has never borne arms against the United States Government or given aid and comfort to its enemies, shall, from and after the first January, eighteen hundred and sixty-three, be entitled to enter one quarter section or a less quantity of unappropriated public lands . . . which shall not, with the land so already owned and occupied, exceed in the aggregate one hundred and sixty acres.

SEC. 2. *And be it further enacted,* That the person applying for the benefit of this act shall, upon application to the register of the land office in which he or she is about to make such entry, make affidavit . . . that said entry is made for the purpose of actual settlement and cultivation, and not either directly or indirectly for the use of benefit of any other person or persons whomsoever; and upon filing the said affidavit with the register or receiver, and on payment of ten dollars, he or she shall thereupon be permitted to enter the quantity of land specified.

2. Pioneer Mary Barnard Aguirre
Marries into the Spanish West, 1863

In September '63 we made preparations for another trip—this time it was to be to unknown lands "across the plains" & by the 19th all was ready & we started from Westport in ambulances—quite a party of us. There was my father & oldest sister, my husband, myself, Pedro (then not quite three months old) & a nursegirl 13 years old, named Angeline. . . . I was like a child with no more knowledge of the responsibilities of life or the care of a baby & only glad to leave that cruel war & the horrors behind me. . . .

. . . That first winter was delightful to us all. The weather was so warm & the constant sunshine so lovely that we States-people enjoyed it to the fullest extent—staying out of doors the most of the time. . . . On New Years day (1864) my husband & myself were invited to be "Padrinos"—(godparents) for the New Years high Mass, which we attended sitting in chairs in front of the altar with highly decorated wax candles in our hands. These were lit & my whole attention was devoted to keeping that candle straight—for I was so interested with the newness of every thing that I'd forget the candle for a moment & it would bob over to the imminent danger of my hat. This was a special attention we were shown because my husband was much beloved in the town.

The Statutes at Large, Treaties, and Proclamations of the United States 1859–1863, vol. 12 (Boston: Little, Brown, 1865), 392.

Mary Barnard Aguirre, " Autobiography," Aguirre Collection, Arizona State Historical Society Library, pp. 7–17 of typed copy.

Next came Pedro's christening which was a grand affair. He being the first grandson in the family an especial celebration was made. For three days before there was a baker & two assistants in the house. They baked no end of cakes & confectionary, roasted fowls & pigs & were highly entertaining to me, on account of the way they made & baked things. Everything was baked in one of those bee hive shaped adobe ovens, that opened into the kitchen. It was heated red hot & then all the coals scraped out & things put in on flat pieces of tin & shallow pans. The number of eggs that were used was a marvel & in fact it was all a wonder to me. There were two hundred guests. People from far & near were invited, some coming from El Paso—60 miles away. . . .

There was something new to see all the time. The annual feasts came on in due time. Each town has its patron saint whose day was celebrated by high mass & then a week of games & bull fights & dancing in the open air by the populace. There were three towns near together—Dona Ana, Las Cruces & La Mesilla & their feasts came in Jan, Feb & March & we attended all of them. At the Mesilla feast which was in March there were much more elaborate preparations made. I was again invited to be the "Madrina" . . . & was dressed in a way that would be astonishing now adays, for part of my attire was an elaborate satin cloak, made in the City of Mexico & embroidered a half a yard wide on three capes, reaching to my feet. I had to go also to the vespers & the evening was cool. It was brown satin & the embroidery white. So you can fancy my astonishing appearance as we sailed up that church, climbing over the kneeling crowds—for there were no seats & all sat on the floor—till we reached the chairs set for us before the altar. Some one remarked that I must be the Virgin Mary.

The next afternoon we all attended a bull fight. The ring was in the church plaza, built of logs tied together with raw hide. Above one side were the private boxes "Palcos" they were called—which were made of boards loosely put together & covered with canvas. These were reached by ladders of the rudest description & the widest apart rungs one could imagine. It was terrible climbing for short folks like me. When we ladies started up that ladder (me in that wonderful cloak) two men held blankets over us as we went up. When we arrived at the top the boards of the floor were so wide apart that we came near stepping thro'. But we all enjoyed the bull fight immensely tho' there were no bulls killed & no blood shed. . . . I lived in Las Cruces seven months & then went to Las Vegas to be with my husband who had what was then called the Interior freight contract from the government to supply all the military posts of the territory with provisions & freight. The shipping point was Ft Union—& Las Vegas was the nearest point. There I lived very happily.

3. The Federal Government Punishes Confederate Indians, 1865

. . . The council assembled at Fort Smith, September 8, and delegates were present in the course of the sittings (though not all in attendance at first) representing the Creeks, Choctaws, Chickasaws, Cherokees, Seminoles, Osages, Senecas, Shawnees,

---

Annual Report of the Commissioner of Indian Affairs, 1865.

Quapaws, Wyandotts, Wichitas, and Comanches. Immediately upon the opening of the proceedings, the tribes were informed generally of the object for which the commission had come to them; that they for the most part, as tribes, had, by violating their treaties—by making treaties with the so-called Confederate States, forfeited all *rights* under them, and must be considered as at the mercy of the government; but that there was every disposition to treat them leniently, and above all a determination to recognize in a signal manner the loyalty of those who had fought upon the side of the government, and endured great sufferings on its behalf. On the next day the delegates were informed that the commissioners were empowered to enter into treaties with the several tribes, upon the basis of the following propositions:

1st. That each tribe must enter into a treaty for permanent peace and amity among themselves, each other as tribes, and with the United States.

2d. The tribes settled in the "Indian country" to bind themselves, at the call of the United States authorities, to assist in compelling the wild tribes of the plains to keep the peace.

3d. Slavery to be abolished, and measures to be taken to incorporate the slaves into the tribes, with their rights guaranteed.

4th. A general stipulation as to final abolition of slavery.

5th. A part of the Indian country to be set apart, to be purchased for the use of such Indians, from Kansas or elsewhere, as the government may desire to colonize therein.

6th. That the policy of the government to unite all the Indian tribes of this region into one consolidated government should be accepted.

7th. That no white persons, except government employees, or officers of employees of internal improvement companies authorized by government, will be permitted to reside in the country, unless incorporated with the several nations.

Printed copies of the address of the commissioners involving the above propositions were placed in the hands of the agents, and of members of the tribes, many of whom were educated men.

On the third day the delegates from the loyal Chickasaws, Choctaws, Senecas, Osages, and Cherokees, principally occupied the time with replies to the address and propositions of the commissioners, the object being partly to express a willingness to accept those propositions, with some modifications, if they had been clothed with sufficient power by their people, but chiefly in explanation of the manner in which their nations became involved with the late confederacy. The address of the Cherokees was especially noteworthy, inasmuch as they attempted to charge the causes of their secession upon the United States, as having violated its treaty obligations, in failing to give the tribe protection, so that it was *compelled* to enter into relations with the confederacy. The next day the loyal Seminoles expressed their willingness to accede to the policy of the government, and to make peace with those of their people who had aided the rebellion. The president of the commission then read a reply to the address of the loyal Cherokees above referred to, showing, from original and official documents, that, *as a tribe,* by the action of their constituted authorities, John Ross being then, as at the time of the council, their head, they had, at the very opening of the rebellion, entered into alliance with it, and raised troops for it, and urged the other tribes to go with them, and that they could not now, under the facts proven, deny their original participation in the rebellion. . . .

The loyal Creeks on this day presented their address of explanation, setting forth the manner in which their nation, by the unauthorized action of its chief, entered into treaty relations with the confederacy, and the terrible sufferings which the loyal Creeks endured in battle and on the march to Kansas seeking protection from the United States, and asking "to be considered not guilty."

4. Katie Bighead (Cheyenne) Remembers Custer and the Battle of Little Big Horn, 1876

I was with the Southern Cheyennes during most of my childhood and young womanhood. I was in the camp beside the Washita river, in the country the white people call Oklahoma, when Custer and his soldiers came there and fought the Indians (November, 1868). Our Chief Black Kettle and other Cheyennes, many of them women and children, were killed that day. It was early in the morning when the soldiers began the shooting. There had been a big storm, and there was snow on the ground. All of us jumped from our beds, and all of us started running to get away. I was barefooted, as were almost all of the others. Our tepees and all of our property we had to leave behind were burned by the white men.

The next spring Custer and his soldiers found us again (March, 1869). We then were far westward, on a branch of what the white people call Red river, I think. That time there was no fighting. Custer smoked the peace pipe with our chiefs. He promised never again to fight the Cheyennes, so all of us followed him to a soldier fort (Fort Sill). Our people gave him the name Hi-es-tzie, meaning Long Hair.

I saw Long Hair many times during those days. One time I was close to where he was mounting his horse to go somewhere, and I took a good look at him. He had a large nose, deep-set eyes, and light-red hair that was long and wavy. He was wearing a buckskin suit and a big white hat. I was then a young woman, 22 years old, and I admired him. All of the Indian women talked of him as being a fine-looking man.

My cousin, a young woman named Me-o-tzi, went often with him to help in finding the trails of Indians. She said he told her his soldier horses were given plenty of corn and oats to eat, so they could outrun and catch the Indians riding ponies that had only grass to eat. All of the Cheyennes liked her, and all were glad she had so important a place in life. After Long Hair went away, different ones of the Cheyenne young men wanted to marry her. But she would not have any of them. She said that Long Hair was her husband, that he had promised to come back to her, and that she would wait for him. She waited seven years. Then he was killed. . . .

I had seen other battles, in past times. I always liked to watch the men fighting. Not many women did that, and I often was teased on account of it. But this time [at the battle of Little Big Horn] I had a good excuse, for White Bull's son, my nephew, named Noisy Walking, had gone. I was but twenty-nine years old, so I had not any son to serve as a warrior, but I would sing strongheart songs for the nephew. He

As told to Thomas B. Marquis, reprinted in Thomas B. Marquis, *Custer on the Little Bighorn* (Algonac, Mich.: Reference Publications, 1986), 35–43.

was eighteen years old. Some women told me he had expected me to be there, and he had wrapped a red scarf about his neck in order that I might know him from a distance. . . .

The Indians were using bows and arrows more than they were using guns. Many of them had no guns, and not many who did have them had also plenty of bullets. But even if they had been well supplied with both guns and bullets, in that fight the bow was better. As the soldier ridge sloped on all sides, and as there were no trees on it nor around it, the smoke from each gun fired showed right where the shooter was hidden. The arrows made no smoke, so it could not be seen where they came from. Also, since a bullet has to go straight out from the end of a gun, any Indian who fired his gun had to put his head up so his eyes could see where to aim it. By doing this his head might be seen by a soldier and hit by a soldier bullet. The Indian could keep himself at all times out of sight when sending arrows. Each arrow was shot far upward and forward, not at any soldier in particular, but to curve down and fall where they were. Bullets would not do any harm if shot in that way. But a rain of arrows from thousands of Indian bows, and kept up for a long time, would hit many soldiers and their horses by falling and sticking into their heads or their backs. . . .

I may have seen Custer at the time of the battle or after he was killed. I do not know, as I did [not] then know of his being there. . . .

But I learned something more about him from our people in Oklahoma. Two of those Southern Cheyenne women who had been in our camp at the Little Bighorn told of having been on the battlefield soon after the fighting ended. They saw Custer lying dead there. They had known him in the South. While they were looking at him some Sioux men came and were about to cut up his body. The Cheyenne women, thinking of Me-o-tzi, made signs, "He is a relative of ours," but telling nothing more about him. So the Sioux men cut off only one joint of a finger. The women then pushed the point of a sewing awl into each of his ears, into his head. This was done to improve his hearing, as it seemed he had not heard what our chiefs in the South said when he smoked the pipe with them. They told him then that if ever afterward he should break that peace promise and should fight the Cheyennes the Everywhere Spirit surely would cause him to be killed.

Through almost sixty years, many a time I have thought of Hi-es-tzie as the handsome man I saw in the South. And I often have wondered if, when I was riding among the dead where he was lying, my pony may have kicked dirt upon his body.

5. Chief Joseph (Nez Percé) Surrenders, 1877

Tell General Howard I know what is in his heart. What he told me before, I have in my heart. I am tired of fighting. Our chiefs are killed. Looking Glass is dead. Tulhul-hutsut is dead. The old men are all dead. It is the young men who say yes or no. He who led the young men is dead. It is cold and we have no blankets. The little children are freezing to death. My people, some of them, have run away to the hills and have no blankets, no food; no one knows where they are—perhaps freezing to death. I

As quoted in Allen P. Slickpoo, *Noon-Nee-Me-Poo: We, the Nez Perce* (Lapwi, Idaho: Nez Perce Tribe, 1973), 193–194.

want to have time to look for my children and see how many of them I can find. Maybe I shall find them among the dead. Hear me, my chiefs. I am tired; my heart is sick and sad. From where the sun now stands I will fight no more, forever.

6. The Dawes Severalty Act Further Reduces Indian Landholdings, 1887

Feb. 8, 1887.

Be it enacted by the Senate and House of Representatives of the United States of America in Congress assembled, That in all cases where any tribe or band of Indians has been, or shall hereafter be, located upon any reservation created for their use, . . . the President of the United States be, and he hereby is, authorized, whenever in his opinion any reservation or any part thereof of such Indians is advantageous for agricultural and grazing purposes, to cause said reservation, or any part thereof, to be surveyed or resurveyed if necessary, and to allot the lands in said reservation in severalty to any Indian located thereon in quantities as follows:

To each head of a family, one-quarter of a section;

To each single person over eighteen years of age, one-eighth of a section;

To each orphan child under eighteen years of age, one-eighth of a section; . . .

. . . *And provided further,* That at any time after lands have been allotted to all the Indians of any tribe as herein provided, or sooner if in the opinion of the President it shall be for the best interests of said tribe, it shall be lawful for the Secretary of the Interior to negotiate with such Indian tribe for the purchase and release by said tribe, in conformity with the treaty or statute under which such reservation is held, of such portions of its reservation not allotted as such tribe shall, from time to time, consent to sell, on such terms and conditions as shall be considered just and equitable between the United States and said tribe of Indians, which purchase shall not be complete until ratified by Congress, and the form and manner of executing such release shall also be prescribed by Congress: *Provided however,* That all lands adapted to agriculture, with or without irrigation so sold or released to the United States by any Indian tribe shall be held by the United States for the sole purpose of securing homes to actual settlers and shall be disposed of by the United States to actual and bona fide settlers only in tracts not exceeding one hundred and sixty acres to any one person. . . . And the sums agreed to be paid by the United States as purchase money for any portion of any such reservation shall be held in the Treasury of the United States for the sole use of the tribe or tribes of Indians; to whom such reservations belonged; and the same, with interest thereon at three per cent per annum, shall be at all times subject to appropriation by Congress for the education and civilization of such tribe or tribes of Indians or the members thereof. . . .

SEC. 6. That upon the completion of said allotments and the patenting of the lands to said allottees, each and every member of the respective bands or tribes of Indians to whom allotments have been made shall have the benefit of and be subject

The Statutes at Large of the United States, From December 1885 to March 1887, and Recent Treaties, Postal Conventions, and Executive Proclamations, vol. 24 (Washington, D.C.: U.S. Government Printing Office, 1887), 388–390.

to the laws, both civil and criminal, of the State or Territory in which they may re-side; and no Territory shall pass or enforce any law denying any such Indian within its jurisdiction the equal protection of the law. And every Indian born within the territorial limits of the United States to whom allotments shall have been made under the provisions of this act, or under any law or treaty, and every Indian born within the territorial limits of the United States who has voluntarily taken up, within said limits, his residence separate and apart from any tribe of Indians therein, and has adopted the habits of civilized life, is hereby declared to be a citizen of the United States, and is entitled to all the rights, privileges, and immunities of such citizens.

7. Wyoming Gunfight: An Attack on Chinatown, 1885

ROCK SPRINGS, WYO., *September 18, 1885.*

HON. HUANG SIH CHUEN,
>   *Chinese Consul:*

YOUR HONOR: We, the undersigned, have been in Rock Springs, Wyoming Terri-tory, for periods ranging from one to fifteen years, for the purpose of working on the railroads and in the coal mines.

Up to the time of the recent troubles we had worked along with the white men, and had not had the least ill-feeling against them. The officers of the companies employing us treated us and the white men kindly, placing both races on the same footing and paying the same wages.

Several times we had been approached by the white men and requested to join them in asking the companies for an increase in the wages of all, both Chinese and white men. We inquired of them what we should do if the companies refused to grant an increase. They answered that if the companies would not increase our wages we should all strike, then the companies would be obliged to increase our wages. To this we dissented, wherefore we excited their animosity against us.

During the past two years there has been in existence in "Whitemen's Town," Rock Springs, an organization composed of white miners, whose object was to bring about the expulsion of all Chinese from the Territory. To them or to their object we have paid no attention. About the month of August of this year notices were posted up, all the way from Evanston to Rock Springs, demanding the expulsion of the Chinese, &c. On the evening of September 1, 1885, the bell of the building in which said organization meets rang for a meeting. It was rumored on that night that threats had been made against the Chinese. . . .

About 2 o'clock in the afternoon [of September 2] a mob, divided into two gangs, came toward "Chinatown," one gang coming by way of the plank bridge, and the other by way of the railroad bridge. The gang coming by way of the railroad bridge was the larger, and was subdivided into many squads, some of which did not cross the bridge, but remained standing on the side opposite to "Chinatown;" others that had already crossed the bridge stood on the right and left at the end of it. Several squads marched up the hill behind Coal-pit No. 3. One squad remained at Coal-shed No. 3, and another at the pump-house. The squad that remained at the pump-house

House, *Providing Indemnity to Certain Chinese Subjects,* 49th Cong., 1st Sess., 1886, 26–29.

fired the first shot, and the squad that stood at Coal-shed No. 3 immediately followed their example and fired. The Chinese by name of Lor Sun Kit was the first
person shot, and fell to the ground. At that time the Chinese began to realize that
the mob were bent on killing. . . .

Whenever the mob met a Chinese they stopped him, and pointing a weapon at
him, asked him if he had a revolver, and then approaching him they searched his
person, robbing him of his watch or any gold or silver that he might have about
him, before letting him go. Some of the rioters would let a Chinese go after depriving him of all his gold and silver, while another Chinese would be beaten with the
butt ends of the weapons before being let go. Some of the rioters, when they could
not stop a Chinese, would shoot him dead on the spot, and then search and rob him.
Some would overtake a Chinese, throw him down and search and rob him before
they would let him go. Some of the rioters would not fire their weapons, but would
only use the butt ends to beat the Chinese with. Some would not beat a Chinese, but
rob him of whatever he had and let him go, yelling to him to go quickly. Some,
who took no part either in beating or robbing the Chinese, stood by, shouting
loudly and laughing and clapping their hands.

There was a gang of women that stood at the "Chinatown" end of the plank
bridge and cheered; among the women, two of them each fired successive shots at
the Chinese. This was done about a little past 3 o'clock p.m. . . .

Some of the Chinese were killed at the bank of Bitter Creek, some near the
railroad bridge, and some in "Chinatown." After having been killed, the dead bodies
of some were carried to the burning buildings and thrown into the flames. Some of
the Chinese who had hid themselves in the houses were killed and their bodies
burned; some, who on account of sickness could not run, were burned alive in the
houses. One Chinese was killed in "Whitemen's Town" in a laundry house, and his
house demolished. The whole number of Chinese killed was twenty-eight and those
wounded fifteen.

8. Southern Freedmen Resolve to Move West, 1879

Fifteen years have elapsed since our emancipation, and though we have made
material advancement as citizens, yet we are forced to admit that obstacles have
been constantly thrown in our way to obstruct and retard our progress. Our toil is
still unrequited, hardly less under freedom than slavery, whereby we are sadly oppressed by poverty and ignorance, and consequently prevented from enjoying the
blessings of liberty, while we are left to the shame and contempt of all mankind.
This unfortunate state of affairs is because of the intolerant spirit exhibited on the
part of the men who control the state governments of the South today. Free speech
in many localities is not tolerated. The lawful exercise of the rights of citizenship is
denied when majorities must be overcome. Proscription meets us on every hand; in
the school-room, in the church that sings praises to that God who made of one
blood all the nations of the earth; in places of public amusement, in the jury box,

W. E. B. DuBois, "Economic Cooperation Among Negro Americans," *Twelfth Annual Atlanta Conference*
(Atlanta: Atlanta University Publications, 1907), 52–53.

and in the local affairs of government we are practically denied the rights and privileges of freemen.

We can not expect to rise to the dignity of true manhood under the system of labor and pay as practically carried out in some portions of the South today. . . .

Resolved, That it is the sense of this conference that the great current of migration which has for the past few months taken so many of our people from their homes in the South, and which is still carrying hundreds to the free and fertile West, should be encouraged and kept in motion until those who remain are accorded every right and privilege guaranteed by the constitution and laws.

Resolved, That we recommend great care on the part of those who migrate. They should leave home well prepared with certain knowledge of localities to which they intend to move; money enough to pay their passage and enable them to begin life in their new homes with prospect of ultimate success.

9. The Jorgensens Long for Other Danes, 1906

[Jorgen:] One would think that we would have been satisfied to settle down where we were but such was not the case. We had constantly longed for fellowship with other Danes in a Danish congregation in a Danish settlement with a Danish school. There was a Danish Church in Waupaca [Wisconsin] but that was a distance of seven miles away. Our neighbors were all native Americans. Most of them were uneducated and not too intellectual. They were congenial and friendly enough but we got little satisfaction or enjoyment from fellowship with them. The language was a handicap too because Kristiane [his wife] had not had as good an opportunity to learn it as I who had mixed with other people more. She could make herself understood alright but has since improved a great deal. She reads English books quite well but when it comes to writing I have to do it.

In the meantime we had managed to get all the land under cultivation that I was able to handle without hired help. All we had to do was to plant potatoes in the spring, dig them up in the fall, and haul them to town during the winter which was a little too tame an existence. I have mentioned two reasons why we wanted to move but there was a third. The older girls were growing up, and what if one of them should come home some day with one of these individuals with a foreign background and present him as her sweetheart. This was unthinkable. (Strangely enough after we came to Montana one of the girls actually did come and present an American as her sweetheart but he was a high class individual. He was a lawyer who later became district judge for Sheridan and other counties.)

When E. F. Madsen's call came in "Dannevirke" in 1906 to establish a Danish colony in eastern Montana, I immediately said, "That's where we are going," and Kristiane immediately agreed. I think people thought we were crazy to abandon what was, as far as people could tell, the comfort and security we had for insecurity and a cold, harsh climate. "You'll freeze to death out there," they said and related terrifying experiences of people who had succumbed in snowstorms. But it didn't

Small Collections 178. Typescripts at Montana Historical Society Archives, 225 N. Roberts Street, Helena, MT 59620.

seem to make much of an impression on us. I was past 50 years of age and if we were to build up another farm it was time to get started.

E. F. Madsen from Clinton, Iowa had been out in Montana on October 6, 1906 to find a place for a new Danish colony and had selected the place where it now is located in the northeast corner of Montana about 25 miles from the Canadian line and close to the Dakota boundary. Madsen named it "Dagmar." Its full name is "Dronning Dagmar's Minde" (Queen Dagmar's Memorial), and is the first such colony in the United States. The land is fertile with smooth rolling prairies. The land was not surveyed but could be claimed by anyone over 21 years of age under Squatter's right. The 160 acres allowed was later increased to 320 acres. . . .

[Otto:] My first recollection of any talk of moving or living anywhere else but where we were, was the folks, setting at the kitchen table one night—it must have been in 1906. Mother was fidgeting with something or other on the table, listening to Pa read aloud from the weekly Danish publication, *Dannevirke,* with a bright, faraway look in her eyes; and when he had finished, she said: "Skul' vi?"(should we?) We kids sat around, I for one, with open mouth, sensing something special was in the wind, and when the word Montana was mentioned,—MONTANA!! Montana to me was a magic word! That's where Falsbuts' were going to go! And Falsbuts' boys had thoroughly briefed me on what could be expected there: buffalo, cowboys, and wild horses—Oh boy! Free land, homesteads, Montana and the West! No one has any idea of what those magic words could conjure up in a 10-year-old boy's mind! . . .

I have often wondered what Pa's reactions were to all this. He never showed anything, outwardly. I remember when we left the farm for the last time, and we were about to get into the wagon. He was buttoning his coat with one hand and with the other, reached down to stroke the big old gray tom-cat, which was to be left behind; and he said, "Kitty, Kitty!" I was dumbfounded, for I had never seen him do a thing like that before. He straightened up and looked around at the good new house and big new red barn; and in his slow, easy-going and deliberate way, climbed into the wagon. I have often wondered what his innermost thoughts were at that moment. But like so many thousands before him who have pulled up stakes for the unknown future in the West, he left little room for sentiment. In tribute to my father, I think this was his staunchest moment. . . . That kind of spirit and courage, I'm afraid, is fast becoming a thing of the past in these United States.

10. Frederick Jackson Turner Articulates the Frontier Thesis, 1893

The American frontier is sharply distinguished from the European frontier—a fortified boundary line running through dense populations. The most significant thing about the American frontier is, that it lies at the hither edge of free land. In the census reports it is treated as the margin of that settlement which has a density of two or more to the square mile. . . .

Reprinted in Ray Allen Billington, ed. *The Frontier Thesis: Valid Interpretation of American History?* (New York: Robert Krieger, 1977), 10–20.

In the settlement of America we have to observe how European life entered the continent, and how America modified and developed that life and reacted on Europe. Our early history is the study of European germs developing in an American environment. Too exclusive attention has been paid by institutional students to the Germanic origins, too little to the American factors. The frontier is the line of most rapid and effective Americanization. The wilderness masters the colonist. It finds him a European in dress, industries, tools, modes of travel, and thought. It takes him from the railroad car and puts him in the birch canoe. It strips off the garments of civilization and arrays him in the hunting shirt and the moccasin. It puts him in the log cabin of the Cherokee and Iroquois and runs an Indian palisade around him. Before long he has gone to planting Indian corn and plowing with a sharp stick; he shouts the war cry and takes the scalp in orthodox Indian fashion. In short, at the frontier the environment is at first too strong for the man. He must accept the conditions which it furnishes, or perish, and so he fits himself into the Indian clearings and follows the Indian trails. Little by little he transforms the wilderness, but the outcome is not the old Europe. . . . The fact is, that here is a new product that is American. At first, the frontier was the Atlantic coast. It was the frontier of Europe in a very real sense. Moving westward, the frontier became more and more American. . . .

But the most important effect of the frontier has been in the promotion of democracy here and in Europe. As has been indicated, the frontier is productive of individualism. Complex society is precipitated by the wilderness into a kind of primitive organization based on the family. The tendency is anti-social. It produces antipathy to control, and particularly to any direct control. . . . The frontier individualism has from the beginning promoted democracy. . . .

From the conditions of frontier life came intellectual traits of profound importance. The works of travelers along each frontier from colonial days onward describe certain common traits, and these traits have, while softening down, still persisted as survivals in the place of their origin, even when a higher social organization succeeded. The result is that to the frontier the American intellect owes its striking characteristics. That coarseness and strength combined with acuteness and inquisitiveness; that practical, inventive turn of mind, quick to find expedients; that masterful grasp of material things, lacking in the artistic but powerful to effect great ends; that restless, nervous energy; that dominant individualism, working for good and for evil, and withal that buoyancy and exuberance which comes with freedom—these are traits of the frontier, or traits called out elsewhere because of the existence of the frontier. . . . But never again will such gifts of free land offer themselves. For a moment, at the frontier, the bonds of custom are broken and unrestraint is triumphant. There is not *tabula rasa*. The stubborn American environment is there with its imperious summons to accept its conditions; the inherited ways of doing things are also there; and yet, in spite of environment, and in spite of custom, each frontier did indeed furnish a new field of opportunity, a gate of escape from the bondage of the past; and freshness, and confidence, and scorn of older society, impatience of its restraints and its ideas, and indifference to its lessons, have accompanied the frontier. What the Mediterranean Sea was to the Greeks, breaking the bond of custom, offering new experiences, calling out new institutions and activities, that, and more, the ever retreating frontier has been to the United States directly, and to the nations of Europe more remotely. And now, four centuries from the discovery of America, at the end of a hundred years of life under the Constitution, the frontier has gone, and with its going has closed the first period of American history.

E S S A Y S

The western frontier looms large in the history of the United States. Historians Frederick Jackson Turner and Theodore Roosevelt helped to create the popular image of the frontier experience by portraying the West as the rough-and-tumble setting in which Americans forged their commitment to political democracy and social equality. Whether one agrees with this may depend on whether one sees the drama as featuring a multiethnic cast, or as being primarily a tale of Anglo-American migration westward. Today, historians debate whether the West was really the cradle of American equality and individualism. Ray Allen Billington, an intellectual heir of Frederick Jackson Turner, shows how the western environment fostered an easy-going social equality among Yankee pioneers. Patricia Nelson Limerick of the University of Colorado at Boulder speaks for a generation of "new western historians" when she argues that western settlement was continuously multiethnic and fundamentally antidemocratic.

Frontier Democracy

RAY ALLEN BILLINGTON

To understand the uniqueness of *American* democracy we must consider not only the form of government and the extent of popular participation, but the way in which the people of the United States view government and society as a whole. Do they regard the state as the master or servant of its citizens? Do they consider their fellow men as equals, or as inferiors and superiors? . . . If the image of the social order common among Americans differs from that usual among Europeans, and if the differences can be explained by the pioneering experience, we can conclude that the frontier has altered the national character as well as institutions.

In this quest, two concepts are especially important: that of "individualism" and that of "equality." Visitors from abroad feel that the people of the United States have endowed these words with distinctive meanings. In no other nation is the equality of all men so loudly proclaimed; in no other country is the right of individual self-assertion (within certain areas) so stoutly defended. . . .

. . . Was frontier individualism a myth, and if not, how did it differ from traditional individualism? One conclusion is obvious: in the social realm the pioneer was a complete traditionalist, leaning on the community no less than his city cousins. Cooperation with his neighbors was commonplace for defense, the accomplishments of essential pioneering tasks, law enforcement, and a host of other necessities. In the economic realm the frontiersman's attitudes were less sharply defined. Consistency

Ray Allen Billington, *America's Frontier Heritage* (New York: Holt, Rinehart and Winston, 1966), 139–157. Reprinted with permission of Wadsworth, an imprint of the Wadsworth Group, a division of Thomson Learning.

was not one of his sins; he favored regulation that seemed beneficial to his interests, and opposed regulation that threatened immediate or potential profits. His views were, in other words, comparable to those of Eastern business leaders who demanded from the government protective tariffs, railroad land grants, and federal subsidies, while mouthing the virtues of "rugged individualism."

Yet in one sense, the frontiersman moved somewhat beyond his counterparts in the East. He was, to a unique degree, living in a land where everyone was a real or potential capitalist. Nowhere could a stake in society be more easily obtained, and nowhere was the belief that this was possible more strongly entrenched. . . .

. . . The widespread property holdings in the West, and the belief that every man would achieve affluence, inclined the Westerner to insist on his right to profits somewhat more stridently than others. His voice spoke for individualism louder than that of his fellows, even though he was equally willing to find haven in coop- eration when danger threatened or need decreed. . . .

Basically, frontier individualism stemmed from the belief that all men were equal (ex- cluding Negroes, Indians, Orientals, and other minority groups), and that all should have a chance to prove their personal capabilities without restraint from society. This seemed fair in a land of plenty, where superabundant opportunity allowed each to rise or fall to his proper level as long as governments did not meddle. Faith in the equality of men was the great common creed of the West. Only an understand- ing of the depth of this belief can reveal the true nature of social democracy on suc- cessive frontiers.

To European visitors, this was the most unique feature of Western life and thought: the attitude that set that region apart from Europe or the East. "There is nothing in America," wrote one, "that strikes a foreigner so much as the real repub- lican equality existing in the Western States, which border on the wilderness." The whole attitude of the people was different; calmly confident of their own future, they looked on all men as their peers and acted accordingly. One Westerner who defined the frontier as a region where a poor man could enter a rich man's house without feeling uneasy or unequal was not far astray. Menial subservience was just as unpopular there as haughty superiority. Dame Shirley, writing from the California gold fields, felt the "I'm as good as you are" spirit all about her, and believed that only an American frontiersman could

> Enter a palace with his old felt hat on—
> To address the King with the title of Mister,
> And ask the price of the throne he sat on.

Everywhere men of all ranks exuded that easy air of confidence that went with complete self-assurance, meeting travelers on terms of equality that charmed those democratically inclined and shocked those of opposite prejudice. "The wealthy man assumes nothing to himself on account of his wealth," marveled one, "and the poor man feels no debasement on account of his poverty, and every man stands on his own individual merits." The spirit of Western democracy was captured by a cowboy addressing a disagreeable scion of British nobility: "You may be a son of a lord back in England, but that ain't what you are out here."

In the give and take of daily life, Western egalitarianism was expressed in the general refusal to recognize the class lines that were forming in every community.

Some of the self-proclaimed "better sort" might hold themselves aloof and put on aristocratic airs, but they were atypical of the great mass of the people. The majority, in evaluating those about them, applied value judgments that differed from those in communities where tradition played a stronger role. Men were weighed on their present and future contributions to society, with total disregard for their background. Each played a role in the developing social order, and as long as he played it well he was respected. "To be useful is here the ruling principle," wrote a Swedish visitor to the West; "it is immaterial what one does so long as he is respected and does his work efficiently." Drones and aristocratic idlers were not bearing their fair share and were outcasts; men of menial rank were contributing to the community welfare and were respected. "There is in the West," noted an unusually acute observer during the 1830s, "a real equality, not merely an equality to talk about, an equality on paper; everybody that has on a decent coat is a gentleman."

Contemporaries speculated often on the reasons for frontier social democracy. Most agreed that the burgeoning Western economy was basically responsible, offering as it did a chance for the lowliest to acquire prestige through accumulated wealth. All had an equal chance to improve themselves, and so all should be treated as equals; conversely, the servant who believed that he would someday be a millionaire saw no reason to be servile to his temporary betters. This was common sense, since every new community boasted dozens of living examples of rags-to-riches success: the tenant farmer who was now a county judge, the mechanic newly elected to the legislature, the farmer grown rich by the sale of lands. As a British traveler saw, "the means of subsistence being so easy in the country, and their dependence on each other consequently so trifling, that spirit of servility to those about them so prevalent in European manners, is wholly unknown to them." Why be servile when the man above today might be the man below tomorrow? Why cling to traditional views of rank when the heir apparent to a British earldom could be seen mowing hay, assisted by two sons of a viscount, while nearby the brother of an earl was feeding grain into a threshing machine? Clearly standards on the frontier were different, and equality more nearly a fact of life.

The common level of wealth encouraged this spirit, for while differences did exist, the gulf between rich and poor was relatively less in frontier regions than in older societies. Poverty was rare in pioneer communities that had graduated from the backwoods stage; one governor complained that the number of dependent paupers in his state was "scarcely sufficient to give exercise to the virtue of charity in individuals." Wealth might and did exist on rural frontiers, but its presence was less obvious than in the East, for money would buy little but land and land was available to all. Ostentatious spending existed but was uncommon, partly because luxuries and leisure were largely unavailable, partly because it would breed hostility in neighbors who resented display. "Their wealth," it was observed, "does very little in the way of purchasing even the outward signs of respect; and as to *adulation,* it is not to be purchased with love or money." This leveling process underlined the sense of equality that was so typical of the frontier.

It was further emphasized by the fact that on the newer frontiers rich and poor lived, dressed, and acted much more alike than in the East. Most owned their own houses, though some might be of logs and some of bricks. Most dressed in homespun clothes and shunned the powdered wigs and knee breeches that were the badge of the gentry in the early nineteenth century; travelers frequently complained that it was impossible to distinguish the well-born from the lowly by the garments they wore. Most bore themselves proudly, scorning the humble mien that marked the lower classes in Europe. "The clumsy gait and bent body of our peasant is hardly ever seen here," wrote an Englishman from Kentucky in 1819; "every one walks erect and easy." When people looked and acted alike, as they did along the frontiers, treating them alike came naturally.

No less important in fanning the spirit of egalitarianism was the newness of the West, and the lack of traditional aristocratic standards there. No entrenched gentry governed social intercourse, setting the practices of those below them and closing their ranks against newcomers. Those who rose in station did not have to surmount the barrier of learning new customs as do those achieving higher status today, for conventions, deferences, and distinctions were rare among the "tree-destroying sovereigns" of the West. A man's ancestry and prior history were less important than the contribution that he could make to a new society badly in need of manpower. One Westerner who remarked: "It's what's above ground, not what's under, that we think on," and another who added: "Not, 'What has he done in the East?' but 'What does he intend to do in Kansas and for Kansas?'" summed up the reasons for much of the social democracy that thrived along the frontiers.

This combination of causal forces—economic equality, commonly shared living standards, and the absence of traditional aristocratic values—enshrined belief in equality as the common faith of Western society. Class distinctions did exist, of course; innate differences in talent, ambition, and skill divided the various strata at an early stage in the evolution of every Western community. But relatively, these distinctions played a lesser role in the West than in the East. Instead belief in equality compelled frontiersmen to uplift the lowly and degrade the superior as they sought a common democratic level.

Elevation of the lowly was most commonly expressed by refusal to use terms designating class distinctions. Every man on the frontier, whatever his status in life, was a "gentleman," and every woman a "lady." Travelers from older societies were frequently amused to find the ragged wagoner or the ill-kempt seller of old bones addressed in this fashion; one who asked a tavern keeper in an infant settlement in New York to find his coachman was delighted when that worthy called out: "Where is the gentleman that brought this man here?" "Ladies" were as carelessly designated; one traveling in the West might hear, as did Mrs. Trollope, references to "the lady over the way that takes in washing," or "that there lady, out by the Gulley, what is making dip-candles." If titles could serve as social escalators, no one on the frontiers need stay long in menial ranks.

The leveling spirit of Western democracy sought not only to elevate the lowly but also to dethrone the elite. Any attempt at "putting on airs," was certain to be met with rude reminders of the equality of all men. New settlers were warned by guidebooks to mingle freely and familiarly with neighbors, and above all to pretend no superiority, if they wished to be accepted. They were told that nothing ruined a man's chances on the frontier so fatally as a suspicion of pride, which, once established, would ruin his reputation. . . . One English newcomer who asked to be addressed as "Esquire" found that within a few days not only his host but the hired hands were calling him "Charlie"; another had the brass buttons unceremoniously ripped from his coat by a frontiersman who objected to such display. Texas rangers gambled or gave away the fancy uniforms issued to them, and stole the gold-braided suits of officers so that these aristocratic evidences of rank would not be seen. "Superiority," observed an English visitor, "is yielded to men of acknowledged talent alone."

Outward signs of social snobbery might arouse resentment in the West, but so did any conduct that seemed to suggest superiority. Families with sizable incomes found themselves better accepted if they lived and dressed as simply as their poorest neighbors; politicians soon realized that for success they must insist on being addressed as "Mister" or "Governor," and not as "Excellency." Even such a born-to-the-purple native aristocrat as Theodore Roosevelt took pains to understate his wealth and ancestry when on his Dakota ranch. When Colonel Thomas Dabney appeared at a frontier cabin raising in the Southwest with twenty slaves to do his work he was ostracized by the community; when a traveler had the good sense to dispose of expensive luggage, he was at last accepted on friendly terms. Natives and visitors alike learned that in the West refusal to drink with a stranger was interpreted as a sign of social superiority; unless they could convince their would-be hosts that they had "sworn off," even redeye whisky was preferable to the trouble that followed if word spread that they were "too good" for the community.

So strong was the spirit of equality along the frontiers that any deviation was met with resentment that was sometimes carried to ludicrous ends. Frontier housewives found themselves in disfavor if they kept their homes neater or cleaner than those of their neighbors; one who had waited three years for her first caller was told: "I woulda come before but I heard you had Brussels carpet on the floor." Another who offered to lend teaspoons for a party was rudely informed that no such luxuries were wanted, for the guests would not be used to them. Even those with a few choice possessions apologized; carpets were excused a "*one* way to hide the dirt," a mahogany table as "dreadful plaguy to scour," and kitchen conveniences as "lumberin' up the house for nothin'." When an Englishman remonstrated about the lack of ceremony in Western life he was told: "Yes, that may be quite necessary in England, in order to overawe a parcel of ignorant creatures, who have no share in making the laws; but with us a man's a man, whether he have a silk gown on him or not." The spirit of Western social democracy could have found no more eloquent expression than that.

In practice this spirit found its most outspoken expression in the attitude of hired workers. A "servant" in the traditional sense was impossible to find in the West because any form of servility was demeaning and hence intolerable; some of the most wealthy hosts and hostesses interrupted their dinner parties to wait on table or busy themselves in the kitchen. When servants could be drafted from the ranks of newly arrived immigrants or the families of less well-to-do pioneers they refused to accept that designation, but insisted on being called "helps," or "hired hands," or "ladies." The term "waiter" was equally unpopular, and was likely to call forth a spirited rejoinder from the person so addressed. Still more insulting was the word *master*. A misguided traveler asking "Is your master at home?" would probably be told "I have no master"; one in the Wyoming cattle country was heatedly informed that "the son of Baliel ain't been born yet." So deep was the resentment against any implication of servility that young men and women preferred to labor at poor pay under bad conditions rather than accept a post as servant.

Those who did so guarded their respectability by abolishing all traditional symbols of servitude. Livery was never used; bells to summon servants in Western inns were unknown because the "helpers" refused to respond. All insisted on being treated as equals, dining with the family, meeting guests, and joining in all social functions under threat of immediate departure. One who had been told she must eat in the kitchen turned up her lip, announced "I guess that's cause you don't think I'm good enough to eat with you," and flounced from the house. Nor was this rebellious spirit peculiar to household help. The oft-heard remark: "If a man is good enough to work for me, he is good enough to eat with me" was literally applied. A family who had hired several carpenters to build a barn made the mistake of an early breakfast without them one day; the next day they left. A honeymooning couple were abandoned by their hired driver when they tried to eat alone just once. In public houses or conveyances the story was the same; travel accounts abound with tales of stewards who joined the card game after serving drinks, of waitresses who leaned over chairs to join in the conversation or borrow a guest's fan, or messengers who seated themselves and demanded a drink while serving their messages, of waiters in inns who joined their patrons when their tasks were done. In the West men felt equal, and acted the part.

Menial tasks were as resented by servants as were menial titles. Travelers were often forced to clean their own boots in frontier inns, or to rub down their own horses while "helpers" looked on disdainfully. One who asked to be awakened in the morning was answered "call yourself and be damned." On another occasion a titled Englishman in the Wyoming wilds was told to take a swim instead of a bath when he asked his hired helper to fill a tub; when he refused the angry helper shot the tub full of holes, shouting: "You ain't quite the top-shelfer you think you is, you ain't even got a shower-bath for cooling your swelled head, but I'll make you a present of one, boss!" Nor did servants alone resent the suggestion of servility. A pioneer Michigan housewife who tired of seeing a guest attack the roast with his own knife and offered to carve was rudely informed: "I'll help myself, I thankye. I never want no waitin' on."

Travelers who were shocked by these evidences of social democracy in the West were equally appalled by the democratic spirit which prevailed in frontier inns. There no "First Class" or "Second Class" accommodations separated patrons; tradesmen, slave dealers, farmers, congressmen, generals, fur trappers, and roustabouts ate side by side at the long tables, and all were treated the same. Sleeping accommodations were allotted on a first-come-first-serve basis, with governors and herdsmen, senators and farmers, rich and poor, clean and unclean, all crowded three or four to a bed. "It has been my lot," recorded an experienced traveler, "to sleep with a diversity of personages; I do believe from the driver of the stage coach, to men of considerable name." Complaints against these arrangements were summarily rejected by pioneer landlords; one visitor from overseas who objected to using a dirt-encrusted wash-bowl with a dozen other guests was told that "one rain bathes the just and the unjust, why not one wash-bowl"; another's protest that the sheets were dirty was answered with: "since *Gentlemen* are all alike, people do not see why they should not sleep in the same sheets." The frontier inn was, as one traveler put it "a most almighty beautiful democratic amalgam."

The social democracy and frontier-type individualism that characterized America's growing period have not persisted unchanged into the twentieth century. . . .

. . . . The United States is no longer a country free of class distinctions and so wedded to egalitarianism that manifestations of wealth arouse public resentment.

But its social democracy does differ from that of older nations, marked by its relative lack of class awareness, and by the brash assurance of the humble that they are as worthy of respect as the elite. The house painter who addresses a client by his first name, the elevator operator who enters into casual conversation with his passengers, the garage mechanic who condescendingly compares his expensive car with your aging model, could exist only in the United States. Their counterparts are unknown in England or on the Continent partly because America's frontiering experience bred into the people attitudes toward democracy that have persisted down to the present.

The Legacy of Conquest: America's Conflicted Frontier

PATRICIA NELSON LIMERICK

In 1871 an informal army of Arizona civilians descended on a peaceful camp and massacred over one hundred Apaches, mostly women and children. Who were the attackers at Camp Grant? The usual images of Western history would suggest one answer: white men. In fact, the attackers were a consortium of Hispanics, Anglo-Americans, and Papago Indians. However different the three groups might have been, they could agree on the matter of Apaches and join in interracial cooperation. Hostility between Apaches and Papagoes, and between Apaches and Hispanics, had in fact begun long before conflict between Apaches and Anglo-Americans.

In the popular imagination, the frontier froze as a biracial confrontation between "whites" and "Indians." More complex questions of race relations seemed to be the terrain of other regions' histories. The history of relations between blacks and whites centered in the South, while "ethnic conflict" suggested the crowded cities of the Northeast, coping with floods of immigrants in the late nineteenth and early twentieth centuries. As blacks moved north and European immigrants crossed the Atlantic, new populations put the adaptability of American society to the test. Could native Americans of northern European stock tolerate these "others"? Was it better to deal with them through assimilation or through exclusion? How could old-stock Americans defend their valued "purity" against these foreign threats?

These are familiar themes in the history of the Southern and Northeastern United States, but ethnic conflict was not exclusive to the East. Western America shared in the transplanted diversity of Europe. Expansion involved peoples of every background: English, Irish, Cornish, Scottish, French, German, Portuguese, Scandinavian, Greek, and Russian. To that diversity, the West added a persistent population of Indians, with a multitude of languages and cultures; an established Hispanic population, as well as one of later Mexican immigrants; Asians, to whom the American West was the East; black people, moving west in increasing numbers in the twentieth century; and Mormons, Americans who lived for a time in isolation, evolving a distinctive culture from the requirements of their new faith. Put the diverse humanity of Western America into one picture, and the "melting pot" of the Eastern United States at the turn of the century begins to look more like a family

Patricia Nelson Limerick, *The Legacy of Conquest: The Unbroken Past of the American West* (New York: Norton, 1987), 259–264, 277–291. Copyright © 1987 by Patricia Nelson Limerick. Used by permission of W. W. Norton & Company, Inc.

reunion, a meeting of groups with an essential similarity—dominantly European, Judeo-Christian, accustomed to the existence of the modern state.

The diversity of the West put a strain on the simpler varieties of racism. In another setting, categories dividing humanity into superior white and inferior black were comparatively easy to steer by. The West, however, raised questions for which racists had no set answers. Were Indians better than blacks—more capable of civilization and assimilation—perhaps even suitable for miscegenation? Were Mexicans essentially Indians? Did their European heritage count for anything? Were "mongrel" races even worse than other "pure" races? Where did Asians fit in the racial ranking? Were they humble, menial workers—or representatives of a great center of civilization, art, and, best of all, trade? Were the Japanese different from, perhaps more tolerable than, the Chinese? What about southern and eastern Europeans? When Greek workers in the mines went on strike and violence followed, was this race war or class war? Western diversity forced racists to think—an unaccustomed activity.

Over the twentieth century, writers of Western history succumbed to the easy temptation, embracing a bipolar West composed of "whites" and "Indians." Relations between the two groups shrank, moreover, to a matter of whites meeting obstacles and conquering them. Fought and refought in books and film, those "colorful" Indian wars raged on. Meanwhile, the sophisticated questions, the true study of American race relations, quietly slipped into the province of historians who studied other parts of the country.

In 1854, in the cast of *People* v. *Hall,* California Supreme Court Chief Justice J. Murray demonstrated the classic dilemma of an American racist wrestling with the questions raised by Western diversity. Ruling on the right of Chinese people to testify in court against white people, Murray took up the white man's burden of forcing an intractable reality back into a unified racist theory.

No statute explicitly addressed the question of Chinese testimony, but Murray found another route to certainty. State law, he argued, already prevented blacks, mulattoes, and Indians from testifying as witnesses "in any action or proceeding in which a white person is a party." Although state law did not refer explicitly to Asians, this was, Murray argued, an insignificant omission. Columbus, he said, had given the name "Indians" to North American natives while under the impression that he was in Asia and the people before him were Asians. "Ethnology," having recently reached a "high point of perfection," disclosed a hidden truth in Columbus's error. It now seemed likely that "this country was first peopled by Asiatics." From Columbus's time, then, "American Indians and the Mongolian, or Asiatic, were regarded as the same type of the human species." Therefore, it could be assumed, the exclusion of "Indians" from testifying applied to Asians as well.

Judge Murray found an even more compelling argument in the essential "degraded" similarity of nonwhite races. The laws excluding "Negroes, mulattoes, and Indians" from giving testimony had obviously been intended to "protect the white person from the influence of all testimony" from another caste. "The use of these terms ["Negro," "mulatto," and "Indian"] must, by every sound rule of construction, exclude everyone who is not of white blood."

Concluding that Asians could not testify, Murray spelled out the "actual and present danger" he had defused. "The same rule which would admit them to testify, would admit them to all the equal rights of citizenship, and we might soon see them at the polls, in the jury box, upon the bench, and in our legislative halls." With a smoke screen of scientific racism, using anthropology, Murray thus declared the essential unity of darker mankind. He did his best to keep power, opportunity, and justice in California in the hands of God's chosen, lighter-skinned people. And he did a good job of it. . . .

To white workingmen, post–gold rush California did not live up to its promise. Facing limited job opportunities and uncertain futures, white laborers looked both for solutions and for scapegoats. Men in California came with high hopes; jobs proved scarce and unrewarding; someone must be to blame. In California, capital had at its command a source of controllable, underpaid labor. White workers, the historian Alexander Saxton has said, "viewed the Chinese as tools of monopoly." The workers therefore "considered themselves under attack on two fronts, or more aptly from above and below." Resenting big business and resenting competition from Chinese labor, frustrated workers naturally chose to attack the more vulnerable target. The slogan "The Chinese must go" could make it through Congress and into federal law; "Big business must go" was not going to earn congressional approval.

The issue of the Chinese scapegoat became a pillar of California politics, a guaranteed vote getter. In 1879, a state referendum on the Chinese question brought out "a margin of 150,000 to 900 favoring total exclusion." Opposition to the Chinese offered unity to an otherwise diverse state; divisions between Protestants and Catholics temporarily healed; Irish immigrants could cross the barrier separating a stigmatized ethnic group from the stigmatizing majority. Popular democratic participation in the rewriting of the California constitution showed this majority at work. "[N]o native of China, no idiot, insane person, or person convicted of any infamous crime," the constitution asserted, ". . . shall ever exercise the privileges of an elector of this State." Moreover, in the notorious Article XIX, the framers went on to prohibit the employment "of any Chinese or Mongolian" in any public works projects below the federal level or by any corporation operating under state laws. These provisions, the historian Mary Roberts Coolidge wrote early in the twentieth century, "were not only unconstitutional but inhuman and silly." They were also directly expressive of the popular will.

"To an American death is preferable to a life on a par with a Chinaman," the manifesto of the California Workingmen's Party declared in 1876. ". . . Treason is better than to labor beside a Chinese slave." Extreme threat justified extreme actions; extralegal, violent harassment followed closely on violent declarations. In harassing the Chinese, white Californians did not seek to violate American ideals and values; they sought to defend them. "They call us a mob," a female organizer said, single-handedly demolishing the image of women as the "gentle tamers" of the West. "It was a mob that fought the battle of Lexington, and a mob that threw the tea overboard in Boston harbor, but they backed their principles. . . . I want to see every Chinaman—white or yellow—thrown out of this state."

California may have "catalyzed and spearheaded the movement for exclusion," but, as Stuart Miller has shown, this was not a matter of a narrow sectional interest pushing the rest of the nation off its preferred course. Negative images gleaned from traders, missionaries, and diplomats in China predisposed the whole country to Sinophobia; the use of Chinese workers as strikebreakers in Eastern industries clinched the question. The 1882 Chinese Exclusion Act, a product of national consensus, met little opposition. . . .

In their anti-Oriental crusading, white Westerners often referred to the South and its "problem." In a search for case studies of discrimination and conflict in black / white relations, they did not need to go so far afield. During the nineteenth century, black people were sparsely represented in the West. Their numerical insignificance, however, did not stop white people from being preoccupied with the issues of black migration. Despite visions of Western fresh starts and new beginnings, the South's "problem" had long ago moved West.

The extension of slavery into the Western territories had, of course, been a prime source of sectional tension before the Civil War. The struggles over the admission of new states, free or slave, had alarmed those concerned with the survival of the Union; "a firebell in the night," Thomas Jefferson called the conflicts preceding the 1820 Missouri Compromise. Fantasies of Western innocence aside, the Western territories were deeply implicated in the national struggle over slavery.

In 1850, California was admitted as a free state; in 1857, Oregon was admitted with a similar status. That fact alone can give the impressions that the Westerners were, in some principled way, opposed to slavery. That impression needs closer examination.

Most white settlers in Oregon opposed the intrusion of slavery into their territory. However, they also opposed the intrusion of free blacks. Following on earlier territorial laws, the 1857 Oregon state constitution included a provision excluding free blacks and received heavy voter support. "The object," one early Oregon leader explained, "is to *keep* clear of this most troublesome class of population. We are in a new world, under most favorable circumstances, and we wish to avoid most of these great evils that have so much afflicted the United States and other countries." To the white Oregonians, this was a principled position. The project was to create and preserve a better social order and to steer clear of the problems and mistakes that plagued other, less pure regions. Oregon's exclusion of blacks thus appeared to be "a clear victory for settlers who came to the Far West to escape the racial troubles of the East."

The particular conditions of Oregon added another reason for black exclusion. The question of the admission of free blacks, Oregon's delegate to Congress explained in 1850,

> is a question of life and death to us in Oregon. . . . The negroes associate with the Indians and intermarry, and, if their free ingress is encouraged or allowed, there would a relationship spring up between them and the different tribes, and a mixed race would ensure inimical to the whites; and the Indians being led on by the negro who is better acquainted with the customs, language, and manners of the whites, than the Indian, these savages would become much formidable than they otherwise would, and long and bloody wars would be the fruits of the comingling of the races. It is the principle of self preservation that justifies the actions of the Oregon legislature.

Beyond actual armed conspiracy, white Westerners saw in black rights the first link in a chain reaction. Permit blacks a place in American political and social life, and Indians, Asians, and Hispanics would be next. Western diversity thus gave an edge of urgency to each form of prejudice; the line had to be held against each group; if the barrier was breached once, it would collapse before all the various "others." White Southerners could specialize, holding off one group; white Westerners fought in a multifront campaign.

Post–Civil War Reconstruction thus posed a challenge to the institutions of the West as well as to those of the South. Western members of Congress could often join in imposing black rights on the South; the South had rebelled, after all, and deserved punishment. One punishment was black suffrage. But imposing black suffrage on Western states that had not rebelled—that was another matter, and the occasion for another round in the westward-moving battle of states' rights.

Confronted with the Fifteenth Amendment, giving blacks the vote, both California and Oregon balked. "If we make the African a citizen," an Oregon newspaper argued in 1865, "we cannot deny the same right to the Indian or the Mongolian. Then how long would we have peace and prosperity when four races separate, distinct and antagonistic should be at the polls and contend for the control of government?" In California, opposition to the Fifteenth Amendment hinged on the prospect that suffrage without regard to "race, color or previous condition of servitude" might include the Chinese. The Fifteenth Amendment became law without ratification by California or Oregon. The Oregon legislature "in a gesture of perverse defiance rejected the amendment in October, 1870, fully six months after its incorporation into the federal Constitution." The amendment, the state senate declared, was "in violation of Oregon's sovereignty, an illegal interference by Congress in Oregon's right to establish voting qualifications, and a change in law forced on the nation by the bayonet." White Southerners might have been reduced to a state of temporary impotence, but they could take comfort in the fact that others had adopted their favored arguments.

In their ongoing preoccupation with purity, various Western state legislatures also moved to hold the line against racial mixing. California, Oregon, and—most extraordinary, in light of its current flexibility in matrimonial matters—Nevada all passed laws against miscegenation. Below the level of law, white Westerners practiced their own, more casual versions of discrimination. Labor unions excluded black workers; owners of restaurants, inns, and hotels limited their clientele; housing segregation was common. Scattered through historical records are incidents in which individual communities abruptly resolved to expel their black residents. "In 1893," Elizabeth McLagan has reported, "the citizens of Liberty, Oregon, requested that all black people leave town." In 1904, facing high unemployment, the town of Reno, Nevada, set out to reduce its problems by "arresting all unemployed blacks and forcing them to leave the city." "There are too many worthless negroes in the city," the Reno police chief explained.

In the twentieth century, as black migration from the South to the West accelerated, Western states' discriminatory laws stayed on the books. Although never consistently enforced, Oregon's prohibition on free blacks was not formally repealed until 1926. California's ban on miscegenation lasted until 1948; Nevada's remained until 1959. Oregon and California finally consented to a symbolic ratification of the Fifteenth Amendment—in 1959 and 1962, respectively. . . .

Race, one begins to conclude, was the key factor in dividing the people of Western America. Its meanings and distinctions fluctuated, but racial feeling evidently guided white Americans in their choice of groups to persecute and exclude. Differences in culture, in language, in religion, meant something; but a physically distinctive appearance seems to have been the prerequisite for full status as a scapegoat. If this conclusion begins to sound persuasive, then the Haun's Mill Massacre restores one to a realistic confusion.

On an October day, the Missouri militia attacked a poorly defended settlement of the enemy, killed seventeen, and wounded fifteen more. One militiaman discovered a nine-year-old boy in hiding and prepared to shoot him. Another intervened. "Nits will make lice," the first man said, and killed the boy.

Is this the classic moment in an Indian massacre? The murdered boy, like the other victims at the 1838 Haun's Mill Massacre, was white—and Mormon.

In the 1830s, Missourians hated Mormons for a variety of reasons. They had unsettling religious, economic, and political practices; they were nonetheless prosperous, did not hold slaves, and could control elections by voting in a bloc. They were a peculiar people, seriously flawed to the Gentile point of view. Mormons were white, but the Missourians still played on most of the usual themes of race hatred. When the governor of Missouri suggested a war of extermination against the Mormons, he made one point clear: the absence of a racial difference could not keep white people from thoroughly hating each other.

Mormonism, moreover, was an American product. In the 1820s, in upstate New York the young Joseph Smith had brooded about American religious diversity. With so many sects making competing claims to certainty, how was the seeker to make the right choice? "I found," Smith said, "that there was a great clash in religious sentiment; if I went to one society they referred me to one plan, and another to another. . . ." It was obvious that "all could not be right" and "that God could not be the author of so much confusion." Wrestling with this chaos, Smith began to experience revelations, he said, leading him to the acquisition of buried golden plates. Translated, the golden plates became the Book of Mormon, and the basis of a new American religion, offering the certainty of direct revelation in modern times. To its believers, Mormonism was not so much a new religion as an old one restored. Over the centuries, true Christianity had become corrupted and factionalized, broken into the competing sects that had once perplexed Smith. The Church of Latter-day Saints of Jesus Christ restored the lost unity.

Against that backdrop of sects and denominations, Mormonism offered its converts certainty and community. In Mormon doctrine, earthly labors carried a direct connection to spiritual progress; one's exertions in the material world directly reflected one's spiritual standing. With nearly every daily action "mormonized," as a later observer put it, Saints clearly had to cluster, constructing communities in which they could keep each other on track. In converting to Mormonism, one converted to a full way of life within a community of believers. In their first decade, Mormons were already on their way to becoming a new ethnic group, something new under the American sun.

As Mormon numbers grew, and the majority of the converts clustered in the Midwest, they came into increasing conflict with their Gentile neighbors. Their novel religion, their occasional experiments in communitarianism, their ability to vote in a bloc, their very separatism, made them targets for suspicion and hostility. When Joseph Smith summarized his people's experience, he could not be accused of much exaggeration: "the injustice, the wrongs, the murders, the bloodshed, the theft, misery and woe that has been caused by the barbarous, inhuman and lawless proceedings" of their enemies, especially in the state of Missouri. . . .

When the "Indian problem" grew heated in the early nineteenth century, the remote and isolated West had presented itself as a geographical solution: place the Indians in locations white people would not want anyway, and end the friction by a strategy of segregation. Geography appeared to offer the same solution to "the Mormon problem." Relocated in the remote and arid Great Basin, the Mormons could escape persecution by a kind of spatial quarantine; the dimensions of the continent itself would guard them. Even when the gold rush broke the quarantine and when Gentiles—and even Missourians—were suddenly provoked into crossing the continent, the Mormons had had the chance to reverse the proportions and become an entrenched majority in the territory of Utah. . . .

The aridity of Utah meant that prosperity depended on a cooperation that the Mormons, uniquely, could provide. Land might be privately held, but water and timber were held in common and allocated by church authorities. The church leadership ordained the founding of towns and farms; communally organized labor could then build the dams and ditches that made irrigation possible. In their prosperity and good order, the settlements of the Mormons impressed even those who could find nothing else to admire in this peculiar people's way of life.

That peculiarity had become suddenly more dramatic. Established in their own territory, far from disapproving neighbors, leaders had felt empowered to bring the church's peculiar domestic practice into the open. In 1852, the Mormons stood revealed as practitioners of polygamy.

For the rest of the nineteenth century, the idea of one man in possession of more than one woman would strike most non-Mormon Americans as deviant, licentious, and *very* interesting—a shocking matter of sexual excess. In fact, Mormon polygamy was a staid and solemn affair. If the patriarchal family was a good thing, if bringing children into the world to be responsibly raised in the right religion was a major goal of life, then it was a logical—and very American—conclusion that more of a good thing could only be better. The Mormon family, properly conducted through this world, would reassemble in the afterlife. Adding more personnel to this sanctified unit gave Mormon patriarchs even greater opportunity to perform their ordained function. . . .

. . . For thirty years, Congress tried to make the Mormons behave. Antipolygamy laws added up to a sustained campaign to change personal behavior, a campaign without parallel except in Indian affairs. . . .

Antipolygamy laws finally drove the Mormon leaders into hiding, concealed—in defiance of federal law—by their loyal followers. The church had been placed in receivership; cohabitation prosecutions went on apace; zealous federal agents pursued the concealed leaders. Then, on September 24, 1890, President Wilford Woodruff of the LDS issued an official manifesto, advising the Latter-day Saints "to refrain from contracting any marriage forbidden by the law of the land." The year was 1890, and one kind of frontier opportunity had indeed closed. . . .

Whatever else it tells us, the Mormon example shows that race was not the only provocation for strong antipathies and prejudices. White people could also become aliens, targets for voyeuristic exploitation, for coercive legislation, even for the use of the U.S. Army. But, the Mormon example also shows that in the long run it paid to be white.

At the Utah statehood convention in 1895, Charles S. Varian gave a speech of reconciliation. Varian had earlier been U.S. district attorney for Utah Territory "and relentless in his prosecution of polygamy." He had, however, found the convention to be an occasion of harmony. Every member, he thought, had "been taught by his fellowmen that, after all, we are very much alike, and that the same passions, and the same motives, actuate us all."

"After all, we are very much alike"—it was a statement no one at the time made to the Chinese or the Japanese. Once polygamy had been formally settled, the "differentness" of Mormons could be subordinated and their essentially American qualities celebrated. . . .

When it came to pitting Western people against each other, politics and economics could work as well as race or religion. When White people appeared to threaten order and prosperity, the lesson was once again clear: race was no protector from vicious conflict. Consider three examples:

• In May 1912, the middle-class citizens of San Diego, California, forcibly expelled the anarchist speakers Emma Goldman and Ben Reitman. San Diego was, in that year, "an established city of more than 40,000 people," "progressive Republican" in politics. In their radicalism and also in their association with the Wobblies, the Industrial Workers of the World, Goldman and Reitman represented a threat that the city's boosters would not tolerate. Goldman "escaped violence only by the narrowest margin," a San Diego newspaper reported. But "treatment that the vigilantes would not give the woman was accorded to the man. Reitman was mysteriously spirited away from the hotel some time near midnight . . . and, it is reported, tarred and feathered and branded on the back with the letters 'I.W.W.' He is furthermore said to have been forced to kneel and kiss the American flag. The branding was done with a lighted cigar, which was traced through the tar. . . ." The concerned citizens and policemen of San Diego were not always so gentle. In other confrontations, "at least two radicals were killed."

• On April 20, 1914, the Colorado militia attacked a tent colony of strikers and their families. Both sides had guns and used them, but bullets were not the major source of injury. In the middle of the battle, the tents burst into flames. Two women and eleven children burned to death. The Ludlow massacre "climaxed a labor struggle in Colorado which erupted into a civil war all over the state."

• On November 5, 1916, two steamboats carrying Wobblies left Seattle for the town of Everett, to support a strike under way against the timber industry. Armed vigilantes and policemen tried to prevent them from landing; in the exchange of bullets, five workers and two vigilantes died, while over fifty were wounded and seven were reported missing. "The water turned crimson," one historian has written, "and corpses were washing ashore for days afterward."

The conventional approach of blaming Western violence on the "frontier environment" does not explain these incidents. Although most of the strikers at Ludlow were of southern or eastern European origin, racial or ethnic explanations of conflict are also of limited help. Judging by the written record alone, a historian blind to actual physical characteristics might think that there were at least eight oppressed races in the West: Indians, Hispanics, Chinese, Japanese, blacks, Mormons, strikers, and radicals.

Exploring the ways in which "Mexicans, Chinese and Indians were shamefully abused by the Yankee majority," Ray Allen Billington in 1956 placed the responsibility on the "corrosive effect of the environment" and "the absence of social pressures." The abuse, he said, represented "a completely undemocratic nativism."

This explanation has an innocent certainty now beyond our grasp. Nativism was only in an ideal sense "undemocratic." The California votes on Chinese exclusion and the Oregon votes on black exclusion made the voice of democracy in these matters clear. Second, blaming "the corrosive effect of the environment" for nativism involved doubtful logic; white Americans brought the raw material for these attitudes with them, with little help from the "environment." And finally, on close examination, over the duration of Western history, the very concept of "the Yankee majority" was a coherent entity only if one retreated to a great distance, from which the divisions simply could not be seen. . . .

When the weight of Southern civilization fell too heavily on Huckleberry Finn, Mark Twain offered the preferred American alternative: "I reckon I got to light out for the Territory ahead of the rest, because Aunt Sally she's going to adopt me and sivilize me, and I can't stand it. I been there before." The West, the theory had gone, was the place where one escaped the trials and burdens of American civilization, especially in its Southern version. Those "trials and burdens" often came in human form. Repeatedly, Americans had used the West as a mechanism for evading these "problems." Much of what went under the rubric "Western optimism" was in fact this faith in postponement, in the deferring of problems to the distant future. Whether in Indian removal or Mormon migration, the theory was the same: the West is remote and vast; its isolation and distance will release us from conflict; this is where we can get away from each other. But the workings of history carried an opposite lesson. The West was not where we escaped each other, but where we all met.

✒ F U R T H E R   R E A D I N G

William Cronon, George Miles, Jay Gitlin, eds., *Under an Open Sky: Rethinking America's Western Past* (1992).
Kenneth M. Hamilton, *Black Towns and Profit: Promotion and Development in the Trans-Appalachian West, 1877–1915* (1991).
Ruth B. Moynihan et al., eds., *So Much to Be Done: Women Settlers on the Mining and Ranching Frontier* (1990).
Theodore Roosevelt, *The Winning of the West* (1889).
Richard Slotkin, *Gunfighter Nation: The Myth of the Frontier in Twentieth Century America* (1992).
Frederick Jackson Turner, *The Frontier in American History* (1920).
Robert M. Utley, *The Indian Frontier of the American West, 1869–1886* (1982).
Richard White, *It's Your Misfortune and None of My Own: A New History of the American West* (1991).

CHAPTER
3

Industrialization, Workers, and the New Immigration

The Industrial Revolution and the migration of Europeans to the Americas were well under way before the American Civil War, but in the years after the war these phenomena restructured the American landscape in ways that would have made it unrecognizable to previous generations. Improvements in steel production allowed architects to design buildings that shot into the sky out of the flat prairie. Railroads built by laborers from China and Ireland linked the East Coast to the West Coast. Huge processing centers took the products of farms and ranches and converted them into consumer goods with a rapidity that made country and city folk alike rub their eyes in disbelief. Industrialists amassed fortunes in a way never before seen in human history, while skilled artisans found their training and judgment less and less called for in an age of mass production. Skilled and unskilled alike competed for jobs that often provided neither security nor salary enough to keep a family from starving.

In the midst of this industrial transformation, a second giant wave of immigration hit the United States. Sometimes called the "new immigration" to distinguish it from the influx of Germans and Irish earlier in the nineteenth century, this wave brought Poles, Italians, Scandinavians, and eastern European Jews. Crowded together in tenements and jostled into factories and sweatshops, these immigrants struggled to adapt their old skills to new working conditions. They also sought to maintain their sense of themselves in the midst of change. They organized labor unions to attempt to create decent working conditions. Outside of work, they gathered in churches, saloons, and public parks, where they could escape the watchful eye of employers and reformers and enjoyed the camaraderie of their "own kind."

At all points on the political and class spectrum, Americans struggled to define the meaning of industrial concentration for democracy and social justice. Unions like the Knights of Labor called for broad reforms to "secure to the laborer the fruits of his toil," including equal pay for women. Organizations like the American Federation of Labor focused more narrowly, but effectively, on specific reforms for particular classes of skilled workers. Industrialists competed to achieve ever more profitable advantages of scale, leading to a rush of corporate mergers between 1897 and 1900. Integrating vertically and horizontally, the largest companies formed "trusts" into which smaller companies disappeared. By 1900, seventy-three such trusts had swallowed up more than 3,000 companies, creating combinations like Standard Oil, U.S. Steel, and the American Tobacco Company. Industrialists defended their actions as the inevitable outcome of "progress" and industrial development. Although they violently resisted the demands of workers for a more equitable sharing of profits, a few also sought to express traditional American concerns for equality and "uplift" through the creation of a new set of institutions—philanthropic foundations and free libraries. Increased immigration, industrialization, and urbanization all contributed to making this a particularly turbulent transition in U.S. history.

Q U E S T I O N S   T O   T H I N K   A B O U T

How did immigrants cope with conditions as they found them in America's brimming cities? Did industry crush immigrants or provide them with new opportunities? In what ways did workers resist the attempts of employers to dictate the terms of life, and were they effective?

D O C U M E N T S

The documents in this chapter present different reactions to the new immigration and industrial changes. Document 1 is a poem by the writer Emma Lazarus, the daughter of a prosperous Jewish family in New York. She wrote it to help raise funds for a pedestal for the Statue of Liberty. The verse appears at the base of the statue, which was often the first thing immigrants saw when they sailed into New York Harbor. Document 2 is a European boy's perspective on the stories of the Golden Country told by returned immigrants. It gives insight into the images that lured immigrants to the New World. Document 3 is another immigrant account, drawn from congressional testimony on the replacement of skilled adult labor with unskilled child labor in factories. It shows graphically the devastating poverty encountered by immigrant and working families. Document 4 outlines the broad objectives of the Knights of Labor, including their more "utopian" goals, such as equal pay for women and the establishment of cooperative institutions. Document 5 reveals the practical emphasis of the American Federation of Labor, which focused its efforts on bettering conditions for skilled labor and giving the working man "eight hours for what we will." Document 6 expresses the Social Darwinism of Andrew Carnegie, a Scottish immigrant and self-made millionaire who during his lifetime gave 90 percent of his wealth to establish free public libraries and a variety of nonprofit foundations. Carnegie's statement helps to explain how some industrialists rationalized to themselves the often-painful consequences of industrialization. In Document 7, the famous efficiency expert Frederick Winslow Taylor details how he persuaded men to work faster by selecting an "ideal worker" and training him to follow instructions slavishly—leaving no room for "unscientific" personal initiative. Document 8 is by the Pulitzer Prize–winning novelist and socialist Upton Sinclair. His masterpiece of muckraking, *The Jungle,* helped Progressive reformers pass the Pure Food and Drug Act, but Sinclair also created one of the most disturbing descriptions of immigrant life ever written. In this selection, the downtrodden Polish immigrant Jurgis Rudkus discovers the saloon.

1. Emma Lazarus Praises the New Colossus, 1883

Not like the brazen giant of Greek fame,
With conquering limbs astride from land to land;
Here at our sea-washed, sunset gates shall stand
A mighty woman with a torch, whose flame
Is the imprisoned lightning, and her name
Mother of Exiles. From her beacon-hand
Glows world-wide welcome; her mild eyes command
The air-bridged harbor that twin cities frame.
"Keep, ancient lands, your storied pomp!" cries she
With silent lips. "Give me your tired, your poor,
Your huddled masses yearning to breathe free,
The wretched refuse of your teeming shore.
Send these, the homeless, tempest-tost to me,
I lift my lamp beside the golden door!"

2. A Slovenian Boy Remembers
Tales of the Golden Country, 1909

As a boy of nine, and even younger, in my native village . . . I experienced a thrill every time one of the men of the little community returned from America.

Five or six years before, as I heard people tell, the man had quietly left the village for the United States, a poor peasant clad in homespun, with a mustache under his nose and a bundle on his back; now, a clean-shaven *Amerikanec,* he sported a blue-serge suit, buttoned shoes very large in the toes and with india-rubber heels, a black derby, a shiny celluloid collar, and a loud necktie made even louder by a dazzling horseshoe pin, which, rumor had it, was made of gold, while his two suit-cases of imitation leather, tied with straps, bulged with gifts from America for his relatives and friends in the village. In nine cases out of ten, he had left in economic desperation, on money borrowed from some relative in the United States; now there was talk in the village that he was worth anywhere from one to three thousand American dollars. And to my eyes he truly bore all the earmarks of affluence. Indeed, to say that he thrilled my boyish fancy is putting it mildly. With other boys in the village, I followed him around as he went visiting his relatives and friends and distributing presents, and hung onto his every word and gesture.

Then, on the first Sunday after his homecoming, if at all possible, I got within earshot of the nabob as he sat in the winehouse or under the linden in front of the winehouse in Blato, surrounded by village folk, ordering wine and *klobase*—Carniolan sausages—for all comers, paying for accordion-players, indulging in tall talk about America, its wealth and vastness, and his own experiences as a worker in

Eve Merriam, *Emma Lazarus: Woman with a Torch!* (New York: Citadel Press, 1956), p. 126. All rights reserved. Reprinted by permission of Citadel Press, Kensington Publishing Corp.

Excerpts (pp. 3–6, 12–17, 19, 20) from *Laughing in the Jungle* by Louis Adamic. Copyright © 1932 by Louis Adamic. Copyright © renewed 1960 by Stella Adamic. Reprinted by permission of HarperCollins Publishers, Inc.

the West Virginia or Kansas coal-mines or Pennsylvania rolling-mills, and comparing notes upon conditions in the United States with other local *Amerikanci* who had returned before him. . . .

I remember that, listening to them, I played with the idea of going to America when I was but eight or nine.

My notion of the United States then, and for a few years after, was that it was a grand, amazing, somewhat fantastic place—the Golden Country—a sort of Paradise—the Land of Promise in more ways than one—huge beyond conception, thousands of miles across the ocean, untellably exciting, explosive, quite incomparable to the tiny, quiet, lovely Carniola; a place full of movement and turmoil, wherein things that were unimaginable and impossible in Blato happened daily as a matter of course.

In America one could make pots of money in a short time, acquire immense holdings, wear a white collar, and have polish on one's boots like a *gospod*—one of the gentry—and eat white bread, soup, and meat on weekdays as well as on Sundays, even if one were but an ordinary workman to begin with. In Blato no one ate white bread or soup and meat, except on Sundays and holidays, and very few then. . . .

In America everything was possible. There even the common people were "citizens," not "subjects," as they were in Austria and in most other European countries. A citizen, or even a non-citizen foreigner, could walk up to the President of the United States and pump his hand. Indeed, that seemed to be a custom in America. There was a man in Blato, a former steel-worker in Pittsburgh, who claimed that upon an occasion he had shaken hands and exchanged words with Theodore Roosevelt, to whom he familiarly referred as "Tedi"—which struck my mother very funny. To her it seemed as if some one had called the Pope of Rome or the Emperor of Austria by a nickname. But the man assured her, in my hearing, that in America everybody called the President merely "Tedi."

Mother laughed about this, off and on, for several days. And I laughed with her. She and I often laughed together.

3. Immigrant Thomas O'Donnell Laments the Plight of the Worker, 1883

BOSTON, MASS., *October 18, 1883*

THOMAS O'DONNELL examined.

By the CHAIRMAN:

Question. Where do you live? *Answer.* At Fall River.

Q. How long have you lived in this country? *A.* Eleven years.

Q. Where were you born? *A.* In Ramsbotham, England.

Q. Have you been naturalized here? *A.* No, sir.

Testimony of Thomas O'Donnell, Fall River mule-spinner, *Report of Senate Committee upon the Relations Between Labor and Capital,* III (1883), 451–457.

Life of a Mule-Spinner

Q. What is your business? *A.* I am a mule-spinner by trade. I have worked at it since I have been in this country—eleven years.

Q. Are you a married man? *A.* Yes, sir; I am a married man; have a wife and two children. I am not very well educated. I went to work when I was young, and have been working ever since in the cotton business; went to work when I was about eight or nine years old. I was going to state how I live. My children get along very well in summer time, on account of not having to buy fuel or shoes or one thing and another. I earn $1.50 a day and can't afford to pay a very big house rent. I pay $1.50 a week for rent, which comes to about $6 a month. . . .

Q. Do you have work right along? *A.* No, sir; since that strike we had down in Fall River about three years ago I have not worked much more than half the time, and that has brought my circumstances down very much.

Q. Why have you not worked more than half the time since then?—*A.* Well, at Fall River if a man has not got a boy to act as "back-boy" it is very hard for him to get along. In a great many cases they discharge men in that work and put in men who have boys.

Q. Men who have boys of their own? *A.* Men who have boys of their own capable enough to work in a mill, to earn 30 or 40 cents a day.

Child Labor Necessary to the Employment of Parents

Q. Is the object of that to enable the boy to earn something for himself?

A. Well, no; the object is this: They are doing away with a great deal of mule-spinning there and putting in ring-spinning, and for that reason it takes a good deal of small help to run this ring work, and it throws the men out of work because they are doing away with the mules and putting these ring-frames in to take their places. For that reason they get all the small help they can to run these ring-frames. There are so many men in the city to work, and whoever has a boy can have work, and whoever has no boy stands no chance. Probably he may have a few months of work in the summer time, but will be discharged in the fall. That is what leaves me in poor circumstances. Our children, of course, are very often sickly from one cause or another, on account of not having sufficient clothes, or shoes, or food, or something. And also my woman; she never did work in a mill; she was a housekeeper, and for that reason she can't help me to anything at present, as many women do help their husbands down there, by working, like themselves. My wife never did work in a mill, and that leaves me to provide for the whole family. I have two children. . . .

Supporting a Family on $133 a Year

. . .

Q. Taking a full year back can you tell how much you have had?—*A.* That would be about fifteen weeks' work. Last winter, as I told you, I got in, and I worked up to about somewhere around Fast Day, or may be New Year's day; anyway, Mr. Howard has it down on his record, if you wish to have an exact answer to that question; he can answer it better than I can, because we have a sort of union there to keep ourselves together.

Q. Do you think you have had $150 within a year? *A.* No, sir.

Q. Have you had $125? *A.* Well, I could figure it up if I had time. The thirteen weeks is all I have had. . . .

Q. That would be somewhere about $133, if you had not lost any time? *A.* Yes, sir.

Q. That is all you have had? *A.* Yes, sir.

Q. To support yourself and wife and two children? *A.* Yes, sir.

Q. Have you had any help from outside? *A.* No, sir.

Q. Do you mean that yourself and wife and two children have had nothing but that for all this time? *A.* That is all. I got a couple dollars' worth of coal last winter, and the wood I picked up myself. I goes around with a shovel and picks up clams and wood. . . .

Too Poor to Go West

Q. Well, I want to know why you do not go out West on a $2,000 farm, or take up a homestead and break it and work it up, and then have it for yourself and family? *A.* I can't see how I could get out West. I have got nothing to go with.

Q. It would not cost you over $1,500. *A.* Well, I never saw over a $20 bill, and that is when I have been getting a month's pay at once. If some one would give me $1,500 I will go. . . .

Q. Are you a good workman? *A.* Yes, sir.

Q. Were you ever turned off because of misconduct or incapacity or unfitness for work? *A.* No, sir.

Q. Or because you did bad work? *A.* No, sir.

Q. Or because you made trouble among the help? *A.* No, sir.

Q. Did you ever have any personal trouble with an employer? *A.* No, sir.

Q. You have not anything now you say? *A.* No, sir.

Q. How old are you? *A.* About thirty.

Q. Is your health good? *A.* Yes, sir. . . .

Q. And there are four of you in the family? *A.* Yes, sir. . . .

Q. What other kinds of meat have you had within a year? *A.* Well, we have had corn beef twice I think that I can remember this year—on Sunday, for dinner.

Q. Twice is all that you can remember within a year? *A.* Yes—and some cabbage.

Q. What have you eaten? *A.* Well, bread mostly, when we could get it; we sometimes couldn't make out to get that, and have had to go without a meal.

Q. Has there been any day in the year that you have had to go without anything to eat? *A.* Yes, sir, several days.

Q. More than one day at a time? *A.* No.

Q. How about the children and your wife—did they go without anything to eat too?

The Children Crying for Food

A. My wife went out this morning and went to a neighbor's and got a loaf of bread and fetched it home, and when she got home the children were crying for something to eat.

Q. Have the children had anything to eat to-day except that, do you think? *A.* They had that loaf of bread—I don't know what they have had since then, if they have had anything.

Q. Did you leave any money at home? *A.* No, sir.

Q. If that loaf is gone, is there anything in the house? *A.* No, sir; unless my wife goes out and gets something; and I don't know who would mind the children while she goes out.

Q. Has she any money to get anything with? *A.* No, sir.

Q. Have the children gone without a meal at any time during the year? *A.* They have gone without bread some days, but we have sometimes got meal and made porridge of it.

Q. What kind of meal? *A.* Sometimes Indian meal, and sometimes oatmeal.

Q. Meal stirred up in hot water? *A.* Yes, sir.

Q. Is it cold weather down there now? *A.* It is very cold now.

4. The Knights of Labor Demand Reform, 1878

The recent alarming development and aggression of aggregated wealth, which, unless checked, will inevitably lead to the pauperization and hopeless degradation of the toiling masses, render it imperative, if we desire to enjoy the blessings of life, that a check should be placed upon its power and upon unjust accumulation, and a system adopted which will secure to the laborer the fruits of his toil; and as this much-desired object can only be accomplished by the thorough unification of labor, and the united efforts of those who obey the divine injunction that "in the sweat of thy brow shalt thou eat bread," we have formed the [*name of local assembly*] with a view to securing the organization and direction, by co-operative effort, of the power of the industrial classes; and we submit to the world the objects sought to be accomplished by our organization, calling upon all who believe in securing "the greatest good to the greatest number" to aid and assist us.

Objectives

I. To bring within the folds of organization every department of productive industry, making knowledge a standpoint for action, and industrial, moral worth, not wealth, the true standard of individual and national greatness.

II. To secure to the toilers a proper share of the wealth that they create; more of the leisure that rightfully belongs to them; more [social] advantages, more of the benefits, privileges, and emoluments of the world; in a word, all those rights and privileges necessary to make them capable of enjoying, appreciating, defending, and perpetuating the blessings of good government.

III. To arrive at the true condition of the producing masses in their educational, moral, and financial condition, by demanding from the various governments the establishment of bureaus of Labor Statistics.

IV. The establishment of co-operative institutions, productive and distributive.

T. V. Powderly, *Thirty Years of Labor* (Columbus, Ohio: Excelssor Publishing House, 1890), 243–246.

V. The reserving of the public lands—the heritage of the people—for the actual settler. Not another acre [is to be allocated] for railroads or speculators.

VI. The abrogation of all laws that do not bear equally upon capital and labor, the removal of unjust technicalities, delays, and discriminations in the administration of justice, and the adopting of measures providing for the health and safety of those engaged in mining, manufacturing, or building pursuits.

VII. The enactment of laws to compel chartered corporations to pay their employees weekly, in full, for labor performed during the preceding week, in the lawful money of the country.

VIII. The enactment of laws giving mechanics and laborers a first lien on their work for their full wages.

IX. The abolishment of the contract system on national, state, and municipal work.

X. The substitution of arbitration for strikes, whenever and wherever employers and employees are willing to meet on equitable grounds.

XI. The prohibition of the employment of children in workshops, mines and factories before attaining their fourteenth year.

XII. To abolish the system of letting out by contract the labor of convicts in our prisons and reformatory institutions.

XIII. To secure for both sexes equal pay for equal work.

XIV. The reduction of the hours of labor to eight per day, so that the laborers may have more time for social enjoyment and intellectual improvement, and be enabled to reap the advantages conferred by the labor-saving machinery which their brains have created.

XV. To prevail upon governments to establish a purely national circulating medium, based upon the faith and resources of the nation, and issued directly to the people, without the intervention of any system of banking corporations, which money shall be a legal tender in payment of all debts, public or private.

5. Unionist Samuel Gompers Asks "What Does the Working Man Want?" 1890

. . . My friends, we have met here today to celebrate the idea that has prompted thousands of working-people of Louisville and New Albany to parade the streets of y[our city]; that prompts the toilers of Chicago to turn out by their fifty or hundred thousand of men; that prompts the vast army of wage-workers in New York to demonstrate their enthusiasm and appreciation of the importance of this idea; that prompts the toilers of England, Ireland, Germany, France, Italy, Spain, and Austria to defy the manifestos of the autocrats of the world and say that on May the first, 1890, the wage-workers of the world will lay down their tools in sympathy with the wage-workers of America, to establish a principle of limitations of hours of labor to eight hours for sleep [applause], eight hours for work, and eight hours for what we will. [Applause.]

"A News Account of an Address in Louisville," in *The Samuel Gompers Papers: The Early Years of the American Federation of Labor, 1887–90,* ed. Stuart Kaufman (Chicago: University of Illinois Press, 1987), 307–314.

It has been charged time and again that were we to have more hours of leisure we would merely devote it to debauchery, to the cultivation of vicious habits—in other words, that we would get drunk. I desire to say this in answer to that charge: As a rule, there are two classes in society who get drunk. One is the class who has no work to do in consequence of too much money; the other class, who also has no work to do, because it can't get any, and gets drunk on its face. [Laughter.] I maintain that that class in our social life that exhibits the greatest degree of sobriety is that class who are able, by a fair number of hours of day's work to earn fair wages—not overworked. The man who works twelve, fourteen, and sixteen hours a day requires some artificial stimulant to restore the life ground out of him in the drudgery of the day. [Applause.] . . .

We ought to be able to discuss this question on a higher ground, and I am pleased to say that the movement in which we are engaged will stimulate us to it. They tell us that the eight-hour movement can not be enforced, for the reason that it must check industrial and commercial progress. I say that the history of this country, in its industrial and commercial relations, shows the reverse. I say that is the plane on which this question ought to be discussed—that is the social question. As long as they make this question an economic one, I am willing to discuss it with them. I would retrace every step I have taken to advance this movement did it mean industrial and commercial stagnation. But it does not mean that. It means greater prosperity; it means a greater degree of progress for the whole people; it means more advancement and intelligence, and a nobler race of people. . . .

They say they can't afford it. Is that true? Let us see for one moment. If a reduction in the hours of labor causes industrial and commercial ruination, it would naturally follow increased hours of labor would increase the prosperity, commercial and industrial. If that were true, England and America ought to be at the tail end, and China at the head of civilization. [Applause.]

Is it not a fact that we find laborers in England and the United States, where the hours are eight, nine and ten hours a day—do we not find that the employers and laborers are more successful? Don't we find them selling articles cheaper? We do not need to trust the modern moralist to tell us those things. In all industries where the hours of labor are long, there you will find the least development of the power of invention. Where the hours of labor are long, men are cheap, and where men are cheap there is no necessity for invention. How can you expect a man to work ten or twelve or fourteen hours at his calling and then devote any time to the invention of a machine or discovery of a new principle or force? If he be so fortunate as to be able to read a paper he will fall asleep before he has read through the second or third line. [Laughter.] . . .

The man who works the long hours has no necessities except the barest to keep body and soul together, so he can work. He goes to sleep and dreams of work; he rises in the morning to go to work; he takes his frugal lunch to work; he comes home again to throw himself down on a miserable apology for a bed so that he can get that little rest that he may be able to go to work again. He is nothing but a veritable machine. He lives to work instead of working to live. [Loud applause.]

My friends, the only thing the working people need besides the necessities of life, is time. Time. Time with which our lives begin; time with which our lives close; time to cultivate the better nature within us; time to brighten our homes. Time, which brings us from the lowest condition up to the highest civilization; time, so that we can raise men to a higher plane. . . .

We want eight hours and nothing less. We have been accused of being selfish, and it has been said that we will want more; that last year we got an advance of ten cents and now we want more. We do want more. You will find that a man generally wants more. Go and ask a tramp what he wants, and if he doesn't want a drink he will want a good, square meal. You ask a workingman, who is getting two dollars a day, and he will say that he wants ten cents more. Ask a man who gets five dollars a day and he will want fifty cents more. The man who receives five thousand dollars a year wants six thousand dollars a year, and the man who owns eight or nine hundred thousand dollars will want a hundred thousand dollars more to make it a million, while the man who has his millions will want every thing he can lay his hands on and then raise his voice against the poor devil who wants ten cents more a day. We live in the latter part of the Nineteenth century. In the age of electricity and steam that has produced wealth a hundred fold, we insist that it has been brought about by the intelligence and energy of the workingmen, and while we find that it is now easier to produce it is harder to live. We do want more, and when it becomes more, we shall still want more. [Applause.] And we shall never cease to demand more until we have received the results of our labor.

6. Steel Magnate Andrew Carnegie Preaches a Gospel of Wealth, 1889

The problem of our age is the proper administration of wealth, that the ties of brotherhood may still bind together the rich and poor in harmonious relationship. The conditions of human life have not only been changed, but revolutionized, within the past few hundred years. In former days there was little difference between the dwelling, dress, food, and environment of the chief and those of his retainers. The Indians are to-day where civilized man then was. When visiting the Sioux, I was led to the wigwam of the chief. It was like the others in external appearance, and even within the difference was trifling between it and those of the poorest of his braves. The contrast between the palace of the millionaire and the cottage of the laborer with us to-day measures the change which has come with civilization. This change, however, is not to be deplored, but welcomed as highly beneficial. It is well, nay, essential, for the progress of the race that the houses of some should be homes for all that is highest and best in literature and the arts, and for all the refinements of civilization, rather than that none should be so. Much better this great irregularity than universal squalor. Without wealth there can be no Mæcenas. The "good old times" were not good old times. Neither master nor servant was as well situated then as to-day. A relapse to old conditions would be disastrous to both—not the least so to him who serves—and would sweep away civilization with it. But whether the change be for good or ill, it is upon us, beyond our power to alter, and, therefore, to be accepted and made the best of. It is a waste of time to criticize the inevitable. . . .

Andrew Carnegie, *Gospel of Wealth* (North American Review, 1889), 1–4, 7, 10–11, 13, 17.

The price we pay for this salutary change is, no doubt, great. We assemble thousands of operatives in the factory, and in the mine, of whom the employer can know little or nothing, and to whom he is little better than a myth. All intercourse between them is at an end. Rigid castes are formed, and, as usual, mutual ignorance breeds mutual distrust. Each caste is without sympathy with the other, and ready to credit anything disparaging in regard to it. Under the law of competition, the employer of thousands is forced into the strictest economies, among which the rates paid to labor figure prominently, and often there is friction between the employer and the employed, between capital and labor, between rich and poor. Human society loses homogeneity.

The price which society pays for the law of competition, like the price it pays for cheap comforts and luxuries, is also great; but the advantages of this law are also greater still than its cost—for it is to this law that we owe our wonderful material development, which brings improved conditions in its train. But, whether the law be benign or not, we must say of it, as we say of the change in the conditions of men to which we have referred: It is here; we cannot evade it; no substitutes for it have been found; and while the law may be sometimes hard for the individual, it is best for the race, because it insures the survival of the fittest in every department. . . .

We start, then, with a condition of affairs under which the best interests of the race are promoted, but which inevitably gives wealth to the few. Thus far, accepting conditions as they exist, the situation can be surveyed and pronounced good. The question then arises,—and if the foregoing be correct, it is the only question with which we have to deal,—What is the proper mode of administering wealth after the laws upon which civilization is founded have thrown it into the hands of the few? And it is of this great question that I believe I offer the true solution. . . .

. . . The budget presented in the British Parliament the other day proposes to increase the death duties; and, most significant of all, the new tax is to be a graduated one. Of all forms of taxation this seems the wisest. Men who continue hoarding great sums all their lives, the proper use of which for public ends would work good to the community from which it chiefly came, should be made to feel that the community, in the form of the State, cannot thus be deprived of its proper share. By taxing estates heavily at death the State marks its condemnation of the selfish millionaire's unworthy life.

It is desirable that nations should go much further in this direction. . . . This policy would work powerfully to induce the rich man to attend to the administration of wealth during his life, which is the end that society should always have in view, as being by far the most fruitful for the people. Nor need it be feared that this policy would sap the root of enterprise and render men less anxious to accumulate, for, to the class whose ambition it is to leave great fortunes and be talked about after their death, it will attract even more attention, and, indeed, be a somewhat nobler ambition, to have enormous sums paid over to the State from their fortunes. . . .

Poor and restricted are our opportunities in this life, narrow our horizon, our best work most imperfect; but rich men should be thankful for one inestimable boon. They have it in their power during their lives to busy themselves in organizing benefactions from which the masses of their fellows will derive lasting advantage, and thus dignify their own lives. . . .

This, then, is held to be the duty of the man of wealth: To set an example of modest, unostentatious living, shunning display or extravagance; to provide moderately for the legitimate wants of those dependent upon him; and, after doing so, to consider all surplus revenues which come to him simply as trust funds, which he is called upon to administer, and strictly bound as a matter of duty to administer in the manner which, in his judgment, is best calculated to produce the most beneficial results for the community—the man of wealth thus becoming the mere trustee and agent for his poorer brethren, bringing to their service his superior wisdom, experience, and ability to administer, doing for them better than they would or could do for themselves. . . .

. . . The day is not far distant when the man who dies leaving behind him millions of available wealth, which was free for him to administer during life, will pass away "unwept, unhonored, and unsung," no matter to what uses he leaves the dross which he cannot take with him. Of such as these the public verdict will then be: "The man who dies thus rich dies disgraced."

Such, in my opinion, is the true gospel concerning wealth, obedience to which is destined some day to solve the problem of the rich and the poor, and to bring "Peace on earth, among men good will."

7. Engineer Frederick Winslow Taylor Fashions the Ideal Worker, 1910

Our first step was the scientific selection of the workman. In dealing with workmen under this type of management, it is an inflexible rule to talk to and deal with only one man at a time, since each workman has his own special abilities and limitations, and since we are not dealing with men in masses, but are trying to develop each individual man to his highest state of efficiency and prosperity. Our first step was to find the proper workman to begin with. We therefore carefully watched and studied these 75 men for three or four days, at the end of which time we had picked out four men who appeared to be physically able to handle pig iron at the rate of 47 tons [as opposed to the customary 12½ tons] per day. A careful study was then made of each of these men. We looked up their history as far back as practicable and thorough inquiries were made as to the character, habits, and the ambition of each of them. Finally we selected one from among the four as the most likely man to start with. He was a little Pennsylvania Dutchman who had been observed to trot back home for a mile or so after his work in the evening about as fresh as he was when he came trotting down to work in the morning. We found that upon wages of $1.15 a day he had succeeded in buying a small plot of ground, and that he was engaged in putting up the walls of a little house for himself in the morning before starting to work and at night after leaving. He also had the reputation of being exceedingly "close," that is, of placing a very high value on a dollar. As one man whom we talked to about him said, "A penny looks about the size of a cart-wheel to him." This man we will call Schmidt.

F. W. Taylor, *Scientific Management* (New York: Harper & Brothers, 1910), 5–8.

The task before us, then, narrowed itself down to getting Schmidt to handle 47 tons of pig iron per day and making him glad to do it. This was done as follows. Schmidt was called out from among the gang of pig-iron handlers and talked to somewhat in this way:

"Schmidt, are you a high-priced man?"

"Vell, I don't know vat you mean."

"Oh yes, you do. What I want to know is whether you are a high-priced man or not."

"Vell, I don't know vat you mean."

"Oh, come now, you answer my questions. What I want to find out is whether you are a high-priced man or one of these cheap fellows here. What I want to find out is whether you want to earn $1.85 a day or whether you are satisfied with $1.15, just the same as all those cheap fellows are getting."

"Did I vant $1.85 a day? Vas dot a high-priced man? Vell, yes, I vas a high-priced man.". . .

"Well, if you are a high-priced man, you will load that pig iron on that car to-morrow for $1.85. Now do wake up and answer my question. Tell me whether you are a high-priced man or not."

"Vell—did I got $1.85 for loading dot pig iron on dot car to-morrow?"

"Yes, of course you do, and you get $1.85 for loading a pile like that every day right through the year. That is what a high-priced man does, and you know it just as well as I do."

"Vell, dot's all right. I could load dot pig iron on the car to-morrow for $1.85, and I get it every day, don't I?"

"Certainly you do—certainly you do."

"Vell, den, I vas a high-priced man."

"Now, hold on, hold on. You know just as well as I do that a high-priced man has to do exactly as he's told from morning till night. You have seen this man here before, haven't you?"

"No, I never saw him."

"Well, if you are a high-priced man, you will do exactly as this man tells you to-morrow, from morning till night. When he tells you to pick up a pig and walk, you pick it up and you walk, and when he tells you to sit down and rest, you sit down. You do that right straight through the day. And what's more, no back talk. Now a high-priced man does just what he's told to do, and no back talk. Do you understand that? When this man tells you to walk, you walk; when he tells you to sit down, you sit down, and you don't talk back at him. Now you come on to work here to-morrow morning and I'll know before night whether you are really a high-priced man or not."

This seems to be rather rough talk. And indeed it would be if applied to an educated mechanic, or even an intelligent laborer. With a man of the mentally sluggish type of Schmidt it is appropriate and not unkind, since it is effective in fixing his attention on the high wages which he wants and away from what, if it were called to his attention, he probably would consider impossibly hard work. . . .

Schmidt started to work, and all day long, and at regular intervals, was told by the man who stood over him with a watch, "Now pick up a pig and walk. Now sit down and rest. Now walk—now rest," etc. He worked when he was told to work, and rested when he was told to rest, and at half-past five in the afternoon had his 47½ tons loaded on the car. And he practically never failed to work at this pace and do the task that was set him during the three years that the writer was at Bethlehem. And throughout this time he averaged a little more than $1.85 per day, whereas before he had never received over $1.15 per day, which was the ruling rate of wages at that time in Bethlehem. That is, he received 60 percent higher wages than were paid to other men who were not working on task work. One man after another was picked out and trained to handle pig iron at the rate of 47½ tons per day until all of the pig iron was handled at this rate, and the men were receiving 60 percent more wages than other workmen around them.

The writer has given above a brief description of three of the four elements which constitute the essence of scientific management: first, the careful selection of the workman, and, second and third, the method of first inducing and then training and helping the workman to work according to the scientific method.

8. Jurgis Rudkus Discovers the Saloon in *The Jungle,* 1905

With one member trimming beef in a cannery, and another working in a sausage factory, the family had a first-hand knowledge of the great majority of Packingtown swindles. For it was the custom, as they found, whenever meat was so spoiled that it could not be used for anything else, either to can it or else to chop it up into sausage. . . .

It was only when the whole ham was spoiled that it came into the department of Elzbieta. Cut up by the two-thousand-revolutions-a-minute flyers, and mixed with half a ton of other meat, no odor that ever was in a ham could make any difference. There was never the least attention paid to what was cut up for sausage; there would come all the way back from Europe old sausage that had been rejected, and that was mouldy and white—it would be dosed with borax and glycerine, and dumped into the hoppers and made over again for home consumption. . . .

Such were the new surroundings in which Elzbieta was placed, and such was the work she was compelled to do. It was stupefying, brutalizing work; it left her no time to think, no strength for anything. She was part of the machine she tended, and every faculty that was not needed for the machine was doomed to be crushed out of existence. There was only one mercy about the cruel grind—that it gave her the gift of insensibility. Little by little she sank into a torpor—she fell silent. She would meet Jurgis and Ona in the evening, and the three would walk home together, often without saying a word. Ona, too, was falling into a habit of silence—Ona, who had once gone about singing like a bird. . . .

Yet the soul of Ona was not dead—the souls of none of them were dead, but only sleeping; and now and then they would waken, and these were cruel times. The gates of memory would roll open—old joys would stretch out their arms to them, old hopes and dreams would call to them, and they would stir beneath the

Upton Sinclair, *The Jungle* (1905), 135–139.

burden that lay upon them, and feel its forever immeasurable weight. They could not even cry out beneath it; but anguish would seize them, more dreadful than the agony of death. It was a thing scarcely to be spoken—a thing never spoken by all the world, that will not know its own defeat.

They were beaten; they had lost the game, they were swept aside. It was not less tragic because it was so sordid, because that it had to do with wages and grocery bills and rents. They had dreamed of freedom; a chance to look about them and learn something; to be decent and clean, to see their child grow up to be strong. And now it was all gone—it would never be! They had played the game and they had lost. Six years more of toil they had to face before they could expect the least respite, the cessation of the payments upon the house; and how cruelly certain it was that they could never stand six years of such a life as they were living! . . .

Jurgis, being a man, had troubles of his own. There was another specter following him. He had never spoken of it, nor would he allow any one else to speak of it—he had never acknowledged its existence to himself. Yet the battle with it took all the manhood that he had—and once or twice, alas, a little more. Jurgis had discovered drink.

He was working in the steaming pit of hell; day after day, week after week—until now there was not an organ of his body that did its work without pain, until the sound of ocean breakers echoes in his head day and night, and the buildings swayed and danced before him as he went down the street. And from all the unending horror of this there was a respite, a deliverance—he could drink! He could forget the pain, he could slip off the burden; he would see clearly again, he would be master of his brain, of his thoughts, of his will. His dead self would stir in him, and he would find himself laughing and cracking jokes with his companions—he would be a man again, and master of his life.

It was not an easy thing for Jurgis to take more than two or three drinks. With the first drink he could eat a meal, and he could persuade himself that that was economy; with the second he could eat another meal—but there would come a time when he could eat no more, and then to pay for a drink was an unthinkable extravagance, a defiance of the age-long instincts of his hunger-haunted class. One day, however, he took the plunge, and drank up all that he had in his pockets, and went home half "piped," as the men phrase it. He was happier than he had been in a year.

E S S A Y S

Immigration history is deeply intertwined with industrialization because workers from Europe provided much of the muscle for the new factories. The great immigration historian Oscar Handlin, retired from Harvard University, articulates convincingly what some have dubbed the "melting pot" theory: that factory work and polyglot cities sheared immigrants of their cultural roots, reduced them to a common human mass, and remolded them in the forms desired by capitalists. In the first essay, an excerpt from Handlin's classic book, *The Uprooted,* he shows how factories simplified their mechanical processes so that they could utilize unskilled peasants and how peasants came to adapt themselves to the new life. He also argues that industrial labor left the immigrant just as vulnerable to poverty as conditions in the Old World, but with considerably less psychic compensation. A generation and more of younger historians have emphasized the ways in which immigrants and other workers resisted the new industrial work discipline. In the second essay, Roy Rosenzweig of George Mason University shifts attention away from the factory to examine other avenues through which the poor and struggling created order out of chaos for themselves in the late nineteenth century. He argues implicitly against the melting pot theory, showing that immigrants never gave up the fight for personal autonomy. First, he shows how immigrants retained a sense of cultural integrity by creating neighborhood enclaves that felt like "home." Second, he asserts that new institutions arose to fulfill new needs. Saloons, in particular, provided an important meeting ground where workers could express their own values rather than the values demanded by employers.

The Uprooted

OSCAR HANDLIN

Let the peasant, now in America, confront his first problem; time enough if ever this is solved to turn to other matters.

How shall a man feed himself, find bread for his family? The condition of man is to till the soil; there is no other wholeness to his existence. True, in retrospect, life on the soil in the old home had not yielded a livelihood. But that was because there was not there soil enough. In consequence, the husbandmen, in their hundreds of thousands, have left their meager plots. They have now come to a New World where open land reaches away in acre after acre of inexhaustible plenty. Arrived, they are ready to work.

Yet only a few, a fortunate few, of these eager hands were destined ever to break the surface of the waiting earth. Among the multitudes that survived the crossing, there were now and then some who survived it intact enough in body and resources to get beyond the port of landing and through the interior cities of transit. Those who were finally able to establish themselves as the independent proprietors of farms of their own made up an even smaller number.

All the others were unable to escape from the cities. Decade after decade, as the Federal government made its count, the census revealed a substantial majority of the immigrants in the urban places; and the margin of that majority grew steadily larger. Always the percentage of the foreign-born who lived in the cities was much higher than that of the total population.

Yet the people who were to live the rest of their days amidst a world of steel and stone and brick were peasants. If they failed to reach the soil which had once been so much a part of their being, it was only because the town had somehow trapped them. . . .

What could the peasant do here? He could not trade or do much to help the traders. There was some room for petty shopkeepers; he lacked the training and the capital. Some handicraftsmen supplied clothes and furniture and a variety of other products to the townsfolk; he lacked the skill and tools. Back on the docks at which he had landed were a number of casual jobs with the stevedores. Here and there in the warehouses and stores were calls for the services of porters. But there was a limit to the amount of lifting and carrying to be done. Wandering about in the first days of their arrival, these immigrants learned that beyond these few opportunities there was, at first, no demand for their capacities.

As time went by, they became restless seekers after employment. Yet many remained unsuccessful in the quest or, drifting about, picked up odd jobs that tided them over from week to week. They joined a growing army of the anxious for work, for they could certainly not remain long without income. Perpetually on the verge of destitution, and therefore of starvation, eager to be hired at any rate, these redundant hands accumulated in a fund of available but unused labor. . . .

In the 1820's and 1830's, factory employment was the province of groups relatively high in social status. North of Boston, the bulk of the labor force was made up of respectable young girls, many the daughters of neighborhood farmers, girls willing to work for a few years in anticipation of the marriageable young man. In southern New England the general practice was to employ whole families of artisans. Everywhere, paternalistic organization and the closely knit communal life of the boarding-houses did not allow the easy entrance of newcomers. The only immigrants who then found a place in industry were the few skilled operatives who had already mastered the craft in the Old Country and were hired for the sake of their skills.

The reservoir of unskilled peasant labor that mounted steadily higher in the cities did not long remain untapped, however. In the 1840's and 1850's came a succession of new inventions that enterprising men of capital used to transform the productive system of the United States. The older industries had disdained the immigrants; but the new ones, high in the risks of innovation and heavy initial investments, drew eagerly on this fund of workers ready to be exploited at attractively low wages. The manufacture of clothing, of machines, and of furniture flourished in the great commercial cities precisely where they could utilize freely the efforts of the newcomers, hire as many as they needed when necessary, lay off any surplus at will. A completely fluid labor supply set the ideal conditions for expansion.

Thereafter, whatever branch of the economy entered upon a period of rapid expansion did so with the aid of the same immigrant labor supply. At midcentury the immigrants went to dig in the mines that pockmarked the great coal and iron fields of Pennsylvania, first experienced Welshmen and Cornishmen, later raw Irishmen and Germans, and still later Slavs—a vague term that popularly took in Bohemians, Slovaks, Hungarians, and also Italians. These people spread with the spread of the fields, southward into West Virginia and westward to Illinois, in a burst of development from which impressive consequences followed.

The wealth of new power extracted from the earth, after 1870, set off a second revolution in American industry. Steam replaced water power. Iron replaced wood in the construction of machines. Factories became larger and more mechanized and the place of unskilled labor more prominent. On the payrolls of new enterprises, immigrant names were almost alone; and the newcomers now penetrated even into the older textile and shoe industries. The former peasants, first taken on for menial duties as janitors and sweepers, found themselves more often placed at machines as the processes of production were divided into ever simpler tasks open to the abilities of the unskilled. . . .

This process, so rich in rewards for the country as a whole, paid mostly dividends of pain for the immigrants involved in it. It cost the peasants this to make the adjustment, that the stifling, brazen factories and the dark, stony pits supplanted the warm, living earth as the source of their daily bread. Year after year they paid the price in innumerable hardships of mind and body.

When he reviewed his grievances the man who went to work said that the conditions of his labor were oppressively harsh. His day was long, he pointed out; not until the 1880's was the ten-hour limit an objective seriously to be struggled for, and for many years more that span remained a pleasing ideal rather than a reality. His week was full, he added; seven days, when they could be had, were not unusual. And, he complained, along with the Sunday there vanished that whole long calendar of holidays that had formerly marked the peasant year. Here the demands of industry and the availability of employment alone determined when a man should work and when he should rest.

These were such wrongs as the ache in his muscles recalled. Others were summoned up by an ache of the spirit. For this matter of time reflected an unhuman lack of concern with human needs that was characteristic of the entire system. In these great concerns, no one seemed troubled with the welfare of the tiny men so cheap to come by who moved uneasily about in the service of the immense expensive machines. A high rate of industrial accidents and a stubborn unwillingness to make the most elementary provisions for the comfort of the employees, to the immigrant were evidence of the same penetrating callousness.

In the terms of his own experience, the laborer could come to understand his total insecurity by recollecting the steady decline in the span of the labor contract. In the Old Country, and in the old America, a man was hired for the year or for the season. But that period was altogether out of place under these conditions. Now it was not even by the month or by the week that the worker was taken on, but by the day or by the hour. Such an arrangement released the employer from the compulsion of paying hands when he had no need of them. But it left the hands uncertain, from moment to moment, as to how much work and how much income they would have.

The ultimate refinement was the shift to piecework in which the laborer, rewarded in accord with his output, received payment only for the instants he was actually at his task. The peasant sometimes conceived of this as an attractive alternative, for he hated the idea of selling his time, of taking directions like a servant, of cringing under the frowns of a foreman who judged all performances inadequate. Piecework brought the consolation of independence—one's time was one's own—and the illusion that additional effort would bring additional returns. But, though the immigrants often clung to the illusion as a token of hope, the reality was inescapably different. There was no independence and rewards would not rise. For the employer who set the rates manipulated them to his own interest while the employee had no choice but to accept. The net effect was to shift from the employer to the employee the whole burden of labor insecurity.

These elements of insecurity, the immigrant learned, were not confined to the conditions of the working day; they pervaded the total relationship of the worker to the economy. The fluid labor supply that gave the employer complete liberty to hire as many workers as he wished, when he wished, also gave him the ability, at will, to dismiss those whose toil he no longer needed. Under such circumstances there were always some men without jobs. Each industry came to have its seasons, peaks and troughs in the level of employment dictated either by the weather as in construction, or, more generally, by the convenience of the managers. It was a rare individual who did not go on the bricks for some part of the year, for periodic unemployment was an expected aspect of the laborer's career.

Then there were the years when unemployment deepened and spread out. The intervals of idleness grew longer and were less frequently interrupted until unemployment was no longer intermittent but continuous. More men appeared on the streets during the day; children were seen, pail in hand, on the way to the police station for the doled-out soup. First in the mill and mining towns where there was only one employer or one industry and where a closing had an immediate cataclysmic effect, then in the cities where the impact was delayed by diversity of occupations, but in time everywhere, the laborer knew a depression was upon him.

At such times, the burdens of his economic role became intolerable. The hunger left behind in Europe was again an intimate of the household, and the cold and raggedness. Endurance stretched to the bursting point, and the misery of regret was overwhelming. It was a golden land here in America as long as there was work, but without work it was worth nothing. In the miry slough of inactivity into which he now sank, the peasant had leisure to meditate upon the meaning of his lot in the New World. . . .

Only by calling upon the earnings of more than one of its members could the immigrant household make ends meet. Not unless it utilized the efforts of wife and child, as well as those of the husband, could the family be certain that there would always be someone working and that the income of the whole would be large enough, secure enough, to withstand the recurrent shocks of American economic life.

It was not the mere fact that wife and child must exert themselves that was hurtful. These were no strangers to toil in the Old World, or in the New. The degradation lay in the *kind* of work. The boys drifted into street occupations, blacked boots or hawked newspapers, missed thus the opportunity to acquire a trade and fell into all sorts of outlandish ways. Or they, and girls too for that matter, entered the shops, where they did men's work at child's wages. For the women, there was "domestic service"—maid's work in strangers' homes or back-breaking laundering in their own; or, more often as time went on, service to industry in the factory or by homework. If it was characteristic of these families that they somehow found the room for a boarder, that was only another method of adding to their ranks another breadwinner.

But in America bread never came without complications. The peasant, new to the means of earning his livelihood, was also new to the means of spending it. To his misfortune he discovered that he himself added to the difficulties in making ends meet through inability to use efficiently whatever money came to his hands. In his old life, he had thought of objects in their individuality and uniqueness; the chair, the hat, the cow. Here he had to learn to think of them as commodities, subject to a common quantitative standard of price. Without a clear conception of the relationship of money to things, every transaction involved a set of totally new conditions. . . .

Often, they would try to understand. They would think about it in the pauses of their work, speculate sometimes as their minds wandered, tired, at the close of a long day.

What had cut short the continuous past, severed it from the unrelated present? Immigration had transformed the entire economic world within which the peasants had formerly lived. From surface forms to inmost functionings, the change was complete. A new setting, new activities, and new meanings forced the newcomers into radically new roles as producers and consumers of goods. In the process, they became, in their own eyes, less worthy as men. They felt a sense of degradation that raised a most insistent question: Why had this happened? . . .

Every element of the immigrants' experience since the day they had left home added to this awareness of their utter helplessness. All the incidents of the journey were bound up with chance. What was the road to follow, what the ship to board, what port to make? These were serious questions. But who knew which were the right answers? Whether they survived the hazards of the voyage, and in what condition, these too were decisions beyond the control of the men who participated in it. The capricious world of the crossing pointed its own conclusion as to the role of chance in the larger universe into which the immigrants plunged.

It was the same with their lives after landing. To find a job or not, to hold it or to be fired, in these matters laborers' wills were of slight importance. Inscrutable, distant persons determined matters on the basis of remote, unknown conditions. The most fortunate of immigrants, the farmers, knew well what little power they had to influence the state of the climate, the yield of the earth, or the fluctuations of the market, all the elements that determined their lot. Success or failure, incomprehensible in terms of peasant values, seemed altogether fortuitous. Time and again, the analogy occurred to them: man was helpless like the driven cog in a great machine.

Loneliness, separation from the community of the village, and despair at the insignificance of their own human abilities, these were the elements that, in America, colored the peasants' view of their world. From the depths of a dark pessimism, they looked up at a frustrating universe ruled by haphazard, capricious forces. Without the capacity to control or influence these forces men could but rarely gratify their hopes or wills. Their most passionate desires were doomed to failure; their lives were those of the feeble little birds which hawks attack, which lose strength from want of food, and which, at last surrendering to the savage blasts of the careless elements, flutter unnoticed to the waiting earth.

Sadness was the tone of life, and death and disaster no strangers. Outsiders would not understand the familiarity with death who had not daily met it in the close quarters of the steerage; nor would they comprehend the riotous Paddy funerals who had no insight of the release death brought. The end of life was an end to hopeless striving, to ceaseless pain, and to the endless succession of disappointments. There was a leaden grief for the ones who went; yet the tomb was only the final parting in a long series of separations that had started back at the village crossroads.

Ethnic Enclaves and the Workers' Saloon

ROY ROSENZWEIG

Worcester is an unlikely industrial city. Lacking the usual prerequisites of antebellum industrial and urban development—a navigable body of water, waterpower, and raw materials—it nevertheless developed into a major industrial center, the twenty-eighth largest city in the United States by 1880. Jonas Rice established a permanent settlement in Worcester in 1713, but it still had fewer than 3,000 residents more than a century later. In the next thirty years, however, this sleepy town was transformed into a burgeoning industrial city. . . .

Stereotypically, the founders of Worcester's industries were poor boys of mechanical ability who migrated to Worcester from the New England countryside and set up shop in one of the factory buildings owned by Stephen Salisbury II or William T. Merrifield. The legends about these inventive Yankee mechanics have sometimes exaggerated their abilities and accomplishments, but the careers of such men as wire manufacturer Ichabod Washburn, loom builder Lucius J. Knowles, wrench makers Loring and A. G. Coes, and railroad-car builder Osgood Bradley lend some credence to this version of Worcester's industrial history. Not only did these men found the city's major industries in the early nineteenth century, but they (or their families) continued to control those industries in the late nineteenth century. An 1884 account, for example, noted that "private capital" dominated Worcester manufacturing to an unusual degree and added that "all these enterprises, large and small, with scarcely an exception are owned by residents of Worcester."

Of course, Worcester was not immune from the trends toward incorporation and concentration of economic power that marked late nineteenth century American industry. Between 1880 and 1919 the average number of wage earners per firm grew two and a half times and the average capitalization of each firm jumped almost seventeen times. As in the rest of the nation, the wave of consolidations surged in the aftermath of the depression of the 1890s. Between 1898 and 1903 five of the city's eight largest companies participated in mergers. Two Worcester companies—Washburn and Moen and Logan, Swift, and Brigham—joined national trusts (U.S. Steel and U.S. Envelope).

These outside take-overs proved exceptional; Worcester generally retained its distinctive pattern of local ownership. More commonly, Worcester mergers involved two or more local companies such as the consolidations of Crompton and Knowles and of Reed and Prince. . . . Worcester industry in the early twentieth century was reorganizing and consolidating, but it was not ceding control to outside corporations. Even a study done in the 1960s found most Worcester industries still under local ownership and management.

In part, the mergers of the early twentieth century formalized a complex web of informal connections that had knit together the city's industrial elite throughout the late nineteenth century. Business ties were one powerful bond uniting different

Roy Rosenzweig, *Eight Hours for What We Will: Workers and Leisure in an Industrial City, 1870–1920* (Cambridge: Cambridge University Press, 1983), 11, 13–14, 16–19, 23–24, 27–31, 35–45, 53–55, 57–64. Reprinted with permission of Cambridge University Press.

parts of industrial Worcester. Wyman and Gordon, for example, initially found its major customers within Worcester—forging parts for Crompton and Knowles looms and producing copper rail bonds for Washburn and Moen. Supporting and reinforcing these business connections as well as a network of interlocking corporate and bank directorates were extensive social and cultural ties. Worcester industrialists worshipped at the same Protestant churches, belonged to the same clubs, attended the same schools, lived in the same West Side neighborhoods, vacationed at the same resorts, and married into each other's families. . . .

. . . These men did not agree on all major issues, nor did they rule every aspect of life in Worcester, but their overwhelming economic power, their close business and social ties, their civic generosity and corporate paternalism made them the preeminent force in late nineteenth and early twentieth century Worcester.

But how far down did this hegemony extend? What organizational structures— political, economic, and cultural—did workers create to combat the power of the city's industrialists? Before we can answer these questions, we need first to survey the composition of Worcester's work force. Although such a quick once-over must inevitably distort complex and changing patterns, two basic characteristics of Worcester's working class stand out: its ethnic diversity and its constantly changing composition.

In 1887 clergyman Samuel Lane Loomis observed that "not every foreigner is a workingman, but in the cities, at least, it may almost be said that every workingman is a foreigner." If Loomis meant to include the children of immigrants in the term "foreigner," then Worcester statistics support his observation. In 1900 first- and second-generation immigrants made up more than 70 percent of every major blue-collar job category. In the least skilled jobs, the dominance was overwhelming: Foreign-stock Worcesterites made up 83 percent of the city's iron- and steelworkers, 89 percent of its domestic servants, and 92 percent of its wireworkers and manual laborers.

This immigrant dominance of Worcester's blue-collar work force only emerged in the second half of the nineteenth century. By 1850 Worcester's newly arrived Irish immigrants already held most of the city's laboring jobs. . . .

The entry into Worcester of large numbers of "new immigrants" from southern and eastern Europe in the years after 1890 crosscut the working class with further ethnic, religious, and linguistic divisions. At the wire mills, for example, Swedes tended to fill the more skilled jobs in the steel rolling mills and the more specialized aspects of wire making, whereas the Irish and the more recently arrived Lithuanians, Poles, Finns, and Armenians took the unskilled positions. Italians also found themselves in unskilled work but less often within factories. In 1875, 88 percent of Worcester Italians were manual laborers, and their share never dropped below 40 percent in the next fifty years. Jews, although predominantly working class, followed a slightly deviant pattern with disproportionate numbers opening small businesses. . . .

Even this cursory summary of industrial and working-class Worcester reveals some of the major obstacles to working-class organization. On the one hand, Worcester manufacturers were well organized, united, and vigorously anti-union. In addition, their local residence, civic responsibility, and paternalistic policies rendered them less vulnerable to attack than were outside, corporate capitalists. On the other hand, Worcester workers (unlike their counterparts in, say, Lynn or Fall

River) were segmented into dissimilar occupations and trades, making it difficult for them to perceive common working-class—rather than occupational—economic and political interests. Ethnic and especially religious differences further fragmented the labor force, inhibiting communication and the development of shared goals. . . .

Local politics in Worcester generally reinforced the power of the industrial elite. In late nineteenth century Lynn, men of working-class backgrounds dominated political office, whereas factory owners "hardly showed their faces." The opposite was true in Worcester. Between 1871 and 1920 factory owners or top officials of manufacturing concerns held the mayor's seat for a total of twenty-two years. During the other years, bankers, lawyers, merchants, and doctors—many of them with close ties to the industrialists—controlled the mayoralty. Blue-collar workers made only slightly greater inroads in the Board of Aldermen and the Common Council. In 1885, 1890, and 1895 workers composed only one-twelfth of the Board of Aldermen and less than one-eighth of the Common Council. Worcester city officials, the *Labor News* repeatedly and bitterly complained, were "corporation owned [and] monopoly bound," "subservient to [the] big business machine," and "extremely antagonistic and positively indifferent" to workers.

In part, the absence of worker-politicians reflects the failure of explicitly pro-labor political movements in Worcester. Although the Knights of Labor in other New England towns and cities captured local governments in the mid-1880s, their Worcester counterparts could claim no local victories. . . .

What explains the weakness of the Worcester labor movement and the city's extraordinary record of labor tranquility? In part, as noted earlier, the strength and power of the city's industrialists inhibited organized working-class resistance. Manufacturers manipulated not only the carrot of paternalism but also the stick of repression to prevent unionization and strikes. Throughout the late nineteenth century Worcester manufacturers of such diverse products as shoes, wire, and pants routinely fired workers suspected of union activity. By the early twentieth century the employers' associations had systematized this procedure through citywide blacklists. The Metal Trades Association maintained a central card file based on reports from employers and their company spies. A typical notation might read: "Joined union, a disturber." "Thru the system of spying and blacklisting in vogue by the employers' association," the *Labor News* commented in 1915, "even the thought of belonging to a union made a man in danger of losing his job." . . .

The failure of Worcester trade unions and the virtual absence of radical or working-class political parties did not give the city's industrialists an unchallenged hegemony over all aspects of working-class life. Instead, Worcester workers created tight ethnic communities with elaborate organizational infrastructures—churches, clubs, kinship networks, saloons—which served as alternatives to trade unions and political parties. These ethnic communities offered Worcester workers a sphere in which they could carry out a mode of life and express values, beliefs, and traditions significantly different from those prescribed by the dominant industrial elite. . . .

In the years after 1880 ethnic Worcester changed in two major ways. First, specific ethnic communities—especially the one created by the Irish—gradually lost some of their old insularity as a new American-born generation matured and increasing numbers of immigrants and their children gained a tenuous hold in the middle class. . . . The second major change affecting ethnic Worcester was the arrival of thousands and thousands of additional immigrants from Europe, Canada, and the Near East. Although the Irish remained the largest single ethnic group in the city, the terms "Irish" and "foreigner" were no longer synonymous in Worcester. . . .

The massive influx of Swedes in the last quarter of the nineteenth century was the most important force in the transformation of Worcester into a multiethnic city. In 1875 only about 166 Swedes resided in Worcester, but within ten years their numbers had increased almost thirteen times to 2,112, and in ten more years tripled again. By the turn of the century, Swedish-stock residents made up about 10 percent of the total population of 118,421. Swedish communities were separatist not only in outlook but also in location. The Irish and French Canadians mingled on the East Side, but the two largest Swedish neighborhoods remained relatively isolated from both other immigrant groups and the city itself. . . .

The diversification of Worcester's ethnic landscape begun by the Swedes in the 1880s and 1890s was accelerated in the next thirty years as large numbers of Jews, Italians, Poles, and Lithuanians, and smaller numbers of Albanians, Armenians, Syrians, Greeks, and Finns entered the city. By 1920 almost 72 percent of Worcester's residents were of foreign birth or parentage. These "newcomers" of the late nineteenth century and early twentieth shared with previous immigrants an affinity for close-knit ethnic neighborhoods. The Italians, the largest contingent among the new immigrants with more than 12,000 residents (first and second generation) in Worcester by 1930, developed along the formerly Irish Shrewsbury Street, a community of stores, churches, and clubs that was, in the words of an ethnic geographer, "virtually a self-contained unit." . . .

The complex interweaving of church, neighborhood, fraternal lodge, and family provided a strong basis for organized immigrant working-class life in Worcester. Yankee industrialists may have dominated the factories and the civic life of the city, but immigrants retained control over their own churches, neighborhoods, clubs, and often schools. And immigrant working-class values, beliefs, and traditions—not those of the manufacturers—governed those areas of life. Still, this ethnic basis of working-class life created strains for the broader working-class community. Although the ethnic groups usually lived in harmony, the harmony was built mainly on lack of contact rather than on mutual respect. Moreover, internecine warfare periodically broke out, particularly between the younger residents of the ethnic neighborhoods. . . .

. . . Consequently, the insularity and separatism of the immigrant communities limited immigrant working-class influence over economic or political issues. On the other hand, these ethnic enclaves not only gave workers a shared basis of experience—similar life-styles, housing, neighborhoods, and jobs—but, more important, provided a refuge and resource for those who confronted the unemployment, poverty, disease, and accidents that accompanied life and work in industrializing America. . . .

The Rise of the Saloon

The large factories of late nineteenth century Worcester would not tolerate the casual informality—the gambling, storytelling, singing, debating, and especially drinking—that had characterized its small workshops in the earlier years of the century or its farms in the previous century. Yet while the factory workers of the 1870s faced a more structured work regimen than the artisans of the 1820s, they also generally had more free time in which to pursue some of the socializing that had been removed from their workday. . . . Thus, it was a response to a complex set of social forces—tightened work discipline, shorter workdays, intensified regulation of public recreation, increased working-class incomes—that the saloon emerged as a center of working-class social life. Although the saloon was a commercial enterprise, its ethnic working-class customers still decisively shaped its ritual and character. Somewhat paradoxically, they infused the saloon with a set of values that differed from those of the dominant industrial capitalist society that had given rise to the saloon in the first place.

. . . Workers in the eighteenth and early nineteenth centuries considered drinking an inextricable, and even mandatory, aspect of work. In the shoe shops of Lynn in the 1820s, a half pint of "white eye" was an expected part of the daily wage and the workers themselves financed further heavy drinking. In Rochester workshops of the same period "drinking was universal" and "was embedded in the pattern of irregular work and easy sociability." This intermingling of work and socializing, of work and drink, marked manual as well as artisanal labor. . . .

The pervasiveness of workplace drinking was hardly surprising in an era when it suffused all areas of life. "Americans between 1790 and 1830," a carefully documented recent study shows, "drank more alcoholic beverages than ever before or since." Even the church was not immune. Under the pulpit of Worcester's Old South Church was a large cupboard containing, "for the accommodation of the congregation, at noon time, a home manufactured beverage from the choicest products of the orchard."

The antebellum temperance crusades, which began in the late 1820s, rapidly undermined the universality of these drinking habits, particularly among the native upper and middle classes. Between 1830 and 1850, according to one estimate, annual per capita consumption of absolute alcohol plummeted from 3.9 gallons to 1 gallon. Testifying before a Massachusetts legislative committee in 1867, Emory Washburn, a Worcester lawyer and a former governor, described the social impact of this new abstinence: "Before 1828 I do not know of any families that pretended to anything like hospitality who did not make a free use of liquor." But by 1867 Washburn noted of these same "respectable" circles that "it was as rare to see liquor offered in a man's house as it would be to see medicine offered."

The early temperance movement appealed particularly to the middle- and upper-class men and women who dined with Emory Washburn. Industrialists and others tied to "the emerging industrial society" led Worcester's temperance movement in the 1830s, according to a recent historian of that movement. And by the 1840s "there was mounting evidence of the broadening appeal of prohibition among not only manufacturers and their allies, but also all respectable and propertied elements in the community." . . .

The prohibitory ordinances passed by local temperance forces were never fully effective, but new workplace bans on drinking had a more direct impact on popular customs. The Worcester Temperance Society reported in 1831 that twenty-six "mechanic shops" and six "manufactories," employing more than 200 workers in all had banned drinking during work hours and had stopped employing intemperate workmen. . . .

Rules against alcohol consumption were the firmest in the most mechanized industries. Where traditional production methods or heavy manual labor prevailed, drinking was more likely to be tolerated. As late as 1898 the superintendent of Worcester's Sewer Department accepted his workers' consumption of "copious amounts of beer" during their noon break, because "the men had a right to drink when off duty if they chose to do so." Drinking, Dr. Samuel Hartwell told the Massachusetts Bureau of Statistics of Labor, was heaviest among those "who perform labor physically exhaustive, and those who are exposed to extremes of heat and cold." . . .

The gradual tightening of workplace discipline—as exemplified by the anti-drink regulations—was accompanied by a more favorable change for the working class: the gradual shortening of the workday. The precise connection between these two developments is difficult to specify, but they appear to have occurred in tandem. Agitation for the ten-hour day, for example, began in the mid-1820s at the same time that men like Washburn were challenging such basic forms of workplace sociability as drinking. Rochester carpenters—"unable," according to one historian, "to control their conditions of work or to mix work and leisure"—struck in 1834 and announced: "We will be faithful to our employers during the ten hours and no longer." Although such other motives as the desire to reduce pervasive unemployment influenced movements for the shorter workday, the growing articulation of a "right to leisure" played an important part. What workers wanted, the Knights of Labor explained, was "more of the leisure that rightfully belongs to them." The "division and specialization of labor" and the "intensity" of work dictated by "modern methods in industry" had reduced "the social opportunities of the masses," an American Federation of Labor pamphlet similarly argued; the only solution was "more leisure, more physical and mental repose, more and larger periods of relief, from the strain which the specialized industrial life imposes."

As early as the 1840s the ten-hour movement had begun to have some impact, particularly in Massachusetts. In 1845, for example, workers at T. K. Earle's Machine Shop and Foundry in Worcester won a two-hour daily reduction to ten hours. Early the following year the Worcester Workingmen's Association invited "the employers of this village to meet us at our weekly meetings and show cause, if they have any, why *men* ought to work more than ten hours a day." And by the early 1850s the ten-hour day was "all but universal" among Worcester's skilled mechanics. . . .

. . . The saloon and similar working-class leisure institutions thus developed in the context of tightening work discipline and decreasing work hours. But just as the saloon owed its existence to the growing temporal separation of drinking and working, of socializing and working, it was also predicated on the growing spatial separation of male sociability from the home.

Formal drink places—taverns—existed in Worcester almost from its first founding in the late seventeenth century. But the 1730s Worcester had five well-regarded taverns with four of the proprietors holding town offices. By the time of the temperance crusades of the 1820s, however, the taverns had begun to lose their social respectability: None of the seventeen tavernkeepers in 1828 held an important town office. Their status declined further with the rise of temperance sentiment among the "respectable" citizens of Worcester and the passage of various prohibitory ordinances, beginning in 1835 and remaining in effect with only temporary break until 1875.

These anti-drink measures had a limited impact on the drink trade. The city's small police force, which consisted of just one watchman before 1851, could not effectively enforce the law. When Mayor Henry Chapin attempted to suppress liquor traffic in 1850, pro-drink protesters responded by bombing his office. Even the use of special police and vigorous prosecutions "did not substantially suppress the sale of liquor," one Worcester mayor admitted. . . .

At least a few of these illicit drink places—the Bay State House, for example— even catered to the city's more "respectable" citizens. But most working-class drinking went on in much less formal and elegant surroundings. As early as the 1830s the city's pioneer Irish laboring community had established a number of popular *shebeens* (unlicensed and home- or kitchen-based liquor sellers) of the type so common in nineteenth century Ireland. In the 1840s and 1850s on the immigrant and working-class East Side of the city, Worcester Irish historian Vincent E. Powers notes, "temperance laws had little effect and illegal shebeens and blind-pigs continue to operate. Irish freighters and railroad crews found an eager market for the liquor they easily smuggled into the city." Throughout Massachusetts those in contact with working-class neighborhoods observed the same close connection of drink selling and home life in the face of official prohibition statutes. A Boston Catholic priest observed that "among the poorer classes . . . in almost every house (and every tenement having a number of families in it) they have some liquor, and they sell it to those in the house." . . .

The centrality of women as both sellers and consumers of liquor in the kitchen grog shops further emphasizes their close connection to immigrant home and family life. Arrest records give ample evidence of the prominence of Irish women drink sellers in Worcester. Whenever temperance-minded Worcester mayors of the 1850s and 1860s decided to crack down on illegal liquor selling, the most immediate impact was that "half a dozen Irish women [would] . . . be sent to the house of correction."

Whereas Worcester officials viewed these female liquor dealers as disreputable and criminal, the Irish community apparently looked at them quite differently. In Ireland the keeping of a shebeen was a "recognized resource of widows," and they had a "privileged" status in the liquor trade. In Worcester Irish immigrants continued to insist on the propriety of this form of communal charity, despite the failure of American laws to recognize it. . . .

Gradually, however, the tighter regulations did have some impact; and Worcester saloons began to emerge from the back rooms and kitchens and take on a more standardized and regulated form. Initially, the Board of Aldermen did not discriminate very carefully in their selection of licensees, issuing an average of 235 licenses yearly over the first four years of licensing. In 1879, however, the Board of Aldermen decided to cut back sharply and so issued only 131 licenses. Although the Board of Aldermen never articulated their motives in the license cutbacks, their targets— women, economically marginal operators, and saloons outside of downtown—reveal their goal of ending the kitchen grog shop and fostering the public working-class saloon. . . .

The effect of the license cutbacks was to eliminate the least public and visible, the hardest-to-regulate, and the least capitalized drink places. In so doing, the board, in effect, endorsed the creation of a more standardized and public institution—the late nineteenth century saloon—as a leisure place clearly separated from both work and home. . . .

The gradual emergence of the saloon as a leisure space clearly distinct from home thus gave workers a more comfortable and appealing place to spend their leisure time. But most working-class women did not share in this modest improvement in working-class life. For married women who did not engage in paid labor, recreation was an integral part of everyday life; in effect, they mixed work and play much in the manner of the early nineteenth century artisan. Thus, despite their home-centered responsibilities, women could have an important place in the kitchen barrooms as both proprietors and customers. However, when leisure was removed from the home or its immediate vicinity, it became predominantly a male privilege. While some women continued to patronize saloons, these public leisure spaces increasingly became male preserves. In this way, the male saloon became a mirror image of the male factory. . . .

What explains the strong ties between the working class and the saloon? Most simply, it effectively met the needs of workers. "The saloon, in relation to the wage-earning classes in America," noted Walter Wyckoff, who had studied it firsthand, "is an organ of high development, adapting itself with singular perfectness to its functions in catering in a hundred ways to the social and political needs of men." Public toilets, food, warmth, clean water, meeting space, check-cashing services, newspapers—often otherwise unavailable to workers in the late nineteenth century city—could be found free of charge in the saloon. Often the saloon served as a communications center, a place where workers picked up their mail, heard the local political gossip, or learned of openings in their trade.

Different types of saloons emphasized different features and functions. The "occupational saloon," which drew on customers from a particular trade or factory, for example, promoted its free lunch and its check-cashing services. Ethnic saloons, which attracted more of an evening business, provided a center for such immigrant communal celebrations as weddings and holidays as well as a meeting place for fraternal orders and gangs. The neighborhood saloon might attract a local multiethnic working-class crowd and provide a constituency for small-time politicians. . . .

The saloonkeeper presided over and fostered this atmosphere of good-hearted, informal socializing. "As a rule," observed the author of the locally published *Saloon Keeper's Companion,* "the saloonkeeper is a jolly, easy going fellow, free with his money." Even Worcester temperance advocate Richard O'Flynn, with his hatred for the "vendors of the deadly cup," found the word "genial" the most appropriate to describe Worcester's rum sellers when he wrote profiles of them: Michael J. Leach was "a genial, generous man"; William Molloy, "a genial, warm hearted man, harmless in all save his calling"; and William H. Foley, "full of fun— always ready with a pleasant anecdote or story." Similarly, when *Light,* a Worcester society weekly, complained in 1890 of "loud and boisterous laughter, obscene pleasantries and curses," it also hinted at the cheerful sociability that prevailed in Worcester saloons. . . .

The singing and storytelling of Worcester barrooms was undoubtedly punctuated by conversations about sports. *The Saloon Keeper's Companion* considered sports rules and the results of major sporting contests as essential knowledge for barkeepers. Patrick Ryan decorated his Mechanic Street saloon "with pictures of pugilists, sprinters, and clogdancers." Sometimes a popular local fighter, like Jack Gray, William H. Foley, or Robert Mahagan, might retire from the ring to become a saloonkeeper, placing his "well-worn boxing gloves" on "the shelf behind the bar" as a reminder of more glorious days. Other saloonkeepers, like Michael Kelley, gained some fame for their intimacy with sporting heroes like John L. Sullivan, whose picture adorned the walls of many, if not most, 1890s saloons. . . .

For these reasons, the saloon remained the axis of the recreational world for large numbers of working-class men. One Saturday night in December 1883, several temperance advocates canvassed fifteen saloons between 6 and 10 P.M. and counted 1,832 patrons, "mostly young men." Thus, even if the city's other ninety-three legal drinking places were only half as popular as these, more than 7,500 Worcesterites would have stopped at the saloon that night—a significant percentage of the city's 30,000 males and easily a majority of its young working-class males.

. . . But did the late nineteenth century saloon hold any significance beyond its role as a social service and recreational center? Does the nature of the late nineteenth century saloon suggest anything about the central values and beliefs of Worcester workers? . . .

Many observers trumpeted the saloon as "the rooster-crow of the spirit of democracy." It was, proclaimed the Reverend George L. McNutt, "the one democratic club in American life," the "great democratic social settlement." Of course, the saloon was much less open and democratic in fact than these commentators would have us believe. Most saloons at least informally barred members of the "wrong" sex, ethnic group, race, neighborhood, or occupation. Still, the commentators were partially right; the saloon was actually a "democracy" of sorts—an *internal* democracy where all who could safely enter received equal treatment and respect. An ethic of mutuality and reciprocity that differed from the market exchange mentality of the dominant society prevailed within the barroom. Although collective and cooperative social relations were not the exclusive property of the immigrant working class, the saloon was one of the few late nineteenth century institutions that publicly and symbolically celebrated these alternative values.

Some understanding of the potential role of drink and the saloon in fostering this ethic of reciprocity and mutuality can be gained by looking at rural Ireland, the birthplace of many Worcester saloon patrons. "Drinking together," notes anthropologist Conrad Arensberg, "is the traditional reaffirmation of solidarity and equality among males" in Ireland. The most important drink custom for fostering such sentiments was "treating"—"a social law in Catholic Ireland enforced with all the vigour of a Coercion Act," according to one commentator. "If a man happens to be in an inn or public-house alone, and if any of his acquaintances come in, no matter how many, it is his duty to 'stand,' that is, to invite them to drink and pay for all they take. . . . It is a deadly insult to refuse to take a drink from a man, unless an elaborate explanation and apology be given and accepted." Treating thus provided the nineteenth-century Irishman with a crucial means of declaring his solidarity and equality with his kin and neighbors. . . .

These treating rituals embodied a resistance of sorts to the transformation of social relationships into "commodities"—a means of preserving reciprocal modes of social interaction within a capitalist world. Jack London, for example, explained his realization of the non-economic mutuality behind treating: "I had achieved a concept. Money no longer counted. It was comradeship that counted." . . .

The saloon clashed with the values of industrial America not just in its communality and mutuality but also in the unwillingness of some patrons to endorse fully the work ethic of that society. Critics of drinking frequently lumped together the very rich and the very poor as unproductive classes "most exposed to the temptation of intemperate drinking." . . .

Not only did drinking and the squandering of wages lead to a loss of work efficiency; it also made it difficult for workers to move ahead in socially approved ways. Temperance advocates repeatedly pointed out that the money spent on drink might instead go toward "a modest working class home." The Worcester Five Cents Savings Bank, "the poor man's bank," claimed a one-third increase in local deposits during one no-license year. "It cannot be emphasized too strongly," Stephan Thernstrom writes in his study of nineteenth-century social mobility, "that the real estate holdings and savings accounts of Newburyport laborers depended on underconsumption. . . . A recreational luxury like drinking, for example, was out of the question." Moreover, it was the sober and thrifty worker who might win the approval of his employer or learn new skills and advance occupationally. It was perhaps no accident that unskilled workers predominated among those arrested for drunkenness. Drinking and saloongoing could represent a rejection—albeit not an articulated rejection—of the dominant social mobility ideology of nineteenth-century America. . . .

In its maleness and gender segregation, the saloon both challenged and affirmed the dominant culture. On the one hand, the saloon was a male institution in an era when the middle-class ideal was increasingly that of family-centered leisure. On the other hand, both the saloon and the bourgeois family mandated subservient roles for women. Thus, whereas saloongoers apparently departed from some of the basic values of industrial America, they nevertheless shared some of its deepest patriarchal assumptions.

In general, however, the saloon stood outside the dominant cultural values of the late nineteenth century, even if neither the saloon nor its patrons mounted an organized or disciplined challenge to those values. . . .

The nineteenth-century ethnic working-class saloon, then, was a form of both accommodation and resistance to the capitalist order that workers faced. Unlike a trade union or a socialist party, the saloon did not openly confront or challenge the dominant society, though neither did it embrace the values and practices of that society. Instead, it offered a space in which immigrants could preserve an alternative, reciprocal value system. This was only partially an act of historical preservation, for the saloon was a new institution and, as such, was a creative response by immigrants to the trials of late nineteenth century urban life.

◤ F U R T H E R   R E A D I N G

Alfred Chandler, Jr., *The Visible Hand: The Managerial Revolution in American Business* (1977).
William Cronon, *Nature's Metropolis: Chicago and the Great West* (1991).
Thomas Kessner, *The Golden Door* (1977).
Thomas J. Misa, *A Nation of Steel: The Making of Modern America* (1995).
David Montgomery, *The Fall of the House of Labor* (1987).
Robert A. Orsi, *The Madonna of 115th Street: Faith and Community in Italian Harlem* (1985).
Kathy Peiss, *Cheap Amusements: Working Women and Leisure in Turn-of-the-Century New York* (1986).
Stephen Thernstrom, *The Other Bostonians* (1973).

CHAPTER
4

Imperialism and
World Power

In 1898 the United States embarked on its first war on behalf of people other than its own. Revolutionaries in Cuba had fought for thirty years (1868–1898) to break Spain's grasp on its last colony in the New World. With U.S. help, they finally succeeded. Eighty years earlier, John Quincy Adams had warned at a similar moment that entanglement in foreign revolutions should be avoided because it would involve the United States "beyond the power of extrication in all the wars of interest and intrigue." No matter how righteous the initial cause, he stated, "the fundamental maxims of her policy would insensibly change from liberty to force. . . . She might become dictatress of the world. She would no longer be the ruler of her own spirit." The war against Spain to secure Cuba's independence, in line with Adams's prediction, in fact did not end there. The United States required Cuba to agree to unilateral American intervention for the next thirty years. More shockingly, in the course of the war the United States took the Philippine Islands, Guam, and Puerto Rico from Spain. The United States had initially collaborated with Filipino independence fighter Emilio Aguinaldo, but then, against his wishes, it transformed the islands into an American colony. When Aguinaldo detected this U.S. treachery, he launched a new rebellion, which the American army brutally suppressed. The U.S.-Philippine war lasted three years. Over four thousand U.S. troops died, along with nearly 200,000 Filipino rebels and civilians.

These first conflicts of the twentieth century contained in full measure the contradictions and danger that were to shape relations between the United States and the rest of the globe for the coming century. Presidents William McKinley, Theodore Roosevelt, and Woodrow Wilson, under whose direction the United States took up a leading role on the world stage, agreed that the time had come to exercise America's tremendous potential for international influence. They disagreed on the reasons and the legitimate means for doing so. Should the United States be an imperial power, or should it fight to eradicate colonialism? Should the United States promote stability and the status quo, or should it promote decolonization and democracy? Should the United States "speak softly and carry a big stick," as Roosevelt argued, or should it exercise a moral diplomacy?

Of course, even the existence of the debate reflected how far the United States had veered from its traditional policy of "nonentanglement," which dated back to George Washington. Any form of intervention involved the United States in disputes beyond its control and often beyond its understanding. Even the process of promoting democracy meant meddling in ways that undermined other peoples' self-determination. The United States did not have to exercise regional, and ultimately global, police power. But at the start of the twentieth century, it did so. Why?

◥ Q U E S T I O N S   T O   T H I N K   A B O U T

How could a nation with democratic values fight a colonial war? What rhetoric or reform aspirations made this undertaking palatable? Was greed the root cause? How did notions of manliness and empire influence the vision of imperialists like Theodore Roosevelt, governor of New York and later president of the United States?

◥ D O C U M E N T S

The documents in this chapter show the many sides to the debate over imperialism within the United States, and some of the ways in which people abroad perceived the American presence. Governor of New York Theodore Roosevelt gave one of his most popular and famous speeches the year after the war in Cuba, where he had commanded a regiment of "Rough Riders." His speech (Document 1) responded to the criticisms of anti-imperialists, charging that it was only "the overcivilized man, who has lost the great fighting, masterful virtues," who distrusted his country's motives. In Document 2, the Filipino revolutionary Emilio Aguinaldo reveals what he thought of the United States in 1899: that it had sent an "army of occupation." The next two documents condemn the policy of the McKinley administration. In Document 3, the Anti-Imperialist League claims that the administration sought "to extinguish the spirit of 1776 in those islands." Mark Twain, author of *Tom Sawyer* and *Huckleberry Finn,* fiercely criticizes the racial and imperial assumptions of the United States in Document 4. In Document 5, a soldier writes that American troops made more enemies than friends in the Philippines by calling the natives "Niggers" and by burning the houses of rebels and peaceful civilians alike. Through Document 6, the Platt Amendment of 1903, the United States forged a neocolonial relationship with Cuba: maximal control, minimal responsibility, and as little conflict as possible with domestic ideals of "liberty and justice for all." Document 7 is the 1904 Roosevelt Corollary to the Monroe Doctrine. Roosevelt's pronouncement expanded the meaning of the Monroe Doctrine of 1823, which had simply warned the great powers of Europe not to intervene in the affairs of, or attempt to recolonize, the independent nations of Latin America. In his annual speech to Congress on December 6, 1904, President Theodore Roosevelt claimed a new role for the United States as "an international police power." In the last reading, Document 8, President Woodrow Wilson condemns a foreign policy that puts economic interest before justice, and swears that the United States will "never again seek one additional foot of territory by conquest." Wilson soon thereafter sent U.S. troops into Mexico, Haiti, and the Dominican Republic, but all in the name of helping to teach Latin Americans to "elect good men."

1. Governor Theodore Roosevelt Praises the Strenuous Life, 1899

In speaking to you, men of the greatest city of the West, men of the state which gave to the country Lincoln and Grant, men who preeminently and distinctly embody all that is most American in the American character, I wish to preach not the doctrine of ignoble ease but the doctrine of the strenuous life; the life of toil and effort; of labor and strife; to preach that highest form of success which comes not to the man who desires mere easy peace but to the man who does not shrink from danger, from hardship, or from bitter toil, and who out of these wins the splendid ultimate triumph. . . .

As it is with the individual so it is with the nation. It is a base untruth to say that happy is the nation that has no history. Thrice happy is the nation that has a glorious history. Far better it is to dare mighty things, to win glorious triumphs, even though checkered by failure, than to take rank with those poor spirits who neither enjoy much nor suffer much because they live in the gray twilight that knows neither victory nor defeat. If in 1861 the men who loved the Union had believed that peace was the end of all things and war and strife a worst of all things, and had acted up to their belief, we would have saved hundreds of thousands of lives, we would have saved hundreds of millions of dollars. Moreover, besides saving all the blood and treasure we then lavished, we would have prevented the heartbreak of many women, the dissolution of many homes; and we would have spared the country those months of gloom and shame when it seemed as if our armies marched only to defeat. We would have avoided all this suffering simply by shrinking from strife. And if we had thus avoided it we would have shown that we were weaklings and that we were unfit to stand among the great nations of the earth. Thank God for the iron in the blood of our fathers, the men who upheld the wisdom of Lincoln and bore sword or rifle in the armies of Grant! Let us, the children of the men who proved themselves equal to the mighty days—let us, the children of the men who carried the great Civil War to a triumphant conclusion, praise the God of our fathers that the ignoble counsels of peace were rejected, that the suffering and loss, the blackness of sorrow and despair, were unflinchingly faced and the years of strife endured; for in the end the slave was freed, the Union restored, and the mighty American Republic placed once more as a helmeted queen among nations.

We of this generation do not have to face a task such as that our fathers faced, but we have our tasks, and woe to us if we fail to perform them! We cannot, if we would, play the part of China, and be content to rot by inches in ignoble ease within our borders, taking no interest in what goes on beyond them; sunk in a scrambling commercialism; heedless of the higher life, the life of aspiration, of toil and risk; busying ourselves only with the wants of our bodies for the day; until suddenly we should find, beyond a shadow of question, what China has already found, that in this world the nation that has trained itself to a career of unwarlike and isolated ease is bound in the end to go down before other nations which have not lost

---

Theodore Roosevelt, *The Strenuous Life and Other Essays* (New York, The Century Company, 1900), 4–10.

the manly and adventurous qualities. If we are to be a really great people, we must strive in good faith to play a great part in the world. We cannot avoid meeting great issues. All that we can determine for ourselves is whether we shall meet them well or ill. Last year we could not help being brought face to face with the problem of war with Spain. All we could decide was whether we should shrink like cowards from the contest or enter into it as beseemed a brave and high-spirited people; and, once in, whether failure or success should crown our banners. So it is now. We cannot avoid the responsibilities that confront us in Hawaii, Cuba, Puerto Rico, and the Philippines. All we can decide is whether we shall meet them in a way that will redound to the national credit, or whether we shall make of our dealings with these new problems a dark and shameful page in our history. To refuse to deal with them at all merely amounts to dealing with them badly. We have a given problem to solve. If we undertake the solution there is, of course, always danger that we may not solve it aright, but to refuse to undertake the solution simply renders it certain that we cannot possibly solve it aright.

The timid man, the lazy man, the man who distrusts his country, the overcivilized man, who has lost the great fighting, masterful virtues, the ignorant man and the man of dull mind, whose soul is incapable of feeling the mighty lift that thrills "stern men with empires in their brains"—all these, of course, shrink from seeing the nation undertake its new duties; shrink from seeing us build a navy and army adequate to our needs; shrink from seeing us do our share of the world's work by bringing order out of chaos in the great, fair tropic islands from which the valor of our soldiers and sailors has driven the Spanish flag. These are the men who fear the strenuous life, who fear the only national life which is really worth leading. . . .

. . . I have scant patience with those who fear to undertake the tasks of governing the Philippines, and who openly avow that they do fear to undertake it, or that they shrink from it because of the expense and trouble; but I have even scanter patience with those who make a pretense of humanitarianism to hide and cover their timidity, and who cant about "liberty" and the "consent of the governed," in order to excuse themselves for their unwillingness to play the part of men. Their doctrines, if carried out, would make it incumbent upon us to leave the Apaches of Arizona to work out their own salvation, and to decline to interfere in a single Indian reservation. Their doctrines condemn your forefathers and mine for ever having settled in these United States. . . .

I preach to you, then, my countrymen, that our country calls not for the life of ease, but for the life of strenuous endeavor. The twentieth century looms before us big with the fate of many nations. If we stand idly by, if we seek merely swollen, slothful ease, and ignoble peace, if we shrink from the hard contests where men must win at hazard of their lives and at the risk of all they hold dear, then the bolder and stronger peoples will pass us by and will win for themselves the domination of the world. Let us therefore boldly face the life of strife, resolute to do our duty well and manfully; resolute to uphold righteousness by deed and by word; resolute to be both honest and brave, to serve high ideals, yet to use practical methods. Above all, let us shrink from no strife, moral or physical, within or without the nation, provided we are certain that the strife is justified; for it is only through strife, through hard and dangerous endeavor, that we shall ultimately win the goal of true national greatness.

2. Filipino Leader Emilio Aguinaldo Rallies His People to Arms, 1899

By my proclamation of yesterday I have published the outbreak of hostilities between the Philippine forces and the American forces of occupation in Manila, unjustly and unexpectedly provoked by the latter.

In my manifest of January 8 [1899] last I published the grievances suffered by the Philippine forces at the hands of the army of occupation. The constant outrages and taunts, which have caused the misery of the people of Manila, and, finally the useless conferences and the contempt shown the Philippine government prove the premeditated transgression of justice and liberty.

I know that war has always produced great losses; I know that the Philippine people have not yet recovered from past losses and are not in the condition to endure others. But I also know by experience how bitter is slavery, and by experience I know that we should sacrifice all on the altar of our honor and of the national integrity so unjustly attacked.

I have tried to avoid, as far as it has been possible for me to do so, armed conflict, in my endeavors to assure our independence by pacific means and to avoid more costly sacrifices. But all my efforts have been useless against the measureless pride of the American Government and of its representatives in these islands, who have treated me as a rebel because I defend the sacred interests of my country and do not make myself an instrument of their dastardly intentions.

Past campaigns will have convinced you that the people are strong when they wish to be so. Without arms we have driven from our beloved country our ancient masters, and without arms we can repulse the foreign invasion as long as we wish to do so. Providence always has means in reserve and prompt help for the weak in order that they may not be annihilated by the strong; that justice may be done and humanity progress.

Be not discouraged. Our independence has been watered by the generous blood of our martyrs. Blood which may be shed in the future will strengthen it. Nature has never despised generous sacrifices.

But remember that in order that our efforts may not be wasted, that our vows may be listened to, that our ends may be gained, it is indispensable that we adjust our actions to the rules of law and of right, learning to triumph over our enemies and to conquer our own evil passions.

3. The American Anti-Imperialist League Denounces U.S. Policy, 1899

We hold that the policy known as imperialism is hostile to liberty and tends toward militarism, an evil from which it has been our glory to be free. We regret that it has become necessary in the land of Washington and Lincoln to reaffirm that all men, of whatever race or color, are entitled to life, liberty and the pursuit of happiness.

Major-General E. S. Otis, *Report on Military Operations and Civil Affairs in the Philippine Islands, 1899* (Washington, D.C.: Government Printing Office, 1899), 95–96.

Frederic Bancroft, ed., *Speeches, Correspondence, and Political Papers of Carl Schurz* (New York: G. P. Putnam's Sons, 1913), VI, 77–79.

We maintain that governments derive their just powers from the consent of the governed. We insist that the subjugation of any people is "criminal aggression" and open disloyalty to the distinctive principles of our Government.

We earnestly condemn the policy of the present National Administration in the Philippines. It seeks to extinguish the spirit of 1776 in those islands. We deplore the sacrifice of our soldiers and sailors, whose bravery deserves admiration even in an unjust war. We denounce the slaughter of the Filipinos as a needless horror. We protest against the extension of American sovereignty by Spanish methods.

We demand the immediate cessation of the war against liberty, begun by Spain and continued by us. We urge that Congress be promptly convened to announce to the Filipinos our purpose to concede to them the independence for which they have so long fought and which of right is theirs.

The United States have always protested against the doctrine of international law which permits the subjugation of the weak by the strong. A self-governing state cannot accept sovereignty over an unwilling people. The United States cannot act upon the ancient heresy that might makes right.

Imperialists assume that with the destruction of self-government in the Philippines by American hands, all opposition here will cease. This is a grievous error. Much as we abhor the war of "criminal aggression" in the Philippines, greatly as we regret that the blood of the Filipinos is on American hands, we more deeply resent the betrayal of American institutions at home. The real firing line is not in the suburbs of Manila. The foe is of our own household. The attempt of 1861 was to divide the country. That of 1899 is to destroy its fundamental principles and noblest ideals.

Whether the ruthless slaughter of the Filipinos shall end next month or next year is but an incident in a contest that must go on until the Declaration of Independence and the Constitution of the United States are rescued from the hands of their betrayers. Those who dispute about standards of value while the foundation of the Republic is undermined will be listened to as little as those who wrangle about the small economies of the household while the house is on fire. The training of a great people for a century, the aspiration for liberty of a vast immigration are forces that will hurl aside those who in the delirium of conquest seek to destroy the character of our institutions.

We deny that the obligation of all citizens to support their Government in times of grave National peril applies to the present situation. If an Administration may with impunity ignore the issues upon which it was chosen, deliberately create a condition of war anywhere on the face of the globe, debauch the civil service for spoils to promote the adventure, organize a truth-suppressing censorship and demand of all citizens a suspension of judgment and their unanimous support while it chooses to continue the fighting, representative government itself is imperiled.

We propose to contribute to the defeat of any person or party that stands for the forcible subjugation of any people. We shall oppose for reelection all who in the White House or in Congress betray American liberty in pursuit of un-American ends. We still hope that both of our great political parties will support and defend the Declaration of Independence in the closing campaign of the century.

We hold, with Abraham Lincoln, that "no man is good enough to govern another man without the other's consent. When the white man governs himself, that is self-government, but when he governs himself and also governs another man, that is more than self-government—that is despotism. Our reliance is in the love of liberty which God has planted in us. Our defense is in the spirit which prizes liberty as the heritage of all men in all lands. Those who deny freedom to others deserve it not for themselves, and under a just God cannot long retain it."

We cordially invite the cooperation of all men and women who remain loyal to the Declaration of Independence and the Constitution of the United States.

4. Mark Twain Satirizes the Battle Hymn of the Republic, 1900

Mine eyes have seen the orgy of the launching of the Sword;
He is searching out the hoardings where the stranger's wealth is stored;
He hath loosed his fateful lightnings, and with woe and death has scored;
   His lust is marching on.

I have seen him in the watch-fires of a hundred circling camps,
They have builded him an altar in the Eastern dews and damps;
I have read his doomful mission by the dim and flaring lamps—
   His night is marching on.

I have read his bandit gospel writ in burnished rows of steel:
"As ye deal with my pretensions, so with you my wrath shall deal;
Let the faithless son of Freedom crush the patriot with his heel;
   Lo, Greed is marching on!"

We have legalized the strumpet and are guarding her retreat;
Greed is seeking out commercial souls before his judgment seat;
O, be swift, ye clods, to answer him! be jubilant my feet!
   Our god is marching on!

In a sordid slime harmonious, Greed was born in yonder ditch,
With a longing in his bosom—and for others' goods an itch—
As Christ died to make men holy, let men die to make us rich—
   Our god is marching on.

5. A Soldier Criticizes American Racism in the Philippines, 1902

Of late by reason of the conduct of the troops such as the extensive burning of the barrios in trying to lay waste the country so that the insurgents cannot occupy it, the torturing of natives by so-called water-cure and other methods to obtain information, the harsh treatment of natives generally, and the failure of inexperienced, lately-appointed lieutenants commanding posts to distinguish between those who

Frederick Anderson, ed., *A Pen Warmed Up in Hell: Mark Twain in Protest* (New York: Harper & Row, 1972).

B. D. Flower, "Some Dead Sea Fruit of Our War Subjugation," *The Arena,* Vol. 27 (1902), 648–649.

are friendly and those unfriendly and to treat every native as if he were, whether or no, an *insurrecto* at heart, . . . and a deep hatred toward us engendered. If these things need be done, they had best be done by native troops, so that the people of the United States will not be credited therewith.

Almost without exception, soldiers and also many officers refer to natives in their presence as "Niggers," and natives are beginning to understand what the word "Nigger" means. The course now being pursued in this province and in the provinces of Batangas, Laguna, and Samar is in my opinion sowing the seeds for a perpetual revolution against us hereafter whenever a good opportunity offers. Under present conditions the political situation in this province is slowly retrograding, the American sentiment is decreasing, and we are daily making permanent enemies. In the course above referred to, troops make no distinction often between the property of those natives who are insurgent or insurgent sympathizers, and the property of those who heretofore have risked their lives by being loyal to the United States and giving us information against their countrymen in arms. Often every house in a barrio is burned. In my opinion the small number of irreconcilable insurgents still in arms, although admittedly difficult to catch, does not justify the means employed, and especially when taking into consideration the suffering that must be undergone by the innocent and its effects upon the relations with these people hereafter.

6. The Platt Amendment Limits Cuban Independence, 1903

Article I.   The Government of Cuba shall never enter into any treaty or other compact with any foreign power or powers which will impair or tend to impair the independence of Cuba, nor in any manner authorize or permit any foreign power or powers to obtain colonization or for military or naval purposes, or otherwise, lodgment in or control over any portion of said island.

Article II.   The Government of Cuba shall not assume or contract any public debt to pay the interest upon which, and to make reasonable sinking-fund provision for the ultimate discharge of which, the ordinary revenues of the Island of Cuba, after defraying the current expenses of the Government, shall be inadequate.

Article III.   The Government of Cuba consents that the United States may exercise the right to intervene for the preservation of Cuban independence, the maintenance of a government adequate for the protection of life, property, and individual liberty, and for discharging the obligations with respect to Cuba imposed by the Treaty of Paris on the United States, now to be assumed and undertaken by the Government of Cuba. . . .

Article V.   The Government of Cuba will execute, and, as far as necessary, extend the plans already devised, or other plans to be mutually agreed upon, for the sanitation

Charles I. Bevans, comp., *Treaties and Other International Agreements of the United States of America, 1776–1949* (Washington, D.C.: Government Printing Office for Department of State, 1971), VI, 1116.

of the cities of the island, to the end that a recurrence of epidemic and infectious diseases may be prevented, thereby assuring protection to the people and commerce of Cuba, as well as to the commerce of the Southern ports of the United States and the people residing therein. . . .

Article VII.   To enable the United States to maintain the independence of Cuba, and to protect the people thereof, as well as for its own defense, the Government of Cuba will sell or lease to the United States lands necessary for coaling or naval stations, at certain specified points, to be agreed upon with the President of the United States.

7. The Roosevelt Corollary Makes the United States the Police of Latin America, 1904

It is not true that the United States feels any land hunger or entertains any projects as regards the other nations of the Western Hemisphere save such as are for their welfare. All that this country desires is to see the neighboring countries stable, orderly, and prosperous. Any country whose people conduct themselves well can count upon our hearty friendship. If a nation shows that it knows how to act with reasonable efficiency and decency in social and political matters, if it keeps order and pays its obligations, it need fear no interference from the United States. Chronic wrongdoing, or an impotence which results in a general loosening of the ties of civilized society, may in America, as elsewhere, ultimately require intervention by some civilized nation, and in the Western Hemisphere the adherence of the United States to the Monroe Doctrine may force the United States, however reluctantly, in flagrant cases of such wrongdoing or impotence, to the exercise of an international police power. If every country washed by the Caribbean Sea would show the progress in stable and just civilization which with the aid of the Platt amendment Cuba has shown since our troops left the island, and which so many of the republics in both Americas are constantly and brilliantly showing, all question of interference by this Nation with their affairs would be at an end. Our interests and those of our southern neighbors are in reality identical. They have great natural riches, and if within their borders the reign of law and justice obtains, prosperity is sure to come to them. While they thus obey the primary laws of civilized society they may rest assured that they will be treated by us in a spirit of cordial and helpful sympathy. We would interfere with them only in the last resort, and then only if it became evident that their inability or unwillingness to do justice at home and abroad had violated the rights of the United States or had invited foreign aggression to the detriment of the entire body of American nations. It is a mere truism to say that every nation, whether in America or anywhere else, which desires to maintain its freedom, its independence, must ultimately realize that the right of such independence can not be separated from the responsibility of making good use of it.

Congressional Record, XXXIX (December 6, 1904), Part I, 19.

8. President Woodrow Wilson Disavows Territorial Conquest, 1913

The future, ladies and gentlemen, is going to be very different for this hemisphere from the past. These States lying to the south of us, which have always been our neighbors, will now be drawn closer to us by innumerable ties, and I hope, chief of all, by the tie of a common understanding of each other. Interest does not tie nations together; it sometimes separates them. But sympathy and understanding does unite them, and I believe that by the new route that is just about to be opened, while we physically cut two continents asunder, we spiritually unite them. It is a spiritual union which we seek. . . .

There is one peculiarity about the history of the Latin American States which I am sure they are keenly aware of. You hear of "concessions" to foreign capitalists in Latin America. You do not hear of concessions to foreign capitalists in the United States. They are not granted concessions. They are invited to make investments. The work is ours, though they are welcome to invest in it. We do not ask them to supply the capital and do the work. It is an invitation, not a privilege; and States that are obliged, because their territory does not lie within the main field of modern enterprise and action, to grant concessions are in this condition—that foreign interests are apt to dominate their domestic affairs, a condition of affairs always dangerous and apt to become intolerable. What these States are going to see, therefore, is an emancipation from the subordination, which has been inevitable, to foreign enterprise. . . .

We must prove ourselves their friends and champions upon terms of equality and honor. You can not be friends upon any other terms than upon the terms of equality. You can not be friends at all except upon the terms of honor. We must show ourselves friends by comprehending their interest, whether it squares with our own interest or not. It is a very perilous thing to determine the foreign policy of a nation in the terms of material interest. It not only is unfair to those with whom you are dealing, but it is degrading as regards your own actions.

Comprehension must be the soil in which shall grow all the fruits of friendship, and there is a reason and a compulsion lying behind all this which is dearer than anything else to the thoughtful men of America. I mean the development of constitutional liberty in the world. Human rights, national integrity, and opportunity as against material interests—that, ladies and gentlemen, is the issue which we now have to face. I want to take this occasion to say that the United States will never again seek one additional foot of territory by conquest. She will devote herself to showing that she knows how to make honorable and fruitful use of the territory she has, and she must regard it as one of the duties of friendship to see that from no quarter are material interests made superior to human liberty and national opportunity. I say this, not with a single thought that anyone will gainsay it, but merely to fix in our consciousness what our real relationship with the rest of America is. It is the relationship of a family of mankind devoted to the development of true constitutional liberty.

This document can be found in Thomas G. Paterson, *Major Problems in American Foreign Policy,* Vol. 1, 3d ed. (Boston: Houghton Mifflin, 1989), pp. 504–506.

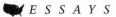

Historians have proposed many explanations for why the United States embarked on a war that spread far from its shores after having so long avoided what were called "foreign entanglements." Scholars have argued variously that it was for economic gain, that it grew out of concern for the Cuban people, that "yellow" journalists created a war hysteria to sell newspapers, and even that the war happened by accident. At bottom, most authors are troubled by a fundamental question: did the United States intend to exploit weaker nations by creating an empire, or did it intend to "spread the American dream"? These essays show two competing explanations: one that emphasizes an intentional will to dominance, and another that suggests a more complex blending of self-interest and intended benevolence. Gail Bederman of Notre Dame University argues that Theodore Roosevelt, a leading proponent of the wars against Spain and the Philippines, was powerfully influenced by images of race and gender. These cultural concepts led him to see imperialism as the next stage in the healthy growth of the republic. As you read Bederman, think about how ideas of gender and race may influence the decisions of leaders. Emily Rosenberg of Macalester College emphasizes very different considerations in the second essay. She asserts that economic interests, intertwined with a belief in America's civilizing "mission," created an impetus toward foreign expansion. President Wilson, for example, scorned imperialism and "dollar diplomacy," but he nonetheless believed that promoting American commerce abroad would advance the interests of the whole world.

Gendering Imperialism: Theodore Roosevelt's Quest for Manhood and Empire

GAIL BEDERMAN

In 1882, a newly elected young state assemblyman arrived in Albany. Theodore Roosevelt, assuming his first elective office, was brimming with self-importance and ambition. He was only twenty-three—the youngest man in the legislature—and he looked forward to a promising career of wielding real political power. Yet Roosevelt was chagrined to discover that despite his intelligence, competence, and real legislative successes, no one took him seriously. The more strenuously he labored to play "a man's part" in politics, the more his opponents derided his manhood.

Daily newspapers lampooned Roosevelt as the quintessence of effeminacy. They nicknamed him "weakling," "Jane-Dandy," "Punkin-Lily," and "the exquisite Mr. Roosevelt." They ridiculed his high voice, tight pants, and fancy clothing. Several began referring to him by the name of the well-known homosexual Oscar Wilde, and one actually alleged (in a less-than-veiled phallic allusion) that Roosevelt was "given to sucking the knob of an ivory cane." While TR might consider himself a manly man, it was becoming humiliatingly clear that others considered him effeminate.

Above all other things, Roosevelt desired power. An intuitive master of public relations, he knew that his effeminate image could destroy any chances for his political future. Nearly forty years before women got the vote, electoral politics was part of a male-only subculture, fraught with symbols of manhood. Besides, Roosevelt,

Gail Bederman, *Manliness and Civilization: A Cultural History of Gender and Race in the U.S., 1880–1917.* © 1995 University of Chicago Press. Reprinted by permission of the University of Chicago Press.

who considered himself a man's man, detested having his virility impugned. Although normally restrained, when he discovered a Tammany legislator plotting to toss him in a blanket, TR marched up to him and swore, "By God! if you try anything like that, I'll kick you, I'll bite you, I'll kick you in the balls, I'll do anything to you—you'd better leave me alone!" Clearly, the effeminate "dude" image would have to go.

And go it did. Roosevelt soon came to embody powerful American manhood. Within five years, he was running for mayor of New York as the "Cowboy of the Dakotas" [in reference to his taking up residence on a South Dakota ranch in 1884]. Instead of ridiculing him as "Oscar Wilde," newspapers were praising his virile zest for fighting and his "blizzard-seasoned constitution." In 1898, after a brief but highly publicized stint as leader of a regiment of volunteers in the Spanish American War, he became known as Colonel Roosevelt, the manly advocate of a virile imperialism. Never again would Roosevelt's name be linked to effeminacy. Even today, historians invoke Roosevelt as the quintessential symbol of turn-of-the-century masculinity.

Roosevelt's great success in masculinizing his image was due, in large part, to his masterful use of the discourse of civilization. As a mature politician, he would build his claim to political power on his claim to manhood. Skillfully, Roosevelt constructed a virile political person for himself as a strong but civilized white man.

Yet Roosevelt's use of the discourse of civilization went beyond mere public relations: Roosevelt drew on "civilization" to help formulate his larger politics as an advocate of both nationalism and imperialism. As he saw it, the United States was engaged in a millennial drama of manly racial advancement, in which American men enacted their superior manhood by asserting imperialistic control over races of inferior manhood. To prove their virility, as a race and a nation, American men needed to take up the "strenuous life" and strive to advance civilization—through imperialistic warfare and racial violence if necessary. . . .

. . . Beginning in 1894, unhappy with President Cleveland's reluctance to annex Hawaii, Roosevelt began to exhort the American race to embrace a manly, strenuous imperialism, in the cause of higher civilization. In Roosevelt's imperialistic pronouncements, as in *The Winning of the West* [a celebratory history of European American westward expansion published between 1889 and 1896], issues of racial dominance were inextricably conflated with issues of manhood. Indeed, when Roosevelt originally coined the term "the strenuous life," in an 1899 speech, he was explicitly discussing only foreign relations: calling on the United States to build up its army and to take imperialistic control of Cuba, Puerto Rico, and the Philippines. Ostensibly, the speech never mentions gender at all. Yet the phrase "the strenuous life" soon began to connote a virile, hard-driving manhood, which might or might not involve foreign relations, at all.

How did the title of an essay calling for American imperialism become a catchphrase to describe vigorous masculinity? To answer this question, we need to understand the logic behind Roosevelt's philosophies about American nationalism and imperialism. For Roosevelt, the purpose of American expansionism and national greatness was always the millennial purpose behind human evolution—human racial advancement toward a higher civilization. And the race that could best achieve this perfected civilization was, by definition, the one with the most superior manhood.

It was not coincidental that Roosevelt's advocacy of manly imperialism in the 1890s was contemporaneous with a widespread cultural concern about effeminacy, overcivilization, and racial decadence. . . . [T]hroughout Europe and Anglo-America intellectuals were worried about the emasculating tendencies of excessive civilization. Roosevelt shared many of his contemporaries' fears about the future of American manly power; and this gave his imperialistic writings an air of especial urgency. . . .

. . . Roosevelt understood decadence in terms of the racial conflict through which he believed civilizations rose and fell. As he had shown in *The Winning of the West,* TR believed that manly racial competition determined which race was superior and deserved to control the earth's resources. A race which grew decadent, then, was a race which had lost the masculine strength necessary to prevail in this Darwinistic racial struggle. Civilized advancement required much more than mere masculine strength, of course; it also required advanced manliness. Intelligence, altruism, and morality were essential traits, possessed by all civilized races and men. Yet, as important as these refined traits were, they were not enough, by themselves, to safeguard civilization's advance and prevent racial decadence. Without the "virile fighting virtues" which allowed a race to continue to expand into new territories, its more civilized racial traits would be useless. If American men lost their primal fighting virtues, a more manful race would strip them of their authority, land, and resources. This effeminate loss of racial primacy and virility was what Roosevelt meant by overcivilized racial decadence. . . .

This concept of overcivilized decadence let Roosevelt construct American imperialism as a conservative way to retain the race's frontier-forged manhood, instead of what it really was—a belligerent grab for a radically new type of nationalistic power. As Roosevelt described it, asserting the white man's racial power abroad was necessary to avoid losing the masculine strength Americans had already established through race war on the frontier. Currently the American race was one of the world's most advanced civilized races. They controlled a rich and mighty continent because their superior manhood had allowed them to annihilate the Indians on the Western frontier. If they retained their manhood, they could continue to look forward to an ever higher civilization, as they worked ever harder for racial improvement and expansion. But if American men ever lost their virile zest for Darwinistic racial contests, their civilization would soon decay. If they ignored the ongoing racial imperative of constant expansion and instead grew effeminate and luxury-loving, a manlier race would inherit their mantle of the highest civilization.

From 1894 until he became president in 1901, Roosevelt wrote and lectured widely on the importance of taking up what Rudyard Kipling, in 1899, would dub "the White Man's burden." Kipling coined this term in a poem written to exhort American men to conquer and rule the Philippines. "The white man". . . simultaneously meant the white race, civilization itself, and white males as a group. In "The White Man's Burden," Kipling used the term in all these senses to urge white males to take up the racial burden of civilization's advancement. "Take up the White Man's burden," he wrote, capitalizing the essential term, and speaking to the manly civilized on behalf of civilization. "Send forth the best ye breed"—quality breeding was essential, because evolutionary development (breeding) was what gave "the White Man" the right and duty to conquer uncivilized races.

> Go bind your sons to exile
>   To serve your captives' need;
> To wait in heavy harness,
>   on fluttered folk and wild—
> Your new-caught, sullen peoples,
>   Half-devil and half-child. . . .

Roosevelt called Kipling's poem "poor poetry but good sense from the expansionist standpoint." Although Roosevelt did not use the term "the white man's burden" in his writings on imperialism, he drew on the same sorts of race and gender linkages which Kipling deployed in his poem. TR's speeches of this period frequently conflate manhood and racial power, and draw extended analogies between the individual American man and the virile American race.

For example, "National Duties," one of TR's most famous speeches, represents both American men and the American race as civilized entities with strong virile characters—in popular parlance, both were "the white man." Roosevelt begins by outlining this racial manhood, which he calls "the essential manliness of the American character." Part of this manliness centered around individual and racial duties to the home. On the one hand, individual men must work to provide for the domestic needs of themselves and their families. On the other hand, the men of the race must work to provide for their collective racial home, their nation. Men who shirked these manly homemaking duties were despicably unsexed; or, as TR put it, "the willfully idle man" was as bad as "the willfully barren woman."

Yet laboring only for his own hearth and nation was not enough to satisfy a real man. Virile manhood also required the manly American nation to take up imperialistic labors outside its borders, just as manhood demanded individual men to labor outside the home: "Exactly as each man, while doing first his duty to his wife and the children within his home, must yet, if he hopes to amount to much, strive mightily in the world outside his home, so our nation, while first of all seeing to its own domestic well-being, must not shrink from playing its part among the great nations without." It would be as unmanly for the American race to refuse its imperialist destiny as it would be for a cowardly man to spend all his time loafing at home with his wife. Imperialist control over primitive races thus becomes a matter of manhood—part of a male-only public sphere, which TR sets in contradistinction to the home.

After setting up imperialism as a manly duty for both man and race, Roosevelt outlines the imperialist's appropriate masculine behavior—or, should we say, his appropriate masculine appendage? Roosevelt immediately brings up the "big stick." It may be a cheap shot to stress the phallic implications of TR's imagery, yet Roosevelt himself explained the meaning of the "big stick" in terms of manhood and the proper way to assert the power of a man: "A good many of you are probably acquainted with the old proverb: 'Speak softly and carry a big stick—you will go far.' If a man continually blusters, if he lacks civility, a big stick will not save him from trouble; and neither will speaking softly avail, if back of the softness there does not lie strength, power." Just as a manly man avoided bluster, relying instead on his self-evident masculine strength and power, so virile American men should build a powerful navy and army, so that when they took up the white man's burden in primitive lands, they would receive the respect due to a masterful, manly race. . . .

Roosevelt was not content merely to make speeches about the need for violent, imperialistic manhood. He always needed to embody his philosophy. The sickly boy had remade himself into an adventure-book hunter-naturalist; the dude politician had remade himself into a heroic Western rancher. The 1898 outbreak of the Spanish-American war—for which he had agitated long and hard—let Roosevelt remake himself into Colonel Roosevelt, the fearless Rough Rider.

Reinventing himself as a charismatic war hero allowed Roosevelt to model the manful imperialism about which he had been writing for four years. TR became a walking advertisement for the imperialistic manhood he desired for the American race. Indeed, from the moment of his enlistment until his mustering out four months later, Roosevelt self-consciously publicized himself as a model of strenuous, imperialistic manhood. In late April 1898, against all advice, Roosevelt resigned as assistant secretary of the navy and enlisted to fight in the just-declared war on Spain. Aged thirty-nine, with an important subcabinet post, a sick wife, and six young children, no one but Roosevelt himself imagined he ought to see active service. Roosevelt's decision to enlist was avidly followed by newspapers all over the country. . . .

The press, fascinated by the undertaking, christened [his] regiment "Roosevelt's Rough Riders." Roosevelt's heroic frontiersman identity thus came full circle, as he no doubt intended. As Richard Slotkin has pointed out, the term "Rough Riders" had long been used in adventure novels to describe Western horsemen. Thus, by nicknaming his regiment the "Rough Riders," the nation showed it understood the historical connections Roosevelt always drew between Indian wars in the American West and virile imperialism in Cuba and the Philippines. . . .

After his mustering out, TR the politician continued to play the role of virile Rough Rider for all he was worth. In November, he was elected governor of New York, campaigning as a war hero and employing ex–Rough Riders to warm up the election crowds. By January 1899, his thrilling memoir, *The Rough Riders,* was appearing serially in *Scribner's Magazine.* And in 1900 his virile popularity convinced Republican party leaders that Roosevelt could counter [Democrat William Jennings] Bryan's populism better than any other vice-presidential candidate. Roosevelt had constructed himself and the Rough Riders as the epitome of civilized, imperialistic manhood, a model for the American race to follow. His success in modeling that imperialistic manhood exceeded even his own expectations and ultimately paved the way for his presidency.

On April 10, 1899, Colonel Roosevelt stood before the men of Chicago's elite, all-male, Hamilton Club and preached the doctrine of "The Strenuous Life." As governor of New York and a fabulously popular ex–Rough Rider, he knew the national press would be in attendance; and though he spoke *at* the Hamilton Club, he spoke *to* men across America. With the cooperation of the press and at the risk of his life, TR had made himself into a national hero—the embodiment of manly virtue, masculine violence, and white American racial supremacy—and the antithesis of overcivilized decadence. Now he urged the men of the American race to live the sort of life he had modeled for them: to be virile, vigorous, and manly, and to reject overcivilized decadence by supporting a strenuously imperialistic foreign policy. When contemporaries ultimately adopted his phrase "the strenuous life" as a synonym for the vigorous, vehement manhood Roosevelt modeled, they showed they correctly understood that his strenuous manhood was inextricably linked to his nationalism, imperialism, and racism.

Ostensibly, "The Strenuous Life" preached the virtues of military prepared-ness and imperialism, but contemporaries understood it as a speech about man-hood. The practical import of the speech was to urge the nation to build up its army, to maintain its strong navy, and to take control of Puerto Rico, Cuba, and the Philippines. But underlying these immediate objectives lay the message that Amer-ican manhood—both the manly race and individual white men—must retain the strength of their Indian-fighter ancestors, or another race would prove itself more manly and overtake America in the Darwinian struggle to be the world's most dominant race.

Roosevelt began by demanding manliness in both the American nation and American men. Slothful men who lacked the "desire and power" to strive in the world were despicable and unmanly. "We do not admire the man of timid peace. We admire the man who embodies victorious effort." If America and its men were not man enough to fight, they would not only lose their place among "the great na-tions of the world," they would become a decadent and effeminate race. Roosevelt held up the Chinese, whom he despised as the most decadent and unmanly of races, as a cautionary lesson: If we "play the part of China, and be content to rot by inches in ignoble ease within our borders," we will "go down before other nations which have not lost the manly and adventurous qualities." If American men lacked the manly fortitude to go bravely and willingly to a foreign war, the race would decay, preached TR, the virile war hero.

In stirring tones, the Rough Rider of San Juan Hill ridiculed the overcivilized anti-imperialists who had lost the "great fighting, masterful virtues." Lacking the masculine impulse toward racial aggression and unmoved by virile visions of em-pire, these men had been sapped of all manhood.

> The timid man, the lazy man, the man who distrusts his country, the over-civilized man, who has lost the great fighting, masterful virtues, the ignorant man, and the man of dull mind, whose soul is incapable of feeling the mighty lift that thrills stern men with em-pires in their brains—all these, of course shrink from seeing the nation undertake its new duties; shrink from seeing us build a navy and an army adequate to our needs; shrink from seeing us do our share of the world's work. These are the men who fear the strenuous life. . . . They believe in that cloistered life which saps the hardy virtues in a nation, as it saps them in the individual.

Like "cloistered" monkish celibates, these "over-civilized" men "shrink, shrink, shrink" from carrying the "big stick." Dishonorably, they refused to do their manly duty by the childish Filipinos. Had the United States followed these anti-imperialists' counsel and refused to undertake "one of the great tasks set modern civilization," Americans would have shown themselves not only unmanly but also racially inferior. "Some stronger, manlier power would have to step in and do the work, and we would have shown ourselves weaklings, unable to carry to successful completion the labors that great and high-spirited nations are eager to undertake." As TR saw it, the man, the race, and the nation were one in their need to possess virile, imperialist manhood.

Then TR got down to brass tacks, dwelling at length on Congress' responsibility to build up the armed forces. After again raising the specter of Chinese decadence, which American men faced if they refused to strengthen their army and navy, Roosevelt stressed America's duty to take up the white man's burden in Cuba, Puerto Rico, and the Philippines. If the American race was "too weak, too selfish, or too foolish" to take on that task, it would be completed by "some stronger and more manful race." He ridiculed anti-imperialists as cowards who "make a pretense of humanitarianism to hide and cover their timidity" and to "excuse themselves for their unwillingness to play the part of men."

"The Strenuous Life" culminates with a Darwinian vision of strife between races for the "dominion of the world," which only the most manful race could win.

> I preach to you then, my countrymen, that our country calls not for the life of ease but for the life of strenuous endeavor. . . . If we stand idly by . . . then the bolder and stronger peoples will pass us by, and will win for themselves the domination of the world. Let us therefore boldly face the life of strife, resolute to do our duty well and manfully.

American men must embrace their manly mission to be the race which dominates the world. Struggle for racial supremacy was inevitable, but the most manful race—the American race—would triumph, if it made the attempt. Its masculine strength was proven by military victories over barbarous brown races. Its manly virtue was evident in its civilized superiority to the primitive childish races it uplifted. White American men must claim their place as the world's most perfect men, the fittest race for the evolutionary struggle toward a perfect civilization. This was the meaning of "The Strenuous Life."

We can now answer the question, "How did the title of an essay calling for American dominance over the brown races become a catchphrase to describe virile masculinity?" Roosevelt's desire for imperial dominance had been, from the first, intrinsically related to his views about male power. As he saw it, the manhood of the American race had been forged in the crucible of frontier race war; and to abandon the virile power of that violence would be to backslide toward effeminate racial mediocrity. Roosevelt wanted American men to be the ultimate in human evolution, the world's most powerful and civilized race. He believed that their victory over the Indians on the frontier proved that the American race possessed the racial superiority and masculine power to overcome any savage race; and he saw a glorious future for the race in the twentieth century, as it pressed on toward international dominance and the perfection of civilization. The only danger which Roosevelt saw menacing this millennial triumph of manly American civilization came from within. Only by surrendering to overcivilized decadence—by embracing unmanly racial sloth instead of virile imperialism—could American men fail. Thus, American men must work strenuously to uphold their civilization. They must refuse a life of ease, embrace their manly task, and take up the white man's burden. Only by living that "strenuous life" could American men prove themselves to be what Roosevelt had no doubt they were—the apex of civilization, evolution's most favored race, masterful men fit to command the barbarous races and the world's "waste spaces"—in short, the most virile and manly of men.

In later years, as Americans came to take international involvement for granted and as imperialism came to seem less controversial, the phrase "the strenuous life" underwent a subtle change of meaning. Always associated with Roosevelt, it came to connote the virile manhood which he modeled for the nation as imperialistic Western hero and Rough Rider—the peculiar combination of moral manliness and aggressive masculinity which he was able to synthesize so well. As Roosevelt's presidency wore on, Americans grew accustomed to taking up the white man's burden, not only in the Philippines, but also in Cuba, Panama, and the Dominican Republic. The "strenuous life" came to be associated with any virile, manly effort to accomplish great work, whether imperialistic or not. Yet on a basic level, "the strenuous life" retained TR's original associations with the evolutionary struggle of the American race on behalf of civilization. "The strenuous life," as it came to be used, meant the opposite of "overcivilized effeminacy." Or, as Roosevelt summed it up himself in his *Autobiography,* the man who lives the strenuous life regards his life "as a pawn to be promptly hazarded whenever the hazard is warranted by the larger interests of the great game in which we are all engaged." That great game, for Roosevelt, was always the millennial struggle for Americans to perfect civilization by becoming the most manly, civilized, and powerful race in the world.

Spreading the American Dream: American Economic and Cultural Expansion, 1890–1945

EMILY S. ROSENBERG

For a number of reasons, the government began to take an active interest in overseas expansion during the 1890s. As American traders and investors enlarged their international stakes, many people argued that the national welfare depended, in part, on continued access to global opportunities. It would, of course, be a mistake to exaggerate the extent of American overseas economic expansion prior to World War I. Compared to Britain's foreign activity, America's efforts seemed slight (except in Mexico and Cuba); by today's standards, the absolute value of exports and investment seems minuscule—export trade and foreign investment comprised only a fraction of domestic economic activity. Yet overseas trade and investment comprised about the same percentages of the United States' GNP at the turn of the century as in recent years, a time when foreign economic activity has certainly been a major governmental concern.

For a variety of reasons, most policymakers of the late nineteenth century, like their more recent counterparts, *did* believe that free participation in international trade and open access to investment opportunities were vital to the nation's well-being. Early multinational companies and the many American firms with international aspirations pressed for greater governmental assistance. Certain important industries, then as later, derived a substantial portion of their profits abroad. By the early twentieth century, Standard Oil, International Harvester, and New York Life—to name only three giant firms—already depended heavily on foreign earnings.

The expansive outlook of these new and powerful international companies gained additional strength from the formation of trade associations. In the late nineteenth and early twentieth centuries most industries developed associations designed to transcend intra-industry rivalry and operate on behalf of the group as a whole. The National Association of Manufacturers (formed in 1895), the American Asiatic Association (1898), the United States Chamber of Commerce (1912), and the American Manufacturers' Export Association (1913) were just a few of the influential offspring of the trade-association movement that urged more governmental support and promoted the identification between foreign commerce and national interest.

But government's new interest in commercial promotion did not stem simply from special pleading. Especially during and after the severe depression that began in 1893, business leaders and policymakers alike became convinced that expansion was needed to avoid overproduction and to maintain prosperity and social cohesion at home.

The reality of overproduction in the 1890s—that is, the validity of any particular ratio placing production higher than consumption—is of little historical importance in assessing the motives behind government's new commercial activism. The so-called crisis of overproduction of the 1890s was rooted less in empirical data than in contemporary attitudes. Twentieth-century Americans have witnessed a process that nineteenth-century analysts could not have imagined: the expansion of domestic demand through techniques such as planned obsolescence, mass advertising, and annual model change. To most American businessmen and policymakers of the 1890s, however, it was domestic production, rather than consumption, that seemed almost infinitely expandable.

Foreign commercial expansion and national prosperity seemed intertwined. The National Association of Manufacturers resolved in 1903: "If, as is claimed, the capacity of our mills and factories is one-third greater than is necessary to supply the home demand, it is obvious that the time is near at hand when we must obtain a broader foreign market, in order to keep the wheels of the factories moving." The *Forum* was more direct: "It is the duty of our government in order to supply remunerative employment to the greatest number of our citizens to take every step possible towards the extension of foreign trade." And farmers also echoed the call for greater governmental assistance. In 1899, the National Grange argued that government had begun to spend "very large sums of money . . . to widen the market for our manufacturing industries in foreign countries" and demanded that it devote "the same energies and efforts" to agricultural marketing. Thus, the overproduction thesis (which mistakenly presumed a fairly inelastic domestic demand) did provoke a reassessment of government's role. Accepting the proposition that government had new responsibilities to enlarge foreign markets, a State Department memo of 1898 stated that the "enlargement of foreign consumption of the products of our mills and workshops has, therefore, become a serious problem of statesmanship as well as of commerce . . . and we can no longer afford to disregard international rivalries now that we ourselves have become a competitor in the world-wide struggle for trade."

Policymakers' social attitudes were also easily compatible with a new role for government. Drawing support from the ideas of Social Darwinism and "scientific" racism, America's dominant groups felt confident of their own superiority. Moreover, they had grown accustomed in domestic affairs to calling upon government to enforce and maintain their prerogatives. In the late nineteenth century, governmental power crushed those ethnic groups that were perceived as threats to social stability. On the frontier, federal troops quashed the last great Indian resistance at Wounded

Knee in 1890; in the South, state governments enforced Jim Crow apartheid against blacks, and the Supreme Court buttressed the system with the separate-but-equal doctrine of *Plessy* v. *Ferguson;* in Northern cities, governmental power clashed with strikers branded as radical "new immigrants"; in the Far West, immigrant restriction laws were enforced against the Chinese.

Concepts of racial mission, so well rehearsed at home, were easily transferred overseas. Editor Theodore Marburg argued: "We have brushed aside 275,000 Indians, and in place of them have this population of 70,000,000 of what we regard as the highest type of modern man . . . [W]e hold to the opinion that we have done more than any other race to conquer the world for civilization in the past few centuries, and we will probably go on holding to this opinion and go on with our conquests." And because governmental power had consistently supported Anglo-Saxon dominance at home in the name of advancing republicanism and progress, so it seemed natural for policymakers to adopt a similar activist role and rationale abroad. Senator Albert Beveridge urged President William McKinley not to shirk the white man's burden. God, he declaimed, "has made us adept in government that we may administer government among savage and senile peoples . . . He has marked the American people as His chosen nation to finally lead in the regeneration of the world." Theodore Roosevelt, who became President in 1901, agreed. Drawing on America's own history, he argued in 1901 that when the United States government fought "wars with barbarous or semi-barbarous peoples" it was not violating the peace but merely exercising "a most regrettable but necessary international police duty which must be performed for the sake of the welfare of mankind."

Crusades to dominate those who were not Anglo-Saxon also found support from the burgeoning Progressive movement, of which Roosevelt, Beveridge, and other imperialists considered themselves a part. Progressivism, a reform impulse that profoundly reshaped American domestic life and foreign relations from the 1890s through World War I, comprised a loose and often contradictory coalition of clean-government crusaders, conservationists, Anglo-Saxon supremacists, muckraking journalists, social-welfare workers, efficiency experts, middle-class professionals, and advocates of business regulation. Although people who adopted the "progressive" label could champion causes as diverse as prohibition, juvenile courts, national parks, and antitrust laws, almost all shared a fundamental faith in professional expertise. Progressives sought to guide the nation and the world away from the social disorders of the late nineteenth century by the scientific application of the problem-solving technique: define the problem, search out relevant facts, deduce a solution, carry it out. Progressives enshrined bureaucratic method and expertise, opening the way for greater governmental action while excluding "irresponsible elements" from decisionmaking. If only they could take charge and attack social problems in a scientific way, the new professionals believed, they would bring order and progress at home and abroad. Such elevation of expertise easily became paternalistic: "expert" and "efficient" people had to dominate lesser breeds in order to uplift them, and, as at home, the force of government might be needed to support, indeed to institutionalize, this effort.

Thus, the entire rationale for overseas expansion was shaped in a domestic crucible. Economic need, Anglo-Saxon mission, and the progressive impulse joined together nicely to justify a more active role for government in promoting foreign expansion.

To say that perceived economic conditions and dominant values supported greater governmental involvement in expansion is not to argue that all, or even most, people favored militant colonialism. Americans differed profoundly over *how* to spread civilization. At home, "undercivilized" peoples were made to conform to Anglo-Saxon standards by many means, ranging from violence to educational persuasion. So, in dealing with foreigners, some believed that "backward nations" could be brought into civilization only by means of force, while others sought to conquer the world peacefully, armed with sewing machines, Bibles, schools, or insights from the new social sciences. Whether the government would promote expansion by brutal domination or peaceful reform (or a mixture of the two) presented a tactical question within a broader consensus that accepted the necessity and ultimate benevolence of American expansion.

Colonialism

Cuban rebellion against Spanish rule stirred Americans into a crusade to free Cuba and, ultimately, to seize an empire at Spain's expense. In 1898 the Republican Administration of William McKinley annexed Hawaii, defeated Spain in a quick war, and acquired Puerto Rico, the Philippines, and Guam as fruits of victory. (Cuba could not be annexed, because Congress had passed the Teller Amendment promising the island independence, but American military occupation dragged on after the war until Cuba agreed to accept protectorate status.) To some people, acquisition of these overseas colonies seemed to offer a way in which the government could both advance its economic interests and fulfill its mission of improving mankind.

The debate over colonialism centered on the issue of acquiring the Philippines. The economic arguments in support of keeping those islands as a possession stressed their importance as a stepping-stone to China. Both farmers and industrialists hoped to open Oriental markets, and yet, after China's defeat in the Sino-Japanese War in 1895, China seemed in imminent danger of being closed off to Americans. A military and political presence in the Philippines, trade expansionists hoped, would give the United States more leverage in dealing with the big-power scramble for concessions and spheres of influence in China. By serving as a coaling station and base for America's newly strengthened navy and as a relay point for an infant communications system, the Philippines would become, one business publication predicted, America's Hong Kong—its gateway to the Orient. McKinley's Assistant Secretary to the Treasury, the prominent banker Frank Vanderlip, stated that the islands would be "pickets of the Pacific, standing guard at the entrances to trade with the millions of China and Korea, French Indo-China, the Malay Peninsula, and the islands of Indonesia."

Possession of the Philippines would also advance American Protestant missionary efforts, both in those Catholic islands and on the Asian mainland. "The Christian view of politics," explained one missionary in 1901, "emphasizes the burden of Government and the responsibility of dominion, and thereby transforms empire from an ambition to an opportunity. Blindly and unworthily, yet, under God, surely and steadily, the Christian nations are subduing the world, in order to make mankind free."

The classic formulation linking American expansion to a militant colonialism was found in Josiah Strong's *Expansion* (1900), written mainly to justify the subjugation of the Philippines. Strong expressed the views of most imperialists when he distinguished between independence and freedom. Because real freedom was possible only under the rule of law, and Anglo-Saxons were the most effective law bringers, spreading freedom into non-Western lands could necessitate violating national independence and imposing Anglo-Saxon colonial governments. Because national independence movements generally supported anarchy or tyranny, America's superior "free" culture probably could be imported only through outright governance. In addition, Strong stressed, the resources of the tropics were underused by their owners, and the well-being of all mankind required interposition by efficient "producer" races. Thus, Strong emphatically defended American suppression of the Filipino independence movement; he believed that the war reflected God's will and furthered the spiritual and economic evolution of mankind. Republican Senator Orville H. Platt advanced the same view when he described Admiral Dewey's warship in Manila Bay as "a new Mayflower . . . the harbinger and agent of a new civilization." And after investigating America's policy, the first Philippine Commission reported: "Only through American occupation, therefore, is the idea of a free, self-governing, and united Philippine commonwealth at all conceivable. And the indispensable need, from the Filipino point of view, of maintaining American sovereignty over the archipelago is recognized by all intelligent Filipinos . . . "

After the seizure of the Philippines, however, the taste for imposing colonial status on an alien people turned sour for most Americans. The costs of colonialism seemed to outstrip potential advantages. The Filipino independence movement, led by Emilio Aguinaldo, allied itself with the United States in the victory over Spain, but when McKinley's imperial policy became clear, Aguinaldo resumed warfare against the United States. By the time American troops had quelled the nationalist resistance, one of every five Filipinos was dead from war or disease, and America's own casualties reached 4,300 men. The American commander in southern Luzon admitted, "it has been necessary to adopt what in other countries would probably be thought harsh measures." Such slaughter in the name of "freedom" fueled the anti-imperialist movement by making humanitarian arguments for colonialism appear ridiculous. Even Dr. Jacob Gould Schurman, president of the Philippine Commission that had so strongly defended American subjugation of the Philippines, publicly confessed his error after touring the battlefields and seeing the horrors there. By 1902, Schurman had become outspoken in denouncing the brutality of the war and in calling for a government based on Filipino consent.

The anti-imperialists also turned concepts of national mission and economic advantage against colonialism. John W. Burgess, the widely read advocate of Anglo-Saxon supremacy, opposed colonialism on the grounds that it incorporated "inferior" people into the American system. Upper-class reformer Carl Schurz and others suggested that the militarism that would inevitably accompany the seizure of colonies would undermine America's best traditions of representative government and equality under the law. Joining the imperial game would tarnish, not spread, the American dream. Even staunch expansionists such as Theodore Roosevelt and Alfred Thayer

Mahan supported acquisition of naval bases but felt grave reservations about annexing large populations of alien peoples. And the prominent anti-imperialist businessman Edward Atkinson attacked the economic argument: "We may not compute the cost of our military control over the Philippine Islands at anything less than 75,000 dollars a day . . . I leave to the advocates . . . to compute how much our export trade must be increased from last year's amount, to cover even the cost of occupation." The expense of empire, Atkinson argued, would always outweigh the benefits.

As the Philippine insurrection demonstrated the moral ambiguity and expense of colonialism, domestic divisions over the issue doomed any further attempts to accumulate an empire. Although most Americans continued to favor expansion, a national consensus never formed to support more acquisition of territory.

The new relationship developed with Cuba—the protectorate—presented fewer problems. After the defeat of Spain, American military officials set up an occupation government in Cuba; in late 1899, General Leonard Wood became military commander and vowed to create a polity "modeled closely upon lines of our great Republic." Wood brought in a host of experts to reshape Cuba. Americans assumed direction of the customhouses (the major source of government revenue), controlled the country's finances, organized a postal service, established telephone and telegraph lines, encouraged railroad and shipping facilities, built roads, carried out sanitation projects (Wood even included "before and after" photos of public toilets in his reports to Washington), established schools (the new Cuban school law closely resembled Ohio's), and invited New York City police to organize their counterparts in Havana. Mark Twain's Connecticut Yankee could not have done more. These measures superficially Americanized and "developed" the island, but Wood bowed to the pressure of the native elite and American landowners and avoided basic changes in land tenure or tax structure—important changes that would have accorded with a liberal, Americanized model. Wood's program further entrenched Cuba's foreign-dominated, export-oriented monoculture of sugar.

America refused to terminate its occupation of Cuba until Cubans accepted the Platt Amendment, which made their country a protectorate. Reluctantly voted by Cubans into their constitution in 1901, the Platt Amendment and its economic counterpart—the Reciprocity Treaty of 1902—gave the United States the right to establish a naval base in Cuba, to intervene against internal or external threats to the country's stability, and to maintain a privileged trading relationship. Under the Platt Amendment, Cuba was independent, but only nominally so.

The protectorate relationship seemed to work economic magic. Trade boomed; American investment in sugar and tobacco shot up; manufacturing sales outlets opened by the score. Integration into America's economy was labeled "development." In 1918, the head of the Latin American Division in the State Department drew this happy conclusion:

> The total trade of Cuba with the United States just prior to the end of the Spanish rule over that island (1897) amounted to about twenty-seven million dollars per annum. During the decade following the termination of our war with Spain the island of Cuba, guided by American influence, increased her trade with us over four hundred and thirty million dollars. This unprecedented *development* of Cuba may serve as an illustration of what probably would take place in the Central American countries provided this government extended to them aid of a practical character as it did to Cuba. [My emphasis.]

Cuba thus became a laboratory for methods of influence that fell short of outright colonialism. Using the Platt Amendment as a model, American Presidents negotiated protectorate treaties with other nations in the strategically and economically important canal area: Panama (1903), Dominican Republic (1905), Nicaragua (1916), Haiti (1916). These protectorates also received a dose of military-directed Americanization. Moreover, the American military and many of the technical advisers who worked to "develop" and Americanize protectorates continued to offer their skills to other foreigners, seldom doubting the universal applicability of their expertise. After a great earthquake in Messina, Italy, in 1909, for example, the navy supervised construction of three thousand new cottages (unfortunately, choosing building materials and styles totally inappropriate to the region). And a great number of American technical and financial missions during the 1920s were staffed by personnel who received their initial foreign experience in Cuba.

With outright colonialism out of fashion, the expansionist debate revolved around other means of control: tutelage under theoretically independent protectorates, or more important, governmental encouragement of private connections, especially economic ones. Increasingly, Americans understood that the extension of American know-how and the expansion of trade and investment could best proceed without formal colonialism. William Graham Sumner, for example, wrote: "What private individuals want is free access, under order and security, to any part of the earth's surface, in order that they may avail themselves of its natural resources for their use, either by investment or commerce." Colonialism was not necessary, or even desirable, to Sumner's ends. If Americans, Sumner added, could have open access to foreign countries but let others actually run the foreign governments, "we should gain all the advantages and escape all the burdens" of colonialism.

⬤ F U R T H E R   R E A D I N G

H. W. Brands, *TR: The Last Romantic* (1997).
Michael Hunt, *Ideology and U.S. Foreign Policy* (1987).
Stanley Karnow, *In Our Image: America's Empire in the Philippines* (1989).
Walter LaFeber, *Inevitable Revolutions* (1993).
Louis Perez, Jr., *On Becoming Cuban: Identity, Nationality, and Culture* (1999).
Robert Rydell, *World of Fairs: The Century-of-Progress Expositions* (1993).
Lars Schoultz, *Beneath the United States: A History of U.S. Policy Towards Latin America* (1999).
William Appleman Williams, *The Tragedy of American Diplomacy* (1959).

CHAPTER
5

The Progressive Movement

*From the turn of the century up to the 1920s, Americans of all backgrounds wrestled
with the notion of "progress." Giant cities peopled by impoverished immigrants,
new technologies of mass production, political machines controlled by party bosses,
and the spectacular concentration of wealth in the hands of the few left many people
wondering, "Is this progress?" The nation had more money and technology, but it
seemed to have more corruption, disease, and poverty as well.*

*A wide spectrum of middle- and upper-class activists throughout the nation
called themselves Progressives. They sought to strengthen the moral fiber of American
society and ameliorate the chaos, corruption, and inequalities of modern life. They
fought successfully for reforms such as woman suffrage, the prohibition of alcohol,
antitrust legislation, laws curtailing child labor, the creation of a national income
tax, conservation of natural resources, and the popular election of senators. But theirs
was not the only definition of progress. Immigrants, politicians, business executives,
and experts in law, economics, engineering, and such newly invented fields as social
work contended over what constituted progress, and on whose terms it would take
place. African Americans, meanwhile, saw the progress contained in the Fourteenth
and Fifteenth Amendments undermined by federal law and local practice. In the
1890s, white mobs on average lynched more than one hundred blacks every year.
In 1896, in* Plessy v. Ferguson, *the Supreme Court legalized segregation by race.
For all their fine words about political virtue, the Progressives mostly ignored the
ugly legacies of slavery. Left to work out their own solutions, African American
leaders also debated the meaning of progress and the methods of obtaining it.*

*Progressives particularly prized the efficient, rational planning of human and
natural resources to promote the "public good," but they often failed to see that
what was good for one public might be bad for another. Cleaning up city politics
made sense to political reformers, who hated to see party bosses buying votes. To
immigrants, cleaning up city government meant losing those politicians who actually
looked out for them. Regulating business to protect public health helped consumers
(as in the Pure Food and Drug Act), but it also gave big corporations an edge over
less efficient small companies. Banning alcohol seemed an urgent moral reform to
nondrinkers; banning cigarettes seemed an urgent moral reform to nonsmokers.
Immigrants and the working class tended to favor both indulgences. Overall, to
Progressives, the great questions concerned how to clean up politics, manage the
nation's natural resources, curb rapacious business practices, eliminate vice, and*

*create a unified "American" nation out of the disparate elements inhabiting the
land from the Atlantic to the Pacific.*

*One outcome was the greatest spate of Constitution rewriting since the adoption
of the Bill of Rights. Through giving women the vote, Progressives doubled the
electorate. Through the direct election of senators, they brought government closer
to the people. By creating the federal income tax, they took money from the wealthy
(and the middle class) and vastly increased the power of government. By prohibiting
the manufacture and sale of alcohol, they imposed their social values and medical
advice on the nation. Progressives came from both political parties, and under former
president Theodore Roosevelt some of them created a third party in 1912. Politically,
they were hard to categorize, but they were nothing if not bold.*

◤ Q U E S T I O N S   T O   T H I N K   A B O U T

What was Progressivism? Was it an inspirational movement to help the nation realize
its democratic ideals, or was it an attempt at social control by self-important, moralistic
busybodies? Considering the assaults on African Americans and the Progressives'
lack of attention to race issues, which approach made more sense: compromise as
advocated by Booker T. Washington, or the continued fight for equal rights as argued
by W. E. B. DuBois?

◤ D O C U M E N T S

The documents in this chapter display different perspectives on Progressivism and the
continuing debate over the concerns of African Americans. Lincoln Steffens, a leading
"muckraking" journalist, found that the American people had only themselves to blame
for their descent into political corruption during the so-called Gilded Age at the end of
the nineteenth century. In *The Shame of the Cities* (Document 1), Steffens urged citizens
to vote according to their consciences, not for the machines. In Document 2, politician
George Washington Plunkitt contradicts reformers' complaints in a famous argument on
behalf of the Tammany machine. Politicians simply provided services, he said, for which
they were compensated by graft. Woman suffrage, a crowning achievement of Progressivism, was the result of political organizing by women going back to 1848. In Document
3, social worker Jane Addams makes what became the winning argument for the vote for
women. The ballot gave them the means to do what she called "civic housekeeping":
cleaning up politics and the cities. Document 4 shows the Progressives' concern with
better management of the environment. Republican President Theodore Roosevelt, like
his successors William Howard Taft and Woodrow Wilson, had enormous confidence in
government regulation. He helped to start the first environmental movement in the
United States, and, as president, he assembled the governors of the states to lecture them
on efficiency and the importance of conserving resources for future generations. Documents 5 and 6 show the Progressives' concern with personal morality, self-control, and
the elimination of vices such as drinking and smoking. From popular songs to the pronouncements of industrialists like Henry Ford, Progressives continuously reiterated the
theme of healthy living. In Document 7, Yale sociology professor William Graham
Sumner vents the annoyance felt by some at the zeal of the Progressives. He criticizes
the Progressives for their extravagant complaints, their attacks on the rights of business,
and their overconfidence in government and legislation. Document 8 attests to the sweep
and efficacy of Progressive reform, despite nay-sayers like Sumner. The Progressive Era
saw more changes to the U.S. Constitution than at any time since the addition of the Bill

of Rights. The last two documents focus on the plight and strategies of African Americans. Born a slave, Booker T. Washington worked in a salt furnace and later a coal mine to earn the money for his own education. He founded the Tuskegee Institute in Alabama in 1881 and became an advocate of vocational training for blacks. In his famous 1895 Atlanta Exposition address to a white audience (Document 9), Washington advocated a compromise that would allow African Americans to better themselves within the context of severe segregation. W. E. B. DuBois, who helped start the National Association for the Advancement of Colored People (NAACP) in 1909, countered that justice has never been achieved by conceding defeat (Document 10). Blacks should pursue higher education and never give up on their civil rights. The disagreement between Washington and DuBois reflected the paucity of options available to blacks in the Progressive period, as white reformers largely turned their backs on questions of racial justice.

1. Journalist Lincoln Steffens Exposes the Shame of Corruption, 1904

. . . The misgovernment of the American people is misgovernment by the American people.

When I set out on my travels, an honest New Yorker told me honestly that I would find that the Irish, the Catholic Irish, were at the bottom of it all everywhere. The first city I went to was St. Louis, a German city. The next was Minneapolis, a Scandinavian city, with a leadership of New Englanders. Then came Pittsburg, Scotch Presbyterian, and that was what my New York friend was. "Ah, but they are all foreign populations," I heard. The next city was Philadelphia, the purest American community of all, and the most hopeless. And after that came Chicago and New York, both mongrel-bred, but the one a triumph of reform, the other the best example of good government that I had seen. The "foreign element" excuse is one of the hypocritical lies that save us from the clear sight of ourselves.

Another such conceit of our egotism is that which deplores our politics and lauds our business. . . .

There is hardly an office from United States Senator down to Alderman in any part of the country to which the business man has not been elected; yet politics remains corrupt, government pretty bad, and the selfish citizen has to hold himself in readiness like the old volunteer firemen to rush forth at any hour, in any weather, to prevent the fire; and he goes out sometimes and he puts out the fire (after the damage is done) and he goes back to the shop sighing for the business man in politics. The business man has failed in politics as he has in citizenship. . . .

But there is hope, not alone despair, in the commercialism of our politics. If our political leaders are to be always a lot of political merchants, they will supply any demand we may create. All we have to do is to establish a steady demand for good government. The bosses have us split up into parties. To him parties are nothing but means to his corrupt ends. He "bolts" his party, but we must not; the bribe-giver changes his party, from one election to another, from one county to another, from one city to another, but the honest voter must not. Why? Because if the honest voter cared no more for his party than the politician and the grafter, then the honest vote would

Lincoln Steffens, *The Shame of the Cities* (New York: Hill and Wang, 1959), 2–7.

govern, and that would be bad—for graft. It is idiotic, this devotion to a machine that is used to take our sovereignty from us. If we would leave parties to the politicians, and would vote not for the party, not even for men, but for the city, and the State, and the nation, we should rule parties, and cities, and States, and nation. If we would vote in mass on the more promising ticket, or, if the two are equally bad, would throw out the party that is in, and wait till the next election and then throw out the other party that is in—then, I say, the commercial politician would feel a demand for good government and he would supply it. . . .

But do the people want good government? Tammany says they don't. Are the people honest? Are the people better than Tammany? Are they better than the merchant and the politician? Isn't our corrupt government, after all, representative? . . .

. . . [T]he corruption that shocks us in public affairs we practice ourselves in our private concerns. There is no essential difference between the pull that gets your wife into society or for your book a favorable review, and that which gets a heeler into office, a thief out of jail, and a rich man's son on the board of directors of a corporation; none between the corruption of a labor union, a bank, and a political machine; none between a dummy director of a trust and the caucus-bound member of a legislature; none between a labor boss like Sam Parks, a boss of banks like John D. Rockefeller, a boss of railroads like J. P. Morgan, and a political boss like Matthew S. Quay. The boss is not a political, he is an American institution, the product of a freed people that have not the spirit to be free.

2. Political Boss George Washington Plunkitt Defends "Honest" Graft, 1905

Everybody is talkin' these days about Tammany men growin' rich on graft, but nobody thinks of drawin' the distinction between honest graft and dishonest graft. . . .

There's an honest graft, and I'm an example of how it works. I might sum up the whole thing by sayin': "I seen my opportunities and I took 'em."

Just let me explain by examples. My party's in power in the city, and it's goin' to undertake a lot of public improvements. Well, I'm tipped off, say, that they're going to lay out a new park at a certain place.

I see my opportunity and I take it. I go to that place and I buy up all the land I can in the neighborhood. Then the board of this or that makes its plan public, and there is a rush to get my land, which nobody cared particular for before.

Ain't it perfectly honest to charge a good price and make a profit on my investment and foresight? Of course, it is. Well, that's honest graft.

Or supposin' it's a new bridge they're goin' to build. I get tipped off and I buy as much property as I can that has to be taken for approaches. I sell at my own price later on and drop some more money in the bank.

Wouldn't you? It's just like lookin' ahead in Wall Street or in the coffee or cotton market. It's honest graft, and I'm lookin' for it every day in the year. I will tell you frankly that I've got a good lot of it, too. . . .

For instance, the city is repavin' a street and has several hundred thousand old granite blocks to sell. I am on hand to buy, and I know just what they are worth.

William L. Riordan, *Plunkitt of Tammany Hall* (New York: McClure, Phillips, 1905), 3–10.

How? Never mind that. I had a sort of monopoly of this business for a while, but once a newspaper tried to do me. It got some outside men to come over from Brooklyn and New Jersey to bid against me.

Was I done? Not much. I went to each of the men and said: "How many of these 250,000 stones do you want?" One said 20,000, and another wanted 15,000, and another wanted 10,000. I said: "All right, let me bid for the lot, and I'll give each of you all you want for nothin."

They agreed, of course. Then the auctioneer yelled: "How much am I bid for these 250,000 fine pavin' stones?"

"Two dollars and fifty cents," says I.

"Two dollars and fifty cents!" screamed the auctioneer. "Oh, that's a joke! Give me a real bid."

He found the bid was real enough. My rivals stood silent. I got the lot for $2.50 and gave them their share. That's how the attempt to do Plunkitt ended, and that's how all such attempts end.

I've told you how I got rich by honest graft. Now, let me tell you that most politicians who are accused of robbin' the city get rich the same way.

They didn't steal a dollar from the city treasury. They just seen their opportunities and took them. That is why, when a reform administration comes in and spends a half million dollars in tryin' to find the public robberies they talked about in the campaign, they don't find them.

The books are always all right. The money in the city treasury is all right. Everything is all right. All they can show is that the Tammany heads of departments looked after their friends, within the law, and gave them what opportunities they could to make honest graft. Now, let me tell you that's never goin' to hurt Tammany with the people. Every good man looks after his friends, and any man who doesn't isn't likely to be popular. If I have a good thing to hand out in private life, I give it to a friend. Why shouldn't I do the same in public life?

Another kind of honest graft. Tammany has raised a good many salaries. There was an awful howl by the reformers, but don't you know that Tammany gains ten votes for every one it lost by salary raisin'?

The Wall Street banker thinks it shameful to raise a department clerk's salary from $1500 to $1800 a year, but every man who draws a salary himself says: "That's all right. I wish it was me." And he feels very much like votin' the Tammany ticket on election day, just out of sympathy.

3. Social Worker Jane Addams Advocates Civic Housekeeping, 1906

It has been well said that the modern city is a stronghold of industrialism quite as the feudal city was a stronghold of militarism, but the modern cities fear no enemies and rivals from without and their problems of government are solely internal. Affairs for the most part are going badly in these great new centres, in which the quickly-congregated population has not yet learned to arrange its affairs satisfactorily.

Jane Addams, "The Modern City and the Municipal Franchise for Women" (speech at the NAWSA Convention, February 1906).

Unsanitary housing, poisonous sewage, contaminated water, infant mortality, the spread of contagion, adulterated food, impure milk, smoke-laden air, ill-ventilated factories, dangerous occupations, juvenile crime, unwholesome crowding, prostitution and drunkenness are the enemies which the modern cities must face and overcome, would they survive. Logically their electorate should be made up of those who can bear a valiant part in this arduous contest, those who in the past have at least attempted to care for children, to clean houses, to prepare foods, to isolate the family from moral dangers; those who have traditionally taken care of that side of life which inevitably becomes the subject of municipal consideration and control as soon as the population is congested. To test the elector's fitness to deal with this situation by his ability to bear arms is absurd. These problems must be solved, if they are solved at all, not from the military point of view, not even from the industrial point of view, but from a third, which is rapidly developing in all the great cities of the world—the human-welfare point of view. . . .

City housekeeping has failed partly because women, the traditional housekeepers, have not been consulted as to its multiform activities. The men have been carelessly indifferent to much of this civic housekeeping, as they have always been indifferent to the details of the household. . . . The very multifariousness and complexity of a city government demand the help of minds accustomed to detail and variety of work, to a sense of obligation for the health and welfare of young children and to a responsibility for the cleanliness and comfort of other people. Because all these things have traditionally been in the hands of women, if they take no part in them now they are not only missing the education which the natural participation in civic life would bring to them but they are losing what they have always had.

4. President Theodore Roosevelt Preaches Conservation and Efficiency, 1908

This Conference on the conservation of natural resources is in effect a meeting of the representatives of all the people of the United States called to consider the weightiest problem now before the Nation; and the occasion for the meeting lies in the fact that the natural resources of our country are in danger of exhaustion if we permit the old wasteful methods of exploiting them longer to continue. . . .

. . . Nature has supplied to us in the United States, and still supplies to us, more kinds of resources in a more lavish degree than has ever been the case at any other time or with any other people. Our position in the world has been attained by the extent and thoroughness of the control we have achieved over nature; but we are more, and not less, dependent upon what she furnishes than at any previous time of history since the days of primitive man. . . .

Since the days when the Constitution was adopted, steam and electricity have revolutionized the industrial world. Nowhere has the revolution been so great as in our own country. The discovery and utilization of mineral fuels and alloys have given us the lead over all other nations in the production of steel. The discovery and utilization of coal and iron have given us our railways, and have led to such industrial

Proceedings of a Conference of Governors in the White House (Washington, D.C.: U.S. Government Printing Office, 1909).

development as has never before been seen. The vast wealth of lumber in our forests, the riches of our soils and mines the discovery of gold and mineral oils, combined with the efficiency of our transportation, have made the conditions of our life unparalleled in comfort and convenience. . . .

The steadily increasing drain on these natural resources has promoted to an extraordinary degree the complexity of our industrial and social life. Moreover, this unexampled development has had a determining effect upon the character and opinions of our people. The demand for efficiency in the great task has given us vigor, effectiveness, decision, and power, and a capacity for achievement which in its own lines has never yet been matched. . . .

We have become great in a material sense because of the lavish use of our resources, and we have just reason to be proud of our growth. But the time has come to inquire seriously what will happen when our forests are gone, when the coal, the iron, and the gas are exhausted, when the soils shall have been still further impoverished and washed into the streams, polluting the rivers, denuding the fields, and obstructing navigation. These questions do not relate only to the next century or to the next generation. One distinguishing characteristic of really civilized men is foresight; we have to, as a nation, exercise foresight for this nation in the future; and if we do not exercise that foresight, dark will be the future! [Applause] We should exercise foresight now, as the ordinarily prudent man exercises foresight in conserving and wisely using the property which contains the assurance of well-being for himself and his children. . . .

Just let me interject one word as to a particular type of folly of which it ought not to be necessary to speak. We stop wasteful cutting of timber; that of course makes a slight shortage at the moment. To avoid that slight shortage at the moment, there are certain people so foolish that they will incur absolute shortage in the future, and they are willing to stop all attempts to conserve the forests, because of course by wastefully using them at the moment we can for a year or two provide against any lack of wood. That is like providing for the farmer's family to live sumptuously on the flesh of the milch cow. [Laughter] Any farmer can live pretty well for a year if he is content not to live at all the year after. [Laughter and applause]

5. Prohibition Poem Castigates the Tyranny of Alcohol, 1910

Vote It Down

IDA M. BUDD

There's a demon in the glass,
    Vote it down!
You can bring the thing to pass;
    Vote it down!
Oh! my brothers, do you know
You can turn to joy its woe,
And its tyranny o'erthrow?
    Vote it down! . . .

Ida M. Budd, "Vote It Down," in *The Curse of Drink,* ed. Elton R. Shaw (1910), 523.

In your manliness arise,
      Vote it down!
Throw aside old party ties,
      Vote it down!
If you love our native land,
Smite this blighting, cursing hand
With your ballot's magic wand,
      Vote it down!

Christian man, we call on you,
      Vote it down!
Are you honest? are you true!
      Vote it down!
Christ, your Saviour crucified,
Then, as though he stood beside,
      Vote it down!

6. Industrialist Henry Ford Lectures Against Cigarettes, 1914

To my friend, the American Boy:

While spending some time in Florida with Mr. Thomas A. Edison, the noted electrical genius, and Mr. John Burroughs, the eminent naturalist, the question of cigarette smoking and its evil effects, particularly upon boys and young men, came up for discussion.

Mr. Edison advanced some pronounced views in condemnation of the cigarette. For several years he had been experimenting with combustion of various substances for the purpose of discovering a suitable filament for use in incandescent lamps, and it was during this research that the harmful effects of acrolein were observed. I asked Mr. Edison to put his conclusions in writing. He did so, and the letter is herewith reproduced in facsimile.

Following receipt of this letter, I authorized an interview in which I went squarely on record as opposed to cigarettes, making it plain that "I do not feel called upon to try to reform any person over 25 years of age because by that time the habit has been formed. Then it is only a question of the strength of will or mind of the smoker which will enable him to stop. He knows the injurious effects and controls his own destiny.

"With the boys it is a different matter. Most boys are told to refrain from many things. Seldom are they given a reason. Boys must be educated so they will know why cigarettes are bad for them.

"If you will study the history of almost any criminal you will find that he is an inveterate cigarette smoker. Boys, through cigarettes, train with bad company. They go with other smokers to the pool rooms and saloons. The cigarette drags

Henry Ford, *The Case Against the Little White Slavery* (Detroit: Henry Ford, 1914), 5, 27–28, 77.

them down. Hence if we can educate them to the dangers of smoking we will perform a service." ...

... Let us ... consider another aspect of the subject—the economic. Let us see whether you as an ambitious American boy can afford to ruin your prospects by doing those things which are disapproved by employers generally, and which in many, many cases must put you out of the running entirely.

If "millions of American men have convinced themselves that cigarettes are good for them" they have not succeeded in convincing their employers of this fact, and this is especially true as regards boys. ...

The world of today needs men, not those whose minds and will power have been weakened or destroyed by the desire and craving for alcohol and tobacco but instead men with initiative and vigor, whose mentality is untainted by ruinous habits.

7. Sociologist William Graham Sumner Denounces Reformers' Fanaticism, 1913

As time runs on it becomes more and more obvious that this generation has raised up for itself social problems which it is not competent to solve, and that this inability may easily prove fatal to it. We have been boasting of the achievements of the nineteenth century, and viewing ourselves and our circumstances in an altogether rose-colored medium. We have not had a correct standard for comparing ourselves with our predecessors on earth, nor for judging soberly what we have done or what men can do. ... We draw up pronunciamentos, every paragraph of which begins with: "we demand," without noticing the difference between the things which we can expect from the society in which we live, and those which we must get either from ourselves or from God and nature.

We believe that we can bring about a complete transformation in the economic organization of society, and not have any incidental social and political questions arise which will make us great difficulty, or that, if such questions arise, they can all be succinctly solved by saying: "Let the State attend to it"; "Make a bureau and appoint inspectors"; "Pass a law." But the plain fact is that the new time presents manifold and constantly varying facts and factors. It is complicated, heterogeneous, full of activity, so that its phases are constantly changing. Legislation and state action are stiff, rigid, inelastic, incapable of adaptation to cases; they are never adopted except under stress of the perception of some one phase which has, for some reason or other, arrested attention. Hence, the higher the organization of society, the more mischievous legislative regulation is sure to be. ...

We think that security and justice are simple and easy things which go without the saying, and need only be recognized to be had and enjoyed; we do not know that security is a thing which men have never yet succeeded in establishing. History is full of instruction for us if we will go to it for instruction. ...

We think that, if this world does not suit us, it ought to be corrected to our satisfaction, and that, if we see any social phenomenon which does not suit our notions,

William Graham Sumner, "Fantasies and Facts," in *Earth-Hunger and Other Essays* (New Brunswick, N.J.: Transaction, Inc., 1980), 207–210.

there should be a remedy found at once. A collection of these complaints and criticisms, however, assembled from the literature of the day, would show the most heterogeneous, contradictory, and fantastic notions.

We think that this is a world in which we are limited by our wants, not by our powers; by our ideals, not by our antecedents.

We think that we are resisting oppression from other men, when we are railing against the hardships of life on this earth. . . .

We think that capital comes of itself, and would all be here just the same, no matter what regulations we might make about the custody, use, and enjoyment of it. . . .

We think that we can impair the rights of landlords, creditors, employers, and capitalists, and yet maintain all other rights intact.

We think that, although A has greatly improved his position in half a lifetime, that is nothing, because B, in the same time, has become a millionaire.

We throw all our attention on the utterly idle question whether A has done as well as B, when the only question is whether A has done as well as he could.

We think that competition produces great inequalities, but that stealing or almsgiving does not.

8. Rewriting the Constitution: Amendments on Income Tax, Election of Senators, Prohibition, and the Vote for Women, 1913–1920

Amendment XVI

The Congress shall have power to lay and collect taxes on incomes, from whatever source derived, without apportionment among the several States, and without regard to any census or enumeration.

Amendment XVII

The Senate of the United States shall be composed of two Senators from each State, elected by the people thereof, for six years; and each Senator shall have one vote. The electors in each State shall have the qualifications requisite for electors of the most numerous branch of the State legislatures.

When vacancies happen in the representation of any State in the Senate, the executive authority of such State shall issue writs of election to fill such vacancies: *Provided,* That the legislature of any State may empower the executive thereof to make temporary appointments until the people fill the vacancies by election as the legislature may direct.

This amendment shall not be so construed as to affect the election or term of any Senator chosen before it becomes valid as part of the Constitution.

Amendment XVIII

Section 1.   After one year from the ratification of this article the manufacture, sale, or transportation of intoxicating liquors within, the importation thereof into,

---

U.S. Constitution, amends. 16–19.

or the exportation thereof from the United States and all territory subject to the jurisdiction thereof for beverage purposes is hereby prohibited.

Section 2. The Congress and the several States shall have concurrent power to enforce this article by appropriate legislation.

Section 3. This article shall be inoperative unless it shall have been ratified as an amendment to the Constitution by the legislatures of the several States, as provided in the Constitution, within seven years from the date of the submission hereof to the States by the Congress.

Amendment XIX

The right of citizens of the United States to vote shall not be denied or abridged by the United States or by any State on account of sex.
Congress shall have power to enforce this article by appropriate legislation.

9. Black Leader Booker T. Washington Advocates Compromise, 1895

A ship lost at sea for many days suddenly sighted a friendly vessel. From the mast of the unfortunate vessel was seen a signal, "Water, water; we die of thirst!" The answer from the friendly vessel at once came back, "Cast down your bucket where you are." A second time the signal, "Water, water; send us water!" ran up from the distressed vessel, and was answered, "Cast down your bucket where you are." And a third and fourth signal for water was answered, "Cast down your bucket where you are." The captain of the distressed vessel, at last heeding the injunction, cast down his bucket, and it came up full of fresh, sparkling water from the mouth of the Amazon River. To those of my race who depend on bettering their condition in a foreign land or who underestimate the importance of cultivating friendly relations with the Southern white man, who is their next-door neighbour, I would say: "Cast down your bucket where you are"—cast it down in making friends in every manly way of the people of all races by whom we are surrounded.

Cast it down in agriculture, mechanics, in commerce, in domestic service, and in the professions. . . . No race can prosper till it learns that there is as much dignity in tilling a field as in writing a poem. It is at the bottom of life we must begin, and not at the top. Nor should we permit our grievances to overshadow our opportunities.

To those of the white race who look to the incoming of those of foreign birth and strange tongue and habits for the prosperity of the South, were I permitted I would repeat what I say to my own race, "Cast down your bucket where you are." Cast it down among the eight millions of Negroes whose habits you know, whose fidelity and love you have tested in days when to have proved treacherous meant the ruin of your firesides. . . . While doing this, you can be sure in the future, as in the past, that you and your families will be surrounded by the most patient, faithful, law-abiding, and unresentful people that the world has seen. As we have proved our loyalty to you

Booker T. Washington, *Up From Slavery* (New York: Doubleday, 1901), 217–227.

in the past, in nursing your children, watching by the sickbed of your mothers and fathers, and often following them with tear-dimmed eyes to their graves, so in the future, in our humble way, we shall stand by you with a devotion that no foreigner can approach. . . . In all things that are purely social we can be as separate as the fingers, yet one as the hand in all things essential to mutual progress. . . .

The wisest among my race understand that the agitation of questions of social equality is the extremest folly, and that progress in the enjoyment of all the privileges that will come to us must be the result of severe and constant struggle rather than an artificial forcing. No race that has anything to contribute to the markets of the world is long in any degree ostracized. It is important and right that all privileges of the law be ours, but it is vastly more important that we be prepared for the exercises of these privileges. The opportunity to earn a dollar in a factory just now is worth infinitely more than the opportunity to spend a dollar in an opera-house.

10. NAACP Founder W. E. B. DuBois Counters Booker T. Washington, 1903

Mr. Washington represents in Negro thought the old attitude of adjustment and submission; but adjustment at such a peculiar time as to make his programme unique. This is an age of unusual economic development, and Mr. Washington's programme naturally takes an economic cast, becoming a gospel of Work and Money to such an extent as apparently almost completely to overshadow the higher aims of life. Moreover, this is an age when the more advanced races are coming in closer contact with the less developed races, and the race-feeling is therefore intensified; and Mr. Washington's programme practically accepts the alleged inferiority of the Negro races. . . . In other periods of intensified prejudice all the Negro's tendency to self-assertion has been called forth; at this period a policy of submission is advocated. In the history of nearly all other races and peoples the doctrine preached at such crises has been that manly self-respect is worth more than lands and houses, and that a people who voluntarily surrender such respect, or cease striving for it, are not worth civilizing.

In answer to this, it has been claimed that the Negro can survive only through submission. Mr. Washington distinctly asks that black people give up, at least for the present, three things,—

First, political power,

Second, insistence on civil rights,

Third, higher education of Negro youth,—

and concentrate all their energies on industrial education, and accumulation of wealth, and the conciliation of the South. This policy has been courageously and insistently advocated for over fifteen years, and has been triumphant for perhaps ten years. As a result of this tender of the palm-branch, what has been the return? In these years there have occurred:

W. E. B. DuBois, *The Souls of Black Folk* (New York: Signet, 1969), 87–89.

1. The disfranchisement of the Negro.
2. The legal creation of a distinct status of civil inferiority for the Negro.
3. The steady withdrawal of aid from institutions for the higher training of the Negro.

These movements are not, to be sure, direct results of Mr. Washington's teachings; but his propaganda has, without a shadow of doubt, helped their speedier accomplishment. The question then comes: Is it possible, and probable, that nine millions of men can make effective progress in economic lines if they are deprived of political rights, made a servile caste, and allowed only the most meager chance for developing their exceptional men? If history and reason give any distinct answer to these questions, it is an emphatic *No*. And Mr. Washington thus faces the triple paradox of his career:

1. He is striving nobly to make Negro artisans business men and property-owners; but it is utterly impossible, under modern competitive methods, for working-men and property-owners to defend their rights and exist without the right of suffrage.
2. He insists on thrift and self-respect, but at the same time counsels a silent submission to civic inferiority such as is bound to sap the manhood of any race in the long run.
3. He advocates common-school and industrial training, and depreciates institutions of higher learning; but neither the Negro common-schools, nor Tuskegee itself, could remain open a day were it not for teachers trained in Negro colleges, or trained by their graduates. . . .

. . . Such men feel in conscience bound to ask of this nation three things:

1. The right to vote.
2. Civic equality.
3. The education of youth according to ability.

ESSAYS

Progressivism was so multidimensional that it has provoked historical arguments about everything from its effect on capitalism to its consequences for women. The following two essays stake out what continues to be a central question: Was Progressivism a movement of people concerned with protecting their own stake in society (under the guise of a concern for all), or was it what it claimed to be, a genuine reawakening of democratic and personal virtue? Richard Hofstadter of City University of New York wrote what stands as one of the most pointed critiques of Progressivism. He argues that the reformers were in essence opportunistic. They sought to shore up their status in the competitive terrain of national politics by elevating their own values. Historian Gerald Woods corroborates Hofstadter's analysis of Progressives as middle-class moralists, but he treats their ideals more gently. Progressives not only fought against the "disreputable pleasures" of gambling, drinking, smoking, dancing, and prostitution, but also helped to create an ideal of nonpartisan public service. Their legacy, Woods argues, shapes modern aspirations for good government to this day.

The Status Revolution and Progressive Leaders

RICHARD HOFSTADTER

Populism had been overwhelmingly rural and provincial. The ferment of the Progressive era was urban, middle-class, and nationwide. . . .

While too sharp a distinction between Populist and Progressive thinking would distort reality, the growth of middle-class reform sentiment, the contributions of professionals and educated men, made Progressive thought more informed, more moderate, more complex than Populist thought had been. . . . The Progressives were more likely to be aware of the complexities of social issues and more divided among themselves. Indeed, the characteristic Progressive was often of two minds on many issues. Concerning the great corporations, the Progressives felt that they were a menace to society and that they were all too often manipulated by unscrupulous men; on the other hand, many Progressives were quite aware that the newer organization of industry and finance was a product of social evolution which had its beneficent side and that it was here to stay. Concerning immigrants, they frequently shared Populist prejudices and the Populist horror of ethnic mixture, but they were somewhat more disposed to discipline their feelings with a sense of some obligation to the immigrant. . . . As for the bosses, the machines, the corruptions of city life, they too found in these things grave evils; but they were ready, perhaps all too ready, to admit that the existence of such evils was in large measure their own fault. Like the Populist the Progressives were full of indignation, but their indignation was more qualified by a sense of responsibility, often even of guilt, and it was supported by a greater capacity to organize, legislate, and administer. . . .

Curiously, the Progressive revolt—even when we have made allowance for the brief panic of 1907 and the downward turn in business in 1913—took place almost entirely during a period of sustained and general prosperity. The middle class, most of which had been content to accept the conservative leadership of Hanna and McKinley during the period of crisis in the mid-nineties, rallied to the support of Progressive leaders in both parties during the period of well-being that followed. This fact is a challenge to the historian. Why did the middle class undergo this remarkable awakening at all, and why during this period of general prosperity in which most of them seem to have shared? What was the place of economic discontents in the Progressive movement? To what extent did reform originate in other considerations?

Of course Progressivism had the adherence of a heterogeneous public whose various segments responded to various needs. But I am concerned here with a large and strategic section of Progressive leadership, upon whose contributions the movement was politically and intellectually as well as financially dependent, and whose members did much to formulate its ideals. It is my thesis that men of this sort, who might be designated broadly as the Mugwump type, were Progressives not because

Richard Hofstadter, *The Age of Reform: From Bryan to F.D.R.* (New York: Vintage, 1955), 131, 133–138, 148–149, 164–167, 182–185. Copyright © 1955 by Richard Hofstadter. Used with permission of Alfred A. Knopf, a division of Random House, Inc.

of economic deprivations but primarily because they were victims of an upheaval in status that took place in the United States during the closing decades of the nineteenth and the early years of the twentieth century. Progressivism, in short, was to a very considerable extent led by men who suffered from the events of their time not through a shrinkage in their means but through the changed pattern in the distribution of deference and power.

Up to about 1870 the United States was a nation with a rather broad diffusion of wealth, status, and power, in which the man of moderate means, especially in the many small communities, could command much deference and exert much influence. The small merchant or manufacturer, the distinguished lawyer, editor, or preacher, was a person of local eminence in an age in which local eminence mattered a great deal. In the absence of very many nationwide sources of power and prestige, the pillars of the local communities were men of great importance in their own right. . . .

In the post–Civil War period all this was changed. The rapid development of the big cities, the building of a great industrial plant, the construction of the railroads, the emergence of the corporation as the dominant form of enterprise, transformed the old society and revolutionized the distribution of power and prestige. During the 1840's there were not twenty millionaires in the entire country; by 1910 there were probably more than twenty millionaires sitting in the United States Senate. By the late 1880's this process had gone far enough to become the subject of frequent, anxious comment in the press. . . .

The newly rich, the grandiosely or corruptly rich, the masters of great corporations, were bypassing the men of the Mugwump type—the old gentry, the merchants of long standing, the small manufacturers, the established professional men, the civic leaders of an earlier era. In a score of cities and hundreds of towns, particularly in the East but also in the nation at large, the old-family, college-educated class that had deep ancestral roots in local communities and often owned family businesses, that had traditions of political leadership, belonged to the patriotic societies and the best clubs, staffed the governing boards of philanthropic and cultural institutions, and led the movements for civic betterment, were being overshadowed and edged aside in the making of basic political and economic decisions. In their personal careers, as in their community activities, they found themselves checked, hampered, and overridden by the agents of the new corporations, the corrupters of legislatures, the buyers of franchises, the allies of the political bosses. In this uneven struggle they found themselves limited by their own scruples, their regard for reputation, their social standing itself. To be sure, the America they knew did not lack opportunities, but it did seem to lack opportunities of the highest sort for men of the highest standards. In a strictly economic sense these men were not growing poorer as a class, but their wealth and power were being dwarfed by comparison with the new eminences of wealth and power. They were less important, and they knew it.

Against the tide of new wealth the less affluent and aristocratic local gentry had almost no protection at all. The richer and better-established among them found it still possible, of course, to trade on their inherited money and position, and their presence as window-dressing was an asset for any kind of enterprise, in business or elsewhere, to which they would lend their sponsorship. Often indeed the new men sought to marry into their circles, or to buy from them social position much as they bought from the bosses legislation and franchises. But at best the gentry could only make a static defense of themselves, holding their own in absolute terms while relatively losing ground year by year. Even this much they could do only in the localities over which they had long presided and in which they were well known. And when everyone could see that the arena of prestige, like the market for commodities, had been widened to embrace the entire nation, eminence in mere localities ceased to be as important and satisfying as once it had been. To face the insolence of the local boss or traction magnate in a town where one's family had long been prominent was galling enough; it was still harder to bear at a time when every fortune, every career, every reputation, seemed smaller and less significant because it was measured against the Vanderbilts, Harrimans, Goulds, Carnegies, Rockefellers, and Morgans. . . .

Whenever an important change takes place in modern society, large sections of the intellectuals, the professional and opinion-making classes, see the drift of events and throw their weight on the side of what they feel is progress and reform. In few historical movements have these classes played a more striking role than in Progressivism. While those intellectuals and professional men who supported Progressive causes no doubt did so in part for reasons that they shared with other members of the middle classes, their view of things was also influenced by marked changes within the professions themselves and by changes in their social position brought about by the growing complexity of society and by the status revolution.

In the previous era, during the industrial and political conflicts of the 1870's and 1880's, the respectable opinion-making classes had given almost unqualified support to the extreme conservative position on most issues. The Protestant ministry, for instance, was "a massive, almost unbroken front in its defense of the status quo." Most college professors preached the great truths of *laissez faire* and the conservative apologetics of social Darwinism, and thundered away at labor unions and social reformers. Lawyers, except for a rare small-town spokesman of agrarian unrest or little business, were complacent. And while an occasional newspaper editor launched an occasional crusade, usually on a local issue, the press was almost as unruffled.

Beginning slowly in the 1890's and increasingly in the next two decades, members of these professions deserted the standpat conservatism of the post–Civil War era to join the main stream of liberal dissent and to give it both moral and intellectual leadership. The reasons for this reversal are complex. But if the professional groups changed their ideas and took on new loyalties, it was not in simple response to changes in the nature of the country's problems—indeed, in many ways the problems of American life were actually less acute after 1897—but rather because they had become disposed to see things they had previously ignored and to agitate themselves about things that had previously left them unconcerned. What interests me here is not the changed external condition of American society, but the inward social and psychological position of the professionals themselves that made so many of them become the advisers and the gadflies of reform movements. The alienation of the professionals was in fact a product of many developments, but among these the effects of the status revolution must be given an important place. Conditions varied from profession to profession, but all groups with claims to learning and skill shared a common sense of humiliation and common grievances against the plutocracy. . . .

What I have said thus far about the impact of the status revolution may help to explain the occurrence of the Progressive movement, but will not account for its location in time. A pertinent question remains to be answered: as the status revolution had been going on at least since the Civil War and was certainly well advanced by the 1890's, why did the really powerful outburst of protest and reform come only with the first fifteen years of the twentieth century? Why did our middle classes, after six years of civic anxieties and three years of acute and ominous depression, give Hanna and McKinley a strong vote of confidence in 1896? And then after this confidence seemed in fact to have been justified by the return of prosperity, when the nation's sense of security and power had been heightened by a quick victory in what John Hay called "our splendid little war," and when a mood of buoyant optimism had again become dominant, why should they have turned about and given ardent support to the forces that were raking American life with criticism?

First, it must be said that in some areas of American life those phenomena that we associate with the Progressive era were already much in evidence before 1900. In a limited and local way the Progressive movement had in fact begun around 1890. On the part of some business interests the movement for cheap transportation and against monopoly had already waxed strong enough to impel a reluctant Congress to pass the Interstate Commerce Act in 1887 and the Sherman Act in 1890. Likewise the crusade for municipal reform was well under way in the 1890's. A very large number of local organizations dedicated to good government and a variety of reforms had sprung into existence, and in some cities they had already achieved more than negligible changes. Finally, the state legislatures had already begun to pass the sort of social legislation—regulation of hours and conditions of labor, for instance—that was later fostered more effectually by the Progressives.

These were the timid beginnings of a movement that did not become nationwide until the years after 1901. One important thing that kept them from going further during the nineties was that the events of that decade frightened the middle classes so thoroughly that they did not dare dream of taking seriously ideas that seemed to involve a more fundamental challenge to established ways of doing things. The Progressive appeal was always directed very largely to people who felt that they did have something to lose. . . .

More pertinent, perhaps, is the fact that the Progressive ferment was the work of the first generation that had been born and raised in the midst of the status revolution. In 1890 the governing generation still consisted of men born in the 1830's and 1840's, who through force of habit still looked upon events with the happier vision of the mid-nineteenth century. . . .

The generation that went Progressive was the generation that came of age in the nineties. . . . The ascension of Theodore Roosevelt to the presidency, the youngest man ever to occupy the White House, was no more than symbolic of the coming-of-age of a generation whose perspectives were sharply demarcated from those of their fathers and who felt the need of a new philosophy and a new politics. T. R. himself had been thirty-two in 1890, Bryan only thirty, La Follette thirty-five, Wilson thirty-four. Most of the Progressive leaders, as well as the muckraking journalists who did so much to form Progressive opinion, were, at the opening of the crucial *fin de siècle* decade, in their early thirties, or perhaps younger, and hence only around forty when the Progressive era got under way. . . .

In politics . . . the immigrant was usually at odds with the reform aspirations of the American Progressive. Together with the native conservative and the politically indifferent, the immigrants formed a potent mass that limited the range and the achievements of Progressivism. The loyalty of immigrant voters to the bosses was one of the signal reasons why the local reform victories were so short-lived. It would be hard to imagine types of political culture more alien to each other than those of the Yankee reformer and the peasant immigrant. The Yankee's idea of political action assumed a popular democracy with widespread participation and eager civic interest. To him politics was the business, the responsibility, the duty of all men. It was an arena for the realization of moral principles of broad application—and even, as in the case of temperance and vice crusades—for the correction of private habits. The immigrant, by contrast, coming as a rule from a peasant environment and from autocratic societies with strong feudal survivals, was totally unaccustomed to the active citizen's role. He expected to be acted on by government, but not to be a political agent himself. To him government meant restrictions on personal movement, the arbitrary regulation of life, the inaccessibility of the law, and the conscription of the able-bodied. To him government was the instrument of the ruling classes, characteristically acting in their interests, which were indifferent or opposed to his own. Nor was government in his eyes an affair of abstract principles and rules of law: it was the actions of particular men with particular powers. Political relations were not governed by abstract principles; they were profoundly personal.

Not being reared on the idea of mass participation, the immigrant was not especially eager to exercise his vote immediately upon naturalization. Nor was he interested in such reforms as the initiative, referendum, and recall, which were intelligible only from the standpoint of the Anglo-American ethos of popular political action. When he finally did assume his civic role, it was either in response to Old World loyalties (which became a problem only during and after the first World War) or to immediate needs arising out of his struggle for life in the American city—to his need for a job or charity or protection from the law or for a street vendor's license. The necessities of American cities—their need for construction workers, street-cleaners, police and firemen, service workers of all kinds—often provided him with his livelihood, as it provided the boss with the necessary patronage. The immigrant in short, looked to politics not for the realization of high principles but for concrete and personal gains, and he sought these gains through personal relationships. And here the boss, particularly the Irish boss, who could see things from the immigrant's angle but could also manipulate the American environment, became a specialist in personal relations and personal loyalties. The boss himself encouraged the immigrant to think of politics as a field in which one could legitimately pursue one's interests. This was, indeed, his own occupational view of it: politics was a trade at which a man worked and for which he should be properly paid. As George Washington Plunkitt, the sage of Tammany Hall, once said, all the machines were agreed "on the main proposition that when a man works in politics, he should get something out of it." The boss, moreover, was astute enough to see that the personal interests that were pursued in politics must be construed broadly enough to include self-respect. Where the reformers and Americanizers tried to prod the immigrant toward the study of American ways, the boss contented himself with studying the immigrant's ways, attending his weddings and christenings (with appropriate gifts) and his funerals, and making himself a sympathetic observer of immigrant life and in a measure a participant in it. Reformers might try on occasion to compete with this, but they lacked the means. The boss, rich with graft, could afford to be more generous; and having doled out many a favor to businessmen, he could draw upon the world of private business as well as the public payroll to provide jobs for his constituents. Where reformers identified patriotism with knowledgeable civic action and self-denial, the bosses were satisfied to confine it to party regularity, and they were not embarrassed by a body of literature purporting to show that to trade one's vote for personal services was a form of civic iniquity.

While the boss, with his pragmatic talents and his immediate favors, quickly appealed to the immigrant, the reformer was a mystery. Often he stood for things that to the immigrant were altogether bizarre, like women's rights and Sunday laws, or downright insulting, like temperance. His abstractions had no appeal within the immigrant's experience—citizenship, responsibility, efficiency, good government, economy, businesslike management. The immigrant wanted humanity, not efficiency, and economies threatened to lop needed jobs off the payroll. The reformer's attacks upon the boss only caused the immigrant to draw closer to his benefactor. Progressives, in return, reproached the immigrant for having no interest in broad principles, in the rule of law or the public good. Between the two, for the most part, the channels of effective communication were closed. Progressive reform drew its greatest support from the more discontented of the native Americans, and on some issues from the rural and small-town constituencies that surrounded the great cities. The insulation of the Progressive from the support of the most exploited sector of the population was one of the factors that, for all his humanitarianism, courage, and vision, reduced the social range and the radical drive of his program and kept him genteel, proper, and safe.

Fighting the Good Fight (Against The Disreputable Pleasures) in San Francisco and Los Angeles

GERALD WOODS

The men and women who created the progressive movement in California and led it to signal victories included people of diverse races, creeds, and colors. The leaders, however, were white, generally born in California of the midwestern states, more likely to be Republican than Democrat, and more likely to be Protestant than any other religion or sect. California progressive leaders tended to be comparatively young—in their thirties and forties—and comparatively successful. Newspaper

Gerald Woods, "A Penchant for Probity: California Progressives and the Disreputable Pleasures, in *California Progressivism Revisited,* ed. William Deverell and Tom Silton (Berkeley: University of California Press, 1994), 99–111. Reprinted by permission of The Regents of the University of California.

owners and editors were well represented, as were lawyers, realtors, bankers, doctors, and other professionals. The large majority of leaders had at least one university degree. As a group they were independent, democratic, somewhat nativist, somewhat anti-labor, generally opposed to monopolies, and committed to free enterprise.

Their external motivation was apparent: to reform the political and social institutions of their society. Their inner motivation has been the subject of speculation. George E. Mowry described California progressivism as "an expression of an older America objecting to the ideological and social drifts of the twentieth century." In the same vein, Richard Hofstadter asserted that the progressives responded defensively to "a changed pattern in the distribution of deference and power"; that they were "victims of an upheaval in status"; and that "the yankee ethos of responsibility [became] transmuted into a sense of guilt." Guilt accounted for the evangelical fervor with which progressives attacked social problems.

These provocative theories seem somehow inadequate. It is difficult to perceive California progressivism in such limited, negative terms, as simply a response to unwanted changes in American society. The progressives were young, educated, confident members of the dominant ethnic group and the dominant political party. They grew up in the post–Civil War period, when enormous fraud permeated every level of government and business; but instead of becoming cynical, they turned to reform.

The ills the progressives set out to cure were of old origin. The struggle to reform the nation had been under way since at least the 1880s, when most of those who became progressives were still in school. Benjamin Parke DeWitt observed in 1915 that "although differences in name, in the specific reforms advocated, and in the emphasis placed upon them, have obscured the identity of the movement, the underlying purposes and ideals of the progressive elements of all parties for the past quarter of a century have been essentially the same." DeWitt then pointed out common interests endorsed by the Democratic, Republican, Progressive, Socialist, and Prohibition parties.

One characteristic of the progressives about which most historians could agree was their abiding antipathy toward saloons, prostitution, gambling, slot machines, horse races, prizefights, dancing (especially in nightclubs where black men played jazz music), and liaisons between black or Asian men and white women. In this regard, Spencer Olin noted that "this penchant for probity, this moral absolutism, was part and parcel of the progressive mind." George Mowry pointed out the "middle-class Christian respectability" implicit in the closing of saloons and gambling halls in Los Angeles at the turn of the century.

Both comments are accurate but say little about motivation. Benjamin DeWitt stated the case from the progressive perspective: "if the American city fails, it will fail not because of the work its people do or the places in which they live, but because of the pleasures which they seek. It is vice, high living, and deterioration of moral fibre more than anything else that destroys cities and democracies." For DeWitt, nothing less was at stake than the soul of America.

In California, the crusade against the disreputable pleasures was essentially a tale of three cities. San Francisco and Los Angeles, the north and the south, proudly embodied the poles, respectively, of civic vice and civic virtue. Sacramento, specifically the state legislature, was a relatively neutral ground where proponents of "personal liberty" did battle with neo-puritans to preserve the lurid entertainments that for decades had characterized West Coast cities. In Washington, D.C., progressives in the Congress also warred against evil and won some significant victories.

During the progressive heyday, from 1909 through 1918, a variety of sumptuary laws were passed. At the national level, these included the Mann Act, directed at the transport of women across state lines for immoral purposes; more restrictive immigration regulations and anti–"white slavery" agreements with European governments, to reduce the remarkable migration of foreign prostitutes into the United States; and national wartime prohibition, the Eighteenth Amendment to the U.S. Constitution, and the Volstead Act, intended to close the saloons and end forever the consumption of beverage alcohol by Americans.

In 1909, the state assembly, described by the *San Francisco Chronicle* as "a legislature of progressive cranks," narrowly passed the Anti–Race Track Gambling Act. The act forbade "wagering or pool selling or bookmaking in any way, shape, form or place." The Local Option Law, allowing prohibition by local option, followed in 1911. This act was known generally as the Gandier Ordinance, after Daniel M. Gandier, legislative superintendent of the Anti-Saloon League. By 1913, nearly one thousand saloons had been closed through the introduction of local prohibition. About half the state went dry. The Red Light Abatement Act, aimed mainly at the owners of properties where brothels were operated, was passed in 1913. It allowed for the padlocking of such premises, thereby denying rental income to the owners.

The progressives did not win easily. Franklin Hichborn, chronicler of state legislative sessions from 1909 until the mid-1920s, declared in 1913 that the Senate Committee on Public Morals (a classic example of progressive thought) was dominated by "the tenderloin element." Although draw poker was added that year to the list of forbidden games, a University Dry Zone Bill, anti-prizefighting bills, and measures against illegal saloons (known as "blind pigs") failed to pass. Eventually, the restrictive bills were guided through the legislature, although the success achieved was less than expected. The reformers could carry state elections and drive legislation through with minimal amendments. Once the laws were in place, however, the state legislature was out of the picture. Local governments could enforce the statutes or ignore them. Hichborn complained in 1915 that, despite the regulations, gambling was wide open during the great San Francisco Exposition. Saloons and brothels also flourished. It had ever been thus in the City by the Bay.

San Francisco had an unsavory municipal government (a "California Tammany") and a wicked demimonde. Brash San Franciscans viewed their town as "the future seat and center of the world's commerce . . . that advertised the notorious Barbary Coast to the world as a symbol of its anti-Puritan tradition." And tradition it had! In the 1880s, the city supported an estimated two thousand saloons and brothels in the Chinatown, Barbary Coast, and tenderloin districts. San Francisco's bawdy reputation was nationwide, and numerous books described the fun to be had in the city that took "uncommon pride in its past sins, real or imagined." Crusades for moral purity might come and go, but, as one prostitute told a reporter, "the police wink at us." When the police did make arrests, judges often dismissed the cases.

Occasionally, San Francisco moral reformers won a round, or thought that they did. After the earthquake and fire of 1906, an enormous brothel housing 133 women was quickly reconstructed. It was described by local wits as "the municipal brothel," because half the profits went to city hall. In 1911, a municipal clinic was established, to ensure that prostitutes maintained good health. For the good progressive folk of San Francisco, this was going too far. Fremont Older, editor of the *Bulletin,* observed that "there was more fuss over the operation of the Municipal Clinic than the Municipal Brothel." The clinic soon was closed. The brothel lasted for several additional years.

In 1913, a reform crusade briefly closed the Barbary Coast and the tenderloin. They soon were back in operation. Herbert Asbury noted that the election of Mayor James Rolph and a new Board of Supervisors put an end to "an unfriendly, if not actively hostile" municipal administration. There were then an estimated 2,800 legal and 2,500 illegal saloons. From 1913 to 1917, "Sunny Jim" Rolph, mayor of San Francisco, and Madam Tessie Wall, the city's most notorious brothel keeper, rode together through the vice districts at the head of an annual parade organized by the entrepreneurs of pleasure. This could not have happened in Los Angeles. . . .

Reformers in San Francisco described themselves as progressives at least as early as 1896. Some of them favored moral reform of the city, including suppression of the vice districts. Associations of Protestants, Catholics, and Jews campaigned against the "adult entertainment" industry for decades. Black and Chinese residents also struggled to suppress open vice in their neighborhoods. Eventually, over a period of four decades, they succeeded. In the short term, they failed. Local-option prohibition was soundly defeated. Legislation such as the Red Light Abatement Act was seldom used. Police would not arrest. Judges would not convict. Vice, per se, apparently was not a serious issue for a majority of voters. As long as the vice districts remained quiet, the tradition of benign neglect could be maintained.

The story was very different in Los Angeles. As with San Francisco, rapid growth in population followed the discovery of gold. Los Angeles became "the toughest town in the West," home to all the traditional frontier amusements. During the 1850s, with a population of fewer than six thousand residents, the city supported about four hundred premises providing gambling, alcohol, and prostitution.

By the 1870s, native-born Protestants had become the dominant political force in Los Angeles. They later boasted that the town contained more churches in relation to population than any other city in the United States. The new middle class exhibited a strong interest in law enforcement and in control of vice operations. They found the town marshals ill-equipped to provide the safe streets and moral order to which they aspired. In 1876, the marshals were replaced by the newly formed Los Angeles Police Department. Thereafter, the police force usually was at the center of local politics, either because it could not be controlled by the municipal government or because it was involved in the protection of illegal enterprises.

At the same time that the LAPD was created, the Los Angeles Common Council issued ordinances limiting the location of vice premises, the type of "personal service" permitted, and the times at which such entertainments could be provided. At first, the ordinances merely forbade vice operations within prescribed boundaries in the central business and residential areas. Later, the council established a legal vice district but soon withdrew the law. An anti-prostitution act forbidding single women to reside on the ground floor of any dwelling was overturned by the state Supreme court. The council also forbade gambling and introduced early-closing hours and Sunday closing for saloons. Consequently, the purveyors of traditional pleasures suddenly made illicit by the council were compelled to bribe the police or the politicians, or both, if they wished to stay in business.

Despite their largely unsuccessful efforts to reform the city, the reformers believed that they might be more successful if the police were removed from politics. (The workings of politics dictated short careers for police chiefs: between 1877 and 1889, at least sixteen men held the post.) To that end, progressives set out to reform the city charter. The Los Angeles city charter was rewritten or revised in 1889, 1902, 1909, 1911, and 1925. In each case, control of the police was a major element. In 1889, the first police commission was established, replacing a council committee, to deal with appointments, promotions, dismissals, and general policy. True to their faith in nonpartisanship, the progressives first tried dividing authority between Republican and Democratic councilmen, who each appointed two members to the commission; the mayor also served but could not be chairman. Depoliticizing lines of authority over the police failed because all the commissioners were political partisans, and their decisions concerning the police force were partisan decisions.

In 1902, progressive voters ratified the initiative, referendum, and recall; established a municipal civil service; and revised the rules governing the police commission and the police. All police jobs were classified except the positions of police chief and secretary to the police chief. Physical and mental entrance standards and competitive promotional examinations were certified. Salaries were mandated by the charter and could not be reduced by the council. The charter further required that any order having to do with the police must be sent directly to the chief for action. The mayor became chairman of the police commission and could remove other commissioners with consent of the council. By these measures, the progressives hoped to raise the caliber and establish the independence of the individual officer, and place day-to-day control of the department in the chief's hands. The mayor, as chief executive officer, was given greater responsibility for the overall management of the police force.

The charter amendments of 1902 outlawed gambling and prostitution within the city limits. Before these amendments were passed, commercial vice had prospered in "the segregated zone"; indeed, directories were printed that identified brothels by address and the name of the madam, often including words of praise for the comely damsels who "assisted" her. Then two churchmen found "the Ballarino," a building of many narrow cells or "cribs," designed for prostitution. Their anti-vice crusade closed the place and brought calumny upon the police force. Afterward, the progressives won a great victory at the polls.

Whether knowledgeable progressives, hoping to gain political support, guided the two ministers to the Ballarino is not known. What is clear is that the anti-vice crusade became the standard election tactic in Los Angeles for half a century afterward. That vice should be the most volatile political issue over a period of five decades spoke volumes about the electorate, although concerns about vice were not entirely misguided. Despite the will of the voting majority, scandal after scandal occurred. Progressives routinely elected "reform" candidates who abandoned reform after the election.

Between 1904 and 1909, the voters rejected, in one way or another, three mayors accused of misconduct involving liquor and prostitution operations. Meredith Snyder was mayor from 1900 to 1904, during which time the vice district flourished. In 1904, Snyder was defeated by Owen McAleer, "the whisky mayor," who opposed further restrictions on saloons. McAleer served two years and declined to run again. The machine Democrat, Arthur Harper, was elected in 1906 but resigned suddenly in 1909 in the midst of a campaign to recall him. Five police chiefs left in disgrace.

Until about 1905, there was still some frontier-style joie de vivre apparent in Los Angeles, but it was soon to disappear. In 1908, the district attorney closed down the brothel of Pearl Morton, the city's best-known madam. The same year, Mayor Arthur Harper boasted that he did not protect vice, he condoned it, notwithstanding the laws against gambling, prostitution, and after-hours saloons. The Municipal League, formed in 1901 by Charles Dwight Willard, then initiated a recall campaign. Other reform clubs joined in, including John R. Haynes's Direct Legislation League, Edward A. Dickson's City Club, and Meyer Lissner's good government organization.

These groups formed the vanguard of the Lincoln-Roosevelt League, which became a powerful, statewide organization. The progressives could depend also on the Anti-Saloon League, the Anti–Race Track Gambling League, the Sunday Rest League, and the League of Justice. Mayor Harper resigned before the recall election. The reason was not made public, but the rumor at the time was that the payoff book detailing the mayor's profits from the tenderloin had been obtained by a local newspaper.

Between 1900 and 1909, Los Angeles's population tripled, to 300,000 residents. Most of the newcomers apparently were native Protestants of progressive sentiments. In the 1909 election, the progressives won all twenty-three elective offices. Subsequently, charter amendments were approved that abolished the ward system and installed nonpartisan election laws. These laws, in effect, eliminated the municipal Democratic party. The great victory of 1911 also initiated the destruction of the movement for political reform, since it witnessed the progressive/conservative coalition built to thwart the challenge from the left. By 1915, although control of the city remained in the hands of Protestant Republicans, the reform coalition was in ruins. With it went the integrity of the police force.

For the six years between 1909 and 1915, nevertheless, vice had been virtually suppressed. In this effort, the police had been aided by a platoon of ministers sworn in as special constables and by the Morals Efficiency League, also staffed by clergymen. Artistic censorship had been introduced, not only for motion pictures but for dance and drama as well. Isadora Duncan had been forbidden to dance. Eugene O'Neill's play *Desire under the Elms* was not allowed to open. Racetrack gambling and prizefighting had been abolished. To ensure the conviction of prostitutes, a local ordinance forbade sexual relations between persons not married to one another.

Willard Huntington Wright, a local author, watched bitterly as the once exciting city was made "chemically pure." Wright described the general atmosphere as "a frenzy of virtue." Pleasure seekers found themselves "thwarted by some ordinance, the primary object of which is to force Middle West moralities on every inhabitant. Puritanism is the inflexible doctrine of Los Angeles." Wright later was echoed by the district attorney, a Roman Catholic, who denounced "pussy-footing, publicity-seeking, religious despots." The ministerial rebuttal praised the Ku Klux Klan "for the enemies they have made."

Worse or better was in store, depending on the point of view. The moral reformers who provided the voting strength of the progressive movement supported a new mid-teens coalition, led mainly by Protestant ministers. They continued the struggle to suppress vice. The various groups were vociferous and determined. They "raided" dance halls and roadhouses, and sometimes had them closed. They held tumultuous press conferences, often in the offices of the mayor or the police commission. They attacked mayors and got police chiefs ousted. They were influential on voting day (for example, the Gandier Ordinance was passed in 1916 with no real difficulty), and they forced further restrictions on anyone whose idea of fun differed from their own.

In the early 1920s, reformers persuaded the police commission to restrict the conduct of dancers. Dancing with the cheek or head touching one's partner was forbidden. The male could place his hand only on his partner's back, between shoulder and waist. The female could place her hand only in her partner's left hand. No music "suggestive of bodily contortions" could be played. Moreover, women were forbidden to smoke in any room or place adjacent to a ballroom or dance academy. One minister led a campaign against a female candidate for the school board because the woman smoked tobacco. The candidate promised to quit if elected, but the reformers were adamant. She was defeated.

For twenty-five years, the second wave of reformers campaigned for civic purity. They constantly harassed the police by publicly identifying premises where various illegal enterprises were operated. They held press conferences and large church meetings. They wrote pamphlets. They sat in court to find out which judges convicted vice operators and which ones did not. They voted overwhelmingly for charter revisions to reform the police department. . . .

The electoral victories of 1902–1915 proved that the numerous and potentially all-powerful reformers could not be ignored. They could be circumvented, nevertheless. Every political candidate of the time styled himself or herself a progressive. Since the reformers would not or could not finance a municipal state of preferred candidates, they were compelled to support the most promising of those who stood for office. Consequently, the venal politicians and purveyors of vice, the so-called underworld combination, regained influence by financing ostensible reformers who, once in office, cooperated with corrupt interests, especially by manipulating the police department. The department operated as a sort of licensing and inspection bureau for organized vice operations. Those approved by the combination were protected; independents were put out of business.

The market for disreputable pleasures grew enormously after 1910. The number of transient males—the most likely "consumers"—increased substantially with the opening of the Panama Canal, the construction of the Los Angeles harbor, and the onset of World War I. The city had a seaport, a naval station, and an army camp. New industries attracted more workers. "Factories in the fields" employed many laborers. The large, continuing migration to the area required thousands of tradesmen to construct houses and services. Transients aside, the population rose from 200,000 in 1900 to 576,000 in 1920, and to 1.3 million in 1930.

Concurrently, local prohibition in 1916, followed by the Eighteenth Amendment, created a law enforcement crisis of unprecedented proportions. Opportunities for graft exceeded anything previously known. The number of police officers and other officials eager to share in the bonanza increased as profits increased. With the vice lords ascendant, the reformers concerned themselves almost entirely with moral issues.

In 1925, the last great progressive city charter went into effect. Again, police administration was an important consideration. The new charter (still in effect in 1992) provided for a five-member board of appointed police commissioners. . . .

Like all previous revisions, the charter of 1925 made no substantive difference. Organized, protected commercial vice remained a staple of nightlife in Los Angeles for another fifteen years. Almost all elected representatives were corrupt. The police force reached unexampled depths of infamy. Between 1915 and 1933, Charles Sebastian, Frederick Woodman, Meredith Snyder, George Cryer, and John Porter took office as reform mayors and left in disgrace. A dozen police chiefs came and went. Only in 1938, when the police intelligence squad tried and failed to murder an investigator hired by reformers, did the significant forces unite to unseat the mayor and reform the police department.

. . . Thus, it could be argued that even in Los Angeles the progressives failed to impose moral order.

On the surface the similarities between San Francisco and Los Angeles were quite marked. Both had manufacturers' associations opposed to organized labor. Both had men's and women's service clubs devoted to economic prosperity and the improvement of public morals. Both accepted municipal socialism with respect to public utilities. Both engaged in successful struggles for charter reform. Both were bumptious, rapidly growing, polyglot communities dominated by white, native-born Republicans. Both were progressive. Both had stringent anti-vice laws, flourishing tenderloin districts protected by police and politicians, and crusading religious leaders opposed to commercial vice.

Why, then, did the two cities diverge so widely where "adult pastimes" were concerned? The reason seems to be that the differences between the two cities, though fewer than the similarities, were far more significant. The simplest but most cogent explanation combines religion and ethnicity: San Francisco was a Catholic and Irish city; Los Angeles was a Protestant and evangelical midwestern city, "the capital of Iowa" moved west.

Catholic churchgoers outnumbered Protestant churchgoers in San Francisco by about a five-to-one margin. Most came from countries where the consumption of wine or beer was a part of the national way of life, or they were descended from immigrants from such countries. These people generally opposed restrictions on personal behavior. The politically active and astute Irish dominated municipal politics. Block and precinct headquarters usually were located in saloons.

The Protestants of San Francisco did favor measures for moral reform and would have passed them if they could. George Kennan (the explorer and journalist) mourned for the prosperous and successful city because it emphasized "material achievement and business prosperity rather than civic virtue and moral integrity. But what shall it profit a city if it gain the whole world and lose its own soul?" Similarly, there were Catholic anti-vice crusaders and Catholic progressives in San Francisco. But no temperance campaign ever succeeded there. San Francisco state representatives voted twelve to one against the Gandier Ordinance. Eighty-three percent of voters opposed local-option prohibition. The city was "wet" during the entire period of national prohibition. Los Angeles voters, on the other hand, voted for local prohibition in 1916 and approved other laws intended to suppress gambling and sexual promiscuity.

In retrospect, it is easy to ridicule the progressives' belief that one can reform a community by changing its laws. In truth, progressives believed more in good people than in good laws. They believed that police officers of good moral character, intelligent, educated, well trained, well paid, with tenure of office and adequate pensions, could and would enforce good laws and rid their communities of moral blight.

This ideal, never completely realized, still sustains civic reformers, as well it should. In Los Angeles, when honorable men and women held municipal office, the police enforced the laws, protected commercial vice was virtually eliminated, and the disreputable pleasures were reduced to an acceptable level. Charters, no matter how well drafted, could not achieve those goals.

The nonpartisan public service is an enduring legacy of the progressive movement. The police in particular have responded to the drive to professionalize every human vocation. Intelligence tests, mental health examinations, educational requirements, competitive promotional examinations that favor candidates with advanced education, physical health and strength regulations, even requirements to employ females and members of ethnic minorities—all these things are in the progressive tradition. When the ideal of impartial public service is violated, it is a matter of personal choice, not the failure of an institution or a law.

Fortunately for their place in history, the California progressives were more than puritanical moralists, although without their religious zeal their movement might have been less significant. A poet has said "When I am sick then I believe in law." The line expresses a very progressive and very American view. The progressives saw that their society was sick, and they moved to cure it with laws prohibiting certain kinds of personal, political, and economic conduct. They succeeded to a limited degree in every area, and their inheritors have generally followed the same path.

FURTHER READING

Leon Fink, *Progressive Intellectuals and the Dilemmas of Democratic Commitment* (1997).
Samuel Hays, *Conservation and the Gospel of Efficiency* (1969).
Gabriel Kolko, *The Triumph of Conservatism: A Re-interpretation of American History, 1900–1916* (1963).
Aileen Kraditor, *Ideas of the Woman Suffrage Movement* (1981).
Christopher Lasch, *The True and Only Heaven: Progress and Its Critics* (1991).
Leon Litwack, *Trouble in Mind: Black Southerners in the Age of Jim Crow* (1998).
Kathryn Kish Sklar, *Florence Kelley and the Nation's Work* (1995).
Louis Warren, *The Hunter's Game: Poachers and Conservationists in Twentieth Century America* (1997).

C H A P T E R
6

America in World War I

In 1917, President Woodrow Wilson broke the precedent of more than one hundred years and sent American soldiers "over there," across the Atlantic. George Washington had declared the "Great Rule" of staying out of Europe's troubles in 1796, and James Monroe had underscored the principle in his famous Monroe Doctrine of 1823. Essentially, the Monroe Doctrine asserted that Europeans should stay out of affairs in the Americas, and that Americans should stay out of political affairs in Europe. Following this venerable tradition, Wilson declared neutrality when the war first broke out on July 28, 1914. But the opportunity to sell food, arms, and other goods to the belligerents gradually led the United States deeper and deeper into the conflict. Britain declared a blockade of all German-occupied territory to prevent food and supplies from getting through to its enemy on the continent. To enforce the blockade, Britain planted underwater mines off the coast of northern Europe. These booby traps sent five U.S. merchant ships to the bottom along with their cargoes and men. Germany retaliated by declaring a war zone around the British Isles, patrolled by the newly developed U-boats, which hunted merchant ships destined for England. When Kaiser Wilhelm of Germany resumed unrestricted submarine warfare in January 1917 in order to break the British blockade, U-boats immediately sank two American merchant ships, bringing the total of German-destroyed American ships to six.

The difference in the number of ships sunk by British mines and by German U-boats is far too slight to explain why President Wilson entered the so-called Great War on the side of the Allies, or even why he took the nation into a European conflict at all. Historians answer these questions in different ways. Some point to the German U-boat, which seemed to Wilson a particularly inhumane and unfair form of warfare, especially after one sank the British passenger liner Lusitania in 1915. Other historians point to Wilson's personality: his religious faith and predilection for moralizing, or his Progressive commitment to political reform and his desire to "make the world safe for democracy." Scholars (and Americans at the time) have also expressed the suspicion that the United States simply followed its economic interests in allying with the British and French. But while they disagree on why the United States went to war, historians concur that this decision set the nation on a course of intervention in world affairs. During the war, Wilson called for a "peace without victory" and a League of Nations that would guarantee the right of all peoples to self-determination. After the war, the U.S. Senate refused to ratify the

148

president's peace treaty. Ever since, historians and politicians have called the notion of an American democratic mission abroad "Wilsonianism."

The consequences of America's new course were profound, both abroad and at home. The Wilson administration fostered hyperpatriotism through a Committee on Public Information, and suppressed free speech through Espionage and Sedition Acts aimed at anyone who opposed the war. Americans rallied around the flag, and over 100,000 soldiers died under its colors. But afterward, disillusionment set in quickly: disillusionment with profiteers who had helped drag the United States into the conflict, with idealists who had sought to remake the world, and with war itself as a patriotic or glorious undertaking. World War I ultimately provided few lessons about when or how the United States should intervene in conflicts beyond its borders. George Washington's Great Rule against foreign entanglements had been broken, but the Senate's vote against the League of Nations showed that it could be restored.

QUESTIONS   TO   THINK   ABOUT

Progressives such as Presidents Woodrow Wilson and Theodore Roosevelt supported American entry into the war. But other Progressives, such as Senator Robert La Follette and Secretary of State William Jennings Bryan, bitterly opposed it. How did the war further the reformers' agenda, and how did the war undermine it? What did the war do to the Progressive movement?

What do you think of Woodrow Wilson's leadership after the war? Was he a hopeless dreamer who bungled the attempt to restore peace, or was he the prescient architect of a new world order?

DOCUMENTS

The documents in this chapter illustrate a variety of attitudes toward the decision to go to war and toward the war itself. In Document 1, President Wilson asks Congress to declare war and pledge "our lives and our fortunes" to make the world free. Progressive Senator Robert La Follette strenuously objected. In a speech to the U.S. Senate (Document 2), he argues that America stands to lose its own freedom through conscription and other measures that take away free speech and free choice. Document 3 is a sworn statement made out by union organizers who were whipped, tarred, and feathered for not buying Liberty Bonds. This selection testifies to the domestic intolerance that grew out of the war, fulfilling La Follette's prophecy. Document 4 is the Espionage Act of 1918, designed to punish pacifists and quell dissent. In a speech on January 8, 1918, Wilson outlined the war aims of the United States, which included self-determination for all peoples. His so-called Fourteen Points (Document 5) spoke to the historic ideals of the United States—ideals that would bedevil the nation's foreign policy for the ensuing century. The next two documents reveal contrasting perceptions of the war itself: as a patriotic opportunity to "make your mother proud of you," or as a senseless slaughter at odds with American values. Document 6 is "Over There," the famous patriotic song by vaudeville performer George M. Cohan that helped stir millions to volunteer. Document 7 is an excerpt from John Dos Passos's antiwar novel *Nineteen Nineteen*, one example of a genre of books (including the works of Ernest Hemingway) that appeared after the war and deplored the slaughter. In Document 8, newspaperman George Creel recounts how the U.S. government used the newest propaganda techniques to "sell" the war and the international crusade for democracy. Document 9 shows cartoons that grappled with the essential choice faced by the United States once the guns went silent: to embrace "foreign entanglements" or to turn its back on the common cause of humanity.

1. President Woodrow Wilson Asks Congress to Declare War, 1917

On the third of February last I officially laid before you the extraordinary announcement of the Imperial German Government that on and after the first day of February it was its purpose to put aside all restraints of law of humanity and use its submarines to sink every vessel that sought to approach either the ports of Great Britain and Ireland or the western coasts of Europe or any of the ports controlled by the enemies of Germany within the Mediterranean. That had seemed to be the object of the German submarine warfare earlier in the war, but since April of last year the Imperial Government had somewhat restrained the commanders of its undersea craft in conformity with its promise then given to us that passenger boats should not be sunk and that due warning would be given to all other vessels which its submarines might seek to destroy, when no resistance was offered or escape attempted, and care taken that their crews were given at least a fair chance to save their lives in their open boats. The precautions taken were meagre and haphazard enough, as was proved in distressing instance after instance in the progress of the cruel and unmanly business, but a certain degree of restraint was observed. The new policy has swept every restriction aside. Vessels of every kind, whatever their flag, their character, their cargo, their destination, their errand, have been ruthlessly sent to the bottom without warning and without thought of help or mercy for those on board, the vessels of friendly neutrals along with those of belligerents. Even hospital ships and ships carrying relief to the sorely bereaved and stricken people of Belgium, though the latter were provided with safe conduct through the proscribed areas by the German Government itself and were distinguished by unmistakable marks of identity, have been sunk with the same reckless lack of compassion or of principle.

I was for a little while unable to believe that such things would in fact be done by any government that had hitherto subscribed to the humane practices of civilized nations. International law had its origin in the attempt to set up some law which would be respected and observed upon the seas, where no nation had right of dominion where lay the free highways of the world. By painful stage after stage has that law been built up, with meagre enough results, indeed, after all was accomplished that could be accomplished, but always with a clear view, at least of what the heart and conscience of mankind demanded. This minimum of right the German Government has swept aside under the plea of retaliation and necessity and because it had no weapons which it could use at sea except these which it is impossible to employ as it is employing them without throwing to the winds all

Congressional Record, LV (April 2, 1917), Part 1, 102–104.

scruples of humanity or of respect for the understandings that were supposed to underlie the intercourse of the world. I am not now thinking of the loss of property involved, immense and serious as that is, but only of the wanton and wholesale destruction of the lives of noncombatants, men, women, and children, engaged in pursuits which have always, even in the darkest periods of modern history, been deemed innocent and legitimate. Property can be paid for; the lives of peaceful and innocent people cannot be. The present German submarine warfare against commerce is a warfare against mankind.

It is a war against all nations. American ships have been sunk, American lives taken, in ways which it has stirred us very deeply to learn of, but the ships and people of other neutral and friendly nations have been sunk and overwhelmed in the waters in the same way. There has been no discrimination. The challenge is to all mankind. Each nation must decide for itself how it will meet it. The choice we make for ourselves must be made with a moderation of counsel and a temperateness of judgment befitting our character and our motives as a nation. We must put excited feeling away. Our motive will not be revenge or the victorious assertion of the physical might of the nation, but only the vindication of right, of human right, of which we are only a single champion. . . .

With a profound sense of the solemn and even tragical character of the step I am taking and of the grave responsibilities which it involves, but in unhesitating obedience to what I deem my constitutional duty, I advise that the Congress declare the recent course of the Imperial German Government to be in fact nothing less than war against the government and people of the United States; that it formally accept the status of belligerent which has thus been thrust upon it; and that it take immediate steps not only to put the country in a more thorough state of defense but also to exert all its power and employ all its resources to bring the Government of the German Empire to terms and end the war. . . .

Does not every American feel that assurance has been added to our hope for the future peace of the world by the wonderful and heartening things that have been happening within the last few weeks in Russia? Russia was known by those who knew it best to have been always in fact democratic at heart, in all the vital habits of her thought, in all the intimate relationships of her people that spoke their natural instinct, their habitual attitude towards life. The autocracy that crowned the summit of her political structure, long as it had stood and terrible as was the reality of its power, was not in fact Russian in origin, character, or purpose; and now it has been shaken off and the great, generous Russian people have been added in all their naive majesty and might to the forces that are fighting for freedom in the world, for justice, and for peace. Here is a fit partner for a League of Honour.

One of the things that has served to convince us that the Prussian autocracy was not and could never be our friends is that from the very outset of the present war it has filled our unsuspecting communities and even our offices of government with spies and set criminal intrigues everywhere afoot against our national unity of counsel, our peace within and without, our industries and our commerce. . . . That it means to stir up enemies against us at our very doors the intercepted note to the German Minister at Mexico City is eloquent evidence.

We are accepting this challenge of hostile purpose because we know that in such a government, following such methods, we can never have a friend; and that in the presence of its organized power, always lying in wait to accomplish we know not what purpose, there can be no assured security for the democratic governments of the world. We are now about to accept gauge of battle with its natural foe to liberty and shall, if necessary, spend the whole force of the nation to check and nullify its pretensions and its power. We are glad, now that we see the facts with no veil of false pretense about them, to fight thus for the ultimate peace of the world and for the liberation of its peoples, the German peoples included: for the rights of nations great and small and the privilege of men everywhere to choose their way of life and of obedience. The world must be made safe for democracy. . . .

It is a distressing and oppressive duty, Gentlemen of the Congress, which I have performed in thus addressing you. There are, it may be, many months of fiery trial and sacrifice ahead of us. It is a fearful thing to lead this great peaceful people into war, into the most terrible and disastrous of all wars, civilization itself seeming to be in the balance. But the right is more precious than peace, and we shall fight for the things which we have always carried nearest our hearts—for democracy, for the right of those who submit to authority to have a voice in their own governments, for the rights and liberties of small nations, for a universal dominion of right by such a concert of free peoples as shall bring peace and safety to all nations and make the world itself at last free. To such a task we can dedicate our lives and our fortunes, everything that we are and everything that we have, with the pride of those who know that the day has come when America is privileged to spend her blood and her might for the principles that gave her birth and happiness and the peace which she has treasured. God helping her, she can do no other.

2. Senator Robert M. La Follette
Voices His Dissent, 1917

The poor, sir, who are the ones called upon to rot in the trenches, have no organized power, have no press to voice their will upon this question of peace or war; but, oh, Mr. President, at some time they will be heard. I hope and I believe they will be heard in an orderly and a peaceful way. I think they may be heard from before long. I think, sir, if we take this step, when the people to-day who are staggering under the burden of supporting families at the present prices of the necessaries of the life find those prices multiplied, when they are raised a hundred percent, or 200 percent, as they will be quickly, aye, sir, when beyond that those who pay taxes come to have their taxes doubled and again doubled to pay the interest on the nontaxable bonds held by Morgan and his combinations, which have been issued to meet this war, there will come an awakening; they will have their day and they will be heard. It will be as certain and as inevitable as the return of the tides, and as resistless, too. . . .

Just a word of comment more upon one of the points in the President's address. He says that this is a war "for the things which we have always carried nearest to our hearts—for democracy, for the right of those who submit to authority to have a voice in their own government." In many places throughout the address is this exalted sentiment given expression. . . .

But the President proposes alliance with Great Britain, which, however liberty-loving its people, is a hereditary monarchy, with a hereditary ruler, with a hereditary House of Lords, with a hereditary landed system, with a limited and restricted suffrage for one class and a multiplied suffrage power for another, and with grinding industrial conditions for all the wageworkers. The President has not suggested that we make our support of Great Britain conditional to her granting home rule to Ireland, or Egypt, or India. We rejoice in the establishment of a democracy in Russia, but it will hardly be contended that if Russia was still an autocratic Government, we would not be asked to enter this alliance with her just the same. Italy and the lesser powers of Europe, Japan in the Orient; in fact all of the countries with whom we are to enter into alliance, except France and newly revolutionized Russia, are still of the old order—and it will be generally conceded that no one of them has done as much for its people in the solution of municipal problems and in securing social and industrial reforms as Germany. . . .

Who has registered the knowledge or approval of the American people of the course this Congress is called upon in declaring war upon Germany? Submit the question to the people, you who support it. You who support it dare not do it, for you know that by a vote of more than ten to one the American people as a body would register their declaration against it.

In the sense that this war is being forced upon our people without their knowing why and without their approval, and that wars are usually forced upon all peoples in the same way, there is some truth in the statement; but I venture to say that the response which the German people have made to the demands of this war shows that it has a degree of popular support which the war upon which we are entering has not and never will have among our people. The espionage bills, the conscription bills, and other forcible military measures which we understand are being ground out of the war machine in this country is the complete proof that those responsible for this war fear that it has no popular support and that armies sufficient to satisfy the demand of the entente allies can not be recruited by voluntary enlistments.

3. A Union Organizer Testifies to Vigilante Attack, 1917

"On the night of November 5, 1917, while sitting in the hall at No. 6 W. Brady Street, Tulsa, Okla. (the room leased and occupied by the Industrial Workers of the World, and used as a union meeting room), at about 8:45 P.M., five men entered the hall, to whom I at first paid no attention, as I was busy putting a monthly stamp in a member's union card book. After I had finished with the member, I walked back to where these five men had congregated at the baggage-room at the back of the hall, and spoke to them, asking if there was anything I could do for them.

"One who appeared to be the leader, answered 'No, we're just looking the place over.' Two of them went into the baggage-room flashing an electric flashlight around the room. The other three walked toward the front end of the hall. I stayed

---

Sworn testimony of the secretary of the Industrial Workers of the World local, Tulsa, Oklahoma, November 1917, from *Liberator,* April 1918.

at the baggage-room door, and one of the men came out and followed the other three up to the front end of the hall. The one who stayed in the baggage-room asked me if I was 'afraid he would steal something.' I told him we were paying rent for the hall, and I did not think anyone had a right to search this place without a warrant. He replied that he did not give a damn if we were paying rent for four places, they would search them whenever they felt like it. Presently he came out and walked toward the front end of the hall, and I followed a few steps behind him.

"In the meantime the other men, who proved to be officers, appeared to be asking some of our members questions. Shortly after, the patrol-wagon came and all the members in the hall—10 men were ordered into the wagon. I turned out the light in the back end of the hall, closed the desk, put the key in the door and told the 'officer' to turn out the one light. We stepped out, and I locked the door, and at the request of the 'leader of the officers,' handed him the keys. He told me to get in the wagon, I being the 11th man taken from the hall, and we were taken to the police station. . . .

"After some argument by both sides the cases were continued until the next night, November 8th, and the case against Gunnard Johnson, one of our men, was called. After four and a half hours' session the case was again adjourned until November 9th at 5 P.M., when we agreed to let the decision in Johnson's case stand for all of us. . . .

"Johnson said he had come into town Saturday, November 3d, to get his money from the Sinclair Oil & Gas Co. and could not get it until Monday, the 5th, and was shipping out Tuesday, the 6th, and that he had $7.08 when arrested. He was reprimanded by the judge for not having a Liberty Bond, and as near as anyone could judge from the closing remarks of Judge Evans, he was found guilty and fined $100 for not having a Liberty Bond.

"Our lawyer made a motion to appeal the case and the bonds were then fixed at $200 each. I was immediately arrested, *as were also five spectators in the open courtroom,* for being I.W.W.'s. One arrested was not a member of ours, but a property-owner and citizen. I was searched and $30.87 taken from me, as also was the receipt for the $100 bond, and we then were all placed back in the cells.

"In about forty minutes, as near as we could judge about 11 P.M., the turnkey came and called 'Get ready to go out you. I.W.W. men.' We dressed as rapidly as possible, were taken out of the cells, and the officer gave us back our possessions, Ingersoll watches, pocketknives and money, with the exception of $3 in silver of mine which they kept, giving me back $27.87. I handed the receipt for the $100 bond I had put up to the desk sergeant and he told me he did not know anything about it, and handed the receipt back to me, which I put in my trousers' pocket with the 87 cents. Twenty-seven dollars in bills was in my coat pocket. We were immediately ordered into automobiles waiting in the alley. Then we proceeded one block north to 1st Street, west one-half block to Boulder Street, north across the Frisco tracks and stopped.

"Then the masked mob came up and ordered everybody to throw up their hands. Just here I wish to state I never thought any man could reach so high as those policemen did. We were then bound, some with hands in front, some with hands behind, and others bound with arms hanging down their sides, the rope being wrapped around the body. Then the police were ordered to 'beat it,' which they did, running, and we started for the place of execution.

"When we arrived there, a company of gowned and masked gunmen were there to meet us standing at 'present arms.' We were ordered out of the autos, told to get in line in front of these gunmen and another bunch of men with automatics and pistols, lined up between us. Our hands were still held up, and those who were bound, in front. Then a masked man walked down the line and slashed the ropes that bound us, and we were ordered to strip to the waist, which we did, threw our clothes in front of us, in individual piles—coats, vests, hats, shirts and undershirts. The boys not having had time to distribute their possessions that were given back to them at the police stations, everything was in the coats, everything we owned in the world.

"Then the whipping began, a double piece of new rope, ⅝ or ¾ hemp, being used. A man, 'the chief' of detectives, stopped the whipping of each man when he thought the victim had had enough. After each one was whipped another man applied the tar with a large brush, from the head to the seat. Then a brute smeared feathers over and rubbed them in.

"After they had satisfied themselves that our bodies were well abused, our clothing was thrown into a pile, gasoline poured on it and a match applied. By the light of our earthly possessions, we were ordered to leave Tulsa, and leave running and never come back. The night was dark, the road very rough, and as I was one of the last two that was whipped, tarred and feathered, and in the rear when ordered to run, I decided to be shot rather than stumble over the rough road. After going forty or fifty feet I stopped and went into the weeds. I told the man with me to get in the weeds also, as the shots were coming very close over us and ordered him to lie down flat. We expected to be killed, but after 150 or 200 shots were fired they got in their autos.

"After the last one had left, we went through a barbed-wire fence, across a field, called to the boys, collected them, counted up, and had all the 16 safe, though sore and nasty with tar. After wandering around the hills for some time—ages it seemed to me—we struck the railroad track. One man, Jack Sneed, remembered then that he knew a farmer in that vicinity, and he and J. F. Ryan volunteered to find the house. I built a fire to keep us from freezing.

"We stood around the fire expecting to be shot, as we did not know but what some tool of the commercial club had followed us. After a long time Sneed returned and called to us, and we went with him to a cabin and found an I.W.W. friend in the shack and 5 gallons of coal oil or kerosene, with which we cleaned the filthy stuff off of each other, and our troubles were over, as friends sent clothing and money to us that day, it being about 3 or 3:30 A.M. when we reached the cabin.

"The men abused, whipped and tarred were Tom McCaffery, John Myers, John Boyle, Charles Walsh, W. H. Walton, L. R. Mitchell, Jos. French, J. R. Hill, Gunnard Johnson, Robt. McDonald, John Fitzsimmons, Jos. Fischer, Gordon Dimikson, J. F. Ryan, E. M. Boyd, Jack Sneed (not an I.W.W.).

"This is a copy of my sworn statement and every word is truth."

"It was very evident that the police force knew what was going to happen when they took us from jail, as there were extra gowns and masks provided *which were put on by the Chief of Police and one detective named Blaine, and the number of blows we received were regulated by the Chief of Police himself, who was easily recognizable by six of us at least.*"

4. The U.S. Government Punishes War Protesters: The Espionage Act, 1918

Be it enacted by the Senate and House of Representatives of the United States of America in Congress assembled, That section three of title one of the Act entitled, "An Act to punish acts of interference with the foreign relations, the neutrality, and the foreign commerce of the United States, to punish espionage, and better to enforce the criminal laws of the United States, and for other purposes," approved June fifteenth, nineteen hundred and seventeen, be, and the same is hereby, amended so as to read as follows:

"SEC. 3. Whoever, when the United States is at war, shall willfully make or convey false reports or false statements with intent to interfere with the operation or success of the military or naval forces of the United States, or to promote the success of its enemies, or shall willfully make or convey false reports or false statements, or say or do anything except by way of bona fide and not disloyal advice to an investor or investors, with intent to obstruct the sale by the United States of bonds or other securities of the United States or the making of loans by or to the United States, and whoever, when the United States is at war, shall willfully cause or attempt to cause, or incite or attempt to incite, insubordination, disloyalty, mutiny, or refusal of duty, in the military or naval forces of the United States, or shall willfully obstruct or attempt to obstruct the recruiting or enlistment service of the United States, and whoever, when the United States is at war, shall willfully utter, print, write, or publish any disloyal, profane, scurrilous, or abusive language about the form of government of the United States, or the Constitution of the United States, or the military or naval forces of the United States, or the flag of the United States, or the uniform of the Army or Navy of the United States, or any language intended to bring the form of government of the United States, or the Constitution of the United States, or the military or naval forces of the United States, or the flag of the United States, or the uniform of the Army or Navy of the United States into contempt, scorn, contumely, or disrepute, or shall willfully utter, print, write, or publish any language intended to incite, provoke, or encourage resistance to the United States, or to promote the cause of its enemies, or shall willfully display the flag of any foreign enemy, or shall willfully by utterance, writing, printing, publication, or language spoken, urge, incite, or advocate any curtailment of production in this country of any thing or things, product or products, necessary or essential to the prosecution of the war in which the United States may be engaged, with intent by such curtailment to cripple or hinder the United States in the prosecution of the war, and whoever shall willfully advocate, teach, defend, or suggest the doing of any of the acts or things in this section enumerated, and whoever shall by word or act support or favor the cause of any country with which the United States is at war or by word or act oppose the cause of the United States therein, shall be punished by a fine of not more than $10,000 or imprisonment for not more than twenty years, or both. . . ."

Espionage Act, U.S. Statutes at Large 40 (1918), 553ff.

Title XII of the said Act of June fifteenth, nineteen hundred and seventeen, be, and the same is hereby, amended by adding thereto the following section:

"Sec. 4. When the United States is at war, the Postmaster General may, upon evidence satisfactory to him that any person or concern is using the mails in violation of any of the provisions of this Act, instruct the postmaster at any post office at which mail is received addressed to such person or concern to return to the postmaster at the office at which they were originally mailed all letters or other matter so addressed, with the words 'Mail to this address undeliverable under Espionage Act' plainly written or stamped upon the outside thereof, and all such letters or other matter so returned to such postmasters shall be by them returned to the senders thereof under such regulations as the Postmaster General may prescribe."

Approved, May 16, 1918.

5. Wilson Proposes a New World Order in the "Fourteen Points," 1918

I. Open covenants of peace, openly arrived at, after which there shall be no private international understandings of any kind but diplomacy shall proceed always frankly and in the public view.

II. Absolute freedom of navigation upon the seas, outside territorial waters, alike in peace and in war, except as the seas may be closed in whole or in part by international action for the enforcement of international covenants.

III. The removal, so far as possible, of all economic barriers and the establishment of an equality of trade conditions among all the nations consenting to the peace and associating themselves for its maintenance.

IV. Adequate guarantees given and taken that national armaments will be reduced to the lowest point consistent with domestic safety.

V. A free, open-minded, and absolutely impartial adjustment of all colonial claims, based upon a strict observance of the principle that in determining all such questions of sovereignty the interests of the populations concerned must have equal weight with the equitable claims of the government whose title is to be determined.

VI. The evacuation of all Russian territory and such a settlement of all questions affecting Russia as will secure the best and freest cooperation of the other nations of the world in obtaining for her an unhampered and unembarrassed opportunity for the independent determination of her own political development and national policy and assure her of a sincere welcome into the society of free nations under institutions of her own choosing; and, more than a welcome, assistance also of every kind that she may need and may herself desire. The treatment accorded Russia by her sister nations in the months to come will be the acid test of their good will, of their comprehension of her needs as distinguished from their own interests, and of their intelligent and unselfish sympathy.

VII. Belgium, the whole world will agree, must be evacuated and restored, without any attempt to limit the sovereignty which she enjoys in common with all other free nations. No other single act will serve as this will serve to restore confidence

Congressional Record, LVI (January 8, 1918), Part 1, 680–682.

among the nations in the laws which they have themselves set and determined for the government of their relations with one another. Without this healing act the whole structure and validity of international law is forever impaired.

VIII. All French territory should be freed and the invaded portions restored, and the wrong done to France by Prussia in 1871 in the matter of Alsace-Lorraine, which has unsettled the peace of the world for nearly fifty years, should be righted, in order that peace may once more be made secure in the interest of all.

IX. A readjustment of the frontiers of Italy should be effected along clearly recognizable lines of nationality.

X. The peoples of Austria-Hungary, whose place among the nations we wish to see safeguarded and assured, should be accorded the freest opportunity of autonomous development.

XI. Rumania, Serbia, and Montenegro should be evacuated; occupied territories restored; Serbia accorded free and secure access to the sea; and the relations of the several Balkan states to one another determined by friendly consul along historically established lines of allegiance and nationality; and international guarantees of the political and economic independence and territorial integrity of the several Balkan states should be entered into.

XII. The Turkish portions of the present Ottoman Empire should be assured a secure sovereignty, but the other nationalities which are now under Turkish rule should be assured an undoubted security of life and an absolutely unmolested opportunity of autonomous development, and the Dardanelles should be permanently opened as a free passage to the ships and commerce of all nations under international guarantees.

XIII. An independent Polish state should be erected which should include the territories inhabited by indisputably Polish populations, which should be assured a free and secure access to the sea, and whose political and economic independence and territorial integrity should be guaranteed by international covenant.

XIV. A general association of nations must be formed under specific covenants for the purpose of affording mutual guarantees of political independence and territorial integrity to great and small states alike.

6. George M. Cohan Sings About Patriotism in "Over There," 1918

> Johnnie, get your gun,
> Get your gun, get your gun,
> Take it on the run,
> On the run, on the run.
> Hear them calling, you and me,
> Every son of liberty.
> Hurry right away,
> No delay, no delay,

George M. Cohan, "Over There."

Make your daddy glad
To have had such a lad.
Tell your sweetheart not to pine,
To be proud her boy's in line.

Chorus

Over there, over there,
Send the word, send the word over there—
That the Yanks are coming,
The Yanks are coming,
The drums rum-tumming
Ev'rywhere.
So prepare, say a pray'r,
Send the word, send the word to beware.
We'll be over, we're coming over,
And we won't come back till it's over
Over there.

Johnnie, get your gun,
Get your gun, get your gun,
Johnnie show the Hun
Who's a son of a gun.
Hoist the flag and let her fly,
Yankee Doodle do or die.
Pack your little kit,
Show your grit, do your bit.
Yankee Doodle fill the ranks,
From the towns and the tanks.
Make your mother proud of you,
And the old Red, White and Blue.

(*repeat chorus twice*)

7. Novelist John Dos Passos: "Remembering the Gray Crooked Fingers," 1919

The Camera Eye (30)

remembering the gray crooked fingers the thick drip of blood off the canvas the bubbling when the lungcases try to breathe the muddy scraps of flesh you put in the ambulance alive and haul out dead

three of us sit in the dry cement fountain of the little garden with the pink walls in Récicourt

John Dos Passos, *Nineteen Nineteen* (New York: Washington Square Press, 1919), 109–110.

No   there must   be   some   way   they   taught   us   Land   of   the
Free   conscience   Give me liberty or give me   Well they give us death
  sunny afternoon   through the faint aftersick of mustardgas I smell the box the
white roses and the white phlox with a crimson eye   three brownandwhitestriped
snails hang with infinite delicacy from a honeysuckle-branch overhead   up in
the blue a sausageballoon grazes drowsily like a tethered cow   there are drunken
wasps clinging to the tooripe pears that fall and squash whenever the near guns
spew their heavy shells that go off rumbling through the sky.
  with a whir that makes you remember walking in the woods and starting a
woodcock
  welltodo country people carefully built the walls and the little backhouse with
the cleanscrubbed seat and the quartermoon in the door like the backhouse of an
old farm at home   carefully planted the garden and savored the fruit and the
flowers and carefully planned this war
  to hell with 'em   Patrick Henry in khaki submits to shortarm inspection and
puts all his pennies in a Liberty Loan   or give me
  arrivés   shrapnel twanging its harps out of tiny powderpuff clouds invites
us delicately to glory   we happy watching the careful movements of the snails
in the afternoon sunlight talking in low voices about
  La Libre Belgique   The Junius papers   Areopagitica   Milton went
blind for freedom of speech   If you hit the words Democracy will under-
stand   even the bankers and the clergymen   I   you   we   must
            When three men hold together
            The kingdoms are less by three
  we are happy talking in low voices in the afternoon sunlight about après la
guerre that our fingers our blood our lungs our flesh under the dirty khaki feldgrau
bleu horizon might go on sweeten grow until we fall from the tree ripe like the
tooripe pears   the arrivés know and singing éclats sizzling gas shells   theirs
is the power and the glory
  or give me death

8. George Creel Recalls Selling the War, 1920

Back of the firing-line, back of armies and navies, back of the great supply-depots,
another struggle waged with the same intensity and with almost equal significance
attaching to its victories and defeats. It was the fight for the *minds* of men, for the
"conquest of their convictions," and the battle-line ran through every home in
every country. . . .
  We strove for the maintenance of our own morale and the Allied morale by
every process of stimulation; every possible expedient was employed to break
through the barrage of lies that kept the people of the Central Powers in darkness
and delusion; we sought the friendship and support of the neutral nations by continuous presentation of facts. We did not call it propaganda, for that word, in

George Creel, *How We Advertised America* (New York: Harper and Brothers, 1920), 3–8.

German hands, had come to be associated with deceit and corruption. Our effort was educational and informative throughout, for we had such confidence in our case as to feel that no other argument was needed than the simple, straightforward presentation of facts.

There was no part of the great war machinery that we did not touch, no medium of appeal that we did not employ. The printed word, the spoken word, the motion picture, the telegraph, the cable, the wireless, the poster, the sign-board— all these were used in our campaign to make our own people and all other peoples understand the causes that compelled America to take arms. All that was fine and ardent in the civilian population came at our call until more than one hundred and fifty thousand men and women were devoting highly specialized abilities to the work of the Committee, as faithful and devoted in their service as though they wore the khaki.

While America's summons was answered without question by the citizenship as a whole, it is to be remembered that during the three and a half years of our neutrality the land had been torn by a thousand divisive prejudices, stunned by the voices of anger and confusion, and muddled by the pull and haul of opposed interests. These were conditions that could not be permitted to endure. What we had to have was no mere surface unity, but a passionate belief in the justice of America's cause that should weld the people of the United States into one white-hot mass instinct with fraternity, devotion, courage, and deathless determination. The *war-will,* the will-to-win, of a democracy depends upon the degree to which each one of all the people of that democracy can concentrate and consecrate body and soul and spirit in the supreme effort of service and sacrifice. What had to be driven home was that all business was the nation's business, and every task a common task for a single purpose. . . .

. . . A speaking division toured great groups like the Blue Devils, Pershing's Veterans, and the Belgians, arranged mass-meetings in the communities, conducted forty-five war conferences from coast to coast, coordinated the entire speaking activities of the nation, and assured consideration to the crossroads hamlet as well as to the city.

The Four Minute Men, an organization that will live in history by reason of its originality and effectiveness, commanded the volunteer services of 75,000 speakers, operating in 5,200 communities, and making a total of 755,190 speeches, every one having the carry of shrapnel.

With the aid of a volunteer staff of several hundred translators, the Committee kept in direct touch with the foreign-language press, supplying selected articles designed to combat ignorance and disaffection. It organized and directed twenty-three societies and leagues designed to appeal to certain classes and particular foreign-language groups, each body carrying a specific message of unity and enthusiasm to its section of America's adopted peoples.

It planned war exhibits for the state fairs of the United States, also a great series of interallied war expositions that brought home to our millions the exact nature of the struggle that was being waged in France. In Chicago alone two million people attended in two weeks, and in nineteen cities the receipts aggregated $1,432,261.36.

The Committee mobilized the advertising forces of the country—press, periodical, car, and outdoor—for the patriotic campaign that gave millions of dollars' worth of free space to the national service.

It assembled the artists of America on a volunteer basis for the production of posters, window-cards, and similar material of pictorial publicity for the use of various government departments and patriotic societies. A total of 1,438 drawings was used.

It issued an official daily newspaper, serving every department of government, with a circulation of one hundred thousand copies a day. For official use only, its value was such that private citizens ignored the supposedly prohibitive subscription price, subscribing to the amount of $77,622.58.

It organized a bureau of information for all persons who sought direction in volunteer war-work, in acquiring knowledge of any administrative activities, or in approaching business dealings with the government. In the ten months of its existence it gave answers to eighty-six thousand requests for specific information.

It gathered together the leading novelists, essayists, and publicists of the land, and these men and women, without payment, worked faithfully in the production of brilliant, comprehensive articles that went to the press as syndicate features.

One division paid particular attention to the rural press and the plate-matter service. Others looked after the specialized needs of the labor press, the religious press, and the periodical press. The Division of Women's War Work prepared and issued the information of peculiar interest to the women of the United States, also aiding in the task of organizing and directing.

Through the medium of the motion picture, America's war progress, as well as the meanings and purposes of democracy, were carried to every community in the United States and to every corner of the world. "Pershing's Crusaders," "America's Answer," and "Under Four Flags" were types of feature films by which we drove home America's resources and determinations, while other pictures, showing our social and industrial life, made our free institutions vivid to foreign peoples.

9. Cartoons for and Against the League of Nations, 1920

INTERRUPTING THE CEREMONY

THE ACCUSER   *March 22, 1920*

E S S A Y S

The stakes at the end of World War I turned out to be very high indeed, since in retro-spect many historians have placed the blame for World War II on the failings of the Treaty of Versailles and the League of Nations. Jan W. Schulte-Nordholt, a Dutch scholar, articulates the view that Wilson ventured into matters far beyond his under-standing. Wilson's idealistic but ill-considered crusade for democracy further unraveled the fabric of European stability. The president made fateful concessions to England and France in return for their agreement on the League and the principle of self-determination, an idea that was itself inflammatory at the time. Tony Smith of Tufts University disagrees. He disputes the notion that there was a more pragmatic, "realistic" direction that Wilson should have chosen. The Wilsonian model of a new world order did not come into being in 1920, but it did become the basis for a more stable interna-tional system after 1945, Smith points out. President Wilson lamented at the end of his career: "I had to negotiate with my back to the wall. Men thought I had all the power. Would to God I had had such power." Considering the powers that Wilson did have, do you think he employed them well?

Wilson as a Peace Advocate Out of Touch with Reality

JAN WILHELM SCHULTE-NORDHOLT

We are in many respects Woodrow Wilson's heirs. That is why it is of great impor-tance to us to make out what kind of man he was, how he came to his exalted and advanced ideas, and why in the end he failed. That is my purpose. . . . I want to ex-amine more closely the life of a man who sought a solution to problems that are still ours, and who was therefore the first great advocate of world peace. He was, as it were, a whole peace movement all by himself.

I almost wrote "apostle of peace," but this phrase is too strong. It makes it seem that I had at least to some extent a work of hagiography in mind. Far from it! History is about people, their dreams and their failures. It would be all too easy to paint Woodrow Wilson as the great prophet who was always wiser than his fellow men. The purpose of a biography ought not to be to turn a human being into a figure of puppetry; to change the metaphor, to press him into flat uniformity. Was Wilson a prophet, an idealist, a dissembler, a practical man, a revolutionary reformer? He was to some small extent all of these. Like most great men, indeed like most people, Wilson was a bundle of contradictions. That is what makes him so fascinating. He was many things: a scholar driven by deep feelings; a poet who found his vocation in politics; a Christian consumed by his need for recognition; a lonely man who thought he understood mankind; a practical man who became fossilized in all too lofty dreams; a reasonable man full of turbulent passions. It is this paradoxical personality that I have tried to respect, . . . the irritating, moving grandeur of a self-willed man who played an immense role in history and whose importance has become extraordi-narily great in our own times, even though he failed so wretchedly. That is why his

From *Woodrow Wilson: A Life for Peace* by Jan W. Schulte-Nordholt, trans. and ed. Herbert Rowen (Berkeley: University of California Press, 1991). Reprinted by permission of The Regents of the Uni-versity of California Press.

life story is a dramatic tale, almost a Greek tragedy, with a catharsis at the end that still drains and raises our emotions. . . .

The outbreak of the war [in 1914] affected the president deeply. It shocked his sensitive nature. We read for example in a letter to [his assistant Edward] House in August: "I feel the burden of the thing almost intolerably from day to day." Two months later he wrote in the same vein but at greater length to Walter Page, the ambassador in London:

> The whole thing is vivid in my mind, painfully vivid, and has been almost ever since the struggle began. I think my thought and imagination contain the picture and perceive its significance from every point of view. I have to force myself not to dwell upon it to avoid the sort of numbness that comes from deep apprehension and dwelling upon elements too vast to be yet comprehended or in any way controlled by counsel.

Here we see once again in Wilson the tension between feeling and detachment.

This only emphasizes the importance of the question of how neutral he really was or wanted to be. His first personal reactions were emotionally favorable to the Allies. He was, after all, imbued with English values and ideals. The French ambassador to Washington, Jules Jusserand, wondered what "the great doctrinaire" in the White House was thinking, but the president soon gave his answer, as it were, to the English ambassador, Sir Cecil Spring-Rice. Spring-Rice informed Sir Edward Grey, the English foreign secretary, that Wilson had admitted to him that everything he held dear was now at stake. The president, he added, spoke with deep emotion. The ambassador, who knew the man he was dealing with, quoted a few lines from Wordsworth's sonnets about English freedom written during the Napoleonic wars. He knew them by heart, Wilson said with tears in his eyes. (Spring-Rice, as it happened, was also playing up to Grey, who, like Wilson, was passionately fond of Wordsworth.)

In his personal feelings Wilson was not in the slightest neutral. House heard him inveigh against everything German—government and people and what he called abstract German philosophy, which lacked spirituality! But he was quite able to separate his personal opinions and his official duties. In the first place, he understood that neutrality was necessary, that the American people were totally set against intervention. But he was also moved by the great goal that he had glimpsed since the beginning of the war, a possibility that fitted his character like a glove. It makes its appearance in his call for neutrality, for he did not merely issue a scrupulously formal official declaration, as any other president would have done. He did more, accompanying this declaration with a personal call to the people to remain truly neutral in thought and words. America, he reminded them, was composed of many peoples and too great sympathy for one or the other side could bring division among them.

Unity was even more necessary for another reason as well. This was the grand ideal that he now made public officially for the first time and which henceforth would inspire him and more and more involve him in international complications. America, he announced, was chosen to mediate, as only America could, just because it was neutral. He spoke in an exalted, religious tone, as he liked to do on so many other occasions. It was as if the war at last made possible things that all his life he had dreamed of—his country as the model and the very leader of the whole world, and himself called and chosen as the leader of his country and the maker of the future. . . .

One thing led to another. The arms shipments [to the Allies] led to loans. [William Jennings] Bryan, the pacifist-minded secretary of state, doubted that this flow of funds, which went almost entirely to the Entente, was really neutral. In good biblical fashion, he saw money as the root of all evil. Was it not written in Scripture that where one's treasure was, one's heart was too? He was able to convince Wilson that steps had to be taken against these loans, and American bankers were therefore warned on August 15, 1914, that such credits were "inconsistent with the true spirit of neutrality." But such a splendid position could not be maintained in the long run. Arms deliveries continued to grow, and the American economy could not do without them. In the spring of 1915 Bryan's idealistic approach was abandoned and one loan after another was floated in the United States. When America entered the war in 1917, the loans to the Allies had risen to more than two billion dollars, while those to the Central Powers amounted to no more than $27,000,000. . . .

War brings all international agreements into question, for war is unpredictable and full of surprises, always different from what anyone could have imagined. This was never so painfully evident as in the question of submarine warfare, since submarines were a weapon without equal, but operated effectively only by surprise. A multitude of notes discussed and debated the question of their surprise attacks. What was the status of the fine agreements about merchant ships in wartime? The answer was clear: a warship might halt, search, seize, and even sink a merchantman, but only after prior warning and giving civilian travelers the opportunity to leave safely. But a submarine that adhered to such rules would of course become defenseless and useless.

When the war broke out, German ships were swept off the seas, Germany was blockaded, and the Germans desperately turned to the submarine as a means of breaking the Allied stranglehold. The initial successes of the U-boats in the autumn of 1914 brought a sudden resurgence of hope, and the German military command slowly realized what a powerful weapon it had in its hands. On February 4, 1915, the German government published an official declaration putting a blockade around the British islands: in a zone around Great Britain, all enemy ships, including merchant vessels, would be attacked without warning. Neutral ships were advised to avoid these regions, since the Allied ships could always be disguised with neutral flags. . . .

The submarine weapon made it much more difficult for the United States, like all nonbelligerents, to remain neutral. Neutrality became a dilemma as never before. Was it neutral to waive fundamental rights of free navigation? Wasn't this itself a serious breach of international law, a grave derogation of morality in a world where morality seemed more and more on the wane?

Wilson, a man of principle, protested but in so doing he reduced his chances for mediation. A sharp note was sent to Berlin, declaring that the policy set forth in the German note was "so unprecedented in naval warfare that this Government is reluctant to believe that the Imperial Government of Germany in this case contemplates it as possible." The American government would hold the German government fully responsible for the consequences. This seemed like plain talk, but what would happen if American rights were really challenged could not be foreseen. It was nonetheless probable that once such a stand on principle was taken, a conflict would result. . . .

Wherever the inspiration for the phrase ["peace without victory"] came from, the address that the president made to the Senate on January 22 [1917] was genuine

Wilson from beginning to end. It was a plea, splendid, grandiose, and vague, for America's involvement in a future world order. That order—an organization of the peoples with its own force—had to come, he said. The question was, what kind of force? This was and remained the point of difficulty. For Wilson, the moralist who knew that without human inspiration and dedication the finest promises are empty, had in mind a "force" that was greater than the force of any country or alliance, which was "the organized major force of mankind." The nations must come to an agreement and then the old system of the "balance of power" would give way to a "community of power." And that could happen only if there was true reconciliation, upon the basis of a "peace without victory," a peace among equals.

That did not bring pleasure to everyone's ears, he realized. But he had to say it, for his intention was "only to face realities and to face them without soft conceal-ments." Dreamers want so much to be taken for realists! . . .

. . . He spoke in the name of the United States of America, the unique and superior country, as he himself liked to call it, forward-looking and in the lead in the service of mankind. All liberal-thinking people everywhere, in Europe and in America, rejoiced at his words. But conservatives (must we call them the realists?) on both sides of the ocean shook their heads over such empty phrases. Among the first of these, as we know, were persons in Wilson's own backyard, his closest ad-visers. [Secretary of State Robert] Lansing had warned against the term "peace without victory." What did it really mean? And, most of all, how would these words be taken in the Allied countries? But, Lansing tells us, Wilson did not want to listen. "I did not argue the matter, especially as I knew his fondness for phrase-making and was sure that it would be useless to attempt to dissuade him." . . .

As was to be expected, [Senator Henry Cabot] Lodge surpassed all the others in his hostility to Wilson. In an angry speech to the Senate he wielded the full resources of his logic to tear apart the arguments of his enemy. What did it mean to say that America had no interest in the peace terms but only in the peace? How can men be required to wage war not to win, so that all their sacrifices were in vain, "a criminal and hideous futility"? . . . How could the "organized major force of mankind" be ap-plied? Voluntarily, or automatically, or compulsorily? When the idea of a league was broached two years earlier, he had been greatly attracted to it, but the more he thought about it, the more problems he saw. It could not be made effective by "high-sounding phrases, which fall so agreeably upon the ear, when there is no thought behind it." Does it mean that the small nations can, by majority vote, involve the large nations in war? "Are we prepared to commit ourselves to a purely general proposition without knowing where we are going or what is to be demanded of us, except that we shall be compelled to furnish our quota of military and naval forces to the service of a league in which we shall have but one voice?" A league for peace meant readiness to wage war against any country that did not obey its decisions. What if it decided that Japan and China should have the right of migration any-where, and Canada, Australia, and New Zealand declined to accept the decision? Or California, for that matter?

The points made by Lodge were fundamental, which is why I present them at such length. Already at this time, in January 1917, the lines of division were drawn which would define the great debate and the great tragedy of 1919. On one side stood the idealist, on the other the realist, and on both sides more than personal ani-mosity was involved. Furthermore, a political alliance was beginning to take shape that slackened during the war years but operated with full force in 1919; it brought together the Republican isolationists from the West, who were also idealists, for the most part from the Progressive camp, and the Republican internationalist realists, [Senator William] Borah on the one side and Lodge on the other. It was an alliance that would bring disaster to Wilson, but in 1917 he could not foresee that. . . .

Wilson shrank from taking the final step [after the German decision in late January 1917 to launch unrestricted submarine warfare], not out of fear, not out of unsullied pacifism, but because his whole conception of mediating between the belligerents (and thereby saving white civilization) would be shattered. This was the principal reason for his hesitation. And so he talked during these weeks in almost pacifist terms about war and imperialism, spoke out in anger against the support for war from right-wing circles, which he described as "Junkerthum trying to creep in under the cover of the patriotic feeling of the moment." . . .

[The journalist] Walter Lippmann, who looked at him with cool rationality and was among those bitterly disappointed with him after 1919, draws for us nonetheless a portrait of Wilson in his book *Men of Destiny,* showing the orator of light learning about darkness. He gazed in March 1917, says Lippmann, "in the bottomless pit." He was "an anguished prophet," full of compassion and doubt, a man who experienced the tragedy of his time and therefore was able, with overwrought absoluteness, to see the league of nations as the only justification of his action.

With this as his justification he went into the war, not out of economic interest, not because of the violation of the neutral rights of the United States, although these played a part, but in order to bring about genuine peace. Only if America took part could it have a voice in the peace. Mediation through participation would be more effective than neutrality, he now believed. To a delegation of pacifists led by Jane Addams, he said on February 28 that "as head of a nation participating in the war, the President of the United States would have a seat at the Peace Table, but that if he remained the representative of a neutral country he could at best only 'call through a crack in the door.'" Personal ambition and general interest concurred in what we may call a mission. The man and his times seemed to fit each other like the two halves of a piece of fruit. . . .

Of all the impressive sermons that Wilson preached to his people and to the world, none became so famous as his "Fourteen Points" speech of January 8, 1918. It attained a breadth and depth, in space and in time, greater than that of all the others. Not that it is his finest address; there are others, such as the "peace without victory" speech of a year earlier and the declaration of war of April 1917, which are more splendid in rhetoric and wider in vision. But this time Wilson was more practical, adding as it were deed to words; he developed a practical program that was of importance for the whole world. . . .

All in all, the Fourteen Points seemed practical and responsible. How lightly they skipped over historical problems would only become evident in Paris. But there was also a fourteenth point, a panacea for all the shortcomings now and later, a League of Nations: "A special association of nations must be formed under specific covenants for the purpose of affording mutual guarantees of political independence and territorial integrity to great and small states alike." This short sentence carried a heavy burden, too heavy as it turned out. In these few words the future world peace was settled, totally and permanently. For Wilson everything revolved around it; he did not see the difficulties and he did not want to see them, and this would in the end bring his downfall. . . .

In general Wilson's principles more and more broke loose from reality and lived their own lives. Self-determination was one such principle. During the war it became one of the major foundations of Wilson's new world order. We shall never subject another people, he had said back in 1915, "because we believe, we passionately believe, in the right of every people to choose their own allegiance and be free of masters altogether."

Only very slowly, as the reality of Europe began to come closer, did he discover the dangerous consequences of the principle. In the discussion with Spring-Rice on January 3 . . . , he wondered whether it was in fact possible to apply it consistently. The example of the threatening dismemberment of Austria-Hungary was probably in his thoughts when he said: "Pushed to its extreme, the principle would mean the disruption of existing governments to an undefinable extent. Logic was a good and powerful thing but apart from the consideration of existing circumstances might well lead to very dangerous results." The Englishman must have heard this with satisfaction, for the British Empire was not about to grant self-determination to all its peoples.

Later, in Paris, many began to realize the difficulties and dangers in this splendid principle. Lansing hit the nail on the head in a confidential memorandum, in which he wondered what self-determination would mean for the Irish, Indians, Egyptians, and South African Boers. What would happen with the Muslims in Syria and Palestine, and how did that fit in with the idea of Zionism, to which Wilson was very sympathetic. "The phrase is simply loaded with dynamite. It will raise hopes which can never be realized." It was the dream of an idealist, he said, and it is clear whom Lansing really had in mind.

As Wilson himself came to see, he had to be very cautious in Paris when trying to put his great principles into practice. He acknowledged that when he had first spoken of self-determination he had not realized that there were so many peoples who would claim it as their right. . . .

Wilson did not underestimate the devastation in Europe, but he retained his nineteenth-century American optimism. His whole existence was tied up with it; he could not live without hope. He clung to the idea of a grand radical cure, to a mystical faith in the mankind of the future, who were purified by events and repented. He had to represent that mankind; he had to make a new peace.

That is why he had to go to Paris [after the German surrender in late 1918]. . . . He was overwhelmed by his mission. His Czech colleague Thomas Masaryk, who understood him well ("now, we were both professors") warned him about the European statesmen: "But he wouldn't listen, for he was too filled with his plan for a League of Nations to take obstacles into account." . . .

Wilson's triumphal tour of Europe took him from Paris to London and then to Rome. Everywhere he was greeted as a savior, as the "Redeemer of Humanity" (*Redentore dell' Humanità*) and "God of Peace" (*Dio di Pace*), in the words of the Italian banners. He spent weeks indulging in this pomp and circumstance, immersed in a sea of flags and songs, carried along by beautiful words that promised so much for the future. Justice! Peace! When we hear Wilson speak in these first weeks, everything is radiant. Sometimes a harsh sound breaks through, as when he replies to [Raymond] Poincaré, the president of France, who wants no reconciliation with the foe, that there exist "eternal principles of right and justice" which bring with them "the certainty of just punishment." But for the most part his outlook is peaceful. He speaks of the peoples who form "the organized moral force of men throughout the world," of the tide of good will: "There is a great tide running in the hearts of men. The hearts of men have never beaten so singularly in unison before. Men have never been so conscious of this brotherhood." . . .

. . . Alas, there was in fact no moral tide that carried all with it. There was rather a divided Europe in which the peoples were driven at least as much by muddled feelings of rage and revenge as by lofty thoughts of right and reason. Wilson himself had experienced the impact of such vindictiveness during the off-year elections in the United States, and it was at least as prevalent in Europe. [French premier Georges] Clemenceau told the Chamber of Deputies at the end of December that he disagreed with Wilson, although he had, he said, the greatest admiration for the American president's "noble candor" (which was changed in the parliamentary journal to "noble grandeur"); he thereupon won a vote of confidence by a majority of 380 to 134. [British prime minister David] Lloyd George triumphed equally convincingly in elections for the House of Commons just before Christmas. His coalition of Liberals and Tories, in which the latter were dominant, ran on an electoral program of hate and revenge against Germany with slogans like "Hang the Kaiser" and "Make Germany Pay," [and] received no less than 526 of the 707 seats. It was not Lloyd George himself but the navy minister Sir Eric Geddes who uttered the notorious words, "We shall squeeze the German lemons until the pips squeak."

Wilson's moral majority therefore existed only in his poetic imagination. He was totally out of touch with reality. The Europeans did not know what to make of his fine words. They asked themselves whether he actually meant what he said. "I am one of the few people who think him honest," said Lloyd George to his friends. But he too was exasperated when the president blew his own horn loudly and gave no sign that he understood the sacrifices England had made: "Not a word of generous appreciation issued from his lips." Wilson, the American, could not establish an accepted character and place in Europe. The Europeans thought he was American, with his smooth, streamlined face, showing no emotion behind his shining glasses. . . .

In a word, the European leaders did not like Woodrow Wilson. From the start there was tension between them. Clemenceau, an old hand in politics, was not the man to come under the influence of Wilson's lofty words. He knew the United States; he had lived there just after the Civil War, spoke English well, and had married an American woman. He had no high opinion of American idealism, as was evident in the witticisms he made at Wilson's expense. God had needed only ten commandments, but Wilson fourteen, he jibed. . . . And, in reaction to the "peace without victory" speech, he wrote: "Never before has any political assembly heard so fine a sermon on what human beings might be capable of accomplishing if only they weren't human." In brief, this was classic realism confronting classic idealism. . . .

Wilson believed in his League of Nations as a remedy for all troubles, a miraculous cure that would work precisely because it was so entwined with the peace treaty itself. The treaty might not be perfect, he said in April, but with the League of Nations as an integral part of the treaty, there was a mechanism to improve its operation.

But actually it worked the other way around, a fact that Wilson completely missed. The delegates of the Allied countries exploited his League of Nations proposal to extract concessions from him; the peace turned out very badly because he repeatedly made compromises in order to save his beloved plan, carrying it through the bustling debates to safe harbor. . . . "The fact is," wrote the deeply disappointed [diplomat Henry] White in May, "that the League of Nations, in which he had been more deeply interested than anything else from the beginning, believing it to be the best if not the only means of avoiding war in the future, has been played to the limit by France and Japan in extracting concessions from him; to a certain extent by the British too, and the Treaty as it stands is the result." . . .

The history of the Versailles peace has called forth a welter of difficult questions. Was it too harsh, a *Diktatfrieden* that automatically elicited a reaction of revanche? Or was it, on the contrary, too mild a settlement, enabling the old forces in Germany to continue? In any case, is there a direct causal link between 1919 and 1933? Does the guilt for the disastrous consequences lie with the men who, in Paris, laid down the rules for the future? These are all questions that in their nature cannot be given a conclusive or logically satisfactory answer. But they are also questions that cannot be evaded. If this peace were not accepted, Wilson said many times on his swing through the West in the fall, there would be another war in twenty years. . . .

How horribly right he proved to be! What he predicted came about just as he said. But was he himself guiltless? Hadn't he written the whole scenario for that future? The defeat [of Germany] was a humiliation, not intended as such by him in his noble naïveté, but nonetheless felt as such by the vanquished. Humiliation led to dreams of revenge; the seeds of a new war were put into the soil. Of course, they would only grow when the climate was favorable, when events, primarily the Great Depression that began in 1929, permitted. But beyond question the seeds were planted by the peace of Versailles. . . .

Historians, in their quest for consistency, have to fit Wilson into some pattern, if need be, one that takes time into account. This provides a way out: in the long run, in the future (but with what a frightful intermezzo!), Wilson would be right. This is the way Arthur Link, Wilson's outstanding biographer, approaches the question. For him, Wilson's vision might seem foolish at first sight, because it clashed with reality, but there is in fact a "higher realism." This adds a wider dimension to the problem of Wilson; his deeds then must be judged within the perspective of the future. In it his deeds accord with his words; if they were failures in the short run, all is reconciled in the perspective of a better future. It is a quite Wilsonian idea, paralleling the way Wilson himself saw the League of Nations as the panacea for all temporary compromises.

But is it possible to separate today and tomorrow from each other in this way? Is this how the relationship between realism and idealism actually works? What is the value of a prophet in politics? These are the questions we constantly encounter. There is a deep tragedy within them. Let me repeat: Wilson himself saw and warned that if there was not a just peace, there would be war again in twenty years. Does it follow from this that he personally shared in the responsibility for the horrors that would break out two decades later? Link's reply is that he did not. At Versailles there was the familiar tension between the ideal and reality, but it is inherent in all human striving. One can only ask why Wilson failed. There are more than enough reasons. After the armistice he had no means to compel France and England; he had been weakened in his own country by the elections; he had formidable opponents in Clemenceau, Lloyd George, [Italian prime minister] Orlando, and [Italian foreign minister Sidney] Sonnino; his ideal of "open covenants" was frustrated. And yet, Link maintains, he gained a reasonable peace that worked and created a new international order. He snaps at the critics:

> It is time to stop perpetuating the myth that the Paris settlement made inevitable the rise to power of Mussolini, the Japanese militarists, and Hitler, and hence the Second World War. That war was primarily the result of the Great Depression.

All the same, questions persist. If the war that came in twenty years was not the consequence of a bad peace, or if it wasn't such a bad peace after all, was Wilson's forecast just a stab in the dark? But then why reproach the others who opposed him?

Wilson as Father and Foreteller of a New World Order

TONY SMITH

Although American efforts to promote democracy abroad have often focused on a single country (as in the case of the Philippines or the Dominican Republic . . .), the presidency of Woodrow Wilson had far more ambitious objectives. His policy toward Latin America had been regional in scope, but with the entry of the United States into war against Germany in 1917, his horizon expanded to Europe, and Wilson stepped forward with specific proposals for a global system of peace and security.

Wilson's recommendations marked the first time that the United States had elaborated a framework for world order. It proposed that governments recognize each other's legitimacy when they were constitutional democracies, and that they should maintain the peace through a system of collective military security and liberal economic exchange. Envisioned as a comprehensive framework for world order, Wilson's program constituted the foundation of what afterward could be called American liberal democratic internationalism or, more simply, Wilsonianism.

Wilson's liberal democratic internationalism was not a radical departure from traditional American national security policy. Thomas Jefferson had insisted that the United States could only participate in a world community dominated by democratic states. With the Monroe Doctrine in 1823, the United States had declared itself opposed to the reimposition of European rule in the Western Hemisphere and so aligned itself with nationalist forces in Latin America, whose states Washington would recognize as sovereign. With the Open Door Notes of the turn of the century, Washington reaffirmed its commitment (as old as the Revolution) to a nondiscriminatory international trading system, hostile to mercantilism and imperialism alike (a position used again in the 1930s, especially to protest Japanese incursions on Chinese sovereignty). While Wilson's proposals to restructure world politics were far more bold than any American leader had ever before laid out, they were

Tony Smith, *America's Mission: The United States and the Worldwide Struggle for Democracy in the Twentieth Century* (Princeton, N.J.: Princeton University Press, 1994), 84–93, 95–97, 102–109. Reprinted by permission of Princeton University Press.

nonetheless quite in line with basic propositions of United States foreign policy set long before his time.

Today we can appreciate more clearly than was possible in 1917–9 the enormous stakes involved by the entry of the United States on the central stage of world history under Wilson's leadership. Nationalism, which had begun to affect world politics in the late eighteenth century with the French Revolution, was now a global force, fueling not only the animosities of World War I but also the breakup of the Russian, Ottoman, and Austro-Hungarian empires thereafter. New states were emerging, struggling to achieve support from their populations through mass based political parties. With the victory of the Russian Revolution in 1917, communism offered itself as an ideology of state building and nationalist consciousness at the very moment Wilson was proposing liberal democracy to the same end. In short order, Mussolini and Hitler would offer yet a third modern alternative with fascism.

Wilson was not fully aware of the magnitude of his undertaking, of course. Like Lincoln during the Civil War, Wilson could only sense that the struggle he was engaged in concerned more than the traditional ends of state policy, and that the character of the peace to be established after the war would be critical to world affairs in a more lasting way than victory in battle often entailed. His reaction to the Bolshevik Revolution was hesitant, and he had left office before fascism took power in Italy. Nonetheless, in his ambitious initiatives of 1917–9, Wilson laid the groundwork for many of the fundamental tenets of American national security policy for the rest of the twentieth century: that nationalism should be respected as one of the most powerful political sentiments of our times; that democracy is the most peace-loving and only legitimate form of modern government, and that the United States has a self-interested as well as a moral obligation to further its prospects abroad; that democracy and capitalism are mutually reinforcing systems of collective action so long as large accumulations of wealth do not control the political process; that in a world destined to be composed of many states, the need for mutual understanding and common purpose calls for a new respect for international law sustained by multilateral institutional arrangements; that a nondiscriminatory world economic system that is antiprotectionist and antimercantilist promotes general prosperity and peace; and that a global system of collective security is necessary to stop aggression. . . .

Wilsonianism in Theory

The essential genius of Wilson's proposals for a new world order after World War I was that it had a vision of the proper ordering of domestic as well as international politics that was well suited to the development of political and economic forces worldwide in the twentieth century. Here was a period in Germany, Russia, and Eastern Europe where social forces were struggling over the modernization of the state, where rival conceptions of national unity were trying to make government responsive through party government to nationalistic appeals for popular sovereignty. In domestic terms, Wilson respected the power of nationalism and favored national self-determination. States were presumed to be legitimate when they were democratically constituted, and it was expected that in most instances ethnic boundaries would make for the frontiers of countries. In the context of the world of

1918, such a proposal was radical; it accepted the dismemberment of empires (those of Austria-Hungary, Russia, and Turkey immediately; those of the Western European powers by implication thereafter), and it worked for the replacement of autocracies with democracies in Germany and the new nation-states to the East.

For international relations, Wilson called for a liberal economic regime and a system of collective security designed to preserve the peace. Again, his initiative was radical for it challenged the competitive mercantilistic practices that dictated much of world commerce with a more open trading system, just as it proposed to replace competitive balance of power thinking politically with what he called "a covenant of cooperative peace."

In short, the foundation of Wilson's order was the democratic nation-state; its superstructure was an international order of economic, military, and moral interdependence. Nationalism wed to democracy; democracies wed in peace, prosperity, and mutual respect embodied in international law and institutions: such was Wilson's essential vision, a form of liberalism he felt to be both necessary and appropriate for his era and essential to guarantee American national security. . . .

. . . As he declared in a celebrated address to the American Congress in January 1917:

> No peace can last, or ought to last, which does not recognize and accept the principle that governments derive all their just powers from the consent of the governed, and that no right anywhere exists to hand peoples about from sovereignty to sovereignty as if they were property. I take it for granted . . . that statesmen everywhere are agreed that there should be a united, independent, and autonomous Poland, and that henceforth inviolable security of life, or worship, and of industrial and social development should be guaranteed to all peoples who have lived hitherto under the power of government devoted to a faith and purpose hostile to their own. . . . I would fain believe that I am speaking for the silent mass of mankind everywhere who have as yet had no place or opportunity to speak their real hearts out . . . no nation should seek to extend its polity over any other nation or people, but every people should be left free to determine its own polity, its own way of development, unhindered, unthreatened, unafraid, the little along with the great and powerful.

As these lines suggest, Wilson was a friend to nationalism everywhere. He endorsed the Balfour Declaration, promising the Jewish people a place in Palestine. He was sympathetic to the needs of the Armenians (and deliberated whether the United States should exercise a mandate over this people). He gave repeated assurances to the Germans that, once their autocratic leaders were deposed, their national integrity would be respected. Czechoslovak patriots quoted Wilson's words of 1898 as their organizing slogan in the United States during World War I: "No lapse of time, no defeat of hopes, seemed sufficient to reconcile the Czechs of Bohemia to incorporation with Austria. Pride of race and the memories of a notable and distinguished history kept them always at odds with the Germans at their gate and the government over their heads." As the president put it in 1919, "self-determination is not a mere phrase. It is an imperative principle of action, which statesmen will henceforth ignore at their peril." . . .

Wilson's faith in popular sovereignty made him the enemy of monarchical rule. In the case of Germany, Wilson repeatedly distinguished between the German people and their government. As he put it to the Congress in his request for a declaration of war:

We have no quarrel with the German people. We have no feeling toward them but one of sympathy and friendship. It was not upon their impulse that their government acted in entering this war. It was not with their previous knowledge or approval. It was a war determined upon as wars used to be determined upon in the old, unhappy days when peoples were nowhere consulted by their rulers and wars were provoked and waged in the interest of dynasties or of little groups of ambitious men who were accustomed to use their fellow men as pawns and tools. . . .

Similarly, Wilson welcomed "the wonderful and heartening things" that transpired in Russia during March, 1917, when the Czar was forced to abdicate to republican forces:

Russia was known by those who knew it best to have been always in fact democratic at heart, in all the vital habits of her thought, in all the intimate relationships of her people that spoke their natural instinct, their habitual attitude toward life. The autocracy that crowned the summit of her political structure, long as it had stood and terrible as was the reality of its power, was not in fact Russian in origin, character or purpose; and now it has been shaken off and the great, generous Russian people have been added in all their naive majesty and might to the forces that are fighting for freedom in the world, for justice, and for peace. . . .

In these politically polarized circumstances, Wilson preached the doctrine of the liberal democratic alternative to reaction and to revolution, a third way forward, which called for clear resolve. In some measure, Wilson understood the full scope of his enormous ambition: "The conservatives do not realize what forces are loose in the world at the present time," he observed in January 1919. "Liberalism is the only thing that can save civilization from chaos. . . . Liberalism must be more liberal than ever before, it must even be radical, if civilization is to escape the typhoon."

Liberalism: here was the touchstone on which Wilson based his hopes for a new order of world peace. Following in the footsteps of British and American liberals before him, Wilson viewed himself as a cosmopolitan as well as an American, a man able to understand and respect the interests of others and to look forward to a structure of world order that would permit nations to work together cooperatively in a system where the self-interest of each would be realized in terms of the common interest of all. Nationalism and democracy were not enough. Only international economic and political cooperation could preserve the peace. "Unless all the right-thinking nations of the world are going to concert their purpose and their power, this treaty is not worth the paper it is written on," he warned in 1919, "because it is a treaty where peace rests upon the right of the weak, and only the power of the strong can maintain the right of the weak." . . .

Given these liberal assumptions, Wilson opposed German mercantilist principles, which implied the necessity of political control over foreign peoples for the advancement of German industry. Speaking before the American Federation of Labor in November 1917, Wilson praised the German success: "The whole world stood at admiration of her wonderful intellectual and material achievements. . . . She had access to all the markets of the world. . . . She had a 'place in the sun.'" But given the structure and attitudes of German business, the president continued, "the authorities of Germany were not satisfied." . . . The point is worth emphasizing, for it would reappear in American conduct toward Germany after 1945: German capitalists were to be obliged to see the world from a liberal Open Door perspective, not from a mercantilist point of view, which implied the necessity of political control over foreign peoples for the advancement of German industry.

Wilson was also outspoken in his distrust of unregulated American trusts. Politics, not economics, should command. Sounding every bit the Progressive, Wilson warned: "Men who are behind any interest always unite in organization, and the danger in every country is that these special interests will be the only things organized, and that the common interest will be unorganized against them. The business of government is to organize the common interest against the special interest." The same logic applied abroad. He broke with Taft's dollar diplomacy, forced American banks out of China, and resisted loans to Latin America, which he felt might compromise national sovereignties in the region. Similarly, writing of the Russian Revolution toward the end of his life, Wilson remarked "that great and widespread reaction like that which is now unquestionably manifesting itself against capitalism do not occur without cause or provocation":

> . . . before we commit ourselves irreconcilably to an attitude of hostility to this movement of the time, we ought frankly to put ourselves the question: Is the capitalistic system unimpeachable? . . . Have capitalists generally used their power for the benefit of the countries in which their capital is employed and for the benefit of their fellow men? Is it not, on the contrary, too true that capitalist[s] have often seemed to regard the men whom they used as mere instruments of profit? . . . if these offenses against high morality and true citizenship have been frequently observable, are we to say that the blame for the present discontent and turbulence is wholly on the side of those who are in revolt against them? . . .

. . . But Wilson's primary concerns were political. . . .

What mattered far more to Wilson, and where his thinking was more original, was in his ambition to build a liberal collective security system centered on Europe after 1918, an idea that was embodied in the League of Nations. As Wilson accurately perceived, the prospects for the survival of the young democracies of Eastern Europe he was working so hard to establish would be greatly enhanced if they could have cooperative relations with a fully democratized Germany and with the more established democracies of Western Europe and the United States in the League. . . .

Wilsonianism in Practice

Nationalism, democracy, a liberal world economic order, a system of collective security, a moral commitment to leadership in such an arrangement on the part of the United States: this was the Wilsonian project of liberalism for world order after 1918. In the interwar years these ambitions came to naught. No way was found to integrate the Soviet Union, born of that war, into the European balance of power, while the threat of communism domestically put a heavy strain on democratic forces throughout the continent. Except in Czechoslovakia, democracy was unable to find fertile soil in Eastern Europe, where a zone of weak states looked with fear alternatively at Berlin and Moscow. After 1929, a weakly structured system of international trade and finance buckled under the weight of the Depression. After fourteen years of effort, democracy collapsed in Germany in 1933 with the rise of Hitler. Democratic forces in France and Britain lost their self-confidence. The United States refused to join the League of Nations and lapsed again into isolationism. . . .

. . . [I]solationism was the regrettable but not surprising result of a style of leadership that was too abstract and too moralistic to anticipate the difficulties of implementing such a visionary policy. This was the essential charge of influential commentators at the time, such as John Maynard Keynes, Harold Nicolson, and Walter Lippmann, all devoted Wilsonians in 1918, who were sorely disappointed by the peace settlement. Keynes's indictment is the most trenchant and famous ever made of Wilson. Under the pressure of quicker, sharper men in Paris who fought for national interests only (especially French Prime Minister Georges Clemenceau), Wilson lost his balance, so Keynes maintained, and permitted a "Carthaginian Peace: . . . if ever the action of a single individual matters, the collapse of the President has been one of the decisive moral events of history." . . .

Yet, suppose that Wilson had been in full possession of his faculties and had built a bipartisan consensus around his ideas. Would the world then have been made safe for democracy? To put the question of Wilsonianism in these terms is to shift the focus of analysis from the president and his program to the world in which it was to operate.

Circumstances in Europe created four major categories of objective difficulties for Wilson's plans: the character of Allied (and especially French) demands for the postwar settlement; the impact of the Bolshevik Revolution on class tensions in Europe (even more than on relations among states); the prospects for democracy over the medium term in Germany; the situation politically in Eastern Europe, a largely agrarian region with ethnically mixed peoples. . . .

To recapitulate: Wilson's effort to create a liberal democratic alternative to the forces of reaction and revolution foundered not so much on his style of leadership as on the social and political reality he faced in Europe. No observation about Eastern Europe could have been more mistaken than that of Thomas Masaryk, saying the war had left the region "a laboratory atop a vast cemetery." Despite the upheavals of the war, Europe was not a tabula rasa, but a continent of social and political forces and in fierce contention. Hence, Wilson's project was thwarted by a French determination to be done with the German menace, by the Bolshevik Revolution, by splits on the left and the resurgence of the right in Germany, by the agrarian social structures of Eastern Europe with class and ethnic antagonisms of great intensity, and by an American nationalist opinion reluctant to see its national security involved in dangerous new foreign entanglements. . . .

Was there a better guide than Wilsonianism as to how America should defend its legitimate concerns in the founding of a stable European order friendly to this country's interests? Between 1940 and the early 1950s, the most influential thinkers in this country on the proper conduct of American foreign policy—Walter Lippmann, George Kennan, Hans Morgenthau, and Reinhold Niebuhr—took special pains to use Wilson as a negative example, a textbook study of how foreign policy should not be formulated. For these analysts, Wilsonianism stands for the American penchant to conduct its foreign conduct by moralizing about it, by assuming that somehow democracy is a panacea for the world's problems. In their eyes, liberal democratic internationalism betrays a vein of naive and utopian idealism ill-fitted to effective participation in global politics. The affliction did not start with Wilson nor end with him, but his presidency marks its high-water point. Realism, the dominant school of international relations theory in the United States, was founded at this time by these men and built its concepts by consciously pitting itself against the basic tenets of Wilsonianism.

Thus, referring to the settlement of 1919, George Kennan wrote:

> This was the sort of peace you got when you allowed war hysteria and impractical idealism to lie down together in your mind, like the lion and the lamb; when you indulged yourself in the colossal conceit of thinking that you could suddenly make international life over into what you believed to be your own image; when you dismissed the past with contempt, rejected the relevance of the past to the future, and refused to occupy yourself with the real problems that a study of the past would suggest. . . .

How, then, should American foreign policy have been formulated? These writers consider themselves realists. They insist that the national interest should be determined rather strictly by calculations of the relative amount of power among states, with a view of preventing threats to the existence or independence of the United States. Seen from this perspective, the only obvious antagonist of the United States in world affairs at that time was Germany, which Washington should forthrightly have mobilized to contain. They have no patience with the "idealism" of a "utopian," "moralistic" crusade to change the character of international relations by making states democratic, such as Wilson advanced, for this talk only put a smokescreen over the essential matter of dealing with German power. . . .

In a word, the realists maintained that Wilson did not adequately appreciate the character of "power politics" or the "balance of power" in his deliberations, by which they meant the need to contain German power so that it would not dominate the continent, a turn of events that would have been seriously threatening to American national security. In Lippmann's view, for example, Wilson failed to explain to the American people why the country went to war: "The reasons he did give were legalistic and moralistic and idealistic reasons, rather than the substantial and vital reasons that the security of the United States demanded that no aggressively expanding imperial power, like Germany, should be allowed to gain the mastery of the Atlantic Ocean."

These charges ask for an indictment that the evidence does not warrant. Thus, Wilson was not a pacifist, and his proposals for disarmament are best understood as confidence-building measures among states, not as a reluctance to back commitments with force, as Lippmann suggested. Again, the League of Nations was not to have either financial or military resources independent of the states that participated in it, and its Council had to act by unanimous agreement; the League was not to be a world government. More, the call for self-determination was not intended as a blank check for secessionist movements. Wilson respected economic, strategic, and historical considerations that had to be weighed against nationalist feelings; it was only toward the end of the war that he finally resigned himself to the dismemberment of the Austro-Hungarian empire rather than to seeing it reconstituted as a democratic federalist structure.

But most importantly, Wilson intended the League to be the vehicle to bind the United States permanently to a management role in world affairs. Whatever the shortcomings of the details in his plan, American membership in the League might well have provided the check on Germany that Wilson's critics allege his naivete and moralizing prevented him from establishing. . . .

. . . But to suggest, as Walter Lippmann did, that the entire liberal peace program was actually little more than an exercise in fomenting the next war is to lay far more of a charge on Wilson's shoulders than is deserved. It is as if the impact on German politics of the Russian Revolution or the Depression of the 1930s were somehow of trivial importance given the blinders Wilson allegedly placed on liberals' appreciation of the German question. . . .

Nor do Wilson's critics—the unreconstructed advocates of balance of power thinking—demonstrate how they would have handled European affairs better. What reason is there to think that a Germany dismembered in 1919 might not have found a way to rise and avenge itself (perhaps in league with the Soviet Union)? Within a few years, the British were beginning to suspect France of hegemonic ambitions in Europe, while no way was found to work with the Soviet Union—tinder enough for another war, one might say, had Wilson's liberal peace program never been mooted. Would a world that denied the power of nationalism, spurned the appeals of democracy, been uninterested in liberal international economic practices, and made a recourse to arms the first duty of states been such an attractive alternative to Wilson's vision? In short, it is far from obvious that Clemenceau's formula for handling Germany was more farsighted than Wilson's. Wilsonianism may have been a failure after 1919, but the realists indicate no more realistic way to proceed.

Fail though it did at the time, the virtues of Wilson's policy for the postwar world were threefold. First, it acknowledged the fundamental political importance of nationalism, seeking to direct rather than to repress its energy. Second, it sought to channel the demands for popular sovereignty contained in nationalism in the direction of democratic government, and away from authoritarian or totalitarian regimes (though the latter—a particular curse of the twentieth century—was not yet clearly visible when Wilson was in office). Third, it attempted to provide a structure of international institutions and agreements to handle military and economic affairs among democratically constituted, capitalist states. In all of these respects, American national security thinking followed Wilson's lead after 1945. . . .

It is commonly observed that politics as an art requires pursuing the desirable in terms of the possible. The dilemma of leadership is to decide when it is weakness to fail to exploit the inevitable ambiguities, and therefore possibilities, of the historical moment, and when it is foolhardy to attempt to overcome immovable constraints set by a combination of forces past and present. Since options are always open to some extent, greatness requires creating opportunities and taking risks within the limits set by history.

While the constraints of history nullified Wilson's hopes, his efforts did not totally contradict the forces of his time. . . . In short, Wilson's gamble on the forces of democracy and collective security (which in practice would have been the balance of power under another name) was not totally unrealistic. And what were his other options? Indeed his greatness as a visionary comes from how close to success his program came. Suppose America had joined the League in good faith, an organization basically of his devising? By that single act, the course of history might have been changed, for it would have committed the United States to the maintenance of a European equilibrium containing Germany.

The best evidence of the power of Wilsonianism, however, comes from its resurgence in American foreign policy in the aftermath of World War II. Bretton

Woods, the initial plans for the United Nations, the hopes for Western Europe integration that lay behind the occupation of Germany and the Marshall Plan—all this was essentially Wilsonian in inspiration (even when operationalized by people like Keynes and Kennan who saw themselves as opponents of Wilson's position in Paris in 1919). . . .

Accordingly, when Czechoslovakia's President Vaclav Havel addressed an emotional joint meeting of Congress on February 21, 1990, the first American he mentioned was Woodrow Wilson, whose "great support" in 1918 for Czech and Slovak nationalists had meant that they "could found our modern independent state." . . . It was in recognition of Wilson's spirit—and not simply his actions—that during the interwar years so many boulevards, statues and parks in Rumania, Poland, Yugoslavia, and especially Czechoslovakia were named after him. In the aftermath of the most terrible war the world had seen, many of the peoples of Eastern Europe regarded Wilson as a liberator, indeed as a founding father of their new-born states.

Unlike most statesmen, then, Wilson deserves to be measured not on the basis of achieving the ends of his policy in their time, but by the magnitude of his efforts and the influence they continued to have in later years. Seen from the perspective of the mid-1990s, three-quarters of a century since he left office, Wilson's concern that nationalism abroad be turned in the direction of democratic government for the sake of the American national interest seems soundly conceived. Writing in 1889 on "Leaders of Men," Wilson had declared:

> Great reformers do not, indeed, observe time and circumstance. Theirs is not a service of opportunity. They have no thought for occasion, no capacity for compromise. They are early vehicles of the Spirit of the Age. They are born of the very times that oppose them. . . .Theirs to hear the inarticulate voices that stir in the night-watches, apprising the lonely sentinel of what the day will bring forth.

FURTHER READING

John Chambers III, *The Tyranny of Change: America in the Progressive Era, 1890–1920* (1992).
John Milton Cooper, Jr., *The Warrior and the Priest: Woodrow Wilson and Theodore Roosevelt* (1983).
Lloyd C. Gardner, *Safe for Democracy* (1984).
Barry Karl, *The Uneasy State: The United States from 1915–1945* (1983).
George F. Kennan, *American Diplomacy, 1900–1950* (1951).
David Kennedy, *Over Here: The First World War and American Society* (1980).
Thomas J. Knock, *To End All Wars: Woodrow Wilson and the Quest for a New World Order* (1992).
Arthur Link, *Woodrow Wilson: Revolution, War, and Peace* (1979).

Crossing a Cultural Divide:
The Twenties

The Nebraska-born novelist Willa Cather famously said of the 1920s that "the world broke in two in 1922 or thereabouts." In that decade, for the first time, more Americans lived in towns than on farms. Mass industrialization, higher wages, and the wide use of credit placed modern products like the car, the vacuum cleaner, and the washing machine at the disposal of millions. Science made new discoveries that appeared to challenge old truths. The vote for women became law in 1920, and though few women became politicians, millions became flappers. In six years, hemlines went from the ankle, where they had been for centuries, to the knee. Film, radio, and advertising came into the lives of everyday Americans, expressing and reshaping their desires and dreams, and reminding them constantly that they lived in a new era.

Cultural change provoked deep conflict over religion, sex, gender roles, and ethnicity. The decade that invented dating also coined the term fundamentalism. The rural vision of America seemed deeply at odds with the urban one, and myriad organizations formed to defend "white Anglo-Saxon Protestant" (WASP) traditions. One such organization was the revitalized Ku Klux Klan, which won legislative and executive elections throughout the Midwest and had nearly 3 million members by 1923. The most famous trial of the decade, the Scopes "monkey trial," epitomized the clash over modernism and the battle to hold the line against "Godless science." Ironically, Progressive icon William Jennings Bryan, leading the prosecution, appeared to stand against progress. Meanwhile, on a day-to-day level, the police struggled and failed to implement the crowning reform of the preceding decade, the prohibition of alcohol. The twenties became known instead for the willful flouting of Progressive-era moralizing: men drank, women smoked, and, worst of all, they did these things in one another's company. Youth culture became distinct from adult culture in this decade, and many young people were discernibly amused by the puritanical streak of the older generation.

The decade also witnessed the culmination of the buildup of xenophobic sentiment that had been going on since the turn of the century. Many Americans concluded that the best way to keep out foreign ideas was to keep out foreigners. In 1924, Congress passed a National Origins Act that was specifically designed to limit Catholic and Jewish immigration and abolish Asian immigration altogether. Proponents sought the triumph of "Nordic" (north European) whites and the

*Protestant religion. But the gates swung closed on a population that was already
enormously diverse in its religious beliefs and ethnic character, and whose face was
turned to the future. The modern era was under way.*

✦ QUESTIONS TO THINK ABOUT

Why was there a great debate in the 1920s about the future? Who won it, the modernists
or the fundamentalists? Would you characterize this period primarily as the Age of Jazz
or as the Age of Prohibition?

✦ DOCUMENTS

The documents in this chapter illustrate many aspects of the cultural changes that took
place in the 1920s. In Document 1, the governor of California decries the economic
competition of the Japanese and their shockingly high fertility. He articulates a commitment to ending Asian immigration that went from the citizenry to the highest levels of
government. Document 2 outlines the program of the Ku Klux Klan and reveals the
extent to which religion, race, and patriotism were inseparably intertwined in the KKK's
definition of "American." In Document 3, novelist Richard Wright recalls growing up in
the twenties, and the rampant hostility toward African Americans and Catholics. Document 4 shows the literary talent that brought Langston Hughes to fame in the Harlem
Renaissance, a cultural movement based in the African American neighborhood of New
York. His poetry expresses the sentiments that propelled African Americans like him and
Richard Wright out of the South on a "One-Way Ticket." Document 5 shows the famous
clash between attorney Clarence Darrow and William Jennings Bryan in the Scopes
"monkey trial." They spoke from opposite sides of the cultural divide noted by Willa
Cather. Former Secretary of State Bryan defended a literal interpretation of the Bible.
Darrow, retained by the American Civil Liberties Union, spoke for modern science.
In Document 6, Bruce Barton, a preacher's son, compliments Jesus as the ultimate
"Madison Avenue" huckster. This reading evokes the bloom of advertising and reveals
a modern sensibility toward the sacred that is quite at odds with the sentiments of
William Jennings Bryan. Document 7 is from a famous sociological study of Muncie,
Indiana (called Middletown), in the 1920s that showed how new mass products like the
automobile reshaped people's values. The changing morality of modern youth is scruti-
nized in Document 8, taken from a survey of high school students sponsored by business
executives in Michigan. The last selection (Document 9) is by F. Scott Fitzgerald, the
handsome, young novelist who epitomized for many the glamour of the Jazz Age. *The
Great Gatsby* reveals the flapper style at its height, the decline in female deference, and
the appeal of racist ideology to men whose world was changing faster than they liked.

1. The Governor of California Tells of the "Oriental Problem," 1920

The Japanese in our midst have indicated a strong trend to land ownership and land
control, and by their unquestioned industry and application, and by standards and
methods that are widely separated from our occidental standards and methods, both
in connection with hours of labor and standards of living, have gradually developed

---

California State Board of Control, *California and the Oriental* (Sacramento: State Printing Office, June
1920), 8–13.

to a control of many of our important agricultural industries. Indeed, at the present time they operate 458,056 acres of the very best lands in California. The increase in acreage control within the last decade, according to these official figures, has been 412.9 per cent. In productive values—that is to say, in the market value of crops produced by them—our figures show that as against $6,235,856 worth of produce marketed in 1909, the increase has been to $67,145,730 approximately tenfold.

More significant than these figures, however, is the demonstrated fact that within the last ten years Japanese agricultural labor has developed to such a degree that at the present time between 80 and 90 per cent of most of our vegetable and berry products are those of the Japanese farms. Approximately 80 per cent of the tomato crop of the state is produced by Japanese; from 80 to 100 per cent of the spinach crop; a greater part of our potato and asparagus crops, and so on. So that it is apparent without much more effective restrictions that in a very short time, historically speaking, the Japanese population within our midst will represent a considerable portion of our entire population, and the Japanese control over certain essential food products will be an absolute one. . . .

These Japanese, by very reason of their use of economic standards impossible to our white ideals—that is to say, the employment of their wives and their very children in the arduous toil of the soil—are proving crushing competitors to our white rural populations. The fecundity of the Japanese race far exceeds that of any other people that we have in our midst. They send their children for short periods of time to our white schools, and in many of the country schools of our state the spectacle is presented of having a few white children acquiring their education in classrooms crowded with Japanese. The deep-seated and often outspoken resentment of our white mothers at this situation can only be appreciated by those people who have struggled with similar problems.

It is with great pride that I am able to state that the people of California have borne this situation and seen its developing menace with a patience and self-restraint beyond all praise. California is proud to proclaim to the nation that despite this social situation her people have been guilty of no excesses and no indignities upon the Japanese within our borders. No outrage, no violence, no insult and no ignominy have been offered to the Japanese people within California. . . .

But with all this the people of California are determined to repress a developing Japanese community within our midst. They are determined to exhaust every power in keeping to maintain this state for its own people. This determination is based fundamentally upon the ethnological impossibility of assimilating the Japanese people and the consequential alternative of increasing a population whose very race isolation must be fraught with the gravest consequences.

2. The Ku Klux Klan Defines Americanism, 1926

The Klan . . . has now come to speak for the great mass of Americans of the old pioneer stock. We believe that it does fairly and faithfully represent them, and our proof lies in their support. To understand the Klan, then, it is necessary to understand the

"The Ku Klux Klan's Fight for Americanism" by Hiram Wesley Evans from *North American Review* (March–May 1926), 38–39, 52–54. Reprinted by permission of *North American Review.*

character and present mind of the mass of old-stock Americans. The mass, it must be remembered, as distinguished from the intellectually mongrelized "Liberals."

These are, in the first place, a blend of various peoples of the so-called Nordic race, the race which, with all its faults, has given the world almost the whole of modern civilization. The Klan does not try to represent any people but these. . . .

. . . The Nordic American today is a stranger in large parts of the land his fathers gave him. Moreover, he is a most unwelcome stranger, one much spit upon, and one to whom even the right to have his own opinions and to work for his own interests is now denied with jeers and revilings. "We must Americanize the Americans," a distinguished immigrant said recently. Can anything more clearly show the state to which the real American has fallen in this country which was once his own? . . .

Thus the Klan goes back to the American racial instincts, and to the common sense which is their first product, as the basis of its beliefs and methods. . . .

There are three of these great racial instincts, vital elements in both the historic and the present attempts to build an America which shall fulfill the aspirations and justify the heroism of the men who made the nation. These are the instincts of loyalty to the white race, to the traditions of America, and to the spirit of Protestantism, which has been an essential part of Americanism ever since the days of Roanoke and Plymouth Rock. They are condensed into the Klan slogan: "Native, white, Protestant supremacy."

First in the Klansman's mind is patriotism—America for Americans. He believes religiously that a betrayal of Americanism or the American race is treason to the most sacred of trusts, a trust from his fathers and a trust from God. He believes, too, that Americanism can only be achieved if the pioneer stock is kept pure. There is more than one race pride in this. Mongrelization has been proven bad. It is only between closely related stocks of the same race that interbreeding has improved men; the kind of interbreeding that went on in the early days of America between English, Dutch, German, Hugenot, Irish and Scotch.

Racial integrity is a very definite thing to the Klansman. It means even more than good citizenship, for a man may be in all ways a good citizen and yet a poor American, unless he has racial understanding of Americanism, and instinctive loyalty to it. It is in no way a reflection on any man to say that he is unAmerican; it is merely a statement that he is not one of us. It is often not even wise to try to make an American of the best of aliens. What he is may be spoiled without his becoming American. The races and stocks of men are as distinct as breeds of animals, and every boy knows that if one tries to train a bulldog to herd sheep, he has in the end neither a good bulldog nor a good collie. . . .

The second word in the Klansman's trilogy is "white." The white race must be supreme, not only in America but in the world. This is equally undebatable, except on the ground that the races might live together, each with full regard for the rights and interests of others, and that those rights and interests would never conflict. Such an idea, of course, is absurd; the colored races today, such as Japan, are clamoring not for equality but for their supremacy. The whole history of the world, on its broader lines, has been one of race conflicts, wars, subjugation or extinction. This is not pretty, and certainly disagrees with the maudlin theories of cosmopolitanism, but it is truth. The world has been so made that each race must fight for its life, must conquer, accept slavery or die. The Klansman believes that the whites will not become slaves, and he does not intend to die before his time. . . .

The third of the Klan principles is that Protestantism must be supreme; that Rome shall not rule America. The Klansman believes this not merely because he is a Protestant, nor even because the Colonies that are now our nation were settled for the purpose of wresting America from the control of Rome and establishing a land of free conscience. He believes it also because Protestantism is an essential part of Americanism; without it America could never have been created and without it she cannot go forward.

3. Author Richard Wright Recalls "Living Jim Crow" in the Twenties, 1937

Negroes who have lived South know the dread of being caught alone upon the streets in white neighborhoods after the sun has set. In such a simple situation as this the plight of the Negro in America is graphically symbolized. While white strangers may be in these neighborhoods trying to get home, they can pass unmolested. But the color of a Negro's skin makes him easily recognizable, makes him suspect, converts him into a defenseless target.

Late one Saturday night I made some deliveries in a white neighborhood. I was pedaling my bicycle back to the store as fast as I could, when a police car, swerving toward me, jammed me into the curbing.

"Get down and put up your hands!" the policemen ordered.

I did. They climbed out of the car, guns drawn, faces set, and advanced slowly.

"Keep still!" they ordered.

I reached my hands higher. They searched my pockets and packages. They seemed dissatisfied when they could find nothing incriminating. Finally, one of them said:

"Boy, tell your boss not to send you out in white neighborhoods this time of night."

As usual, I said:

"Yes, sir." . . .

[Later] . . . my Jim Crow education assumed quite a different form. It was no longer brutally cruel, but subtly cruel. Here I learned to lie, to steal, to dissemble. I learned to play that dual role which every Negro must play if he wants to eat and live.

For example, it was almost impossible to get a book to read. It was assumed that after a Negro had imbibed what scanty schooling the state furnished he had no further need for books. I was always borrowing books from men on the job. One day I mustered enough courage to ask one of the men to let me get books from the library in his name. Surprisingly, he consented. I cannot help but think that he consented because he was a Roman Catholic and felt a vague sympathy for Negroes, being himself an object of hatred. Armed with a library card, I obtained books in the following manner: I would write a note to the librarian, saying: "Please let this nigger boy have the following books." I would then sign it with the white man's name.

When I went to the library, I would stand at the desk, hat in hand, looking as unbookish as possible. When I received the books desired I would take them home.

Richard Wright, "The Ethics of Living Jim Crow," in *American Stuff: An Anthology of Prose and Verse by Members of the Federal Writers' Project,* ed. Henry G. Alsberg. Copyright 1937 by the Guilds' Committee for Federal Writers' Publications, Inc. Used by permission of Viking Penguin, a division of Penguin Putnam.

If the books listed in the note happened to be out, I would sneak into the lobby and forge a new one. I never took any chances guessing with the white librarian about what the fictitious white man would want to read. No doubt if any of the white patrons had suspected that some of the volumes they enjoyed had been in the home of a Negro, they would not have tolerated it for an instant.

4. Langston Hughes: Poet of the 1920s Harlem Renaissance

One-Way Ticket

I pick up my life
And take it with me
And I put it down in
Chicago, Detroit,
Buffalo, Scranton,
Any place that is
North and East—
And not Dixie.

I pick up my life
And take it on the train
To Los Angeles, Bakersfield,
Seattle, Oakland, Salt Lake,
Any place that is
North and West—
And not South.

I am fed up
With Jim Crow laws,
People who are cruel
And afraid,
Who lynch and run,
Who are scared of me
And me of them.

I pick up my life
And take it away
On a one-way ticket—
Gone up North,
Gone out West,
Gone!

5. Clarence Darrow Interrogates
William Jennings Bryan in the Monkey Trial, 1925

Examination of W. J. Bryan by Clarence Darrow, of counsel for the defense:

Q—You have given considerable study to the Bible, haven't you, Mr. Bryan?

A—Yes, sir, I have tried to. . . .

Q—Do you claim that everything in the Bible should be literally interpreted?

A—I believe everything in the Bible should be accepted as it is given there; some of the Bible is given illustratively. For instance: "Ye are the salt of the earth." I would not insist that man was actually salt, or that he had flesh of salt, but it is used in the sense of salt as saving God's people.

Q—But when you read that Jonah swallowed the whale—or that the whale swallowed Jonah—excuse me please—how do you literally interpret that?

A—When I read that a big fish swallowed Jonah—it does not say whale.

Q—Doesn't it? Are you sure?

A—That is my recollection of it. A big fish, and I believe it, and I believe in a God who can make a whale and can make a man and make both do what He pleases. . . .

Q—You don't know whether it was the ordinary run of fish, or made for that purpose? . . .

Q—Do you believe Joshua made the sun stand still?

A—I believe what the Bible says. I suppose you mean that the earth stood still?

Q—I don't know. I am talking about the Bible now.

A—I accept the Bible absolutely.

Q—The Bible says Joshua commanded the sun to stand still for the purpose of lengthening the day, doesn't it, and you believe it?

A—I do.

Q—Do you believe at that time the entire sun went around the earth?

A—No, I believe that the earth goes around the sun.

Q—Do you believe that the men who wrote it thought that the day could be lengthened or that the sun could be stopped?

A—I don't know what they thought.

Q—You don't know?

A—I think they wrote the fact without expressing their own thoughts. . . .

Mr. Darrow—Have you an opinion as to whether—whoever wrote the book, I believe it is, Joshua, the Book of Joshua, thought the sun went around the earth or not?

A—I believe that he was inspired.

Mr. Darrow—Can you answer my question?

A—When you let me finish the statement. . . .

Q—Now, Mr. Bryan, have you ever pondered what would have happened to the earth if it had stood still?

A—No.

Q—You have not?

The World's Most Famous Trial: Tennessee Evolution Case (Cincinnati: National Book Co.), 284–291.

A—No; the God I believe in could have taken care of that, Mr. Darrow.

Q—I see. Have you ever pondered what would naturally happen to the earth if it stood still suddenly?

A—No.

Q—Don't you know it would have been converted into a molten mass of matter?

A—You testify to that when you get on the stand, I will give you a chance.

Q—Don't you believe it?

A—I would want to hear expert testimony on that.

Q—You have never investigated that subject?

A—I don't think I have ever had the question asked.

Q—Or ever thought of it?

A—I have been too busy on things that I thought were of more importance than that.

Q—You believe the story of the flood to be a literal interpretation?

A—Yes, sir.

Q—When was that flood?

A—I would not attempt to fix the date. The date is fixed, as suggested this morning.

Q—About 4004 B. C. ?

A—That has been the estimate of a man that is accepted today. I would not say it is accurate.

Q—That estimate is printed in the Bible?

A—Everybody knows, at least, I think most of the people know, that was the estimate given.

Q—But what do you think that the Bible, itself, says? Don't you know how it was arrived at?

A—I never made a calculation.

Q—A calculation from what?

A—I could not say.

Q—From the generations of man?

A—I would not want to say that.

Q—What do you think?

A—I do not think about things I don't think about.

Q—Do you think about things you do think about?

A—Well, sometimes. . . .

Mr. Darrow—How long ago was the flood, Mr. Bryan? . . .

The Witness—It is given here, as 2348 years B. C.

Q—Well, 2348 years B. C. You believe that all the living things that were not contained in the ark were destroyed.

A—I think the fish may have lived. . . .

Q—Don't you know there are any number of civilizations that are traced back to more than 5,000 years?

A—I know we have people who trace things back according to the number of ciphers they have. But I am not satisfied they are accurate. . . .

Mr. Darrow—You do know that there are thousands of people who profess to be Christians who believe the earth is much more ancient and that the human race is much more ancient?

A—I think there may be.

Q—And you never have investigated to find out how long man has been on the earth?

A—I have never found it necessary. . . .

Q—Don't you know that the ancient civilizations of China are 6,000 or 7,000 years old, at the very least?

A—No; but they would not run back beyond the creation, according to the Bible, 6,000 years.

Q—You don't know how old they are, is that right?

A—I don't know how old they are, but probably you do. (Laughter in the court-yard.) I think you would give the preference to anybody who opposed the Bible, and I give the preference to the Bible.

6. Bruce Barton Sees Jesus as an Advertising Man, 1925

Every advertising man ought to study the parables of Jesus . . . , schooling himself in their language and learning these four big elements of their power.

1. First of all they are marvelously condensed, as all good advertising must be. . . . A single sentence grips your attention; three or four more tell the story; one or two more and the application is driven home. When he wanted a new disciple he said simply "Follow me." When he sought to explain the deepest philosophic mystery— the personality and character of God—he said, "A king made a banquet and invited many guests. God is that king and you are the guests; the Kingdom of Heaven is happiness—a banquet to be enjoyed." . . .

2. His language was marvelously simple—a second great essential. There is hardly a sentence in his teaching which a child can not understand. His illustrations were all drawn from the commonest experiences of life; "a sower went forth to sow"; "a certain man had two sons"; "a man built his house on the sands"; "the kingdom of heaven is like a grain of mustard seed." The absence of adjectives is striking. . . .

Jesus used few qualifying words and no long ones. . . . [Recall] those three literary masterpieces, The Lord's Prayer, The Twenty-Third Psalm, The Gettysburg Address. Recall their phraseology:

Our Father which art in Heaven, hallowed be thy name

The Lord is my shepherd; I shall not want

Four score and seven years ago

Not a single three-syllable word; hardly any two-syllable words. All the greatest things in human life are one-syllable things—love, joy, hope, home, child, wife, trust, faith, God—and the great advertisements generally speaking, are those in which the most small words are found.

Reprinted with the permission of Simon & Schuster from *The Man Nobody Knows* by Bruce Barton. Copyright © 1925 by The Bobbs-Merrill Company, Inc., renewed 1953 by Bruce Barton.

3. Sincerity glistened like sunshine through every sentence he uttered; sincerity is the third essential. . . . The public has a sixth sense for detecting insincerity; they know instinctively when words ring true. . . .

Jesus was notably tolerant of almost all kinds of sinners. . . . But for one sin he had no mercy. He denounced the *insincerity* of the Pharisees in phrases which sting like the lash of a whip. They thought they had a first mortgage on the Kingdom of Heaven, and he told them scornfully that only those who become like little children have any chance of entering in. . . .

Much brass has been sounded and many cymbals tinkled in the mane of advertising; but the advertisements which persuade people to act are written by men who have an abiding respect for the intelligence of their readers, and a deep sincerity regarding the merits of the goods they have to sell. . . .

4. Finally he knew the necessity for repetition and practised it. . . .

It has been said that "reputation is repetition." No important truth can be impressed upon the minds of any large number of people by being said only once. The thoughts which Jesus had to give the world were revolutionary, but they were few in number. "God is your father," he said, "caring more for the welfare of every one of you than any human father can possibly care for his children. His Kingdom is happiness! his rule is love." This is what he had to teach, but he knew the necessity of driving it home from every possible angle. So in one of his stories God is the shepherd searching the wilds for one wandering sheep; in another, the Father welcoming home a prodigal boy; in another a King who forgives his debtors large amounts and expects them to be forgiving in turn—*many* stories, *many* advertisements, but the same big Idea.

7. The Automobile Comes to Middletown, U.S.A., 1929

The first real automobile appeared in Middletown in 1900. About 1906 it was estimated that "there were probably 200 in the city and county." At the close of 1923 there were 6,221 passenger cars in the city, one for every 6.1 persons, or roughly two for every three families. . . . For some of the workers and some of the business class, use of the automobile is a seasonal matter, but the increase in surfaced roads and in closed cars is rapidly making the car a year-round tool for leisure-time as well as getting-a-living activities. As, at the turn of the century, business class people began to feel apologetic if they did not have a telephone, so ownership of an automobile has now reached the point of being an accepted essential of normal living. . . .

Group-sanctioned values were disturbed by the inroads of the automobile upon the family budget. A case in point is the not uncommon practice of mortgaging a

Excerpts from *Middletown: A Study in American Culture* by Robert S. Lynd and Helen M. Lynd. Copyright © 1929 by Harcourt Brace & Company, and renewed in 1957 by Robert S. and Helen M. Lynd. Reprinted by permission of the publisher.

home to buy an automobile. Data on automobile ownership were secured from 123 working class families. Of these, sixty have cars. Forty-one of the sixty own their homes. Twenty-six of these forty-one families have mortgages on their homes. Forty of the sixty-three families who do not own a car own their homes. Twenty-nine of these have mortgages on their homes. Obviously other factors are involved in many of Middletown's mortgages. That the automobile does represent a real choice in the minds of some at least is suggested by the acid retort of one citizen to the question about car ownership: "No, sir we've *not* got a car. *That's* why we've got a home." According to an officer of a Middletown automobile financing company, 75 to 90 per cent of the cars purchased locally are bought on time payment, and a working man earning $35.00 a week frequently plans to use one week's pay each month as payment for his car. . . .

Many families feel that an automobile is justified as an agency holding the family group together. "I never feel as close to my family as when we are all together in the car," said one business class mother, and one or two spoke of giving up Country Club membership or other recreations to get a car for this reason. "We don't spend anything on recreation except for the car. We save every place we can and put the money into the car. It keeps the family together," was an opinion voiced more than once. Sixty-one per cent of 337 boys and 60 per cent of 423 girls in the three upper years of the high school say that they motor more often with their parents than without them.

But this centralizing tendency of the automobile may be only a passing phase; sets in the other direction are almost equally prominent. "Our daughters [eighteen and fifteen] don't use our car much because they are always with somebody else in their car when we go out motoring," lamented one business class mother. And another said, "The two older children [eighteen and sixteen] never go out when the family motors. They always have something else on." "In the nineties we were all much more together," said another wife. "People brought chairs and cushions out of the house and sat on the lawn evenings. We rolled out a strip of carpet and put cushions on the porch step to take care of the unlimited overflow of neighbors that dropped by. We'd sit out so all evening. The younger couples perhaps would wander off for half an hour to get a soda but come back to join in the informal singing or listen while somebody strummed a mandolin or guitar." "What on earth *do* you want me to do? Just sit around home all evening!" retorted a popular high school girl of today when her father discouraged her going out motoring for the evening with a young blade in a rakish car waiting at the curb. The fact that 348 boys and 382 girls in the three upper years of the high school placed "use of automobile" fifth and fourth respectively in a list of twelve possible sources of disagreement between them and their parents suggests that this may be an increasing decentralizing agent. . . .

The threat which the automobile presents to some anxious parents is suggested by the fact that of thirty girls brought before the juvenile court in the twelve months preceding September 1, 1924, charged with "sex crime," for whom the place where the offense occurred was given in the records, nineteen were listed as having committed the offense in an automobile. Here again the automobile appears to some as an "enemy" of the home and society.

8. A Survey Examines the Morals
of High School Students, 1924

Excerpts from a Questionaire relative to Moral Problems in the High Schools as judged by the students, North Central Association of Colleges and Schools, covering 19 States.

The chief moral qualities exhibited by pupils:
  Honesty 30%
  Fellowship 12%
  Clean habits 19%
  Courtesy lowest with only 9%

The most regretable practices of boys in school:
  Smoking 38%
  Swearing 19%
  Drinking 8%
  Telling vulgar stories 5%

The most regretable practices of girls in school:
  Cosmetics 17%
  Flirting & petting 14%
  Profane language 12%

Factors tending to develope high moral qualities among pupils:
  Teacher 31%
  School Organization 18%
  Athletics 17%

Invidious factors tending to undermine right conduct:
  Certain low minded people 63%
  Poor discipline 11%
  Immoral parties 11%

How could school help to develope morality among pupils?
  Course in morals 32%
  Stricter Rules 21%
  Talks 19%

Is a course in moral education desirable?
  61% of replies said "Yes."
  39% of replies said "No."

Some forces which are the most helpful:
  Mother 20%
  Father 17%
  Teacher 11%

Influences which made pupils do what they should not have done:
  Evil companions 55%
  Personal weakness 10%
  Immoral movies 9%
  Wish to be popular & desire for a good time 6%

Highest school ambitions:
  To be all around capable person 62%
  Excellent student 31%

Thing pupils are proud of:
  The High School spirit 22%
  Athletic Activities 20%
  Moral strength 12%

What change in class procedure advocated?
  More class discussions 23%
  More recitations by pupils 20%
  More explanations 23%

Things making a boy popular:
  Athletics 21%
  Scholarship 14%
  Good looks 10%
  Dependability has 1%
  Capability only 2%
  Character only 2% & takes 12th place of 18 questions asked.

National Archives and Records Administration and National Council for the Social Studies, *Teaching with Documents: Using Primary Sources from the National Archives* (Washington, D.C.: National Archives, 1989), 124.

Things that make a girl popular:
  Appearance 17%
  Scholarship 13%
  Personality 9%
  Morality 4%
  Character only 3% & takes 15th
  place of 18 questions asked. . . .

Present causes of worry:
  Choice of vocation 27%
  Money matters 21%
  Studies 16%
  Religious matters 2%
  (lowest of ten questions).

9. F. Scott Fitzgerald Reveals Attitudes About Gender and Race in *The Great Gatsby*, 1925

Tom Buchanan who had been hovering restlessly about the room stopped and rested his hand on my shoulder.

"What you doing, Nick?"

"I'm a bond man."

"Who with?"

I told him.

"Never heard of them," he remarked decisively.

This annoyed me.

"You will," I answered shortly. "You will if you stay in the East."

"Oh, I'll stay in the East, don't you worry," he said, glancing at Daisy and then back at me as if he were alert for something more. "I'd be a God Damn fool to live anywhere else."

At this point Miss Baker said "Absolutely!" with such suddenness that I started—it was the first word she had uttered since I came into the room. Evidently it surprised her as much as it did me, for she yawned and with a series of rapid, deft movements stood up into the room.

"I'm stiff," she complained. "I've been lying on that sofa for as long as I can remember."

"Don't look at me," Daisy retorted. "I've been trying to get you to New York all afternoon."

"No thanks," said Miss Baker to the four cocktails just in from the pantry, "I'm absolutely in training."

Her host looked at her incredulously.

"You are?" He took down his drink as if it were a drop in the bottom of a glass. "How you ever get anything done is beyond me."

I looked at Miss Baker wondering what it was she "got done." I enjoyed looking at her. She was a slender, small-breasted girl with an erect carriage which she accentuated by throwing her body backward at the shoulders like a young cadet. Her grey sun-strained eyes looked back at me with polite reciprocal curiosity out of a wan, charming discontented face. It occurred to me now that I had seen her, or a picture of her, somewhere before.

"You live in West Egg," she remarked contemptuously. "I know somebody there."

"I don't know a single——"

"You must know Gatsby."

"Gatsby?" demanded Daisy. "What Gatsby?"

Before I could reply that he was my neighbor dinner was announced; wedging his tense arm imperatively under mine Tom Buchanan compelled me from the room as though he were moving a checker to another square.

Slenderly, languidly, their hands set lightly on their hips the two young women preceded us out onto a rosy-colored porch open toward the sunset where four candles flickered on the table in the diminished wind. . . .

"Civilization's going to pieces," broke out Tom violently. "I've gotten to be a terrible pessimist about things. Have you read 'The Rise of the Coloured Empires' by this man Goddard?"

"Why, no," I answered, rather surprised by his tone.

"Well, it's a fine book and everybody ought to read it. The idea is if we don't look out the white race will be—will be utterly submerged. It's all scientific stuff, it's been proved."

"Tom's getting very profound," said Daisy with an expression of unthoughtful sadness. "He reads deep books with long words in them. What was that word we——"

"Well, these books are all scientific," insisted Tom, glancing at her impatiently. "This fellow has worked out the whole thing. It's up to us who are the dominant race to watch out or these other races will have control of things."

"We've got to beat them down," whispered Daisy, winking ferociously toward the fervent sun.

"You ought to live in California——" began Miss Baker but Tom interrupted her by shifting heavily in his chair.

"This idea is that we're Nordics. I am and you are and you are and——" After an infinitesimal hesitation he included Daisy with a slight nod and she winked at me again, "——and we've produced all the things that go to make civilization—oh, science and art and all that. Do you see?"

There was something pathetic in his concentration as if his complacency, more acute than of old, was not enough to him any more. . . .

There was dancing now on the canvas in the garden, old men pushing young girls backward in eternal graceless circles, superior couples holding each other tortuously, fashionably and keeping in the corners—and a great number of single girls dancing individualistically or relieving the orchestra for a moment of the burden of the banjo or the traps. By midnight the hilarity had increased. A celebrated tenor had sung in Italian and a notorious contralto had sung in jazz and between the numbers people were doing "stunts" all over the garden while happy vacuous bursts of laughter rose toward the summer sky. A pair of stage "twins"—who turned out to be the girls in yellow—did a baby act in costume and champagne was served in glasses bigger than finger bowls. The moon had risen higher, and floating in the Sound was a triangle of silver scales, trembling a little to the stiff, tinny drip of the banjoes on the lawn.

I was still with Jordan Baker. We were sitting at a table with a man of about my age and a rowdy little girl who gave way upon the slightest provocation to uncontrollable laughter. I was enjoying myself now. I had taken two finger bowls of champagne and the scene had changed before my eyes into something significant, elemental and profound. . . .

Gatsby's butler was suddenly standing beside us.

"Miss Baker?" he inquired. "I beg your pardon but Mr. Gatsby would like to speak to you alone."

"With me?" she exclaimed in surprise.

"Yes, madame."

She got up slowly, raising her eyebrows at me in astonishment, and followed the butler toward the house. I noticed that she wore her evening dress, all her dresses, like sports clothes—there was a jauntiness about her movements as if she had first learned to walk upon golf courses on clean, crisp mornings.

 *E S S A Y S*

Like most periods characterized by rapid cultural change, the twenties are a bundle of contradictions. Paula S. Fass of the University of California, Berkeley, examines the social behavior of college youth in the 1920s, who, she asserts, changed gender roles and relationships between men and women. They invented "dating" (courtship not tied to marriage), "petting" (erotic interactions not tied to intercourse), and provocative fashions not expected to provoke outrage. The author looks at the range of behaviors that young people redefined as socially acceptable, from petting to smoking to drinking. What gave college youth this much power and influence? In the second essay, Edward J. Larson of the University of Georgia places the Scopes trial—easily caricatured as a clash between "backward" yokels and sophisticated city slickers—in the context of the struggle to reconcile science with faith. The term *fundamentalism* was coined in the 1920s to symbolize the fight against theological liberalism and the updating (or diluting) of the old-time religion in view of new scientific information. Both of these authors look at phenomena linked to schools: textbook controversies and the attitudes of college undergraduates. Clearly, education was one battleground in the cultural conflicts of the twenties. But although the state of Tennessee won its skirmish against teacher John Scopes, it is less clear who won the culture war.

Sex and Youth in the Jazz Age

PAULA S. FASS

"Most of 'em pet, I guess."

"All the pretty ones."

"Some do one night and don't the next—goddam funny."

"ALL of 'em pet. Good women. Poor women. All of 'em."

"If a girl doesn't pet, a man can figure he didn't rush 'er right."

> *Lynn Montross and Lois Montross,* Town and Gown (1923)

Students of modern sexual behavior have quite correctly described the twenties as a turning point, a critical juncture between the strict double standard of the age of Victoria and the permissive sexuality of the age of Freud. Too often, however, the

Paula S. Fass, *The Damned and the Beautiful: American Youth in the 1920s* (New York: Oxford University Press, 1977), 260–265, 268–269, 279–284, 287–288, 292–293, 297–298, 300–301, 310–314, 316–318, 326. Used by permission of Oxford University Press.

sexual revolution of the twenties has been described exclusively in terms of scattered data suggesting an increase in premarital sexual intercourse on the part of women. One is tempted to picture investigators hunting for that special morning between 1919 and 1929 when 51% of the young unmarried women in America awoke to find that they were no longer virgins. Instead, of course, investigators are forced to deduce revolutionary changes from small, though important, increases in what remained a minority pattern of behavior. This kind of thinking, not unlike the Victorian concept of all or nothing, overlooks the fact that changes in sexual habits, as in most other areas of social relations, are evolutionary. . . .

College youth of the 1920's redefined the relationship between men and women. In good part this resulted from a simple rediscovery—love is erotic. The remainder drew on an old assumption—that the goal of relations between men and women was marriage. Together the new insight and the old tradition resulted in a significant restructuring of premarital forms of sexual behavior as relationships were charged by a new sexual dynamism and a vigorous experimentalism. Sex for middle-class youths of the 1920's had become a significant premarital experience, but it continued to be distinctly marriage-oriented and confined by stringent etiquettes and sharply etched definitions. In the process of defining their future roles in the new society and within the context of already potent changes, the young helped to create the sexual manners of the twentieth century. . . .

Dating was something definitely new in the ritual of sexual interaction. It was unlike the informal get-togethers that characterized youth socializing in the village or small town of the nineteenth century, for at such events there was no pairing early in an acquaintance. It was also unlike courting, which implied a commitment between two people. Dating permitted a paired relationship without implying a commitment to marriage and encouraged experimental relations with numerous partners. Dating emerged in response to a modern environment in which people met casually and irregularly, and in response to new kinds of recreations like movies, dance halls, and restaurants, where pairing was the most convenient form of boy-girl relation. Moreover, it developed as youths were increasingly freed from the direct supervision of family and community and allowed the freedom to develop private, intimate, and isolated associations. Dating opened the way for experimentation in mate compatibility. The lack of commitment permitted close and intimate associations and explorations of personality, and isolation and privacy laid the ground for sexual experimentation, both as a means for testing future compatibility and as an outlet for present sexual energies.

With the isolation of relations, the young were forced to rely on their own judgment in determining the degree and limits of permissible eroticism. It was this latitude for self-determination that produced the haunting fear of sexual promiscuity in the jeremiads of the twenties. The fear was unfounded. The young were thrown back on their own resources, but they were not free, either from the influence of childhood training or, more immediately, from the controls and sanctions of their peers. Basing their actions on an unyielding taboo against sexual intercourse and an elaborate network of peer norms and standards, they proceeded to open up the possibilities of sexual play without overstepping the bounds of family prohibition and peer propriety. After investigating female conduct in the late twenties, Phyllis Blanchard and Carlyn Manasses concluded that "very many girls draw a distinct line between the exploratory activities of the petting party and complete yielding of sexual favors to men." In the behavior of young men and women in the twenties, this charting of distinctions was as important as the exploration. The two ran a parallel course, for the young experimented with eroticism within a clear sense of limits, thus tasting a little of the fruit and enjoying the naughtiness of their bravery without seriously endangering the crop.

"Petting" described a broad range of potentially erotic physical contacts, from a casual kiss to more intimate caresses and physical fondling. Even such limited eroticism would have automatically defined a woman as loose and disreputable in the nineteenth century. To the Victorians, who divided good women from bad, revered ideal purity, and were suspicious of female sexuality, all forms of eroticism on the part of women could be equated with total submission. Even in the twenties, it was not unknown for reformers to introduce legislation that would prohibit petting and define it along with fornication as illegal as well as immoral. But the young drew distinct boundaries between what was acceptable erotic behavior and what was not. Petting was the means to be safe and yet not sorry, and around this form of sexual activity they elaborated a code of permissible eroticism. . . . A casual first date might thus entail a good-night kiss, but greater intimacies and a certain amount of erotic play were permitted and expected of engaged couples. "Erotic play," as Ira Wile rightfully observed, had "become an end rather than a means," and the strong "distinctions made in petting recognize that erotic activity may or may not have coitus as a goal." The young first sanctioned eroticism and then imposed degrees and standards of acceptability. . . .

Dating and petting were, moreover, distinctly marriage-oriented in the twenties. Since mating was one of the chief aims of both rituals, immediate sexual satisfactions had to be carefully weighed in view of long-term goals. And while virginity in a bride was no longer an absolute prerequisite for most men, it was still considered desirable. For men, female chastity appears to have taken a back seat to considerations of compatibility, but there was still some ambiguity on this point, and the devaluation of virginity in the bride was probably related to a growing acceptance of intercourse among engaged couples rather than to a tolerance of casual promiscuity. Women too continued to display considerable anxiety about the consequences of lost virginity. These multiple ambivalences reinforced the sense of acceptable limitations on sexual indulgence.

For most youths, this meant an acceptance of eroticism with very clear limits of permissible expression. Petting established a norm that deviated from that of the family but was still not antagonistic to its basic taboo. The majority could pet because it filled the need for response in a specific relationship, and in filling that need they believed they had the security of peer-group opinion. Of course, many ambivalences remained. But by the 1930's these sexual definitions had congealed into a dependable norm, a norm which, in the words of one investigation, provided ample room for "spontaneous demonstrations of affection." In their study of sexual behavior on the thirties campus, Dorothy Bromley and Florence Britten discovered that the fact "that a girl should feel she can give within limits or permit exploratory intimacies without compromising her essential virginity is one of the phenomena of the contemporary younger generation's mores." During the twenties, peer pressure to pet was still strong, and behavior patterns were, as a result, less stable, more inhibiting, altogether more full of anxieties. Probably many youths petted less to express personal needs than to conform to group standards and to demonstrate what Ernest Burgess called "the outstanding attitude of modern youth"—their "self-consciousness and sophistication about sex." . . .

Not surprisingly, the new attention to sexuality colored a whole range of related behavior. Language became more candid and conversations more frank as the fact of freer association between the sexes was accompanied by a basic commitment to freedom of expression. As women became companions to men in work and play, it was easier to see them as "pals" and partners, and the informal access between the sexes radically affected ideas of *de facto* equality and the manners that reflected that equality. At the same time, this access encouraged a pronounced attention to sexual attractiveness and to the cultivation of styles that operated on a purely sexual level.

What is at first glance enigmatic in the fashions and manners of young women in the twenties—the apparent conflict between those modes that emphasized her boyish characteristics, her gamin quality, and those that consciously heightened her sexual piquancy—must be understood in terms of the two distinct but related consequences of this new access between the sexes. They express not conflict but a well-poised tension between the informal boyish companion and the purposefully erotic vamp. They served at once a symbolic and a functional role in the new variety of relationships between the sexes. Bobbed hair, for example, which was the prevailing style for women on all campuses, was enthusiastically defended on the grounds that it was carefree and less troublesome to care for than the long ponderous mane, which was *de rigueur* in the prewar period. It facilitated indulgence in ad-hoc and informal activities like sports and made it easier for women to remain well-groomed during an increasingly busy campus or work day. It was indeed liberating, as it emphasized the woman's more informal existence and behavior. It allowed her to feel equal with men and unencumbered by a traditional symbol of her different role.

At the same time, the short hair was carefully marcelled, a process that occasioned no end of campus humor. The well-sculpted head was, in fact, in the context of the twenties, more self-consciously erotic than fluffy long hair that was girlish and young. Long hair was often inimical to real sexual allure because it was necessary to wear it carefully tied in a bun or chignon. Hair worn loose had for a long time been restricted to very young girls. Older girls, forced to compose it because it was improper to wear hair so informally and because it was unmanageable in an active day, often appeared staid and sedate. Short hair, on the other hand, could be worn freely and the possibility of prudish compactness averted. Bobbed hair was often attacked as a symbol of female promiscuity, of explicit sexuality, and of a self-conscious denial of respectability and the domestic ideal. Once we suspend absolute definitions of sexual attractiveness, we can begin to see the sexuality implicit in bobbed hair in the context of the period. It was not mannish but liberating, and that liberation implied a renunciation of sexual stereotypes. . . .

Short skirts, which became increasingly abbreviated as the decade progressed, were defined on the same grounds of comfort and practicality. Again, women could feel less encumbered and freer to engage in all the purportedly male activities. But the provocation of bared calves and knees was not overlooked. One outraged observer, a divinity student at Duke University, was so repelled by the bared knees of coeds that he was provoked to write a disgusted letter to the school paper. What really offended him, more even than the fashion, was the women's manipulation of the fashions. The coed, he observed, "would look every now and then to assure herself that they [her knees] were exposed to the nth degree." . . .

. . . To accompany the trend in skirt lengths and form-revealing silhouettes, there was a keen calorie-consciousness among young women. Dieting became so popular that newspapers often cited the calorie value of foods and gave nutritional advice about the amount of food intake that would help to sustain or shed weight. Young women were conscious of the new vamp silhouette and sought to imitate the lean, honed-down proportions of the movie queens. . . .

Cosmetics were used to increase attractiveness, but they were more than that—they were provocative. The use of cosmetics symbolized the woman's open acceptance of her own sexuality. Whatever the long history of cosmetics and their general use, the reference point for women in the twenties was not ancient Egypt or India but the America of the late nineteenth and early twentieth centuries. And by the mores of that period, cosmetics were immoral. They were associated with prostitutes. By appropriating the right to use such sexual aids, respectable women proclaimed that they too were endowed with a sexual personality. They had taken on themselves as potential wives all the characteristics of lovers. The two kinds of women were no longer separate and distinguishable at first glance but one and the same.

Young women did not generally abuse their new-found cosmetic allies. They used powder, rouge, and lip color in moderation with an eye to increasing allure without offending propriety. The moderate use was in conformity with the standards and expectations of their peers, who had incorporated cosmetics as a permissible part of fashion. That the peer group that encouraged the use of cosmetics also limited its over-indulgence was lost on adults. The adult world, its eyes still fixed on an older standard, stood aghast. But among the young the moderate use of cosmetics was encouraged and recognized for what it was, an attempt to increase physical attractiveness and to score points in the game of rating within the rules set by the peer group. . . .

So too, the male "line" was a conscious extension of the cultivated attention to sexual manners. A line was a well-rehearsed and oft-repeated set of phrases used by men when introduced to women. The line was a mark of sophistication, a demonstration of worldliness, a touch of cynicism that made a man more attractive by making him more dangerous. "As for the co-eds," remarked a solicitous Trinity editor, "don't the young sweet things know that the senior law students have a line so long and slippery that it can't be caught?" But it was the very slipperiness that made the line effective. It was a staged ritual, a self-conscious and even a self-protective form of sexual aggression in the new and potentially dangerous sexual explorations in which the young were engaged. It was well known that the line was not spontaneous but used as a staged approach in meeting and cultivating female company. It identified a man as experienced, so the approval of the line reflected the desirability of "experience" in meeting respectable women. A man without a line was an innocent, basically not savvy in the ways of the world. Like a woman without her cosmetics, a man without his line went out naked into the frightening wilderness of a newly sexual world. With its barely veiled sexual naughtiness, the line pointed up the ways in which conscious sexuality had been incorporated into the rituals of attack and protection that governed male and female interaction. . . .

Smoking was perhaps the one most potent symbol of young woman's testing of the elbow room provided by her new sense of freedom and equality. Prostitutes and women in liberated bohemian and intellectual sets had been known to flaunt their cigarettes publicly and privately before the twenties. But in respectable middle-class circles, and especially among young women, smoking, like rouging, was simply not done. Throughout the twenties, smoking could still provoke heated commentary, and for many young women, to smoke in public was a welcome form of notoriety. Although young women in college did not initiate the smoking habit, they increasingly took advantage of the cigarette as a symbol of liberation and as a means of proclaiming their equal rights with men. More importantly, within the college community they had the support of peer-group opinion. Among the young, smoking for women became widely accepted during the twenties, and while smoking remained an issue, as the decade wore on it became an acceptable and familiar habit among college women.

Smoking is not a sexual activity in itself. In the abstract, it is morally neutral. In the context of the specific values of American society, however, it was both morally value-laden and sexually related. Like cosmetics, smoking was sexually suggestive and associated with disreputable women or with bohemian types who self-consciously rejected traditional standards of propriety and morality. College administrators objected to smoking because it undermined an ideal of proper female behavior and decency. As the Dean of Women at Ohio State University noted, smoking was simply not "done in the best circles," and it was, in the words of the Dean of Rhode Island State College, "an unladylike act." . . .

Women and men on the campuses of the twenties proclaimed that women had a right to smoke if they pleased: "If a man can enjoy his coke more by smoking as he drinks it, why isn't it logical to assume that a woman can enjoy hers more when it is accompanied by a cigarette?" asked one woman correspondent at Illinois. "Why shouldn't a woman have a taste for cigarettes just as a man has? It is not the smoking that breaks down the bonds of convention between men and women . . . a woman can command just as much respect with a cigarette in her mouth as without." At New York University women claimed their rights by announcing that they would hold a smoker rather than a traditional tea. The Dean was outraged and prohibited the event, but the women went ahead with their plans anyway. Blanchard and Manasses found that 80% of the young women they questioned approved of smoking for women. In marked contrast, only 26% of the parents approved. . . .

In the twenties, young men and women danced whenever the opportunity presented itself. Unquestionably the most popular social pastime, dancing was, of all potentially questionable and morally related behaviors, the least disreputable in the view of the young. For most youths dancing was not even questionable but a thoroughly respectable and almost compulsory form of socializing. Even at denominational schools, where dancing continued to be regarded as morally risky by officials, students clamored for a relaxation of the older bans as they asked officials to give up outdated "prejudiced feelings" and respond to "the bending of current public opinion." A dance was an occasion. It was a meeting ground between young men and women. It was a pleasurable recreation. But above all it was a craze.

The dancers were close, the steps were fast, and the music was jazz. And because popular forms of dancing were intimate and contorting, and the music was rhythmic and throbbing, it called down upon itself all the venom of offended respectability. Administrative officials as well as women's clubs and city fathers found the dancing provocative and indecent and tried at least to stop the young from engaging in its most egregious forms, if not from the dances entirely. But the young kept on dancing.

They started during the war years, and they danced through the decade. Dancing would leave its stamp on the twenties forever, and jazz would become the lingering symbol for an era. But whatever its symbolic value during the twenties and thereafter, dancing and jazz were forms of recreation, even a means of peer-group communication, that youth appropriated to itself. . . .

Drinking for youth in the twenties was unlike sex, smoking, or dancing, because the young labored under a specific legal ordinance forbidding alcoholic indulgence of any kind. Prohibition was an anomaly in an age of increasing freedoms. Students had been permitted to drink at least off-campus before the passage of the Eighteenth Amendment and the Volstead Act, and beer drinking had been a regular form of celebration and socializing among male students. Prohibition cut off a former freedom. Moreover, unlike the other moral issues of the twenties, drinking was a male-centered problem that secondarily involved women. Drinking had always been a male prerogative. Respectable women were effectively barred from indulgence by tradition. Drinking among youths during the twenties therefore involved a number of distinct issues: the attitude toward the moral code, the attitude toward the law, and the question of female roles. . . .

It is difficult to determine how many students actually drank during the twenties and what the significance of their behavior was. By the end of the decade, the polls of the Congressional Hearing on the Repeal of the Prohibition Amendment presented overwhelming evidence that men and women students drank in a proportion close to two drinkers to every non-drinker. This was the case in all parts of the nation. . . . Of the total number of ballots cast in the nationwide congressional poll, 29,794 in all, only 34% of the students claimed not to be drinkers. By 1930, at least, drinking appears to have been very common among the majority of all students.

Coming to the end of the decade, the Congressional survey reflected the campus situation when anti-Prohibition sentiment had reached a peak. But the college newspapers suggest that there were changes over the course of the decade in the amount and style of drinking. Drinking among the young appears to have been greatest at the very beginning and again in the second half of the twenties. There was a short period between 1921 and 1924 when the amount of drinking was kept to a minimum, the result of initial attempts by the young spurred on by the administration to control drinking, especially at official university parties and at fraternity dances. At this time, the papers, after important events like proms and homecomings, were filled with self-congratulations on the commendable way in which the students were controlling the drinking problem and enforcing the national and school anti-drinking laws. In 1921, the *Cornell Sun,* for example, which noted that the previous year had been especially wet, observed, "The low point has been passed in regard to the liquor situation, and the upward swing is beginning. All evidence, at least, points to a slowly growing public sentiment against drinking at dances—which is the crux of the whole matter. The parties in the last three or four weeks have had a different tone from those of a year ago." Even homecomings, usually the wettest weekends of the year because returning alumni brought liquor in abundance, were reported to be relatively dry. At Madison, Wisconsin, as at most schools, there was reported to be "a determined effort . . . to stamp out drinking." In the second half of the decade, however, there was a marked increase in the agitation for repeal or modification of Prohibition and a general decrease in the commitment with which the now formal injunctions against drinking were issued. This happened first at the Eastern schools, which appear to have had a shorter dry spell, and gradually affected the Midwest.

In the early period, some editors observed that Prohibition needed time to prove its efficacy and that slowly the public would be educated toward a self-imposed abstinence. On this assumption, students were urged to give Prohibition a chance. But most arguments supporting Prohibition were based on the law rather than on the social or moral objection to drinking. The injunction that the law should be obeyed was a constant aspect of the formally expressed attitudes toward drinking. This remained true throughout the decade. At Cornell, where editorial comment was consistently hostile to Prohibition and to all attempts to impose morality, the editor of the *Sun* nevertheless maintained that in respect to the law, there was but one answer, "to enforce the law . . . it is one thing for a citizen of the United States to be in doubt on the question of prohibition and it is another for him to be in doubt on the question of the dignity and power of the Constitution." . . .

At the same time, students were openly contemptuous of the kind of moral reformers who had succeeded in passing Prohibition. Self-righteous moralists trying to impose their own standards on everyone were the butt of derision. The *Daily Princetonian* struck just the right tone of contempt: "If the projects of the crusaders for virtue and purity are realized . . . once more the tottering world and western civilization will be made safe for unsullied virgins and old ladies above sixty. The absurdity of such efforts is second only to the presumption with which they are undertaken by . . . certain self-styled upholders of public morals. . . . To presume that one can define decency or legislate virtue is folly." . . .

These two very distinct and clearly articulated attitudes—the strong sentiment supporting the law and the hostility toward the idea of Prohibition—were accompanied by a less clearly enunciated ethic that made drinking an unofficially sanctioned peer activity. The editorials reflected this view. While always serious when denouncing law-breaking, editors were rarely serious about drinking. Usually drinking and Prohibition were fair game for humor and "smartness." The informal approval demonstrated by making Prohibition a joke cannot possibly have done other than undercut the effectiveness of the formal injunctions to obey the law contained in the very same papers. In this sense the spirit of Prohibition, if not the letter of the law, was officially denied. Drinking jokes were a staple of the humor columns and, more insidiously, of the side comments of the purportedly serious editorial columns. Even when intending to scold, editorials came off as shoulder-shrugging at the antics of college youths. . . .

In the early twenties, there was a clear code of limitations on drinking that reflected traditional attitudes toward propriety in drinking. Thus, drinking at athletic events and with other men was permissible, but drinking at dances and in the presence of women was not. When editors denounced drinking with alumni or at athletic events, for example, they usually invoked the law rather than the moral code. But the same editors were disturbed by drinking at dances, where it was believed to be improper because it was public and in the presence of women. The *Cornell Sun* called such drinking "an offense to good manners and against decency," and the *Sun* noted that while there was never a time in Cornell history when students did not drink, "there are times, when it is considered bad manners." So too, at the University of Wisconsin 2000 women students signed a pledge to boycott any social function where men were under the influence of liquor. The action reflected the prevailing ethic that drinking in the presence of women was improper.

The code also drew a fundamental distinction between drinking and drunkenness. In 1921, the editor of the *Daily Illini* noted that "The number of persons who object to an individual taking a drink of intoxicating liquor is probably in the minority," but that the student public strenuously objected to drinking to the point of intoxication. The editor concluded his message by advising that drinking "must not become open or offensive to student society." When the young drank according to these self-limiting rules, they were, in effect, conforming to the traditional standard of adult society that operated in the days before the Prohibition law went into effect.

During the twenties, however, the young increasingly deviated from these unofficial codes of conduct. There was a subterranean ethic developing that worked counter to these self-limiting rules. In this ethic, one drank to become drunk or, failing that, to appear drunk. Thus the *Cornell Sun* noted that where once it had been the aim to see how much one could drink without appearing drunk, it had now become part of "the game" to get as drunk as possible on whatever drink was available and to see who "can get the Greatest Publicity while in a state of Pseudo Ginification." "Contrary to the rabid assertions of matronly sewing circles and pessimistic male reformers," the *Dartmouth* declared, "the college student of today is sober ninety-nine one hundredths of the time. When he does drink, it is usually to parade his drunkenness—at a football game, at a dance, during a vacation, at a social gathering—and it is on such occasions that a shocked older generation is most liable to see youth in action." In addition, one drank in the company and together with women. It was not until the middle of the decade when this new ethic began to jell that drinking among women became an issue. Before then it was considered a strictly male-centered problem. Drinking at dances, with women, and to excess had become, by the latter twenties, a new code of permissible behavior among college students because it was sanctioned by peer opinion.

"Terpsichordian tippling," as the *Cornell Sun* called it, had become commonplace on most campuses and the editor explained quite accurately why this was so. "'Is it the smart thing to be drunk at a college function?' 'Yes,' reply the undergraduates by their indulgence in liquor consumption at dances, house parties and the like, and by their tolerance of it by others. Right there we believe lies the solution of the drinking problem at colleges in general. . . . Campus leaders set the style by drinking openly and laughingly approving the drunken actions of fellow students." A similar situation prevailed at Duke, where "a dance among the younger set can hardly be called a success nowadays unless most of the boys get 'high,' not to mention the occasional girl who cannot be outdone by her masculine companions." . . .

Did the young use sex and morals as a basis for conscious generational revolt? On the whole the answer would appear to be no, although their sexual attitudes and practices did distinguish them from their elders and made them appear rebellious. They welcomed the lingering naughtiness of which they were accused, but more in the spirit of play than with any serious display of anger. As eager capitalists, the young were anything but rebellious in social and political questions. They emphasized style in personal matters and severely demarcated the personal from the social sphere. In so doing they were in the advance guard of twentieth-century American culture.

Fundamentalists vs. Modernists in the Scopes Monkey Trial

EDWARD J. LARSON

Fossil discoveries provided persuasive new evidence for human evolution and as such provoked a response from antievolutionists. Henry Fairfield Osborn threw down the gauntlet in his reply to [William Jennings] Bryan's 1922 plea in the *New York Times* for restrictions on teaching evolution. Bryan had argued that "neither Darwin nor his supporters have been able to find a fact in the universe to support their hypothesis," prompting Osborn to cite "the Piltdown man" and other recent hominid fossil finds. "All this evidence is today within reach of every schoolboy," Osborn wrote. "It will, we are convinced, satisfactorily answer in the negative [Bryan's] question, 'Is it not more rational to believe in the creation of man by separate act of God than to believe in evolution without a particle of evidence?'" Of course, the fact that all this evidence *was* within the reach of every public-school student constituted the nub of Bryan's concern, and Osborn further baited antievolutionists by stressing how it undermined belief in the special creation of humans.

During the years leading up to the Scopes trial, antievolutionists responded to such evidence in various ways. . . .

The culprit, they all agreed, was a form of theological liberalism known as "modernism" that was gaining acceptance within most mainline Protestant denominations. Modernists viewed their creed as a means to save Christianity from irrelevancy in the face of recent developments in literary higher criticism and evolutionary thinking in the social sciences. Higher criticism, especially as applied by German theologians, subjected the Bible to the same sort of literary analysis as any other religious text, interpreting its "truths" in light of its historical and cultural context. The new social sciences, particularly psychology and anthropology, assumed that Judaism and Christianity were natural developments in the social evolution of the Hebrew people. Modernists responded to these intellectual developments by viewing God as immanent in history. Conceding human (rather than divine) authorship for scripture and evolutionary development (rather than revelational truth) for Christianity, modernists nevertheless claimed that the Bible represented valid human perceptions of how God acted. Under this view, the precise historical and scientific accuracy of scripture did not matter. Judeo–Christian ethical teachings and individual religious sentiments could still be "true" in a realm beyond the "facts" of history and science. "In belief," the modernist leader Shailer Mathews of the University of Chicago divinity school wrote in 1924, "the use of scientific, historical, and social methods in understanding and applying evangelical Christianity to the needs of living persons, is Modernism."

Conservative Christians drew together across denominational lines to fight for the so-called fundamentals of their traditional faith against the perceived heresy of modernism, and in so doing gave birth to the fundamentalist movement and antievolution crusade. Certainly modernism had made significant inroads within divinity schools and among the clergy of mainline Protestant denominations in the North and West, and fundamentalism represented a legitimate theological effort to counter these advances. Biblical higher criticism and an evolutionary world view, as twin pillars of this opposing creed, stood as logical targets of a conservative counterattack. A purely theological effort, however, rarely incites a mass movement, at least in pluralistic America; much more stirred up fundamentalism—and turned its fury against teaching evolution in public schools.

The First World War played a pivotal role. American intervention, as part of a progressive effort to defeat German militarism and make the world "safe for democracy," was supported by many of the modernists, who revered the nation's wartime leader, Woodrow Wilson, himself a second-generation modernist academic. A passionate champion of peace, William Jennings Bryan opposed this position and in 1915 resigned his post as Wilson's secretary of state in protest over the drift toward war. He spent the next two years criss-crossing the country campaigning against American intervention. . . .

When a horribly brutal war led to an unjust and uneasy peace, the rise of international communism, worldwide labor unrest, and an apparent breakdown of traditional values, the cultural crisis worsened for conservative Christians in the United States. "One indication that many premillennialists were shifting their emphasis—away from just evangelizing, praying, and waiting for the end time, toward more intense concern with retarding [social] degenerative trends—was the role they played in the formation of the first explicitly fundamentalist organization," [historian of religion George M.] Marsden noted. "In the summer of 1918, under the guidance of William B. Riley, a number of leaders in the Bible school and prophetic conference movement conceived of the idea of the World's Christian Fundamentals Association."

During the preceding two decades, Riley had attracted a 3,000-member congregation to his aging Baptist church in downtown Minneapolis through a distinctive combination of conservative dispensational-premillennialist theology and politicized social activism. "When the Church is regarded as the body of God-fearing, righteous-living men, then, it ought to be in politics, and as a powerful influence," he proclaimed in a 1906 book that urged Christians to promote social justice for the urban poor and workers. During the next decade, Riley focused his social activism on outlawing liquor, which he viewed as a key source of urban problems. By the twenties, he turned against teaching evolution in public schools. Later, he concentrated on attacking communism. Following the First World War and flushed with success upon ratification of the Eighteenth Amendment authorizing Prohibition, he was ideally suited to lead premillennialists into the cultural wars of the twenties.

In 1919, Riley welcomed some 6,000 conservative Christians to the World's Christian Fundamentals Association (WCFA) inaugural conference with the warning that their Protestant denominations were "rapidly coming under the leadership of the new infidelity, known as 'modernism.'" One by one, seventeen prominent ministers from across the country—the future high priests of fundamentalism—took the podium to denounce modernism as, in the words of one speaker, "the product of Satan's lie," and to call for a return to biblical fundamentals in church and culture. "It is ours to stand by our guns," Riley proclaimed in closing the conference. "God forbid that we should fail him in the hour when the battle is heavy." Participants then returned to their separate denominations, ready to battle the modernists. . . . Indeed, it was during the ensuing intradenominational strife within the Northern Baptist Convention that conservative leader Curtis Lee Laws coined the word *fundamentalist* to identify those willing "to do battle royal for the Fundamentals." Use of the term quickly spread to include all conservative Christians militantly opposed to modernism. . . .

Bryan's crusade against teaching evolution capped a remarkable thirty-five-year-long career in the public eye. He entered Congress in 1890 as a 30-year-old populist Democratic politician committed to roll back the Republican tariff for the dirt farmers of his native Nebraska. His charismatic speaking ability and youthful enthusiasm quickly earned him the nickname The Boy Orator of the Platte. Bryan's greatest speech occurred at the 1896 Democratic National Convention, where he defied his party's conservative incumbent president, Grover Cleveland, and the eastern establishment that dominated both political parties by demanding an alternative silver-based currency to help debtors cope with the crippling deflation caused by exclusive reliance on limited gold-backed money. Using a potent mix of radical majoritarian arguments and traditional religious oratory, he demanded, "You shall not press down upon the brow of labor this crown of thorns, you shall not crucify mankind upon a cross of gold." The speech electrified the convention and secured the party's presidential nomination for Bryan. For many, he became known as the Great Commoner; for some, the Peerless Leader.

. . . After helping Woodrow Wilson secure the White House in 1912, Bryan became secretary of state and idealistically (some said naively) set about negotiating a series of international treaties designed to avert war by requiring the arbitration of disputes among nations. This became more of a religious mission than a political task for Bryan, who called on America to "exercise Christian forbearance" in the face of increasing German aggression and vowed, "There will be no war while I am Secretary of State." Of course, he had to resign from office to keep this promise. . . .

Bryan's antievolutionism was compatible with his progressive politics because both supported reform, appealed to majoritarianism, and sprang from his Christian convictions. Bryan alluded to these issues in his first public address dealing with Darwinism, which he composed in 1904 at the height of his political career. From this earliest point, he described Darwinism as "dangerous" for both religious and social reasons. "I object to the Darwinian theory," Bryan said with respect to the religious implications of a naturalistic explanation for human development, "because I fear we shall lose the consciousness of God's presence in our daily life, if we must accept the theory that through all the ages no spiritual force has touched the life of man and shaped the destiny of nations." Turning to the social consequences of the theory, Bryan added, "But there is another objection. The Darwinian theory represents man as reaching his present perfection by the operation of the law of hate—the merciless law by which the strong crowd out and kill off the weak."

The Great Commoner was no more willing to defer to ivy tower scientists on this issue than to Wall Street bankers on monetary matters. "I have a right to assume," he declared in this early speech, "a Designer back of the design [in nature]—a Creator back of the creation; and no matter how long you draw out the process of creation; so long as God stands back of it you can not shake my faith in Jehovah." This last comment allowed for an extended geologic history and even for limited theistic evolution; but Bryan dug in his heels regarding the supernatural creation of humans and described it as "one of the test questions with the Christian." Although Bryan regularly delivered this speech on the Chautauqua circuit during the early years of the century, he said little else against Darwinism until the twenties, when he began blaming it for the First World War and an apparent decline in religious faith among educated Americans.

As a devout believer in peace, Bryan could scarcely understand how supposedly Christian nations could engage in such a brutal war until two scholarly books attributed it to misguided Darwinian thinking. In *Headquarters Nights,* the renowned Stanford University zoologist Vernon Kellogg, who went to Europe as a peace worker, recounted his conversations with German military leaders. "Natural selection based on violent and fatal competitive struggle is the gospel of the German intellectuals," he reported, and served as their justification "why, for the good of the world, there should be this war." Whereas Kellogg used this evidence to promote his own non-Darwinian view of evolutionary development through mutual aid, Bryan saw it as a reason to suppress Darwinian teaching. The philosopher Benjamin Kidd's *The Science of Power* further explored the link between German militarism and Darwinian thinking by examining Darwin's influence on the German philosopher Friedrich Nietzsche. Bryan regularly referred to both books when speaking and writing against teaching evolution. . . .

A third book had an even greater impact on Bryan and touched an even more sensitive nerve. In 1916, the Bryn Mawr University psychologist James H. Leuba published an extensive survey of religious belief among college students and professors. The result confirmed Bryan's worst fears. "The deepest impression left by these records," Leuba concluded, "is that . . . Christianity, as a system of belief, has utterly broken down." Among students, Leuba reported, "the proportion of disbelievers in immortality increases considerably from the freshman to the senior year in college." Among scientists, he found disbelief higher among biologists than physicists, and higher among scientists of greater than lesser distinction, such that "the smallest percentage of believers is found among the greatest biologists; they count only 16.9 per cent of believers in God." Leuba did not identify teaching evolution as the cause for this rising tide of disbelief among educated Americans, but Bryan did. "Can Christians be indifferent to such statistics?" Bryan asked in one speech. "What shall it profit a man if he shall gain all the learning of the schools and lose his faith in God?" This became his ultimate justification for the Scopes trial. . . .

The campaign for restrictive legislation spread quickly and all but commandeered the antievolution movement. Fundamentalist leader John Roach Straton began advocating antievolution legislation for his home state of New York in February 1922. J. Frank Norris, pastor of the largest church in the Dallas-Fort Worth area, soon took up the cause in Texas. The evangelist T. T. Martin carried the message throughout the South. By fall 1922, William Bell Riley was offering to debate evolutionists on the issue as he traveled around the nation battling modernism in the church. "The whole country is seething on the evolution question," he reported to Bryan in early 1923. Three years later, these same four ministers became the most prominent church figures to actively support the prosecution of John Scopes. . . .

Individual rights lost out under this political philosophy. "If it is contended that an instructor has a right to teach anything he likes, I reply that the parents who pay the salary have a right to decide what shall be taught," Bryan maintained. "A scientific soviet is attempting to dictate what is taught in our schools," he warned. "It is the smallest, the most impudent, and the most tyrannical oligarchy that ever attempted to exercise arbitrary power." He gave a similarly facile response to charges that antievolution laws infringed on the rights of nonfundamentalist parents and students. Protestants, Catholics, and Jews shared a creationist viewpoint, Bryan believed, and he sought to enlist all of them into his crusade. As for nontheists, he asserted, "The Christians who want to teach religion in their schools furnish the money for denominational institutions. If atheists want to teach atheism, why do they not build their own schools and employ their own teachers?" Such a position assumed that the separation of church and state precluded teaching the Genesis account in public schools. "We do not ask that teachers paid by taxpayers shall teach the Christian religion to students," Bryan told West Virginia lawmakers, "but we do insist that they shall not, under the guise of either science or philosophy, teach evolution as a fact." He apparently expected them to skip the topic of organic origins altogether, or to teach evolution as a hypothesis. . . .

"Fundamentalism drew first blood in Tennessee today," a January 20, 1925 article in the *Commercial Appeal* reported, "in the introduction of a bill in the Legislature by Senator [John A.] Shelton of Savannah to make it a felony to teach evolution in the public schools of the state." A day later, John W. Butler offered similar legislation in the House of Representatives. Both legislators had campaigned on the issue and their actions were predictable. Butler justified his proposal on Bryanesque grounds: "If we are to exist as a nation the principles upon which our Government is founded must not be destroyed, which they surely would be if . . . we set the Bible aside as being untrue and put evolution in its place." Butler was a little-known Democratic farmer-legislator and Primitive Baptist lay leader. For him, public schools served to promote citizenship based on biblical concepts of morality. Evolutionary beliefs undermined those concepts. Driven by such reasoning, Butler proposed making it a misdemeanor, punishable by a maximum fine of $500, for a public school teacher "to teach any theory that denies the story of the Divine Creation of man as taught in the Bible, and to teach instead that man had descended from a lower order of animal." Most of Butler's colleagues apparently agreed with this proposal, because six days later the House passed it without any amendments. The vote was seventy-one to five. Although three of the dissenters came from Memphis and one from Nashville, the bill gained the support of both rural and urban representatives, including most delegates from every major city in the state. . . .

Outnumbered Senate opponents of the legislation countered with pleas for individual rights. "It isn't a question of whether you believe in the Book of Genesis, but whether you think the church and state should be kept separate," one senator asserted. "No law can shackle human thought," another declared. A Republican lawmaker quoted passages on religious freedom from the state constitution, and blamed the entire controversy on "that greatest of all disturbers of the political and public life from the last twenty-eight or thirty years, I mean William Jennings Bryan." But a proponent countered, "This bill does not attempt to interfere with religious freedom or dictate the beliefs of any man, for it simply endeavors to carry out the wishes of the great majority of the people." Such sentiments easily carried the Senate.

State and national opponents of antievolution laws appealed to Governor Peay to veto the legislation. Owing to the governor's national reputation as a progressive who championed increased support for public education and a longer school year—efforts that later led to the naming of a college in his honor—those writing from out of state probably entertained some hope for success. Urged on by the California science writer Maynard Shipley and his Science League of America, a new organization formed to oppose antievolutionism, letters of protest poured in from across America. For example, taking the line of Draper and White, a New Yorker asked, "The Middle Ages gave us heretics, witches burnt at the stake, filth and ignorance. Do we want to return to the same?" From within Tennessee, some concerned citizens appealed for a veto. The dean of the state's premiere African-American college, Fisk University, wrote, "As a clergyman and educator, I hope that you will refuse to give your support to the Evolution Bill. It would seem most unfortunate to me should the State of Tennessee legislate against the beliefs of liberal Christianity." The Episcopal bishop of Tennessee added, "I consider such restrictive legislation not only unfortunate but calamitous."

Yet most letters to the governor from Tennesseans supported the measure, and two potentially significant opponents kept silent. The University of Tennessee's powerful president Harcourt A. Morgan, who privately opposed the antievolution bill, held his tongue so long as Peay's proposal for expanding the university still awaited action in the state legislature—and admonished his faculty to do likewise. In a confidential note, he assured the governor, "The subject of Evolution so intricately involves religious belief, which the University has no disposition to dictate, that the University declines to engage in the controversy." Only after the legislature adjourned and the new law became the primary subject of ridicule at the annual student parade did the depth of university opposition to it become apparent. . . .

The governor explained his decision to sign the bill in a curious message to the legislature. On one hand, Peay firmly asserted for proponents, "It is the belief of our people and they say in this bill that any theory of man's descent from lower animals, . . . because a denial of the Bible, shall not be taught in our public schools." On the other hand, he assured opponents that this law "will not put our teachers in any jeopardy." Indeed, even though the most cursory review of Tennessee high school biology textbooks should have shown him otherwise, Peay wrote, "I can find nothing of consequence in the books now being taught in our schools with which this bill will interfere in the slightest manner." Nevertheless, he went on to hail the measure as "a distinct protest against an irreligious tendency to exalt *so-called* science, and deny the Bible in some schools and quarters—a tendency fundamentally wrong and fatally mischievous in its effects on our children, our institutions and our country."

Peay, whose progressivism grew out of his traditional religious beliefs, simply could not accept a conflict between public education and popular religion. . . . Yet he could not totally ignore the tension between a fundamentalist's fear of modern education and a progressive's faith in it. In his message to the legislature on the antievolution bill, he fell back on Bryan's populist refrain: "The people have a right and must have the right to regulate what is taught in their schools." Trapped between fundamentalism and progressivism, Peay may have viewed majoritarianism as an excuse for the law. Caught in the same bind, Bryan saw it as the law's ultimate justification. . . .

Activists with the American Civil Liberties Union did not dismiss the enactment of the Tennessee law against teaching evolution as an insignificant occurrence in some remote intellectual backwater. More critically, they did not view the antievolution crusade in isolation; if they had, they probably would have ignored it along with countless other laws and movements to advance Protestant culture then prevalent throughout the United States. Prior to the Scopes trial, the ACLU did not display any particular interest in challenging government efforts to protect or promote religious beliefs. To the contrary, Quakers played a major role in founding and financing the organization during the First World War as a vehicle to protect religiously motivated pacifists from compulsory military service. Yet ACLU leaders saw the new Tennessee statute in a different light, one that made it stand out as a threat to freedom and individual liberty in the broader American society.

A fashionable new book of the era, *The Mind in the Making* by James Harvey Robinson of the left-wing New School for Social Research in New York City, captured the reactionary mood of the times as perceived by many of the socially prominent, politically radical New Yorkers who led the ACLU during the early twenties. According to this book, which incorporated an evolutionary view of intellectual and social history, a systematic assault on personal liberty in the United States began during the First World War; various state and local authorities had limited freedom prior to this period, to be sure, but these earlier restrictions represented isolated incidents and could be dealt with accordingly. The war changed everything.

"It is a terrible thing to lead this great and peaceful people into war," President Wilson declared in his 1917 war message to Congress. He then added to the terror of some by warning that "a firm hand of stern repression" would curtail domestic disloyalty during wartime. At Wilson's request, Congress imposed a military draft, enacted an Espionage Act that outlawed both obstructing the recruitment of troops and causing military insubordination, and authorized the immigration service to denaturalize and deport foreign-born radicals. The federal Justice Department broadly construed the Espionage Act to cover statements critical of the war effort, while the postal service revoked mailing privileges for publications it considered to "embarrass or hamper the government in conducting the war." . . .

Proponents of civil liberties expected conditions to improve after the armistice in 1918, but to them the repression appeared only to intensify. "The war brought with it a burst of unwanted and varied animation. . . . It was common talk that when the foe, whose criminal lust for power had precipitated the mighty tragedy, should be vanquished, things would 'no longer be the same,'" Robinson wrote. "Never did bitter disappointment follow such high hopes. All the old habits of nationalistic policy reasserted themselves at Versailles. . . . Then there emerged from the autocracy of the Tsars the dictatorship of the proletariat, and in Hungary and Germany various startling attempts to revolutionize hastily and excessively." From these developments the so-called Red Scare ensued. "War had naturally produced its machinery for dealing with dissenters, . . . and it was the easiest thing in the world to extend the repression to those who held exceptional or unpopular views, like the Socialists and members of the I.W.W.," Robinson reasoned. . . .

The government reacted swiftly. Most states outlawed the possession or display of either the red flag of communism or the black flag of anarchism. They also enacted the strictly enforced tough new "criminal syndicalism" laws against organized violent or unlawful activities designed to disrupt commercial or governmental activities. . . .

"Well, of course, it was a time of tremendous labor unrest, highlighted by the two general strikes in the steel mills and coal mines. And it was also, and I guess above all, a time of intense radical agitation, brought on by the Russian Revolution," Roger Baldwin later recalled. "So by the time the World War was over we had a new war on our hands—a different one. Then, instead of arresting and persecuting opponents of the war, we were arresting and persecuting friends of Russia." Thus events stood when Baldwin . . . reassumed leadership of the National Civil Liberties Bureau. He promptly concluded, as he stated in a memorandum to the executive committee, that the bureau should be "reorganized and enlarged to cope more adequately with the invasions of civil liberties incident to the industrial struggle which had followed the war." Direct action to protect labor unions would replace legal maneuvers on behalf of pacifists as the bureau's principal focus. The bureau assumed a new name to go with its new mission: the American Civil Liberties Union. "The cause we now serve is labor," Baldwin proclaimed at the time, and labor included public school teachers. . . .

Academic freedom had been an ongoing concern of the ACLU from the organization's inception; naturally, it related to free speech, yet the interest ran even deeper. The pacifists who helped form the National Civil Liberties Bureau abhorred wartime efforts to promote patriotism and militarism in the schools. They defended teachers fired for opposing American involvement in the war and fought against efforts to purge the public school curriculum of German influences. After the war, when the ACLU turned its attention to defending unpopular speakers, its efforts widened to include fighting classroom restrictions on unpopular ideas. "The attempts to maintain a uniform orthodox opinion among teachers should be opposed," the ACLU's initial position statement declared. "The attempts of education authorities to inject into public schools and colleges instruction propaganda in the interest of any particular theory of society to the exclusion of others should be opposed."

This statement primarily reflected the ACLU's opposition to school patriotism programs. Building on wartime developments in New York, the Lusk Committee proposed legislation in 1920 to dismiss public school teachers who "advocated, either by word of mouth or in writing, a form of government other than the government of the United States." The ACLU helped persuade New York governor Al Smith to veto this bill in 1921, but Smith's successor signed similar legislation into law a year later. Dozens of other states required public school teachers and college professors to sign loyalty oaths. Powerful patriotic organizations, including the

American Legion, lobbied for promoting "Americanism" in the public schools by mandatory patriotic exercises (typically a flag salute) and through classroom use of education materials that praised the military and disparaged all things "foreign" (often including the international labor movement). Publicity generated by the ACLU forestalled these programs in some places, but an ACLU lawsuit challenging compulsory military training for male students attending the state University of California at Los Angeles failed. The rise of a militantly anti-Catholic Ku Klux Klan during the early 1920s led to ACLU efforts to protect both Catholic teachers from mass firings in Klan-dominated school districts and the free-speech rights of the Klan in Catholic communities. Repeatedly, the ACLU was drawn into courtrooms over education. Indeed, during the 1920s, it had to go to court to protect its own right to sponsor programs in New York City schools after the local board of education barred all ACLU representatives from "talking in school buildings" under a general regulation requiring classroom speakers to "be loyal to American institutions." . . .

This approach to education led to a de facto establishment of Christianity within American public schools. About the time of the Scopes trial, for example, the Georgia Supreme Court dismissed a Jewish taxpayer's complaint against Christian religious exercises in public schools with the observation, "The Jew may complain to the court as a taxpayer just exactly when and only when a Christian may complain to the court as a taxpayer, *i.e.,* when the Legislature authorizes such reading of the Bible or such instruction in the Christian religion in the public schools as give one Christian sect a preference over others." The Tennessee legislature codified a similar practice in 1915 when it mandated the daily reading of ten Bible verses in public schools but prohibited any comment on the readings. This suggestion that constitutional limits on the establishment of religion simply forbad the government from giving preference to any one church denomination reflected a traditional view of religious freedom that dated at least as far back as the great federalist U.S. Supreme Court justice Joseph Story. By the 1920s, however, an increasing number of liberally educated Americans, including leaders of the ACLU, rejected the idea that public education should promote any particular political, economic, or religious viewpoint—even one broadly defined as democratic, capitalistic, or Christian. . . .

The ACLU press release offering to challenge the Tennessee law appeared in its entirety on May 4 in the *Chattanooga Times,* which had opposed enactment of the antievolution statute. "We are looking for a Tennessee teacher who is willing to accept our services in testing this law in the courts," the release stated. "Our lawyers think a friendly test case can be arranged without costing a teacher his or her job. Distinguished counsel have volunteered their services. All we need now is a willing client." Pursuing the story, a *Chattanooga Times* reporter inquired whether city schools taught evolution. "That depends on what is meant by evolution. If you have reference to the Darwinian theory, which, I suppose, was aimed at in the law passed by the Tennessee legislature, it is not," the city school superintendent assured the reporter. "It is recognized by all our teachers that this is a debatable theory and, as such, has no place in our curriculum." Earlier, in making similar assurances regarding his schools, the Knoxville superintendent had noted, "Our teachers have a hard enough time teaching the children how to distinguish between plant and animal life." These urban school officials clearly did not want to test the new law, but midway between these cities enterprising civic boosters in Dayton craved some attention for their struggling community, and accepted the ACLU offer. They got more than they bargained for. Powerful social forces converged on Dayton that summer: populist majoritarianism and traditional evangelical faith versus scientific secularism and modern concepts of individual liberty. America would never be the same again—or perhaps it had changed already from the country that had nurtured Bryan and Darrow in its heartland.

FURTHER READING

Kathleen Blee, *Women of the Klan: Racism and Gender in the 1920s* (1991).
Stanley Coben, *Rebellion Against Victorianism: The Impetus for Cultural Change in 1920s America* (1991).
Ann Daly, *Done into Dance: Isadora Duncan in America* (1995).
John Higham, *Strangers in the Land: Patterns of American Nativism* (1963).
David Levering Lewis, *When Harlem Was in Vogue* (1989).
Roland Marchand, *Advertising the American Dream: Making Way for Modernity* (1985).
Carole Marks, *Farewell—We're Good and Gone: The Great Black Migration* (1989).
Ronald Takaki, *Strangers from a Different Shore: A History of Asian-Americans* (1989).

C H A P T E R
8

The Depression, the New Deal, and Franklin D. Roosevelt

In the "Dirty Thirties," as sufferers of the Dust Bowl called the decade, it seemed that everything that could go wrong, did go wrong. The stock market crash of 1929, terrifying as it was to investors, who saw their shares fall by 40 percent, was only a harbinger of the international economic collapse and natural calamities to come. The run on banks that began in 1930 ultimately forced more than five thousand financial institutions to shut their doors. With no insurance on deposits, families lost their life savings. Industrial production fell to 20 percent of capacity. Unemployment zoomed to nearly 25 percent in the worst year. With no money to make mortgage payments, millions lost their homes. Local governments that tried to provide relief quickly exhausted their resources, and some went bankrupt. The federal government, which could have provided broad relief, largely refused to do so, as President Herbert Hoover feared creating a welfare-dependent class. Mismanagement by banks, corporations, and the titans of the stock market—combined with a lack of management by government—created the fear that capitalism had rotted from within, and the nation with it.

Farmers were the first to see the Depression coming. Economic stagnation had afflicted agriculture throughout the twenties. To feed the hungry of World War I, farmers had broken the sod of millions of acres of prairie soil in areas with unreliable rainfall. An end to the war and economic instability in Europe in the twenties lessened the demand for their bountiful crops. A persistent drought beginning in 1932, combined with poor farming practices, left soil exposed. Farmers everywhere saw prices for their products plummet as the Depression deepened, but few were more deeply afflicted than those who inhabited the five states making up the "Dust Bowl" (Oklahoma, Texas, Kansas, Colorado, and New Mexico). Winds caught at the dry, loosened dirt, blowing up storms of topsoil that blacked out the sky, asphyxiated animals, choked children and old people, and swept grit all the way to New York City. Foreclosures on desolated lands stimulated an exodus of desperate, starving families to more fertile areas, particularly California. And even where crops would still grow, they rotted on the ground for a lack of buyers. Angry farmers, angry workers, and angry veterans cried out for relief.

Franklin D. Roosevelt came into office prepared to experiment broadly with measures to "fix" some of the most egregious failings of the nation's economic system.

214

The New Deal, as Roosevelt called his programs, aimed at all elements of the crisis, from the stock market on Wall Street to hog markets in Nebraska. The New Deal established the first federal minimum wage, the first government system of unemployment compensation, the first system of old-age pensions (Social Security), the first protections for labor unions, the first regulatory agency for stocks and bonds (the Securities and Exchange Commission), and a host of other institutions. Some of the Roosevelt administration's relief programs were fleeting, but many endure today. The New Deal did not end the Depression, which continued until World War II, nor did it eliminate all the social inequities; these had existed long before the thirties and continued after them. But the New Deal did dramatically recast the role of Washington by giving it a responsibility for the general social welfare. "Big government," like big business, was here to stay.

QUESTIONS TO THINK ABOUT

Who was Franklin D. Roosevelt? Was he a man of the people, or did he simply save the systems of government and business that had made families like his wealthy? What were the strengths and what were the shortcomings of the New Deal?

DOCUMENTS

The documents in this chapter illustrate the various ways in which people experienced the Depression and some of the responses to it. In Document 1, President Herbert Hoover warns the American people that too great a federal role in fighting the Depression might destroy the moral "character" of the nation's citizens and undermine their freedom. In Document 2, the editors of *The Nation* scathingly denounce Hoover's concern for citizens' moral character when many of them were near starvation. In Document 3, auto manufacturer Henry Ford agrees with President Hoover that "self-help" is the best remedy for unemployment, assuming that Americans will volunteer to help one another out. In Document 4, from John Steinbeck's epic *The Grapes of Wrath,* the Joad family is forced to migrate to California, where they learn a hard lesson about being unwelcome in their own country. Steinbeck's novel helped to publicize the plight of the "Okies," landless refugees from Oklahoma and other parts of the Dust Bowl. Document 5 is folk singer Woody Guthrie's famous protest song of the Great Depression, "This Land Is Your Land." It speaks to the frustrations of people like the Joads, who starved in the midst of plenty. Document 6 is Roosevelt's second inaugural address, which he gave at the Capitol on January 20, 1937. In it he called for national attention to the needs of every citizen, especially the poorest. Yet the New Deal did not achieve this ideal in all cases, as Document 7 makes plain. To ensure its passage by Congress, the authors of the Social Security Act wrote it in such a way that the states would not be punished if they discriminated against African Americans in old-age assistance. Document 8 further illustrates the uneven distribution of economic security: widows needed less money than widowers, according to the authors of the Social Security Act. Document 9 is from the National Labor Relations Act, also called the Wagner Act, which for the first time in American history placed the federal government on the side of labor unions. The last selection (Document 10) is a speech by Nelson Rockefeller, wealthy heir to Standard Oil, lecturing corporate executives on the need for big business to revamp its thinking in order to survive the New Deal era.

1. President Herbert Hoover Applauds Limited Government, 1931

The Federal Government has assumed many new responsibilities since Lincoln's time, and will probably assume more in the future when the states and local communities can not alone cure abuse or bear the entire cost of national programs, but there is an essential principle that should be maintained in these matters. I am convinced that where Federal action is essential then in most cases it should limit its responsibilities to supplement the states and local communities, and that it should not assume the major role or the entire responsibility, in replacement of the states or local government. To do otherwise threatens the whole foundations of local government, which is the very basis of self-government.

The moment responsibilities of any community, particularly in economic and social questions, are shifted from any part of the Nation to Washington, then that community has subjected itself to a remote bureaucracy with its minimum of understanding and of sympathy. It has lost a large part of its voice and its control of its own destiny. Under Federal control the varied conditions of life in our country are forced into standard molds, with all their limitations upon life, either of the individual or the community. Where people divest themselves of local government responsibilities they at once lay the foundation for the destruction of their liberties.

And buried in this problem lies something even deeper. The whole of our governmental machinery was devised for the purpose that through ordered liberty we give incentive and equality of opportunity to every individual to rise to that highest achievement of which he is capable. At once when government is centralized there arises a limitation upon the liberty of the individual and a restriction of individual opportunity. The true growth of the Nation is the growth of character in its citizens. The spread of government destroys initiative and thus destroys character. Character is made in the community as well as in the individual by assuming responsibilities, not by escape from them. Carried to its logical extreme, all this shouldering of individual and community responsibility upon the Government can lead but to the superstate where every man becomes the servant of the State and real liberty is lost. Such was not the government that Lincoln sought to build.

There is an entirely different avenue by which we may both resist this drift to centralized government and at the same time meet a multitude of problems. That is to strengthen in the Nation a sense and an organization of self-help and cooperation to solve as many problems as possible outside of government. We are today passing through a critical test in such a problem arising from the economic depression.

Due to lack of caution in business and to the impact of forces from an outside world, one-half of which is involved in social and political revolution, the march of our prosperity has been retarded. We are projected into temporary unemployment, losses, and hardships. In a Nation rich in resources, many people were faced with hunger and cold through no fault of their own. Our national resources are not only material supplies and material wealth but a spiritual and moral wealth in kindliness, in compassion, in a sense of obligation of neighbor to neighbor and a realization of

Herbert Hoover, "Radio Address on Lincoln's Birthday" (February 12, 1931), in *The State Papers and Other Public Writings of Herbert Hoover,* collected and edited by William Starr Myers (Garden City, N.Y.: Doubleday, 1934), Vol. 1, 503–505.

responsibility by industry, by business, and the community for its social security and its social welfare.

The evidence of our ability to solve great problems outside of Government action and the degree of moral strength with which we emerge from this period will be determined by whether the individuals and the local communities continue to meet their responsibilities.

Throughout this depression I have insisted upon organization of these forces through industry, through local government and through charity, that they should meet this crisis by their own initiative, by the assumption of their own responsibilities. The Federal Government has sought to do its part by example in the expansion of employment, by affording credit to drought sufferers for rehabilitation, and by cooperation with the community, and thus to avoid the opiates of Government charity and stifling of our national spirit of mutual self-help. . . .

We are going through a period when character and courage are on trial, and where the very faith that is within us is under test. Our people are meeting this test. And they are doing more than the immediate task of the day. They are maintaining the ideals of our American system. By their devotion to these ideals we shall come out of these times stronger in character, in courage, and in faith.

2. *The Nation* Asks "Is It to Be Murder, Mr. Hoover?" 1932

Is it to be mass murder, Herbert Hoover? Murder by starvation, murder by disease, murder by killing all hope—and the soul? We ask, Mr. President, because this terrible fate is now staring multitudes in the face in the sight of plenty and because the responsibility now rests entirely upon you. Congress has adjourned after voting only $300,000,000 for direct relief—and that only for the States. No one can call it together again for five months except you. Day by day more cities approach the line of bankruptcy; day by day the plight of the individual States of the Union gets worse. In community after community the authorities and the leading citizens can see no hope whatever of heading off the starvation of innocents. And that is murder, Mr. President, cold-blooded and utterly unnecessary murder, far worse than if the victims were to be stood up against a wall and shot down by firing squads. Every death by starvation today—and there are men, women, and children perishing daily because of plain lack of food and undernourishment—must be charged up against the government of the United States, and in the last analysis against *you*. That is not merely because you are President, but because you as an individual have from the first set your face against direct federal relief to those who through no fault of their own are without work and food. You are deeply and sincerely convinced that if necessary it is better that some should starve than that multitudes should have their characters wrecked and their initiative killed by a dole.

But Mr. President, are you living in the United States? Do you know what is happening? Do you know that it is no longer starvation of a few which is at hand? We ask these questions because your statement to the press on July 17 indicates that you are living entirely detached from the actual situation, that you do not know what is

---

"Is It to Be Murder, Mr. Hoover?" by *The Nation*'s editors, *The Nation*, Aug. 3, 1932, 96–97. Cartoon by Edmund Duffy. Text and cartoon reproduced with permission.

happening under the flag of which you are the chief guardian. You stated on that day that you would sign the so-called relief bill granting $300,000,000 for temporary loans by the Reconstruction Finance Corporation "to such States as are absolutely unable to finance the relief of distress." You then went on to say that, through this provision, "We have a solid back log of assurance that there need be no hunger and cold in the United States." You added that these loans were to be based only upon "absolute need and evidence of financial exhaustion," and concluded with the statement: "I do not expect any State to resort to it except as a last extremity." . . . Is it any wonder that we ask you if you know what is happening in the United States today?

. . . Have you not heard that city authorities in St. Louis and the charitable agencies have just turned adrift 13,000 families which they can no longer support, while the city of Detroit has dropped 18,000 who now have nowhere to turn, no assurance that even a single crust of bread will be forthcoming for their support? Have you not learned that the city of Bridgeport, and other cities and towns in Connecticut have let it be known that if the State does not come to their aid at once they have no hope whatever of caring further for their unemployed, their own resources being entirely exhausted? Did you read that eight hundred men marched into the Indiana State Capitol last week demanding food, declaring that if they were not given help they would return 300,000 strong? Have you learned that the police in St. Louis have already fired on a mob demanding bread? Have you not read of the town of Clinton, Mass., where on July 7 "more than three hundred men, women, and crying children crowded the corridors of the Town Hall appealing for food"—only

to learn that the town treasury has been exhausted, that it is unable to borrow a cent from any bank, and that it has been, and still is, trying to support one out of every six residents of the town who are destitute? These are not exceptional cases; they can be multiplied a hundredfold and from almost every section of the country. Is it any wonder, Mr. President, that thirty States moved at once? And how long do you think the $300,000,000 is going to last in the face of this?

3. Business Leader Henry Ford Advocates Self-Help, 1932

I have always had to work, whether any one hired me or not. For the first forty years of my life, I was an employe. When not employed by others, I employed myself. I found very early that being out of hire was not necessarily being out of work. The first means that your employer has not found something for you to do; the second means that you are waiting until he does.

We nowadays think of work as something that others find for us to do, call us to do, and pay us to do. No doubt our industrial growth is largely responsible for that. We have accustomed men to think of work that way. . . .

But something entirely outside the workshops of the nation has affected this hired employment very seriously. The word "unemployment" has become one of the most dreadful words in the language. The condition itself has become the concern of every person in the country. . . .

I do not believe in routine charity. I think it a shameful thing that any man should have to stoop to take it, or give it. I do not include human helpfulness under the name of charity. My quarrel with charity is that it is neither helpful nor human. The charity of our cities is the most barbarous thing in our system, with the possible exception of our prisons. What we call charity is a modern substitute for being personally kind, personally concerned and personally involved in the work of helping others in difficulty. True charity is a much more costly effort than money-giving. . . .

Methods of self-help are numerous and great numbers of people have made the stimulating discovery that they need not depend on employers to find work for them—they can find work for themselves. I have more definitely in mind those who have not yet made that discovery, and I should like to express certain convictions I have tested.

The land! That is where our roots are. There is the basis of our physical life. The farther we get away from the land, the greater our insecurity. From the land comes everything that supports life, everything we use for the service of physical life. The land has not collapsed or shrunk in either extent or productivity. It is there waiting to honor all the labor we are willing to invest in it, and able to tide us across any dislocation of economic conditions.

No unemployment insurance can be compared to an alliance between a man and a plot of land. With one foot in industry and another foot in the land, human society is firmly balanced against most economic uncertainties. With a job to supply him with cash, and a plot of land to guarantee him support, the individual is doubly secure. Stocks may fall, but seedtime and harvest do not fail.

Literary Digest, June 18, 1932. Reprinted courtesy of Ford Motor Company.

I am not speaking of stop-gaps or temporary expedients. Let every man and every family at this season of the year cultivate a plot of land and raise a sufficient supply for themselves or others. Every city and village has vacant space whose use would be permitted. Groups of men could rent farms for small sums and operate them on the co-operative plan. Employed men, in groups of ten, twenty or fifty, could rent farms and operate them with several unemployed families. Or, they could engage a farmer with his farm to be their farmer this year, either as employe or on shares. There are farmers who would be glad to give a decent indigent family a corner of a field on which to live and provide against next winter. Industrial concerns everywhere would gladly make it possible for their men, employed and unemployed, to find and work the land. Public-spirited citizens and institutions would most willingly assist in these efforts at self-help.

I do not urge this solely or primarily on the ground of need. It is a definite step to the restoration of normal business activity. Families who adopt self-help have that amount of free money to use in the channels of trade. That in turn means a flow of goods, an increase in employment, a general benefit.

4. John Steinbeck Portrays the Outcast Poor in *The Grapes of Wrath,* 1939

Two men dressed in jeans and sweaty blue shirts came through the willows and looked toward the naked men. They called, "How's the swimmin'?"

"Dunno," said Tom. "We ain't tried none. Sure feels good to set here, though."

"Mind if we come in an' set?"

"She ain't our river. We'll len' you a little piece of her."

The men shucked off their pants, peeled their shirts, and waded out. The dust coated their legs to the knee; their feet were pale and soft with sweat. They settled lazily into the water and washed listlessly at their flanks. Sun-bitten, they were, a father and a boy. They grunted and groaned with the water.

Pa asked politely, "Goin' west?"

"Nope. We come from there. Goin' back home. We can't make no livin' out there."

"Where's home?" Tom asked.

"Panhandle, come from near Pampa."

Pa asked, "Can you make a livin' there?"

"Nope. But at leas' we can starve to death with folks we know. Won't have a bunch a fellas that hates us to starve with."

Pa said, "Ya know, you're the second fella talked like that. What makes 'em hate you?"

"Dunno," said the man. He cupped his hands full of water and rubbed his face, snorting and bubbling. Dusty water ran out of his hair and streaked his neck.

"I like to hear some more 'bout this," said Pa.

"Me too," Tom added. "Why these folks out west hate ya?"

The man looked sharply at Tom. "You jus' goin' wes'?"

"Jus' on our way."

"You ain't never been in California?"

"No, we ain't."

"Well, don' take my word. Go see for yourself."

"Yeah," Tom said, "but a fella kind a likes to know what he's gettin' into."

"Well, if you truly wanta know, I'm a fella that's asked questions an' give her some thought. She's a nice country. But she was stole a long time ago. You git acrost the desert an' come into the country aroun' Bakersfield. An' you never seen such purty country—all orchards an' grapes, purtiest country you ever seen. An' you'll pass lan' flat an' fine with water thirty feet down, and that lan's layin' fallow. But you can't have none of that lan'. That's a Lan' and Cattle Company. An' if they don't want ta work her, she ain't gonna git worked. You go in there an' plant you a little corn, an' you'll go to jail!"

"Good lan', you say? An' they ain't workin' her?"

"Yes, sir. Good lan' an' they ain't! Well, sir, that'll get you a little mad, but you ain't seen nothin'. People gonna have a look in their eye. They gonna look at you an' their face says, 'I don't like you, you son-of-a-bitch.' Gonna be deputy sheriffs, an' they'll push you aroun'. You camp on the roadside, an' they'll move you on. You gonna see in people's face how they hate you. An'—I'll tell you somepin. They hate you 'cause they're scairt. They know a hungry fella gonna get food even if he got to take it. They know that fallow lan's a sin an' somebody' gonna take it. What the hell! You never been called 'Okie' yet."

Tom said, "Okie? What's that?"

"Well, Okie use' ta mean you was from Oklahoma. Now it means you're a dirty son-of-a-bitch. Okie means you're scum. Don't mean nothing itself, it's the way they say it. But I can't tell you nothin'. You got to go there. I hear there's three hunderd thousan' of our people there—an' livin' like hogs, 'cause ever'thing in California is owned. They ain't nothin' left. An' them people that owns it is gonna hang on to it if they got ta kill ever'body in the worl' to do it. An' they're scairt, an' that makes 'em mad. You got to see it. You got to hear it. Purtiest goddamn country you ever seen, but they ain't nice to you, them folks. They're so scairt an' worried they ain't even nice to each other."

Tom looked down into the water, and he dug his heels into the sand. "S'pose a fella got work an' saved, couldn' he get a little lan'?"

The older man laughed and he looked at his boy, and his silent boy grinned almost in triumph. And the man said, "You ain't gonna get no steady work. Gonna scrabble for your dinner ever' day. An' you gonna do her with people lookin' mean at you." . . .

. . . Ma turned over on her back and crossed her hands under her head. She listened to Granma's breathing and to the girl's breathing. She moved a hand to start a fly from her forehead. The camp was quiet in the blinding heat, but the noises of hot grass—of crickets, the hum of flies—were a tone that was close to silence. Ma sighed deeply and then yawned and closed her eyes. In her half-sleep she heard footsteps approaching, but it was a man's voice that started her awake.

"Who's in here?"

Ma sat up quickly. A brown-faced man bent over and looked in. He wore boots and khaki pants and a khaki shirt with epaulets. On a Sam Browne belt a pistol holster hung, and a big silver star was pinned to his shirt at the left breast. A loose-crowned military cap was on the back of his head. He beat on the tarpaulin with his hand, and the tight canvas vibrated like a drum.

"Who's in here?" he demanded again.

Ma asked, "What is it you want, mister?"

"What you think I want? I want to know who's in here."

"Why, they's jus' us three in here. Me an' Granma an' my girl."

"Where's your men?"

"Why, they went down to clean up. We was drivin' all night."

"Where'd you come from?"

"Right near Sallisaw, Oklahoma."

"Well, you can't stay here."

"We aim to get out tonight an' cross the desert, mister."

"Well, you better. If you're here tomorra this time I'll run you in. We don't want none of you settlin' down here."

Ma's face blackened with anger. She got slowly to her feet. She stooped to the utensil box and picked out the iron skillet. "Mister," she said, " you got a tin button an' a gun. Where I come from, you keep your voice down." She advanced on him with the skillet. He loosened the gun in the holster. "Go ahead," said Ma. "Scarin' women. I'm thankful the men folks ain't here. They'd tear ya to pieces. In my country you watch your tongue."

The man took two steps backward. "Well, you ain't in your country now. You're in California, an' we don't want you god-damn Okies settlin' down."

Ma's advance stopped. She looked puzzled. "Okies?" she said softly. "Okies."

"Yeah, Okies! An' if you're here when I come tomorra, I'll run ya in."

5. Woody Guthrie Sings "This Land Is Your Land," 1940

This land is your land, This land is my land,
From California to the New York island;
From the redwood forest to the Gulf Stream waters:
This land was made for you and me.

As I was walking that ribbon of highway,
I saw above me that endless skyway:
I saw below me that golden valley:
This land was made for you and me.

I've roamed and rambled and I followed my footsteps
To the sparkling sands of her diamond deserts;
And all around me a voice was sounding:
This land was made for you and me.

When the sun came shining, and I was strolling,
And the wheat fields waving and the dust clouds rolling,
As the fog was lifting a voice was chanting:
This land was made for you and me.

As I went walking, I saw a sign there,
And on the sign it said "No Trespassing."
But on the other side it didn't say nothing,
That side was made for you and me.

In the shadow of the steeple I saw my people,
By the relief office I seen my people;
As they stood there hungry, I stood there asking
Is this land made for you and me?

Nobody living can ever stop me,
As I go walking that freedom highway;
Nobody living can ever make me turn back,
This land was made for you and me.

6. President Franklin Roosevelt Seeks Justice for "One-Third of a Nation," 1937

In this nation I see tens of millions of its citizens—a substantial part of its whole population—who at this very moment are denied the greater part of what the very lowest standards of today call the necessities of life.

I see millions of families trying to live on incomes so meager that the pall of family disaster hangs over them day by day.

I see millions whose daily lives in city and on farm continue under conditions labeled indecent by a so-called polite society half a century ago.

I see millions denied education, recreation, and the opportunity to better their lot and the lot of their children.

I see millions lacking the means to buy the products of farm and factory and by their poverty denying work and productiveness to many other millions.

I see one-third of a nation ill-housed, ill-clad, ill-nourished.

It is not in despair that I paint you that picture. I paint it for you in hope—because the Nation, seeing and understanding the injustice in it, proposes to paint it out. We are determined to make every American citizen the subject of his country's interest and concern; and we will never regard any faithful law-abiding group within our borders as superfluous. The test of our progress is not whether we add more to the abundance of those who have much; it is whether we provide enough for those who have too little.

7. An Architect of Social Security Recalls the Southern Concession, 1935

In the congressional hearings and in the executive sessions of the Committee on Ways and Means, as well as in the House debate, the major interest was in old age assistance. Very important changes were made in this part of the bill, principally by the House committee.

The Public Papers and Addresses of Franklin Delano Roosevelt (New York: Random House, 1937), 1–6.

Edwin E. Witte, *The Development of the Social Security Act,* © 1962. Reprinted by permission of The University of Wisconsin Press.

Title I of the original bill was very bitterly attacked, particularly by Senator Byrd, on the score that it vested in a federal department the power to dictate to the state to whom pensions should be paid and how much. In this position, Senator Byrd was supported by nearly all of the southern members of both committees, it being very evident that at least some southern senators feared that this measure might serve as an entering wedge for federal interference with the handling of the Negro question in the South. The southern members did not want to give authority to anyone in Washington to deny aid to any state because it discriminated against Negroes in the administration of old age assistance.

It was my position in the prolonged questioning which I underwent from Senator Byrd that there was no intention of federal dictation. The fact is that it had never occurred to any person connected with the Committee on Economic Security that the Negro question would come up in this connection. After the first days of the committee hearings, however, it was apparent that the bill could not be passed as it stood and that it would be necessary to tone down all clauses relating to supervisory control by the federal government.

The principal changes which were made by the Ways and Means Committee to this end were the following:

1. The conditions for the approval of state plans for old age assistance were stated negatively, with the effect that states might impose other conditions for old age assistance than those dealt with in the bill. Under the original bill, states could not impose any income or property restrictions, nor bar from old age assistance persons with criminal records or any other group of persons. Under the House bill, states were free to impose any conditions they saw fit, with the limitation that if they prescribed conditions as to age, residence, citizenship, etc., their restrictions might not be more stringent than those stipulated in the bill.

2. The House bill eliminated the provision that states must furnish assistance sufficient to provide, "when added to the income of the aged recipient, a reasonable subsistence compatible with decency and health." This provision was copied from the Massachusetts and New York laws and was very objectionable to southern members of Congress. The elimination of this provision left the states free to pay pensions of any amount, however small, and yet recover 50 per cent of their costs from the federal government.

3. The provision that the methods of administration in the states must be satisfactory to the federal department was toned down by adding the qualification, "other than those relating to selection, tenure of office and compensation of personnel." This limitation was inserted because it was feared that the federal administrative agency would require the states to select their personnel on a merit basis, as had been done by the United States Employment Service. The members of Congress did not want any dictation by the federal government in this respect and inserted this limitation for the express purpose of allowing the states to appoint whomever they wished to administer old age assistance.

4. The provisions relating to the withdrawal of approval of state plans were somewhat toned down by inserting provisions to the effect that withdrawal of

approval may occur only after notice to the state authorities, a fair hearing, and a finding that "in a substantial number of cases" the requirements of the federal act were being violated.

8. Social Security Advisers Consider Male and Female Pensioners, 1938

Mr. Myers One very good solution would be to require that the woman must be married to an annuitant for at least five years before she receives any benefits. If a man who is 65 retires and he has been married for three years, he receives 110% for the next two years and following that they will be married five years and they will receive 150% thereafter. Under the plan as it is here they are supposed to be married five years and would receive 100%. Under the plan she would have to be married five years before he retired. He would receive nothing for two years and after that he would receive 150%. Under this plan he would receive 100% for the two-year period and then 150%. . . .

Mr. Mowbray It seems to me that the restriction on the marital period and the period of waiting is only desirable to keep out the designing woman. That wouldn't affect things at all. I made the remark that I thought a two-year period was long enough in a life insurance policy, but I was not at all sure that a five-year period was long enough as a defense against a designing woman.

Mr. Brown How far should those in need be kept in need to protect the system against designing women and old fools? Do you think it ought to be longer than five years? . . .

Miss Dewson I am confused about one point. The single man or single person gets less than the married person. Supposing that the man who is married, say at 66, loses his wife and becomes a single man, would that change his annuity?

Mr. Brown He would drop back. He drops back to the 100%. He no longer gets wife allowance, whereas if the wife survives him it would drop back to the 75%.

Miss Dewson That is what makes it more for the married man?

Mr. Brown Yes, on the principle that it is more costly for the single man to live than for the single woman if she is able to avail herself of the home of the child. A woman is able to fit herself into the economy of the home of the child much better than the single man; that is, the grandmother helps in the raising of the children and helps in home affairs, whereas the aged grandfather is the man who sits out on the front porch and can't help much in the home. . . .

Mr. Brown Are there any other points? In regard to the widows' benefits at 75% of the base we could put in a corollary as to whether 75% of the base is proper.

Mr. Linton I wonder why we didn't make the widows' benefit the regular individual annuity without cutting it down 25%. . . . Why not cut it 50%. Why should you pay the widow less than the individual himself gets if unmarried?

Federal Advisory Council Minutes (April 29, 1938), morning session, 18. File 025, Box 12, Chairman's Files, RG 47, Records of the Social Security Administration, National Archives.

Mr. Williamson She can look after herself better than he can.

Mr. Linton Is that a sociological fact?

Mr. Brown Can a single woman adjust herself to a lower budget on account of the fact that she is used to doing her own housework whereas the single man has to go out to a restaurant?

9. The Wagner Act Allows Workers to Unionize, 1935

. . . The denial by employers of the right of employees to organize and the refusal by employers to accept the procedure of collective bargaining lead to strikes and other forms of industrial strife or unrest, which have the intent or the necessary effect of burdening or obstructing commerce by (a) impairing the efficiency, safety, or operation of the instrumentalities of commerce; (b) occurring in the current of commerce; (c) materially affecting, restraining, or controlling the flow of raw materials or manufactured or processed goods from or into the channels of commerce, or the prices of such materials or goods in commerce; or (d) causing diminution of employment and wages in such volume as substantially to impair or disrupt the market for goods flowing from or into the channels of commerce.

The inequality of bargaining power between employees who do not possess full freedom of association or actual liberty of contract, and employers who are organized in the corporate or other forms of ownership association substantially burdens and affects the flow of commerce, and tends to aggravate recurrent business depressions, by depressing wage rates and the purchasing power of wage earners in industry and by preventing the stabilization of competitive wage rates and working conditions within and between industries.

Experience has proved that protection by law of the right of employees to organize and bargain collectively safeguards commerce from injury, impairment, or interruption, and promotes the flow of commerce by removing certain recognized sources of industrial strife and unrest, by encouraging practices fundamental to the friendly adjustment of industrial disputes arising out of differences as to wages, hours, or other working conditions, and by restoring equality of bargaining power between employers and employees.

It is hereby declared to be the policy of the United States to eliminate the causes of certain substantial obstructions to the free flow of commerce and to mitigate and eliminate these obstructions when they have occurred by encouraging the practice and procedure of collective bargaining and by protecting the exercise by workers of full freedom of association, self-organization, and designation of representatives of their own choosing, for the purpose of negotiating the terms and conditions of their employment or other mutual aid or protection.

National Labor Relations Act, in *Public Laws of the United States of America, 1935–1936*, vol. 49, pt. 1 (Washington, D.C.: U.S. Government Printing Office, 1936), 449–450.

10. Nelson Rockefeller Lectures Standard Oil on Social Responsibility, 1937

The Standard Oil Company of New Jersey has established a unique record by maintaining its supremacy throughout the world despite constantly changing conditions. The adaptability and elasticity of the various departments in devising improved methods of research, production, refining, transportation, and marketing, with constantly increasing efficiency and lower cost is a wonderful tribute to the ability of the management. Unfortunately, today this is no longer enough. . . .

Throughout the world today the rights of the individual or corporation to possess property are being challenged. In many areas here and abroad these rights have already been destroyed. While their defense may rest in legal process fundamentally the preservation of these property rights will be established only by the demonstration of their value to the people. If, as and when the people become convinced—rightly or wrongly—that the owners have disregarded the responsibilities of their stewardship, they can withdraw through legislative action or otherwise these privileges of private ownership. This can apply to corporations individually or industry as a whole. Therefore, if we wish to continue our present system of individual initiative and private ownership, management must conduct its affairs with a sense of moral and social responsibility in such a way as to contribute to the general welfare of society. . . .

. . . When the collapse came in 1929, industry was not sufficiently established in the good will of the country to receive credit for the constructive things it had done and it became a target for public indignation. President Roosevelt and his administration have taken advantage of this opportunity to enact measures to correct some of the situations which industry should never have permitted to develop. Many of the fundamentally important reforms which have been enacted have been the subject of political regulation but should have come as a natural outgrowth of industry's own recognition and acceptance of economic and social changes. If these reforms are to last and become a permanent part of our democratic system they must be accepted wholeheartedly by industry and put on a practical and workable basis.

E S S A Y S

Franklin D. Roosevelt excited both admirers and detractors in his own day, and still does. Herbert Hoover called him a "chameleon on plaid," implying that Roosevelt adjusted his temperament and policies as the situation dictated, without regard to any core values or personal vision. David M. Kennedy of Stanford University, whose book on this era won the Pulitzer Prize, describes a man of immense complexity, whose own experience of crippling disease gave him exceptional fortitude and empathy for others' plight. Roosevelt's leadership, Kennedy states, contrasted markedly with that of Hoover and made the New Deal what it was. Barton Bernstein, also of Stanford University, mostly ignores Roosevelt's personal role. Bernstein's essay is sharply critical of the New Deal. He argues that the New Deal served capitalism better than it served laborers,

Speech of Nelson A. Rockefeller, Rockefeller Archive Center, RFA, R.G. 2, Business Interests Series, box 134, folder 1004. Reprinted by permission of the Rockefeller Archive Center.

small farmers, or African Americans. According to Bernstein, Roosevelt was a paternalist whose humanitarianism remained unengaged by the plight of workers. Bernstein's argument fails to explain, however, how Roosevelt got himself elected to the office of the presidency four times. As you read these two authors, think about how the New Deal may have rewritten government's contract with the people.

FDR: Advocate for the American People

DAVID M. KENNEDY

Hoover brought a corporate executive's sensibility to the White House. Roosevelt brought a politician's. Hoover as president frequently dazzled visitors with his detailed knowledge and expert understanding of American business. "His was a mathematical brain," said his admiring secretary, Theodore Joslin. "Let banking officials, for instance, come into his office and he would rattle off the number of banks in the country, list their liabilities and assets, describe the trend of fiscal affairs, and go into the liquidity, or lack of it, of individual institutions, all from memory." Roosevelt, in contrast, impressed his visitors by asking them to draw a line across a map of the United States. He would then name, in order, every county through which the line passed, adding anecdotes about each locality's political particularities. Where Hoover had a Quaker's reserve about the perquisites of the presidency, Roosevelt savored them with gusto. By 1932 Hoover wore the mantle of office like a hair shirt that he could not wait to doff. Roosevelt confided to a journalist his conviction that "no man ever willingly gives up public life—no man who has ever tasted it." Almost preternaturally self-confident, he had no intimidating image of the presidential office to live up to, it was said, since his untroubled conception of the presidency consisted quite simply of the thought of himself in it.

Hoover's first elected office was the presidency. Roosevelt had been a professional politician all his life. He had spent years charting his course for the White House. To a remarkable degree, he had followed the career path blazed by his cousin Theodore Roosevelt—through the New York legislature and the office of assistant secretary of the navy to the governor's chair in Albany. In 1920 he had been the vice-presidential candidate on the losing Democratic ticket.

The following year, while vacationing at his family's summer estate on Campobello Island, in the Canadian province of New Brunswick, he had been stricken with poliomyelitis. He was thirty-nine years of age. He would never again be able to stand without heavy steel braces on his legs. Through grueling effort and sheer will power, he eventually trained himself to "walk" a few steps, an odd shuffle in which, leaning on the strong arm of a companion, he threw one hip, then the other, to move his steel-cased legs forward. His disability was no secret, but he took care to conceal its extent. He never allowed himself to be photographed in his wheelchair or being carried.

David M. Kennedy, *Freedom from Fear: The American People in Depression and War* (New York: Oxford University Press, 1999), 94–96, 115–117, 133–137, 144–146, 160–163, 168, 258, 261–263, 372, 377–379. Used by permission of Oxford University Press, Inc.

Roosevelt's long struggle with illness transformed him in spirit as well as body. Athletic and slim in his youth, he was now necessarily sedentary, and his upper body thickened. He developed, in the manner of many paraplegics, a wrestler's torso and big, beefy arms. His biceps, he delighted in telling visitors, were bigger than those of the celebrated prizefighter Jack Dempsey. Like many disabled persons, too, he developed a talent for denial, a kind of forcefully willed optimism that refused to dwell on life's difficulties. Sometimes this talent abetted his penchant for duplicity, as in the continuing love affair he carried on with Lucy Mercer, even after he told his wife in 1918 that the relationship was ended. At other times it endowed him with an aura of radiant indomitability, lending conviction and authority to what in other men's mouths might have been banal platitudes, such as "all we have to fear is fear itself." Many of Roosevelt's acquaintances also believed that his grim companionship with paralysis gave to this shallow, supercilious youth the precious gift of a purposeful manhood. . . .

Though Roosevelt was never a systematic thinker, the period of lonely reflection imposed by his convalescence allowed him to shape a fairly coherent social philosophy. By the time he was elected governor, the distillate of his upbringing, education, and experience had crystallized into a few simple but powerful political principles. [Raymond] Moley summarized them this way: "He believed that government not only could, but should, achieve the subordination of private interests to collective interests, substitute co-operation for the mad scramble to selfish individualism. He had a profound feeling for the underdog, a real sense of the critical imbalance of economic life, a very keen awareness that political democracy could not exist side by side with economic plutocracy." As Roosevelt himself put it:

> [O]ur civilization cannot endure unless we, as individuals, realize our responsibility to and dependence on the rest of the world. For it is literally true that the "self-supporting" man or woman has become as extinct as the man of the stone age. Without the help of thousands of others, any one of us would die, naked and starved. Consider the bread upon our table, the clothes upon our backs, the luxuries that make life pleasant; how many men worked in sunlit fields, in dark mines, in the fierce heat of molten metal, and among the looms and wheels of countless factories, in order to create them for our use and enjoyment. . . . In the final analysis, the progress of our civilization will be retarded if any large body of citizens falls behind.

Perhaps deep within himself Roosevelt trembled occasionally with the common human palsies of melancholy or doubt or fear, but the world saw none of it. On February 15, 1933, he gave a memorable demonstration of his powers of self-control. Alighting in Miami from an eleven-day cruise aboard Vincent Astor's yacht *Nourmahal,* FDR motored to Bay Front Park, where he made a few remarks to a large crowd. At the end of the brief speech, Mayor Anton J. Cermak of Chicago stepped up to the side of Roosevelt's open touring car and said a few words to the president-elect. Suddenly a pistol barked from the crowd. Cermak doubled over. Roosevelt ordered the Secret Service agents, who were reflexively accelerating his car away from the scene, to stop. He motioned to have Cermak, pale and pulseless, put into the seat beside him. "Tony, keep quiet—don't move. It won't hurt you if you keep quiet," Roosevelt repeated as he cradled Cermak's limp body while the car sped to the hospital.

Cermak had been mortally wounded. He died within weeks, the victim of a deranged assassin who had been aiming for Roosevelt. On the evening of February 15, after Cermak had been entrusted to the doctors, Moley accompanied Roosevelt back to the *Nourmahal,* poured him a stiff drink, and prepared for the letdown now that Roosevelt was alone among his intimates. He had just been spared by inches from a killer's bullet and had held a dying man in his arms. But there was nothing—"not so much as the twitching of a muscle, the mopping of a brow, or even the hint of a false gaiety—to indicate that it wasn't any other evening in any other place. Roosevelt was simply himself—easy, confident, poised, to all appearances unmoved." The episode contributed to Moley's eventual conclusion "that Roosevelt had no nerves at all." He was, said Frances Perkins, "the most complicated human being I ever knew." . . .

Roosevelt began inaugural day by attending a brief service at St. John's Episcopal Church. His old Groton School headmaster, Endicott Peabody, prayed the Lord to "bless Thy servant, Franklin, chosen to be president of the United States." After a quick stop at the Mayflower Hotel to confer urgently with his advisers on the still-worsening banking crisis, Roosevelt donned his formal attire and motored to the White House. There he joined a haggard and cheerless Hoover for the ride down Pennsylvania Avenue to the inaugural platform on the east side of the Capitol.

Braced on his son's arm, Roosevelt walked his few lurching steps to the rostrum. Breaking precedent, he recited the entire oath of office, rather than merely repeating "I do" to the chief justice's interrogation. Then he began his inaugural address, speaking firmly in his rich tenor voice. Frankly acknowledging the crippled condition of the ship of state he was now to captain, he began by reassuring his countrymen that "this great nation will endure as it had endured, will revive and will prosper. . . . The only thing we have to fear," he intoned, "is fear itself." The nation's distress, he declared, owed to "no failure of substance." Rather, "rulers of the exchange of mankind's goods have failed through their own stubbornness and their own incompetence, have admitted their failure, and have abdicated. . . . The money changers have fled from their high seats in the temple of our civilization. We may now restore that temple to the ancient truths." The greatest task, he went on, "is to put people to work," and he hinted at "direct recruiting by the Government" on public works projects as the means to do it. . . .

Just weeks before his inaugural, while on his way to board the *Nourmahal* in Florida, Roosevelt had spoken restlessly of the need for "action, action." President at last, he now proceeded to act with spectacular vigor.

The first and desperately urgent item of business was the banking crisis. Even as he left the Mayflower Hotel to deliver his inaugural condemnation of the "money changers," he approved a recommendation originating with the outgoing treasury secretary, Ogden Mills, to convene an emergency meeting of bankers from the leading financial centers. The next day, Sunday, March 5, Roosevelt issued two proclamations, one calling Congress into special session on March 9, the other invoking the Trading with the Enemy Act to halt all transactions in gold and declare a four-day national banking holiday—both of them measures that Hoover had vainly urged him to endorse in the preceding weeks. Hoover's men and Roosevelt's now began an intense eighty hours of collaboration to hammer out the details of an emergency banking measure that could be presented to the special session of Congress. Haunting the corridors of the Treasury Department day and night, private bankers and government officials both old and new toiled frantically to rescue the moribund corpse of American finance. In that hectic week, none led normal lives, Moley remembered. "Confusion, haste, the dread of making mistakes, the consciousness of responsibility for the economic well-being of millions of people, made mortal inroads on the health of some of us . . . and left the rest of us ready to snap at our images in the mirror. . . . Only Roosevelt," Moley observed, "preserved the air of a man who'd found a happy way of life."

Roosevelt's and Hoover's minions "had forgotten to be Republicans or Democrats," Moley commented. "We were just a bunch of men trying to save the banking system." William Woodin, the new treasury secretary, and Ogden Mills, his predecessor, simply shifted places on either side of the secretary's desk in the Treasury Building. Otherwise, nothing changed in the room. The kind of bipartisan collaboration for which Hoover had long pleaded was now happening, but under Roosevelt's aegis, not Hoover's—and not, all these men hoped, too late. When the special session of Congress convened at noon on March 9, they had a bill ready—barely.

The bill was read to the House at 1:00 P.M., while some new representatives were still trying to locate their seats. Printed copies were not ready for the members. A rolled-up newspaper symbolically served. After thirty-eight minutes of "debate," the chamber passed the bill, sight unseen, with a unanimous shout. The Senate approved the bill with only seven dissenting votes—all from agrarian states historically suspicious of Wall Street. The president signed the legislation into law at 8:36 in the evening. "Capitalism," concluded Moley, "was saved in eight days." . . .

On Monday the thirteenth the banks reopened, and the results of Roosevelt's magic with the Congress and the people were immediately apparent. Deposits and gold began to flow back into the banking system. The prolonged banking crisis, acute since at least 1930, with roots reaching back through the 1920s and even into the days of Andrew Jackson, was at last over. And Roosevelt, taking full credit, was a hero. William Randolph Hearst told him: "I guess at your next election we will make it unanimous." Even Henry Stimson, who so recently had thought FDR a "peanut," sent his "heartiest congratulations."

The common people of the country sent their congratulations as well—and their good wishes and suggestions and special requests. Some 450,000 Americans wrote to their new president in his first week in office. Thereafter mail routinely poured in at a rate of four to seven thousand letters per day. The White House mailroom, staffed by a single employee in Hoover's day, had to hire seventy people to handle the flood of correspondence. Roosevelt had touched the hearts and imaginations of his countrymen like no predecessor in memory. . . .

Meanwhile, the steady legislative drumbeat of the Hundred Days continued. Relishing power and wielding it with gusto, Roosevelt next sent to Congress, on March 21, a request for legislation aimed at unemployment relief. Here he departed most dramatically from Hoover's pettifogging timidity, and here he harvested the greatest political rewards. He proposed a Civilian Conservation Corps (CCC) to employ a quarter of a million men on forestry, flood control, and beautification projects. Over the next decade, the CCC became one of the most popular of all the New Deal's innovations. By the time it expired in 1942, it had put more than three million idle youngsters to work at a wage of thirty dollars a month, twenty-five of which they were required to send home to their families. CCC workers built fire-breaks and lookouts in the national forests and bridges, campgrounds, trails, and museums in the national parks. Roosevelt also called for a new agency, the Federal Emergency Relief Administration (FERA), to coordinate and eventually increase direct federal unemployment assistance to the states. And he served notice, a bit half-heartedly, that he would soon be making recommendations about a "broad public works labor-creating program."

The first two of these measures—CCC and FERA—constituted important steps along the road to direct federal involvement in unemployment relief, something that Hoover had consistently and self-punishingly resisted. Roosevelt showed no such squeamishness, just as he had not hesitated as governor of New York to embrace relief as a "social duty" of government in the face of evident human suffering. As yet, Roosevelt did not think of relief payments or public works employment as means of significantly increasing purchasing power. He proposed them for charitable reasons, and for political purposes as well, but not principally for economic ones. . . .

These first modest steps at a direct federal role in welfare services also carried into prominence another of Roosevelt's associates from New York, Harry Hopkins, whom Roosevelt would soon name as federal relief administrator. A chain-smoking, hollow-eyed, pauper-thin social worker, a tough-talking, big-hearted blend of the sardonic and sentimental, Hopkins represented an important and durable component of what might be called the emerging political culture of the New Deal. In common with Brain Truster Adolf Berle, future treasury secretary Henry Morgenthau Jr., and Labor Secretary Frances Perkins, Hopkins was steeped in the Social Gospel tradition. Ernest, high-minded, and sometimes condescending, the Social Gospelers were middle-class missionaries to America's industrial proletariat. Inspired originally by late nineteenth-century Protestant clergymen like Walter Rauschenbusch and Washington Gladden, they were committed to the moral and material uplift of the poor, and they had both the courage and the prejudices of their convictions. Berle and Morgenthau had worked for a time at Lillian Wald's Henry Street settlement house in New York, Perkins at Jane Addams's Hull House in Chicago, and Hopkins himself at New York's Christadora House. Amid the din and squalor of thronged immigrant neighborhoods, they had all learned at first hand that poverty could be an exitless way of life, that the idea of "opportunity" was often a mockery in the precarious, threadbare existence of the working class. Together with Franklin Roosevelt, they meant to do something about it. . . .

"What I want you to do," said Harry Hopkins to Lorena Hickok in July 1933, "is to go out around the country and look this thing over. I don't want statistics from you. I don't want the social-worker angle. I just want your own reaction, as an ordinary citizen.

"Go talk with preachers and teachers, businessmen, workers, farmers. Go talk with the unemployed, those who are on relief and those who aren't. And when you talk with them don't ever forget that but for the grace of God you, I, any of our friends might be in their shoes. Tell me what you see and hear. All of it. Don't ever pull your punches."

The Depression was now in its fourth year. In the neighborhoods and hamlets of a stricken nation millions of men and women languished in sullen gloom and looked to Washington with guarded hope. Still they struggled to comprehend the nature of the calamity that had engulfed them. Across Hopkins's desk at the newly created Federal Emergency Relief Administration flowed rivers of data that measured the Depression's impact in cool numbers. But Hopkins wanted more—to touch the human face of the catastrophe, taste in his mouth the metallic smack of the fear and hunger of the unemployed, as he had when he worked among the immigrant poor at New York's Christadora settlement house in 1912. Tied to his desk in Washington, he dispatched Lorena Hickok in his stead. In her he chose a uniquely gutsy and perceptive observer who could be counted on to see without illusion and to report with candor, insight, and moxie. . . .

From the charts and tables accumulating on his desk even before Hickok's letters began to arrive, Hopkins could already sketch the grim outlines of that history. Stockholders, his figures confirmed, had watched as three-quarters of the value of their assets had simply evaporated since 1929, a colossal financial meltdown that blighted not only the notoriously idle rich but struggling neighborhood banks, hard-earned retirement nest eggs, and college and university endowments as well. The more than five thousand bank failures between the Crash and the New Deal's rescue operation in March 1933 wiped out some $7 billion in depositors' money. Accelerating foreclosures on defaulted home mortgages—150,000 homeowners lost their property in 1930, 200,000 in 1931, 250,000 in 1932—stripped millions of people of both shelter and life savings at a single stroke and menaced the balance sheets of thousands of surviving banks. Several states and some thirteen hundred municipalities, crushed by sinking real estate prices and consequently shrinking tax revenues, defaulted on their obligations to creditors, pinched their already scant social services, cut payrolls, and slashed paychecks. Chicago was reduced to paying its teachers in tax warrants and then, in the winter of 1932–33, to paying them nothing at all.

Gross national product had fallen by 1933 to half its 1929 level. Spending for new plants and equipment had ground to a virtual standstill. Businesses invested only $3 billion in 1933, compared with $24 billion in 1929. . . . Residential and industrial construction shriveled to less than one-fifth of its pre-Depression volume, a wrenching contraction that spread through lumber camps, steel mills, and appliance factories, disemploying thousands of loggers, mill hands, sheet-metal workers, engineers, architects, carpenters, plumbers, roofers, plasterers, painters, and electricians. Mute shoals of jobless men drifted through the streets of every American city in 1933.

Nowhere did the Depression strike more savagely than in the American countryside. On America's farms, income had plummeted from $6 billion in what for farmers was the already lean year of 1929 to $2 billion in 1932. The net receipts from the wheat harvest in one Oklahoma county went from $1.2 million in 1931 to just $7,000 in 1933. Mississippi's pathetic $239 per capita income in 1929 sank to $117 in 1933.

Unemployment and its close companion, reduced wages, were the most obvious and the most wounding of all the Depression's effects. The government's data showed that 25 percent of the work force, some thirteen million workers, including nearly four hundred thousand women, stood idle in 1933. . . .

Hickok set out in quest of the human reality of the Depression. She found that and much more besides. In dingy working-class neighborhoods in Philadelphia and New York, in unpainted clapboard farmhouses in North Dakota, on the ravaged cotton farms of Georgia, on the dusty mesas of Colorado, Hickok uncovered not just the effects of the economic crisis that had begun in 1929. She found herself face to face as well with the human wreckage of a century of pell-mell, buccaneer-ing, no-holds-barred, free-market industrial and agricultural capitalism. As her travels progressed, she gradually came to acknowledge the sobering reality that for many Americans the Great Depression brought times only a little harder than usual. She discovered, in short, what historian James Patterson has called the "old poverty" that was endemic in America well before the Depression hit. By his esti-mate, even in the midst of the storied prosperity of the 1920s some forty million Americans, including virtually all nonwhites, most of the elderly, and much of the rural population, were eking out unrelievedly precarious lives that were scarcely visible and practically unimaginable to their more financially secure countrymen. "The researches we have made into standards of living of the American family," Hopkins wrote, "have uncovered for the public gaze a volume of chronic poverty, unsuspected except by a few students and by those who have always experienced it." From this perspective, the Depression was not just a passing crisis but an episode that revealed deeply rooted structural inequities in American society.

The "old poor" were among the Depression's most ravaged victims, but it was not the Depression that had impoverished them. They were the "one-third of a na-tion" that Franklin Roosevelt would describe in 1937 as chronically "ill-housed, ill-clad, ill-nourished." By suddenly threatening to push millions of other Amer-icans into their wretched condition, the Depression pried open a narrow window of political opportunity to do something at last on behalf of that long-suffering one-third, and in the process to redefine the very character of America. . . .

. . . The Emergency Relief Appropriation Act addressed only the most immediate of his [FDR's] goals. Most of the agencies it spawned were destined to survive less than a decade. The longer-term features of Roosevelt's grand design—unemployment insurance and old-age pensions—were incorporated in a separate piece of legisla-tion, a landmark measure whose legacy endured and reshaped the texture of Ameri-can life: the Social Security Act.

No other New Deal measure proved more lastingly consequential or more emblematic of the very meaning of the New Deal. Nor did any other better reveal the tangled skein of human needs, economic calculations, idealistic visions, political pressures, partisan maneuverings, actuarial projections, and constitutional constraints out of which Roosevelt was obliged to weave his reform program. Tortuously thread-ing each of those filaments through the needle of the legislative process, Roosevelt began with the Social Security Act to knit the fabric of the modern welfare state. It would in the end be a peculiar garment, one that could have been fashioned only in America and perhaps only in the circumstances of the Depression era.

No one knew better the singular possibilities of that place and time than Secre-tary of Labor Frances Perkins. To her the president in mid-1934 assigned the task of chairing a cabinet committee to prepare the social security legislation for submission to Congress. (Its other members were Treasury Secretary Henry Morgenthau, Attor-ney General Homer Cummings, Agriculture Secretary Henry Wallace, and Relief Administrator Harry Hopkins.) "[T]his was the time, above all times," Perkins wrote, "to be foresighted about future problems of unemployment and unprotected old age." The president shared this sense of urgency—and opportunity. Now is the time, he said to Perkins in 1934, when "we have to get it started, or it will never start." . . .

At the outset the president entertained extravagantly far-reaching ideas about the welfare system he envisioned. "[T]here is no reason why everybody in the United States should not be covered," he mused to Perkins on one occasion. "I see no reason why every child, from the day he is born, shouldn't be a member of the social security system. When he begins to grow up, he should know he will have old-age benefits direct from the insurance system to which he will belong all his life. If he is out of work, he gets a benefit. If he is sick or crippled, he gets a benefit. . . . And there is no reason why just the industrial workers should get the benefit of this," Roosevelt went on. "Everybody ought to be in on it—the farmer and his wife and his family. I don't see why not," Roosevelt persisted, as Perkins shook her head at this presidential woolgathering. "I don't see why not. Cradle to the grave—from the cradle to the grave they ought to be in a social insurance system."

That may have been the president's ideal outcome, but he knew as well as anyone that he would have to temper that vision in the forge of political and fiscal reality. Much of the country, not least the southern Democrats who were essential to his party's congressional majority, remained suspicious about all forms of social insurance. So Perkins, with dour Yankee prudence, went to work in a more practical vein. In the summer of 1934 she convened the Committee on Economic Security (CES), an advisory body of technical experts who would hammer out the precise terms of the social security legislation. She instructed the CES in words that spoke eloquently about her sensitivity to the novelties and difficulties of what they were about to undertake. "I recall emphasizing," she later wrote, "that the President was already in favor of a program of social insurance, but that it remained for them to make it practicable. We expected them," she recollected, in a passage that says volumes about her shrewd assessment of American political culture in the 1930s, "to remember that this was the United States in the years 1934–35. We hoped they would make recommendations based upon a practical knowledge of the needs of our country, the prejudices of our people, and our legislative habits."

The needs of the country were plain enough. But what of those prejudices and habits? What, in particular, of that phrase "under state laws" in the Democratic platform? Few items more deeply vexed the CES planners. Given the mobility of American workers and the manifest desirability of uniformity in national laws, most of the CES experts insisted that a centralized, federally administered system of social insurance would be the most equitable and the easiest to manage. They deemed a miscellany of state systems to be utterly impractical. Yet deeply ingrained traditions of states' rights challenged that commonsense approach, as did pervasive doubts about the federal government's constitutional power to act in this area.

Thomas Eliot, the young, Harvard-educated general counsel to the CES who played a major role in drafting the final bill, worried above all about "the omnipresent question of constitutionality." The lower federal courts, Eliot knew, had already handed down hundreds of injunctions against other New Deal measures. Constitutional tests of NRA and AAA were working their way to the Supreme Court. There, four justices—the "Battalion of Death" that included Justices McReynolds, Butler, VanDevanter, and Sutherland—were notoriously hostile to virtually any expansion of federal power over industry and commerce, not to mention the far bolder innovation of federal initiatives respecting employment and old age. Eliot brooded that "I could not honestly assure the committee that a national plan . . . would be upheld by the Supreme Court." . . .

Against their better judgment, the CES experts therefore resigned themselves to settling for a mixed federal-state system. Perkins took what comfort she could from the reflection that if the Supreme Court should declare the federal aspects of the law to be unconstitutional, at least the state laws would remain. Though they would not be uniform, they would be better than nothing. . . .

The pattern of economic reforms that the New Deal wove arose out of concrete historical circumstances. It also had a more coherent intellectual underpinning than is customarily recognized. Its cardinal aim was not to destroy capitalism but to devolatilize it, and at the same time to distribute its benefits more evenly. . . .

. . . And ever after, Americans assumed that the federal government had not merely a role, but a major responsibility, in ensuring the health of the economy and the welfare of citizens. That simple but momentous shift in perception was the newest thing in all the New Deal, and the most consequential too.

Humankind, of course, does not live by bread alone. Any assessment of what the New Deal did would be incomplete if it rested with an appraisal of New Deal economic policies and failed to acknowledge the remarkable array of social innovations nourished by Roosevelt's expansive temperament. . . .

For all his alleged inscrutability, Franklin Roosevelt's social vision was clear enough. "We are going to make a country," he once said to Frances Perkins, "in which no one is left out." In that unadorned sentence Roosevelt spoke volumes about the New Deal's lasting historical meaning. Like his rambling, comfortable, and unpretentious old home on the bluff above the Hudson River, Roosevelt's New Deal was a welcoming mansion of many rooms, a place where millions of his fellow citizens could find at last a measure of the security that the patrician Roosevelts enjoyed as their birthright.

Perhaps the New Deal's greatest achievement was its accommodation of the maturing immigrant communities that had milled uneasily on the margins of American society for a generation and more before the 1930s. In bringing them into the Democratic Party and closer to the mainstream of national life, the New Deal, even without fully intending to do so, also made room for an almost wholly new institution, the industrial union. To tens of millions of rural Americans, the New Deal offered the modern comforts of electricity, schools, and roads, as well as unaccustomed financial stability. To the elderly and the unemployed it extended the promise of income security, and the salvaged dignity that went with it.

To black Americans the New Deal offered jobs with CCC, WPA, and PWA and, perhaps as important, the compliment of respect from at least some federal officials. The time had not come for direct federal action to challenge Jim Crow and put right at last the crimes of slavery and discrimination, but more than a few New Dealers made clear where their sympathies lay and quietly prepared for a better future. Urged on by Eleanor Roosevelt, the president brought African-Americans into the government in small but unprecedented numbers. By the mid-1930s they gathered periodically as an informal "black cabinet," guided often by the redoubtable Mary McLeod Bethune. Roosevelt also appointed the first black federal judge, William Hastie. Several New Deal Departments and agencies, including especially Ickes's Interior Department and Aubrey Williams's National Youth Administration, placed advisers for "Negro affairs" on their staffs. . . .

Above all, the New Deal gave to countless Americans who had never had much of it a sense of security, and with it a sense of having a stake in their country. And it did it all without shredding the American Constitution or sundering the American people. At a time when despair and alienation were prostrating other peoples under the heel of dictatorship, that was no small accomplishment.

FDR: Savior of Capitalism

BARTON J. BERNSTEIN

The liberal reforms of the New Deal did not transform the American system; they conserved and protected American corporate capitalism, occasionally by absorbing parts of threatening programs. There was no significant redistribution of power in American society, only limited recognition of other organized groups, seldom of unorganized peoples. Neither the bolder programs advanced by New Dealers nor the final legislation greatly extended the beneficence of government beyond the middle classes or drew upon the wealth of the few for the needs of the many. Designed to maintain the American system, liberal activity was directed toward essentially conservative goals. Experimentalism was most frequently limited to means; seldom did it extend to ends. Never questioning private enterprise, it operated within safe channels, far short of Marxism or even of native American radicalisms that offered structural critiques and structural solutions.

All of this is not to deny the changes wrought by the New Deal—the extension of welfare programs, the growth of federal power, the strengthening of the executive, even the narrowing of property rights. But it is to assert that the elements of continuity are stronger, that the magnitude of change has been exaggerated. The New Deal failed to solve the problem of depression, it failed to raise the impoverished, it failed to redistribute income, it failed to extend equality and generally countenanced racial discrimination and segregation. It failed generally to make business more responsible to the social welfare or to threaten business's pre-eminent political power. In this sense, the New Deal, despite the shifts in tone and spirit from the earlier decade, was profoundly conservative and continuous with the 1920s. . . .

. . . Using the federal government to stabilize the economy and advance the interests of the groups, Franklin D. Roosevelt directed the campaign to save large-scale corporate capitalism. Though recognizing new political interests and extending benefits to them, his New Deal never effectively challenged big business or the organization of the economy. In providing assistance to the needy and by rescuing them from starvation, Roosevelt's humane efforts also protected the established system: he sapped organized radicalism of its waning strength and of its potential constituency among the unorganized and discontented. Sensitive to public opinion and fearful of radicalism, Roosevelt acted from a mixture of motives that rendered his liberalism cautious and limited, his experimentalism narrow. Despite the flurry

Barton J. Bernstein, "New Deal: Conservative Achievements of Liberal Reform," in *Towards a New Past: Dissenting Essays in American History* (New York: Random House, 1968), 264–265, 267–275, 278–282. Used by permission of Pantheon Books, a division of Random House, Inc.

of activity, his government was more vigorous and flexible about means than goals, and the goals were more conservative than historians usually acknowledge.

Roosevelt's response to the banking crisis emphasizes the conservatism of his administration and its self-conscious avoidance of more radical means that might have transformed American capitalism. Entering the White House when banks were failing and Americans had lost faith in the financial system, the President could have nationalized it—"without a word of protest," judged Senator Bronson Cutting. "If ever there was a moment when things hung in the balance," later wrote Raymond Moley, a member of the original "brain trust," it was on March 5, 1933—when unorthodoxy would have drained the last remaining strength of the capitalistic system." To save the system, Roosevelt relied upon collaboration between bankers and Hoover's Treasury officials to prepare legislation extending federal assistance to banking. So great was the demand for action that House members, voting even without copies, passed it unanimously, and the Senate, despite objections by a few Progressives, approved it the same evening. "The President," remarked a cynical congressman, "drove the money-changers out of the Capitol on March 4th—and they were all back on the 9th."

Undoubtedly the most dramatic example of Roosevelt's early conservative approach to recovery was the National Recovery Administration (NRA). It was based on the War Industries Board (WIB) which had provided the model for the campaign of Bernard Baruch, General Hugh Johnson, and other former WIB officials during the twenties to limit competition through industrial self-regulation under federal sanction. As trade associations flourished during the decade, the FTC encouraged "codes of fair competition" and some industries even tried to set prices and restrict production. Operating without the force of law, these agreements broke down. When the depression struck, industrial pleas for regulation increased. After the Great Crash, important business leaders including Henry I. Harriman of the Chamber of Commerce and Gerard Swope of General Electric called for suspension of antitrust laws and federal organization of business collaboration. Joining them were labor leaders, particularly those in "sick" industries—John L. Lewis of the United Mine Workers and Sidney Hillman of Amalgamated Clothing Workers.

Designed largely for industrial recovery, the NRA legislation provided for minimum wages and maximum hours. It also made concessions to pro-labor congressmen and labor leaders who demanded some specific benefits for unions—recognition of the worker's right to organization and to collective bargaining. In practice, though, the much-heralded Section 7a was a disappointment to most friends of labor. (For the shrewd Lewis, however, it became a mandate to organize: "The President wants you to join a union.") To many frustrated workers and their disgusted leaders, NRA became "National Run Around." The clause, unionists found (in the words of Brookings economists), "had the practical effect of placing NRA on the side of anti-union employers in their struggle against trade unions. . . . [It] thus threw its weight against labor in the balance of bargaining power." And while some far-sighted industrialists feared radicalism and hoped to forestall it by incorporating unions into the economic system, most preferred to leave their workers unorganized or in company unions. To many businessmen, large and independent unions as such seemed a radical threat to the system of business control.

Not only did the NRA provide fewer advantages than unionists had anticipated, but it also failed as a recovery measure. It probably even retarded recovery by supporting restrictionism and price increases, concluded a Brookings study. Placing effective power for code-writing in big business, NRA injured small businesses and contributed to the concentration of American industry. It was not the government-business partnership as envisaged by Adolf A. Berle, Jr., nor government managed as Rexford Tugwell had hoped, but rather, business managed, as Raymond Moley had desired. Calling NRA "industrial self-government," its director, General Hugh Johnson, had explained that "NRA is exactly what industry organized in trade associations makes it." Despite the annoyance of some big businessmen with Section 7a, the NRA reaffirmed and consolidated their power at a time when the public was critical of industrialists and financiers.

Viewing the economy as a "concert of organized interests," the New Deal also provided benefits for farmers—the Agricultural Adjustment Act. Reflecting the political power of larger commercial farmers and accepting restrictionist economics, the measure assumed that the agricultural problem was overproduction, not underconsumption. Financed by a processing tax designed to raise prices to parity, payments encouraged restricted production and cutbacks in farm labor. With benefits accruing chiefly to the larger owners, they frequently removed from production the lands of sharecroppers and tenant farmers, and "tractored" them and hired hands off the land. In assisting agriculture, the AAA, like the NRA, sacrificed the interests of the marginal and the unrecognized to the welfare of those with greater political and economic power.

In large measures, the early New Deal of the NRA and AAA was a "broker state." Though the government served as a mediator of interests and sometimes imposed its will in divisive situations, it was generally the servant of powerful groups. "Like the mercantilists, the New Dealers protected vested interests with the authority of the state," acknowledges William Leuchtenburg. But it was some improvement over the 1920s when business was the only interest capable of imposing its will on the government. While extending to other groups the benefits of the state, the New Deal, however, continued to recognize the pre-eminence of business interests.

The politics of the broker state also heralded the way of the future—of continued corporate dominance in a political structure where other groups agreed generally on corporate capitalism and squabbled only about the size of the shares. Delighted by this increased participation and the absorption of dissident groups, many liberals did not understand the dangers in the emerging organization of politics. They had too much faith in representative institutions and in associations to foresee the perils— of leaders not representing their constituents, of bureaucracy diffusing responsibility, of officials serving their own interests. Failing to perceive the dangers in the emerging structure, most liberals agreed with Senator Robert Wagner of New York: "In order that the strong may not take advantage of the weak, every group must be equally strong." His advice then seemed appropriate for organizing labor, but it neglected the problems of unrepresentative leadership and of the many millions to be left beyond organization.

In dealing with the organized interests, the President acted frequently as a broker, but his government did not simply express the vectors of external forces. The New Deal state was too complex, too loose, and some of Roosevelt's subordinates were following their own inclinations and pushing the government in directions of their own design. The President would also depart from his role as a broker and act to secure programs he desired. As a skilled politician, he could split coalitions, divert the interests of groups, or place the prestige of his office on the side of desired legislation.

In seeking to protect the stock market, for example, Roosevelt endorsed the Securities and Exchange measure (of 1934), despite the opposition of many in the New York financial community. His advisers split the opposition. Rallying to support the administration were the out-of-town exchanges, representatives of the large commission houses, including James Forrestal of Dillon, Read, and Robert Lovett of Brown Brothers, Harriman, and such commission brokers as E. A. Pierce and Paul Shields. Opposed to the Wall Street "old guard" and their companies, this group included those who wished to avoid more radical legislation, as well as others who had wanted earlier to place trading practices under federal legislation which they could influence.

Though the law restored confidence in the securities market and protected capitalism, it alarmed some businessmen and contributed to the false belief that the New Deal was threatening business. But it was not the disaffection of a portion of the business community, nor the creation of the Liberty League, that menaced the broker state. Rather it was the threat of the Left—expressed, for example, in such overwrought statements as Minnesota Governor Floyd Olson's: "I am not a liberal . . . I am a radical. . . . I am not satisfied with hanging a laurel wreath on burglars and thieves . . . and calling them code authorities or something else." While Olson, along with some others who succumbed to the rhetoric of militancy, would back down and soften their meaning, their words dramatized real grievances: the failure of the early New Deal to end misery, to re-create prosperity. The New Deal excluded too many. Its programs were inadequate. While Roosevelt reluctantly endorsed relief and went beyond Hoover in support of public works, he too preferred self-liquidating projects, desired a balanced budget, and resisted spending the huge sums required to lift the nation out of depression.

For millions suffering in a nation wracked by poverty, the promises of the Left seemed attractive. Capitalizing on the misery, Huey Long offered Americans a "Share Our Wealth" program—a welfare state with prosperity, not subsistence, for the disadvantaged, those neglected by most politicians. "Every Man a King": pensions for the elderly, college for the deserving, homes and cars for families—that was the promise of American life. Also proposing minimum wages, increased public works, shorter work weeks, and a generous farm program, he demanded a "soak-the-rich" tax program. Despite the economic defects of his plan, Long was no hayseed, and his forays into the East revealed support far beyond the bayous and hamlets of his native South. In California discontent was so great that Upton Sinclair, food faddist and former socialist, captured the Democratic nomination for governor on a platform of "production-for-use"—factories and farms for the unemployed. "In a cooperative society," promised Sinclair, "every man, woman, and child would have the equivalent of $5,000 a year income from labor of the able-bodied young men for three or four hours per day." . . .

Challenged by the Left, and with the new Congress more liberal and more willing to spend, Roosevelt turned to disarm the discontent. "Boys—this is our hour," confided Harry Hopkins. "We've got to get everything we want—a works program, social security, wages and hours, everything—now or never. Get your minds to work on developing a complete ticket to provide security for all the folks of this country up and down and across the board." Hopkins and the associates he addressed were not radicals: they did not seek to transform the system, only to make it more humane. They, too, wished to preserve large-scale corporate capitalism, but unlike Roosevelt or Moley, they were prepared for more vigorous action. Their commitment to reform was greater, their tolerance for injustice far less. Joining them in pushing the New Deal left were the leaders of industrial unions, who, while also not wishing to transform the system, sought for workingmen higher wages, better conditions, stronger and larger unions, and for themselves a place closer to the fulcrum of power.

The problems of organized labor, however, neither aroused Roosevelt's humanitarianism nor suggested possibilities of reshaping the political coalition. When asked during the NRA about employee representation, he had replied that workers could select anyone they wished—the Ahkoond of Swat, a union, even the Royal Geographical Society. As a paternalist, viewing himself (in the words of James MacGregor Burns) as a "partisan and benefactor" of workers, he would not understand the objections to company unions or to multiple unionism under NRA. Nor did he foresee the political dividends that support of independent unions could yield to his party. Though presiding over the reshaping of politics (which would extend the channels of power to some of the discontented and redirect their efforts to competition within a limited framework), he was not its architect, and he was unable clearly to see or understand the unfolding design.

When Senator Wagner submitted his labor relations bill, he received no assistance from the President and even struggled to prevent Roosevelt from joining the opposition. The President "never lifted a finger," recalls Miss Perkins. ("I, myself, had very little sympathy with the bill," she wrote.) But after the measure easily passed the Senate and seemed likely to win the House's endorsement, Roosevelt reversed himself. Three days before the Supreme Court invalidated the NRA, including the legal support for unionization, Roosevelt came out for the bill. Placing it on his "must" list, he may have hoped to influence the final provisions and turn an administration defeat into victory.

Responding to the threat from the left, Roosevelt also moved during the Second Hundred Days to secure laws regulating banking, raising taxes, dissolving utility-holding companies, and creating social security. Building on the efforts of states during the Progressive Era, the Social Security Act marked the movement toward the welfare state, but the core of the measure, the old-age provision, was more important as a landmark than for its substance. While establishing a federal-state system of unemployment compensation, the government, by making workers contribute to their old-age insurance, denied its financial responsibility for the elderly. The act excluded more than a fifth of the labor force leaving, among others, more than five million farm laborers and domestics without coverage.

Though Roosevelt criticized the tax laws for not preventing "an unjust concentration of wealth and economic power," his own tax measure would not have significantly redistributed wealth. Yet his message provoked an "amen" from Huey Long and protests from businessmen. Retreating from his promises, Roosevelt failed to support the bill, and it succumbed to conservative forces. They removed the inheritance tax and greatly reduced the proposed corporate and individual levies. The final law did not "soak the rich." But it did engender deep resentment among the wealthy for increasing taxes on gifts and estates, imposing an excess-profits tax (which Roosevelt had not requested), and raising surtaxes. When combined with such regressive levies as social security and local taxes, however, the Wealth Tax of 1935 did not drain wealth from higher-income groups, and the top one percent even increased their shares during the New Deal years. . . .

While slum dwellers received little besides relief from the New Deal, and their needs were frequently misunderstood, Negroes as a group received even less assistance— less than they needed and sometimes even less than their proportion in the population would have justified. Under the NRA they were frequently dismissed and their wages were sometimes below the legal minimum. The Civilian Conservation Corps left them "forgotten" men—excluded, discriminated against, segregated. In general, what the Negroes gained—relief, WPA jobs, equal pay on some federal projects— was granted them as poor people, not as Negroes. To many black men the distinction was unimportant, for no government had ever given them so much. "My friends, go home and turn Lincoln's picture to the wall," a Negro publisher told his race. "That debt has been payed in full."

Bestowing recognition on some Negro leaders, the New Deal appointed them to agencies as advisers—the "black cabinet." Probably more dramatic was the advocacy of Negro rights by Eleanor Roosevelt. Some whites like Harold Ickes and Aubrey Williams even struggled cautiously to break down segregation. But segregation did not yield, and Washington itself remained a segregated city. The white South was never challenged, the Fourteenth Amendment never used to assist Negroes. Never would Roosevelt expend political capital in an assault upon the American caste system. Despite the efforts of the NAACP to dramatize the Negroes' plight as second-class citizens, subject to brutality and often without legal protection, Roosevelt would not endorse the anti-lynching bill. ("No government pretending to be civilized can go on condoning such atrocities," H. L. Mencken testified. "Either it must make every possible effort to put them down or it must suffer the scorn and contempt of Christendom.") Unwilling to risk schism with Southerners ruling committees, Roosevelt capitulated to the forces of racism.

Even less bold than in economic reform the New Deal left intact the race relations of America. Yet its belated and cautious recognition of the black man was great enough to woo Negro leaders and even to court the masses. One of the bitter ironies of these years is that a New Dealer could tell the NAACP in 1936: "Under our new conception of democracy, the Negro will be given the chance to which he is entitled. . . ." But it was true, Ickes emphasized, that "The greatest advance [since Reconstruction] toward assuring the Negro that degree of justice to which he is entitled and that equality of opportunity under the law which is implicit in his American citizenship, has been made since Franklin D. Roosevelt was sworn in as President. . . ."

It was not in the cities and not among the Negroes but in rural America that [the] Roosevelt administration made its (philosophically) boldest efforts: creation of the Tennessee Valley Authority and the later attempt to construct seven little valley authorities. Though conservation was not a new federal policy and government-owned utilities were sanctioned by municipal experience, federal activity in this area constituted a challenge to corporate enterprise and an expression of concern about the poor. A valuable example of regional planning and a contribution to regional prosperity, TVA still fell far short of expectations. The agency soon retreated from social planning. ("From 1936 on," wrote Tugwell, "the TVA should have been called the Tennessee Valley Power Production and Flood Control Corporation.") Fearful of antagonizing the powerful interests, its agricultural program neglected the tenants and the sharecroppers.

To urban workingmen the New Deal offered some, but limited, material benefits. Though the government had instituted contributory social security and unemployment insurance, its much-heralded Fair Labor Standards Act, while prohibiting child labor, was a greater disappointment. It exempted millions from its wages-and-hours provisions. So unsatisfactory was the measure that one congressman cynically suggested, "Within 90 days after appointment of the administrator, she should report to Congress whether anyone is subject to this bill." Requiring a minimum of twenty-five cents an hour ($11 a week for 44 hours), it raised the wages of only about a half-million at a time when nearly twelve million workers in interstate commerce were earning less than forty cents an hour.

More important than these limited measures was the administration's support, albeit belated, of the organization of labor and the right of collective bargaining. Slightly increasing organized workers' share of the national income, the new industrial unions extended job security to millions who were previously subject to the whim of management. Unionization freed them from the perils of a free market.

By assisting labor, as well as agriculture, the New Deal started the institutionalization of larger interest groups into a new political economy. Joining business as tentative junior partners, they shared the consensus on the value of large-scale corporate capitalism, and were permitted to participate in the competition for the division of shares. While failing to redistribute income, the New Deal modified the political structure at the price of excluding many from the process of decision making. To many what was offered in fact was symbolic representation, formal representation. It was not the industrial workers necessarily who were recognized, but their unions and leaders; it was not even the farmers, but their organizations and leaders. While this was not a conscious design, it was the predictable result of conscious policies. It could not have been easily avoided, for it was part of the price paid by a large society unwilling to consider radical new designs for the distribution of power and wealth.

In the deepest sense, this new form of representation was rooted in the liberal's failure to endorse a meaningful egalitarianism which would provide actual equality of opportunity. It was also the limited concern with equality and justice that accounted for the shallow efforts of the New Deal and left so many Americans behind. The New Deal was neither a "third American Revolution," as Carl Degler suggests, nor even a "half-way revolution," as William Leuchtenburg concludes. Not only was the extension of representation to new groups less than full-fledged partnership, but the New Deal neglected many Americans—sharecroppers, tenant farmers, migratory workers and farm laborers, slum dwellers, unskilled workers, and the unemployed Negroes. They were left outside the new order. As Roosevelt asserted in 1937 (in a classic understatement), one third of the nation was "ill-nourished, ill-clad, ill-housed."

Yet, by the power of rhetoric and through the appeals of political organization, the Roosevelt government managed to win or retain the allegiance of these peoples. Perhaps this is one of the crueller ironies of liberal politics, that the marginal men trapped in hopelessness were seduced by rhetoric, by the style and movement, by the symbolism of efforts seldom reaching beyond words. In acting to protect the institution of private property and in advancing the interests of corporate capitalism, the New Deal assisted the middle and upper sectors of society. It protected them, sometimes, even at the cost of injuring the lower sectors. Seldom did it bestow much of substance upon the lower classes. Never did the New Deal seek to organize these groups into independent political forces. Seldom did it risk antagonizing established interests. For some this would constitute a puzzling defect of liberalism; for some, the failure to achieve true liberalism. To others it would emphasize the inherent shortcomings of American liberal democracy.

F U R T H E R   R E A D I N G

Alan Brinkley, *Voices of Protest: Huey Long, Father Coughlin, and the Great Depression* (1982).
Colin Gordon, *New Deals: Business, Labor, and Politics in America* (1994).
William Leuchtenburg, *Franklin D. Roosevelt and the New Deal* (1963).
Gwendolyn Mink, *The Wages of Motherhood: Inequality in the Welfare State* (1995).
James Olson, *Saving Capitalism* (1988).
Harvard Sitkoff, *Fifty Years Later: The New Deal Evaluated* (1985).
Patricia Sullivan, *Days of Hope: Race and Democracy in the New Deal Era* (1996).
Studs Terkel, *Hard Times: An Oral History of the Great Depression* (1970).

CHAPTER
9

The Ordeal of World War II

The Japanese bombing of American warships at Pearl Harbor, Hawaii, on December 7, 1941, brought the United States into a series of wars that had been under way, first in Asia and then in Europe as well, for nearly a decade. In 1931, the Japanese Imperial Army had begun a program of expansion and conquest that eventually reached from the cold far north of China down to the tropical jungles of Indochina. The United States consistently opposed Japan's military aggressiveness. Then, in 1933, Adolf Hitler seized dictatorial power in Germany, determined to rebuild his country. This would require, he decided, eliminating what he called the "parasites" within the nation (Jews), putting "inferior human material" (Poles, Russians, and other Slavs) to work for Germany, and obtaining the territory of other European nations for the enlargement of what he named the Third Reich. England and France went to war against Germany when Hitler invaded and occupied Poland in September 1939, following his previous annexation of Austria and Czechoslovakia. The following spring, Hitler's massive army and air force attacked Norway, Denmark, Holland, Belgium, and France, all of which fell within a few weeks and remained occupied until the Allied invasion, which began on the French beaches of Normandy four years later. The bombing of Pearl Harbor finally brought the United States into the war on the side of Britain and Russia, the last nations with any capacity to resist Hitler, who had allied himself with both Japan and the fascist government of Italy in a "Triple Axis." The United States, Britain, and Soviet Russia formed the nucleus of a worldwide, fifty-nation Grand Alliance, which eventually forced the Axis to surrender. The war culminated in the discovery of the Nazi death camps, where 6 million Jews and millions of Slavs had perished, and in the dropping of atomic bombs by the United States on the Japanese cities of Hiroshima and Nagasaki.

The war transformed America and the world. After resisting the Axis, Great Britain and France found a process set in motion that led to the collapse of their overseas empires. The Soviet Union came to control nations that had been traditionally hostile to it, and used the process of liberating central Europe from the Nazis to create a new security zone for itself. The United States, which had entered both world wars late, found itself the most powerful and wealthy nation on earth following the war, blessed with the opportunity and burdened with the responsibility of restructuring world politics, resurrecting the world economy, and preventing future wars. The Grand Alliance created a new organization called the United Nations designed to mediate all subsequent conflicts. The task was Herculean, but the effort to find rational alternatives to global self-destruction had begun.

Franklin D. Roosevelt and the Grand Alliance announced at the start of American participation in World War II that the war was being fought on behalf of elemental human freedoms—the "four freedoms." Hitler's deliberate slaughter of peoples who did not belong to the Aryan "race" helped to stir revulsion toward racism. One of the unforeseen consequences of the war for the United States was to highlight the extent to which the "land of the free" itself violated the dignity of citizens who were not white or Protestant. The war reinforced American liberalism, strengthened the hand of advocates for civil rights, brought women into the work force in greater numbers than ever before, ended the Great Depression, and heralded what the publisher of Time *and* Life *called "the American Century."*

⬛ Q U E S T I O N S   T O   T H I N K   A B O U T

How did the war change Americans' expectations of their nation's role in the world? In what ways did participation in World War II differ from participation in World War I, and what were the consequences of these differences? How did the war transform the nation internally?

⬛ D O C U M E N T S

The documents in this chapter reflect the global character of the war. What people said and did thousands of miles away from the United States mattered deeply to the history of the nation. German and Japanese actions not only brought the United States into the war but cast a new light on issues of human rights in the United States. Document 1 is drawn from *Mein Kampf* (My Battle), Hitler's blueprint for the resurgence of German power. Race and nationality were inseparable, he argued, eerily echoing sentiments that had been expressed in the United States in the twenties. Only the Aryan race could be true Germans. This book set the stage not only for German aggression and the Holocaust of the European Jews, but also for a new global definition of human rights after the war. Document 2 reveals the perspective of Japanese leaders, who assert that by expanding they are bringing stability and progress to East Asia. They expressed confidence that the Chinese (whom they conquered) would understand their "true intentions." The Chinese didn't see it that way, nor did the Americans. In Document 3, President Franklin D. Roosevelt calls for war following the surprise bombing of Pearl Harbor by the Japanese on December 7, 1941, a "date which will live in infamy." In Document 4, British prime minister Winston Churchill recounts the moment at which he learned of the attack on Hawaii. American entry into the war marked the end of a lonely and desperate struggle for Great Britain, the only western European nation that had not yet been conquered by or allied itself with Nazi Germany. The alliance with Britain proved crucial to Allied victory, as the final great assault was launched from its shores. Early in the war, Roosevelt declared that the United States was fighting on behalf of what he called the "four freedoms." His statements in Document 5 helped to raise expectations at home and abroad that the nation struggled to measure up to in the following decades. Document 6 shows the connection that African American citizens drew between Roosevelt's goals for the world and their own aspirations for greater freedom. Soldiers stationed at segregated bases and consigned to nonfighting units complained that there was a "lack of democracy" right at home. Japanese Americans found themselves the target of suspicion, discrimination, and finally imprisonment. In Document 7, Stanford University history professor Yamato Ichihashi writes to his former colleagues. Like thousands of

Japanese Americans from the states of California, Oregon, and Washington, Ichihashi faced internment for the duration of the war. Document 8 reveals the strategic complexities of the war and the compromises Roosevelt made between an ideal world and the real world. In addition to creating a United Nations, he and Soviet Premier Josef Stalin agreed, the largest states would have to act as "policemen" after the war to ensure future peace. Reinhold Niebuhr, an influential theologian from Princeton University, reveals in Document 9 a similar blend of optimism and pessimism regarding the potential for world order. In the last selection, Document 10, Dwight D. Eisenhower reports to General George C. Marshall about his discoveries at the German concentration camps. The Holocaust of the Jews would later contribute to American support for the creation of Israel and come to symbolize the worst excesses of unchecked aggression.

1. Nazi Leader Adolf Hitler Links Race and Nationality, 1927

There are numberless examples in history, showing with terrible clarity how each time Aryan blood has become mixed with that of inferior peoples the result has been an end of the culture-sustaining race. North America, the population of which consists for the most part of Germanic elements, which mixed very little with inferior coloured nations, displays humanity and culture very different from that of Central and South America, in which the settlers, mainly Latin in origin, mingled their blood very freely with that of the aborigines. Taking the above as an example, we clearly recognize the effects of racial intermixture. The man of Germanic race on the continent of America having kept himself pure and unmixed, has risen to be its master; and he will remain master so long as he does not fall into the shame of mixing the blood.

Perhaps the pacifist-humane idea is quite a good one in cases where the man at the top has first thoroughly conquered and subdued the world to the extent of making himself sole master of it. Then the principle when applied in practice, will not affect the mass of the people injuriously. Thus first the struggle and then pacifism. Otherwise, it means that humanity has passed the highest point in its development, and the end is not domination by any ethical idea, but barbarism, and chaos to follow. Some will naturally laugh at this, but this planet travelled through the ether for millions of years devoid of humanity, and it can only do so again if men forget that they owe their higher existence, not to the ideas of a mad ideologue, but to understanding and ruthless application of age-old natural laws.

All that we admire on this earth—science, art, technical skill and invention— is the creative product of only a small number of nations, and originally, perhaps, of one single race. All this culture depends on them for its very existence. If they are ruined, they carry with them all the beauty of this earth into the grave.

If we divide the human race into three categories—founders, maintainers, and destroyers of culture—the Aryan stock alone can be considered as representing the first category.

Adolf Hitler, *My Battle,* abridged and translated by E. T. S. Dugdale (Boston: Houghton Mifflin, 1933), 121–127, 136–137. Copyright renewed 1971 by Houghton Mifflin Company. All rights reserved.

The Aryan races—often in absurdly small numbers—overthrow alien nations, and, favoured by the numbers of people of lower grade who are at their disposal to aid them, they proceed to develop, according to the special conditions for life in the acquired territories—fertility, climate, etc.—the qualities of intellect and organization which are dormant in them. In the course of a few centuries they create cultures, originally stamped with their own characteristics alone, and develop them to suit the special character of the land and the people which they have conquered. As time goes on, however, the conquerors sin against the principle of keeping the blood pure (a principle which they adhered to at first), and begin to blend with the original inhabitants whom they have subjugated, and end their own existence as a peculiar people; for the sin committed in Paradise was inevitably followed by expulsion. . . .

For the development of the higher culture it was necessary that men of lower civilization should have existed, for none but they could be a substitute for the technical instruments, without which higher development was inconceivable. In its beginnings human culture certainly depended less on the tamed beast and more on employment of inferior human material. . . .

The exact opposite of the Aryan is the Jew. . . .

The Jew's intellectual qualities were developed in the course of centuries. Today we think him "cunning," and in a certain sense it was the same at every epoch. But his intellectual capacity is not the result of personal development, but of education by foreigners.

Thus, since the Jew never possessed a culture of his own, the bases of his intellectual activity have always been supplied by others. His intellect has in all periods been developed by contact with surrounding civilizations. Never the opposite.

. . . His propagation of himself throughout the world is a typical phenomenon with all parasites; he is always looking for fresh feeding ground for his race.

His life within other nations can be kept up in perpetuity only if he succeeds in convincing the world that with him it is not a question of a race, but of a 'religious bond,' one however peculiar to himself. This is the first great lie!

In order to continue existing as a parasite within the nation, the Jew must set to work to deny his real inner nature. The more intelligent the individual Jew is, the better will he succeed in his deception—to the extent of making large sections of the population seriously believe that the Jew genuinely is a Frenchman or an Englishman, a German or an Italian, though of a different religion. . . .

It was clear to us, even in 1919, that the chief aim of the new movement must be to awaken a sentiment of nationality in the masses. From the tactical standpoint a number of requirements arise out of this.

1. No social sacrifice is too great in order to win the masses over to the national movement. But a movement whose aim is to recover the German worker for the German nation must realize that economic sacrifices are not an essential factor in it, so long as the maintenance and independence of the nation's economic life are not menaced by them.

2. Nationalizing of the masses can never be effected by half-measures or by mild expression of an 'objective standpoint,' but by determined and fanatical concentration

on the object aimed at. The mass of the people do not consist of professors or diplomats. A man who desires to win their adherence must know the key which will unlock the door to their hearts. This is not objectivity—i.e., weakness—but determination and strength.

3. There can only be success in winning the soul of the people if, while we are conducting the political struggle for our own aim, we also destroy those who oppose it.

The masses are but a part of nature, and it is not in them to understand mutual hand-shakings between men whose desires are nominally in direct opposition to each other. What they wish to see is victory for the stronger and destruction of the weaker.

2. Japan Announces a "New Order" in Asia, 1938

What Japan seeks is the establishment of a new order which will insure the permanent stability of East Asia. In this lies the ultimate purpose of our present military campaign.

This new order has for its foundation a tripartite relationship of mutual aid and co-ordination between Japan, Manchoukuo [the name Japan gave to Manchuria in February 1932], and China in political, economic, cultural and other fields. Its object is to secure international justice, to perfect the joint defence against Communism, and to create a new culture and realize a close economic cohesion throughout East Asia. This indeed is the way to contribute toward the stabilization of East Asia and the progress of the world.

What Japan desires of China is that that country will share in the task of bringing about this new order in East Asia. She confidently expects that the people of China will fully comprehend her true intentions and that they will respond to the call of Japan for their co-operation. Even the participation of the Kuomintang Government would not be rejected, if, repudiating the policy which has guided it in the past and remolding its personnel, so as to translate its re-birth into fact, it were to come forward to join in the establishment of the new order.

Japan is confident that other Powers will on their part correctly appreciate her aims and policy and adapt their attitude to the new conditions prevailing in East Asia. For the cordiality hitherto manifested by the nations which are in sympathy with us, Japan wishes to express her profound gratitude.

The establishment of a new order in East Asia is in complete conformity with the very spirit in which the Empire was founded; to achieve such a task is the exalted responsibility with which our present generation is entrusted. It is, therefore, imperative to carry out all necessary internal reforms, and with a full development of the aggregate national strength, material as well as moral, fulfill at all costs this duty incumbent upon our nation.

Such the Government declare to be the immutable policy and determination of Japan.

U.S. Department of State, *Papers Relating to the Foreign Relations of the United States, Japan: 1931–1941* (Washington, D.C.: U.S. Government Printing Office, 1943), I, 477–478.

3. President Franklin D. Roosevelt Asks Congress to Declare War, 1941

Yesterday, December 7, 1941—a date which will live in infamy—the United States of America was suddenly and deliberately attacked by naval and air forces of the Empire of Japan.

The United States was at peace with that Nation and, at the solicitation of Japan, was still in conversation with its Government and its Emperor looking toward the maintenance of peace in the Pacific. Indeed, one hour after Japanese air squadrons had commenced bombing in Oahu, the Japanese Ambassador to the United States and his colleague delivered to the Secretary of State a formal reply to a recent American message. While this reply stated that it seemed useless to continue the existing diplomatic negotiations, it contained no threat or hint of war or armed attack.

It will be recorded that the distance of Hawaii from Japan makes it obvious that the attack was deliberately planned many days or even weeks ago. During the intervening time the Japanese Government has deliberately sought to deceive the United States by false statements and expressions of hope for continued peace.

The attack yesterday on the Hawaiian Islands has caused severe damage to American naval and military forces. Very many American lives have been lost. In addition American ships have been reported torpedoed on the high seas between San Francisco and Honolulu.

Yesterday the Japanese Government also launched an attack against Malaya.

Last night Japanese forces attacked Hong Kong.

Last night Japanese forces attacked Guam.

Last night Japanese forces attacked the Philippine Islands.

Last night the Japanese attacked Wake Island.

This morning the Japanese attacked Midway Island.

Japan has, therefore, undertaken a surprise offensive extending throughout the Pacific area. The facts of yesterday speak for themselves. The people of the United States have already formed their opinions and well understand the implications to the very life and safety of our Nation.

As Commander-in-Chief of the Army and Navy I have directed that all measures be taken for our defense.

Always will we remember the character of the onslaught against us.

No matter how long it may take us to overcome this premeditated invasion, the American people in their righteous might will win through to absolute victory.

I believe I interpret the will of the Congress and of the people when I assert that we will not only defend ourselves to the uttermost but will make very certain that this form of treachery shall never endanger us again.

Hostilities exist. There is no blinking at the fact that our people, our territory, and our interests are in grave danger.

With confidence in our armed forces—with the unbounded determination of our people—we will gain the inevitable triumph—so help us God.

U.S. Department of State, *Papers Relating to the Foreign Relations of the United States, Japan: 1931–1941* (Washington, D.C.: Government Printing Office, 1943), II, 793–794.

I ask that the Congress declare that since the unprovoked and dastardly attack by Japan on Sunday, December seventh, a state of war has existed between the United States and the Japanese Empire.

4. British Prime Minister Winston Churchill Reacts to Pearl Harbor, 1941

It was Sunday evening, December 7, 1941. Winant and Averell Harriman were alone with me at the table at Chequers. I turned on my small wireless set shortly after the nine o'clock news had started. There were a number of items about the fighting on the Russian front and on the British front in Libya, at the end of which some few sentences were spoken regarding an attack by the Japanese on American shipping at Hawaii, and also Japanese attacks on British vessels in the Dutch East Indies. There followed a statement that after the news Mr. Somebody would make a commentary, and that the Brains Trust programme would then begin, or something like this. I did not personally sustain any direct impression, but Averell said there was something about the Japanese attacking the Americans, and, in spite of being tired and resting, we all sat up. By now the butler, Sawyers, who had heard what had passed, came into the room, saying, "It's quite true. We heard it ourselves outside. The Japanese have attacked the Americans." There was a silence. At the Mansion House luncheon on November 11 I had said that if Japan attacked the United States a British declaration of war would follow "within the hour." I got up from the table and walked through the hall to the office, which was always at work. I asked for a call to the President. The Ambassador followed me out, and, imagining I was about to take some irrevocable step, said, "Don't you think you'd better get confirmation first?"

In two or three minutes Mr. Roosevelt came through. "Mr. President, what's this about Japan?" "It's quite true," he replied. "They have attacked us at Pearl Harbour. We are all in the same boat now." I put Winant onto the line and some interchanges took place, the Ambassador at first saying, "Good," "Good"—and then, apparently graver, "Ah!" I got on again and said, "This certainly simplifies things. God be with you," or words to that effect. We then went back into the hall and tried to adjust our thoughts to the supreme world event which had occurred, which was of so startling a nature as to make even those who were near the centre gasp. My two American friends took the shock with admirable fortitude. We had no idea that any serious losses had been inflicted on the United States Navy. They did not wail or lament that their country was at war. They wasted no words in reproach or sorrow. In fact, one might almost have thought they had been delivered from a long pain. . . .

No American will think it wrong of me if I proclaim that to have the United States at our side was to me the greatest joy. I could not foretell the course of events. I do not pretend to have measured accurately the martial might of Japan, but now at this very moment I knew the United States was in the war, up to the neck and in to the death. So we had won after all! Yes, after Dunkirk; after the fall of France; after the horrible episode of Oran; after the threat of invasion, when, apart from the Air and the Navy, we were an almost unarmed people; after the deadly struggle of the U-boat war—the first Battle of the Atlantic, gained by a hand's-breadth; after seventeen months of lonely fighting and nineteen months of my responsibility in dire stress. We had won the war. England would live; Britain would live; the Commonwealth of Nations and the Empire would live. How long the war would last or in what fashion it would end no man could tell, nor did I at this moment care. Once again in our long island history we should emerge, however mauled or mutilated, safe and victorious. We should not be wiped out. Our history would not come to an end. We might not even have to die as individuals. Hitler's fate was sealed. Mussolini's fate was sealed. As for the Japanese, they would be ground to powder. All the rest was merely the proper application of overwhelming force. The British Empire, the Soviet Union, and now the United States, bound together with every scrap of their life and strength, were, according to my lights, twice or even thrice the force of their antagonists. . . .

Silly people, and there were many, not only in enemy countries, might discount the force of the United States. Some said they were soft, others that they would never be united. They would fool around at a distance. They would never come to grips. They would never stand blood-letting. Their democracy and system of recurrent elections would paralyse their war effort. They would be just a vague blur on the horizon to friend or foe. Now we should see the weakness of this numerous but remote, wealthy, and talkative people. But I had studied the American Civil War, fought out to the last desperate inch. American blood flowed in my veins. I thought of a remark which Edward Grey had made to me more than thirty years before—that the United States is like "a gigantic boiler. Once the fire is lighted under it there is no limit to the power it can generate." Being saturated and satiated with emotion and sensation, I went to bed and slept the sleep of the saved and thankful.

5. President Franklin D. Roosevelt Identifies the "Four Freedoms" at Stake in the War, 1941

. . . There is nothing mysterious about the foundations of a healthy and strong democracy. The basic things expected by our people of their political and economic systems are simple. They are:

Equality of opportunity for youth and for others.

Jobs for those who can work.

Security for those who need it.

The ending of special privilege for the few.

The preservation of civil liberties for all.

The enjoyment of the fruits of scientific progress in a wider and constantly rising standard of living.

The Public Papers and Addresses of Franklin D. Roosevelt (New York: Macmillan, 1941), Vol. 9, 671–672.

These are the simple, basic things that must never be lost sight of in the turmoil and unbelievable complexity of our modern world. The inner and abiding strength of our economic and political systems is dependent upon the degree to which they fulfill these expectations.

Many subjects connected with our social economy call for immediate improvement.

As examples:

We should bring more citizens under the coverage of old-age pensions and unemployment insurance.

We should widen the opportunities for adequate medical care.

We should plan a better system by which persons deserving or needing gainful employment may obtain it.

I have called for personal sacrifice. I am assured of the willingness of almost all Americans to respond to that call.

A part of the sacrifice means the payment of more money in taxes. In my Budget Message I shall recommend that a greater portion of this great defense program be paid for from taxation than we are paying today. No person should try, or be allowed, to get rich out of this program; and the principle of tax payments in accordance with ability to pay should be constantly before our eyes to guide our legislation.

If the Congress maintains these principles, the voters, putting patriotism ahead of pocketbooks, will give you their applause.

In the future days, which we seek to make secure, we look forward to a world founded upon four essential human freedoms.

The first is freedom of speech and expression—everywhere in the world.

The second is freedom of every person to worship God in his own way—everywhere in the world.

The third is freedom from want—which, translated into world terms, means economic understandings which will secure to every nation a healthy peacetime life for its inhabitants—everywhere in the world.

The fourth is freedom from fear—which, translated into world terms, means a world-wide reduction of armaments to such a point and in such a thorough fashion that no nation will be in a position to commit an act of physical aggression against any neighbor—anywhere in the world.

That is no vision of a distant millennium. It is a definite basis for a kind of world attainable in our own time and generation. That kind of world is the very antithesis of the so-called new order of tyranny which the dictators seek to create with the crash of a bomb.

To that new order we oppose the greater conception—the moral order. A good society is able to face schemes of world domination and foreign revolutions alike without fear.

Since the beginning of our American history, we have been engaged in change—in a perpetual peaceful revolution—a revolution which goes on steadily, quietly adjusting itself to changing conditions—without the concentration camp or the quicklime in the ditch. The world order which we seek is the cooperation of free countries, working together in a friendly, civilized society.

This nation has placed its destiny in the hands and heads and hearts of millions of free men and women; and its faith in freedom under the guidance of God. Freedom means the supremacy of human rights everywhere. Our support goes to those who struggle to gain those rights or keep them. Our strength is our unity of purpose.

To that high concept there can be no end save victory.

6. An African American Soldier Notes the "Strange Paradox" of the War, 1944

33rd AAF Base Unit (CCTS(H))
Section C
President Franklin Delano Roosevelt   DAVIS-MONTHAN FIELD
White House   Tucson, Arizona
Washington, D.C.   9 May 1944.

Dear President Roosevelt:

It was with extreme pride that I, a soldier in the Armed Forces of our country, read the following affirmation of our war aims, pronounced by you at a recent press conference:

"The United Nations are fighting to make a world in which tyranny, and aggression cannot exist; a world based upon freedom, equality, and justice; a world in which all persons, regardless of race, color and creed, may live in peace, honor and dignity." . . .

But the picture in our country is marred by one of the strangest paradoxes in our whole fight against world fascism. The United States Armed Forces, to fight for World Democracy, is within itself undemocratic. The undemocratic policy of jim crow and segregation is practiced by our Armed Forces against its Negro members. Totally inadequate opportunities are given to the Negro members of our Armed Forces, nearly one tenth of the whole, to participate with "equality" . . . "regardless of race and color" in the fight for our war aims. In fact it appears that the army intends to follow the very policy that the FEPC [Fair Employment Practices Commission] is battling against in civilian life, the pattern of assigning Negroes to the lowest types of work.

Let me give you an example of the lack of democracy in our Field, where I am now stationed. Negro soldiers are completely segregated from the white soldiers on the base. And to make doubly sure that no mistake is made about this, the barracks and other housing facilities (supply room, mess hall, etc.) of the Negro Section C are covered with black tar paper, while all other barracks and housing facilities on the base are painted white.

It is the stated policy of the Second Air Force that "every potential fighting man must be used as a fighting man. If you have such a man in a base job, you have no choice. His job must be eliminated or be filled by a limited service man, WAC, or

Taps for a Jim Crow Army: Letters from Black Soldiers in World War II, ABC-CLIO, © 1983, 134–139. Reprinted by permission of The University Press of Kentucky.

civilian." And yet, leaving out the Negro soldiers working with the Medical Section, fully 50% of the Negro soldiers are working in base jobs, such as, for example, at the Resident Officers' Mess, Bachelor Officers' Quarters, and Officers' Club, as mess personnel, BOQ orderlies, and bar tenders. Leaving out the medical men again, based on the section C average only 4% of this 50% would not be "potential fighting men." . . .

How can we convince nearly one tenth of the Armed Forces, the Negro members, that your pronouncement of the war aims of the United Nations means what it says, when their experience with one of the United Nations, the United States of America, is just the opposite? . . .

With your issuance of Executive Order 8802, and the setting up of the Fair Employment Practices Committee, you established the foundation for fighting for democracy in the industrial forces of our country, in the interest of victory for the United Nations. In the interest of victory for the United Nations, another Executive Order is now needed. An Executive Order which will lay the base for fighting for democracy in the Armed Forces of our country. An Executive Order which would bring about the result here at Davis-Monthan Field whereby the Negro soldiers would be integrated into all of the Sections on the base, as fighting men, instead of in the segregated Section C as housekeepers.

Then and only then can your pronouncement of the war aims of the United Nations mean to *all* that we "are fighting to make a world in which tyranny, and aggression cannot exist; a world based upon freedom, equality and justice; a world in which all persons, regardless of race, color and creed, may live in peace, honor and dignity."

Respectfully yours,

Charles F. Wilson, 36794590
Private, Air Corps.

7. Stanford Professor Yamato Ichihashi Writes of His Internment, 1942

June 7, 1942

Dear Friends: . . .

This is our 12th day here, and of course I have used all my spare time (very limited because of numerous visitors) in looking over the Camp as well as in obtaining as much reliable information possible. I have already learned a great many interesting things concerning the community life, including even gambling and commercial vice, which are said to have now been suppressed. One has to be even careful of his own immediate neighbors. Here goes my first story touching on matters which, I think, will interest you.

First of all, whether it was so intended or not, the Wartime Civil Control Administration under the Army's authority, has established in this Center a truly classless community (a Soviet ideal unrealized as yet in Russia). Residents (inmates more appropriately) are not recognized as individuals; we are numbered for identification and are treated exactly alike, except babies one year and younger as regards foods. We are fed, quartered and forced to do our own washing, including sheets, shirts, and what not. Washing facilities are wholly inadequate. They do not allow to have washing done by a laundry outside. Why I do not know. Criticisms relative [to] any matter are not tolerated by the management; a few days [ago] a doctor was railroaded from here because he, as a scientist, has tried to bring about improvements. It is very dangerous for any individual to try [not to go] along the line.

The Camp has a population of 18,400, each of which is numbered for identification; for instance I am No. 5561A, which is required for every transaction in the Camp; of course aside from mails, we have no contact with the outside world. The above number [of residents] has been mostly drawn from Southern California; the first batch reached here on April 3rd from San Diego and Long Beach; others followed from southern counties, and a month later from San Francisco; those from Santa Clara were the last to arrive here thus far. More are said to be coming, but from what places I do not know. At no time was the Camp prepared to receive evacuees; each arrival faced many hardships which could have been avoided; in particular their feeding was undescribably bad, and that was our experience, although we are informed by older residents that general conditions have been vastly improved in more recent days. The population is mixed: citizens and enemy aliens; they are differentiated in the Camp; it is an impossible combination. Many of the youngsters have been appointed [to administrative positions], and they act like petty bureaucrats—the word most commonly heard is *order.* More on this later.

In management of the classless community, the government has apparently adopted the lowest conceivable standard of treating human beings; thousands are still housed in stables; a stable for one animal is now occupied from five to six persons. They are still odorous and poor of ventilation. Of course, barracks are constructed exactly like our old fashioned wood-shed; each barrack is partitioned into six sections so that inmates have 4 walls, all constructed of rough pine boards nailed in a manner so that on the average [there is] ½ inch spaces between these wall boards; you can not only hear what goes on in the barrack, but can see, if you want, what goes on next door. There is no privacy anywhere; we have become veritable animals as far as our living is concerned. In addition, to be thrown into a community mostly composed of lowly, uncouth rustics, is in itself very painful for cultured persons. Some times these intangibles are more difficult to bear; but despite all, we are determined to be philosophic about everything; this is easy to talk about, but extremely difficult to face as realities.

A little more prosaically, meals served consist mostly of vegetables and rice, and meat or fish is very rarely served; when the latter is served it is done in very small quantities. Butter is not used with bread; nor do we get fats and oils and already our skin shows the result. Because of the coarseness of foods, digestive organs have a hard time in functioning properly. Diarrhoea is very prevalent, often causing panics in the lavatories, and this is no exaggeration. . . .

There naturally exist a number of things which require reform or elimination in order to correct the general condition. But politics and graft prevent any efforts along these lines, according to older residents; for the time being, these must be seen as rumors; I have no means of verifying one way or other. They say that the Army allows 54 cents per diem for the food, if this be true, the residents are getting the benefit of such an appropriation.

I must now proceed to the mess hall ½ hour ahead [of time] so as to join the line in order to get into the hall on time, so I had better to put an abrupt end here, since there is no real end no matter [what] you write.

Very affectionately.
Yamato

8. Roosevelt and Soviet Premier Josef Stalin Plan the United Nations, 1943

The President then said the question of a post-war organization to preserve peace had not been fully explained and dealt with and he would like to discuss with the Marshal the prospect of some organization based on the United Nations.

The President then outlined the following general plan:

1. There would be a large organization composed of some 35 members of the United Nations which would meet periodically at different places, discuss and make recommendations to a smaller body.

Marshal Stalin inquired whether this organization was to be world-wide or European, to which the President replied, world-wide.

The President continued that there would be set up an executive committee composed of the Soviet Union, the United States, United Kingdom and China, together with two additional European states, one South American, one Near East, one Far Eastern country, and one British Dominion. He mentioned that Mr. Churchill did not like this proposal for the reason that the British Empire only had two votes. This Executive Committee would deal with all non-military questions such as agriculture, food, health, and economic questions, as well as the setting up of an International Committee. This Committee would likewise meet in various places.

Marshal Stalin inquired whether this body would have the right to make decisions binding on the nations of the world.

The President replied, yes and no. It could make recommendations for settling disputes with the hope that the nations concerned would be guided thereby, but that, for example, he did not believe the Congress of the United States would accept as binding a decision of such a body. The President then turned to the third organization which he termed "The Four Policemen," namely, the Soviet Union, United States, Great Britain, and China. This organization would have the power to deal immediately with any threat to the peace and any sudden emergency which requires this action. He went on to say that in 1935, when Italy attacked Ethiopia, the only machinery in existence was the League of Nations. He personally had begged France to close the Suez Canal, but they instead referred it to the League which disputed the question and in the end did nothing. The result was that the Italian Armies went through the Suez Canal and destroyed Ethiopia. The President pointed out that had the machinery of the Four Policemen, which he had in mind, been in existence, it would have been possible to close the Suez Canal. The President then summarized briefly the idea that he had in mind.

U.S. Department of State, *Foreign Relations of the United States: Diplomatic Papers, The Conferences at Cairo and Teheran, 1943* (Washington, D.C.: U.S. Government Printing Office, 1961), 530–532.

Marshal Stalin said that he did not think that the small nations of Europe would like the organization composed of the Four Policemen. He said, for example, that a European state would probably resent China having the right to apply certain machinery to it. And in any event, he did not think China would be very powerful at the end of the war. He suggested as a possible alternative, the creation of a European or a Far Eastern Committee and a European or a Worldwide organization. He said that in the European Commission there would be the United States, Great Britain, the Soviet Union and possibly one other European state.

The President said that the idea just expressed by Marshal Stalin was somewhat similar to Mr. Churchill's idea of a Regional Committee, one for Europe, one for the Far East, and one for the Americas. Mr. Churchill had also suggested that the United States be a member of the European Commission, but he doubted if the United States Congress would agree to the United States' participation in an exclusively European Committee which might be able to force the dispatch of American troops to Europe.

The President added that it would take a terrible crisis such as at present before Congress would ever agree to that step.

Marshal Stalin pointed out that the world organization suggested by the President, and in particular the Four Policemen, might also require the sending of American troops to Europe.

The President pointed out that he had only envisaged the sending of American planes and ships to Europe, and that England and the Soviet Union would have to handle the land armies in the event of any future threat to the peace. He went on to say that if the Japanese had not attacked the United States, he doubted very much if it would have been possible to send any American forces to Europe.

9. Theologian Reinhold Niebuhr Warns of American Naivete, 1944

A sober approach to the world situation must begin with the assumption that the initial basis of unity for the world must be laid in a stable accord between the great powers. . . .

Since no constitutional checks, which may be placed upon the power of the great hegemonic nations, will be fully adequate, it is particularly important that the strongest possible moral restraints be placed upon their power. . . .

Since China is only potentially, and not yet actually, one of these great powers, the peace of the world will depend particularly upon the policies of the three other great powers, Britain, Russia and America. Of these three Russia will have the greatest difficulty in establishing inner moral checks upon its will-to-power. This will be the case not because it is communistic or materialistic; but rather because it is informed by a simple religion and culture which makes self-criticism difficult and self-righteousness inevitable. . . . The tendency toward self-righteousness is accentuated in Russia by the absence of democratic institutions through which, in other nations, sensitive minorities may act as the conscience of the nation and subject its actions and pretensions to criticism.

Excerpt from Reinhold Niebuhr, *Children of Light and Children of Darkness* (New York: Charles Scribner's Sons, 1944), 177, 182–186. Reprinted by permission of The Estate of Reinhold Niebuhr.

The so-called democratic and "Christian" nations have a culture which demands self-criticism in principle; and institutions which make it possible in practice. We must not assume, however, that any modern nation can easily achieve the high virtue of humility; or establish moral checks upon its power lusts. Britain has certain advantages over America in this realm for two reasons. The national interest of Britain is more completely identical with the interests of the nations than is the case with the United States; because Britain is more desperately in need of world security for its survival than America. Secondly, Britain has had longer experience in wielding power in world affairs than America. Through this experience Britain has learned to exercise restraint upon its power impulses to a larger degree than its critics realize. . . .

. . . America is potentially more powerful than Britain; but it has had little moral consciousness of its own power. As a result it alternates between moods of complete irresponsibility and of cynicism. In the one mood it would disavow the responsibilities of power because it fears its corruptions. In the other mood it displays an adolescent pride of power and a cynical disregard of its responsibilities.

These moods are marks of a lack of political and moral maturity. They are, in addition to certain constitutional difficulties, the cause of the unpredictable character of American foreign policy. If America achieves maturity, the primary mark of it must be the willingness to assume continuing responsibility in the world community of nations. We must seek to maintain a critical attitude toward our own power impulses; and our self-criticism must be informed by the humble realization of the fact that the possession of great power is a temptation to injustice for any nation. Relative innocency or inexperience in wielding power is no guarantee of virtue. It is on the contrary a hazard to the attainment of virtue. The possession of power on the other hand creates responsibilities which must not be evaded, even though it is known that they cannot be fulfilled without some egoistic corruption.

The field of politics is not helpfully tilled by pure moralists; and the realm of international politics is particularly filled with complexities which do not yield to the approach of a too simple idealism. On the other hand the moral cynicism and defeatism which easily results from a clear-eyed view of the realities of international politics is even more harmful. The world community must be built by men and nations sufficiently mature and robust to understand that political justice is achieved, not merely by destroying, but also by deflecting, beguiling and harnessing residual self-interest and by finding the greatest possible concurrence between self-interest and the general welfare.

10. General Dwight Eisenhower Reports to General George Marshall on the German Concentration Camps, 1945

To George Catlett Marshall   *April 15, 1945*
Secret

Dear General: . . .

On a recent tour of the forward areas in First and Third Armies, I stopped momentarily at the salt mines to take a look at the German treasure. There is a lot

The Papers of Dwight D. Eisenhower, vol. 4, *The War Years,* ed. Alfred D. Changler, Jr. (Baltimore: Johns Hopkins Press, 1970), 2615–2617, 2623.

of it. But the most interesting—although horrible—sight that I encountered during the trip was a visit to a German internment camp near Gotha. The things I saw beggar description. While I was touring the camp I encountered three men who had been inmates and by one ruse or another had made their escape. I interviewed them through an interpreter. The visual evidence and the verbal testimony of starvation, cruelty and bestiality were so overpowering as to leave me a bit sick. In one room, where they [there] were piled up twenty or thirty naked men, killed by starvation, George Patton would not even enter. He said he would get sick if he did so. I made the visit deliberately, in order to be in position to give *first-hand* evidence of these things if ever, in the future, there develops a tendency to charge these allegations merely to "propaganda." . . .

April 19, 1945

From Eisenhower to General Marshall for eyes only: We continue to uncover German concentration camps for political prisoners in which conditions of indescribable horror prevail. I have visited one of these myself and I assure you that whatever has been printed on them to date has been understatement. If you would see any advantage in asking about a dozen leaders of Congress and a dozen prominent editors to make a short visit to this theater in a couple of C-54's, I will arrange to have them conducted to one of these places where the evidence of bestiality and cruelty is so overpowering as to leave no doubt in their minds about the normal practices of the Germans in these camps. I am hopeful that some British individuals in similar categories will visit the northern area to witness similar evidence of atrocity.

☞ E S S A Y S

World War II is sometimes called "the good war"—even though it is widely recognized that all war is "hell." The bombing of Pearl Harbor created a broader consensus of support for this war than for any other war in the nation's history, including the Revolution. Historians have thus tended to debate the consequences of the war more than its origins. The following two essays look at the experience of the war from different vantage points: that of the soldier fighting for his own elemental survival as well as for his country, and that of the society back home. Stephen Ambrose, retired from the University of New Orleans, writes about D-Day, the June 1944 assault on German-occupied France. This selection evokes the terrifying siege of Omaha Beach and explains the military strategy (and misadventures) that went into the landing. The war transformed those who survived. Put yourself in their boots: think about how such battles might have affected that generation's view of life afterward, and of their nation's role in the world. In the second essay, Alan Brinkley of Columbia University discusses the effects of World War II on the domestic character of the United States. The war, he shows, not only brought the Great Depression to an end and established the nation as a superpower, but also reshaped race relations, gender roles, and the ideology of liberalism itself. At the same time, it fostered a peculiar blend of optimism and fear in popular culture. Reading Ambrose and Brinkley together may lead you to wonder whom the war affected most: the soldiers who fought it, or the society they left behind at home.

Visitors to Hell: Omaha Beach on D-Day

STEPHEN E. AMBROSE

The Allied problem was to land, penetrate the Atlantic Wall, and secure a lodgment in an area suitable for reinforcement and expansion. The sine qua non of the operation was to achieve surprise. If the Germans knew where and when the attack was coming they could surely concentrate enough men, concrete, tanks, and artillery at the spot to defeat the assault.

It was going to be difficult enough even with surprise. Amphibious operations are inherently the most complicated in war; few have ever been successful. Julius Caesar and William the Conqueror had managed it, but nearly every other invasion attempted against organized opposition had failed. Napoleon had not been able to cross the English Channel, nor had Hitler. The Mongols were defeated by the weather when they tried to invade Japan, as were the Spanish when they tried to invade England. The British were frustrated in the Crimea in the nineteenth century and defeated at Gallipoli in World War I.

In World War II, the record got better. By the end of 1943 the Allies had launched three successful amphibious attacks—North Africa (November 8, 1942), Sicily (July 10, 1943), and Salerno (September 9, 1943), all involving British and American land, sea, and air forces under the command of Gen. Dwight D. Eisenhower. None of the coastlines, however, had been fortified. (The only attack against a fortified coast, by the Canadians at Dieppe in northern France in August 1942, had been decisively defeated.) In North Africa, the Allies had achieved surprise when they attacked a French colonial army without a declaration of war, and even then they encountered many difficulties. At Sicily the opposition had been mainly dispirited Italian troops; nevertheless, there were some horrendous foul-ups, including the shooting down by Allied naval craft of Allied transport planes carrying the U.S. 82nd Airborne Division into battle. At Salerno, the Germans had quickly recovered from the twin surprises of the Italian double cross and the seaborne landings and come awfully close to driving the Anglo-American troops back into the sea, despite being outnumbered and outgunned.

Going into 1944, in short, there was precious little in the way of precedent or historic example the Allies could look to for inspiration. What they were about to attempt had not been done before.

But it had to be done. U.S. Army chief of staff George C. Marshall had wanted to invade France in late 1942, and even more in mid-1943. British hesitation and political necessity had forced a diversion to the Mediterranean. At the end of 1943, however, the British overcame their doubts and the Allies committed themselves to a cross-Channel attack as the decisive effort for 1944.

There were manifold reasons, of which the overriding one was the obvious point that wars are won by offensive action. For all his hesitation about when the offensive should begin, British prime minister Winston Churchill always knew that

From Stephen E. Ambrose, *D-Day, June 6, 1944: The Climactic Battle of World War II* (New York: Simon & Schuster, 1994), excerpts from pp. 39–42, 48–49, 320–326, 337–338, 344–345. Reprinted with the permission of Simon & Schuster from *D-Day* by Stephen Ambrose. Copyright © 1994 by Ambrose-Tubbs, Inc.

it must happen. As early as October 1941, he had told Capt. Lord Louis Mountbatten, head of Combined Operations, "You are to prepare for the invasion of Europe, for unless we can go and land and fight Hitler and beat his forces on land, we shall never win this war."

To precisely that end, Marshall had transformed the U.S. Army from a cadre of 170,000 men in 1940 to an army three years later that numbered 7.2 million (2.3 million in the Army Air Force). It was the best equipped, most mobile, with the most firepower, of any army on earth. This achievement was one of the greatest accomplishments in the history of the Republic.

To use that army only in Italy was unacceptable. Failure to mount an assault to create a second front would be a double cross to Stalin and might lead to precisely the political consequence—a separate Nazi-Soviet armistice—Hitler was counting on. Or, perhaps worse, a Red Army liberation (and thus postwar occupation) of Western Europe. At a minimum, no cross-Channel attack in 1944 would put off victory against the Nazis until at least late 1945, possibly until 1946. Meanwhile, the political pressure to say to the British "To hell with it, if you won't fight in France, we will take our army to the Pacific" would become all but irresistible.

So there had to be an assault. And for all the difficulties, for all the German advantages—land lines of communication, fighting on the defensive, fixed fortifications—the Allies had the decisive edge. Thanks to their control of the sea and air, and to the mass production of a bewildering variety of landing craft, the Allies had unprecedented mobility. They would choose the time and place the battle would be fought.

As soon as the battle began, however, the advantage would shift to the Germans. Once in France, the Allied paratroops and seaborne troops would be relatively immobile. Until the beachhead had been expanded to allow self-propelled artillery and trucks to come ashore, movement would be by legs rather than half-tracks or tires. The Germans, meanwhile, could move to the sound of the guns by road and rail—and by spring 1944 they would have fifty infantry and eleven armored divisions in France. The Allies could hardly hope to put much more than five divisions into the attack on the first day, enough to give them local superiority to be sure, but all reinforcements, plus every bullet, every bandage, every K ration, would have to cross the English Channel to get into the battle.

So the Allies really had two problems—getting ashore, and winning the battle of the buildup. Once they had established a secure beachhead and won room to deploy inland, the weapons being produced in massive quantity in the United States could be brought into France, sealing the German fate. It would then be only a question of when and at what cost unconditional surrender was achieved. But if the Wehrmacht could bring ten divisions of infantry and armor into the battle by the end of the first week to launch a coordinated counterattack, its local manpower and firepower advantages could be decisive. Long-term, the Allied problem appeared to be even greater, for there would be sixty-plus German divisions in France in the spring of 1944 while the Allies would need seven weeks after D-Day to complete the commitment of the forty-odd divisions they would gather in Britain.

To win the battle of the buildup, the Allies could count on their vast air fleet to hamper German movement—but interdiction would be effective only in daylight and good weather. Far more effective would be to immobilize the panzer divisions through trickery—fooling the Germans not only in advance of the attack, but making them believe that the real thing was a feint. That requirement would be *the* key factor in selecting the invasion site.

Whatever site was selected, the assault would be a direct frontal attack against prepared positions. How to do that successfully at an acceptable cost was a problem that had stumped generals on all sides between 1914 and 1918 and had not been solved by the end of 1943. The Wehrmacht had outflanked and outmaneuvered its opponents in Poland in 1939, in France in 1940, and in Russia in 1941. Direct frontal attacks by the Red Army against the Wehrmacht in 1943, and by the British and Americans in Italy that same year, had been costly and relatively ineffective. And the frontal attack on D-Day would be from sea to land.

In World War I, all frontal attacks had been preceded by tremendous artillery bombardments, sometimes a week or more long. Thanks to their enormous fleet, the Allies had the firepower to duplicate such artillery preparation. But the Allied planners decided that surprise was more important than a lengthy bombardment, so they limited the pre-assault bombardment to a half hour or so, in order to ensure surprise.

(Later, critics charged that the heavy losses suffered at the beach called Omaha would have been less had there been a pre-invasion air and sea bombardment of several days, as was done later in the Pacific at Iwo Jima and Okinawa. What the criticism missed was the central point. As Samuel Eliot Morison wrote in his official history of the U.S. Navy, "The Allies were invading a continent where the enemy had immense capabilities for reinforcement and counterattack, not a small island cut off by sea power from sources of supply. . . . Even a complete pulverizing of the Atlantic Wall at Omaha would have availed us nothing, if the German command had been given 24 hours' notice to move up reserves for counterattack. We had to accept the risk of heavy casualties on the beaches to prevent far heavier ones on the plateau and among the hedgerows.") . . .

The U.S. Army's infantry divisions were not elite, by definition, but they had some outstanding characteristics. Although they were made up, primarily, of conscripted troops, there was a vast difference between American draftees and their German counterparts (not to mention *Ost* battalions). The American Selective Service System was just that, selective. One-third of the men called to service were rejected after physical examinations, making the average draftee brighter, healthier, and better educated than the average American. He was twenty-six years old, five feet eight inches tall, weighed 144 pounds, had a thirty-three-and-a-half-inch chest, and a thirty-one-inch waist. After thirteen weeks of basic training, he'd gained seven pounds (and converted many of his original pounds from fat to muscle) and added at least an inch to his chest. Nearly half the draftees were high-school graduates; one in ten had some college. As Geoffrey Perret puts it in his history of the U.S. Army in World War II, "These were the best-educated enlisted men of any army in history."

At the end of 1943 the U.S. Army was the greenest army in the world. Of the nearly fifty infantry, armored, and airborne divisions selected for participation in the campaign in northwest Europe, only two—the 1st Infantry and the 82nd Airborne— had been in combat.

Nor had the bulk of the British army seen action. Although Britain had been at war with Germany for four years, only a small number of divisions had been in combat, and none of those designated for the assault had more than a handful of veterans.

This posed problems and caused apprehension, but it had a certain advantage. According to Pvt. Carl Weast of the U.S. 5th Ranger Battalion, "A veteran infantryman is a terrified infantryman." Sgt. Carwood Lipton of the 506th Parachute Infantry Regiment (PIR) of the 101st Airborne commented, "I took chances on D-Day I would never have taken later in the war."

In *Wartime*, Paul Fussell writes that men in combat go through two stages of rationalization followed by one of perception. Considering the possibility of a severe wound or death, the average soldier's first rationalization is: "It *can't* happen to me. I am too clever/agile/well-trained/good-looking/beloved/tightly laced, etc." The second rationalization is: "It *can* happen to me, and I'd better be more careful. I can avoid the danger by watching more prudently the way I take cover/dig in/ expose my position by firing my weapon/keep extra alert at all times, etc." Finally, the realization is "It *is going to* happen to me, and only my not being there is going to prevent it."

For a direct frontal assault on a prepared enemy position, men who have not seen what a bullet or a land mine or an exploding mortar round can do to a human body are preferable to men who have seen the carnage. Men in their late teens or early twenties have a feeling of invulnerability, as seen in the remark of Charles East of the 29th Division. Told by his commanding officer on the eve of D-Day that nine out of ten would become casualties in the ensuing campaign, East looked at the man to his left, then at the man to his right, and thought to himself, You poor bastards. . . .

Men like Sergeant Lipton and Private East—and there were thousands of them in the American army—could overcome the problem of inexperience with their zeal and daredevil attitude. . . .

If the Germans were going to stop the invasion anywhere, it would be at Omaha Beach. It was an obvious landing site, the only sand beach between the mouth of the Douve to the west and Arromanches to the east, a distance of almost forty kilometers. On both ends of Omaha the cliffs were more or less perpendicular.

The sand at Omaha Beach is golden in color, firm and fine, perfect for sunbathing and picnicking and digging, but in extent the beach is constricted. It is slightly crescent-shaped, about ten kilometers long overall. At low tide, there is a stretch of firm sand of 300 to 400 meters in distance. At high tide, the distance from the waterline to the one- to three-meter bank of shingle (small round stones) is but a few meters.

In 1944 the shingle, now mostly gone, was impassable to vehicles. On the western third of the beach, beyond the shingle, there was a part-wood, part-masonry seawall from one to four meters in height (now gone). Inland of the seawall there was a paved, promenade beach road, then a V-shaped antitank ditch as much as two meters deep, then a flat swampy area, then a steep bluff that ascended thirty meters or more. A man could climb the bluff, but a vehicle could not. The grass-covered slopes appeared to be featureless when viewed from any distance, but in fact they contained many small folds or irregularities that proved to be a critical physical feature of the battlefield.

There were five small "draws" or ravines that sloped gently up to the tableland above the beach. A paved road led off the beach at exit D-1 to Vierville; at Les

Moulins (exit D-3) a dirt road led up to St.-Laurent; the third draw, exit E-1, had only a path leading up to the tableland; the fourth draw, E-3, had a dirt road leading to Colleville; the last draw had a dirt path at exit F-1.

No tactician could have devised a better defensive situation. A narrow, enclosed battlefield, with no possibility of outflanking it; many natural obstacles for the attacker to overcome; an ideal place to build fixed fortifications and a trench system on the slope of the bluff and on the high ground looking down on a wide, open killing field for any infantry trying to cross no-man's-land.

The Allied planners hated the idea of assaulting Omaha Beach, but it had to be done. This was as obvious to Rommel as to Eisenhower. Both commanders recognized that if the Allies invaded in Normandy, they would have to include Omaha Beach in the landing sites; otherwise the gap between Utah and the British beaches would be too great.

The waters offshore were heavily mined, so too the beaches, the promenade (which also had concertina wire along its length), and the bluff. Rommel had placed more beach obstacles here than at Utah. He had twelve strong points holding 88s, 75s, and mortars. He had dozens of Tobruks and machine-gun pillboxes, supported by an extensive trench system.

Everything the Germans had learned in World War I about how to stop a frontal assault by infantry Rommel put to work at Omaha. He laid out the firing positions at angles to the beach to cover the tidal flat and beach shelf with crossing fire, plunging fire, and grazing fire, from all types of weapons. He prepared artillery positions along the cliffs at either end of the beach, capable of delivering enfilade fire from 88s all across Omaha. The trench system included underground quarters and magazines connected by tunnels. The strong points were concentrated near the entrances to the draws, which were further protected by large cement roadblocks. The larger artillery pieces were protected to the seaward by concrete wing walls. There was not one inch of the beach that had not been presighted for both grazing and plunging fire.

Watching the American landing craft approach, the German defenders could hardly believe their eyes. "Holy smoke—here they are!" Lieutenant Frerking declared. "But that's not possible, that's not possible." He put down his binoculars and rushed to his command post in a bunker near Vierville.

"Landing craft on our left, off Vierville, making for the beach," Cpl. Hein Severloh in *Widerstandsnesten* 62 called out. "They must be crazy," Sergeant Krone declared. "Are they going to swim ashore? Right under our muzzles?"

The colonel of the artillery regiment passed down a strict order: "Hold your fire until the enemy is coming up to the waterline."

All along the bluff, German soldiers watched the landing craft approach, their fingers on the triggers of machine guns, rifles, artillery fuses, or holding mortar rounds. In bunker 62, Frerking was at the telephone, giving the range to gunners a couple of kilometers inland: "Target Dora, all guns, range four-eight-five-zero, basic direction 20 plus, impact fuse." . . .

Four things gave the Allies the notion that they could successfully assault this all-but-impregnable position. First, Allied intelligence said that the fortifications and trenches were manned by the 716th Infantry Division, a low-quality unit made up of Poles and Russians with poor morale. At Omaha, intelligence reckoned that there was only one battalion of about 800 troops to man the defenses.

Second, the B-17s assigned to the air bombardment would hit the beach with everything they had, destroying or at least neutralizing the bunkers and creating craters on the beach and bluff that would be usable as foxholes for the infantry. Third, the naval bombardment, culminating with the LCT(R)s' rockets, would finish off anything left alive and moving after the B-17s finished. The infantry from the 29th and 1st divisions going into Omaha were told that their problems would begin when they got to the top of the bluff and started to move inland toward their D-Day objectives.

The fourth cause for confidence that the job would be done was that 40,000 men with 3,500 motorized vehicles were scheduled to land at Omaha on D-Day.

In the event, none of the above worked. The intelligence was wrong; instead of the contemptible 716th Division, the quite-capable 352nd Division was in place. Instead of one German battalion to cover the beach, there were three. The cloud cover and late arrival caused the B-17s to delay their release until they were as much as five kilometers inland; not a single bomb fell on the beach or bluff. The naval bombardment was too brief and generally inaccurate, and in any case it concentrated on the big fortifications above the bluff. Finally, most of the rockets fell short, most of them landing in the surf, killing thousands of fish but no Germans.

Captain Walker, on an LCI, recalled that just before H-Hour, "I took a look toward the shore and my heart took a dive. I couldn't believe how peaceful, how untouched, and how tranquil the scene was. The terrain was green. All buildings and houses were intact. The church steeples were proudly and defiantly standing in place. 'Where,' I yelled to no one in particular, 'is the damned Air Corps?'" . . .

Eisenhower's little aphorism that plans are everything before the battle, useless once it is joined, was certainly the case at Omaha. Nothing worked according to plan, which was indeed useless the moment the Germans opened fire on the assault forces, and even before.

With the exception of Company A, 116th , no unit landed where it was supposed to. Half of E Company was more than a kilometer off target, the other half more than two kilometers to the east of its assigned sector. This was a consequence of winds and tide. A northwest wind of ten to eighteen knots created waves of three to four feet, sometimes as much as six feet, which pushed the landing craft from right to left. So did the tidal current, which with the rising tide (dead low tide at Omaha was 0525) ran at a velocity of 2.7 knots.

By H-Hour, not only were the boats out of position, but the men in them were cramped, seasick, miserable. Most had climbed down their rope nets into crafts four hours or more earlier. The waves came crashing over the gunwales. Every LCVP and LCA (landing craft assault, the British version of the Higgins boat) shipped water. In most of them, the pumps could not carry the load, so the troops had to bail with their helmets.

At least ten of the 200 boats in the first wave swamped; most of the troops were picked up later by Coast Guard rescue craft, often after hours in the water; many drowned. Another disheartening sight to the men in the surviving boats was the glimpse of GIs struggling in life preservers and on rafts, personnel from the foundered DD tanks.

In general, the men of the first wave were exhausted and confused even before the battle was joined. Still, the misery caused by the spray hitting them in the face with each wave and by their seasickness was such that they were eager to hit the beach, feeling that nothing could be worse than riding on those damned Higgins boats. The only comforting thing was those tremendous naval shells zooming over their heads—but even they were hitting the top of the bluff or further inland, not the beach or the slope. At H minus five minutes the fire lifted.

Chief Electrician's Mate Alfred Sears was in the last LCVP of sixteen in the first wave. Going in, the ensign had told him "all the German strong points will be knocked out by the time we hit the beach." Sears went on, "We were so confident of this, that on the way in most of my men and I were sitting on top of the engine room decking of the landing craft, enjoying the show, fascinated by the barrage from the rocket ships. About one thousand rockets shattered the beach directly where we were to land. It looked pretty good."

Lt. Joe Smith was a Navy beachmaster. His job was to put up flags to guide the landing craft from A Company, 116th Regiment. His Higgins boat may have been the first to hit the beach. "The Germans let us alone on the beach. We didn't know why, we could see the Germans up there looking down on us; it was a weird feeling. We were right in front of a German 88 gun emplacement, but fortunately for us they were set to cover down the beach and not toward the sea, so they could not see us."

A Higgins boat carrying an assault team from A Company came in behind Smith. The men in it figured that what they had been told to expect had come true: the air and naval bombardments had wiped out the opposition. The ramp went down.

"Target Dora—fire!" Lieutenant Frerking shouted into the telephone. When the battery opened fire, eager German gunners throughout the area pulled their triggers. To Frerking's left there were three MG-42 positions; to his front a fortified mortar position; on the forward slopes of the bluff infantrymen in trenches. They exploded into action.

"We hit the sandbar," Electrician's Mate Sears recalled, "dropped the ramp, and then all hell poured loose on us. The soldiers in the boat received a hail of machine-gun bullets. The Army lieutenant was immediately killed, shot through the head."

In the lead Company A boat, LCA 1015, Capt. Taylor Fellers and every one of his men were killed before the ramp went down. It just vaporized. No one ever learned whether it was the result of hitting a mine or getting hit by an 88.

"They put their ramp down," Navy beachmaster Lt. Joe Smith said of what he saw, "and a German machine gun or two opened up and you could see the sand kick up right in front of the boat. No one moved. The coxswain stood up and yelled and for some reason everything was quiet for an instant and you could hear him as clear as a bell, he said, 'For Christ's sake, fellas, get out! I've got to go get another load.'"

All across the beach, the German machine guns were hurling fire of monstrous proportions on the hapless Americans. (One gunner with Lieutenant Frerking at strong point 62 fired 12,000 rounds that morning.) Because of the misplaced landings, the GIs were bunched together, with large gaps between groups, up to a kilometer in length, which allowed the Germans to concentrate their fire. As the Higgins boats and larger LCIs approached the beach, the German artillery fired at will, from the Tobruks and fortifications up the draws and on top of the bluff and from the emplacements on the beach. . . .

As what was left of A, F, G, and E companies of the 116th huddled behind obstacles or the shingle, the following waves began to come in: B and H companies at 0700, D at 0710, C, K, I, and M at 0720. Not one came in on target. The coxswains were trying to dodge obstacles and incoming shells, while the smoke drifted in and out and obscured the landmarks and what few marker flags there were on the beach.

On the command boat for B Company, the CO, Capt. Ettore Zappacosta, heard the British coxswain cry out, "We can't go in there. We can't see the landmarks. We must pull off."

Zappacosta pulled his Colt .45 and ordered, "By God, you'll take this boat straight in."

The coxswain did. When the ramp dropped, Zappacosta was first off. He was immediately hit. Medic Thomas Kenser saw him bleeding from hip and shoulder. Kenser, still on the ramp, shouted, "Try to make it in! I'm coming." But the captain was already dead. Before Kenser could jump off the ramp he was shot dead. Every man in the boat save one (Pvt. Robert Sales) was either killed or wounded before reaching the beach.

Nineteen-year-old Pvt. Harold Baumgarten of B Company got a bullet through the top of his helmet while jumping from the ramp, then hit the receiver of his M-1 as he carried it at port arms. He waded through the waist-deep water as his buddies fell alongside him.

"I saw Pvt. Robert Ditmar of Fairfield, Connecticut, hold his chest and heard him yell, 'I'm hit, I'm hit!' I hit the ground and watched him as he continued to go forward about ten more yards. He tripped over an obstacle and, as he fell, his body made a complete turn and he lay sprawled on the damp sand with his head facing the Germans, his face looking skyward. He was yelling, 'Mother, Mom.'

"Sgt. Clarence 'Pilgrim' Robertson had a gaping wound in the upper right corner of his forehead. He was walking crazily in the water. Then I saw him get down on his knees and start praying with his rosary beads. At this moment, the Germans cut him in half with their deadly crossfire."

Baumgarten had drawn a Star of David on the back of his field jacket, with "The Bronx, New York" written on it—that would let Hitler know who he was. He was behind an obstacle. He saw the reflection from the helmet of one of the German riflemen on the bluff "and took aim and later on I found out I got a bull's eye on him." That was the only shot he fired because his damaged rifle broke in two when he pulled the trigger.

Shells were bursting about him. "I raised my head to curse the Germans when an 88 shell exploded about twenty yards in front of me, hitting me in my left cheek. It felt like being hit with a baseball bat only the results were much worse. My upper jaw was shattered, the left cheek blown open. My upper lip was cut in half. The roof of my mouth was cut up and teeth and gums were laying all over my mouth. Blood poured freely from the gaping wound."

The tide was coming in. Baumgarten washed his face with the cold, dirty Channel water and managed not to pass out. The water was rising about an inch a minute (between 0630 and 0800 the tide rose eight feet) so he had to get moving or drown. He took another hit, from a bullet, in the leg. He moved forward in a dead man's float with each wave of the incoming tide. He finally reached the seawall where a medic dressed his wounds. Mortars were coming in, "and I grabbed the medic by the shirt to pull him down. He hit my hand away and said, 'You're injured now. When I get hurt you can take care of me.'"

Sgt. Benjamin McKinney was a combat engineer attached to C Company. When his ramp dropped, "I was so seasick I didn't care if a bullet hit me between the eyes and got me out of my misery." As he jumped off the ramp, "rifle and machine-gun fire hit it like rain falling." Ahead, "it looked as if all the first wave were dead on the beach." He got to the shingle. He and Sergeant Storms saw a pillbox holding a machine gun and a rifleman about thirty meters to the right, spraying the beach with their weapons. Storms and McKinney crawled toward the position. McKinney threw hand grenades as Storms put rifle fire into it. Two Germans jumped out; Storms killed them. The 116th was starting to fight back. . . .

This was the critical moment in the battle. It was an ultimate test: could a democracy produce young men tough enough to take charge, to lead? As Pvt. Carl Weast put it, "It was simple fear that stopped us at that shingle and we lay there and we got butchered by rocket fire and by mortars for no damn reason other than the fact that there was nobody there to lead us off that goddamn beach. Like I say, hey man, I did my job, but somebody had to lead me."

Sgt. William Lewis remembered cowering behind the shingle. Pvt. Larry Rote piled in on top of Lewis. He asked, "Is that you shaking, Sarge?"

"Yeah, damn right!"

"My God," Rote said. "I thought it was me!" Lewis commented, "Rote was shaking all right."

They huddled together with some other men, "just trying to stay alive. There was nothing we could do except keep our butts down. Others took cover behind the wall."

All across Omaha, the men who had made it to the shingle hid behind it. Then Cota, or Canham, or a captain here, a lieutenant there, a sergeant someplace else, began to lead. They would cry out, "Follow me!" and start moving up the bluff.

In Sergeant Lewis's case, "Lt. Leo Van de Voort said, 'Let's go, goddamn, there ain't no use staying here, we're all going to get killed!' The first thing he did was to run up to a gun emplacement and throw a grenade in the embrasure. He returned with five or six prisoners. So then we thought, hell, if he can do that, why can't we. That's how we got off the beach."

That was how most men got off the beach. Pvt. Raymond Howell, an engineer attached to D Company, described his thought process. He took some shrapnel in helmet and hand. "That's when I said, bullshit, if I'm going to die, to hell with it I'm not going to die here. The next bunch of guys that go over that goddamn wall, I'm going with them. If I'm gonna be infantry, I'm gonna be infantry. So I don't know who else, I guess all of us decided well, it is time to start."

Over Here: World War II and American Liberalism

ALAN BRINKLEY

Few would disagree that World War II changed the world as profoundly as any event of this century, perhaps any century. What is less readily apparent, perhaps, is how profoundly the war changed America—its society, its politics, and . . . its image of itself. Except for the combatants themselves, Americans experienced the war at a remove of several thousand miles. They endured no bombing, no invasion, no massive dislocations, no serious material privations. Veterans returning home in 1945 and 1946 found a country that looked very much like the one they had left—something that clearly could not be said of veterans returning home to Britain, France, Germany, Russia, or Japan.

But World War II did transform America in profound, if not immediately visible, ways. Not the least important of those transformations was in the nature of American liberalism, a force that would play a central role in shaping the nation's postwar political and cultural life. Liberalism in America rests on several consistent and enduring philosophical assumptions: the high value liberals believe society should attribute to individual rights and freedoms and the importance of avoiding rigid and immutable norms and institutions. But in the half century since the New Deal, liberalism in America has also meant a prescription for public policy and political action; and in the 1940s this "New Deal liberalism" was in a state of considerable uncertainty and was undergoing significant changes. Several broad developments of the war years helped lay the foundations for the new liberal order that followed the war.

Among those developments was a series of important shifts in the size, distribution, and character of the American population. Not all the demographic changes of the 1940s were a result of the war, nor were their effects on liberal assumptions entirely apparent until well after 1945. But they were a crucial part of the process that would transform American society and the way liberals viewed their mission in that society.

Perhaps the most conspicuous demographic change was the single biggest ethnic migration in American history: the massive movement of African Americans from the rural South to the urban North, a migration much larger than the "great migration" at the time of World War I. Between 1910 (when the first great migration began) and 1940, approximately 1.5 million blacks moved from the South to the North. In the 1940s alone, 2 million African Americans left the South, and 3 million more moved in the twenty years after that. The migration brought substantial numbers of them closer to the center of the nation's economic, cultural, and institutional life. The number of blacks employed in manufacturing more than doubled during the war. There were major increases in the number of African Americans employed as skilled craftsmen or enrolled in unions. There was a massive movement of African American women out of domestic work and into the factory and the shop. Much of this would have occurred with or without World War II, but the war

The War in American Culture by Brinkley, Erenberg, & Hirsch (Chicago: University of Chicago Press, 1996), 314–323, 326–327. Reprinted by permission of The University of Chicago Press.

greatly accelerated the movement by expanding industrial activity and by creating a labor shortage that gave African American men and women an incentive to move into industrial cities.

This second great migration carried the question of race out of the South and into the North, out of the countryside and into the city, out of the field and into the factory. African American men and women encountered prejudice and discrimination in the urban, industrial world much as they had in the agrarian world; but in the city they were far better positioned to organize and protest their condition, as some were beginning to do even before the fighting ended. World War II therefore began the process by which race would increase its claim on American consciousness and, ultimately, transform American liberalism.

Just as the war helped lay the groundwork for challenges to racial orthodoxies, so it contributed to later challenges to gender norms. Three million women entered the paid workforce for the first time during the war, benefiting—like black workers— from the labor shortage military conscription had created. Many women performed jobs long considered the exclusive province of men. Women had been moving into the workforce in growing numbers before the war began, to be sure, and almost certainly they would have continued to do so even had the United States remained at peace. Many of their wartime gains, moreover, proved short lived. Female factory workers in particular were usually dismissed as soon as male workers returned to take their places, even though many wanted to remain in their jobs.

Still, most women who had begun working during the war continued working after 1945 (if not always in the same jobs). And while popular assumptions about women's roles (among both women and men) were slow to change, the economic realities of many women's lives were changing dramatically and permanently—in ways that would eventually help raise powerful challenges to ideas about gender. The war, in short, accelerated a critical long-term shift in the role of women in society that would produce, among other things, the feminist movements of the 1960s and beyond.

Similar, if less dramatic, changes were affecting other American communities during the war. Men and women who had long lived on the margins of American life—because of prejudice or geographical isolation or both—found their lives transformed by the pressures of war. Asian Americans, Latino Americans, Native Americans, and others served in the military, worked in factories, moved into diverse urban neighborhoods, and otherwise encountered the urban-industrial world of the midtwentieth century. Life was not, perhaps, much better for many such people in their new roles than it had been in traditional ones. For Japanese Americans on the West Coast, who spent much of the war in internment camps, victims of popular and official hysteria, it was considerably worse. But for many such communities the changes helped erode the isolation that had made it difficult to challenge discrimination and demand inclusion.

No one living in the era of multiculturalism will be inclined to argue with the proposition that the changing composition of the American population over the past fifty years—and the changing relations among different groups within the population—is one of the most important events in the nation's recent history. Those changes have reshaped America's economy, its culture, its politics, and its intellectual life. They have forced the nation to confront its increasing diversity in more direct and painful ways than at any time since the Civil War. They have challenged America's conception of itself as a nation and a society. And they have transformed American liberalism. In the 1930s, most liberals considered questions of racial, ethnic, or gender difference of distinctly secondary importance (or in the case of gender, virtually no importance at all). Liberal discourse centered much more on issues of class and the distribution of wealth and economic power. By 1945 that was beginning to change. One sign of that change was the remarkable reception among liberals of Gunnar Myrdal's *An American Dilemma,* published in 1944. Myrdal identified race as the one issue most likely to shape and perplex the American future. The great migration of the 1940s helped ensure that history would vindicate Myrdal's prediction and that American liberals would adjust their outlook and their goals in fundamental ways in the postwar years.

Perhaps the most common and important observation about the domestic impact of World War II is that it ended the Great Depression and launched an era of unprecedented prosperity. Between 1940 and 1945 the United States experienced the greatest expansion of industrial production in its history. After a decade of depression, a decade of growing doubts about capitalism, a decade of high unemployment and underproduction, suddenly, in a single stroke, the American economy restored itself and—equally important—seemed to redeem itself. Gross national product in the war years rose from $91 billion to $166 billion; 15 million new jobs were created, and the most enduring problem of the depression—massive unemployment—came to an end; industrial production doubled; personal incomes rose (depending on location) by as much as 200 percent. The revival of the economy is obviously important in its own right. But it also had implications for the future of American political economy, for how liberals in particular conceived of the role of the state in the postwar United States.

One of the mainstays of economic thought in the late 1930s was the belief that the United States had reached what many called "economic maturity": the belief that the nation was approaching, or perhaps had reached, the end of its capacity to grow, that America must now learn to live within limits. This assumption strengthened the belief among many reformers that in the future it would be necessary to regulate the economy much more closely and carefully for the benefit of society as a whole. America could not rely any more on a constantly expanding pie; it would have to worry about how the existing pie was to be divided.

The wartime economic experience—the booming expansion, the virtual elimination of unemployment, the creation of new industries, new "frontiers"—served as a rebuke to the "mature economy" idea and restored the concept of growth to the center of liberal hopes. The capitalist economy, liberals suddenly discovered, was not irretrievably stagnant. Economic expansion could achieve, in fact had achieved, dimensions beyond the wildest dreams of the 1930s. Social and economic advancement could proceed, therefore, without structural changes in capitalism, without continuing, intrusive state management of the economy. It could proceed by virtue of growth.

Assaults on the concept of economic maturity were emerging as early as 1940 and gathered force throughout the war. Alvin Hansen, one of the most prominent champions in the 1930s of what he called "secular stagnation," repudiated the idea in 1941. "All of us had our sights too low," he admitted. The *New Republic* and the

Nation, both of which had embraced the idea of economic maturity in 1938 and 1939, openly rejected it in the 1940s—not only rejected it, but celebrated its demise. The country had achieved a "break," exulted the *Nation,* "from the defeatist thinking that held us in economic thraldom through the thirties, when it was assumed that we could not afford full employment or full production in this country."

But along with this celebration of economic growth came a new and urgent fear: that the growth might not continue once the war was over. What if the depression came back? What if there was a return to massive unemployment? What could be done to make sure that economic growth continued? That was the great liberal challenge of the war years—not to restructure the economy, not to control corporate behavior, not to search for new and more efficient forms of management, but to find a way to keep things going as they were.

And in response to that challenge, a growing number of liberal economists and policymakers became interested in a tool that had begun to attract their attention in the 1930s and that seemed to prove itself during the war: government spending. That was clearly how the economy had revived—in response to the massive increase in the federal budget in the war years, from $9 billion in 1939 to $100 billion in 1945. And that was how the revival could be sustained—by pumping more money into the economy in peacetime. What government needed to do, therefore, was to "plan" for postwar full employment.

Those who called themselves "planners" in the 1940s did not talk much anymore, as planners had talked in earlier years, about the need for an efficient, centrally planned economy in which the government would help direct the behavior of private institutions. They talked instead about fiscal planning—about public works projects, about social welfare programs, about the expansion of the Social Security system. The National Resource Planning Board, the central "planning" agency of the New Deal since 1933, issued a report in 1942 called *Security, Work, and Relief Policies.* In the past, the NRPB had been preoccupied largely with older ideas of planning— regional planning, resource management, government supervision of production and investment. Now, in their 1942 report, the members turned their attention to the new kind of planning. The government should create a "shelf" of public works projects, so that after the war—whenever the economy showed signs of stagnating—it could pull projects off the shelf and spend the money on them to stimulate more growth. The government should commit itself to more expansive Social Security measures so that after the war—if the economy should slow down—there would be welfare mechanisms in place that would immediately pick up the slack and start paying out benefits, which would increase purchasing power and stimulate growth.

All of this reflected, among other things, the increasing influence in American liberal circles of Keynesian economics. The most important liberal economist of the war years—Alvin Hansen of Harvard, who contributed to many NRPB reports— was also the leading American exponent of Keynesianism. Keynesianism provided those concerned about the future of the American economy with an escape from their fears of a new, postwar depression. Economic growth, it taught them, did not require constant involvement in the affairs of private institutions—which the 1930s (and the war itself) had shown to be logistically difficult and politically controversial. Growth could be sustained through the *indirect* manipulation of the economy by fiscal and monetary levers.

The wartime faith in economic growth led, in other words, to several developments of great importance to the future of American liberalism. It helped relegitimize capitalism among people who had, in the 1930s, developed serious doubts about its viability. It helped rob the "administrative" reform ideas of the late 1930s—the belief in ever greater regulation of private institutions—of their urgency. It helped elevate Keynesian ideas about indirect management of the economy to the center of reform hopes. And it made the idea of the welfare state—of Social Security and public works and other social welfare efforts—come to seem a part of the larger vision of sustaining economic growth by defining welfare as a way to distribute income and stimulate purchasing power. It helped channel American liberalism into a new, less confrontational direction—a direction that would produce fewer clashes with capitalist institutions; that tried to define the interests of capitalists and the interests of the larger public in identical terms; that emphasized problems of consumption over problems of production; that shaped the liberal agenda for more than a generation and helped shape the next great episode in liberal policy experiments: the Great Society of the 1960s.

World War II had other important and more purely ideological effects on American liberalism—some of them in apparent conflict with others, but all of them important in determining the permissible range of liberal aspirations for the postwar era. First, the war created, or at least greatly reinforced, a set of anxieties and fears that would become increasingly central to liberal thought in the late 1940s and 1950s. It inflamed two fears in particular: a fear of the state and a fear of the people. Both were a response, in large part, to the horror with which American liberals (and most other Americans as well) regarded the regimes the United States was fighting in World War II. Both would be sustained and strengthened by the similar horror with which most Americans came to view the regime the nation was beginning to mobilize against in peacetime even before the end of the war: the Soviet Union.

The fear of the state emerged directly out of the way American liberals (and the American people generally) defined the nature of their enemy in World War II. During World War I many Americans had believed the enemy was a race, a people: the Germans, the beastlike "Huns," and their presumably savage culture. In World War II racial stereotypes continued to play an important role in portrayals of the Japanese; but in defining the enemy in Europe—always the principal enemy in the 1940s to most Americans—the government and most of the media relied less on racial or cultural images than on political ones. Wartime propaganda in World War II did not personify the Germans and Italians as evil peoples. It focused instead on the Nazi and fascist states.

The war, in other words, pushed a fear of totalitarianism (and hence a general wariness about excessive state power) to the center of American liberal thought. In particular, it forced a reassessment of the kinds of associational and corporatist arrangements that many had found so attractive in the aftermath of World War I. Those, after all, were the kinds of arrangements Germany and Italy had claimed to be creating. But it also created a less specific fear of state power that made other kinds of direct planning and management of the economy of society seem unappealing as well. "The rise of totalitarianism," Reinhold Niebuhr noted somberly in 1945, "has prompted the democratic world to view all collectivist answers to our social problems with increased apprehension." Virtually all experiments in state supervision of private institutions, he warned, contained "some peril of compounding economic and political power." Hence "a wise community will walk warily and test the effect of each new adventure before further adventures." To others the lesson was even starker. *Any* steps in the direction of state control of economic institutions were (to use the title of Friedrich A. Hayek's celebrated antistatist book of 1944) steps along "the road to serfdom." This fear of the state was one of many things that lent strength to the emerging Keynesian–welfare state liberal vision of political economy, with its much more limited role for government as a manager of economic behavior.

Along with this fear of the state emerged a related fear: a fear of "mass politics" or "mass man"; a fear, in short, of the people. Nazi Germany, facist Italy, even the Soviet Union, many liberals came to believe, illustrated the dangers inherent in trusting the people to control their political life. The people, the "mass," could too easily be swayed by demagogues and tyrants. They were too susceptible to appeals to their passions, to the dark, intolerant impulses that in a healthy society remained largely repressed and subdued. Fascism and communism were not simply the products of the state or of elite politics, many liberals believed; they were the products of mass movements, of the unleashing of the dangerous and irrational impulses within every individual and every society.

This fear of the mass lay at the heart of much liberal cultural and intellectual criticism in the first fifteen years after World War II. It found expression in the writings of Hannah Arendt, Theodor Adorno, Richard Hofstadter, Lionel Trilling, Daniel Bell, Dwight Macdonald, and many others. Like the fear of the state, with which it was so closely associated, it reinforced a sense of caution and restraint in liberal thinking; a suspicion of ideology, a commitment to pragmatism, a wariness about moving too quickly to encourage or embrace spontaneous popular movements; a conviction that one of the purposes of politics was to defend the state against popular movements and their potentially dangerous effects.

There were, in short, powerful voices within American liberalism during and immediately after World War II arguing that the experience of the war had introduced a dark cloud of doubt and even despair to human society. A world that could produce so terrible a war; a world that could produce Hiroshima, Nagasaki, the Katyn Forest, Auschwitz; a world capable of profound evil and inconceivable destruction: such a world, many American liberals argued, must be forever regarded skeptically and suspiciously. Humankind must move cautiously into its uncertain future, wary of unleashing the dark impulses that had produced such horror.

Some liberal intellectuals went further. Americans, they argued, must resist the temptation to think of themselves, in their hour of triumph, as a chosen people. No people, no nation, could afford to ignore its own capacity for evil. Reinhold Niebuhr spoke for many liberals when he wrote of the dangers of the "deep layer of Messianic consciousness in the mind of America" and warned of liberal culture's "inability to comprehend the depth of evil to which individuals and communities may sink, particularly when they try to play the role of God in history." Americans, he said, would do well to remember that "no nation is sacred and unique. . . . Providence has not set Americans apart from lesser breeds. We too are part of history's seamless web."

But Niebuhr's statements were obviously written to refute a competing assumption. And as it suggests, there was in the 1940s another, very different ideological force at work in America, another form of national self-definition that affected liberal thought and behavior, at home and in the world, at least as much as the somber assessments of Niebuhr and others. Indeed even many liberal intellectuals attracted to Niebuhr's pessimistic ideas about human nature and mass politics were simultaneously drawn to this different and, on the surface at least, contradictory assessment of the nation's potential. For in many ways the most powerful ideological force at work in postwar American liberalism, and in the postwar United States generally, was the view of America as an anointed nation; America as a special moral force in the world; America as a society with a unique mission, born of its righteousness. This is an ideological tradition that is often described as the tradition of American innocence. But innocence is perhaps too gentle a word for what has often been an aggressive and intrusive vision, a vision that rests on the belief that America is somehow insulated from the sins and failures and travails that affect other nations, that America stands somehow outside of history, protected from it by its own strength and virtue.

World War II did not create those beliefs. They are as old as the nation itself. But the American experience in the conflict, and the radically enhanced international stature and responsibility of the United States in the aftermath of the war, strengthened such ideas and gave them a crusading quality that made them as active and powerful as they had been at any moment in the nation's history. . . .

The war left other ideological legacies for American liberalism as well. In the glow of the nation's victory, in the sense of old orders shattered and a new world being born, came an era of exuberant innovation, an era in which, for a time, nothing seemed more appealing than the new. The allure of the new was visible in the brave new world of architectural modernism, whose controversial legacy is so much a part of the postwar American landscape. It was visible in the explosive growth of the innovative and iconoclastic American art world, which made New York in the 1940s and 1950s something of what Paris had been in the nineteenth century. It was visible in the increased stature and boldness of the American scientific community, and in the almost religious faith in technological progress that came to characterize so much of American life.

Above all, perhaps, it was visible in the way it excited, and then frustrated, a generation of American liberals as they imagined new possibilities for progress and social justice. That is what Archibald MacLeish meant in 1943 when he spoke about the America of the imagination, the society that the war was encouraging Americans to create:

> We have, and we know we have, the abundant means to bring our boldest dreams to pass—to create for ourselves whatever world we have the courage to desire. . . . We have the tools and the skill and the intelligence to take our cities apart and put them together, to lead our roads and rivers where we please to lead them, to build our houses where we want our houses, to brighten the air, to clean the wind, to live as men in this Republic, free men, should be living. We have the power and the courage and the resources of good-will and decency and common understanding . . . to create a nation such as men have never seen. . . . We stand at the moment of the building of great lives, for the war's end and our victory in the war will throw that moment and the means before us.

There was, of course, considerable naïveté, and even arrogance, in such visions. But there was also an appealing sense of hope and commitment—a belief in the possibility of sweeping away old problems and failures, of creating "great lives." Out of such visions came some of the postwar crusades of American liberals—the battle for racial justice, the effort to combat poverty, the expansion of individual rights. And although all of those battles had some ambiguous and even unhappy consequences, they all reflected a confidence in the character and commitment of American society—and the possibility of creating social justice within it—that few people would express so blithely today. Postwar liberalism had suffered many failures and travails in the half century since 1945. But surely its postwar faith in the capacity of America to rebuild—and perhaps even redeem—itself remains one of its most appealing legacies.

FURTHER READING

Michael Adams, *The Best War Ever: America and World War II* (1994).

James Atleson, *Labor and the Wartime State* (1998).

Robert Dallek, *Franklin D. Roosevelt and American Foreign Policy* (1979).

John Dower, *War Without Mercy: Race and Power in the Pacific War* (1986).

Marilynn Johnson, *The Second Gold Rush: Oakland and the East Bay in World War II* (1993).

David M. Kennedy, *Freedom from Fear: The American People in Depression and War* (1999).

Martin J. Sherwin, *A World Destroyed: The Atomic Bomb and the Grand Alliance* (1975).

John Tateishi, *And Justice for All: An Oral History of the Japanese American Detention Camps* (1984).

C H A P T E R
10

The Cold War and
the Nuclear Age

Winning the peace can be more difficult than winning the war, as both the United States and the Soviet Union learned in the decade following V-E Day (Victory-Europe). "We may not get 100 percent of what we want in the postwar world, but I think we can get 85 percent," President Harry Truman optimistically told his advisers. Yet the United States was not the only victor, and more importantly not the only superpower, to arise from the ashes. The Soviet Union had lost more than 20 million of its people, compared with American losses of less than half a million. The Soviet resolve to maintain a security zone in eastern Europe after the war clashed with American expectations, as well as with the wishes of most eastern Europeans. Some historians contend that the Cold War began with the initial American decision to keep the atomic bomb a secret from its Soviet ally, stirring Stalin's suspicions. Others cite the influence of people like diplomat George Kennan, who saw no end to Soviet ambition and gave advice that helped to crystallize the policy called containment. Still other historians cite the actions of the Russian army, which made the Soviet Union thoroughly unpopular in the zones where the USSR hoped to maintain a sphere of influence.

Whatever its causes, discord between the two most powerful members of the former Grand Alliance created a Cold War that lasted more than forty years. With the Truman Doctrine of 1947, the United States adopted the role of "global policeman." With the Marshall Plan of 1948, the United States adopted the role of economic caretaker of Europe. Both actions originated as attempts to stop the perceived communist threat to world peace and stability. When the Korean War broke out in 1950, the Truman administration approved a policy drafted by the National Security Council (NSC), NSC-68. This policy drastically expanded American defense expenditures, placed the nation on a permanent war footing, and created what President Eisenhower later dubbed "the military-industrial complex."

Two of the most important effects of the Cold War for the United States were the "Red Scare" at home and the nuclear arms race. Unable to understand why the United States could not better control the outcomes of World War II, many Americans readily believed critics who charged that traitors in government were responsible. Senator Joseph McCarthy was not the first to make these claims, but he became the most famous. McCarthy's subcommittee in the Senate publicly interrogated citizens on their loyalty, as did the Un-American Activities Committee of the House of Representatives. These congressional initiatives coincided with the prosecution of suspected communists under a new federal loyalty program created by Truman in 1947. Between 1947 and 1952, 6.6 million federal employees were investigated for disloyalty. No cases of espionage within government came to light, but thousands of people lost their jobs and sometimes their freedom as a result of tenuous connections to leftist causes or ideas.

The nuclear buildup went into full swing when the Soviet Union tested its first nuclear weapon in 1949. The United States immediately began construction of the more powerful hydrogen bomb, and scientists who opposed the arms race, including J. Robert Oppenheimer, the "father" of the atom bomb, were run out of government on grounds of disloyalty. Under President Dwight D. Eisenhower, the U.S. government gradually developed a policy of nuclear deterrence—backed up by immense lethal arsenals—which later developed into MAD, or mutual assured destruction. The potential for nuclear annihilation contrasted bizarrely with a booming economy and with the happy families portrayed on television in the 1950s. Some Americans wondered what to believe: that life was wonderful, or that the world might be destroyed the next day. Ironically, both things could be true.

QUESTIONS TO THINK ABOUT

Why was there a Cold War? Did Soviet aggression make conflict inevitable, or did the United States overreact to the battered Soviet Union's quest for security? What was the effect of the Cold War on the worldview and psychology of American citizens?

DOCUMENTS

The documents in this chapter provide various perspectives on the Cold War. At the end of World War II, the United States was the only nation with atomic bombs. In Document 1, Henry Stimson, a member of the Republican Party who was secretary of state under Hoover and secretary of war under Roosevelt, cautions against using this as a subtle threat against the Soviets. He argues that if the United States does not act on the basis of trust, it will create mistrust and a consequent arms race. Document 2 is American diplomat George Kennan's famous 1946 telegram from Moscow to Washington, in which he states that the Russians cannot be trusted, and must be met with force before they destroy "our traditional way of life." In Document 3, Henry Wallace, secretary of commerce and former vice president, states that Americans should try to understand how their attempts to reshape the world order (and build an atomic arsenal) might appear to the Soviets. Soon thereafter Wallace, the last of the New Dealers in Truman's cabinet, was forced to resign. Document 4 gives a Soviet perspective: that of Ambassador to the U.S. Nikolai Novikov, who tells his superiors that the United States seems bent on world dominance. In Document 5, the president outlines to Congress what came to be known as the Truman Doctrine: the commitment of the United States to police the world to ensure that free peoples are able to "work out their own destinies in their own way." Although the Truman Doctrine initially authorized the government to aid only Greece and Turkey, the commitment soon spread to all areas of the globe. Document 6 outlines the Marshall Plan, a $12 billion program to reconstruct the economies of the countries of western Europe after the war to ensure that these countries remained allied with the United States. NSC-68, Document 7, placed the United States on a semipermanent war footing. Approved at the start of the Korean War, this National Security Council (NSC) plan committed the United States to a militarized Cold War. The next two documents show some of the consequences of Truman's campaign to enlist Americans in fighting communism worldwide. In his famous Wheeling, West Virginia, speech (Document 8), Senator Joseph McCarthy claimed that the international communist threat was actually the result of treason at home, especially within the U.S. Department of State. The Truman administration's own campaign against subversion lent credence to McCarthy's claims, having stirred up doubts about numerous federal employees, often on the basis of flimsy evidence. In Document 9, a temporary postal clerk loses his job because, among other things, a college professor once required him to read *Das Kapital,* the nineteenth-century economics book by Karl Marx. Document 10 shows President Dwight Eisenhower warning that the vast military-industrial complex created to fight the Cold War may eventually "endanger our liberties."

1. Secretary of War Henry Stimson Appeals for Atomic Talks with the Soviets, 1945

In many quarters it [atomic bomb] has been interpreted as a substantial offset to the growth of Russian influence on the continent. We can be certain that the Soviet Government has sensed this tendency and the temptation will be strong for the Soviet political and military leaders to acquire this weapon in the shortest possible time. Britain in effect already has the status of a partner with us in the development of this weapon. Accordingly, unless the Soviets are voluntarily invited into the partnership upon a basis of cooperation and trust, we are going to maintain the Anglo-Saxon bloc over against the Soviet in the possession of this weapon. Such a condition will almost certainly stimulate feverish activity on the part of the Soviet toward the development of this bomb in what will in effect be a secret armament race of a rather desperate character. There is evidence to indicate that such activity may have already commenced. . . .

To put the matter concisely, I consider the problem of our satisfactory relations with Russia as not merely connected with but as virtually dominated by the problem of the atomic bomb. Except for the problem of the control of that bomb, those relations, while vitally important, might not be immediately pressing. The establishment of relations of mutual confidence between her and us could afford to await the slow progress of time. But with the discovery of the bomb, they became immediately emergent. Those relations may be perhaps irretrievably embittered by the way in which we approach the solution of the bomb with Russia. For if we fail to approach them now and merely continue to negotiate with them, having this weapon rather ostentatiously on our hip, their suspicions and their distrust of our purposes and motives will increase. . . .

If the atomic bomb were merely another though more devastating military weapon to be assimilated into our pattern of international relations, it would be one

---

Henry L. Stimson, Memorandum for the President, 11 September 1945, "Proposed Actions for Control of Atomic Bombs," Harry S. Truman Papers, PSF: General File, Folder: Atomic Bomb, Box 112, Harry S. Truman Presidential Library, Independence, MO. This document can also be found in Henry L. Stimson and McGeorge Bundy, *On Active Service in Peace and War* (New York: Harper & Brothers, 1948), 642–646.

thing. We could then follow the old custom of secrecy and nationalistic military superiority relying on international caution to prescribe the future use of the weapon as we did with gas. But I think the bomb instead constitutes merely a first step in a new control by man over the forces of nature too revolutionary and dangerous to fit into the old concepts. . . .

My idea of an approach to the Soviets would be a direct proposal after discussion with the British that we would be prepared in effect to enter an arrangement with the Russians, the general purpose of which would be to control and limit the use of the atomic bomb as an instrument of war and so far as possible to direct and encourage the development of atomic power for peaceful and humanitarian purposes. Such an approach might more specifically lead to the proposal that we would stop work on the further improvement in, or manufacture of, the bomb as a military weapon, provided the Russians and the British would agree to do likewise. It might also provide that we would be willing to impound what bombs we now have in the United States provided the Russians and the British would agree with us that in no event will they or we use a bomb as an instrument of war unless all three Governments agree to that use. . . .

I emphasize perhaps beyond all other considerations the importance of taking this action with Russia as a proposal of the United States—backed by Great Britain but peculiarly the proposal of the United States.

2. Diplomat George F. Kennan Advocates Containment, 1946

At bottom of Kremlin's neurotic view of world affairs is traditional and instinctive Russian sense of insecurity. Originally, this was insecurity of a peaceful agricultural people trying to live on vast exposed plain in neighborhood of fierce nomadic peoples. To this was added, as Russia came into contact with economically advanced West, fear of more competent, more powerful, more highly organized societies in that area. . . . For this reason they have always feared foreign penetration, feared direct contact between Western world and their own, feared what would happen if Russians learned truth about world without or if foreigners learned truth about world within. And they had learned to seek security only in patient but deadly struggle for total destruction of rival power, never in compacts and compromises with it.

It was no coincidence that Marxism, which had smouldered ineffectively for half a century in Western Europe, caught hold and blazed for first time in Russia. Only in this land which had never known a friendly neighbor or indeed any tolerant equilibrium of separate powers, either internal or international, could a doctrine thrive which viewed economic conflicts of society as insoluble by peaceful means. After establishment of Bolshevist regime, Marxist dogma, rendered even more truculent and intolerant by Lenin's interpretation, became a perfect vehicle for sense of insecurity with which Bolsheviks, even more than previous Russian rulers, were afflicted. In this dogma, with its basic altruism of purpose, they found justification for their instinctive fear of outside world, for the dictatorship without which they

---

U.S. Department of State, *Foreign Relations of the United States, 1946, Eastern Europe: The Soviet Union* (Washington, D.C.: U.S. Government Printing Office, 1969), VI, 699–701, 706–707.

did not know how to rule, for cruelties they did not dare not to inflict, for sacrifices they felt bound to demand. In the name of Marxism they sacrificed every single ethical value in their methods and tactics. Today they cannot dispense with it. It is fig leaf of their moral and intellectual respectability. . . .

In summary, we have here a political force committed fanatically to the belief that with US there can be no permanent *modus vivendi,* that it is desirable and necessary that the internal harmony of our society be disrupted, our traditional way of life be destroyed, the international authority of our state be broken, if Soviet power is to be secure. This political force has complete power of disposition over energies of one of world's greatest peoples and resources of world's richest national territory, and is borne along by deep and powerful currents of Russian nationalism. In addition, it has an elaborate and far flung apparatus for exertion of its influence in other countries, an apparatus of amazing flexibility and versatility, managed by people whose experience and skill in underground methods are presumably without parallel in history. . . . Problem of how to cope with this force [is] undoubtedly greatest task our diplomacy has ever faced and probably greatest it will ever have to face. It should be point of departure from which our political general staff work at present juncture should proceed. It should be approached with same thoroughness and care as solution of major strategic problem in war, and if necessary, with no smaller outlay in planning effort. I cannot attempt to suggest all answers here. But I would like to record my conviction that problem is within our power to solve—and that without recourse to any general military conflict. And in support of this conviction there are certain observations of a more encouraging nature I should like to make:

1. Soviet power, unlike that of Hitlerite Germany, is neither schematic nor adventuristic. It does not work by fixed plans. It does not take unnecessary risks. Impervious to logic of reason, and it is highly sensitive to logic of force. For this reason it can easily withdraw—and usually does—when strong resistance is encountered at any point. Thus, if the adversary has sufficient force and makes clear his readiness to use it, he rarely has to do so. If situations are properly handled there need be no prestige-engaging showdowns.
2. Gauged against Western World as a whole, Soviets are still by far the weaker force. Thus, their success will really depend on degree of cohesion, firmness and vigor which Western World can muster. And this is factor which it is within our power to influence.
3. Success of Soviet system, as form of internal power, is not yet finally proven. It has yet to be demonstrated that it can survive supreme test of successive transfer of power from one individual group to another.

3. Democrat Henry A. Wallace Questions the "Get Tough" Policy, 1946

How do American actions since V-J Day appear to other nations? I mean by actions the concrete things like $13 million for the War and Navy Departments, the Bikini tests of the atomic bomb and continued production of bombs, the plan to arm Latin America with our weapons, production of B-29s and planned production of B-36s,

Henry A. Wallace, "The Path to Peace with Russia," *New Republic,* 115 (1946), 401–406.

and the effort to secure air bases spread over half the globe from which the other half of the globe can be bombed. I cannot but feel that these actions must make it look to the rest of the world as if we were only paying lip service to peace at the conference table. These facts rather make it appear either (1) that we are preparing ourselves to win the war which we regard as inevitable or (2) that we are trying to build up a pre-dominance of force to intimidate the rest of mankind. How would it look to us if Russia had the atomic bomb and we did not, if Russia had ten thousand-mile bombers and air bases within a thousand miles of our coast lines and we did not?

Some of the military men and self-styled "realists" are saying: "What's wrong with trying to build up a predominance of force? The only way to preserve peace is for this country to be so well armed that no one will dare attack us. We know that America will never start a war."

The flaw in this policy is simply that it will not work. In a world of atomic bombs and other revolutionary new weapons, such as radioactive poison gases and biological warfare, a peace maintained by a predominance of force is no longer possible. . . .

Insistence on our part that the game must be played our way will only lead to a deadlock. The Russians will redouble their efforts to manufacture bombs, and they may also decide to expand their "security zone" in a serious way. Up to now, despite all our outcries against it, their efforts to develop a security zone in Eastern Europe and in the Middle East are small change from the point of view of military power as compared with our air bases in Greenland, Okinawa and many other places thousands of miles from our shores. We may feel very self-righteous if we refuse to budge on our plan and the Russians refuse to accept it, but that means only one thing—the atomic armament race is on in deadly earnest. . . .

I should list the factors which make for Russian distrust of the United States and of the Western world as follows: The first is Russian history, which we must take into account because it is the setting in which Russians see all actions and policies of the rest of the world. Russian history for over a thousand years has been a succession of attempts, often unsuccessful, to resist invasion and conquest—by the Mongols, the Turks, the Swedes, the Germans and the Poles. The scant thirty years of the existence of the Soviet government has in Russian eyes been a contin-uation of their historical struggle for national existence. . . .

Second, it follows that to the Russians all of the defense and security measures of the Western powers seem to have an aggressive intent. Our actions to expand our military security system—such steps as extending the Monroe Doctrine to include the arming of the Western Hemisphere nations, our present monopoly of the atomic bomb, our interest in outlying bases and our general support of the British Empire—appear to them as going far beyond the requirements of defense. . . .

Finally, our resistance to her attempts to obtain warm water ports and her own security system in the form of "friendly" neighboring states seems, from the Russian point of view, to clinch the case. After twenty-five years of isolation and after having achieved the status of a major power, Russia believes that she is en-titled to recognition of her new status. Our interest in establishing democracy in Eastern Europe, where democracy by and large has never existed, seems to her an attempt to reestablish the encirclement of unfriendly neighbors which was created after the last war and which might serve as a springboard of still another effort to destroy her.

If this analysis is correct, and there is ample evidence to support it, the action to improve the situation is clearly indicated. The fundamental objective of such action should be to allay any reasonable Russian grounds for fear, suspicions and distrust. We must recognize that the world has changed and that today there can be no "one world" unless the United States and Russia can find some way of living together.

4. Soviet Ambassador Nikolai Novikov Sees a U.S. Bid for World Supremacy, 1946

The foreign policy of the United States, which reflects the imperialist tendencies of American monopolistic capital, is characterized in the postwar period by a striving for world supremacy. This is the real meaning of the many statements by President Truman and other representatives of American ruling circles: that the United States has the right to lead the world. All the forces of American diplomacy—the army, the air force, the navy, industry and science—are enlisted in the service of this foreign policy. . . .

The foreign policy of the United States is not determined at present by the circles in the Democratic party that (as was the case during Roosevelt's lifetime) strive to strengthen the cooperation of the three great powers that constituted the basis of the anti-Hitler coalition during the war. The ascendance to power of President Truman, a politically unstable person but with certain conservative tendencies, and the subsequent appointment of [James F.] Byrnes as Secretary of State meant a strengthening of the influence on U.S. foreign policy of the most reactionary circles of the Democratic party. . . .

At the same time, there has been a decline in the influence on foreign policy of those who follow Roosevelt's course for cooperation among peace-loving countries. Such persons in the government, in Congress, and in the leadership of the Democratic party are being pushed farther and farther into the background. The contradictions in the field of foreign policy existing between the followers of [Henry] Wallace and [Claude] Pepper, on the one hand, and the adherents of the reactionary "bi-partisan" policy, on the other, were manifested with great clarity recently in the speech by Wallace that led to his resignation from the post of Secretary of Commerce. . . .

In the summer of 1946, for the first time in the history of the country, Congress passed a law on the establishment of a peacetime army, not on a volunteer basis but on the basis of universal military service. The size of the army, which is supposed to amount to about one million persons as of July 1, 1947, was also increased significantly. The size of the navy at the conclusion of the war decreased quite insignificantly in comparison with wartime. At the present time, the American navy occupies first place in the world, leaving England's navy far behind, to say nothing of those of other countries.

Expenditures on the army and navy have risen colossally, amounting to 13 billion dollars according to the budget for 1946–47 (about 40 percent of the total budget

Origins of the Cold War: The Novikov, Kennan, and Roberts "Long Telegram" of 1946, ed. Kenneth M. Jensen (Washington, D.C.: United States Institute of Peace, 1991). Translated by Kenneth M. Jensen and John Glad. Reprinted by permission of the United States Institute of Peace.

of 36 billion dollars). This is more than ten times greater than corresponding expenditures in the budget for 1938, which did not amount to even one billion dollars. . . .

The "hard-line" policy with regard to the USSR announced by [Secretary of State James F.] Byrnes after the rapprochement of the reactionary Democrats with the Republicans is at present the main obstacle on the road to cooperation of the Great Powers. It consists mainly of the fact that in the postwar period the United States no longer follows a policy of strengthening cooperation among the Big Three (or Four) but rather has striven to undermine the unity of these countries. The objective has been to impose the will of other countries on the Soviet Union.

5. The Truman Doctrine Calls for the United States to Become the World's Police, 1947

The gravity of the situation which confronts the world today necessitates my appearance before a joint session of the Congress.

The foreign policy and the national security of this country are involved.

One aspect of the present situation, which I present to you at this time for your consideration and decision, concerns Greece and Turkey.

The United States has received from the Greek Government an urgent appeal for financial and economic assistance. Preliminary reports from the American Economic Mission now in Greece and reports from the American Ambassador in Greece corroborate the statement of the Greek Government that assistance is imperative if Greece is to survive as a free nation. . . .

The British Government has informed us that, owing to its own difficulties, it can no longer extend financial or economic aid to Turkey.

As in the case of Greece, if Turkey is to have the assistance it needs, the United States must supply it. We are the only country able to provide that help.

I am fully aware of the broad implications involved if the United States extends assistance to Greece and Turkey, and I shall discuss these implications with you at this time.

One of the primary objectives of the foreign policy of the United States is the creation of conditions in which we and other nations will be able to work out a way of life free from coercion. This was a fundamental issue in the war with Germany and Japan. Our victory was won over countries which sought to impose their will, and their way of life, upon other nations. . . .

The peoples of a number of countries of the world have recently had totalitarian regimes forced upon them against their will. The Government of the United States has made frequent protests against coercion and intimidation, in violation of the Yalta agreement, in Poland, Rumania, and Bulgaria. I must also state that in a number of other countries there have been similar developments. . . .

I believe that it must be the policy of the United States to support free peoples who are resisting attempted subjugation by armed minorities or by outside pressures.

Public Papers of the Presidents of the United States: Harry S. Truman, 1947 (Washington, D.C.: U.S. Government Printing Office, 1963), 176–180.

I believe that we must assist free peoples to work out their own destinies in their own way.

I believe that our help should be primarily through economic and financial aid which is essential to economic stability and orderly political processes. . . .

I therefore ask the Congress to provide authority for assistance to Greece and Turkey in the amount of $400,000,000 for the period ending June 30, 1948. . . .

In addition to funds, I ask the Congress to authorize the detail of American civilian and military personnel to Greece and Turkey, at the request of those countries, to assist in the tasks of reconstruction, and for the purpose of supervising the use of such financial and material assistance as may be furnished. I recommend that authority also be provided for the instruction and training of selected Greek and Turkish personnel. . . .

This is a serious course upon which we embark.

I would not recommend it except that the alternative is much more serious. The United States contributed $341,000,000,000 toward winning World War II. This is an investment in world freedom and world peace.

The assistance that I am recommending for Greece and Turkey amounts to little more than 1/10 of 1 percent of this investment. It is only common sense that we should safeguard this investment and make sure that it was not in vain.

6. The Marshall Plan Seeks to Rebuild Europe, 1948

Recognizing the intimate economic and other relationships between the United States and the nations of Europe, and recognizing that disruption following in the wake of war is not contained by national frontiers, the Congress finds that the existing situation in Europe endangers the establishment of a lasting peace, the general welfare and national interest of the United States, and the attainment of the objectives of the United Nations. The restoration or maintenance in European countries of principles of individual liberty, free institutions, and genuine independence rests largely upon the establishment of sound economic conditions, stable international economic relationships, and the achievement by the countries of Europe of a healthy economy independent of extraordinary outside assistance. The accomplishment of these objectives calls for a plan of European recovery, open to all such nations which cooperate in such plan, based upon a strong production effort, the expansion of foreign trade, the creation and maintenance of internal financial stability, and the development of economic cooperation, including all possible steps to establish and maintain equitable rates of exchange and to bring about the progressive elimination of trade barriers. Mindful of the advantages which the United States has enjoyed through the existence of a large domestic market with no internal trade barriers, and believing that similar advantages can accrue to the countries of Europe, it is declared to be the policy of the people of the United States to encourage these countries through a joint organization to exert sustained common efforts as set forth in the report of the Committee of European Economic Cooperation signed at Paris on September 22,

United States Statutes at Large, 1948 (Washington, D.C.: U.S. Government Printing Office, 1949), Vol. 62, p. 137.

1947, which will speedily achieve that economic cooperation in Europe which is essential for lasting peace and prosperity. It is further declared to be the policy of the people of the United States to sustain and strengthen principles of individual liberty, free institutions, and genuine independence in Europe through assistance to those countries of Europe which participate in a joint recovery program based upon self-help and mutual cooperation.

7. National Security Council Paper No. 68 (NSC-68) Arms America, 1950

Within the past thirty-five years the world has experienced two global wars of tremendous violence. It has witnessed two revolutions—the Russian and the Chinese—of extreme scope and intensity. It has also seen the collapse of five empires—the Ottoman, the Austro-Hungarian, German, Italian, and Japanese—and the drastic decline of two major imperial systems, the British and the French. During the span of one generation, the international distribution of power has been fundamentally altered. For several centuries it had proved impossible for any one nation to gain such preponderant strength that a coalition of other nations could not in time face it with greater strength. The international scene was marked by recurring periods of violence and war, but a system of sovereign and independent states was maintained, over which no state was able to achieve hegemony.

Two complex sets of factors have now basically altered this historical distribution of power. First, the defeat of Germany and Japan and the decline of the British and French Empires have interacted with the development of the United States and the Soviet Union in such a way that power has increasingly gravitated to these two centers. Second, the Soviet Union, unlike previous aspirants to hegemony, is animated by a new fanatic faith, antithetical to our own, and seeks to impose its absolute authority over the rest of the world. Conflict has, therefore, become endemic and is waged, on the part of the Soviet Union, by violent or nonviolent methods in accordance with the dictates of expediency. With the development of increasingly terrifying weapons of mass destruction, every individual faces the ever-present possibility of annihilation should the conflict enter the phase of total war. . . .

Our overall policy at the present time may be described as one designed to foster a world environment in which the American system can survive and flourish. It therefore rejects the concept of isolation and affirms the necessity of our positive participation in the world community.

This broad intention embraces two subsidiary policies. One is a policy which we would probably pursue even if there were no Soviet threat. It is a policy of attempting to develop a healthy international community. The other is the policy of "containing" the Soviet system. These two policies are closely interrelated and interact on one another. Nevertheless, the distinction between them is basically valid and contributes to a clearer understanding of what we are trying to do. . . .

U.S. Department of State, *Foreign Relations of the United States, 1950. National Security Affairs; Foreign Economic Policy* (Washington, D.C.: U.S. Government Printing Office, 1977), I, 237, 252–253, 262–263, 264, 282, 290.

As for the policy of "containment," it is one which seeks by all means short of war to (1) block further expansion of Soviet power, (2) expose the falsities of Soviet pretentions, (3) induce a retraction of the Kremlin's control and influence and (4) in general, so foster the seeds of destruction within the Soviet system that the Kremlin is brought at least to the point of modifying its behavior to conform to generally accepted international standards.

It was and continues to be cardinal in this policy that we possess superior overall power in ourselves or in dependable combination with other like-minded nations. One of the most important ingredients of power is military strength. In the concept of "containment," the maintenance of a strong military posture is deemed to be essential for two reasons: (1) as an ultimate guarantee of our national security and (2) as an indispensable backdrop to the conduct of the policy of "containment." Without superior aggregate military strength, in being and readily mobilizable, a policy of "containment"—which is in effect a policy of calculated and gradual coercion—is no more than a policy of bluff. . . .

Our position as the center of power in the free world places a heavy responsibility upon the United States for leadership. We must organize and enlist the energies and resources of the free world in a positive program for peace which will frustrate the Kremlin design for world domination by creating a situation in the free world to which the Kremlin will be compelled to adjust. . . .

. . . The analysis shows that this will be costly and will involve significant domestic financial and economic adjustments.

8. Senator Joseph McCarthy Describes the Internal Communist Menace, 1950

Five years after a world war has been won, men's hearts should anticipate a long peace, and men's minds should be free from the heavy weight that comes with war. But this is not such a period—for this is not a period of peace. This is a time of the "cold war." This is a time when all the world is split into two vast, increasingly hostile armed camps—a time of a great armaments race. . . .

Six years ago, at the time of the first conference to map out the peace—Dumbarton Oaks—there was within the Soviet orbit 180,000,000 people. Lined up on the antitotalitarian side there were in the world at that time roughly 1,625,000,000 people. Today, only 6 years later, there are 800,000,000 people under the absolute domination of Soviet Russia—an increase of over 400 percent. On our side, the figure has shrunk to around 500,000,000. In other words, in less than 6 years the odds have changed from 9 to 1 in our favor to 8 to 5 against us. This indicates the swiftness of the tempo of Communist victories and American defeats in the cold war. As one of our outstanding historical figures once said, "When a great democracy is destroyed, it will not be because of enemies from without, but rather because of enemies from within." . . .

The reason why we find ourselves in a position of impotency is not because our only powerful potential enemy has sent men to invade our shores, but rather because of the traitorous actions of those who have been treated so well by this Nation. It has

Congressional Record, 81 Cong., 2d Sess., pp. 1954–1957.

not been the less fortunate or members of minority groups who have been selling this Nation out, but rather those who have had all the benefits that the wealthiest nation on earth has had to offer—the finest homes, the finest college education, and the finest jobs in Government we can give.

This is glaringly true in the State Department. There the bright young men who are born with silver spoons in their mouths are the ones who have been the worst. . . . In my opinion the State Department, which is one of the most important government departments, is thoroughly infested with Communists.

I have in my hand 57 cases of individuals who would appear to be either card carrying members or certainly loyal to the Communist Party, but who nevertheless are still helping to shape our foreign policy. . . .

As you know, very recently the Secretary of State proclaimed his loyalty to a man guilty of what has always been considered as the most abominable of all crimes—of being a traitor to the people who gave him a position of great trust. The Secretary of State in attempting to justify his continued devotion to the man who sold out the Christian world to the atheistic world, referred to Christ's Sermon on the Mount as a justification and reason therefore, and the reaction of the American people to this would have made the heart of Abraham Lincoln happy.

When this pompous diplomat in striped pants, with a phony British accent, proclaimed to the American people that Christ on the Mount endorsed communism, high treason, and betrayal of a sacred trust, the blasphemy was so great that it awakened the dormant indignation of the American people.

He has lighted the spark which is resulting in a moral uprising and will end only when the whole sorry mess of twisted, warped thinkers are swept from the national scene so that we may have a new birth of national honesty and decency in government.

9. The Federal Loyalty-Security Program Questions a Postal Clerk, 1954

In late February 1954, the employee was working in a clerical capacity as a substitute postal employee. He performed no supervisory duties. His tasks were routine in nature.

One year prior to the initiation of proceedings, the employee had resigned from his position as an executive officer of a local union whose parent union had been expelled from the CIO in 1949 as Communist dominated. The employee had served as an officer for one year prior to the expulsion, had helped to lead his local out of the expelled parent and back into the CIO, and had thereafter remained in an executive capacity until his resignation in 1953. He resigned from that position upon being appointed a substitute clerk with the United States Post Office in early 1953. . . .

In the last week of February 1954, the employee received notice, by mail, that he was under investigation by the Regional Office of the United States Civil Service Commission. . . .

Case Studies in Personnel Security, ed. Adam Yarmolinsky (Washington, D.C.: Bureau of National Affairs, 1955), 142–149.

[The employee immediately answered the first set of charges against him only to be suspended without pay at the end of March on the following charges.————Ed.]

"3. In January 1948, your name appeared on a general mailing list of the Spanish Refugee Appeal of the Joint Anti-Fascist Refugee Committee. . . .

"5. Your wife . . . was a member of the . . . Club of the Young Communist League.

"6. In 1950, Communist literature was observed in the bookshelves and Communist art was seen on the walls of your residence in ————.

"7. Your signature appeared on a Communist Party nominating petition in the November 1941 Municipal Elections in ————." . . .

The employee had a hearing four months later, in July 1954. The members of the Board were three (3) civilian employees of military installations. None of them were attorneys. The Post Office establishment was represented by an Inspector, who administered the oath to the employee and his witnesses, but did not otherwise participate in the proceedings. There was no attorney-adviser to the Board. There was no testimony by witnesses hostile to the employee, nor was any evidence introduced against him. . . .

. . . Before the employee testified, he submitted a nine-page autobiography to the Hearing Board. . . .

. . . The autobiography set forth in some detail the employee's activities as an officer of his local union, and discussed particularly his role therein as an anti-Communist, and his opposition to the pro-Communist policies of the National Organization with which his local was affiliated. The autobiography recited that when his National Union was expelled from the CIO, he and his supporters successfully won a struggle within his local and as a direct result thereof, caused the said local to disaffiliate from the expelled parent, and affiliate with a new organization established within the CIO. The employee's autobiography recited that the aforesaid struggle directly involved the question of Communist domination of the local's parent union, that the victory of the employee and his supporters represented a victory over Communist adherents in the local, and that the employee was the frequent target of threats and slander by the pro-Communist faction of his local. . . .

With respect to the third charge against the employee (that his name had been on a general mailing list of the Spanish Refugee Appeal of the Joint Anti-Fascist Refugee Committee), the employee reiterated his denial of any knowledge concerning it, and his counsel reminded the Board that no Attorney General's list existed in January 1948—the date contained in the charge. The employee testified, further, that he had no recollection of ever having received any mail from the organization involved. . . .

With respect to charge No. 5 against the employee (that his wife had been a member of the Young Communist League), the Chairman of the Hearing Board advised the employee that the date involved was March 1944. The employee testified that he and his wife were married in February 1944, and that the charge was ridiculous. He testified, further, that he had no independent recollection that his wife was ever a member of the said organization. In addition, the employee testified that he had never lived in the neighborhood in which the organization was alleged to have existed, and that he had never heard of said organization. . . .

The Chairman then read charge No. 6 in which it was alleged that Communist literature was observed in the employee's bookshelves at home. . . .

Counsel for the employee then questioned him concerning his courses in college, and the books which he was there required to read for those courses. In this connection, counsel for the employee asked whether books had been recommended as part of study courses by instructors, and whether one of these books had been *Das Kapital* by Karl Marx, and whether the employee had bought *Das Kapital,* following such a recommendation. The employee responded that certain books had been recommended by his instructors, that *Das Kapital* was one, and that he had bought the Modern Library Giant Edition of *Das Kapital.* . . .

Thereafter, in response to counsel's question, the employee testified that he had not read *Das Kapital* in its entirety, that he had been required to read "a chapter or two for classwork," and that "he had found it a little dull and tedious." . . .

The Chairman read charge No. 7, in which it was alleged that the employee's signature appeared on a Communist Party nominating petition in 1941 municipal elections in the employee's home city.

The employee had answered this charge by stating that he had signed such a petition; that in 1941, the Communist Party appeared on the initial ballot; that his recollection was that on the cover page of the petition it stated that the signers were not members of the Communist Party, and that prior to 1941 and at all times thereafter, the employee had been registered as a member of one of the two major political parties, and that he had no recollection of voting for any political party other than one of the two major political parties. . . .

Thereafter, counsel for the employee objected to the charge on the ground that the signing of a petition for a party which had a legal place on the ballot in 1941 had no relationship to present security. The Chairman then asked the employee to recall the circumstances in which his signature had been solicited in 1941. The employee responded by stating that, so far as he could recall, someone came down the street and seeing him working on the premises asked him to sign the petition, after explaining the petition to him. In response to a question by a member of the Board, the employee stated that he did not know the person who had solicited his signature, and that he had never seen or heard from him thereafter, nor had he thereafter heard from the Communist Party. . . .

. . . In early September, 1954, and without notice as to whether the Board had reached a decision in his case, the employee received notice from the Post Office Department that the Postmaster General had ordered the employee's removal. . . . The employee [also] received a letter from the Regional Office of the United States Civil Service Commission. This letter advised the employee that he had been rated ineligible for Civil Service appointment, and that he was barred from competing in Federal Civil Service Examinations for a period of three years.

10. President Eisenhower Warns of the Military-Industrial Complex, 1961

A vital element in keeping the peace is our military establishment. Our arms must be mighty, ready for instant action, so that no potential aggressor may be tempted to risk his own destruction.

Public Papers of the Presidents of the United States: Dwight D. Eisenhower, 1961 (Washington, D.C.: U.S. Government Printing Office, 1961), 1037–1040.

Our military organization today bears little relation to that known by any of my predecessors in peacetime, or indeed by the fighting men of World War II or Korea.

Until the latest of our world conflicts, the United States had no armaments industry. American makers of plowshares could, with time and as required, make swords as well. But now we can no longer risk emergency improvisation of national defense; we have been compelled to create a permanent armaments industry of vast proportions. Added to this, three and a half million men and women are directly engaged in the defense establishment. We annually spend on military security more than the net income of all United States corporations.

This conjunction of an immense military establishment and a large arms industry is new in the American experience. The total influence—economic, political, even spiritual—is felt in every city, every State house, every office of the Federal government. We recognize the imperative need for this development. Yet we must not fail to comprehend its grave implications. Our toil, resources and livelihood are all involved; so is the very structure of our society.

In the councils of government, we must guard against the acquisition of unwarranted influence, whether sought or unsought, by the military-industrial complex. The potential for the disastrous rise of misplaced power exists and will persist.

We must never let the weight of this combination endanger our liberties or democratic processes. We should take nothing for granted. . . .

Today, the solitary inventor, tinkering in his shop, has been overshadowed by task forces of scientists in laboratories and testing fields. In the same fashion, the free university, historically the fountainhead of free ideas and scientific discovery, has experienced a revolution in the conduct of research. Partly because of the huge costs involved, a government contract becomes virtually a substitute for intellectual curiosity. For every old blackboard there are now hundreds of new electronic computers.

The prospect of domination of the nation's scholars by Federal employment, project allocations, and the power of money is ever present—and is gravely to be regarded.

Yet, in holding scientific research and discovery in respect, as we should, we must also be alert to the equal and opposite danger that public policy could itself become the captive of a scientific-technological elite.

It is the task of statesmanship to mold, to balance, and to integrate these and other forces, new and old, within the principles of our democratic system—ever aiming toward the supreme goals of our free society.

E S S A Y S

The Cold War had tremendous costs for both the United States and the Soviet Union. It helped justify domestic repression in both nations, led to enormous expenditures on weapons that could destroy the earth many times over, and involved both countries in costly "proxy" wars at the margins of their spheres of influence. (For the United States, Korea and Vietnam are the best examples.) Thus, for many scholars, the question of who started the Cold War prompts passionate debate. Walter LaFeber of Cornell University makes the argument that the United States unintentionally, but quite clearly, provoked the conflict. President Harry Truman came into office an insecure and uninformed man who was determined not to appear soft and therefore took the advice of hard-liners in his administration. Strategists who held opposite views and who had earlier advised President Roosevelt were largely shunted aside. John Lewis Gaddis of Yale University takes a different tack. Gaddis acknowledges that both superpowers sought to mold the world in their own images, but he asserts that the system advocated by the United States was inherently more benign. In the second essay he contrasts the ways in which the Soviets and the Americans acted abroad. He argues that the American "empire" was more attractive and thus enduring because it consulted its allies and promised security. The Soviets provoked the Cold War by treating their neighbors in eastern Europe so harshly that they could be kept "friendly" only through coercion, and thus scared western Europeans into a military alliance with the United States. Soviet behavior, far more than American, he argues, gradually led to the creation of two hostile blocs.

Truman's Hard-Line Policy

WALTER LAFEBER

Truman entered the White House a highly insecure man. ("I felt like the moon, the stars, and all the planets had fallen on me," he told reporters.) And he held the world's most responsible job in a world that was changing radically. Truman tried to compensate for his insecurity in several ways. First, he was extremely jealous of his presidential powers and deeply suspicious of anyone who challenged those powers. Truman made decisions rapidly not only because that was his character but also because he determined "the buck stopped" at his desk. There would be no more sloppy administration or strong, freewheeling bureaucrats as in FDR's later years.

Second, and more dangerously, Truman was determined that these decisions would not be tagged as "appeasement." He would be as tough as the toughest. After only twenty-four hours in the White House, the new President confidently informed his secretary of state, "We must stand up to the Russians," and he implied "We had been too easy with them." In foreign policy discussions during the next two weeks, Truman interrupted his advisors to assure them he would certainly be "tough."

His determination was reinforced when he listened most closely to such advisors as [Averell] Harriman, [William] Leahy, and Secretary of the Navy James Forrestal, who urged him to take a hard line. Warning of a "barbarian invasion of Europe," Harriman declared that postwar cooperation with the Soviets, especially economically, must depend on their agreement to open Poland and Eastern Europe. In a decisive meeting on April 23, Secretary of War Henry Stimson argued with Harriman. Stimson declared that peace must never be threatened by an issue such as Poland, for free elections there were impossible, Russia held total control, and Stalin was "not likely to yield . . . in substance." Stimson was not an amateur; he had been a respected Wall Street lawyer and distinguished public servant for forty years, including a term as Herbert Hoover's secretary of state.

But Truman dismissed Stimson's advice, accepted Harriman's, and later that day berated Soviet Foreign Minister [Vyacheslav] Molotov "in words of one syllable"

From Walter LaFeber, *America, Russia, and the Cold War, 1945–1984* (New York: Alfred A. Knopf, 1985), excerpts from 16–18, 20–27, 38–39, 44, 49, 57–59, 61–63, 68–69, 71–74, 82, 84–85, 96–97. Reprinted by permission of The McGraw-Hill Companies.

for breaking the Yalta agreements on Poland. Truman demanded the Soviets agree to a "new" (not merely "reorganized") Polish government. An astonished Molotov replied, "I have never been talked to like that in my life." "Carry out your agreements," Truman supposedly retorted, "and you won't get talked to like that."

The next day Stalin rejected Truman's demand, observing that it was contrary to the Yalta agreement. The dictator noted that "Poland borders with the Soviet Union, what [*sic*] cannot be said of Great Britain and the United States." After all, Stalin continued, the Soviets do not "lay claim to interference" in Belgium and Greece where the Americans and British made decisions without consulting the Russians. . . . Truman's toughness had only stiffened Russian determination to control Poland.

An "iron fence" was falling around Eastern Europe, Churchill blurted out to Stalin in mid-1945. "All fairy-tales," the Soviet leader blandly replied. But it was partly true. The crises over Rumania and Poland only raised higher the fence around those two nations. In other areas, however, the Soviet approach varied. A Russian-sponsored election in Hungary produced a noncommunist government. In Bulgaria the Soviet-conducted elections satisfied British observers, if not Americans. Stalin agreed to an independent, noncommunist regime in Finland if the Finns would follow a foreign policy friendly to Russia. An "iron fence" by no means encircled all of Eastern Europe. There was still room to bargain if each side wished to avoid a confrontation over the remaining areas.

But the bargaining room was limited. Stalin's doctrine and his determination that Russia would not again be invaded from the west greatly narrowed his diplomatic options. So too did the tremendous devastation of the war. Rapid rebuilding required security, access to resources in Eastern and Central Europe, and justified continued tight control over the Russian people. The experience of war was indelible. Russians viewed almost everything in their lives through their "searing experience of World War II," as one psychologist has phrased it. The conflict had destroyed 1700 towns, 70,000 villages, and left 25 million homeless. Twenty million died; 600,000 starved to death at the single siege of Leningrad. . . .

Some scholars have examined Stalin's acts of 1928 to 1945, pronounced them the work of a "paranoid," and concluded that the United States had no chance to avoid a cold war since it was dealing with a man who was mentally ill. . . . If he and other Soviets were suspicious of the West, they were realistic, not paranoid: the West had poured thousands of troops into Russia between 1917 and 1920, refused to cooperate with the Soviets during the 1930s, tried to turn Hitler against Stalin in 1938, reneged on promises about the second front, and in 1945 tried to penetrate areas Stalin deemed crucial to Soviet security.

American diplomats who frequently saw Stalin understood this background. In January 1945 Harriman told the State Department, "The overriding consideration in Soviet foreign policy is the preoccupation with 'security,' as Moscow sees it." The problem was that Americans did not see "security" the same way. They believed their security required an open world, including an open Eastern Europe. . . .

By mid-1945 Stalin's policies were brutally consistent, while Truman's were confused. The confusion became obvious when the United States, opposed to a sphere of interest in Europe, strengthened its own sphere in the Western Hemisphere. Unlike its policies elsewhere, however, the State Department did not use economic weapons. The economic relationship with Latin America and Canada could simply be assumed. . . .

But Latin America was not neglected politically. A young assistant secretary of state for Latin American affairs, Nelson Rockefeller, and Senator Arthur Vandenberg (Republican from Michigan) devised the political means to keep the Americas solidly within Washington's sphere. Their instrument was Article 51 of the United Nations Charter. This provision was largely formulated by Rockefeller and Vandenberg at the San Francisco conference that founded the United Nations in the spring of 1945. The article allowed for collective self-defense through special regional organizations to be created outside the United Nations but within the principles of the charter. In this way, regional organizations would escape Russian vetoes in the Security Council. The United States could control its own sphere without Soviet interference. . . .

The obvious confusion in that approach was pinpointed by Secretary of War Stimson when he condemned Americans who were "anxious to hang on to exaggerated views of the Monroe Doctrine and at the same time butt into every question that comes up in Central Europe." Almost alone, Stimson argued for an alternative policy. Through bilateral U.S.-U.S.S.R. negotiations (and not negotiations within the United Nations, where the Russians would be defensive and disagreeable because the Americans controlled a majority), Stimson hoped each side could agree that the other should have its own security spheres. But as he had lost the argument over Poland, so Stimson lost this argument. Truman was prepared to bargain very little. He might not get 100 percent, the President told advisors, but he would get 85 percent. Even in Rumania, where the Russians were particularly sensitive, the State Department secretly determined in August 1945, "It is our intention to attain a position of equality with the Russians." When, however, the Americans pressed, the Soviets only tightened their control of Rumania. . . .

Although Truman did not obtain his "85 percent" at Potsdam [the last wartime conference], en route home he received the news that a weapon of unimaginable power, the atomic bomb, had obliterated Hiroshima, Japan, on August 6. Eighty thousand had died. This was some 20,000 fewer than had been killed by a massive American fire bombing of Tokyo earlier in the year, but it was the newly opened secret of nature embodied in a single bomb that was overwhelming. Since Roosevelt had initiated the atomic project in 1941, American policy makers had never doubted they would use the weapon if it could be rapidly developed. Roosevelt, moreover, had decided at least by late 1944 not to share information about the bomb with the Soviets, even though he knew Stalin had learned about the project. By the summer of 1945 this approach, and the growing Soviet-American confrontation in Eastern Europe, let Truman and Byrnes to discuss securing "further *quid pro quos*" in Rumania, Poland, and Asia from Stalin before the Russians could share the secret of atomic energy. . . .

. . . Stimson, about to retire from the War Department, made one final attempt to stop an East-West confrontation. In a September 11 memorandum to Truman, Stimson prophesied "that it would not be possible to use our possession of the atomic bomb as a direct lever to produce the change" desired inside Eastern Europe. If Soviet-American negotiations continue with "this weapon rather ostentatiously on our hip, their suspicions and their distrust of our purposes and motives will increase." He again urged direct, bilateral talks with Stalin to formulate control of the bomb and to write a general peace settlement. Stimson's advice was especially notable because several months before he himself had hoped to use the bomb to pry the Soviets out of Eastern Europe. Now he had changed his mind.

Truman again turned Stimson's advice aside. A month later the President delivered a speech larded with references to America's monopoly of atomic power, then attacked Russia's grip on Eastern Europe. Molotov quickly replied that peace could not be reconciled with an armaments race advocated by "zealous partisans of the imperialist policy." In this connection, he added, "We should mention the discovery of . . . the atomic bomb."

With every utterance and every act, the wartime alliance further disintegrated. . . .

During early 1946 Stalin and Churchill issued their declarations of Cold War. In an election speech of February 9, the Soviet dictator announced that Marxist-Leninist dogma remained valid, for "the unevenness of development of the capitalist countries" could lead to "violent disturbance" and the consequent splitting of the "capitalist world into two hostile camps and war between them." War was inevitable as long as capitalism existed. The Soviet people must prepare themselves for a replay of the 1930s by developing basic industry instead of consumer goods and, in all, making enormous sacrifices demanded in "three more Five-Year Plans, I should think, if not more." There would be no peace, internally or externally. These words profoundly affected Washington. Supreme Court Justice William Douglas, one of the reigning American liberals, believed that Stalin's speech meant "The Declaration of World War III."

Winston Churchill delivered his reply at Fulton, Missouri, on March 5. The former prime minister exalted American power with the plea that his listeners recognize that "God has willed" the United States, not "some Communist or neo-Fascist state" to have atomic bombs. To utilize the "breathing space" provided by these weapons, Churchill asked for "a fraternal association of the English-speaking peoples" operating under the principles of the United Nations, but not inside that organization, to reorder the world. This unilateral policy must be undertaken because "From Stettin in the Baltic to Trieste in the Adriatic, an iron curtain has descended across the Continent" allowing "police government" to rule Eastern Europe. The Soviets, he emphasized, did not want war: "What they desire is the fruits of war and the indefinite expansion of their power and doctrines."

The "iron curtain" phrase made the speech famous, but, as Churchill himself observed, the "crux" of the message lay in the proposal that the Anglo-Americans, outside the United Nations and with the support of atomic weaponry (the title of the address was "The Sinews of Peace"), create "a unity in Europe from which no nation should be permanently outcast." The Soviets perceived this as a direct challenge to their power in Eastern Europe. Within a week Stalin attacked Churchill and his "friends" in America, whom he claimed resembled Hitler by holding a "racial theory" that those who spoke the English language "should rule over the remaining nations of the world." This, Stalin warned, is "a set-up for war, a call to war with the Soviet Union."

Within a short period after the Churchill speech, Stalin launched a series of policies which, in retrospect, marks the spring and summer of 1946 as a milestone in the Cold War. During these weeks the Soviets finally rejected the terms of a $1 billion American loan after having worked for such a loan during the previous fifteen months. They also refused to become a member of the World Bank and the International Monetary Fund. . . . Control of their border areas was worth more to the Russians than $1 billion, or even $10 billion. . . .

. . . Truman's difficulties came into the open during the autumn of 1946, when he was attacked by liberals for being too militaristic and by conservatives for his economic policies.

The liberal attack was led by Henry Agard Wallace, a great secretary of agriculture during the New Deal, Vice President from 1941 to 1945, maneuvered out of the vice-presidential nomination in 1944 so Harry Truman could be FDR's running mate, and finally secretary of commerce in 1945. Here he devoted himself to the cause of what he liked to call the "Common Man," by extending increased loans to small businessmen and, above all, enlarging the economic pie by increasing foreign trade. Wallace soon discovered that Truman threatened to clog the trade channels to Russia, Eastern Europe, perhaps even China, with his militant attitude toward the Soviets.

At a political rally in New York on September 12, 1946, Wallace delivered a speech, cleared personally, and too rapidly, by Truman. The address focused on the necessity of a political understanding with Russia. This, Wallace declared, would require guaranteeing Soviet security in Eastern Europe. . . . At the moment Byrnes and Vandenberg were in Paris, painfully and unsuccessfully trying to negotiate peace treaties with Molotov. They immediately demanded Wallace's resignation. . . .

On March 12, 1947, President Truman finally issued his own declaration of Cold War. Dramatically presenting the Truman Doctrine to Congress, he asked Americans to join in a global commitment against communism. The nation responded. A quarter of a century later, Senator J. William Fulbright declared, "More by far than any other factor the anti-communism of the Truman Doctrine has been the guiding spirit of American foreign policy since World War II." . . .

The Truman Doctrine was a milestone in American history for at least four reasons. First, it marked the point at which Truman used the American fear of communism both at home and abroad to convince Americans they must embark upon a Cold War foreign policy. This consensus would not break apart for a quarter of a century. Second, . . . Congress was giving the President great powers to wage this Cold War as he saw fit. Truman's personal popularity began spiraling upward after his speech. Third, for the first time in the postwar era, Americans massively intervened in another nation's civil war. Intervention was justified on the basis of anti-communism. In the future, Americans would intervene in similar wars for supposedly the same reason and with less happy results. . . .

Finally, and perhaps most important, Truman used the doctrine to justify a gigantic aid program to prevent a collapse of the European and American economies. Later such programs were expanded globally. The President's arguments about anti-communism were confusing, for the Western economies would have been in grave difficulties whether or not communism existed. The complicated problems of reconstruction and the United States dependence on world trade were not well understood by Americans, but they easily comprehended anticommunism. So Americans embarked upon the Cold War for the good reasons given in the Truman Doctrine, which they understood, and for real reasons, which they did not understand. . . .

The President's program evolved naturally into the Marshall Plan. Although the speech did not limit American effort, Secretary of State Marshall did by concentrating the administration's attention on Europe. Returning badly shaken from a Foreign Ministers conference in Moscow, the secretary of state insisted in a nationwide broadcast that Western Europe required immediate help. "The patient is sinking," he declared, "while the doctors deliberate." Personal conversations with Stalin had convinced Marshall that the Russians believed Europe would collapse. Assuming that the United States must lead in restoring Europe, Marshall appointed a policy planning staff under the direction of George Kennan to draw up policies. . . .

Building on this premise, round-the-clock conferences in May 1947 began to fashion the main features of the Marshall Plan. Kennan insisted that any aid, particularly military supplies, be limited and not given to just any area where communists seemed to be enjoying some success. The all-important question then became how to handle the Russians. Ostensibly, Marshall accepted Kennan's advice to "play it straight" by inviting the Soviet bloc. In reality, the State Department made Russian acceptance improbable by demanding that economic records of each nation be open for scrutiny. For good measure Kennan also suggested that the Soviets' devastated economy, weakened by the war and at that moment suffering from drought and famine, participate in the plan by shipping Soviet goods to Europe. Apparently no one in the State Department wanted the Soviets included. Russian participation would vastly multiply the costs of the program and eliminate any hope of its acceptance by a purse-watching Republican Congress, now increasingly convinced by Truman that communists had to be fought, not fed. . . .

The European request for a four-year program of $17 billion of American aid now had to run the gauntlet of a Republican Congress, which was dividing its attention between slashing the budget and attacking Truman, both in anticipation of the presidential election only a year away. In committee hearings in late 1947 and early 1948, the executive presented its case. Only large amounts of government money which could restore basic facilities, provide convertibility of local currency into dollars, and end the dollar shortage would stimulate private investors to rebuild Europe, administration witnesses argued. . . .

The Marshall Plan now appears not the beginning but the end of an era. It marked the last phase in the administration's use of economic tactics as the primary means of tying together the Western world. The plan's approach . . . soon evolved into military alliances. Truman proved to be correct in saying that the Truman Doctrine and the Marshall Plan "are two halves of the same walnut." Americans willingly acquiesced as the military aspects of the doctrine developed into quite the larger part. . . .

The military and personal costs of the Truman Doctrine . . . would be higher than expected. And the cost became more apparent as Truman and J. Edgar Hoover (director of the Federal Bureau of Investigation) carried out the President's Security Loyalty program. . . .

. . . The House Un-American Activities Committee began to intimate that Truman was certainly correct in his assessment of communism's evil nature but lax in destroying it. In March 1948 the committee demanded the loyalty records gathered by the FBI. Truman handled the situation badly. Unable to exploit the committee's distorted view of the internal communist threat, he accused it of trying to cover up the bad record of the Republican Congress. He refused to surrender the records, ostensibly because they were in the exclusive domain of the executive, more probably because of his fear that if the Republicans saw the FBI reports, which accused some federal employees of disloyalty on the basis of hearsay, unproved allegations, and personal vendettas, November might be an unfortunate month for Truman's political aspirations. Not able to discredit the loyalty program he had set in motion, trapped by his own indiscriminating anticommunist rhetoric designed to "scare hell" out of the country, Truman stood paralyzed as the ground was carefully plowed around him for the weeds of McCarthyism. . . .

And then came the fall of Czechoslovakia. The Czechs had uneasily coexisted with Russia by trying not to offend the Soviets while keeping doors open to the West. This policy had started in late 1943, when Czech leaders signed a treaty with Stalin that, in the view of most observers, obligated Czechoslovakia to become a part of the Russian bloc. President Eduard Beneš and Foreign Minister Jan Masaryk, one of the foremost diplomatic figures in Europe, had nevertheless successfully resisted complete communist control. Nor had Stalin moved to consolidate his power in 1946 after the Czech Communist party emerged from the parliamentary elections with 38 percent of the vote, the largest total of any party. By late 1947 the lure of Western aid and internal political changes began to pull the Czech government away from the Soviets. At this point Stalin, who like Truman recalled the pivotal role of Czechoslovakia in 1938, decided to put the 1943 treaty into effect. Klement Gottwald, the Czech Communist party leader, demanded the elimination of independent parties. In mid-February 1948 Soviet armies camped on the border as Gottwald ordered the formation of a wholly new government. A Soviet mission of top officials flew to Prague to demand Beneš's surrender. The communists assumed full control on February 25. Two weeks later Masaryk either committed suicide, or, as Truman believed, was the victim of "foul play."

Truman correctly observed that the coup "sent a shock throughout the civilized world." He privately believed "We are faced with exactly the same situation with which Britain and France was faced in 1938–9 with Hitler." . . . Two days before, on March 14, the Senate had endorsed the Marshall Plan by a vote of 69 to 17. As it went to the House for consideration, Truman, fearing the "grave events in Europe [which] were moving so swiftly," decided to appear before Congress.

In a speech remarkable for its repeated emphasis on the "increasing threat" to the very "survival of freedom," the President proclaimed the Marshall Plan "not enough." Europe must have "some measure of protection against internal and external aggression." He asked for Universal Military Training, the resumption of Selective Service (which he had allowed to lapse a year earlier), and speedy passage of the Marshall Plan. Within twelve days the House approved authorization of the plan's money. . . .

During the spring of 1948 a united administration, enjoying strong support on foreign policy from a Republican Congress, set off with exemplary single-mindedness to destroy the communist threat that loomed over Europe. Within two years this threat had been scotched, but the officials who created the policy had split, the Congress that ratified the policy had turned against the executive, the administration had fought off charges that it had been infiltrated by communists, and the United States found itself fighting a bloody war not in Europe but in Asia. These embarrassments did not suddenly emerge in 1950 but developed gradually from the policies of 1948–1949. . . .

The world in which NATO was to be born was undergoing rapid change. . . .

The Senate ratified the treaty 82 to 13. On the day he added his signature in mid-July 1949, Truman sent Congress a one-year Mutual Defense Assistance (MDA) bill providing for $1.5 billion for European military aid. This was the immediate financial price for the NATO commitment. A memorandum circulating through the executive outlined the purpose of MDA: "to build up our own military industry," to "create a common defense frontier in Western Europe" by having the Allies pool "their industrial and manpower resources," and particularly, to subordinate "nationalistic tendencies." In the House, however, the bill encountered tough opposition from budget-cutting congressmen. On September 22 President Truman announced that Russia had exploded an atomic bomb. Within six days the NATO appropriations raced through the House and went to the President for approval.

Although publicly playing down the significance of the Russian test, the administration painfully realized that, in Vandenberg's words, "This is now a different world." Few American officials had expected the Soviet test this early. Because it was simultaneous with the fall of China, the American diplomatic attitude further stiffened. . . .

. . . A grim President, pressed by domestic critics and the new Soviet bomb, demanded a wide-ranging reevaluation of American Cold War policies. In early 1950 the National Security Council began work on a highly secret document (declassified only a quarter of a century later, and then through an accident) that would soon be known as NSC-68. Truman examined the study in April, and it was ready for implementation when Korea burst into war.

NSC-68 proved to be the American blueprint for waging the Cold War during the next twenty years. It began with two assumptions that governed the rest of the document. First, the global balance of power had been "fundamentally altered" since the nineteenth century so that the Americans and Russians now dominated the world: "What is new, what makes the continuing crisis, is the polarization of power which inescapably confronts the slave society with the free." It was us against them. Second, "the Soviet Union, unlike previous aspirants to hegemony, is animated by a new fanatic faith, antithetical to our own, and seeks to impose its absolute authority," initially in "the Soviet Union and second in the areas now under [its] control." Then the crucial sentence: "In the minds of the Soviet leaders, however, achievement of this design requires the dynamic extension of their authority and the ultimate elimination of any effective opposition to their authority. . . . To that end Soviet efforts are now directed toward the domination of the Eurasian land mass." . . .

In conclusion, therefore, NSC-68 recommended (1) against negotiations with Russia since conditions were not yet sufficient to force the Kremlin to "change its policies drastically"; (2) development of hydrogen bombs to offset possible Soviet possession of an effective atomic arsenal by 1954; (3) rapid building of conventional military forces to preserve American interests without having to wage atomic war; (4) a large increase in taxes to pay for this new, highly expensive military establishment; (5) mobilization of American society, including a government-created "consensus" on the necessity of "sacrifice" and "unity" by Americans; (6) a strong alliance system directed by the United States; (7) and—as the topper—undermining the "Soviet totalitariat" from within by making "the Russian people our allies in this enterprise." How this was to be done was necessarily vague. But no matter. The assumptions and recommendations of NSC-68 were not overburdened with modesty. Truman and [Secretary of State Dean] Acheson were no longer satisfied with containment. They wanted Soviet withdrawal and an absolute victory.

Two Cold War Empires: Friendly Persuasion vs. Brute Force

JOHN LEWIS GADDIS

Leaders of both the United States and the Soviet Union would have bristled at having the appellation "imperial" affixed to what they were doing after 1945. But one need not send out ships, seize territories, and hoist flags to construct an empire: "informal" empires are considerably older than, and continued to exist alongside, the more "formal" ones Europeans imposed on so much of the rest of the world from the fifteenth through the nineteenth centuries. During the Cold War years Washington and Moscow took on much of the character, if never quite the charm, of old imperial capitals like London, Paris, and Vienna. And surely American and Soviet influence, throughout most of the second half of the twentieth century, was at least as ubiquitous as that of any earlier empire the world had ever seen. . . .

Let us begin with the structure of the Soviet empire, for the simple reason that it was, much more than the American, deliberately designed. It has long been clear that, in addition to having had an authoritarian vision, [Joseph] Stalin also had an imperial one, which he proceeded to implement in at least as single-minded a way. No comparably influential builder of empire came close to wielding power for so long, or with such striking results, on the Western side.

It was, of course, a matter of some awkwardness that Stalin came out of a revolutionary movement that had vowed to smash, not just tsarist imperialism, but all forms of imperialism throughout the world. The Soviet leader constructed his own logic, though, and throughout his career he devoted a surprising amount of attention to showing how a revolution and an empire might coexist. Bolsheviks could never be imperialists, Stalin acknowledged in one of his earliest public pronouncements on this subject, made in April 1917. But surely in a *revolutionary* Russia nine-tenths of the non-Russian nationalities would not *want* their independence. Few among those minorities found Stalin's reasoning persuasive after the Bolsheviks did seize power later that year, however, and one of the first problems [Vladimir] Lenin's new government faced was a disintegration of the old Russian empire not unlike what happened to the Soviet Union after communist authority finally collapsed in 1991.

John Lewis Gaddis, *We Now Know: Rethinking Cold War History* (New York: Oxford University Press, 1997). Copyright © 1997 by John Lewis Gaddis. Reprinted by permission of Oxford University Press.

Whether because of Lenin's own opposition to imperialism or, just as plausibly, because of Soviet Russia's weakness at the time, Finns, Estonians, Latvians, Lithuanians, Poles, and Moldavians were allowed to depart. Others who tried to do so—Ukrainians, Belorussians, Caucasians, Central Asians—were not so fortunate, and in 1922 Stalin proposed incorporating these remaining (and reacquired) nationalities into the Russian republic, only to have Lenin as one of his last acts override this recommendation and establish the multi-ethnic Union of Soviet Socialist Republics. After Lenin died and Stalin took his place it quickly became clear, though, that whatever its founding principles the USSR was to be no federation of equals. Rather, it would function as an updated form of empire even more tightly centralized than that of the Russian tsars. . . .

Stalin's fusion of Marxist internationalism with tsarist imperialism could only reinforce his tendency, in place well before World War II, to equate the advance of world revolution with the expanding influence of the Soviet state. . . .

Stalin had been very precise [after World War II] about where he wanted Soviet boundaries changed; he was much less so on how far Moscow's sphere of influence was to extend. He insisted on having "friendly" countries around the periphery of the USSR, but he failed to specify how many would have to meet this standard. He called during the war for dismembering Germany, but by the end of it was denying that he had ever done so: that country would be temporarily divided, he told leading German communists in June 1945, and they themselves would eventually bring about its reunification. He never gave up on the idea of an eventual world revolution, but he expected this to result—as his comments to the Germans suggested—from an expansion of influence emanating from the Soviet Union itself. "[F]or the Kremlin," a well-placed spymaster recalled, "the mission of communism was primarily to consolidate the might of the Soviet state. Only military strength and domination of the countries on our borders could ensure us a superpower role."

But Stalin provided no indication—surely because he himself did not know—of how rapidly, or under what circumstances, this process would take place. He was certainly prepared to stop in the face of resistance from the West: at no point was he willing to challenge the Americans or even the British where they made their interests clear. . . .

What all of this suggests, though, is not that Stalin had limited ambitions, only that he had no timetable for achieving them. [Foreign minister Vyacheslav] Molotov retrospectively confirmed this: "Our ideology stands for offensive operations when possible, and if not, we wait." Given this combination of appetite with aversion to risk, one cannot help but wonder what would have happened had the West tried containment earlier. To the extent that it bears partial responsibility for the coming of the Cold War, the historian Vojtech Mastny has argued, that responsibility lies in its failure to do just that. . . .

. . . The fact that Stalin was able to *expand* his empire when others were contracting and while the Soviet Union was as weak as it was required explanation. Why did opposition to this process, within and outside Europe, take so long to develop?

One reason was that the colossal sacrifices the Soviet Union had made during the war against the Axis had, in effect, "purified" its reputation: the USSR and its leader had "earned" the right to throw their weight around, or so it seemed. Western governments found it difficult to switch quickly from viewing the Soviet Union as a glorious wartime ally to portraying it as a new and dangerous adversary. President Harry S. Truman and his future Secretary of State Dean Acheson—neither of them sympathetic in the slightest to communism—nonetheless tended to give the Soviet Union the benefit of the doubt well into the early postwar era. . . .

Resistance to Stalin's imperialism also developed slowly because Marxism-Leninism at the time had such widespread appeal. It is difficult now to recapture the admiration revolutionaries outside the Soviet Union felt for that country before they came to know it well. "[Communism] was the most rational and most intoxicating, all-embracing ideology for me and for those in my disunited and desperate land who so desired to skip over centuries of slavery and backwardness and to bypass reality itself," [Milovan] Djilas recalled, in a comment that could have been echoed throughout much of what came to be called the "third world." Because the Bolsheviks themselves had overcome one empire and had made a career of condemning others, it would take decades for people who were struggling to overthrow British, French, Dutch, or Portuguese colonialism to see that there could also be such a thing as Soviet imperialism. European communists—notably the Yugoslavs—saw this much earlier, but even to most of them it had not been apparent at the end of the war. . . .

One has the impression that Stalin and the Eastern Europeans got to know one another only gradually. The Kremlin leader was slow to recognize that Soviet authority would not be welcomed everywhere beyond Soviet borders; but as he did come to see this he became all the more determined to impose it everywhere. The Eastern Europeans were slow to recognize how confining incorporation within a Soviet sphere was going to be; but as they did come to see this they became all the more determined to resist it, even if only by withholding, in a passive but sullen manner, the consent any regime needs to establish itself by means other than coercion. Stalin's efforts to consolidate his empire therefore made it at once more repressive and less secure. Meanwhile, an alternative vision of postwar Europe was emerging from the other great empire that established itself in the wake of World War II, that of the United States, and this too gave Stalin grounds for concern.

The first point worth noting, when comparing the American empire to its Soviet counterpart, is a striking reversal in the sequence of events. Stalin's determination to create his empire preceded by some years the conditions that made it possible: he had first to consolidate power at home and then defeat Nazi Germany, while at the same time seeing to it that his allies in that enterprise did not thwart his long-term objectives. With the United States, it was the other way around: the conditions for establishing an empire were in place long before there was any clear intention on the part of its leaders to do so. Even then, they required the support of a skeptical electorate, something that could never quite be taken for granted.

The United States had been poised for global hegemony at the end of World War I. Its military forces played a decisive role in bringing that conflict to an end. Its economic predominance was such that it could control both the manner and the rate of European recovery. Its ideology commanded enormous respect, as Woodrow Wilson found when he arrived on the Continent late in 1918 to a series of rapturous public receptions. The Versailles Treaty fell well short of Wilson's principles, to be sure, but the League of Nations followed closely his own design, providing an explicit legal basis for an international order that was to have drawn, as much as anything else, upon the example of the American constitution itself. If there was ever a point at which the world seemed receptive to an expansion of United States influence, this was it.

Americans themselves, however, were not receptive. The Senate's rejection of membership in the League reflected the public's distinct lack of enthusiasm for international peace-keeping responsibilities. Despite the interests certain business, labor, and agricultural groups had in seeking overseas markets and investment opportunities, most Americans saw few benefits to be derived from integrating their economy with that of the rest of the world. . . .

This isolationist consensus broke down only as Americans began to realize that a potentially hostile power was once again threatening Europe: even their own hemisphere, it appeared, might not escape the consequences this time around. After September 1939, the Roosevelt administration moved as quickly as public Congressional opinion would allow to aid Great Britain and France by means short of war; it also chose to challenge the Japanese over their occupation of China and later French Indochina, thereby setting in motion a sequence of events that would lead to the attack on Pearl Harbor. . . .

It did not automatically follow, though, that the Soviet Union would inherit the title of "first enemy" once Germany and Japan had been defeated. A sense of vulnerability preceded the identification of a source of threat in the thinking of American strategists: innovations in military technology—long-range bombers, the prospect of even longer-range missiles—created visions of future Pearl Harbors before it had become clear from where such an attack might come. Neither in the military nor the political-economic planning that went on in Washington during the war was there consistent concern with the USSR as a potential future adversary. The threat, rather, appeared to arise from war itself, whoever might cause it, and the most likely candidates were thought to be resurgent enemies from World War II.

The preferred solution was to maintain preponderant power for the United States, which meant a substantial peacetime military establishment and a string of bases around the world from which to resist aggression if it should ever occur. But equally important, a revived international community would seek to remove the fundamental causes of war through the United Nations, a less ambitious version of Wilson's League, and through new economic institutions like the International Monetary Fund and the World Bank, whose task it would be to prevent another global depression and thereby ensure prosperity. The Americans and the British assumed that the Soviet Union would want to participate in these multilateral efforts to achieve military and economic security. The Cold War developed when it became clear that Stalin either could not or would not accept this framework.

Did the Americans attempt to impose their vision of the postwar world upon the USSR? No doubt it looked that way from Moscow: both the Roosevelt and Truman administrations stressed political self-determination and economic integration with sufficient persistence to arouse Stalin's suspicions—easily aroused, in any event—as to their ultimate intentions. But what the Soviet leader saw as a challenge to his hegemony the Americans meant as an effort to salvage multilateralism. At no point prior to 1947 did the United States and its Western European allies abandon the hope that the Russians might eventually come around; and indeed negotiations aimed at bringing them around would continue at the foreign minister's level, without much hope of success, through the end of that year. The American attitude was less that of expecting to impose a system than one of puzzlement as to why its merits were not universally self-evident. It differed significantly, therefore, from Stalin's point of view, which allowed for the possibility that socialists in other countries might come to see the advantages of Marxism-Leninism as practiced in the Soviet Union, but never capitalists. They were there, in the end, to be overthrown, not convinced. . . .

At the same time, though, it is difficult to see how a strategy of containment could have developed—with the Marshall Plan as its centerpiece—had there been nothing to contain. . . . The American empire arose *primarily,* therefore, not from internal causes, as had the Soviet empire, but from a perceived external danger powerful enough to overcome American isolationism.

Washington's wartime vision of a postwar international order had been premised on the concepts of political self-determination and economic integration. It was intended to work by assuming a set of *common* interests that would cause other countries to *want* to be affiliated with it rather than to resist it. The Marshall Plan, to a considerable extent, met those criteria. . . .

The test of any empire comes in administering it, for even the most repressive tyranny requires a certain amount of acquiescence among its subjects. Coercion and terror cannot everywhere and indefinitely prop up authority: sooner or later the social, economic, and psychological costs of such measures begin to outweigh the benefits. . . .

It is apparent now, even if it was not always at the time, that the Soviet Union did not manage its empire particularly well. Because of his personality and the structure of government he built around it, Stalin was—shall we say—less than receptive to the wishes of those nations that fell within the Soviet sphere. He viewed departures from his instructions with deep suspicion, but he also objected to manifestations of independent behavior where instructions had not yet been given. As a result, he put his European followers in an impossible position: they could satisfy him only by seeking his approval for whatever he had decided they should do—even, at times, before he had decided that they should do it.

An example occurred late in 1944 when the Yugoslavs—then the most powerful but also the most loyal of Stalin's East European allies—complained politely to Soviet commanders that their troops had been raping local women in the northern corner of the country through which they were passing. Stalin himself took note of this matter, accusing the Yugoslavs—at one point tearfully—of showing insufficient respect for Soviet military sacrifices and for failing to sympathize when "a soldier who has crossed thousands of kilometers through blood and fire and death has fun with a woman or takes some trifle." The issue was not an insignificant one: the Red Army's behavior was a problem throughout the territories it occupied, and did much to alienate those who lived there. . . .

The United States, in contrast, proved surprisingly adept at managing an empire. Having attained their authority through democratic processes, its leaders were experienced—as their counterparts in Moscow were not—in the arts of persuasion, negotiation and compromise. Applying domestic political insights to foreign policy could produce embarrassing results, as when President Truman likened Stalin to his old Kansas City political mentor, Tom Pendergast, or when Secretary of State James F. Byrnes compared the Russians to the US Senate: "You build a post office in their state, and they'll build a post office in our state." But the habits of democracy had served the nation well during World War II: its strategists had assumed that their ideas would have to reflect the interests and capabilities of allies; it was also possible for allies to advance proposals of their own and have them taken seriously. That same pattern of mutual accommodation persisted after the war, despite the fact that all sides acknowledged—as they had during most of the war itself—the disproportionate power of the United States could ultimately bring to bear.

Americans so often deferred to the wishes of allies during the early Cold War that some historians have seen the Europeans—especially the British—as having managed *them.* The new Labour government in London did encourage the Truman administration to toughen its policy toward the Soviet Union; Churchill—by then out of office—was only reinforcing these efforts with his March 1946 "Iron Curtain" speech. The British were ahead of the Americans in pressing for a consolidation of Western occupation zones in Germany, even if this jeopardized prospects for an overall settlement with the Russians. Foreign Secretary Ernest Bevin determined the timing of the February 1947 crisis over Greece and Turkey when he ended British military and economic assistance to those countries. . . .

But one can easily make too much of this argument. Truman and his advisers were not babes in the woods. They knew what they were doing at each stage, and did it only because they were convinced their actions would advance American interests. They never left initiatives entirely up to the Europeans: they insisted on an integrated plan for economic recovery and quite forcefully reined in prospective recipients when it appeared that their requests would exceed what Congress would approve. "[I]n the end we would not *ask* them," Kennan noted, "we would just *tell* them, what they would get." The Americans were flexible enough, though, to accept and build upon ideas that came from allies; they also frequently let allies determine the timing of actions taken. . . .

The Americans simply did not find it necessary, in building a sphere of influence, to impose unrepresentative governments or brutal treatment upon the peoples that fell within it. . . . It was as if the Americans were projecting abroad a tradition they had long taken for granted at home: that civility made sense; that spontaneity, within a framework of minimal constraint, was the path to political and economic robustness; that to intimidate or to overmanage was to stifle. The contrast to Stalin's methods of imperial administration could hardly have been sharper.

Stalin saw the need, after learning of the Marshall Plan, to improve his methods of imperial management. He therefore called a meeting of the Soviet and East European communist parties, as well as the French and the Italian communists, to be held in Poland in September 1947, ostensibly for the purpose of exchanging ideas on fraternal cooperation. Only after the delegations had assembled did he reveal his real objective, which was to organize a new coordinating agency for the international communist movement. . . .

Even with the Cominform in place, the momentary independence Czechoslovakia demonstrated must have continued to weigh on Stalin's mind. That country, more than any other in Eastern Europe, had sought to accommodate itself to Soviet hegemony. Embittered by how easily the British and French had betrayed Czech interests at the Munich conference in 1938, President Eduard Beneš welcomed the expansion of Soviet influence while reassuring Marxist-Leninists that they had nothing to fear from the democratic system the Czechs hoped to rebuild after the war. "If you play it well," he told Czech Communist Party leaders in 1943, "you'll win."

But Beneš meant "win" by democratic means. Although the Communists had indeed done well in the May 1946 parliamentary elections, their popularity began to drop sharply after Stalin forbade Czech participation in the Marshall Plan the following year. Convinced by intelligence reports that the West would not intervene, they therefore took advantage of a February 1948 government crisis to stage a *coup d' état*—presumably with Stalin's approval—that left them in complete control, with no further need to resort to the unpredictabilities of the ballot box. . . .

Because of its dramatic impact, the Czech coup had consequences Stalin could hardly have anticipated. It set off a momentary—and partially manufactured—war scare in Washington. It removed the last Congressional objections to the Marshall Plan, resulting in the final approval of that initiative in April 1948. It accelerated plans by the Americans, the British, and the French to consolidate their occupation zones in Germany and to proceed toward the formation of an independent West German state. And it caused American officials to begin to consider, much more seriously than they had until this point, two ideas Bevin had begun to advance several months earlier: that economic assistance alone would not restore European self-confidence, and that the United States would have to take on direct military responsibilities for defending that portion of the Continent that remained outside Soviet control.

Stalin then chose the late spring of 1948 to attempt a yet further consolidation of the Soviet empire, with even more disastrous results. . . .

West Europeans were meanwhile convincing themselves that they had little to lose from living within an American sphere of influence. The idea of a European "third force" soon disappeared, not because Washington officials lost interest in it, but because the Europeans themselves rejected it. The North Atlantic Treaty Organization, which came into existence in April 1949, had been a European initiative from the beginning: it was as explicit an invitation as has ever been extended from smaller powers to a great power to construct an empire and include them within it. When Kennan, worried that NATO would divide Europe permanently, put forward a plan later that spring looking toward an eventual reunification and neutralization of Germany as a way of ending both the Soviet and American presence on the continent, British and French opposition quickly shot it down. . . .

. . . Why were allies of the United States willing to give up so much autonomy in order to enhance their own safety? How did the ideas of sovereignty and security, which historically have been difficult to separate, come to be so widely seen as divisible in this situation?

The answer would appear to be that despite a postwar polarization of authority quite at odds, in its stark bilateralism, from what wartime planners had expected, Americans managed to retain the multilateral conception of security they had developed during World War II. They were able to do this because Truman's foreign policy—like Roosevelt's military strategy—reflected the habits of domestic democratic politics. Negotiation, compromise, and consensus building abroad came naturally to statesmen steeped in the uses of such practices at home: in this sense, the American political tradition served the country better than its realist critics—Kennan definitely among them—believed it did. . . .

It would become fashionable to argue, in the wake of American military intervention in Vietnam, the Soviet invasions of Czechoslovakia and Afghanistan, and growing fears of nuclear confrontation that developed during the early 1980s, that there were no significant differences in the spheres of influence Washington and Moscow had constructed in Europe after World War II: these had been, it was claimed, "morally equivalent," denying autonomy quite impartially to all who lived under them. Students of history must make their own judgments about morality, but even a cursory examination of the historical record will show that these imperial structures could hardly have been more different in their origins, their composition, their tolerance of diversity, and as it turned out their durability. It is important to specify just what these differences were. . . .

One empire arose . . . by invitation, the other by imposition. *Europeans* made this distinction, very much as they had done during the war when they welcomed armies liberating them from the west but feared those that came from the east. They did so because they saw clearly at the time—even if a subsequent generation would not always see—how different American and Soviet empires were likely to be. It is true that the *extent* of the American empire quickly exceeded that of its Soviet counterpart, but this was because *resistance* to expanding American influence was never as great. The American empire may well have become larger, paradoxically, because the American *appetite* for empire was less that of the USSR. The United States had shown, throughout most of its history, that it could survive and even prosper without extending its domination as far as the eye could see. The logic of Lenin's ideological internationalism, as modified by Stalin's Great Russian nationalism and personal paranoia, was that the Soviet Union could not.

✔ F U R T H E R   R E A D I N G

Margot Henriksen, *Dr. Strangelove's America: Society and Culture in the Atomic Age* (1997).
Melvyn Leffler, *A Preponderance of Power* (1992).
Vojtech Mastny, *The Cold War and Soviet Insecurity* (1996).
Thomas Paterson, *On Every Front: The Making and Unmaking of the Cold War* (1992).
Ellen Schrecker, *Many Are the Crimes: McCarthyism in America* (1998).
Martin Sherwin, *A World Destroyed: The Atomic Bomb and the Grand Alliance* (1975).
Reinhold Wagnleitner, *Coca-Colonization and the Cold War* (1994).
Vladislav Zubok and Constantine Pleshakov, *Inside the Kremlin's Cold War* (1996).

CHAPTER
11

The 1950s "Boom":
Affluence and Anxiety

In the 1950s, everything about America seemed to get bigger: families, towns, highways, shopping centers, corporations, and government. Americans' wealth grew along with the domestic economy, and American power expanded with the Cold War. After the trials of the Great Depression and World War II, Americans appeared to revel in the stability and normalcy of the fifties. The G.I. Bill, passed by Congress in 1944, paid millions of former soldiers to go to college, lent them money to buy homes, and helped finance their new careers. Although some people thought President Eisenhower bland, many more embraced the cheerful Republican slogan "I Like Ike." Patriotism soared, along with belief in the superiority of the so-called American Way. With political and economic confidence high, well-off consumers fueled a spectacular economic expansion. Middle-class families could afford to, and did, purchase most of the conveniences offered by mass production— including mass-produced homes in sprawling new suburbs. They had more babies than their parents' generation to fill these homes, and affluence enabled women to stay home in droves to take care of this special "baby-boom" generation. Parents sought to give their children all the things they had not had growing up in the Depression and during the war.

Affluence sparked anxiety, however. Some critics asserted that the United States was becoming too complacent, and its citizens too coddled. Parents especially worried about the effect of abundance on their children's character development. Novelists and social commentators harped on the emergence of a new phenomenon that some called "juvenile delinquency." Blockbuster films such as Rebel Without a Cause, West Side Story, Splendor in the Grass, *and* Blackboard Jungle *told of a genera-tion run wild: sophisticated, perhaps, but lost. Adult roles also occasioned commen-tary. The fifties witnessed an ongoing preoccupation with the lack of creative or "manly" jobs for men in mass society, and with women's place in the family.*

Television contributed to the social ferment. At the start of the decade, only a small fraction of the population (roughly 3 million Americans) owned the new technology. By 1960, 50 million households had TV sets. More Americans had TVs than had running water and indoor toilets. Television helped to create a more uniform culture than had ever before existed in the United States. Coal miners in rural Appalachia could hear the bubbling Cuban accent of Desi Arnaz on I Love Lucy. *Schoolchildren in southern California could identify the nasal twang of the Boston Irish in the 1960 TV appearances of John Kennedy. Overtaking all of these regional speech patterns was the uniform, "accentless" cadence of a new generation of television performers and news announcers, whose dialect and appearance set the norm for "middle America." The new television shows also brought regions, classes, and ethnic groups together by giving them a common subject: 50 million households could laugh at the same jokes and pratfalls. Because the content of many shows focused on optimistic, happy portrayals of suburban life, these shows also helped to set a standard—rarely attainable—of the ideal postwar family. And, by establishing an ideal, television offered viewers a chance to compare their own lives with those of others, creating an anxiety about why they might not match the model.*

Although "traditional" by reputation, the fifties were a time of great flux. Pervasive television imagery, booming suburbs, and growing incomes dramatically changed how Americans lived and what they thought about it.

QUESTIONS TO THINK ABOUT

Were the fifties really *Happy Days,* as a television show once characterized the era, or is the period more accurately described as an era of psychological, social, and political tensions? Why do the fifties prompt (as they have) such nostalgia for poodle skirts, sock hops, hula hoops, stay-at-home moms, and Fourth of July parades?

DOCUMENTS

The documents in this chapter reveal a number of aspects of the postwar boom. Near the close of World War II, the U.S. Congress passed a bill that transformed the lives of millions, and the American economy as well. Document 1, the Servicemen's Readjustment Act—also known as the G.I. Bill of Rights—outlines the many benefits that would come to those who fought in World War II. In Document 2, *Science News Letter* observes a startling new trend: a sharp upswing in the birth rate among college-educated Americans. The fifties, indeed, was the key decade of what became known as the "baby boom." Combined with increased affluence, the baby boom helped to create an immense new market for retail sales: teenagers. As we see in Document 3, some people complained that "teen-agers are spoiled to death these days," but business boomed along with this new generation. Document 4 is from Ron Kovic's memoir, *Born on the Fourth of July.* The author later lost the use of his legs (and his trust in government) in Vietnam, but his fifties childhood helps to explain the boundless love he felt for his country while he was growing up. Document 5 shows congressional and presidential concern for instilling such patriotism in the young. In 1954, at the urging of President Dwight D. Eisenhower, Congress inserted the words "under God" into the pledge of allegiance to the flag, and outlined the proper behavior to accompany the pledge. Document 6 illustrates the conflict between some baby-boom adolescents and their "permissive" parents. Actor James Dean, who died in a high-speed car crash shortly before the release of the movie *Rebel Without a Cause,* came to symbolize the angst of his generation, who wanted to be "men" but were treated as spoiled children. In Document 7, famed social critic Paul Goodman talks about "growing up absurd"—the consequence of a mass society that no longer calls for creativity, bravery, or even hard work from its young people. Governor Adlai Stevenson, in Document 8, addresses women at Smith, the elite Massachusetts women's college. He suggests that there is nothing more fulfilling for a woman than helping her husband to remember the values of Western civilization as he goes to work each day to a job that, in effect, reduces him to a cog in a machine. In the final selection, Document 9, feminist author Betty Friedan asks the question that helped to start a revolution among women: "Is this all?"

1. Congress Passes the G.I. Bill of Rights, 1944

AN ACT

To provide Federal Government aid for the readjustment in civilian life of returning World War II veterans.

Be it enacted by the Senate and House of Representatives of the United States of America in Congress assembled, That this Act may be cited as the "Servicemen's Readjustment Act of 1944."

Title I

The Veterans' Administration is hereby declared to be an essential war agency and entitled, second only to the War and Navy Departments, to priorities in personnel, equipment, supplies, and material under any laws, Executive orders, and regulations pertaining to priorities, and in appointments of personnel from civil-service registers the Administrator of Veterans' Affairs is hereby granted the same authority and discretion as the War and Navy Departments and the United States Public Health Service: *Provided,* That the provisions of this section as to priorities for materials shall apply to any State institution to be built for the care or hospitalization of veterans.

Sec. 101. The Administrator of Veterans' Affairs and the Federal Board of Hospitalization are hereby authorized and directed to expedite and complete the construction of additional hospital facilities for war veterans, and to enter into agreements and contracts for use by or transfer to the Veterans' Administration of suitable Army and Navy hospitals after termination of hostilities in the present war of after such institutions are no longer needed by the armed services; and the Administrator of Veterans' Affairs is hereby authorized and directed to establish necessary regional offices, suboffices, branch offices, contact units, or other subordinate offices in centers of population where there is no Veterans' Administration. . . .

Title II—Education of Veterans

Any person who served in the active military or naval service on or after September 16, 1940, and prior to the termination of the present war, and who shall have been discharged or released therefrom under conditions other than dishonorable, and whose education or training was impeded, delayed, interrupted, or interfered with by reason of his entrance into the service, . . . shall be eligible for and entitled to receive

United States Statutes at Large, 58 (1944): 284–294.

education or training under this part: *Provided*, That such course shall be initiated not later than two years after either the date of discharge or the termination of the present war, whichever is the later: *Provided further*, That no such education or training shall be afforded beyond seven years after the termination of the present war: *And provided further*, That any such person who was not over 25 years of age at the time he entered the service shall be deemed to have had his education or training impeded, delayed, interrupted, or interfered with. . . .

The Administrator shall pay to the education or training institution, for each person enrolled in full time or part time course of education or training, the customary cost of tuition, and such laboratory, library, health, infirmary, and other similar fees as are customarily charged, and may pay for books, supplies, equipment, and other necessary expenses, exclusive of board, lodging, other living expenses, and travel, as are generally required for the successful pursuit and completion of the course by other students in the institution. . . .

While enrolled in and pursuing a course under this part, such person, upon application to the Administrator, shall be paid a subsistence allowance of $50 per month, if without a dependent or dependents, or $75 per month, if he has a dependent or dependents, including regular holidays and leave not exceeding thirty days in a calendar year. . . .

Title III—Loans for the Purchase or Construction of Homes, Farms, and Business Property

Any person who shall have served in the active military or naval service of the United States at any time on or after September 16, 1940, and prior to the termination of the present war . . . shall be eligible for the benefits of this title. Any such veteran may apply within two years after separation from the military or naval forces, or two years after termination of the war, whichever is the later date, but in no event more than five years after the termination of the war, to the Administrator of Veterans' Affairs for the guaranty by the Administrator of not to exceed 50 per centum of a loan or loans for any of the purposes specified in sections 501, 502 and 503. . . .

Purchase or Construction of Homes.   Sec. 501. (a) Any application made by a veteran under this title for the guaranty of a loan to be used in purchasing residential property, or in constructing a dwelling on unimproved property owned by him to be occupied as his home may be approved by the Administrator of Veterans' Affairs. . . .

Purchase of Farms and Farm Equipment.   Sec. 502. Any application made under this title for the guaranty of a loan to be used in purchasing any land, buildings, livestock, equipment, machinery, or implements, or in repairing, altering, or improving any building or equipment, to be used in farming operations conducted by the applicant, may be approved by the Administrator of Veterans' Affairs. . . .

Purchase of Business Property.   Sec. 503. Any application made under this title for the guaranty of a loan to be used in purchasing any business, land, buildings, supplies, equipment, machinery, or tools, to be used by the applicant in pursuing a gainful occupation (other than farming) may be approved by the Administrator of Veterans' Affairs. . . .

Title IV—Employment of Veterans

Sec. 600. (a) In the enactment of the provisions of this title Congress declares as its intent and purpose that there shall be an effective job counseling and employment placement service for veterans and that, to this end, policies shall be promulgated and administered, so as to provide for them the maximum of job opportunity in the field of gainful employment. For the purpose there is hereby created to cooperate with and assist the United States Employment Service, as established by the provisions of the Act of June 6, 1933, a Veterans' Placement Service Board.

2. *Science News Letter* Reports a Baby Boom, 1954

The trend toward larger families among married college graduates is still continuing, the Population Reference Bureau reports.

For the last eight years, since 1946, the number of babies per graduate has been going up. The increase is greater for men graduates than for women.

"There is even a possibility," says a report in the Population Bulletin, "that members of the class of 1944 will replace themselves in the new generation." Statisticians figure that each graduate must have an average of 2.1 children to be sure that one will live to grow up, marry and have children to carry on the chain unbroken.

The low was reached by men graduates in the class of 1922 with 1.70 children per graduate; by women in the class of 1926 with 1.18.

For many years in the United States the tendency among white women of child-bearing age has been for those with the most education to have the fewest children. The figure in 1940 was 1.23 for college graduates as compared with 4.33 for women who had not gone beyond fourth grade.

The institution leading in number of children per graduate, for men of both the class 1944 and the class 1929 and women for the class 1929, is Brigham Young University in Utah. But this university is outdistanced by the 1944 women graduates of St. Mary's College in Indiana.

The increasing fertility of recent college graduates is attributed to an improvement in economic conditions and to changing attitudes toward marriage. In the 20's and early 30's, marriage and birth rates were both low. People were marrying later in life.

Now that it is easier for young couples to set up their home and start families, they are marrying younger. Births are not deferred as often nor as long as they were 15 years ago.

3. *Life* Magazine Identifies the New Teen-age Market, 1959

To some people the vision of a leggy adolescent happily squealing over the latest fancy present from Daddy is just another example of the way teen-agers are spoiled to death these days. But to a growing number of businessmen the picture spells out

---

"Baby Boom Continues Among College Grads," *Science News Letter*, June 19, 1954. Reprinted with permission of *Science News*, the weekly magazine of science. Copyright 1954 by Science Service, Inc.

"A Young $10 Billion Power: The US Teen-age Consumer Has Become a Major Factor in the Nation's Economy," *LIFE* (August 31, 1959), 78–84. Courtesy of *LIFE* MAGAZINE. Reprinted with permission.

the profitable fact that the American teen-agers have emerged as a big-time consumer in the U.S. economy. They are multiplying in numbers. They spend more and have more spent on them. And they have minds of their own about what they want.

The time is past when a boy's chief possession was his bike and a girl's party wardrobe consisted of a fancy dress worn with a string of dime-store pearls. What Depression-bred parents may still think of as luxuries are looked on as necessities by their offspring. Today teen-agers surround themselves with a fantastic array of garish and often expensive baubles and amusements. They own 10 million phonographs, over a million TV sets, 13 million cameras. Nobody knows how much parents spend on them for actual necessities nor to what extent teen-agers act as hidden persuaders on their parents' other buying habits. Counting only what is spent to satisfy their special teen-age demands, the youngsters and their parents will shell out about $10 billion this year, a billion more than the total sales of GM. . . .

At 17 Suzie Slattery of Van Nuys, Calif. fits any businessman's dream of the ideal teen-age consumer. The daughter of a reasonably well-to-do TV announcer, Suzie costs her parents close to $4,000 a year, far more than average for the country but not much more than many of the upper middle income families of her town. In an expanding economy more and more teen-agers will be moving up into Suzie's bracket or be influenced as consumers by her example.

Last year $1,500 was spent on Suzie's clothes and $550 for her entertainment. Her annual food bill comes to $900. She pays $4 every two weeks at the beauty parlor. She has her own telephone and even has her own soda fountain in the house. On summer vacation days she loves to wander with her mother through fashionable department stores, picking out frocks or furnishings for her room or silver and expensive crockery for the hope chest she has already started.

As a high school graduation present, Suzie was given a holiday cruise to Hawaii and is now in the midst of a new clothes-buying spree for college. Her parents' constant indulgence has not spoiled Suzie. She takes for granted all the luxuries that surround her because she has had them all her life. But she also has a good mind and some serious interests. A top student in her school, she is entering Occidental College this fall and will major in political science. . . .

Some Fascinating Facts About a Booming Market

FOOD: Teen-agers eat 20% more than adults. They down 3 ½ billion quarts of milk every year, almost four times as much as is drunk by infant population under 1. Teen-agers are a main prop of the ice cream industry, gobble 145 million gallons a year.

BEAUTY CARE: Teen-agers spent $20 million on lipstick last year, $25 million on deodorants (a fifth of total sold), $9 million on home permanents. Male teen-agers own 2 million electric razors.

ENTERTAINMENT: Teen-agers lay out more than $1.5 billion a year for entertainment. They spend about $75 million on single pop records. Although they create new musical idols, they are staunchly faithful to the old. Elvis Presley, still their favorite, has sold 25 million copies of single records in four years, an all-time high.

HOMEMAKERS: Major items like furniture and silver are moving into the teen-age market because of growing number of teen-age marriages. One third of all 18- and 19-year-old girls are already married. More than 600,000 teen-agers will be married this year. Teen-agers are now starting hope chests at 15.

4. A Young American Is
"Born on the Fourth of July," 1946

For me it began in 1946 when I was born on the Fourth of July. The whole sky lit up in a tremendous fireworks display and my mother told me the doctor said I was a real firecracker. Every birthday after that was something the whole country celebrated. It was a proud day to be born on. . . .

The whole block grew up watching television. There was Howdy Doody and Rootie Kazootie, Cisco Kid and Gabby Hayes, Roy Rogers and Dale Evans. The Lone Ranger was on Channel 7. We watched cartoons for hours on Saturdays—Beanie and Cecil, Crusader Rabbit, Woody Woodpecker—and a show with puppets called Kukla, Fran, and Ollie. I sat on the rug in the living room watching Captain Video take off in his spaceship and saw thousands of savages killed by Ramar of the Jungle.

I remember Elvis Presley on the Ed Sullivan Show and my sister Sue going crazy in the living room jumping up and down. He kept twanging this big guitar and wiggling his hips, but for some reason they were mostly showing just the top of him. My mother was sitting on the couch with her hands folded in her lap like she was praying, and my dad was in the other room talking about how the Church had advised us all that Sunday that watching Elvis Presley could lead to sin.

I loved God more than anything else in the world back then and I prayed to Him and the Virgin Mary and Jesus and all the saints to be a good boy and a good American. Every night before I went to sleep I knelt down in front of my bed, making the sign of the cross and cupping my hands over my face, sometimes praying so hard I would cry. I asked every night to be good enough to make the major leagues someday. With God anything was possible. I made my first Holy Communion with a cowboy hat on my head and two six-shooters in my hands. . . .

Every Saturday afternoon we'd all go down to the movies in the shopping center and watch gigantic prehistoric birds breathe fire, and war movies with John Wayne and Audie Murphy. Bobbie's mother always packed us a bagful of candy. I'll never forget Audie Murphy in *To Hell and Back*. At the end he jumps on top of a flaming tank that's just about to explode and grabs the machine gun blasting it into the German lines. He was so brave I had chills running up and down my back, wishing it were me up there. There were gasoline flames roaring around his legs, but he just kept firing that machine gun. It was the greatest movie I ever saw in my life.

[My best friend Richie] Castiglia and I saw *The Sands of Iwo Jima* together. The Marine Corps hymn was playing in the background as we sat glued to our seats, humming the hymn together and watching Sergeant Stryker, played by John Wayne, charge up the hill and get killed just before he reached the top. And then they showed the men raising the flag on Iwo Jima with the marines' hymn still playing, and Castiglia and I cried in our seats. . . .

We'd go home and make up movies like the ones we'd just seen or the ones that were on TV night after night. We'd use our Christmas toys—the Matty Mattel

Ron Kovic, *Born on the Fourth of July* (New York: Pocket Books, 1976), excerpt from pp. 47–63. Reprinted with permission of The McGraw-Hill Companies.

machine guns and grenades, the little green plastic soldiers with guns and flamethrowers in their hands. My favorites were the green plastic men with bazookas. They blasted holes through the enemy. They wiped them out at thirty feet just above the coffee table. They dug in on the front lawn and survived countless artillery attacks. . . .

We joined the cub scouts and marched in parades on Memorial Day. We made contingency plans for the cold war and built fallout shelters out of milk cartons. We wore spacesuits and space helmets. We made rocket ships out of cardboard boxes. . . . And the whole block watched a thing called the space race begin. On a cold October night Dad and I watched the first satellite, called *Sputnik,* moving across the sky above our house like a tiny bright star. I still remember standing out there with Dad looking up in amazement at that thing moving in the sky above Massapequa. It was hard to believe that this thing, this *Sputnik,* was so high up and moving so fast around the world, again and again. Dad put his hand on my shoulder that night and without saying anything I quietly walked back inside and went to my room thinking that the Russians had beaten America into space and wondering why we couldn't even get a rocket off the pad. . . .

We were still trying to catch up with the Russians when I heard on the radio that the United States was going to try and launch its first satellite, called *Vanguard,* into outer space. That night Mom and Dad and me and the rest of the kids watched the long pencil-like rocket on the television screen as it began to lift off after the countdown. It lifted off slowly at first. And then, almost as if in slow motion, it exploded into a tremendous fireball on the launching pad. It had barely gotten off the ground, and I cried that night in my living room. . . .

When *Vanguard* finally made it into space, I was in junior high school, and right in the middle of the class the loudspeaker interrupted us and the principal in a very serious voice told us that something very important was about to happen. He talked about history, and how important the day was, how America was finally going to launch its first satellite and we would remember it for a long time. . . .

And now America was finally beginning to catch up with the Russians and each morning before I went to school I was watching "I Led Three Lives" on television about this guy who joins the Communists but is actually working for us. And I remember thinking how brave he was, putting his life on the line for his country, making believe he was a Communist, and all the time being on our side, getting information from them so we could keep the Russians from taking over our government. He seemed like a very serious man, and he had a wife and a kid and he went to secret meetings, calling his friends comrades in a low voice, and talking through newspapers on park benches.

The Communists were all over the place back then. And if they weren't trying to beat us into outer space, Castiglia and I were certain they were infiltrating our schools, trying to take over our classes and control our minds. We were both certain that one of our teachers was a secret Communist agent and in our next secret club meeting we promised to report anything new he said during our next history class. We watched him very carefully that year. One afternoon he told us that China was going to have a billion people someday. "One billion!" he said, tightly clenching his fist. "Do you know what that means?" he said, staring out the classroom window. "Do you know what that's going to mean?" he said in almost a whisper. He never finished what he was saying and after that Castiglia and I were convinced he was definitely a Communist.

About that time I started doing push-ups in my room and squeezing rubber balls until my arms began to ache, trying to make my body stronger and stronger. . . .

I wanted to be a hero.

5. Congress Adds God to the Pledge of Allegiance, 1954

Resolved by the Senate and House of Representatives of the United States of America in Congress assembled, . . .

"The following is designated as the pledge of allegiance to the flag: 'I pledge allegiance to the flag of the United States of America and to the Republic for which it stands, one Nation under God, indivisible, with liberty and justice for all.' Such pledge should be rendered by standing with the right hand over the heart. However, civilians will always show full respect to the flag when the pledge is given by merely standing at attention, men removing the headdress. Persons in uniform shall render the military salute."

Approved June 14, 1954.

6. Parental Indulgence Is Criticized in *Rebel Without a Cause,* 1955

[MOTHER, FATHER *and* GRANDMA *are framed in entrance, frozen. They are all well dressed in party clothes.* MOTHER *is a very chic but rather hard-faced woman.* FATHER *is a man always unsure of himself.* GRANDMA *is the smallest, also very chic and very bright-eyed.* RAY *has paused by upstage side of desk again.*]

JIM [*facing them*]. Happy Easter.
MOTHER [*as she,* FATHER, *and* GRANDMA *move toward him*].Where were you tonight? They called us at the club, and I got the fright of my life! [*Silence.*]
FATHER. Where were you tonight, Jimbo? [JIM *says nothing.* FATHER *laughs uncomfortably.*]
JIM [*nodding toward* RAY (a juvenile officer)]. Ask him.
FATHER [*to* RAY]. Was he drinking? I don't see what's so bad about taking a little drink.
RAY. You don't?
FATHER. No. I definitely don't. I did the sa——
RAY. He's a minor, Mr. Stark, and he hasn't been drinking. He was picked up on suspicion at the scene of a stomping.
FATHER. A what?
RAY. A gang of teen-agers beat up a man. . . .

United States Statutes at Large, 68 (1954), part 1, p. 249.

Rebel Without a Cause, A Play in Three Acts (Woodstock, Ill.: Dramatic Publishing Company, 1955), pp. 18–20, 23–24. MCMLVIII by Warner Bros. Pictures, Inc. Copyright renewed © MCMLXXXVI. Based upon the motion picture "Rebel Without a Cause," produced and copyright 1955 by Warner Bros. Pictures, Inc. Screenplay by Stewart Stern, adaptation by Irving Shulman, James Dean and Natalie Wood. Printed in the United States of America. All rights reserved.

FATHER. But Jim hasn't done anything. You said so.

RAY. That's right.

FATHER. After all, a little drink isn't much. I cut pretty loose in my day, too.

MOTHER. [*needling him*]. Really, Frank? When was that?

FATHER [*blowing up*]. Listen, *can't you wait till we get home?*

RAY [*holding up his hand*]. Whoa! Whoa! I know you're a little upset, but——

FATHER. Sorry.

RAY. What about you, Jim? Got anything to say for yourself? [JIM *stops humming and shrugs.*] Not interested, huh? [JIM *shakes his head.*]

MOTHER. Can't you answer? What's the matter with you?

FATHER. He's in one of his moods.

MOTHER [*to* FATHER]. I was talking to *Jim.*

FATHER. [*crossing to* RAY]. Let me explain. We just moved here, y'understand? The kid has no friends yet and——

JIM. Tell him why we moved here.

FATHER. Hold it, Jim.

JIM. You can't protect me.

FATHER. [*to* JIM]. You mind if I *try?* You have to slam the door in my face? [*To* RAY.] I try to get to him. What happens? [*To* JIM.] Don't I give you everything you want? A bicycle—you get a bicycle. A car——

JIM. You buy me many things. [*A little mock bow.*] Thank you.

FATHER. Not just buy! You hear all this talk about not loving your kids enough. We give you love and affection, don't we? [*Silence.* JIM *is fighting his emotion.*] Then what is it? I can't even touch you any more but you pull away. I want to understand you. You must have reasons. [JIM *stares straight ahead, trying not to listen.*] Was it because we went to that party? [*Silence.*] You know what kind of drunken brawls those parties turn into. It's no place for kids.

MOTHER. A minute ago you said you didn't care if *he* drinks.

GRANDMA. He said a *little* drink.

JIM [*exploding*]. Let me alone! [*Moves down right in* L *area.*]

MOTHER. What?

JIM. Stop tearing me apart! You say one thing, and he says another, and then everybody changes back——

MOTHER. That's a fine way to talk!

GRANDMA [*smiling*]. Well, you know whom he takes after! . . .

[MOTHER, JIM, FATHER, *and* GRANDMA *go out* D L, RAY *looking after them.* RAY *lights a cigarette and shakes his head as he stands in front of desk.*]

OFFICER. What a way to raise a kid.

RAY. How do you mean that?

OFFICER. Give him everything he wants and nothing he needs.

RAY. What does he need?

OFFICER. It's too late now, but instead of throwing bikes and cars at him, a strap on the behind when he got uppity would've saved them a lot of grief.

RAY. You figure he'll be back?

OFFICER. Hell, yes! He's got modern parents.

7. Author Paul Goodman Describes
Growing Up Absurd, 1956

In every day's newspaper there are stories about the two subjects that I have brought together in this book, the disgrace of the Organized System of semimonopolies, government, advertisers, etc., and the disaffection of the growing generation. Both are newsworthily scandalous, and for several years now both kinds of stories have come thicker and faster. It is strange that the obvious connections between them are not played up in the newspapers; nor, in the rush of books on the follies, venality, and stifling conformity of the Organization, has there been a book on Youth Problems in the Organized System.

Those of the disaffected youth who are articulate, however—for instance, the Beat or Angry young men—are quite clear about the connection: their main topic is the "system" with which they refuse to co-operate. They will explain that the "good" jobs are frauds and sells, that it is intolerable to have one's style of life dictated by Personnel, that a man is a fool to work to pay installments on a useless refrigerator for his wife, that the movies, TV, and Book-of-the-Month Club are beneath contempt, but the Luce publications make you sick to the stomach; and they will describe with accuracy the cynicism and one-upping of the "typical" junior executive. They consider it the part of reason and honor to wash their hands of all of it.

Naturally, grown-up citizens are concerned about the beatniks and delinquents. The school system has been subjected to criticism. And there is a lot of official talk about the need to conserve our human resources lest Russia get ahead of us. The question is why the grownups do not, more soberly, draw the same connections as the youth. Or, since no doubt many people *are* quite clear about the connection that the structure of society that has become increasingly dominant in our country is disastrous to the growth of excellence and manliness, why don't more people speak up and say so, and initiate a change? . . .

This brings me to another proposition about growing up, and perhaps the main theme of this book. *Growth, like any ongoing function, requires adequate objects in the environment* to meet the needs and capacities of the growing child, boy, youth, and young man, until he can better choose and make his own environment. It is not a "psychological" question of poor influences and bad attitudes, but an objective question of real opportunities for worth-while experience. . . .

(I say the "young men and boys" rather than the "young people" because the problems I want to discuss in this book belong primarily, in our society, to the boys: how to be useful and make something of oneself. A girl does not *have* to, she is not expected to, "make something" of herself. Her career does not have to be self-justifying, for she will have children, which is absolutely self-justifying, like any other natural or creative act. With this background, it is less important, for instance, what job an average young woman works at till she is married.) . . .

Paul Goodman, *Growing Up Absurd: Problems of Youth in the Organized System,* excerpts from pp. ix–14, © copyright 1956, 1957, 1958, 1959, 1960. Used by permission of Random House, Inc.

. . . In our society, bright lively children, with the potentiality for knowledge, noble ideals, honest effort, and some kind of worth-while achievement, are transformed into useless and cynical bipeds, or decent young men trapped or early resigned, whether in or out of the organized system. My purpose is a simple one: to show how it is desperately hard these days for an average child to grow up to be a man, for our present organized system of society does not want men. They are not safe. They do not suit.

8. Governor Adlai Stevenson Tells College Women About Their Place in Life, 1955

I think there is much you can do about our crisis in the humble role of housewife.

The peoples of the West are still struggling with the problems of a free society and just now are in dire trouble. For to create a free society is at all times a precarious and audacious experiment. Its bedrock is the concept of man as an end in himself. But violent pressures are constantly battering away at this concept, reducing man once again to subordinate status, limiting his range of choice, abrogating his responsibility and returning him to his primitive status of anonymity in the social group. I think you can be more helpful in identifying, isolating and combatting these pressures, this virus, than you perhaps realize.

Let me put it this way: individualism has promoted technological advance, technology promoted increased specialization, and specialization promoted an ever closer economic interdependence between specialties. . . .

Thus this typical Western man, or typical Western husband, operates well in the realm of means, as the Romans did before him. But outside his specialty, in the realm of ends, he is apt to operate poorly or not at all. And this neglect of the cultivation of more mature values can only mean that his life, and the life of the society he determines, will lack valid purpose, however busy and even profitable it may be.

And here's where you come in: to restore valid, meaningful purpose to life in your home; to beware of instinctive group reaction to the forces which play upon you and yours, to watch for and arrest the constant gravitational pulls to which we are all exposed—your workaday husband especially—in our specialized, fragmented society, that tend to widen the breach between reason and emotion, between means and ends. . . .

You may be hitched to one of these creatures we call "Western man" and I think part of your job is to keep him Western, to keep him truly purposeful, to keep him whole. In short—while I have had very little experience as a wife or mother— I think one of the biggest jobs for many of you will be to frustrate the crushing and corrupting effects of specialization, to integrate means and ends, to develop that balanced tension of mind and spirit which can be properly called "integrity."

This assignment for you, as wives and mothers, has great advantages. In the first place, it is home work—you can do it in the living-room with a baby in your lap or in the kitchen with a can opener in your hand. If you're really clever, maybe

Adlai Stevenson, "A Purpose for Modern Woman," excerpted from Commencement Address, Smith College, 1955, in *Women's Home Companion* (September 1955).

you can even practice your saving arts on that unsuspecting man while he's watching television!

And, secondly, it is important work worthy of you, whoever you are, or your education, whatever it is, because we will defeat totalitarian, authoritarian ideas only by better ideas; we will frustrate the evils of vocational specialization only by the virtues of intellectual generalization. Since Western rationalism and Eastern spiritualism met in Athens and that mighty creative fire broke out, collectivism in various forms has collided with individualism time and again. This twentieth-century collision, this "crisis" we are forever talking about, will be won at last not on the battlefield but in the head and heart. . . .

Women, especially educated women, have a unique opportunity to influence us, man and boy, and to play a direct part in the unfolding drama of our free society. But I am told that nowadays the young wife or mother is short of time for such subtle arts, that things are not what they used to be; that once immersed in the very pressing and particular problems of domesticity, many women feel frustrated and far apart from the great issues and stirring debates for which their education has given them understanding and relish. Once they read Baudelaire. Now it is the Consumer's Guide. Once they wrote poetry. Now it's the laundry list. Once they discussed art and philosophy until late in the night. Now they are so tired they fall asleep as soon as the dishes are finished. There is, often, a sense of contraction, of closing horizons and lost opportunities. They had hoped to play their part in the crisis of the age. . . .

The point is that whether we talk of Africa, Islam or Asia, women "never had it so good" as you do. And in spite of the difficulties of domesticity, you have a way to participate actively in the crisis in addition to keeping yourself and those about you straight on the difference between means and ends, mind and spirit, reason and emotion—not to mention keeping your man straight on the differences between Botticelli and Chianti.

9. Feminist Betty Friedan Describes the Problem That Has No Name, 1959

The problem lay buried, unspoken, for many years in the minds of American women. It was a strange stirring, a sense of dissatisfaction, a yearning that women suffered in the middle of the twentieth century in the United States. Each suburban wife struggled with it alone. As she made the beds, shopped for groceries, matched slip-cover material, ate peanut butter sandwiches with her children, chauffeured Cub Scouts and Brownies, lay beside her husband at night—she was afraid to ask even of herself the silent question—"Is this all?"

For over fifteen years there was no word of this yearning in the millions of words written about women, for women, in all the columns, books and articles by experts telling women their role was to seek fulfillment as wives and mothers. Over and over women heard in voices of tradition and of Freudian sophistication that they could desire no greater destiny than to glory in their own femininity. Experts told

Betty Friedan, *The Feminine Mystique* (New York: Norton, 1963), 15–17, 19–20. Copyright © 1983, 1974, 1973, 1963 by Betty Friedan. Used by permission of W. W. Norton & Company, Inc.

them how to catch a man and keep him, how to breastfeed children and handle their toilet training, how to cope with sibling rivalry and adolescent rebellion; how to buy a dishwasher, bake bread, cook gourmet snails, and build a swimming pool with their own hands; how to dress, look, and act more feminine and make marriage more exciting; how to keep their husbands from dying young and their sons from growing into delinquents. They were taught to pity the neurotic, unfeminine, unhappy women who wanted to be poets or physicists or presidents. They learned that truly feminine women do not want careers, higher education, political rights—the independence and the opportunities that the old-fashioned feminists fought for. Some women, in their forties and fifties, still remembered painfully giving up those dreams, but most of the younger women no longer even thought about them. A thousand expert voices applauded their femininity, their adjustment, their new maturity. All they had to do was devote their lives from earliest girlhood to finding a husband and bearing children.

By the end of the nineteen-fifties, the average marriage age of women in America dropped to 20, and was still dropping, into the teens. Fourteen million girls were engaged by 17. The proportion of women attending college in comparison with men dropped from 47 per cent in 1920 to 35 per cent in 1958. A century earlier, women had fought for higher education; now girls went to college to get a husband. By the mid-fifties, 60 per cent dropped out of college to marry, or because they were afraid too much education would be a marriage bar. Colleges built dormitories for "married students," but the students were almost always husbands. A new degree was instituted for the wives—"Ph.T." (Putting Husband Through).

Then American girls began getting married in high school. And the women's magazines, deploring the unhappy statistics about these young marriages, urged that courses on marriage, and marriage counselors, be installed in the high schools. Girls started going steady at twelve and thirteen, in junior high. Manufacturers put out brassieres with false bosoms of foam rubber for little girls of ten. And an advertisement for a child's dress, sizes 3–6x, in the *New York Times* in the fall of 1960, said: "She Too Can Join the Man-Trap Set."

By the end of the fifties, the United States birthrate was overtaking India's. The birth-control movement, renamed Planned Parenthood, was asked to find a method whereby women who had been advised that a third or fourth baby would be born dead or defective might have it anyhow. Statisticians were especially astounded at the fantastic increase in the number of babies among college women. Where once they had two children, now they had four, five, six. Women who had once wanted careers were now making careers out of having babies. So rejoiced *Life* magazine in a 1956 paean to the movement of American women back to the home.

In a New York hospital, a woman had a nervous breakdown when she found she could not breastfeed her baby. In other hospitals, women dying of cancer refused a drug which research had proved might save their lives: its side effects were said to be unfeminine. "If I have only one life, let me live it as a blonde," a larger-than-life-sized picture of a pretty, vacuous woman proclaimed from newspaper, magazine, and drugstore ads. And across America, three out of every ten women dyed their hair blonde. . . .

If a woman had a problem in the 1950's and 1960's, she knew that something must be wrong with her marriage, or with herself. Other women were satisfied with their lives, she thought. What kind of a woman was she if she did not feel this mysterious fulfillment waxing the kitchen floor? She was so ashamed to admit her dissatisfaction that she never knew how many other women shared it. If she tried to tell her husband, he didn't understand what she was talking about. She did not really understand it herself. For over fifteen years women in America found it harder to talk about this problem than about sex. Even the psychoanalysts had no name for it. . . .

But on an April morning in 1959, I heard a mother of four, having coffee with four other mothers in a suburban development fifteen miles from New York, say in a tone of quiet desperation, "the problem." And the others knew, without words, that she was not talking about a problem with her husband, or her children, or her home. Suddenly they realized they all shared the same problem, the problem that has no name. They began, hesitantly, to talk about it. Later, after they had picked up their children at nursery school and taken them home to nap, two of the women cried, in sheer relief, just to know they were not alone.

E S S A Y S

Historians debate whether the fifties was America at its best, or whether that is an illusion created by hindsight. In the first essay, John Patrick Diggins of the University of California, Irvine, charts social and economic change in the fifties. He characterizes the era as one of bountiful lifestyles, traditional values, and remarkable stability for families. Diggins further argues that the fifties were not an aberration, but represent "the steady norm of America's political temper." In the second essay, Stephanie Coontz, a professor at Evergreen State College, articulates almost the reverse argument: the fifties transformed the nuclear family, trapped men and women in roles they came to loathe, and created a stereotype of the "perfect fifties family" that clouds political debate to the present. This stereotype, she insists, is "the way we never were."

A Decade to Make One Proud

JOHN PATRICK DIGGINS

Although McCarthyism, the cold war, Korea and politics dominated front pages in the fifties, opinion polls profiled the American people as preoccupied with their own lives and largely nonpolitical. To most white, middle-class Americans the fifties meant television; bobby sox and the bunny hop; bermuda shorts and gray flannel suits; "I Love Lucy"; Marlon Brando astride a motorcycle and Elvis belting out "Hound Dog"; Lolita the nymphet; crew cut and duck's ass hairstyles; Marilyn Monroe; James Dean; cruising and panty raids; preppies and their cashmeres and two-toned saddle shoes; Willie Mays; Rocky Graziano; drive-in movies and restaurants; diners with chrome-leg tables and backless stools; suburbia; barbecued steaks; Billy Graham and the way to God without sacrifice; the Kinsey Report and the way to sex without sin. Few items in this list would strike one as serious, but many of them have proved durable. Indeed, such subjects fascinate even members

Reprinted from *The Proud Decades, America in War and Peace, 1941–1960,* by John Patrick Diggins, 177–178, 194–199, 204–207, 219, 348–350. By permission of W. W. Norton & Company, Inc. Copyright © 1988 by John Patrick Diggins.

of the post-fifties generation. In the seventies and eighties mass magazines like *Newsweek* and *Life* devoted special issues to the fifties as "The Good Old Days" and Hollywood produced *The Last Picture Show*, *American Graffiti*, and *The Way We Were*. Nostalgia even succeeded in trivializing the Korean War, as with the immensely popular "M*A*S*H."

Nostalgia is one way to ease the pain of the present. Those who survived the sixties, a decade that witnessed the turmoils of the Vietnam War and the tragedies of political assassination, looked back wistfully on the fifties as a period of peace and prosperity. Many of those who survived the fifties, however, particularly writers and professors, passed a different verdict. "Good-by to the fifties—and good riddance," wrote the historian Eric Goldman, "the dullest and dreariest in all our history." "The Eisenhower years," judged columnist William Shannon, "have been years of flabbiness and self-satisfaction and gross materialism. . . . The loudest sound in the land has been the oink-and-grunt of private hoggishness. . . . It has been the age of the slob." The socialist Michael Harrington called the decade "a moral disaster, an amusing waste of time," and the novelist Norman Mailer derided it as "one of the worst decades in the history of man." The poet Robert Lowell summed up his impatience in two lines: "These are the tranquil Fifties, and I am forty./Ought I to regret my seedtime?"

On the other side of the political spectrum, conservative writers tended to praise the fifties as "the happiest, most stable, most rational period the western world has ever known since 1914." They point to the seemingly pleasant fact that in the fifties, in contrast to the sixties, many nations like India and Burma achieved independence without resorting to armed force. The same era enjoyed a postwar prosperity and overcame a massive unemployment that had haunted the depression generation, and did it without raising inflation. Yet even conservatives conceded that the fifties were not a "creative time" in the realm of high culture. This was all right for many of them since "creative periods have too often a way of coinciding with periods of death and destruction."

Whatever the retrospective of writers and intellectuals, those who lived through the fifties looked upon them as a period of unbounded possibility. This was especially true of the beginning of the decade when the lure and novelty of material comforts seemed irresistible. Toward the end of the decade a barely noticeable undercurrent of dissatisfaction emerged and by the early sixties a minority of women and men would rebel against the conditions of the fifties and wonder what had gone wrong with their lives. A sweet decade for the many, it became a sour experience for the few who would go on to question not only the feminine mystique but the masculine as well. In dealing with the fifties one must deal with its contented and its discontents. . . .

The economic context is crucial. Between 1950 and 1958, the economy expanded enormously. A steady high growth rate of 4.7 percent heralded remarkable increases in living standards and other conditions of life. This prosperity derived from a combination of factors: (a) the lingering postwar back-up demand for consumer goods together with increased purchasing power as a result of savings; (b) the expansion of plant and machine tool capacity, and other technological advances left by the war and revived by the cold war and Korean conflict; (c) the appearance of new and modernized industries ranging from electronics to plastics; (d) population growth and the expansion of large cities; (e) increases in the productivity, or output per man-hour, of the working force; and (f) the commitment to foreign aid, which made possible overseas credits and American exports.

America experienced three mild recessions in the fifties, but through them all the rate of personal income grew and reached a record high of a 3.9 percent rise in 1960. If few became rich, the great majority lived more comfortably than ever before and enjoyed shorter hours on the job, as America moved to the five-day work week. Prior to the Second World War only 25 percent of the farming population had electricity. By the end of the fifties more than 80 percent had not only lighting but telephones, refrigerators, and televisions.

The generation that had borne the depression and the war was now eager to put politics behind and move into a bountiful new world. One strong indicator of confidence in the future was a sudden baby boom. Demographers had been predicting a postwar relative decline in fertility rates and no expansion of immigration quotas. Instead, population leaped from 130 million in 1940 to 165 million by the mid-fifties, the biggest increase in the history of the Republic. Population migrated as well as grew, spreading into the region that came to be called "the sun belt," states like Florida, Texas, Arizona, and California. Farms and small towns lost population. Many big cities, while still growing with lower-class and minority inhabitants, witnessed the flight of the middle class to the periphery. The massive phenomenon of suburbia would rip apart and remake the texture of social life in America.

Suburbia met a need and fulfilled a dream. During the depression and the war most Americans lived in apartments, flats, or small houses within an inner city. After the war, with GIs returning and the marriage rate doubling, as many as two million young couples had to share a dwelling with their relatives. Some settled for a cot in the living room, while married college students often had to live in off-campus quonset huts. Their immediate need for space in which to raise a family was answered by the almost overnight appearance of tracts, subdivisions, and other developments that sprawled across the landscape. Ironically, while suburban growth cut into the natural environment, felling trees and turning fields into asphalt streets, the emotional appeal of suburbia lay in a desire to recapture the greenness and calm of rural life. Thus eastern tracts featured such names as "Crystal Stream," "Robin Meadows," and "Stonybrook," while in the West the Spanish motif of "Villa Serena" and "Tierra Vista" conveyed the ambience of old, preindustrial California. In California the tracts were developed by Henry J. Kaiser and Henry Doelger, who drew on their war-time skills for mass production to provide ranch-style homes complete with backyards and front lawns. In the Northeast William Levitt offered New Yorkers and Pennsylvanians houses with shuttered windows and steep pitched roofs to mimic the cozy Cape Cod look. Levitt had never liked cities. Having no patience with people who did, he saw his opportunity after the war when the government agreed to guarantee to banks the entire amount of a veteran's mortgage, making it possible for him to move in with no down payment, depending on the Veteran Administration's assessment of the value of the specific property. To keep building costs down, Levitt transformed the housing industry by using prefabricated walls and frames assembled on the site. In an effort to foster community spirit, he and other builders added schools, swimming pools, tennis courts, and athletic fields with Little League diamonds. For young members of the aspiring middle class, suburbia was a paradise of comfort and convenience.

Others were not so sure. "Is this the American dream, or is it a nightmare?" asked *House Beautiful*. Architectural and cultural critics complained of the monotony of house after house with the same façade, paint, and lawn inhabited by people willing to sign an agreement to keep them the same. One song writer would call them "little boxes made of ticky-tacky." Some children who grew up in them would agree, rebelling in the following decade against all that was sterile and standardized. The most angry critic was the cultural historian Lewis Mumford, author of *The City in History*. Mumford feared that Levitt was doing more to destroy the modern city than did the World War II aerial bombings. He also feared that suburbia was transforming the American character, rendering it dreary and conformist when it should be daring and courageous. "In the mass movement into suburban areas a new kind of community was produced, which caricatured both the historic city and the archetypal suburban refuge, a multitude of uniform, unidentifiable houses, lined up inflexibly at uniform distances, on uniform roads, in a treeless communal waste, inhabited by people in the same class, the same income, the same age group, witnessing the same television performances, eating the same tasteless pre-fabricated foods from the same freezers, conforming in every outward and inward respect to a common mold."

Admonishments aside, Americans were falling in love with suburbia—at least at first; some would have second thoughts and later wonder what they had bought, the theme of the cheerless film *No Down Payment* (1957). By the end of the fifties one-fourth of the population had moved to such areas. If not beautiful, suburbia was affordable, and thousands of homeless veterans were grateful to have their place in the sun for $65 per month on a full purchase price of $6,990 that included separate bedrooms for the children and a kitchen full of glittering gadgets. Such amenities also enabled housewives to be free of some domestic chores as they became involved in community affairs while their husbands commuted to work in the cities. A frequent event was the Tupperware party, arranged by wives ostensibly to sell household conveniences but also to overcome isolation and boredom. The most serious drawback of suburbia was that its planners envisaged no need for public transportation. As a result, suburbanites became forever dependent upon the automobile. When their children reached driving age, some households became three- or even four-car families. But in the fifties, when gasoline was relatively cheap and the promising new freeways wide and uncongested, the car was seen as a solution, not a problem. Indeed, for proud teenagers it was the supreme status symbol, the one possession that with its "souped-up" carburetors and lowered chassis and various metallic colors, answered the need for freedom and diversity in a community of flatness and conformity.

In the fifties, car was king. Freeways, multilevel parking lots, shopping centers, motels, and drive-in restaurants and theaters all catered to the person behind the wheel. By 1956 an estimated seventy-five million cars and trucks were on American roads. One out of every seven workers held a job connected to the automobile industry. In suburbia the station wagon became a common sight. But really to fulfill the American dream one needed a Cadillac, or so advertisers informed the arriviste of new wealth with such effectiveness that one had to wait a year for delivery. Almost all American automobiles grew longer and wider. Their supersize and horsepower, together with more chrome and bigger tailfins, served no useful transportation purpose but were powerful enhancers of self-esteem. At the end of the decade, when many rich Texans, some country-western singers, salesmen, and even gangsters and pimps owned a Cadillac, it became what it always was, gauche, and its image declined from the sublime to the ridiculous.

In the fifties the spectacle of waste, once regarded by the older morality as a sign of sin, had become a sign of status. It was no coincidence that Americans junked almost as many cars as Detroit manufactured, thereby fulfilling Thorstein Veblen's earlier prediction that modern man would be more interested in displaying and destroying goods than in producing them. Veblen's insight into "conspicuous consumption" also took on real meaning in this era as Americans rushed out to buy the latest novelty, whether it was a convertible, TV set, deep-freeze, electric carving knife, or the "New Look" Christian Dior evening dress. The postwar splurge of consumption had been made possible by the $100 billion of savings Americans had banked during the war. Immediately after the war, household appliances were in demand, then luxuries like fashionable clothes and imported wines. For those who bought homes for $8,000 or more, luxuries were seen as necessities. The middle-class suburbanite looked out his window and "needed" what his neighbor had—a white Corvette or a swimming pool. Travel to Europe, once regarded as the "Grand Tour" only for the rich and famous, became accessible to millions of Americans in the fifties. For the masses who remained at home and took to the road, new tourist attractions sprang up, like Disneyland. Mass recreational mobility changed the nation's eating habits. In 1954 in San Bernardino, California, Ray Kroc, a high-school dropout, devised a precision stand for turning out French fries, beverages, and fifteen-cent hamburgers that grew rapidly into a fast-food empire: McDonald's.

Spending less time cooking and eating, Americans had more time for shopping. Discount houses such as Korvette's and Grant's opened up for the lower-middle class while the prestigious Neiman-Marcus catered to the needs of oil-rich Texans. Parents raised in the depression naturally felt that more was better, not only for themselves but particularly for their children. Teenagers splurged on phonograph records, bedroom decorations, cashmere sweaters, trips to Hawaii, motor-scooters, and hot rods. The seemingly infinite indulgence of the young worried many parents even as they contributed to it. In a survey 94 percent of the mothers interviewed reported that their children had asked them to buy various goods they had seen on television.

Television in America, unlike in England and much of Western Europe, was supported by the advertising industry, which did more than any other institution to fill the viewer's eyes with images of abundance. Advertisers spent $10 billion a year to persuade, not to say manipulate, the people into buying products that promised to improve their lives, whether frozen peas or French perfume. Professional football, the prime target for beer ads, invented the "two-minute warning" in the last quarter to accommodate commercials. Confronted by a medical report linking smoking to lung cancer, tobacco companies increased their ad campaigns with jingles like "Be Happy Go Lucky!" Television bloomed with romantic scenes of a dashing young man offering a cigarette to a seductively beautiful woman under a full moon. As violins rose, the match was lit, and her face turned into that of a goddess—young, eager, divine. Partial take-offs from the Bogart-Bacall films of the early forties, Madison Avenue could readily exploit such scenes, perhaps realizing that desire can always be tempted precisely because it can never be completely fulfilled.

What facilitated the illusion of fulfillment was a little rectangle of plastic dubbed the credit card. In 1950 Diner's Club distributed credit cards to select wealthy New Yorkers to give them the privilege of eating at swank restaurants without fumbling for money. By the end of the decade Sears Roebuck alone had more than ten million accounts for those who chose to live on credit or, more bluntly, to be in debt. Installment buying shot consumer indebtedness up to $196 billion, so high that certain department stores offered "debt counselors" for worried customers. One soothing nostrum was a good stiff martini, the favorite drink of suburbia and the commuters' circle. Drinking rose sharply in the fifties. So did prescription-drugs use. Sales of "tranquilizers" soared; by 1959, 1,159,000 pounds had been consumed. The following decade the Food and Drug Administration discovered that the once-popular pill "miltown" had no medicinal value. But for the fifties generation, coping with the boss's demands at work and the children's at home, popping tranquilizing drugs became a respectable adult addiction. That mental anxiety should accompany material abundance is no surprise. For centuries moralists had warned that people become unhappy when they get what they want—or think they want. Suburbia offered Americans the cleanliness and safety of a planned community, but nothing is more hopeless than planned happiness. . . .

During the forties and fifties music became widely accessible to the masses of people. Elaborate hi-fi sets replaced the simple victrola and the jukebox lifted the spirits of the lonely, the tense, and the bored. Light operas like "Oklahoma," "South Pacific," and "My Fair Lady" played to packed theaters, and Americans listened to Mary Martin and Ethel Merman belt out popular songs.

One of the most curious shifts in popular musical tastes that separated the forties and the fifties involved the careers of Frank Sinatra and Elvis Presley. During World War II Sinatra suddenly became the idol of hordes of bobby soxers who were mysteriously mesmerized by his crooning serenades, some shrieking and swooning, others fainting or possibly pretending to. . . . Yet the hysteria ended almost as suddenly as it began, and by the early fifties Sinatra could not land even a Hollywood film contract. Then another singer captured the youth's imagination and another mode of music determined the nation's sound and rhythm for years to come—Elvis and rock 'n' roll.

. . . Unlike Sinatra, who appeared so emaciated as to be starving, Presley exuded raw strength and sensuality. Parents brought up on the mawkish music of Bing Crosby tried in vain to shield their children from contamination by the new phenomenon sweeping the country. They were aghast watching "Elvis the Pelvis" with his tight pants, full, pouting lips, and shoulder-length black hair, grip the microphone and buck his hips in gestures so lewd that some TV producers would only film him from the waist up. Magnetic but aloof, self-possessed yet sad, Presley stood before screaming crowds as the icon of the fifties, charging teenagers with energy and emotion in scores like "I Want You, I Need You, I Love You," "Don't Be Cruel," and "Love Me Tender."

Commentators in the fifties often compared Presley to Marlon Brando, James Dean, and Montgomery Clift, three new film stars who revolutionized acting methods and left audiences emotionally drained and confused. . . . All were actors who conveyed complex emotions more felt than understood in an attempt to express what could not be voiced. In *On the Waterfront*, *East of Eden*, and *From Here to Eternity*, Brando, Dean, and Clift displayed a sensitivity and depth of pure feeling that rendered them almost defenseless against the world. Indeed the film *Rebel Without A Cause* is haunted by tragedy. All of its four stars—Dean, Natalie Wood, Sal Mineo, and Vic Morrow—would suffer tragic deaths.

To the fifties generation, James Dean communicated the emotions of a crippled romantic, a moody idealist whose dreams about the world have already been destroyed by his resentment toward it. "My mother died on me when I was nine years old," he complained of his broken home. "What does she expect me to do? Do it all myself?" Raised in Indiana by a father and step-mother, Dean had little interest in school except for basketball, track, and dramatics. After dropping out of college in California, he held a string of odd jobs before heading for New York and acting school. There he was discovered and immediately compared to Brando in *The Wild One*: the same wandering, lonely eyes, the scornful lip, the inarticulate mumblings, and the controlled rage that made being "cool" the strategy of survival. . . . Dean also played the restless, searching youth, hungering for innocence, knowing too much about the compromises and complacencies of the world. Thus in films he appeared both wiser and sadder than the older characters. Yet he would make no reconciliation with reality. To do so was to adjust and settle down, precisely what society demanded of the fifties generation. "Whoso would be a man," wrote Emerson a century earlier, "must be a nonconformist." On September 30, 1955, Dean's speeding white Porsche-Spider collided with another car; the steering wheel went right through him. Lost and lovable, the symbol of troubled youth, James Dean was dead at the age of twenty-four. . . .

"Live fast, die young, and have a good-looking corpse." The lines by the novelist Willard Motley haunted sensitive youths of the fifties generation, many of whom experienced the era with more unease than did their parents. As children they had come to know the horrors of the bomb from the media; in school they were taught "duck-and-cover" exercises in case of attack; at home some of the affluent heard their parents speak of building bomb shelters in the backyards. Teenagers often knew someone who had been killed in an auto accident or drag race. A best-selling novel, Irving Shulman's *The Amboy Dukes*, intended to expose the brutality of urban street gangs; for young males it had the opposite effect of glorifying courage in the face of violence. A similar response could be felt after watching such films as *Rebel Without A Cause, The Wild One,* and *Blackboard Jungle,* where the opening scene thunders with the theme song, "Rock-Around-the-Clock," a shrill of seething rebellion. Asked what he was rebelling against, Brando replied: "What've ya got?" Perhaps the quest for security on the part of the parents drove their children to desire risk and adventure all the more. Boys cruising in hot rods and quaffing six-packs of beer knew they were flirting with danger, as did those girls who risked pregnancy to discover the secret pleasures of the body. Why not? The fifties was the first generation in modern history to know that the world could end tomorrow. . . .

The amount of attention the media devoted to sex in the fifties may be misleading since there is reason to doubt significant changes in behavior actually occurred. Sex was then an emotion more felt than fulfilled. It was also a fantasy, and if fantasies reflect what people desire and not necessarily what they do, desires nonetheless are a large part of the human secrets of life.

During the decade, while teachers and professors were lamenting the decline in educational standards and ministers and priests the decline of morality, teenagers and college students were awakening to something stirring in their own bodies, something at once new, at least to them, and exciting and confusing, a subject more seen and felt than heard and understood. It could be seen in *Playboy*, which started publishing in 1955, exposing more naked angles to the female body than male students could ever imagine, fleshy images that aroused erotic fantasies and made one forget Somerset Maugham's witty warning about sex: the pleasure is momentary, the price damnable, and the position ridiculous. . . .

Their curiosities were met by two postwar publications, *Sexual Behavior in the Human Male* (1948) and *Sexual Behavior in the Human Female* (1953), both by Alfred Kinsey and his colleagues of the Institute for Sexual Research at Indiana University. . . .

Fifty percent of American husbands had committed adultery and 85 percent had sexual intercourse before marriage. Ninety-five percent of males had been sexually active before the age of fifteen and by the ages sixteen and seventeen the activity was at a peak. The average unmarried male had three or four orgasms a week. Nearly 90 percent of men had relationships with prostitutes by their thirty-fifth birthday, and one out of six American farm boys had copulated with farm animals. As to females, two out of three had engaged in premarital petting. Fifty percent were non-virgins before marriage. One out of every six girls had experienced orgasm prior to adolescence, and one in four by the age of fifteen. . . .

No one knew how accurate Kinsey's figures were and no one knew what to make of them. Fearing the worst, a few politicians persuaded the Rockefeller Foundation to withdraw support of Kinsey's Institute for Sexual Research. A double standard prevailed. The male study aroused relatively little objection, but when the female document emerged a few years later some Americans regarded it as a threat to women's virtue. . . . Very acceptable, however, were big breasts, and those who had them—Jayne Mansfield, Jane Russell, Mamie Van Doren, Marilyn Monroe, Elizabeth Taylor. These desirables covered magazines in poses that defied the laws of geometry.

But even these monuments to photography could mislead by confusing fantasy for reality. Was there a sexual revolution in the fifties? Hardly. . . .

Among the lower classes uninvestigated by Kinsey and perhaps untouched by *Playboy*, sex still had more to do with having a lot of children than having multiple orgasms. Married middle-class adults probably enjoyed more sexual intimacy with their marital partners than their parents or grandparents ever contemplated. . . .

The striking thing about the fifties was not the coming crisis of the modern family but its enduring stability. True, the rising divorce rate alarmed Americans in the immediate postwar years. But it soon leveled off and then decreased so that at the end of the fifties the rate was near that of the forties—1.4 percent versus 2.5 percent. Neither marriage nor the family had been threatened by the Kinsey report. Monogamy may have been strained by the freeing effect of carnal knowledge, but most Americans remained inhibited and feared their sexual feelings as soon as they felt them. "Sex is Fun—or Hell," was how J. D. Salinger put it in one of his short stories. In the words of one memoirist, women in particular vacillated between "titillation and terror." Ultimately most married men and women accepted their situation, for better or for worse. Society said they should, and in the fifties the pressures of society, not the risqué pleasures of the body, dictated the conduct of life. . . .

The mixed messages were only part of the many paradoxes of the fifties. It was an age of stable nuclear families and marital tension, of student conformity on the campus and youth rebellion on the screen and phonograph, of erotic arousal before the visual and sexual hesitancy before the actual, of suburban contentment with lawns and station wagons and middle-class worry about money and status, of high expectations of upward mobility and later some doubts about the meaning and value of the age's own achievements. Members of the fifties generation were unique. They had more education and aspirations. They married younger and produced more babies. They possessed more buying power and enjoyed more material pleasure than any generation of men and women in American history. And it is a measure of the complexity of the fifties that its members could reach no consensus about the meaning of their accomplishments and disappointments. Looking back from the eighties, one male member, a building contractor and multimillionaire, put it this way:

> If you had a college diploma, a dark suit, and anything between the ears, it was like an escalator; you just stood there and you moved up. . . .

The Truman and Eisenhower years gave Americans a sense of pride in themselves and confidence in the future. It is questionable whether either sentiment survived the fifties intact. The America that emerged victorious from World War II was not the same America fifteen years later. The decline of confidence resulted in part from the changing nature of warfare brought by modern technology. After the Second World War Americans could take pride in the performance of their soldiers. With the increasing complexity of the cold war, which offered the possibility of either covert CIA operations or nuclear attack and retaliation, warfare seemed more and more a choice between the dishonorable and the suicidal; and if new inventions in sophisticated missile weaponry would make some Americans feel proud of their technological achievements, it was a pride born of fear.

The cold war itself, however, is not the only explanation for the decline of self-assurance that came to be felt at the end of the Eisenhower years. Equally troubling was the sense of unease and discontent. No one had predicted it. In 1950, for example, *Fortune* published a book with the curious title, *U.S.A., the Permanent Revolution*. The title, taken from Leon Trotsky, was meant to depict a new way of life founded on unlimited prosperity, active citizen participation, winning friends abroad with generous foreign aid and free-trade policies, and proudly accepting the burdens of history as a great world power. America must be understood not as a nation of definite goals but of indefinite growth. "Americans wish that other people could see their country as it really is: not as an achievement but as a *process*—a process of becoming." But can there be growth without conscious direction and meaning? "Why should we assume that America has *any* meaning?" the editors asked. "Rightly understood, the principles that embody the meaning of America are the very forces that have done most to change America."

By 1960, all confidence that America could simply be accepted as a process of continual growth and change came to be questioned and in many instances rejected. "What is wrong with America?" queried the *U.S. News and World Report*. "What shall we do with our greatness?" asked the editors of *Life*. President Eisenhower set up a "Commission on National Goals" and Walter Lippmann analyzed the "Anatomy of Discontent," which he specified as a willingness to fulfill them. The Reverend Billy Graham thought Americans overextended themselves in more concrete ways. "We overeat, overdrink, oversex, and overplay. . . . We have tried to fill ourselves with science and education, with better living and pleasure . . . but we are still empty and bored." Adlai Stevenson doubted that America's "permanent revolution" would have any impact on the rest of the world. "With the supermarket as our temple and the singing commercial as our litany, are we likely to fire the world with an irresistible vision of America's exalted purpose and inspiring way of life?" "Something has gone wrong in America," complained the novelist John Steinbeck of his fellow people. "Having too many things, they spend their hours and money on the couch searching for a soul." Everywhere Americans were engaged in the "great debate" about "the national purpose." Americans have become worried, journalists concluded, because they feel they lack inspiring ideals and because they have been led to believe that they do not need them. "The case of the missing purpose," wrote a philosopher in *The Nation*, "is a case of human beings missing the purpose of life." The proud decades were over.

Or were they? Several months before Eisenhower's farewell and Kennedy's inauguration, things were changing. Within a few years America would be addressing problems it never knew existed and some people would be singing "We Shall Overcome!" Yet even before the sixties ended America would be more divided than ever, the two Kennedys and King dead, and the Republicans back in office. Now it was Nixon who promised to bring Americans "back together again." Henceforth, the period of the fifties, once regarded as a dreadful aberration standing between the more compassionate thirties and activist sixties, would seem more and more the steady norm of America's political temper. The generation of the sixties experienced the previous decade as a burden that had to be radically transformed, and some of its worst aspects were confronted and eradicated. But as the radical sixties petered out, it became all the more clear that the two decades beginning with the Second World War shaped the nation's environment and consciousness in more enduring ways than had once been expected. The forties and perhaps especially the fifties are still living in the present, and the assumptions and values of the two decades have become ingrained in our habits and institutions. "What is the national purpose?" asked Dean Acheson in response to the great debate of the late fifties. "To survive and, perchance, to prosper." In doing both well, America still had good reason to be proud of itself.

Families in the Fifties: The Way We Never Were

STEPHANIE COONTZ

Our most powerful visions of traditional families derive from images that are still delivered to our homes in countless reruns of 1950s television sit-coms. When liberals and conservatives debate family policy, for example, the issue is often framed in terms of how many "Ozzie and Harriet" families are left in America. Liberals compute the percentage of total households that contain a breadwinner father, a

Stephanie Coontz, *The Way We Never Were: American Families and the Nostalgia Trap*, pp. 23–33, 36–41. Copyright 1992 by Basic Books, a Division of HarperCollins Publishers, Inc. Reprinted by permission of Basic Books, a member of Perseus Books, LLC.

full-time homemaker mother, and dependent children, proclaiming that fewer than 10 percent of American families meet the "Ozzie and Harriet" or "Leave It to Beaver" model. Conservatives counter that more than half of all mothers with preschool children either are not employed or are employed only part-time. They cite polls showing that most working mothers would like to spend more time with their children and periodically announce that the Nelsons are "making a comeback," in popular opinion if not in real numbers.

Since everyone admits that nontraditional families are now a majority, why this obsessive concern to establish a higher or a lower figure? Liberals seem to think that unless they can prove the "Leave It to Beaver" family is on an irreversible slide toward extinction, they cannot justify introducing new family definitions and social policies. Conservatives believe that if they can demonstrate the traditional family is alive and well, although endangered by policies that reward two-earner families and single parents, they can pass measures to revive the seeming placidity and prosperity of the 1950s, associated in many people's minds with the relative stability of marriage, gender roles, and family life in that decade. If the 1950s family existed today, both sides seem to assume, we would not have the contemporary social dilemmas that cause such debate.

At first glance, the figures seem to justify this assumption. The 1950s was a profamily period if there ever was one. Rates of divorce and illegitimacy were half what they are today; marriage was almost universally praised; the family was everywhere hailed as the most basic institution in society; and a massive baby boom, among all classes and ethnic groups, made America a "child-centered" society. Births rose from a low of 18.4 per 1,000 women during the Depression to a high of 25.3 per 1,000 in 1957. "The birth rate for third children doubled between 1940 and 1960, and that for fourth children tripled."

In retrospect, the 1950s also seem a time of innocence and consensus: Gang warfare among youths did not lead to drive-by shootings; the crack epidemic had not yet hit; discipline problems in the schools were minor; no "secular humanist" movement opposed the 1954 addition of the words *under God* to the Pledge of Allegiance; and 90 percent of all school levies were approved by voters. Introduction of the polio vaccine in 1954 was the most dramatic of many medical advances that improved the quality of life for children.

The profamily features of this decade were bolstered by impressive economic improvements for vast numbers of Americans. Between 1945 and 1960, the gross national product grew by almost 250 percent and per capita income by 35 percent. Housing starts exploded after the war, peaking at 1.65 million in 1955 and remaining above 1.5 million a year for the rest of the decade; the increase in single-family homeownership between 1946 and 1956 outstripped the increase during the entire preceding century and a half. By 1960, 62 percent of American families owned their own homes, in contrast to 43 percent in 1940. Eighty-five percent of the new homes were built in the suburbs, where the nuclear family found new possibilities for privacy and togetherness. While middle-class Americans were the prime beneficiaries of the building boom, substantial numbers of white working-class Americans moved out of the cities into affordable developments, such as Levittown.

Many working-class families also moved into the middle class. The number of salaried workers increased by 61 percent between 1947 and 1957. By the mid-1950s, nearly 60 percent of the population had what was labeled a middle-class income level (between $3,000 and $10,000 in constant dollars), compared to only 31 percent in the "prosperous twenties," before the Great Depression. By 1960, thirty-one million of the nation's forty-four million families owned their own home, 87 percent had a television, and 75 percent possessed a car. The number of people with discretionary income doubled during the 1950s.

For most Americans, the most salient symbol and immediate beneficiary of their newfound prosperity was the nuclear family. The biggest boom in consumer spending, for example, was in household goods. Food spending rose by only 33 percent in the five years following the Second World War, and clothing expenditures rose by 20 percent, but purchases of household furnishings and appliances climbed 240 percent. "Nearly the entire increase in the gross national product in the mid-1950s was due to increased spending on consumer durables and residential construction," most of it oriented toward the nuclear family.

Putting their mouths where their money was, Americans consistently told pollsters that home and family were the wellsprings of their happiness and self-esteem. Cultural historian David Marc argues that prewar fantasies of sophisticated urban "elegance," epitomized by the high-rise penthouse apartment, gave way in the 1950s to a more modest vision of utopia: a single-family house and a car. The emotional dimensions of utopia, however, were unbounded. When respondents to a 1955 marriage study "were asked what they thought they had sacrificed by marrying and raising a family, an overwhelming majority of them replied, 'Nothing.'" Less than 10 percent of Americans believed that an unmarried person could be happy. As one popular advice book intoned: "The family is the center of your living. If it isn't, you've gone far astray."

In fact, the "traditional" family of the 1950s was a qualitatively new phenomenon. At the end of the 1940s, all the trends characterizing the rest of the twentieth century suddenly reversed themselves: For the first time in more than one hundred years, the age for marriage and motherhood fell, fertility increased, divorce rates declined, and women's degree of educational parity with men dropped sharply. In a period of less than ten years, the proportion of never-married persons declined by as much as it had during the entire previous half century.

At the time, most people understood the 1950s family to be a new invention. The Great Depression and the Second World War had reinforced extended family ties, but in ways that were experienced by most people as stultifying and oppressive. As one child of the Depression later put it, "The Waltons" television series of the 1970s did not show what family life in the 1930s was really like: "It wasn't a big family sitting around a table radio and everybody saying goodnight while Bing Crosby crooned 'Pennies from Heaven.'" On top of Depression-era family tensions had come the painful family separations and housing shortages of the war years: By 1947, six million American families were sharing housing, and postwar family counselors warned of a widespread marital crisis caused by conflicts between the generations. A 1948 *March of Time* film, "Marriage and Divorce," declared: "No home is big enough to house two families, particularly two of different generations, with opposite theories on child training."

During the 1950s, films and television plays, such as "Marty," showed people working through conflicts between marital loyalties and older kin, peer group, or community ties; regretfully but decisively, these conflicts were almost invariably "resolved in favor of the heterosexual couple rather than the claims of extended kinship networks, . . . homosociability and friendship." Talcott Parsons and other sociologists argued that modern industrial society required the family to jettison traditional productive functions and wider kin ties in order to specialize in emotional nurturance, childrearing, and production of a modern personality. Social workers "endorsed nuclear family separateness and looked suspiciously on active extended-family networks."

Popular commentators urged young families to adopt a "modern" stance and strike out on their own, and with the return of prosperity, most did. By the early 1950s, newlyweds not only were establishing single-family homes at an earlier age and a more rapid rate than ever before but also were increasingly moving to the suburbs, away from the close scrutiny of the elder generation.

For the first time in American history, moreover, such average trends did not disguise sharp variations by class, race, and ethnic group. People married at a younger age, bore their children earlier and closer together, completed their families by the time they were in their late twenties, and experienced a longer period living together as a couple after their children left home. The traditional range of acceptable family behaviors—even the range in the acceptable number and timing of children—narrowed substantially.

The values of 1950s families also were new. The emphasis on producing a whole world of satisfaction, amusement, and inventiveness within the nuclear family had no precedents. Historian Elaine Tyler May comments: "The legendary family of the 1950s . . . was not, as common wisdom tells us, the last gasp of 'traditional' family life with deep roots in the past. Rather, it was the first wholehearted effort to create a home that would fulfill virtually all its members' personal needs through an energized and expressive personal life."

Beneath a superficial revival of Victorian domesticity and gender distinctions, a novel rearrangement of family ideals and male-female relations was accomplished. For women, this involved a reduction in the moral aspect of domesticity and an expansion of its orientation toward personal service. Nineteenth-century middle-class women had cheerfully left housework to servants, yet 1950s women of all classes created makework in their homes and felt guilty when they did not do everything for themselves. The amount of time women spent doing housework actually *increased* during the 1950s, despite the advent of convenience foods and new, labor-saving appliances; child care absorbed more than twice as much time as it had in the 1920s. By the mid-1950s, advertisers' surveys reported on a growing tendency among women to find "housework a medium of expression for . . . [their] femininity and individuality."

For the first time, men as well as women were encouraged to root their identity and self-image in familial and parental roles. The novelty of these family and gender values can be seen in the dramatic postwar transformation of movie themes. Historian Peter Biskind writes that almost every major male star who had played tough loners in the 1930s and 1940s "took the roles with which he was synonymous and transformed them, in the fifties, into neurotics or psychotics." In these films, "men belonged at home, not on the streets or out on the prairie, . . . not alone or hanging out with other men." The women who got men to settle down had to promise enough sex to compete with "bad" women, but ultimately they provided it only in the marital bedroom and only in return for some help fixing up the house.

Public images of Hollywood stars were consciously reworked to show their commitment to marriage and stability. After 1947, for example, the Actors' Guild organized "a series of unprecedented speeches . . . to be given to civic groups around the country, emphasizing that the stars now embodied the rejuvenated family life unfolding in the suburbs." Ronald Reagan's defense of actors' family values was especially "stirring," noted one reporter, but female stars, unlike Reagan and other male stars, were obliged to *live* the new values as well as propagandize them. Joan Crawford, for example, one of the brash, tough, independent leading ladies of the prewar era, was now pictured as a devoted mother whose sex appeal and glamour did not prevent her from doing her own housework. She posed for pictures mopping floors and gave interviews about her childrearing philosophy.

The "good life" in the 1950s, historian Clifford Clark points out, made the family "the focus of fun and recreation." The ranch house, architectural embodiment of this new ideal, discarded the older privacy of the kitchen, den, and sewing room (representative of separate spheres for men and women) but introduced new privacy and luxury into the master bedroom. There was an unprecedented "glorification of self-indulgence" in family life. Formality was discarded in favor of "livability," "comfort," and "convenience." A contradiction in terms in earlier periods, "the sexually charged, child-centered family took its place at the center of the postwar American dream."

On television, David Marc comments, all the "normal" families moved to the suburbs during the 1950s. Popular culture turned such suburban families into capitalism's answer to the Communist threat. In his famous "kitchen debate" with Nikita Khrushchev in 1959, Richard Nixon asserted that the superiority of capitalism over communism was embodied not in ideology or military might but in the comforts of the suburban home, "designed to make things easier for our women."

Acceptance of domesticity was the mark of middle-class status and upward mobility. In sit-com families, a middle-class man's work was totally irrelevant to his identity; by the same token, the problems of working-class families did not lie in their economic situation but in their failure to create harmonious gender roles. Working-class and ethnic men on television had one defining characteristic: They were unable to control their wives. The families of middle-class men, by contrast, were generally well behaved.

Not only was the 1950s family a new invention; it was also a historical fluke, based on a unique and temporary conjuncture of economic, social, and political factors. During the war, Americans had saved at a rate more than three times higher than that in the decades before or since. Their buying power was further enhanced by America's extraordinary competitive advantage at the end of the war, when every other industrial power was devastated by the experience. This privileged economic position sustained both a tremendous expansion of middle-class management occupations and a new honeymoon between management and organized labor: During the 1950s, real wages increased by more than they had in the entire previous half century.

The impact of such prosperity on family formation and stability was magnified by the role of government, which could afford to be generous with education benefits, housing loans, highway and sewer construction, and job training. All this allowed most middle-class Americans, and a large number of working-class ones, to adopt family values and strategies that assumed the availability of cheap energy, low-interest home loans, expanding educational and occupational opportunities, and steady employment. . . .

Even aside from the exceptional and ephemeral nature of the conditions that supported them, 1950s family strategies and values offer no solution to the discontents that underlie contemporary romanticization of the "good old days." The reality of these families was far more painful and complex than the situation-comedy reruns or the expurgated memories of the nostalgic would suggest. Contrary to popular opinion, "Leave It to Beaver" was not a documentary.

In the first place, not all American families shared in the consumer expansion that provided Hotpoint appliances for June Cleaver's kitchen and a vacuum cleaner for Donna Stone. A full 25 percent of Americans, forty to fifty million people, were poor in the mid-1950s, and in the absence of food stamps and housing programs, this poverty was searing. Even at the end of the 1950s, a third of American children were poor. Sixty percent of Americans over sixty-five had incomes below $1,000 in 1958, considerably below the $3,000 to $10,000 level considered to represent middle-class status. A majority of elders also lacked medical insurance. Only half the population had savings in 1959; one-quarter of the population had no liquid assets at all. Even when we consider only native-born, white families, one-third could not get by on the income of the household head.

In the second place, real life was not so white as it was on television. Television, comments historian Ella Taylor, increasingly ignored cultural diversity, adopting "the motto 'least objectionable programming,' which gave rise to those least objectionable families, the Cleavers, the Nelsons and the Andersons." Such families were so completely white and Anglo-Saxon that even the Hispanic gardener in "Father Knows Best" went by the name of Frank Smith. But contrary to the all-white lineup on the television networks and the streets of suburbia, the 1950s saw a major transformation in the ethnic composition of America. More Mexican immigrants entered the United States in the two decades after the Second World War than in the entire previous one hundred years. Prior to the war, most blacks and Mexican-Americans lived in rural areas, and three-fourths of blacks lived in the South. By 1960, a majority of blacks resided in the North, and 80 percent of both blacks and Mexican-Americans lived in cities. Postwar Puerto Rican immigration was so massive that by 1960 more Puerto Ricans lived in New York than in San Juan. . . .

The happy, homogeneous families that we "remember" from the 1950s were thus partly a result of the media's denial of diversity. But even among sectors of the population where the "least objectionable" families did prevail, their values and behaviors were not entirely a spontaneous, joyful reaction to prosperity. If suburban ranch houses and family barbecues were the carrots offered to white middle-class families that adopted the new norms, there was also a stick. . . .

Vehement attacks were launched against women who did not accept [the prevailing] self-definitions. In the 1947 bestseller, *The Modern Woman: The Lost Sex*, Marynia Farnham and Ferdinand Lundberg described feminism as a "deep illness," called the notion of an independent woman a "contradiction in terms," and accused women who sought educational or employment equality of engaging in symbolic "castration" of men. As sociologist David Riesman noted, a woman's failure to bear children went from being "a social disadvantage and sometimes a personal tragedy" in the nineteenth century to being a "quasi-perversion" in the 1950s. The conflicting messages aimed at women seemed almost calculated to demoralize: At the same time as they labeled women "unnatural" if they did not seek fulfillment in motherhood, psychologists and popular writers insisted that most modern social ills could be traced to domineering mothers who invested too much energy and emotion in their children. Women were told that "no other experience in life . . . will provide the same sense of fulfillment, of happiness, of complete pervading contentment" as motherhood. But soon after delivery they were asked, "Which are you first of all, Wife or Mother?" and warned against the tendency to be "too much mother, too little wife." . . .

Men were also pressured into acceptable family roles, since lack of a suitable wife could mean the loss of a job or promotion for a middle-class man. Bachelors were categorized as "immature," "infantile," "narcissistic," "deviant," or even "pathological." Family advice expert Paul Landis argued: "Except for the sick, the badly crippled, the deformed, the emotionally warped and the mentally defective, almost everyone has an opportunity [and, by clear implication, a duty] to marry."

Families in the 1950s were products of even more direct repression. Cold war anxieties merged with concerns about the expanded sexuality of family life and the commercial world to create what one authority calls the domestic version of George F. Kennan's containment policy toward the Soviet Union: A "normal" family and vigilant mother became the "front line" of defense against treason; anticommunists linked deviant family or sexual behavior to sedition. The FBI and other government agencies instituted unprecedented state intrusion into private life under the guise of investigating subversives. Gay baiting was almost as widespread and every bit as vicious as red baiting.

The Civil Service Commission fired 2,611 persons as "security risks" and reported that 4,315 others resigned under the pressure of investigations that asked leading questions of their neighbors and inquired into the books they read or the music to which they listened. In this atmosphere, movie producer Joel Schumacher recalls, "No one told the truth. . . . People pretended they weren't unfaithful. They pretended that they weren't homosexual. They pretended that they weren't horrible."

Even for people not directly coerced into conformity by racial, political, or personal repression, the turn toward families was in many cases more a defensive move than a purely affirmative act. Some men and women entered loveless marriages in order to forestall attacks about real or suspected homosexuality or lesbianism. Growing numbers of people saw the family, in the words of one husband, as the one "group that in spite of many disagreements internally always will face its external enemies together." Conservative families warned children to beware of communists who might masquerade as friendly neighbors; liberal children learned to confine their opinions to the family for fear that their father's job or reputation might be threatened. . . .

A successful 1950s family, moreover, was often achieved at enormous cost to the wife, who was expected to subordinate her own needs and aspirations to those of both her husband and her children. In consequence, no sooner was the ideal of the postwar family accepted than observers began to comment perplexedly on how discontented women seemed in the very roles they supposedly desired most. In 1949, *Life* magazine reported that "suddenly and for no plain reason" American women were "seized with an eerie restlessness." Under a "mask of placidity" and an outwardly feminine appearance, one physician wrote in 1953, there was often "an inwardly tense and emotionally unstable individual seething with hidden aggressiveness and resentment.". . .

Although Betty Friedan's bestseller *The Feminine Mystique* did not appear until 1963, it was a product of the 1950s, originating in the discontented responses Friedan received in 1957 when she surveyed fellow college classmates from the class of 1942. The heartfelt identification of other 1950s women with "the problem that has no name" is preserved in the letters Friedan received after her book was published, letters now at the Schlesinger Library at Radcliffe.

Men tended to be more satisfied with marriage than were women, especially over time, but they, too, had their discontents. Even the most successful strivers after the American dream sometimes muttered about "mindless conformity." The titles of books such as *The Organization Man*, by William Whyte (1956), and *The Lonely Crowd*, by David Riesman (1958), summarized a widespread critique of 1950s culture. Male resentments against women were expressed in the only partly humorous diatribes of *Playboy* magazine (founded in 1953) against "money-hungry" gold diggers or lazy "parasites" trying to trap men into commitment.

Happy memories of 1950s family life are not all illusion, of course—there were good times for many families. But even the most positive aspects had another side. One reason that the 1950s family model was so fleeting was that it contained the seeds of its own destruction. . . . It was during the 1950s, not the 1960s, that the youth market was first produced, then institutionalized into the youth culture. It was through such innocuous shows as "Howdy Doody" and "The Disney Hour" that advertisers first discovered the riches to be gained by bypassing parents and appealing directly to youth. It was also during this period that advertising and consumerism became saturated with sex. . . .

Whatever its other unexpected features, the 1950s family does appear, at least when compared to families in the last two decades, to be a bastion of "traditional" sexual morality. Many modern observers, accordingly, look back to the sexual values of this decade as a possible solution to what they see as the peculiarly modern "epidemic" of teen pregnancy. On closer examination, however, the issue of teen pregnancy is a classic example of both the novelty and the contradictions of the 1950s family.

Those who advocate that today's youth should be taught abstinence or deferred gratification rather than sex education will find no 1950s model for such restraint. "Heavy petting" became a norm of dating in this period, while the proportion of white brides who were pregnant at marriage more than doubled. Teen birth rates soared, reaching highs that have not been equaled since. In 1957, 97 out of every 1,000 girls aged fifteen to nineteen gave birth, compared to only 52 of every 1,000 in 1983. A surprising number of these births were illegitimate, although 1950s census codes made it impossible to identify an unmarried mother if she lived at home with her parents. The incidence of illegitimacy was also disguised by the new emphasis on "rehabilitating" the white mother (though not the black) by putting her baby up for adoption and encouraging her to "start over"; there was an 80 percent increase in the number of out-of-wedlock babies placed for adoption between 1944 and 1955.

The main reason that teenage sexual behavior did not result in many more illegitimate births during this period was that the age of marriage dropped sharply. Young people were not taught how to "say no"—they were simply handed wedding rings. In fact, the growing willingness of parents to subsidize young married couples and the new prevalence of government educational stipends and home ownership loans for veterans undermined the former assumption that a man should be able to support a family before embarking on marriage. . . .

Contemporary teenage motherhood . . . in some ways represents a *continuation* of 1950s values in a new economic situation that makes early marriage less viable. Of course, modern teen pregnancy also reflects the rejection of some of those earlier values. The values that have broken down, however, have little to do with sexual restraint. What we now think of as 1950s sexual morality depended not so much on stricter sexual control as on intensification of the sexual double standard. Elaine Tyler May argues that sexual "repression" gave way to sexual "containment." The new practice of going steady "widened the boundaries of permissible sexual activity," creating a "sexual brinksmanship" in which women bore the burden of "drawing the line," but that line was constantly changing. Popular opinion admitted, as the *Ladies' Home Journal* put it in 1956, that "sex suggestiveness" was here to stay, but insisted that it was up to women to "put the brakes on."

This double standard led to a Byzantine code of sexual conduct: "Petting" was sanctioned so long as one didn't go "too far" (though this was an elastic and ambiguous prohibition); a woman could be touched on various parts of her body (how low depended on how serious the relationship was) but "nice girls" refused to fondle the comparable male parts in return; mutual stimulation to orgasm was compatible with maintaining a "good" reputation so long as penetration did not occur.

The success of sexual containment depended on sexual inequality. Men no longer bore the responsibility of "saving themselves for marriage"; this was now exclusively a woman's job. In sharp contrast to the nineteenth century, when "oversexed" or demanding men were considered to have serious problems, it was now considered "normal" or "natural" for men to be sexually aggressive. The "average man," advice writers for women commented indulgently, "will go as far as you let him go." When women succeeded in "holding out" (a phrase charged with moral ambiguity), they sometimes experienced problems "letting go," even after marriage; when they failed, they were often reproached later by their husbands for having "given in." The contradictions of this double standard could not long withstand the period's pressures for companionate romance: By 1959, a more liberal single standard had already gained ground among older teenagers across America.

People who romanticize the 1950s, or any model of the traditional family, are usually put in an uncomfortable position when they attempt to gain popular support. The legitimacy of women's rights is so widely accepted today that only a tiny minority of Americans seriously propose that women should go back to being full-time housewives or should be denied educational and job opportunities because of their family responsibilities. Yet when commentators lament the collapse of traditional family commitments and values, they almost invariably mean the uniquely female duties associated with the doctrine of separate spheres for men and women.

Karl Zinsmeister of the American Enterprise Institute, for example, bemoans the fact that "workaholism and family dereliction have become equal-opportunity diseases, striking mothers as much as fathers." David Blankenhorn of the Institute for American Values expresses sympathy for the needs of working women but warns that "employed women do not a family make. The goals of women (and of men, too) in the workplace are primarily individualistic: social recognition, wages, opportunities for advancement, and self-fulfillment. But the family is about collective goals . . . , building life's most important bonds of affection, nurturance, mutual support, and long-term commitment."

In both statements, a seemingly gender-neutral indictment of family irresponsibility ends up being directed most forcefully against women. For Blankenhorn, it is not surprising that *men's* goals should be individualistic; this is a parenthetical aside. For Zinsmeister, the problem with the disease of family dereliction is that it has spread to women. So long as it was confined to men, evidently, there was no urgency about finding a cure.

F U R T H E R   R E A D I N G

Lizabeth Cohen, "From Town Center to Shopping Center," *American Historical Review,*
    October 1996.
David Halberstam, *The Fifties* (1993).
Kenneth T. Jackson, *Crabgrass Frontier: The Suburbanization of America* (1985).
David Mark, *Democratic Vistas: Television in American Culture.*
Elaine Tyler May, *Homeward Bound: American Families in the Cold War Era* (1988).
William O'Neill, *American High* (1989).
Richard Pells, *The Liberal Mind in a Conservative Age: American Intellectuals in the*
    1940s and 1950s (1985).
Benjamin Rader, *In Its Own Image: How Television Has Transformed Sports* (1985).

Making the Great Society:
Civil Rights

The "American Way" meant something very different to blacks in the 1950s from what it did to people like Ron Kovic (Born on the Fourth of July). For blacks in the South, the American Way was "Jim Crow," a system of segregation that included separate schools, separate drinking fountains, separate beaches, separate neighborhoods, separate public accommodations. African Americans in the South could not vote, marry whites, sit in the front of buses, attend state colleges, or even try on clothes and hats in major department stores. Beyond the inconvenience and embarrassment lurked the potential for violence. Women and men who "stepped out of line" could expect the full force of the law—and perhaps even brutal vigilantes like the Ku Klux Klan or White Citizens Council—to turn upon them. It took incalculable bravery to confront this system, and in the 1950s a grassroots movement of men, women, and children did just this.

People like Rosa Parks and Martin Luther King, Jr., helped to start the Civil Rights Movement, which led finally to the implementation of the Fourteenth and Fifteenth Amendments to the Constitution, placed on the books almost one hundred years earlier. The Civil Rights Act of 1964 outlawed segregation in public establishments and discrimination in employment. It extended equal protection under the law to all citizens, which had been the intent of the Fourteenth Amendment. The Civil Rights Act of 1965 guaranteed the right to vote, and the Civil Rights Act of 1968 prohibited discrimination in housing. But the movement did not stop at legal reforms, nor did it pertain only to African Americans. Racial prejudice itself came under attack, and other groups whose rights had been abridged grabbed hold of the new, empowering rhetoric to proclaim their inalienable right to "life, liberty, and the pursuit of happiness." Women, American Indians, Chicanos, Asian Americans, gays, the elderly, and, by 1990, the disabled all sought remedies for discrimination and inequality. They echoed one another's statements and demands, each asserting in turn that freedoms guaranteed to one group of people could not be denied to another.

Although none of these groups achieved their ultimate goal of creating a perfectly just society—what President Lyndon Baines Johnson called the Great Society—they changed many laws and practices within the United States. Legal segregation came to an end. No ethnic or racial group could be paid less than another, and women could no longer legally be paid less than men (or be beaten by their husbands). The very words that people spoke, and the jokes that they told, changed as the legacy of racism, sexism, ageism, and all the other "isms" came under attack.

Of course, the problem was as old as slavery, the solution as old as the Declaration of Independence. Almost two hundred years before the Civil Rights Movement, Jefferson had written the immortal words, "We hold these truths to be self-evident, that all men are created equal." In the 1950s and 1960s, for arguably the first time, the nation sought to put these words into practice across the board. Why then? There are many places to look for the answer to this question, including beyond the United States. The holocaust of World War II and the role of the United States as world leader helped to reshape thinking about the place of discrimination in the "land of the free, home of the brave." This new thinking was the most important legacy of the 1950s and 1960s.

QUESTIONS TO THINK ABOUT

Why were Jefferson's "self-evident" truths finally put into practice at this time? What was more important in bringing about these fundamental changes: charismatic leadership at home, the new world role of the United States, or economic change and prosperity?

DOCUMENTS

The documents in this chapter illustrate a variety of aspects of the Civil Rights Movement. Document 1 is the Universal Declaration of Human Rights passed by the United Nations in 1948. Arising out of the genocide of World War II, this was the first global concord in human history that articulated the premise "All human beings are born free and equal in dignity and rights." Eleanor Roosevelt, a champion of civil rights in the United States, chaired the tumultuous U.N. committee that drafted the declaration. Document 2 is the Supreme Court's famous reversal of *Plessy* v. *Ferguson* (1896). Separate is not equal, the Court ruled in *Brown* v. *Board of Education.* Document 3 is from Martin Luther King, Jr.'s first speech on behalf of Rosa Parks at the Holt Street Baptist Church in Montgomery, Alabama. Returning home from work, Parks refused to give up her seat on a bus so that a white person would not have to occupy the same row as she. This 1955 sermon following Rosa Parks's arrest helped to launch the Montgomery bus boycott, as well as King's career as a civil rights leader. In Document 4, Henry Louis Gates, Jr., now a professor at Harvard University, remembers growing up in the segregated South and learning about civil rights on TV. This selection shows the ways in which different generations perceived the movement. Document 5 is the Civil Rights Act of 1964, one of the milestones of American history. In Document 6, black Muslim leader Malcolm X draws on the imagery of the American Revolution to encourage the nation to live up to its promises. This selection speaks sharply to the alternative to the ballot, which, as in 1776, was "the bullet." The Voting Rights Act of 1965 (Document 7) answered Malcolm's demands and those of 22 million African Americans. Document 8 is the founding statement of the National Organization for Women. The women's rights movement gathered force quickly in the 1960s, encouraged by the Civil Rights Movement and spurred by female activists. Document 9 describes the United Farm Workers Movement, La Raza Unida, the leadership of Cesar Chavez, and the inspiration that Chicanos (Mexican Americans) drew from black civil rights as well as from the Cuban revolution. Document 10 is a satirical manifesto sent to "the Great White Father" by the founders of the American Indian Movement after their occupation of Alcatraz Island in San Francisco Bay. The Indians offered to pay $24 in glass beads and red cloth for the sixteen acres. Document 11, the last reading, connects the post–World War II human rights movement with today. The 1990 Americans with Disabilities Act is a clear outcome of the commitment made back in 1948 to respect the rights, dignity, and abilities of all humans regardless of condition.

1. The United Nations Approves a Universal Declaration of Human Rights, 1948

PREAMBLE

Whereas recognition of the inherent dignity and of the equal and inalienable rights of all members of the human family is the foundation of freedom, justice and peace in the world,

Whereas disregard and contempt for human rights have resulted in barbarous acts which have outraged the conscience of mankind, and the advent of a world in which human beings shall enjoy freedom of speech and belief and freedom from fear and want has been proclaimed as the highest aspiration of the common people,

Whereas it is essential, if man is not to be compelled to have recourse, as a last resort, to rebellion against tyranny and oppression, that human rights should be protected by the rule of law,

Whereas it is essential to promote the development of friendly relations between nations,

Whereas the peoples of the United Nations have in the Charter reaffirmed their faith in fundamental human rights, in the dignity and worth of the human person and in the equal rights of men and women and have determined to promote social progress and better standards of life in larger freedom,

Whereas Member States have pledged themselves to achieve, in co-operation with the United Nations, the promotion of universal respect for and observance of human rights and fundamental freedoms,

Whereas a common understanding of these rights and freedoms is of the greatest importance for the full realization of this pledge,

Now, Therefore THE GENERAL ASSEMBLY proclaims THIS UNIVERSAL DECLARATION OF HUMAN RIGHTS as a common standard of achievement for all peoples and all nations, to the end that every individual and every organ of society, keeping this Declaration constantly in mind, shall strive by teaching and education to promote respect for these rights and freedoms and by progressive measures, national and international, to secure their universal and effective recognition

United Nations web site, www.un.org/Overview/rights.html.

and observance, both among the peoples of Member States themselves and among the peoples of territories under their jurisdiction.

Article 1.

All human beings are born free and equal in dignity and rights. They are endowed with reason and conscience and should act towards one another in a spirit of brotherhood.

Article 2.

Everyone is entitled to all the rights and freedoms set forth in this Declaration, without distinction of any kind, such as race, colour, sex, language, religion, political or other opinion, national or social origin, property, birth or other status. . . .

Article 3.

Everyone has the right to life, liberty and security of person.

Article 4.

No one shall be held in slavery or servitude; slavery and the slave trade shall be prohibited in all their forms.

Article 5.

No one shall be subjected to torture or to cruel, inhuman or degrading treatment or punishment.

Article 6.

Everyone has the right to recognition everywhere as a person before the law.

2. The Supreme Court Rules on
Brown v. *Board of Education,* 1954

These cases come to us from the States of Kansas, South Carolina, Virginia, and Delaware. They are premised on different facts and different local conditions, but a common legal question justifies their consideration together in this consolidated opinion.

In each of the cases, minors of the Negro race, through their legal representatives, seek the aid of the courts in obtaining admission to the public schools of their community on a nonsegregated basis. In each instance, they had been denied admission to schools attended by white children under laws requiring or permitting

---

Brown v. *Board of Education,* 324, U.S. 483–496 (1954).

segregation according to race. This segregation was alleged to deprive the plaintiffs of the equal protection of the laws under the Fourteenth Amendment. In each of the cases other than the Delaware case, a three-judge federal district court denied relief to the plaintiffs on the so-called "separate but equal" doctrine announced by this Court in *Plessy* v. *Ferguson,* 163 U.S. 537. Under that doctrine, equality of treatment is accorded when the races are provided substantially equal facilities, even though these facilities be separate. . . .

The plaintiffs contend that segregated public schools are not "equal" and cannot be made "equal," and that hence they are deprived of the equal protection of the laws. . . .

In approaching this problem, we cannot turn the clock back to 1868 when the Amendment was adopted, or even to 1896 when *Plessy* v. *Ferguson* was written. We must consider public education in the light of its full development and its present place in American life throughout the Nation. Only in this way can it be determined if segregation in public schools deprives these plaintiffs of the equal protection of the laws.

Today, education is perhaps the most important function of state and local governments. Compulsory school attendance laws and the great expenditures for education both demonstrate our recognition of the importance of education to our democratic society. It is required in the performance of our most basic public responsibilities, even service in the armed forces. It is the very foundation of good citizenship. Today it is a principal instrument in awakening the child to cultural values, in preparing him for later professional training, and in helping him to adjust normally to his environment. In these days, it is doubtful that any child may reasonably be expected to succeed in life if he is denied the opportunity of an education. Such an opportunity, when the state has undertaken to provide it, is a right which must be made available to all on equal terms.

We come then to the question presented: Does segregation of children in public schools solely on the basis of race, even though the physical facilities and other "tangible" factors may be equal, deprive the children of the minority group of equal educational opportunities? We believe that it does.

. . . To separate them from others of similar age and qualifications solely because of their race generates a feeling of inferiority as to their status in the community that may affect their hearts and minds in a way unlikely ever to be undone. The effect of this separation on their educational opportunities was well stated by a finding in the Kansas case by a court which nevertheless felt compelled to rule against the Negro plaintiffs:

> "Segregation of white and colored children in public schools has a detrimental effect upon the colored children. The impact is greater when it has the sanction of the law; for the policy of separating the races is usually interpreted as denoting the inferiority of the negro group. A sense of inferiority affects the motivation of a child to learn. Segregation with the sanction of law, therefore, has a tendency to [retard] the educational and mental development of negro children and to deprive them of some of the benefits they would receive in a racial[ly] integrated school system."

Whatever may have been the extent of psychological knowledge at the time of *Plessy* v. *Ferguson,* this finding is amply supported by modern authority. Any language in *Plessy* v. *Ferguson* contrary to this finding is rejected.

We conclude that in the field of public education the doctrine of "separate but equal" has no place. Separate educational facilities are inherently unequal. Therefore, we hold that the plaintiffs and others similarly situated for whom the actions have been brought are, by reason of the segregation complained of, deprived of the equal protection of the laws guaranteed by the Fourteenth Amendment.

3. Reverend Martin Luther King, Jr., Defends Seamstress Rosa Parks, 1955

We are here this evening for serious business. We are here in a general sense because first and foremost we are American citizens, and we are determined to apply our citizenship to the fullness of its means. We are here because of our love for democracy, because of our deep-seated belief that democracy transformed from thin paper to thick action is the greatest form of government on earth. But we are here in a specific sense, because of the bus situation in Montgomery. We are here because we are determined to get the situation corrected.

This situation is not at all new. The problem has existed over endless years. For many years now Negroes in Montgomery and so many other areas have been inflicted with the paralysis of crippling fear on buses in our community. On so many occasions, Negroes have been intimidated and humiliated and oppressed because of the sheer fact that they were Negroes. I don't have time this evening to go into the history of these numerous cases. . . . But at least one stands before us now with glaring dimensions. Just the other day, just last Thursday to be exact, one of the finest citizens in Montgomery—not one of the finest Negro citizens but one of the finest citizens in Montgomery—was taken from a bus and carried to jail and arrested because she refused to get up to give her seat to a white person. . . . Mrs. Rosa Parks is a fine person. And since it had to happen I'm happy it happened to a person like Mrs. Parks, for nobody can doubt the boundless outreach of her integrity. Nobody can doubt the height of her character, nobody can doubt the depth of her Christian commitment and devotion to the teachings of Jesus. . . .

And just because she refused to get up, she was arrested. . . . You know my friends there comes a time when people get tired of being trampled over by the iron feet of oppression. There comes a time my friends when people get tired of being flung across the abyss of humiliation where they experience the bleakness of nagging despair. There comes a time when people get tired of being pushed out of the glittering sunlight of life's July and left standing amidst the piercing chill of an Alpine November.

We are here, we are here this evening because we're tired now. Now let us say that we are not here advocating violence. We have overcome that. I want it to be known throughout Montgomery and throughout this nation that we are Christian people. We believe in the Christian religion. We believe in the teachings of Jesus. The only weapon that we have in our hands this evening is the weapon of protest.

Excerpt from speech delivered by Martin Luther King, Jr., at Holt Street Baptist Church, Montgomery, Alabama, December 5, 1955, as reprinted in *The Eyes on the Prize Civil Rights Reader* (New York: Viking, 1991), 48–51. Reprinted by arrangement with the Estate of Martin Luther King, Jr., c/o Writers House as agent for the proprietor. Copyright 1955 Martin Luther King, Jr., copyright renewed 1991 Coretta Scott King.

And secondly, this is the glory of America, with all its faults. This is the glory of our democracy. If we were incarcerated behind the iron curtains of a Communistic nation we couldn't do this. If we were trapped in the dungeon of a totalitarian regime we couldn't do this. But the great glory of American democracy is the right to protest for right.

My friends, don't let anybody make us feel that we ought to be compared in our actions with the Ku Klux Klan or with the White Citizens' Councils. There will be no crosses burned at any bus stops in Montgomery. There will be no white persons pulled out of their homes and taken out to some distant road and murdered. There will be nobody among us who will stand up and defy the Constitution of this nation. We only assemble here because of our desire to see right exist.

My friends, I want it to be known that we're going to work with grim and firm determination to gain justice on the buses in this city. And we are not wrong, we are not wrong in what we are doing. If we are wrong, then the Supreme Court of this Nation is wrong. If we are wrong, the Constitution of the United States is wrong. If we are wrong, God Almighty is wrong. If we are wrong, Jesus of Nazareth was merely a utopian dreamer and never came down to earth. If we are wrong, justice is a lie. And we are determined here in Montgomery to work and fight until justice runs down like water and righteousness like a mighty stream. . . .

And as we stand and sit here this evening, and as we prepare ourselves for what lies ahead, let us go out with a grim and bold determination that we are going to stick together. We are going to work together. Right here in Montgomery when the history books are written in the future, somebody will have to say "There lived a race of people, black people, fleecy locks and black complexion, of people who had the moral courage to stand up for their rights." And thereby they injected a new meaning into the veins of history and of civilization. And we're gonna do that. God grant that we will do it before it's too late.

4. Henry Louis Gates, Jr., Remembers Civil Rights on TV, 1957

Civil rights took us all by surprise. Every night we'd wait until the news to see what "Dr. King and dem" were doing. It was like watching the Olympics or the World Series when somebody colored was on. The murder of Emmett Till was one of my first memories. He whistled at some white girl, they said; that's all he did. He was beat so bad they didn't even want to open the casket, but his mama made them. She wanted the world to see what they had done to her baby.

In 1957, when I was in second grade, black children integrated Central High School in Little Rock, Arkansas. We watched it on TV. All of us watched it. I don't mean Mama and Daddy and Rocky. I mean *all* the colored people in America watched it, together, with one set of eyes. We'd watch it in the morning, on the *Today* show on NBC, before we'd go to school; we'd watch it in the evening, on the news, with Edward R. Murrow on CBS. We'd watch the Special Bulletins at night, interrupting our TV shows.

Henry Louis Gates, Jr., *Colored People: A Memoir*, pp. 25–27. Copyright © 1994 by Henry Louis Gates, Jr. Used with permission of Alfred A. Knopf, a division of Random House, Inc.

The children were all well scrubbed and greased down, as we'd say. Hair short and closely cropped, parted, and oiled (the boys); "done" in a "permanent" and straightened, with turned-up bangs and curls (the girls). Starched shirts, white, and creased pants, shoes shining like a buck private's spit shine. Those Negroes were *clean.* The fact was, those children trying to get the right to enter that school in Little Rock looked like black versions of models out of *Jack & Jill* magazine, to which my mama had subscribed for me so that I could see what children outside the Valley were up to. "They hand-picked those children," Daddy would say. "No dummies, no nappy hair, heads not too kinky, lips not too thick, no disses and no dats." At seven, I was dismayed by his cynicism. It bothered me somehow that those children would have been chosen, rather than just having shown up or volunteered or been nearby in the neighborhood.

Daddy was jaundiced about the civil rights movement, and especially about the Reverend Dr. Martin Luther King, Jr. He'd say all of his names, to drag out his scorn. By the mid-sixties, we'd argue about King from sunup to sundown. Sometimes he'd just mention King to get a rise from me, to make a sagging evening more interesting, to see if I had *learned* anything real yet, to see how long I could think up counter arguments before getting so mad that my face would turn purple. I think he just liked the color purple on my face, liked producing it there. But he was not of two minds about those children in Little Rock.

The children would get off their school bus surrounded by soldiers from the National Guard and by a field of state police. They would stop at the steps of the bus and seem to take a very deep breath. Then the phalanx would start to move slowly along this gulley of sidewalk and rednecks that connected the steps of the school bus with the white wooden double doors of the school. All kinds of crackers would be lining that gulley, separated from the phalanx of children by rows of state police, who formed a barrier arm in arm. Cheerleaders from the all-white high school that was desperately trying to stay that way were dressed in those funny little pleated skirts, with a big red *C* for "Central" on their chests, and they'd wave their pom-poms and start to cheer: "Two, four, six, eight—We don't want to integrate!" And all those crackers and all those rednecks would join in that chant as if their lives depended on it. Deafening, it was: even on our twelve-inch TV, a three-inch speaker buried along the back of its left side.

The TV was the ritual arena for the drama of race. In our family, it was located in the living room, where it functioned like a fireplace in the proverbial New England winter. I'd sit in the water in the galvanized tub in the middle of our kitchen, watching the TV in the next room while Mama did the laundry or some other chore as she waited for Daddy to come home from his second job. We watched people getting hosed and cracked over their heads, people being spat upon and arrested, rednecks siccing fierce dogs on women and children, our people responding by singing and marching and staying strong. Eyes on the prize. Eyes on the prize. George Wallace at the gate of the University of Alabama, blocking Autherine Lucy's way. Charlayne Hunter at the University of Georgia. President Kennedy interrupting our scheduled program with a special address, saying that James Meredith will *definitely* enter the University of Mississippi; and saying it like he believed it (unlike Ike), saying it like the big kids said "It's our turn to play" on the basketball court and walking all through us as if we weren't there.

5. Congress Passes the Civil Rights Act of 1964

Injunctive Relief Against Discrimination in Places of Public Accommodation

Sec. 201. (a) All persons shall be entitled to the full and equal enjoyment of the goods, services, facilities, privileges, advantages, and accommodations of any place of public accommodation, as defined in this section, without discrimination or segregation on the ground of race, color, religion, or national origin.

(b) Each of the following establishments which serves the public is a place of public accommodation within the meaning of this title if its operations affect commerce, or if discrimination or segregation by it is supported by State action:

(1) any inn, hotel, motel, or other establishment which provides lodging to transient guests, other than an establishment located within a building which contains not more than five rooms for rent or hire and which is actually occupied by the proprietor of such establishment as his residence;

(2) any restaurant, cafeteria, lunchroom, lunch counter, soda fountain, or other facility principally engaged in selling food for consumption on the premises, including, but not limited to, any such facility located on the premises of any retail establishment; or any gasoline station;

(3) any motion picture house, theater, concert hall, sports arena, stadium or other place of exhibition or entertainment. . . .

Discrimination Because of Race, Color, Religion, Sex, or National Origin

Sec. 703. (a) It shall be an unlawful employment practice for an employer—

(1) to fail or refuse to hire or to discharge any individual, or otherwise to discriminate against any individual with respect to his compensation, terms, conditions, or privileges of employment, because of such individual's race, color, religion, sex, or national origin; or

(2) to limit, segregate, or classify his employees in any way which would deprive or tend to deprive any individual of employment opportunities or otherwise adversely affect his status as an employee, because of such individual's race, color, religion, sex, or national origin.

6. Black Muslim Malcolm X Warns: The Ballot or the Bullet, 1964

Our People, 22,000,000 African-Americans, are fed up with America's hypocritical democracy and today we care nothing about the odds that are against us. Every time a black man gets ready to defend himself some Uncle Tom tries to tell us, how can you win? That's Tom talking. Don't listen to him. This is the first thing we hear: the odds are against you. You're dealing with black people who don't care anything about odds. We care nothing about odds.

U.S. Statutes at Large 78 (1964), pp. 243, 255.

Again I go right back to the people who founded and secured the independence of this country from the colonial power of England. When George Washington and the others got ready to declare or come up with the Declaration of Independence, they didn't care anything about the odds of the British Empire. They were fed up with taxation without representation. And you've got 22,000,000 black people in this country today, 1964, who are fed up with taxation without representation, and will do the same thing. Who are ready, willing and justified to do the same thing today to bring about independence for our people that your forefathers did to bring about independence for your people. . . .

So 1964 will see the Negro revolt evolve and merge into the world-wide black revolution that has been taking place on this earth since 1945. The so-called revolt will become a real black revolution. Now the black revolution has been taking place in Africa and Asia and in Latin America. Now when I say black, I mean non-white. Black, brown, red or yellow. Our brothers and sisters in Asia, who were colonized by the Europeans, our brothers and sisters in Africa, who were colonized by the Europeans, and in Latin America, the peasants, who were colonized by the Europeans, have been involved in a struggle since 1945 to get the colonialists, or the colonizing powers, the Europeans, off their land, out of their country.

This is a real revolution. Revolution is always based on land. Revolution is never based on begging somebody for an integrated cup of coffee. Revolutions are never fought by turning the other cheek. Revolutions are never based upon love your enemy, and pray for those who spitefully use you. And revolutions are never waged singing, "We Shall Overcome." Revolutions are based upon bloodshed. . . . Revolutions overturn systems, and there is no system on this earth which has proven itself more corrupt, more criminal than this system, that in 1964 still colonizes 22,000,000 African-Americans, still enslaves 22,000,000 Afro-Americans. . . .

All of our people have the same goals. The same objective. That objective is freedom, justice, eqality. All of us want recognition and respect as human beings. We don't want to be integrationists. Nor do we want to be separationists. We want to be human beings. Integration is only a method that is used by some groups to obtain freedom, justice, equality and respect as human beings. Separation is only a method that is used by other groups to obtain freedom, justice, equality or human dignity. . . .

So in my conclusion in speaking about the black revolution, America today is at a time or in a day or at an hour where she is the first country on this earth that can actually have a bloodless revolution. In the past revolutions have been bloody. Historically you just don't have a peaceful revolution. Revolutions are bloody, revolutions are violent, revolutions cause bloodshed and death follows in their paths. America is the only country in history in a position to bring about a revolution without violence and bloodshed. But America is not morally equipped to do so.

Why is America in a position to bring about a bloodless revolution? Because the Negro in this country holds the balance of power and if the Negro in this country were given what the Constitution says he is supposed to have, the added power of the Negro in this country would sweep all of the racists and the segregationists out of office. It would change the entire political structure of the country. It would wipe out the Southern segregationism that now controls America's foreign policy, as well as America's domestic policy.

And the only way without bloodshed that this can be brought about is that the black man has to be given full use of the ballot in every one of the 50 states. But if the black man doesn't get the ballot, then you are going to be faced with another man who forgets the ballot and starts using the bullet.

7. Congress Approves the Voting Rights Act, 1965

Be it enacted by the Senate and House of Representatives of the United States of America in Congress assembled, That this Act shall be known as the "Voting Rights Act of 1965."

Sec. 2. No voting qualification or prerequisite to voting, or standard, practice, or procedure shall be imposed or applied by any State or political subdivision to deny or abridge the right of any citizen of the United States to vote on account of race or color.

Sec. 3. (a) Whenever the Attorney General institutes a proceeding under any statute to enforce the guarantees of the fifteenth amendment in any State or political subdivision the court shall authorize the appointment of Federal examiners by the United States Civil Service Commission . . . to enforce the guarantees of the fifteenth amendment . . . : *Provided,* That the court need not authorize the appointment of examiners if any incidents of denial or abridgement of the right to vote on account of race or color (1) have been few in number and have been promptly and effectively corrected by State or local action, (2) the continuing effect of such incidents has been eliminated, and (3) there is no reasonable probability of their recurrence in the future. . . .

(2) No person who demonstrates that he has successfully completed the sixth primary grade in a public school in, or a private school accredited by, any State or territory, the District of Columbia, or the Commonwealth of Puerto Rico in which the predominant classroom language was other than English, shall be denied the right to vote in any Federal, State, or local election because of his inability to read, write, understand, or interpret any matter in the English language. . . .

Sec. 10. (a) The Congress finds that the requirement of the payment of a poll tax as a precondition to voting (i) precludes persons of limited means from voting or imposes unreasonable financial hardship upon such persons as a precondition to their exercise of the franchise, (ii) does not bear a reasonable relationship to any legitimate State interest in the conduct of elections, and (iii) in some areas has the purpose or effect of denying persons the right to vote because of race or color. Upon the basis of these findings, Congress declares that the constitutional right of citizens to vote is denied or abridged in some areas by the requirement of the payment of a poll tax as a precondition to voting.

U.S. Statutes at Large 79 (1965), pp. 437, 439, 442.

8. The National Organization for Women Calls for Equality, 1966

We, men and women who hereby constitute ourselves as the National Organization for Women, believe that the time has come for a new movement toward true equality for all women in America, and toward a fully equal partnership of the sexes, as part of the world-wide revolution of human rights now taking place within and beyond our national borders.

The purpose of NOW is to take action to bring women into full participation in the mainstream of American society now, exercising all the privileges and responsibilities thereof in truly equal partnership with men. . . .

NOW is dedicated to the proposition that women first and foremost are human beings, who, like all other people in our society, must have the chance to develop their fullest human potential. We believe that women can achieve such equality only by accepting to the full challenges and responsibilities they share with all other people in our society, as part of the decision-making mainstream of American political, economic and social life. . . .

There is no civil rights movement to speak for women, as there has been for Negroes and other victims of discrimination. The National Organization for Women must therefore begin to speak.

WE BELIEVE that the power of American law, and the protection guaranteed by the U.S. Constitution to the civil rights of all individuals, must be effectively applied and enforced to isolate and remove patterns of sex discrimination, to ensure equality of opportunity in employment and education, and equality of civil and political rights and responsibilities on behalf of women, as well as for Negroes and other deprived groups.

We realize that women's problems are linked to many broader questions of social justice; their solution will require concerted action by many groups. Therefore, convinced that human rights for all are indivisible, we expect to give active support to the common cause of equal rights for all those who suffer discrimination and deprivation, and we call upon other organizations committed to such goals to support our efforts toward equality for women.

WE DO NOT ACCEPT the token appointment of a few women to high-level positions in government and industry as a substitute for a serious continuing effort to recruit and advance women according to their individual abilities. To this end, we urge American government and industry to mobilize the same resources of ingenuity and command with which they have solved problems of far greater difficulty than those now impeding the progress of women.

WE BELIEVE that this nation has a capacity at least as great as other nations, to innovate new social institutions which will enable women to enjoy true equality of opportunity and responsibility in society, without conflict with their responsibilities as mothers and homemakers. In such innovations, America does not lead the Western world, but lags by decades behind many European countries. We do not

NOW Statement of Purpose, 1966. Reprinted by permission of the National Organization for Women. This is a historical document and does not reflect the current language or priorities of the organization.

354   *Major Problems in American History*

accept the traditional assumption that a woman has to choose between marriage
and motherhood, on the one hand, and serious participation in industry or the professions on the other. We question the present expectation that all normal women
will retire from job or profession for ten or fifteen years, to devote their full time to
raising children, only to reenter the job market at a relatively minor level. . . .

WE BELIEVE that it is as essential for every girl to be educated to her full
potential of human ability as it is for every boy—with the knowledge that such
education is the key to effective participation in today's economy and that, for a
girl as for a boy, education can only be serious where there is expectation that it
will be used in society. We believe that American educators are capable of devising
means of imparting such expectations to girl students. Moreover, we consider the
decline in the proportion of women receiving higher and professional education to
be evidence of discrimination. . . . We believe that the same serious attention must be
given to high school dropouts who are girls as to boys.

WE REJECT the current assumptions that a man must carry the sole burden of
supporting himself, his wife, and family, and that a woman is automatically entitled
to lifelong support by a man upon her marriage, or that marriage, home and family
are primarily woman's world and responsibility—hers, to dominate, his to support.
We believe that a true partnership between the sexes demands a different concept
of marriage, an equitable sharing of the responsibilities of home and children and of
the economic burdens of their support. We believe that proper recognition should be
given to the economic and social value of homemaking and child care. To these ends,
we will seek to open a reexamination of laws and mores governing marriage and
divorce, for we believe that the current state of "half-equality" between the sexes
discriminates against both men and women, and is the cause of much unnecessary
hostility between the sexes.

WE BELIEVE that women must now exercise their political rights and responsibilities as American citizens. They must refuse to be segregated on the basis of sex
into separate-and-not-equal ladies' auxiliaries in the political parties, and they must
demand representation according to their numbers in the regularly constituted party
committees—at local, state, and national levels—and in the informal power structure,
participating fully in the selection of candidates and political decision-making, and
running for office themselves.

IN THE INTERESTS OF THE HUMAN DIGNITY OF WOMEN, we will
protest and endeavor to change the false image of women now prevalent in the
mass media, and in the texts, ceremonies, laws, and practices of our major social
institutions. . . .

NOW WILL HOLD ITSELF INDEPENDENT OF ANY POLITICAL PARTY
in order to mobilize the political power of all women and men intent on our goals.
We will strive to ensure that no party, candidate, President, senator, governor, congressman, or any public official who betrays or ignores the principle of full equality between the sexes is elected or appointed to office. If it is necessary to mobilize
the votes of men and women who believe in our cause, in order to win for women
the final right to be fully free and equal human beings, we so commit ourselves.

WE BELIEVE THAT women will do most to create a new image of women by
acting now, and by speaking out in behalf of their own equality, freedom, and
human dignity—not in pleas for special privilege, nor in enmity toward men, who
are also victims of the current half-equality between the sexes—but in an active,

self-respecting partnership with men. By so doing, women will develop confidence in their own ability to determine actively, in partnership with men, the conditions of their life, their choices, their future and their society.

9. Mexican Americans Form "La Raza Unida," 1968

1. What is LA RAZA UNIDA? It is a ground swell movement of Mexican-American solidarity throughout the Southwest comprising a loose fellowship of some two or three hundred civic, social, cultural, religious, and political groups.

2. What has brought it about? The need deeply felt among Mexican-Americans to dramatize their plight as a disadvantaged minority, to assert their rights as first-rate citizens, and to assume their rightful share of the social, economic, educational, and political opportunities guaranteed by the American democratic system.

3. Are Mexican-Americans a disadvantaged minority? The most recent study, the Mexican-American Study Project conducted at UCLA and funded by the Ford Foundation, has disclosed that in the Southwest, as compared to the Negro, the Mexican-American is on generally the same level economically, but substantially below educationally. As for dilapidated housing and unemployment, the Mexican-American is not too much better off than the Negro.

4. Why this sudden awakening? Actually, it is not as sudden as it looks. Its first manifestations begin in the period following the Second World War. Mexican-Americans emerged from that conflict with a new determination to make their sacrifice count. No ethnic group has received a larger proportion of decorations, and few had sustained as large a share of casualties. These veterans challenged in and out of court the blatant legacy of discrimination still prevailing in the Southwest, often displayed by the glaring signs or the brutal words "No Mexicans allowed." The G.I. Bill made it possible for quite a few to obtain college degrees, better jobs, and positions of leadership. . . .

Since then Latin America has been rediscovered south and north of the Rio Grande, following the tremors set off by the Cuban revolution. Spanish is once again a prestige language, and being bilingual somehow is no longer un-American. Then came the radiation fall-out of the Negro civil rights struggle which made even the most disillusioned Mexican-American begin to dream large dreams again. But if anyone thought the new vision borrowed from this struggle would give way to violence, there emerged in 1965 the most inspirational of all, Cesar Chavez. It is he, more than anyone else, who has contributed to LA RAZA UNIDA the mystique of the pursuit of justice through non-violent means. His recent 24-day penitential fast was undertaken to signify the Christian determination of himself and his followers not to be driven into acts of violence by the obdurate grape-growing firms near Delano, California, which refuse to enter into contract negotiations with his fledgling union, while using every conceivable means to discredit it.

5. Are all members of LA RAZA UNIDA non-violent? The vast majority abhor violence. Indeed, one of their most persistent criticisms is that they have been the victims of too much violence, and they are sick of it. . . . An unbiased look at this vigorous awakening of the Mexican-American will make us realize it is a tremendous affirmation of

"What Is La Raza?" by Jorge Lara Braud, in *La Raza Yearbook,* Sept. 1968. This document can also be found in Luis Valdez and Stan Steiner (eds.), *Aztlan: An Anthology of Mexican-American Literature* (New York: Vintage, 1972), pp. 222–224.

faith in the American dream. They actually believe, unlike many other sectors, that this society is still capable of undergoing a reformation of "freedom and justice for all."

10. A Proclamation from the Indians of All Tribes, Alcatraz Island, 1969

To the Great White Father and All His People—

We, the native Americans, re-claim the land known as Alcatraz Island in the name of all American Indians by right of discovery.

We wish to be fair and honorable in our dealings with the Caucasian inhabitants of this land, and hereby offer the following treaty:

We will purchase said Alcatraz Island for twenty-four dollars (24) in glass beads and red cloth, a precedent set by the white man's purchase of a similar island about 300 years ago. We know that $24 in trade goods for these 16 acres is more than was paid when Manhattan Island was sold, but we know that land values have risen over the years. Our offer of $1.24 per acre is greater than the 47 cents per acre the white men are now paying the California Indians for their land.

We will give to the inhabitants of this island a portion of the land for their own to be held in trust by the American Indian Affairs and by the bureau of Caucasian Affairs to hold in perpetuity—for as long as the sun shall rise and the rivers go down to the sea. We will further guide the inhabitants in the proper way of living. We will offer them our religion, our education, our life-ways, in order to help them achieve our level of civilization and thus raise them and all their white brothers up from their savage and unhappy state. We offer this treaty in good faith and wish to be fair and honorable in our dealings with all white men.

We feel that this so-called Alcatraz Island is more than suitable for an Indian reservation, as determined by the white man's own standards. By this we mean that this place resembles most Indian reservations in that:

1. It is isolated from modern facilities, and without adequate means of transportation.
2. It has no fresh running water.
3. It has inadequate sanitation facilities.
4. There are no oil or mineral rights.
5. There is no industry and so unemployment is very great.
6. There are no health care facilities.
7. The soil is rocky and non-productive, and the land does not support game.
8. There are no educational facilities.
9. The population has always exceeded the land base.
10. The population has always been held as prisoners and kept dependent upon others.

Further, it would be fitting and symbolic that ships from all over the world, entering the Golden Gate, would first see Indian land, and thus be reminded of the true history of this nation. This tiny island would be a symbol of the great lands once ruled by free and noble Indians.

Peter blue cloud, ed., *Alcatraz Is Not an Island,* by Indians of All Tribes (Berkeley, Calif.: Wingbow Press, 1972), pp. 40–42.

What use will we make of this land?

Since the San Francisco Indian Center burned down, there is no place for Indians to assemble and carry on tribal life here in the white man's city. Therefore, we plan to develop on this island several Indian institutions:

1. A Center for Native American Studies which will educate them to the skills and knowledge relevant to improve the lives and spirits of all Indian peoples.
2. An American Indian Spiritual Center which will practice our ancient tribal religious and sacred healing ceremonies. . . .
3. An Indian Center of Ecology which will train and support our young people in scientific research and practice to restore our lands and waters to their pure and natural state. . . .
4. A Great Indian Training School will be developed to teach our people how to make a living in the world, improve our standard of living, and to end hunger and unemployment among all our people. . . .

Some of the present buildings will be taken over to develop an American Indian Museum which will depict our native food & other cultural contributions we have given to the world. Another part of the museum will present some of the things the white man has given to the Indians in return for the land and life he took: disease, alcohol, poverty and cultural decimation (As symbolized by old tin cans, barbed wire, rubber tires, plastic containers, etc.). . . .

In the name of all Indians, therefore, we re-claim this island for our Indian nations.

> Signed,
> Indians of All Tribes
> November 1969
> San Francisco, California

11. Americans with Disabilities Act, 1990

The Congress finds that—

(1) some 43,000,000 Americans have one or more physical or mental disabilities, and this number is increasing as the population as a whole is growing older;

(2) historically, society has tended to isolate and segregate individuals with disabilities, and, despite some improvements, such forms of discrimination against individuals with disabilities continue to be a serious and pervasive social problem;

(3) discrimination against individuals with disabilities persists in such critical areas as employment, housing, public accommodations, education, transportation, communication, recreation, institutionalization, health services, voting, and access to public services;

(4) unlike individuals who have experienced discrimination on the basis of race, color, sex, national origin, religion, or age, individuals who have experienced discrimination on the basis of disability have often had no legal recourse to redress such discrimination. . . .

Statutes of the United States 104 (1990): 327–378.

It is the purpose of this Act—

(1) to provide a clear and comprehensive national mandate for the elimination of discrimination against individuals with disabilities;

(2) to provide clear, strong, consistent, enforceable standards addressing discrimination against individuals with disabilities;

(3) to ensure that the Federal Government plays a central role in enforcing the standards established in this Act on behalf of individuals with disabilities; and

(4) to invoke the sweep of congressional authority, including the power to enforce the fourteenth amendment and to regulate commerce, in order to address the major areas of discrimination faced day-to-day by people with disabilities.

✦ E S S A Y S

One might well ponder how and why Americans woke up when they did to the implications of their nation's founding principles. Historians have examined conditions external to the South, as well as the charismatic leadership of southerners like Martin Luther King, Jr., who persevered despite the constant threat of violence. Harvard Sitkoff of Columbia University emphasizes external events. He argues that economic, political, and ideological "preconditions" set the stage for the movement, including the advent of television, the booming postwar economy, decolonization in Africa and Asia, and the emergence of the United States as leader of the Free World. David Garrow of Emory University focuses on the leadership of Martin Luther King, Jr. In this selection from his Pulitzer Prize–winning biography, Garrow reveals the depth of King's commitment to a role he did not ask for. King's sacrifice is made more poignant by the fact that he knew full well that he was making one. The willingness of King, and many others, to "bear the cross" testifies to the critical place of individuals in history.

The Preconditions for Racial Change

HARVARD SITKOFF

Of the interrelated causes of progress in race relations since the start of the Great Depression, none was more important than the changes in the American economy. No facet of the race problem was untouched by the elephantine growth of the Gross National Product, which rose from $206 billion in 1940 to $500 billion in 1960, and then in the 1960s increased by an additional 60 percent. By 1970, the economy topped the trillion dollar mark. This spectacular rate of economic growth produced some 25 million new jobs in the quarter of a century after World War II and raised real wage earnings by at least 50 percent. It made possible the increasing income of blacks; their entry into industries and labor unions previously closed to them; gains for blacks in occupational status; and created a shortage of workers that necessitated a slackening of restrictive promotion policies and the introduction of scores of government and private industry special job training programs for Afro-Americans. It also meant that the economic progress of blacks did not have to

Excerpted and revised by the author in William Chafe and Harvard Sitkoff, eds., *A History of Our Time*, 4th ed. (New York: Oxford University Press, 1995), pp. 155–164. Reprinted by permission of the author.

côme at the expense of whites, thus undermining the most powerful source of white resistance to the advancement of blacks.

The effect of economic changes on race relations was particularly marked in the South. The rapid industrialization of the South since 1940 ended the dominance of the cotton culture. With its demise went the need for a vast underclass of unskilled, subjugated laborers. Power shifted from rural areas to the cities, and from tradition-oriented landed families to the new officers and professional workers in absentee-owned corporations. The latter had neither the historical allegiances nor the nonrational attachment to racial mores to risk economic growth for the sake of tradition. The old system of race relations had no place in the new economic order. Time and again in the 1950s and 1960s, the industrial and business elite took the lead in accommodating the South to the changes sought by the civil rights movement.

The existence of an "affluent society" boosted the fortunes of the civil rights movement itself in countless ways. Most obviously, it enabled millions of dollars in contributions from wealthy liberals and philanthropic organizations to pour into the coffers of the NAACP, Urban League, Southern Christian Leadership Conference, and countless other civil rights groups. Without those funds it is difficult to comprehend how the movement could have accomplished those tasks so essential to its success: legislative lobbying and court litigation; nationwide speaking tours and the daily mailings of press releases all over the country; the organization of mass marches, demonstrations, and rallies; constant, rapid communication and traveling over long distances; and the convocation of innumerable public conferences and private strategy sessions.

Prosperity also increased the leisure time of many Americans and enabled them to react immediately to the changing times. The sons and daughters of the newly affluent increasingly went to college. By 1970, five times as many students were in college as in 1940. What they learned helped lead to pronounced changes in white attitudes toward racial discrimination and segregation. Other whites learned from the TV sets in their homes. By the time Lyndon Johnson signed the Voting Rights Act of 1965, some 95 percent of all American families owned at least one television. The race problem entered their living rooms. Tens of millions nightly watched the drama of the Negro Revolution. The growing majority of Americans favoring racial equality and justice had those sentiments reinforced by TV shots of snarling police dogs attacking black demonstrators, rowdy white hoods molesting young blacks patiently waiting to be served at a lunch counter, and hate-filled white faces in a frenzy because of the effrontery of little black children entering a previously all-white school.

Blacks viewed the same scenes on their TV sets, and the rage these scenes engendered helped transform isolated battles into a national campaign. Concurrently, the conspicuous display of white affluence on TV vividly awakened blacks to a new sense of their relative deprivation. That, too, aroused black anger. And now something could be done about it. The growing black middle and working classes put their money and bodies on the line. In addition, because the consumer economy depended on consumer purchasing, black demands had to be taken seriously. By 1970, black buying power topped $25 billion, a large enough sum to make the threat of boycotts an effective weapon for social change. Afro-American economic advances also made blacks less patient in demanding alterations in their social status. They desired all the decencies and dignity they believed their full paycheck promised. Lastly, nationwide prosperity contributed to more blacks entering college, which stimulated higher expectations and a heightened confidence that American society need not be static.

Most importantly, changes in the economy radically affected black migration. Cotton mechanization pushed blacks off the farms, and the lure of jobs pulled them to the cities. In 1930, three-quarters of the Afro-Americans lived in or near the rural black belt. By 1973, over half the blacks lived outside the South, and nationally, nearly 80 percent resided in urban areas. Indeed, in the two decades prior to 1970, the black population in metropolitan areas rose by more than seven million—a number greater than the total immigration by any single nationality group in American history. Such a mass migration, in conjunction with prosperity, fundamentally altered the whole configuration of the race problem. First, the issue of race became national in scope. No longer did it affect only one region, and no longer could it be left in the hands of Southern whites. Second, it modified the objective conditions of life for blacks and changed their perception of what was right and how to get it. For the first time in American history the great mass of blacks were freed from the confines of a rigid caste structure. Now subject to new formative experiences, blacks developed new norms and beliefs. In the relative anonymity and freedom of the North and the big city, aggression could be turned against one's oppressor rather than against one's self; more educational and employment opportunities could be secured; and political power could be mobilized. Similarly, as expectations of racial equality increased with the size of black migration from the rural South, so the religious faith that had for so long sustained Afro-Americans working on plantations declined. The promise of a better world in the next one could not suffice. The urban black would not wait for his rewards until the afterlife.

Because blacks could vote in the North, they stopped believing they would have to wait. Enfranchisement promised all in this life that religion did in the next. The heavenly city, to put it mildly, was not achieved; but vital legislative and legal accomplishments did flow from the growing black vote. Without the presence of black political power in the North, the demonstrations in the South would not have led to the civil rights laws and presidential actions necessary to realize the objectives of those protesting against Jim Crow in Montgomery, Greensboro, Birmingham, Jackson, and Selma. Although the claim of black publicists that the concentration of Northern black votes in the industrial cities made the Afro-American electorate a "balance of power" in national politics was never wholly accepted by either major party, the desire of every president from Franklin Roosevelt to Lyndon Johnson to win and hold the black vote became a factor in determining public policy. And as the Democratic party became less dependent upon Southern electoral votes, and less able to garner them, it had to champion civil rights more in order to win the populous states of the North and Midwest where blacks were increasingly becoming an indispensable component of the liberal coalition.

The prominence of the United States as a world power further pushed politicians into making race relations a matter of national concern. During World War II millions of Americans became aware for the first time of the danger of racism to national security. The costs of racism went even higher during the Cold War. The Soviet Union continuously undercut American appeals to the nations of Africa and Asia by publicizing American ill-treatment of blacks. As the competition between the United

States and international Communism intensified, foreign-policy makers came to recognize racism as the American's own worst enemy. President Harry Truman justified his asking Congress for civil rights legislation squarely on the world-wide implications of American race relations. Rarely in the next twenty years did a plea for civil rights before the Supreme Court, on the floor of Congress, and emanating from the White House, fail to emphasize that point. In short, fear forced the nation to hasten the redefining of the black status. The more involved in world affairs the United States became, the more imperative grew the task of setting its racial affairs in order.

The rapid growth of nationalistic independence movements among the world's colored peoples had special significance for Afro-Americans. In 1960 alone, sixteen African nations emerged from under white colonial rule. Each proclamation of independence in part shamed blacks in the United States to intensify their struggle for equality and justice, and in part caused a surge of racial pride in Afro-Americans, an affirmation of blackness. The experience of African independence proved the feasibility of change and the vulnerability of white supremacy, while at the same time aiding Afro-Americans to see themselves as members of a world majority rather than as just a hopelessly outnumbered American minority.

The decline in intellectual respectability of ideas used to justify segregation and discrimination similarly provided Afro-Americans with new weapons and shields. The excesses of Nazism and the decline of Western imperialism combined with internal developments in the academic disciplines of anthropology, biology, history, psychology, and sociology to discredit notions of inherent racial differences or predispositions. First in the 1930s, then with accelerating rapidity during World War II and every year thereafter, books and essays attacking racial injustice and inequality rolled off the presses. As early as 1944, Gunnar Myrdal in his monumental *An American Dilemma* termed the pronounced change in scholarship about race "the most important of all social trends in the field of interracial relations." This conclusion overstated the power of the word, but undoubtedly the mountain of new data, theory, and exposition at least helped to erode the pseudo-scientific rationalizations once popularly accepted as the basis for white supremacy.

In such an atmosphere, young blacks could mature without "the mark of oppression." Blacks could safely abandon the "nigger" role. To the extent that textbooks, sermons, declarations by governmental officials, advertising, and movies and TV affirmed the need to transform relationships between the races and to support black demands for full citizenship, blacks could confidently and openly rebel against the inequities they viewed as the sources of their oppression. They could publicly express the rage their parents had been forced to internalize; they could battle for what they deemed their birthright rather than wage war against themselves. Thus, in conjunction with the migration to cities, these new cultural processes helped to produce the "New Negro" hailed by essayists ever since the Montgomery bus boycott in 1956 inaugurated a more aggressive stage in the Afro-American's quest for equality.

In sum, changes in the American economy after 1940 set in motion a host of developments which made possible a transformation in race relations. The increasing income and number of jobs available to blacks and whites, and black migration and social mobility, coalesced with converging trends in politics, foreign affairs, and the mass media to endow those intent on improving race relations with both the resources and consciousness necessary to challenge the status quo. Objective conditions that had little to do with race in a primary sense thus created a context in which organizations and leaders could press successfully for racial changes. This is not to suggest that individuals do not matter in history or that the civil rights movement did not make an indispensable contribution to progress in race relations. It is, however, to emphasize the preconditions for such an endeavor to prevail. Desire and will are not enough. Significant and long-lasting alterations in society flow neither from the barrel of a gun nor from individual conversions. Mass marches, demonstrations, and rhetoric alone cannot modify entrenched behavior and values. Fundamental social change is accomplished only when individuals seize the moment to mobilize the latent power inherent in an institutional structure in flux.

Beginning in the 1930s, blacks, no longer facing a monolithic white power structure solidly arrayed against them, demanded with numbers and a unity that had never existed before the total elimination of racial inequality in American life. For three decades, the tactics and goals of the movement steadily grew more militant as the organization, protests, and power of blacks jumped exponentially. Each small triumph held out the promise of a greater one, heightening expectations and causing blacks to become ever more anxious about the pace of progress.

The first stage centered on securing the enforcement of the Fourteenth and Fifteenth Amendments. Supported mainly by white liberals and upper-middle-class blacks, the civil rights movement in the 1930s and 1940s relied on publicity, agitation, litigation in the courts, and lobbying in the halls of political power to gain the full inclusion of blacks in American life. Advances came in the legal and economic status of blacks, and in the minor social, political, and cultural concessions afforded Afro-Americans in the North, but the all-oppressive system of Jim Crow in the South remained virtually intact.

First in the court system, then in executive actions, and finally in Congress, this unceasing and mounting pressure from the civil rights movement prodded the government consistently in the direction of *real* racial equality. In the 1930s, the black movement failed to secure its two major legislative goals—anti-poll tax and anti-lynching laws—but it did manage to get Franklin D. Roosevelt and other members of his official family to speak on behalf of racial justice, to increase the numbers of blacks in government, to establish a Civil Rights Section in the Justice Department, and to ensure blacks a share of the relief and recovery assistance.

The gains during the New Deal, however, functioned primarily as a prelude to the take-off of the civil rights movement during World War II. The ideological character of the war and the government's need for the loyalty and manpower of all Americans stimulated blacks to expect a better deal from the government; this led to a militancy never before seen in black communities. Membership in the NAACP multiplied nearly ten times; the Congress of Racial Equality, organized in 1942, experimented with various forms of nonviolent direct action confrontations to challenge segregation; and A. Philip Randolph attempted to build his March-on-Washington Committee into an all-black mass protest movement. In 1941, his threat of a march on Washington, combined with the growth of the black vote and the exigencies of a foreign threat to American society, forced Roosevelt to issue Executive Order 8802 (the first such order dealing with race since Reconstruction), establishing the first President's Committee on Fair Employment Practices (FEPC). And, with increasing firmness, liberal politicians pressed for civil rights legislation and emphasized that the practices of white supremacy brought into disrepute America's stated war aims. Minimal gains to be sure, but the expectations they aroused set the stage for the greater advances in the postwar period. By 1945, Afro-Americans had benefited enough from the expansion in jobs and income, service in the armed forces and the massive migration to Northern cities to know better what they now wanted; and they had developed enough political influence, white alliances, and organizational skills to know how to go about getting their civil rights.

Equally vital, the Supreme Court began to dismantle the separate-but-equal doctrine in 1938. That year, the high court ruled that Missouri could not exclude a Negro from its state university law school when its only alternative was a scholarship to an out-of-state institution. Other Supreme Court decisions prior to World War II whittled away at discrimination in interstate travel, in employment, in judicial and police practices, and in the exclusion of blacks from jury service. During the war, the Court outlawed the white primary, holding that the nominating process of a political party constituted "state action." In other decisions handed down during the Truman presidency, the Supreme Court moved vigorously against all forms of segregation in interstate commerce, decided that states and the federal government cannot enforce restrictive racial covenants on housing, and so emphasized the importance of "intangible factors" in quality education that the demise of legally segregated schooling for students at all levels became a near certainty.

Meanwhile, the Truman administration emerged as an ally of the cause of civil rights. Responding to the growth of the black vote, the need to blunt the Soviet Union's exploitation of the race issue, and the firmly organized campaign for the advancement of blacks, Harry Truman acted where Roosevelt had feared to. In late 1946, the President appointed a Committee on Civil Rights to recommend specific measures to safeguard the civil rights of minorities. This was the first such committee in American history, and its 1947 report, *To Secure These Rights,* eloquently pointed out all the inequities of life in Jim Crow America and spelled out the moral, economic, and international reasons for government action. It called for the end of segregation and discrimination in public education, employment, housing, the armed forces, public accommodations, and interstate transportation. Other commissions appointed by Truman stressed the need for racial equality in the armed services and the field of education. Early in 1948, Truman sent the first presidential message on civil rights to Congress. Congress failed to pass any of the measures he proposed, but Truman later issued executive orders ending segregation in the military and barring discrimination in federal employment and in work done under government contract. In addition, his Justice Department prepared *amicus curiae* briefs to gain favorable court decisions in civil rights cases, and Truman's rhetoric in behalf of racial justice helped legitimize goals of the civil rights movement. However small the meaningful accomplishment remained, the identification of the Supreme Court and the Presidency with the cause of racial equality further aroused the expectations of blacks that they would soon share in the American Dream.

No single event did more to quicken black hopes than the coup de grâce to segregated education delivered by a unanimous Supreme Court on May 17, 1954. The *Brown* ruling that separate educational facilities "are inherently unequal" struck at the very heart of white supremacy in the South. A year later, the Court called for compliance "with all deliberate speed," mandating the lower federal courts to require from local school boards "a prompt and reasonable start toward full compliance." The end of legally mandated segregation in education started a chain reaction which led the Supreme Court even further down the road toward the total elimination of all racial distinctions in the law. For all practical purposes, the legal quest for equality had succeeded: the emphasis on legalism had accomplished its goals. Constitutionally, blacks had become first-class citizens.

But in the decade after the *Brown* decision, the promise of change far outran the reality of it. While individual blacks of talent desegregated most professions, the recessions of the Fifties caused black unemployment to soar and the gap between black and white family income to widen. And despite the rulings of the Supreme Court and the noble gestures and speeches of politicians, massive resistance to desegregation throughout the South proved the rule. This was the context for the second stage of the civil rights movement. When the nation's attempt to forestall integration and racial equality collided with both the Afro-Americans' leaping expectations and their dissatisfaction with the speed of change, blacks took to the streets in a wave of non-violent, direct-action protests against every aspect of racism still humiliating them.

A Leader for His Time: Martin Luther King, Jr.

DAVID J. GARROW

Thursday had been busy and tiring for Mrs. Raymond A. Parks. Her job as a tailor's assistant at the Montgomery Fair department store had left her neck and shoulder particularly sore, and when she left work at 5:30 P.M. that December 1, 1955, she went across the street to a drugstore in search of a heating pad. Mrs. Parks didn't find one, but she purchased a few other articles before recrossing the street to her usual bus stop on Court Square. The buses were especially crowded this cold, dark evening, and when she boarded one for her Cleveland Avenue route, only one row of seats—the row immediately behind the first ten seats that always were reserved for whites only—had any vacancies. She took an aisle seat, with a black man on her right next to the window, and two black women in the parallel seat across the way.

As more passengers boarded at each of the two next stops, the blacks moved to the rear, where they stood, and the whites occupied their exclusive seats at the front of the bus. At the third stop, more passengers got on, and one, a white male, was left standing after the final front seat was taken. The bus driver, J. F. Blake, looked back and called out to Mrs. Parks and her three colleagues, "All right you folks, I want those two seats." Montgomery's customary practice of racial preference demanded that all four blacks would have to stand in order to allow one white man to sit, since no black was allowed to sit parallel with a white. No one moved at first. Blake spoke out again: "You all better make it light on yourselves and let me have those seats." At that, the two women across from Mrs. Parks rose and moved to the rear; the man beside her rose also, and she moved her legs to allow him out into the aisle. She remained silent, but shifted to the window side of the seat.

David J. Garrow, *Bearing the Cross: Martin Luther King, Jr., and the Southern Christian Leadership Conference* (New York, Vintage, 1988), pp. 11–24, 32, 54–58, 71. Copyright © 1986 by David J. Garrow. Reprinted by permission of HarperCollins Publishers, Inc., and William Morrow.

Blake could see that Mrs. Parks had not arisen. "Look, woman, I told you I wanted the seat. Are you going to stand up?" At that, Rosa Lee McCauley Parks uttered her first word to him: "No." Blake responded, "If you don't stand up, I'm going to have you arrested." Mrs. Parks told him to go right ahead, that she was not going to move. Blake said nothing more, but got off the bus and went to a phone. No one spoke to Mrs. Parks, and some passengers began leaving the bus, not wanting to be inconvenienced by the incident. . . .

Word of Mrs. Parks's arrest began to spread even before that phone call. One passenger on the bus told a friend of Mrs. Parks's about the event, and that friend, Mrs. Bertha Butler, immediately called the home of longtime black activist E. D. Nixon, a past president of Montgomery's National Association for the Advancement of Colored People (NAACP) chapter and the most outspoken figure in the black community. Nixon was not at home, but his wife, Arlet, was, and she phoned his small downtown office. Nixon was out at the moment, but when he returned a few moments later, he saw the message to call home. "What's up?" he asked his wife. She told him of Mrs. Parks's arrest, but couldn't tell him what the charge was. Nixon hung up and immediately called the police station.

The desk officer rudely told Nixon that the charges against Mrs. Parks were none of his business. Determined to pursue the matter, but knowing that Montgomery's principal black lawyer, Fred Gray, was out of town, Nixon called the home of a white lawyer, Clifford Durr, one of the city's few racial liberals. . . .

Mrs. Parks, Mr. Nixon, and the Durrs all had known each other for a number of years. Mrs. Parks, forty-two years old at the time of her arrest, had been an active member and occasional officer of Montgomery's NAACP chapter since 1943, and had worked with Nixon on a number of voter registration efforts. Nixon, a Pullman porter whose job regularly took him to Chicago and other northern cities, had been a stalwart member of A. Philip Randolph's Brotherhood of Sleeping Car Porters, as well as a local activist, since the 1920s. The Durrs, Alabama natives who had returned to the state several years earlier following Clifford's service on the Federal Communications Commission, had become friendly with Nixon through his political activism. . . .

Over the years, the Durrs had heard distressing stories of how Montgomery bus drivers regularly insulted black passengers. Mrs. Parks once told them about how she had been physically thrown off a bus some ten years earlier when, after paying her fare at the front of the bus, she had refused to get off and reenter by the back door—a custom often inflicted on black riders. . . .

On their way to the jail Nixon and the Durrs discussed the possibility of Mrs. Parks being a test case. . . .

Throughout the early 1950s the Women's Political Council, sometimes in conjunction with Nixon or Nixon's chief rival for active leadership in the black community, businessman and former Alabama State football coach Rufus Lewis, who headed the Citizens Steering Committee, repeatedly complained to Montgomery's three popularly elected city commissioners about how the municipally chartered Montgomery City Lines mistreated its black customers. The commissioners politely, but consistently, brushed aside the WPC's entreaties concerning drivers' behavior and how blacks had to stand while whites-only seats remained vacant. In early 1954 Mrs. [Jo Ann] Robinson suggested to the commissioners "a city law that would make it possible for Negroes to sit from back toward front, and whites from front toward back until all seats were taken," so that no one would have to stand over a vacant seat, but again the officials were unresponsive.

Then, on May 17, 1954, the U.S. Supreme Court handed down its widely heralded school desegregation decision in *Brown* v. *Board of Education of Topeka,* which explicitly held that the segregationist doctrine of "separate but equal" was unconstitutional. Her spirits lifted, Mrs. Robinson four days later sent a firm declaration to Montgomery Mayor W. A. Gayle. . . . Other Alabama cities, such as Mobile, were using the front-to-back and back-to-front seating policy without any problems, Mrs. Robinson reminded Gayle. Why could not Montgomery do the same? "Please consider this plea," she wrote him, "and if possible, act favorably upon it, for even now plans are being made to ride less, or not at all, on our buses. We do not want this."

Robinson's hints about a boycott were not supported by any unified sentiment in the black community. One mid-1954 meeting of community leaders had found a majority opposed to any boycott at that time. The stalemate continued into early 1955 as Nixon and the WPC privately discussed the possibility of mounting a legal challenge to Montgomery's bus seating practices. Then, on March 2, 1955, an incident occurred that galvanized the long-smoldering black sentiments. A fifteen-year-old high school student, Claudette Colvin, refused a driver's demand that she give up her bus seat, well toward the rear of the vehicle, to allow newly boarding whites to sit down. Policemen dragged Colvin from the bus, and word spread quickly. Mrs. Robinson and Nixon thought they might have an ideal legal test case. Colvin had been active in the NAACP Youth Council, and the group's advisor, Mrs. Rosa Parks, along with her friend Virginia Durr, began soliciting contributions toward the legal fees. Almost immediately, however, problems developed. First, Colvin's resistance to the arresting officers had resulted in her being charged with assault and battery as well as violating city and state segregation statutes. Second, both Robinson and Nixon learned in independent interviews with Colvin and her family that the young unmarried woman was several months pregnant. Both leaders concluded that Colvin would be neither an ideal candidate for symbolizing the abuse heaped upon black passengers nor a good litigant for a test suit certain to generate great pressures and publicity. . . .

When Mrs. Robinson learned of the [Rosa Parks's] arrest late that Thursday night from Fred Gray, she immediately phoned Nixon, who had just gotten home from Mrs. Parks's house. Together they agreed that this was just what they had been waiting for. "We had planned the protest long before Mrs. Parks was arrested," Mrs. Robinson emphasized years later. "There had been so many things that happened, that the black women had been embarrassed over, and they were ready to explode." Also, "Mrs. Parks had the caliber of character we needed to get the city to rally behind us." Robinson told Nixon that she and her WPC colleagues would begin producing boycott leaflets immediately, and the two agreed that the flyers would call on all black people to stay off the buses on Monday, the day of Mrs. Parks's trial. They also agreed that the black community leadership should assemble on Friday. Nixon would organize that meeting, while Robinson would see to the leafletting.

Robinson alerted several of her WPC colleagues, then sat down and drafted the leaflet. She called a friend who had access to Alabama State's mimeograph room, and they rendezvoused at the college and began running off thousands of copies. They worked all night, and when morning came, WPC members, helped by some of Robinson's students, began distributing the announcements to every black neighborhood in Montgomery. . . . The long-discussed boycott was about to get under way.

After a fitful night, E. D. Nixon arose early Friday morning to begin assembling the black leadership. Nixon knew that a mass boycott of Montgomery's buses could not be accomplished simply by the WPC and the few regular activists such as himself. Although the women had been the driving force behind all of the black community efforts of the last few years, a mass protest would succeed only if they could obtain the enthusiastic support of Montgomery's black ministers. With that in mind, Nixon made his first call to one of the youngest and most outspoken of the city's pastors, Ralph D. Abernathy.

Abernathy, the secretary of the Baptist Ministers' Alliance, told Nixon he would support the effort. . . . Abernathy also advised Nixon to phone one of Abernathy's best friends, the Reverend M. L. King, Jr., pastor of Dexter Avenue Baptist Church, and ask if the meeting could be held there. In the meantime, Abernathy would begin contacting other ministers.

Nixon quickly secured [President of the Baptist Ministers' Alliance Reverend H. H.] Hubbard's approval. He then called King. Nixon related the events of the previous evening, told King of the emerging consensus to begin a boycott on Monday, and asked if the young pastor would join in supporting the effort. King hesitated. He had a newborn daughter, less than one month old, and heavy responsibilities at his church. Only a few weeks earlier he had declined to be considered for president of the local NAACP chapter because of these other demands on his time. He wasn't sure he could handle any additional responsibilities. "Brother Nixon," he said, "let me think about it awhile, and call me back." Nixon told King that he and Abernathy already were telling people to meet at King's church that evening. "That's all right," King replied. "I just want to think about it and then you call me back." Nixon agreed.

King hadn't had long to mull over Nixon's request before Abernathy called. Abernathy had heard from Nixon about his friend's hesitation, and wanted to stress to King the opportunity that the Parks arrest represented. King acknowledged that Abernathy was correct; he had no quarrel with the boycott plan. So long as he did not have to do the organizational work, he would be happy to support the effort and host the evening meeting at Dexter church. . . .

Early Friday evening, as Mrs. Robinson's leaflets circulated throughout Montgomery, some seventy black leaders assembled in the basement meeting room of Dexter Avenue Baptist Church. After a brief prayer by Hubbard, [Reverend L. Roy] Bennett took the floor and told the influential group that he did not see much need for any extended discussion because he, Bennett, knew full well how to organize a boycott.

Bennett lectured on. As the minutes passed, more and more people became frustrated and angry. Despite repeated requests, Bennett refused to yield the floor. When Bennett's monologue reached the half-hour mark, some people began walking out. Among those to leave was Alabama State Professor James E. Pierce, one of Nixon's closest allies. Earlier that day Pierce had tried to dissuade his friend from the boycott plan on the grounds that many black citizens might not support it. This session had only strengthened Pierce's doubts about the effort, and his fear that many individual leaders, like Bennett, would be unable to put aside their rivalries and desires for self-advancement long enough to agree on a unified community effort.

Heading out the door, Pierce paused and whispered to King, "This is going to fizzle out. I'm going." King was unhappy too, and told Pierce, "I would like to go too, but it's in my church."

Finally, Ralph Abernathy stood up and took over the meeting from Bennett, insisting that all of the twenty or so people who remained be given an opportunity to speak. Jo Ann Robinson seconded Abernathy's demand, and proposed that all present endorse the Monday boycott. A mass meeting would be called for Monday night at the large Holt Street Baptist Church to determine whether community sentiment would support extending the boycott beyond Monday. A new version of Robinson's leaflet would be prepared, adding the news about the mass meeting. Some ministers, hesitant about even a one-day boycott, went along so that some unity would emerge despite Bennett's performance. It was agreed that those who remained would meet again Monday afternoon, after Mrs. Parks's trial, to plan the mass meeting.

Abernathy and King stayed at Dexter church until almost midnight, mimeographing the new leaflets. Early Saturday the distribution began, with two hundred or more volunteers giving out the handbills in door-to-door visits. Meanwhile, a taxi committee headed by Rev. W. J. Powell was winning agreement from all the black cab firms to carry riders on Monday for only the standard bus fare of ten cents. Then, Saturday evening, King, Abernathy, and others visited nightclubs to spread further the news of the upcoming boycott. . . .

The first public word of the impending boycott appeared, however, in the Saturday afternoon edition of Montgomery's smaller paper, the *Alabama Journal.* It quoted the bus company's Bagley as saying he was "sorry that the colored people blame us for any state or city ordinance which we didn't have passed," and reported that he had discussed the news with company attorney Jack Crenshaw. Montgomery City Lines, Bagley stressed, felt it had no choice in the matter. "We have to obey all laws." . . .

Although happy with the public coverage, the black leaders discussed Bennett's disastrous performance and the need to move the protest out from under the mantle of his Interdenominational Ministerial Alliance. There were few options. The leadership of the Women's Political Council knew that any public revelation of their central role would cost many of them their jobs at publicly controlled Alabama State. No other existing organization, including the NAACP chapter, had sufficient breadth of membership to represent all those who already had taken a hand in organizing the boycott. A new organization, with freshly chosen leaders, would have to be formed.

Abernathy and King agreed that creating a new organization would be the best way to oust Bennett without openly insulting him. Abernathy thought that Nixon would be the obvious choice for president of the new group, but King had doubts, arguing that Rufus Lewis would be better suited for the job. Only one month earlier King had tried to persuade Abernathy to take the NAACP presidency, but he had said no. He was thinking of returning to graduate school. Abernathy knew that King also had declined the NAACP post.

In addition to King and Abernathy, . . . Rufus Lewis and one of his closest friends, P. E. Conley, spent the weekend discussing what they could do. They also wanted to be rid of Bennett, and Lewis felt that the unschooled Nixon would be equally unacceptable. An ideal candidate who should be acceptable to all the different groups, Lewis told Conley, was his own pastor, Reverend King. True, Lewis conceded, the twenty-six-year-old King did look "more like a boy than a man," but he was extremely well educated and an articulate speaker. Those qualities would appeal strongly to the wealthier, professional segment of the black community, people who otherwise might be ambivalent about conditions on public buses that they rarely patronized. Likewise, the fact that King was a minister, and a Baptist minister, should help to draw the more conservative clergy into what had begun as a secularly led effort. . . . King, he told Conley, would be an ideal choice; both men agreed to put him forward at the Monday meeting.

Early Monday morning the attention of the black leadership shifted to the question of how successful the boycott would be. Nixon, Robinson, King, and others arose early to begin their own individual surveys of bus ridership. King watched several nearly empty buses pass his South Jackson Street home and then set out by car to observe others. In one hour's worth of driving, King spied only *eight* black riders. Hundreds of others could be seen headed toward their jobs on foot, or gathering for rides with friends and acquaintances. The black leaders were pleased; the first hours of the boycott represented a grand success. . . .

That afternoon, several dozen black leaders assembled at Reverend Bennett's Mt. Zion AME Church. Bennett immediately took charge. "We are not going to have any talking. I am not going to let anybody talk; we came here to work and to outline our program." As Ralph Abernathy recalled the scene, "I tried to get the floor, but he said, 'Well, Ab, although you're my good friend, I'm not going to even let you talk—so sit down.'" At that point, an objection was raised that some "stool pigeons" representing city officials might be present, and that a smaller group should meet in private to map their course of action. That idea was adopted, and a committee of eighteen persons was chosen to meet in the pastor's study. . . .

The group also accepted Abernathy's recommendation of "Montgomery Improvement Association" as a name for the new organization. Then Bennett called for nominations for officers, beginning with president. Without a moment's pause, Rufus Lewis's voice rang out. "Mr. Chairman, I would like to nominate Reverend M. L. King for president." P. E. Conley, Lewis's friend, immediately seconded it. No other candidates were put forward, and King was asked if he would accept the position. Abernathy, seated beside him, fully expected King to decline. Instead, after a pause, King told his colleagues, "Well, if you think I can render some service, I will," and accepted the presidency. . . .

The newly chosen president returned home less than an hour before the meeting at which he would deliver the major speech. . . .

As 7:00 P.M. approached, the area around Holt Street Baptist Church became increasingly crowded with cars and people. Thousands of Montgomery's black citizens were intent upon attending the mass meeting. The building itself was full to capacity long before seven, but Reverend Wilson quickly arranged for loudspeakers to be set up outside. King and Abernathy had to make their way slowly through the growing crowd, which was solemn and dignified almost to the point of complete silence. Though perhaps unwieldy, the number of people was gratifying to the leaders, and answered the question that had been left open that afternoon. As King put it, "my doubts concerning the continued success of our venture" were dispelled by the mass turnout. "The question of calling off the protest was now academic."

When the program got under way, one thousand people were inside the church and four thousand were gathered outside for at least a block in every direction. Contrary to E. D. Nixon's desire, no speakers were introduced by name as one pastor led a prayer and a second read a selection of Scripture. Then King stepped forward to tell the people why and how they must protest the arrest and conviction of Mrs. Parks and the continuing indignities that hundreds of them regularly suffered on Montgomery's buses. King gave a lengthy testimonial to Mrs. Parks's character, and reminded his listeners that she, and they, suffered these insults only on account of their race. "First and foremost we are American citizens," he continued. "We are not here advocating violence. We have overcome that. . . . The only weapon that we have . . . is the weapon of protest," and "the great glory of American democracy is the right to protest for right." He referred twice to the commands of the U.S. Constitution, and once to the Supreme Court's prior vindication of blacks' demands for truly equal rights. But protest and legal demands were only part of what was required, King went on. "We must keep God in the forefront. Let us be Christian in all of our action.". . . Rising to their feet, the people applauded heartily.

King's MIA colleague and subsequent biographer, L. D. Reddick, later observed that "during this early period, King's philosophy of nonviolent resistance was only gradually taking form. When he made his debut as president of the MIA at the initial mass meeting, December 5, he did not mention Gandhi or anything directly relating to the Mahatma's theory or practice of social change. His speech was just one more appeal to principles of Christianity and democracy, to fair play and compassion for those in the opposite camp." By Christmas, however, an emerging emphasis on nonviolence was clear. The statement of the MIA position, set forth in the mimeographed brochure, observed that "this is a movement of passive resistance, depending on moral and spiritual forces. We, the oppressed, have no hate in our hearts for the oppressors, but we are, nevertheless, determined to resist until the cause of justice triumphs." Though *"passive* resistance" was a misnomer, the conscious desire to combine Gandhian precepts with Christian principles was growing in both King and the MIA. . . .

Within the private councils of the MIA, there was growing appreciation both for King's ability as the boycott's principal public spokesman and for his skillful leadership of the executive board. "King knew how to get along with all types and classes of people. He also persuaded them to get along with each other," MIA historian Lawrence Reddick later recalled. King's "democratic, patient and optimistic" approach to things impressed everyone. . . .

. . . On Monday, [January 23, 1956] Mayor Gayle announced that the city was adopting a new, tougher stance. Calling the MIA "a group of Negro radicals who have split asunder the fine relationships" between Montgomery's blacks and whites, Gayle declared that "we have pussyfooted around on this boycott long enough." No further negotiations would take place while the protest remained in force. "Until they are ready to end it, there will be no more discussions." White people, Gayle emphasized, must realize that far more was at stake in the MIA's demands than merely the question of seating practices. "What they are after is the destruction of our social fabric."

The meaning of the new city policy quickly became clear. Sellers ordered policemen to disperse groups of blacks waiting for car pool rides on street corners, and Gayle asked white housewives to stop giving rides to their black domestic workers. Giving a lift to any black person would merely aid "the Negro radicals who lead the boycott." City police also began tailing drivers from the MIA car pool, issuing tickets for trivial or nonexistent traffic violations. The official harassment made some protest supporters pause. "The voluntary pick-up system began to weaken," one MIA leader reported, and "for a moment the protest movement seemed to be wavering."

One of the first motorists to fall victim to this new policy of traffic enforcement was King himself. On Thursday, January 26, King left Dexter church in midafternoon, accompanied by one of his best friends, Robert Williams, and his church secretary, Mrs. Lillie Thomas. Before heading home, King stopped at the MIA's central transportation point to give three other persons a lift. When King pulled out, two motorcycle officers began tailing him. After several blocks, King stopped to drop off the riders. The officers pulled up beside him and told him he was under arrest. . . .

King was placed in a filthy group cell with various black criminals. Several minutes later he was taken out and fingerprinted. It was the first time King had been locked in a jail, and the first time he had been fingerprinted. . . .

Meanwhile, word of King's arrest had spread rapidly through the black community. Even before Abernathy returned, several dozen others—members of Dexter, MIA colleagues, and friends—began arriving at the jail. The growing crowd worried the white jailers, and while the fingerprinting ink was still being wiped from King's hands, the chief jailer told him he was free to leave upon his own signature. His trial would be Saturday morning. In hardly a moment's time, King was escorted out and driven back to town.

The emotional trauma of the arrest heightened the growing personal tensions King was feeling. He had not wanted to be *the* focal point of the protest in the first place, and he had erroneously assumed that a negotiated settlement would be obtained in just a few weeks time. With no end in sight, and more attention coming his way, King wondered whether he was up to the rigors of the job. He stressed to everyone that he as an individual was not crucial to the protest, that if something happened to him, or should he step aside, the movement would go on. "If M. L. King had never been born this movement would have taken place," the young minister told one mass meeting. "I just happened to be here. You know there comes a time when time itself is ready for change. That time has come in Montgomery, and I had nothing to do with it."

. . . That night, for the first time in his life, King felt . . . an experience [with God] as he sought to escape the pressures the MIA presidency had placed upon him.

He thought more about how trouble-free his life had been until the movement began. . . .

And then we started our struggle together. Things were going well for the first few days but then, about ten or fifteen days later, after the white people in Montgomery knew that we meant business, they started doing some nasty things. They started making nasty telephone calls, and it came to the point that some days more than forty telephone calls would come in, threatening my life, the life of my family, the life of my child. I took it for a while, in a strong manner.

But that night, unable to be at peace with himself, King feared he could take it no longer. It was the most important night of his life, the one he always would think back to in future years when the pressures again seemed to be too great.

"It was around midnight," he said, thinking back on it. "You can have some strange experiences at midnight." The threatening caller had rattled him deeply. "Nigger, we are tired of you and your mess now. And if you aren't out of this town in three days, we're going to blow your brains out, and blow up your house."

> I sat there and thought about a beautiful little daughter who had just been born. . . . She was the darling of my life. I'd come in night after night and see that little gentle smile. And I sat at that table thinking about that little girl and thinking about the fact that she could be taken away from me any minute. . . .
>
> And I discovered then that religion had to become real to me, and I had to know God for myself. And I bowed down over that cup of coffee. I never will forget it . . . I prayed a prayer, and I prayed out loud that night. I said, "Lord, I'm down here trying to do what's right. I think I'm right. I think the cause that we represent is right. But Lord, I must confess that I'm weak now, I'm faltering. I'm losing my courage. And I can't let the people see me like this because if they see me weak and losing my courage, they will begin to get weak."

Then it happened:

> And it seemed at that moment that I could hear an inner voice saying to me, "Martin Luther, stand up for righteousness. Stand up for justice. Stand up for truth. And lo I will be with you, even until the end of the world." . . . I heard the voice of Jesus saying still to fight on. He promised never to leave me, never to leave me alone. No never alone. No never alone. He promised never to leave me, never to leave me alone.

That experience gave King a new strength and courage. "Almost at once my fears began to go. My uncertainty disappeared." He went back to bed no longer worried about the threats of bombings. . . .

King's sense of history and the broader meaning of the protest was striking. "Whether we want to be or not, we are caught in a great moment of history," King told one mass meeting. "It is bigger than Montgomery. . . . The vast majority of the people of the world are colored. . . . Up until four or five years ago" most of them "were exploited by the empires of the west. . . . Today many are free. . . . And the rest are on the road. . . . We are part of that great movement." The target was larger than just segregation. "We must oppose all exploitation. . . . We want no classes and castes. . . . We want to see everybody free."

F U R T H E R   R E A D I N G

Taylor Branch, *Parting the Waters* (1988) and *Pillar of Fire* (1998).

Clayborne Carson, *In Struggle: SNCC and the Black Awakening of the 1960s* (1981).

Vine Deloria, Jr., *Custer Died for Your Sins: An Indian Manifesto* (1969).

John D'Emilio, *Sexual Politics, Sexual Communities: The Making of a Homosexual Minority in the United States, 1940–1970* (1983).

David Gutiérrez, *Walls and Mirrors: Mexican Americans, Mexican Immigrants, and the Politics of Ethnicity* (1995).

Alex Haley, comp., *The Autobiography of Malcolm X* (1965).

Manning Marable, *Race, Reform, and Rebellion: The Second Reconstruction in Black America* (1984).

Ruth Rosen, *The World Split Open: How the Modern Women's Movement Changed America* (2000).

C H A P T E R
13

The Sixties: Left, Right, and the Culture Wars

Like the psychedelic music and drugs that were popular during the decade, the history of the sixties can be a mind-altering experience. Colorful reform movements shift, reshape, and overlap as in a kaleidoscope. Consumer advocacy, environmental reform, organic foods, communal living, the sexual revolution, personal growth groups, feminism, civil rights, the antiwar crusade, and dozens of other issues clamored for attention (and some of them still do). In fact, it was precisely this bewildering hubbub that defined the sixties as a captivating and, for some, maddening period of time. Everything seemed open to question: politics, manners, sexual relations, and even the meaning of America.

Of course the sixties did not begin on New Year's Day 1960 and end on New Year's Eve 1969. As we have seen, the sources of unrest reached back into the 1950s for both liberals and conservatives. Liberals looked out on the political landscape and optimistically asked themselves, how can we enable the greatest nation on earth to live up to its full potential for social justice? They did not have to look far beyond the Mason-Dixon line to see one set of answers. John Kennedy, in fact, said explicitly in the campaign debates that led to his election, "I think we can do better." As president, he consistently emphasized the theme of citizen responsibility, exhorting Americans: "ask not what your country can do for you—ask what you can do for your country." Conservatives posed a different question to their constituencies: where did we go wrong? Brash new leaders like Barry Goldwater and Ronald Reagan repudiated moderate "Eisenhower Republicanism," seeing it as an unholy compromise with a set of disturbing trends unleashed by Roosevelt during the New Deal. They wanted "big government" out, "states' rights" in, and a return to so-called traditional values at all levels. As the decade wore on, activists on both the right and the left became more assertive in their rhetoric and more radical in their demands.

But many of the social forces at work in the period were beyond the control of any political group, liberal or conservative. The invention of the birth control pill at Stanford University in 1960, for example, fundamentally altered the behavior of millions of women and men, regardless of religion, politics, or economic privilege; the so-called Sexual Revolution had begun. And issues like civil rights were not something many politicians took up willingly—they pushed up from the grassroots.

Even prosperity, as we saw in the fifties, invited discontent. Suddenly millions of Americans became worried about their "potential." The Human Potential Movement of the 1960s, centered in California, asked Americans not what they could do for their country, but what they could do for themselves. Gestalt therapy, encounter groups, and Transactional Analysis—to name but a few of the best known therapeutic approaches—were so far outside the ken of official Washington that California was ridiculed as "la-la land."

The period continues to excite debate in part because we are still not entirely sure of its legacy. By the end of the sixties, the liberal administrations of John F. Kennedy and Lyndon Johnson had implemented a number of reforms, but lost the presidency for the Democratic Party. Four of the greatest reformers ended their lives in pools of blood: John Kennedy, Robert Kennedy, Martin Luther King, Jr., and Malcolm X. In the end, it was difficult to say who had won: the advocates of change or the defenders of tradition.

Q U E S T I O N S   T O   T H I N K   A B O U T

Did the sixties, on balance, create a more liberal or a more conservative America? If liberals or leftists defined the sixties, as conservatives sometimes say, why did it end so badly for them? Which changes initiated in the sixties are still with us today?

D O C U M E N T S

The documents in this chapter reflect a variety of views on the sixties. Document 1 is from John F. Kennedy's inaugural speech, given January 20, 1961. As journalist Bill Moyers recalls in Document 2, the effect of this speech and others like it was to galvanize idealistic Americans. Shortly after the inaugural, Moyers became deputy director of the Peace Corps, an organization started by Kennedy to send young American volunteers to the Third World. In Document 3, less than two months after Kennedy's assassination on November 22, 1963, in Dallas, Lyndon Baines Johnson declares a "war on poverty" in the name of the martyred president. Document 4 states the goals of the Young Americans for Freedom (YAF), a conservative youth group on what was then the right-wing fringe of the moderate Republican Party. Their generation provided support for Senator Barry Goldwater of Arizona and California governor Ronald Reagan, and helped to steer the party in a new direction. In Document 5, the Students for a Democratic Society proclaim goals opposite to those of YAF, foreshadowing the clash of ideals between left and right that characterized the era. In Document 6, Alabama governor George Wallace pledges "segregation forever." Wallace spoke for millions of Americans who staunchly opposed the Civil Rights Movement and any kind of "outside intervention" by the federal government in the South. Document 7 reveals what was sometimes called the generation gap. Parents and children often found themselves at odds during the sixties, when values were changing so rapidly. In this selection, a nineteen-year-old participant in "sit-ins" at Columbia University in 1968 recalls conversations with his father about long hair and the meaning of the student protest. The Columbia protest was sparked by the university's decision to convert an adjacent park used by Harlem residents into a new campus gymnasium, as well as by the university's participation in military research related to the Vietnam War. In Document 8, Vice President Spiro Agnew attacks student demonstrators as "impudent snobs" bent upon the destruction of the country. In Document 9, San Francisco folk singer Malvina Reynolds expresses the critique made by the sixties counterculture that the effect of mass society, including mass housing, had been to put people into "little boxes" and to make them "all look just the same." In the last reading, Document 10, California psychologist Carl Rogers describes the alternative: focusing inward to find the "real" you. Encounter groups probably reached more citizens than protest groups. Their wide popularity reflects the transition from President Kennedy's "we" generation to the "me" generation, as more and more Americans came to value "getting in touch with their feelings."

1. President John Kennedy Tells Americans to Ask "What You Can Do," 1961

We observe today not a victory of party but a celebration of freedom—symbolizing an end as well as a beginning—signifying renewal as well as change. For I have sworn before you and Almighty God the same solemn oath our forebears prescribed nearly a century and three-quarters ago.

The world is very different now. For man holds in his mortal hands the power to abolish all forms of human poverty and all forms of human life. And yet the same revolutionary beliefs for which our forebears fought are still at issue around the globe—the belief that the rights of man come not from the generosity of the state but from the hand of God.

We dare not forget today that we are the heirs of that first revolution. Let the word go forth from this time and place, to friend and foe alike, that the torch has been passed to a new generation of Americans—born in this century, tempered by war, disciplined by a hard and bitter peace, proud of our ancient heritage—and unwilling to witness or permit the slow undoing of those human rights to which this nation has always been committed, and to which we are committed today at home and around the world.

Let every nation know, whether it wishes us well or ill, that we shall pay any price, bear any burden, meet any hardship, support any friend, oppose any foe to assure the survival and the success of liberty.

This much we pledge—and more. . . .

In your hands, my fellow citizens, more than mine, will rest the final success or failure of our course. Since this country was founded, each generation of Americans has been summoned to give testimony to its national loyalty. The graves of young Americans who answered the call to service surround the globe.

Now the trumpet summons us again—not as a call to bear arms, though arms we need,—not as a call to battle, though embattled we are—but a call to bear the burden of a long twilight struggle, year in and year out, "rejoicing in hope, patient in tribulation"—a struggle against the common enemies of man: tyranny, poverty, disease, and war itself.

Can we forge against these enemies a grand and global alliance, North and South, East and West, that can assure a more fruitful life for all mankind? Will you join in that historic effort?

Public Papers of the Presidents of the United States: John F. Kennedy, 1961 (Washington, D.C.: U.S. Government Printing Office, 1962), p. 1.

In the long history of the world, only a few generations have been granted the role of defending freedom in its hour of maximum danger. I do not shrink from this responsibility—I welcome it. I do not believe that any of us would exchange places with any other people or any other generation. The energy, the faith, the devotion which we bring to this endeavor will light our country and all who serve it—and the glow from that fire can truly light the world.

And so, my fellow Americans: ask not what your country can do for you—ask what you can do for your country.

My fellow citizens of the world: ask not what America will do for you, but what together we can do for the freedom of man.

Finally, whether you are citizens of America or citizens of the world, ask of us here the same high standards of strength and sacrifice which we ask of you. With a good conscience our only sure reward, with history the final judge of our deeds, let us go forth to lead the land we love, asking His blessing and His help, but knowing that here on earth God's work must truly be our own.

2. Bill Moyers Remembers Kennedy's Effect on His Generation (1961), 1988

Of the private man John Kennedy I knew little. I saw him rarely. Once, when the 1960 campaign was over and he was ending a post-election visit to the LBJ Ranch, he pulled me over into a corner to urge me to abandon my plans for graduate work at the University of Texas and to come to Washington as part of the New Frontier. I told him that I had already signed up to teach at a Baptist school in Texas while pursuing my doctorate. Anyway, I said, "You're going to have to call on the whole faculty at Harvard. You don't need a graduate of Southwestern Baptist Theological Seminary." In mock surprise he said, "Didn't you know that the first president of Harvard was a Baptist? You'll be right at home."

And so I was.

So I remember John Kennedy not so much for what he was or what he wasn't but for what he empowered in me. We all edit history to give some form to the puzzle of our lives, and I cherish the memory of him for awakening me to a different story for myself. He placed my life in a larger narrative than I could ever have written. One test of a leader is knowing, as John Stuart Mill put it, that "the worth of the state, in the long run, is the worth of the individuals composing it." Preserving civilization is the work not of some miracle-working, superhuman personality but of each one of us. The best leaders don't expect us just to pay our taxes and abdicate, they sign us up for civic duty and insist we sharpen our skills as citizens. . . .

Public figures either make us feel virtuous about retreating into the snuggeries of self or they challenge us to act beyond our obvious capacities. America is always up for grabs, can always go either way. The same culture that produced the Ku Klux Klan, Lee Harvey Oswald, and the Jonestown massacre also produced Martin Luther King, Archibald MacLeish, and the Marshall Plan.

Bill Moyers, *To Touch the World: The Peace Corps Experience* (Washington, D.C.: Peace Corps, 1995), pp. 152–153.

A desperate and alienated young man told me in 1970, after riots had torn his campus and town: "I'm just as good as I am bad. I think all of us are. But nobody's speaking to the good in me." In his public voice John Kennedy spoke to my generation of service and sharing; he called us to careers of discovery through lives open to others. . . .

. . . It was for us not a trumpet but a bell, sounding in countless individual hearts that one clear note that said: "You matter. You can signify. You can make a difference." Romantic? Yes, there was romance to it. But we were not then so callous toward romance.

3. President Lyndon B. Johnson Declares War on Poverty, 1964

Let this session of Congress be known as the session which did more for civil rights than the last hundred sessions combined; as the session which enacted the most far-reaching tax cut of our time; as the session which declared all-out war on human poverty and unemployment in these United States; as the session which finally recognized the health needs of all our older citizens; as the session which reformed our tangled transportation and transit policies; as the session which achieved the most effective, efficient foreign aid program ever; and as the session which helped to build more homes, more schools, more libraries, and more hospitals than any single session of Congress in the history of our Republic. . . .

This budget, and this year's legislative program, are designed to help each and every American citizen fulfill his basic hopes—his hopes for a fair chance to make good; his hopes for fair play from the law; his hopes for a full-time job on full-time pay, his hopes for a decent home for his family in a decent community; his hopes for a good school for his children with good teachers; and his hopes for security when faced with sickness or unemployment or old age.

Unfortunately, many Americans live on the outskirts of hope—some because of their poverty, and some because of their color, and all too many because of both. Our task is to help replace their despair with opportunity.

This administration today, here and now, declares unconditional war on poverty in America. I urge this Congress and all Americans to join with me in that effort. . . .

Our aim is not only to relieve the symptom of poverty, but to cure it and, above all, to prevent it. No single piece of legislation, however, is going to suffice.

We will launch a special effort in the chronically distressed areas of Appalachia.

We must expand our small but our successful area redevelopment program.

We must enact youth employment legislation to put jobless, aimless, hopeless youngsters to work on useful projects.

We must distribute more food to the needy through a broader food stamp program.

We must create a National Service Corps to help the economically handicapped of our own country as the Peace Corps now helps those abroad.

Public Papers of the Presidents of the United States: Lyndon B. Johnson, 1964 (Washington, D.C.: U.S. Government Printing Office, 1965), pp. 704–707.

We must modernize our unemployment insurance and establish a high-level commission on automation. If we have the brain power to invent these machines, we have the brain power to make certain that they are a boon and not a bane to humanity.

We must extend the coverage of our minimum wage laws to more than 2 million workers now lacking this basic protection of purchasing power.

We must, by including special school aid funds as part of our education program, improve the quality of teaching, training, and counseling in our hardest hit areas.

We must build more libraries in every area and more hospitals and nursing homes under the Hill-Burton Act, and train more nurses to staff them.

We must provide hospital insurance for our older citizens financed by every worker and his employer under Social Security, contributing no more than $1 a month during the employee's working career to protect him in his old age in a dignified manner without cost to the Treasury, against the devastating hardship of prolonged or repeated illness.

We must, as a part of a revised housing and urban renewal program, give more help to those displaced by slum clearance, provide more housing for our poor and our elderly, and seek as our ultimate goal in our free enterprise system a decent home for every American family.

We must help obtain more modern mass transit within our communities as well as low-cost transportation between them.

Above all, we must release $11 billion of tax reduction into the private spending stream to create new jobs and new markets in every area of this land.

4. Young Americans for Freedom Draft a Conservative Manifesto, 1960

In this time of moral and political crisis, it is the responsibility of the youth of America to affirm certain eternal truths.

We, as young conservatives, believe:

That foremost among the transcendent values is the individual's use of his God-given free will, whence derives his right to be free from the restrictions of arbitrary force;

That liberty is indivisible, and that political freedom cannot long exist without economic freedom;

That the purposes of government are to protect these freedoms through the preservation of internal order, the provision of national defense, and the administration of justice;

That when government ventures beyond these rightful functions, it accumulates power which tends to diminish order and liberty;

That the Constitution of the United States is the best arrangement yet devised for empowering government to fulfill its proper role, while restraining it from the concentration and abuse of power;

Buckley Papers, Box 12, Sterling Library, Yale University. Reprinted in John A. Andrew III, *The Other Side of the Sixties: Young Americans for Freedom and the Rise of Conservative Politics* (New Brunswick, N.J.: Rutgers University Press, 1997), pp. 221–222. Copyright © 1997 by John A. Andrew III. Reprinted by permission of Rutgers University Press.

That the genius of the Constitution—the division of powers—is summed up in the clause which reserves primacy to the several states, or to the people, in those spheres not specifically delegated to the Federal Government;

That the market economy, allocating resources by the free play of supply and demand, is the single economic system compatible with the requirements of personal freedom and constitutional government, and that it is at the same time the most productive supplier of human needs;

That when government interferes with the work of the market economy, it tends to reduce the moral and physical strength of the nation; that when it takes from one man to bestow on another, it diminishes the incentive of the first, the integrity of the second, and the moral autonomy of both;

That we will be free only so long as the national sovereignty of the United States is secure: that history shows periods of freedom are rare, and can exist only when free citizens concertedly defend their rights against all enemies;

That the forces of international Communism are, at present, the greatest single threat to these liberties;

That the United States should stress victory over, rather than coexistence with, this menace; and

That American foreign policy must be judged by this criterion: does it serve the just interests of the United States?

5. Students for a Democratic Society Advance a Reform Agenda, 1962

We are people of this generation, bred in at least modest comfort, housed now in universities, looking uncomfortably to the world we inherit.

When we were kids the United States was the wealthiest and strongest country in the world; the only one with the atom bomb, the least scarred by modern war, an initiator of the United Nations that we thought would distribute Western influence throughout the world. Freedom and equality for each individual, government of, by, and for the people—these American values we found good, principles by which we could live as men. Many of us began maturing in complacency.

As we grew, however, our comfort was penetrated by events too troubling to dismiss. First, the permeating and victimizing fact of human degradation, symbolized by the Southern struggle against racial bigotry, compelled most of us from silence to activism. Second, the enclosing fact of the Cold War, symbolized by the presence of the Bomb, brought awareness that we ourselves, and our friends, and millions of abstract "others" we knew more directly because of our common peril, might die at any time. We might deliberately ignore, or avoid, or fail to feel all other human problems, but not these two, for these were too immediate and crushing in their impact, too challenging in the demand that we as individuals take the responsibility for encounter and resolution.

While these and other problems either directly oppressed us or rankled our consciences and became our own subjective concerns, we began to see complicated and disturbing paradoxes in our surrounding America. The declaration "all men are

---

Excerpt from The Port Huron Statement, 1962. State Historical Society of Wisconsin.

created equal . . . " rang hollow before the facts of Negro life in the South and the big cities of the North. The proclaimed peaceful intentions of the United States contradicted its economic and military investments in the Cold War status quo.

We witnessed, and continue to witness, other paradoxes. With nuclear energy whole cities can easily be powered, yet the dominant nation-states seem more likely to unleash destruction greater than that incurred in all wars of human history. Although our own technology is destroying old and creating new forms of social organization, men still tolerate meaningless work and idleness. While two-thirds of mankind suffers undernourishment, our own upper classes revel amidst superfluous abundance. Although world population is expected to double in forty years, the nations still tolerate anarchy as a major principle of international conduct and uncontrolled exploitation governs the sapping of the earth's physical resources. Although mankind desperately needs revolutionary leadership, America rests in national stalemate, its goals ambiguous and tradition-bound instead of informed and clear, its democratic system apathetic and manipulated rather than "of, by, and for the people." . . .

Our work is guided by the sense that we may be the last generation in the experiment with living. But we are a minority—the vast majority of our people regard the temporary equilibriums of our society and world as eternally-functional parts. In this is perhaps the outstanding paradox: we ourselves are imbued with urgency, yet the message of our society is that there is no viable alternative to the present. Beneath the reassuring tones of the politicians, beneath the common opinion that America will "muddle through," beneath the stagnation of those who have closed their minds to the future, is the pervading feeling that there simply are no alternatives, that our times have witnessed the exhaustion not only of Utopias, but of any new departures as well. . . .

Some would have us believe that Americans feel contentment amidst prosperity—but might it not be better called a glaze above deeply-felt anxieties about their role in the new world? And if these anxieties produce a developed indifference to human affairs, do they not as well produce a yearning to believe there *is* an alternative to the present, that something *can* be done to change circumstances in the school, the workplaces, the bureaucracies, the government? It is to this latter yearning, at once the spark and engine of change, that we direct our present appeal. The search for truly democratic alternatives to the present, and a commitment to social experimentation with them, is a worthy and fulfilling human enterprise, one which moves us and, we hope, others today.

6. Alabama Governor George Wallace Pledges "Segregation Forever," 1963

Today I have stood, where once Jefferson Davis stood, and took an oath to my people. It is very appropriate then that from this Cradle of the Confederacy, this very Heart of the Great Anglo-Saxon Southland, that today we sound the drum for freedom as have our generations of forebears before us done, time and time again through history. Let us rise to the call of freedom-loving blood that is in us and send our answer to

Inaugural speech, January 14, 1963, Alabama Department of Historical Archives.

the tyranny that clanks its chains upon the South. In the name of the greatest people that have ever trod this earth, I draw the line in the dust and toss the gauntlet before the feet of tyranny . . . and I say . . . segregation today . . . segregation tomorrow . . . segregation forever. . . .

Let us send this message back to Washington by our representatives who are with us today . . . that from this day we are standing up, and the heel of tyranny does not fit the neck of an upright man . . . that we intend to take the offensive and carry our fight for freedom across the nation, wielding the balance of power we know we possess in the Southland . . . that WE, not the insipid bloc of voters of some sections . . . will determine in the next election who shall sit in the White House of these United States. . . . That from this day, from this hour . . . from this minute . . . we give the word of a race of honor that we will tolerate their boot in our face no longer . . . and let those certain judges put *that* in their opium pipes of power and smoke it for what it is worth. . . .

. . . We can no longer hide our head in the sand and tell ourselves that the ideology of our free fathers is not being attacked and is not being threatened by another idea . . . for it is. We are faced with an idea that if a centralized government assumes enough authority, enough power over its people, that it can provide a utopian life . . . that if given the power to dictate, to forbid, to require, to demand, to distribute, to edict and to judge what is best and enforce that will produce only "good" . . . and it shall be our father . . . and our God. It is an idea of government that encourages our fears and destroys our faith. . . . It is a system that is the very opposite of Christ for it feeds and encourages everything degenerate and base in our people as it assumes the responsibilities that we ourselves should assume. Its pseudo-liberal spokesmen and some Harvard advocates have never examined the logic of its substitution of what it calls "human rights" for individual rights, for its propaganda play on words has appeal for the unthinking. . . .

This nation was never meant to be a unit of one . . . but a united of the many . . . that is the exact reason our freedom loving forefathers established the states, so as to divide the rights and powers among the states, insuring that no central power could gain master government control.

In united effort we were meant to live under this government . . . whether Baptist, Methodist, Presbyterian, Church of Christ, or whatever one's denomination or religious belief . . . each respecting the others' right to a separate denomination. . . .

And so it was meant in our racial lives . . . each race, within its own framework has the freedom to teach . . . to instruct . . . to develop . . . to ask for and receive deserved help from others of separate racial stations. This is the great freedom of our American founding fathers . . . but if we amalgamate into the one unit as advocated by the communist philosophers . . . then the enrichment of our lives . . . the freedom for our development . . . is gone forever. We become, therefore, a mongrel unit of one under a single all powerful government . . . and we stand for everything . . . and for nothing. . . .

We invite the negro citizens of Alabama to work with us from his separate racial station . . . as we will work with him . . . to develop, to grow in individual freedom and enrichment. . . .

The liberals' theory that poverty, discrimination and lack of opportunity is the cause of communism is a false theory . . . if it were true the South would have been the biggest single communist bloc in the western hemisphere long ago . . . for after the great War Between the States, our people faced a desolate land of burned universities, destroyed crops and homes, with manpower depleted and crippled, and even the mule, which was required to work the land, was so scarce that whole communities shared one animal to make the spring plowing. There were no government handouts, no Marshall Plan aid, no coddling to make sure that *our* people would not suffer; instead the South was set upon by the vulturous carpetbagger and federal troops, all loyal Southerners were denied the vote at the point of bayonet, so that the infamous, illegal 14th Amendment might be passed. There was no money, no food and no hope of either. But our grandfathers bent their knee only in church and bowed their head only to God. . . .

And that is why today, I stand ashamed of the fat, well-fed whimperers who say that it is inevitable . . . that our cause is lost. I am ashamed *of* them . . . and I am ashamed *for* them. They do not represent the people of the Southland. . . .

We remind all within hearing of this Southland that a *Southerner,* Peyton Randolph, presided over the Continental Congress in our nation's beginning . . . that a *Southerner,* Thomas Jefferson, wrote the Declaration of Independence, that a *Southerner,* George Washington, is the Father of our country . . . that a *Southerner,* James Madison, authored our Constitution, that a *Southerner,* George Mason, authored the Bill of Rights and it was a Southerner who said, "Give me liberty . . . or give me death," Patrick Henry.

Southerners played a most magnificent part in erecting this great divinely inspired system of freedom . . . and as God is our witness, Southerners will save it.

7. A Protester at Columbia University Speaks on Long Hair and Revolution, 1969

Columbia used to be called King's College. They changed the name in 1784 because they wanted to be patriotic and *Columbia* means *America.* This week we've been finding out what America means.

Every morning now when I wake up I have to run through the whole thing in my mind. I have to do that because I wake up in a familiar place that isn't what it was. I wake up and I see blue coats and brass buttons all over the campus. ("Brass buttons, blue coat, can't catch a nanny goat" goes the Harlem nursery rhyme.) I start to go off the campus but then remember to turn and walk two blocks uptown to get to the only open gate. There I squeeze through the three-foot "out" opening in the police barricade, and I feel for my wallet to be sure I've got the two I.D.'s necessary to get back into my college. I stare at the cops. They stare back and see a red armband and long hair and they perhaps tap their night sticks on the barricade. They're looking at a radical leftist. . . .

At the sundial are 500 people ready to follow Mark Rudd (whom they don't particularly like because he always refers to President Kirk as "that shithead") into the Low Library administration building to demand severance from IDA [Institute

A memoir of the protest at Columbia, 1966, from James S. Kunen, *The Strawberry Statement—Notes of a College Revolutionary,* Brandywine Press, 1995, pp. 19, 20, 22, 72, 149–151. Reprinted by permission of Sterling Lord Literistic, Inc. Copyright by James S. Kunen.

for Defense Analysis], an end to gym construction, and to defy Kirk's recent edict prohibiting indoor demonstrations. . . .

I go upstairs to reconnoiter and there is none other than Peter Behr of Linda LeClair fame* chalking on the wall, "'Up against the wall, motherfucker, . . .' from a poem by LeRoi Jones." I get some chalk and write "I am sorry about defacing the walls, but babies are being burned and men are dying, and this University is at fault quite directly."

. . . Medical science has yet to discover any positive correlation between hair length and anything—intelligence, virility, morality, cavities, cancer—anything.

Long hair on men, however, has been known to make some people sick.

My father, for instance. On July 8, 1968, he alleged that long hair on his sons made him sick. "You look like a woman," he said. "I'll get a haircut," I said. That threw him off, but only for a moment. "If I were a girl," he continued, "I wouldn't like the way you look." "You are not a girl," I said, "and anyway, I said I'd get a haircut." "I don't see how your hair could possibly get any longer," he added. "Would you agree," I asked, "that if I let it grow for another two months, it would get longer?" "Maybe," he conceded, "but it just couldn't possibly be any longer."

My father talks about the bad associations people make when they see someone with hair. I come back with the bad associations people make when they see someone replete with a shiny new Cadillac that looks like it should have a silk-raimented coachman standing at each fender. But as for bad vibrations emanating from my follicles, I say great. I want the cops to sneer and the old ladies swear and the businessmen worry. I want everyone to see me and say "There goes an enemy of the state," because that's where I'm at, as we say in the Revolution biz.

Also, I like to have peace people wave me victory signs and I like to return them, and for that we've got to be able to recognize each other. And hair is an appropriate badge. Long hair should be associated with peace, because the first time American men wore short hair was after World War I, the first time great numbers of American men had been through the military. . . .

Explanatory Note

At Columbia University in the City of New York, in the spring of 1968, there was an uprising of students against the administration of their school.

Columbia is an Ivy League school. Ivy League schools are known for good scholarship and poor football teams, a situation which shows signs of reversing. They are also known for being stodgily proper, populated by nice people.

It came as a shock, then, to everyone, that the administration of an Ivy League school should be so un-nice as to involve their institution in racism and war, and that the students should be so ill-mannered as to do something about it. . . .

At Columbia a lot of students simply did not like their school commandeering a park and they rather disapproved of their school making war, and they told other

---

*Peter Behr and Linda LeClair were students from Columbia and Barnard—both single-sex schools—who flouted university rules by living together off campus while unmarried.

students who told others and we saw that Columbia is our school and we will have something to say for what it does.

8. Vice President Spiro Agnew Warns of the Threat to America, 1969

A little over a week ago, I took a rather unusual step for a Vice President. I said something. Particularly, I said something that was predictably unpopular with the people who would like to run the country without the inconvenience of seeking public office. I said I did not like some of the things I saw happening in this country. I criticized those who encouraged government by street carnival and suggested it was time to stop the carousel. . . .

Think about it. Small bands of students are allowed to shut down great universities. Small groups of dissidents are allowed to shout down political candidates. Small cadres of professional protestors are allowed to jeopardize the peace efforts of the President of the United States.

It is time to question the credentials of their leaders. And, if in questioning we disturb a few people, I say it is time for them to be disturbed. If, in challenging, we polarize the American people, I say it is time for a positive polarization.

It is time for a healthy in-depth examination of policies and constructive realignment in this country. It is time to rip away the rhetoric and to divide on authentic lines. It is time to discard the fiction that in a country of 200 million people, everyone is qualified to quarterback the government. . . .

Now, we have among us a glib, activist element who would tell us our values are lies, and I call them impudent. Because anyone who impugns a legacy of liberty and dignity that reaches back to Moses, is impudent.

I call them snobs for most of them disdain to mingle with the masses who work for a living. They mock the common man's pride in his work, his family and his country. . . .

Abetting the merchants of hate are the parasites of passion. These are the men who value a cause purely for its political mileage. These are the politicians who temporize with the truth by playing both sides to their own advantage. They ooze sympathy for "the cause" but balance each sentence with equally reasoned reservations. Their interest is personal, not moral. They are ideological eunuchs whose most comfortable position is straddling the philosophical fence, soliciting votes from both sides. . . .

This is what is happening in this nation. We *are* an effete society if we let it happen here. . . .

Because on the eve of our nation's 200th birthday, we have reached the crossroads. Because at this moment totalitarianism's threat does not necessarily have a foreign accent. Because we have a home-grown menace, made and manufactured in the U.S.A. Because if we are lazy or foolish, this nation could forfeit its integrity, never to be free again.

Alexander Bloom and Wini Breines, eds., *Takin' It to the Streets: A Sixties Reader* (New York: Oxford University Press, 1995), pp. 355–358.

9. Folk Singer Malvina Reynolds Sees Young People in "Little Boxes," 1963

Little boxes on the hillside, little boxes made of ticky tacky
Little boxes on the hillside, little boxes all the same
There's a green one and a pink one and a blue one and a yellow one
And they're all made out of ticky tacky and they all look just the same.

And the people in the houses
All went to the university,
Where they were put in boxes
And they came out all the same,
And there's doctors and there's lawyers,
And business executives,
And they're all made out of ticky tacky
And they all look just the same.
And they all play on the golf course
And drink their martinis dry,
And they all have pretty children
And the children go to school,
And the children go to summer camp
And then to the university,
Where they are put in boxes and they come out all the same.

And the boys go into business
and marry and raise a family
In boxes made of ticky tacky
And they all look just the same.

10. Carl Rogers Describes "What Really Goes On in an Encounter Group," 1970

I think of one government executive, a man with high responsibility and excellent technical training as an engineer. At the first meeting of the group he impressed me, and I think others, as being cold, aloof, somewhat bitter, resentful, cynical. When he spoke of how he ran his office he appeared to administer it "by the book" without warmth or human feeling entering in. In one of the early sessions, when he spoke of his wife a group member asked him, "Do you love your wife?" He paused for a long time, and the questioner said, "OK, that's answer enough." The executive said, "No, wait a minute! The reason I didn't respond was that I was wondering if I ever loved anyone. I don't think I have *ever* really *loved* anyone." It seemed quite dramatically clear to those of us in the group that he had come to accept himself as an unloving person.

"Little Boxes," words and music by Malvina Reynolds. Copyright 1962 by Schroder Music Company (ASCAP. Renewed 1990). Used with permission. All rights reserved.

Carl R. Rogers, *Carl Rogers on Encounter Groups* (New York: Harper & Row, 1970), 25–28. Reprinted by permission of HarperCollins Publishers, Inc.

A few days later he listened with great intensity as one member of the group expressed profound personal feelings of isolation, loneliness, pain, and the extent to which he had been living behind a mask, a façade. The next morning the engineer said, "Last night I thought and thought about what Bill told us. I even wept quite a bit by myself. I can't remember how long it has been since I've cried and I really *felt* something. I think perhaps what I felt was love."

It is not surprising that before the week was over he had thought through new ways of handling his growing son, on whom he had been placing extremely rigorous demands. He had also begun genuinely to appreciate his wife's love for him, which he now felt he could in some measure reciprocate. . . .

Still another person reporting shortly after his workshop experience says, "I came away from the workshop feeling much more deeply that 'It's all right to be me with all my strengths and weaknesses.' My wife told me that I seem more authentic, more real, more genuine."

This feeling of greater realness and authenticity is a very common experience. It would appear that the individual is learning to accept and to *be* himself and is thus laying the foundation for change. He is closer to his own feelings, hence they are no longer so rigidly organized and are more open to change. . . .

. . . As the sessions continue, so many things tend to occur together that it is hard to know which to describe first. It should again be stressed that these different threads and stages interweave and overlap. One of the threads is the increasing impatience with defenses. As time goes on the group finds it unbearable that any member should live behind a mask or front. The polite words, the intellectual understanding of each other and of relationships, the smooth coin of tact and cover-up—amply satisfactory for interactions outside—are just not good enough. The expression of self by some members of the group has made it very clear that a deeper and more basic encounter is *possible,* and the group appears to strive intuitively and unconsciously, toward this goal. Gently at times, almost savagely at others, the group *demands* that the individual be himself, that his current feelings not be hidden, that he remove the mask of ordinary social intercourse. In one group there was a highly intelligent and quite academic man who had been rather perceptive in his understanding of others but revealed himself not at all. The attitude of the group was finally expressed sharply by one member when he said, "Come out from behind that lectern, Doc. Stop giving us speeches. Take off your dark glasses. We want to know *you.*"

E S S A Y S

How one assesses the legacy of the sixties depends partly on which aspect of the era one looks at. Social values represent a triumph of the left; politics represent a triumph of the right. In the first essay, Kenneth Cmiel of the University of Iowa shows how the sixties reshaped popular notions of civility—what it meant to be "nice." How could one be polite, for instance, when being polite to white people meant yielding one's seat on a bus or quietly absorbing deliberate insults? Cmiel traces the effects of civil rights, the counterculture, the New Left, feminism, and the rulings of the Supreme Court on how Americans treated one another in the sixties and how they treat one another today. The second essay, by Dan Carter of the University of South Carolina, examines the political outcomes of the sixties. His essay helps to explain how the Republican Party triumphed in 1968, and why it continued to veer to the right for decades afterward.

Sixties Liberalism and the Revolution in Manners

KENNETH CMIEL

As the 1960s opened, civility was, quite literally, the law of the land. In 1942 the U.S. Supreme Court had declared that certain words were not protected by the First Amendment. Not only fighting words, but also the "lewd," "obscene," and "profane" were all excluded from protection. A statute declaring that "no person shall address any offensive, derisive or annoying word to any other person who is lawfully in any street" was upheld by the Court as perfectly legal. This decision, although modified in later years, was still law in 1960, and statutes like the one mentioned above continued to be on the books and enforced. They implied that free speech was possible only in what eighteenth-century writers had called "civil society." Civility, in other words, had to precede civil rights.

One part of the contentious politics of the sixties, however, was a fight over this notion. From a number of perspectives, prevailing attitudes toward social etiquette were attacked. African Americans argued that civil society as constructed by whites helped structure racial inequality. Counterculturalists insisted that civil politeness suppressed more authentic social relations. Some student radicals infused the strategic disruption of civility with political meaning. And finally, there was a moderate loosening of civil control at the center of society. Under this onslaught, the nation's courts struggled to redefine the relationship between law and civil behavior.

. . . This essay charts the shift within the United States from one sense of order to another. In reaction to various social changes and pressures, federal courts, most importantly the Supreme Court, altered the law of decorum. From the belief that civility took precedence over civil rights, the Supreme Court decided that in public forums, incivility was protected by the First Amendment. But this major change was qualified. No incivility, the Court argued, could disrupt the normal workings of a school, workplace, or courtroom. . . .

The civil rights movement's nonviolent efforts to alter the social order marked the first powerful sortie into the politics of civility during the 1960s. As the sixties opened, nonviolent direct action was the tactic of choice for organizations like the Congress of Racial Equality (CORE), the Southern Christian Leadership Conference (SCLC), and the Student Nonviolent Coordinating Committee (SNCC). . . .

Nonviolent resistance asked demonstrators to peaceably and lovingly call attention to the inequities of the social system. For those believing in direct nonviolent action, the path of protest was a complicated and patient one, moving through four distinct stages—the investigation of a problem, efforts to negotiate a solution, public protest, and then further negotiation. One never proceeded to the next stage without warrant. Henry David Thoreau's "Civil Disobedience" was often cited as a precursor to direct action. Another important source was Mahatma Gandhi. Indeed, Gandhi's 1906 campaign in South Africa was seen as the first example of a mass direct nonviolent action.

But while Gandhi and Thoreau were sources, for both black and white activists committed to direct nonviolent action there was something far more important—the Gospel's injunction to love one's enemies. All the early leaders of CORE, SCLC, and SNCC were deeply influenced by the Christian message of hope and redemption. SNCC's statement of purpose on its founding in May 1960 called attention to those "Judaic-Christian traditions" that seek "a social order permeated by love." . . .

Civil rights protest took a number of characteristic forms—the boycott, the sit-in, the freedom ride, and the mass march. At all, efforts were made to keep the protest civil. In 1960, when four neatly dressed black college students sat down at a white-only lunch counter in a downtown Woolworth's in Greensboro, North Carolina, one began the protest by turning to a waitress and saying, "I'd like a cup of coffee, please." Although the students were not served, they continued to be well mannered, sitting "politely" at the counter for days on end. This first effort set off a wave of sit-ins to desegregate southern restaurants. Typical were the instructions given in Nashville: "Do show yourself friendly on the counter at all times. Do sit straight and always face the counter. Don't strike back or curse back if attacked." Candie Anderson, one of the students at the Nashville sit-in, recalled: "My friends were determined to be courteous and well-behaved. . . . Most of them read or studied while they sat at the counters, for three or four hours. I heard them remind each other not to leave cigarette ashes on the counter, to take off their hats, etc." . . .

The meaning of the polite protests was complicated. Rosa Parks, who refused to move to the back of the bus in Montgomery, Alabama, the students integrating lunch counters in Greensboro, and the marchers at Selma were all not only acting with decorum, they were also all breaking the law, calling attention to the inadequacy of the present system, and violating long-standing white/black custom of the South. The southern caste system was reinforced through an elaborate etiquette. Blacks stepped aside on the street to let whites pass, they averted their eyes from whites, and even adult African Americans were called by a diminutive first name ("Charlie" or "Missie") while addressing all whites with the formal titles of "Sir," "Ma'am," "Mr.," or "Mrs." No distinctions in economic status changed this. Black ministers tipped their hats to white tradesmen. To the overwhelming majority of white southerners, the assertion of civil equality by civil rights protesters was in fact a radical *break* in decorum.

The protest, indeed, highlights some of the complexities of civility itself. On the one hand, politeness is a means of avoiding violence and discord. It is a way of *being nice*. One of sociologist Norbert Elias's great insights was to see that the introduction of civil etiquette in the early modern West was part of an effort to reduce the amount of interpersonal violence prevalent during the Middle Ages." At some time or other, all of us are polite to people we do not like simply because we do not want to live in an overly contentious world. On the other hand, however, civility *also* reaffirms established social boundaries. And when there are huge inequities in the social order, polite custom ratifies them in everyday life.

Direct nonviolent action attempted to undermine southern etiquette. It did so not by attacking civility pure and simple but by using polite behavior to challenge social inequality. More precisely, the first function of politeness (being nice) attacked the second (the caste system). The determined civility of the protesters dramatized the inequities of the South and at the same time signaled to the nation and world the "worthiness" (that is, civility) of African Americans.

Most southern whites did not see it this way. Even those who were called moderates in the early sixties often viewed the polite protests as an attack on civility. Sit-ins, boycotts, and marches openly challenged the caste system and, moderates argued, too easily slipped into violence. To the *Nashville Banner,* the sit-ins were an "incitation to anarchy." . . .

In Greensboro, it was *white* children who were the first to be arrested for disorderly conduct, who harassed blacks at the lunch counter, who got angry. At Selma, it was the white police who waded into crowds of protesters and began clubbing them. Black activists, in fact, had expected this to happen. Martin Luther King was typical, noting that nonviolent resistance forced "the oppressor to commit his brutality openly—in the light of day—with the rest of the world looking on." . . .

This style of protest was under assault almost as the sixties started. As early as 1961, and certainly by 1964, those partisans of "civil" protest were faced with a growing mass movement that was more assertive, less polite, and more willing to defend itself. A host of reasons explain this shift. The fiercely violent reaction of so many whites made nonviolent decorum extremely hard and dangerous to maintain. Black nationalism, grass roots activism, a growing sense of frustration, and burgeoning antiestablishment sentiment in the culture at large all helped throw bourgeois misrule on the defensive. It would be just a few more steps to the Black Panther party or the calls to violence by people like Stokely Carmichael and H. Rap Brown. . . .

One place we can spot the erosion of polite protest is in the Freedom Summer of 1964. Among an important group of young SNCC activists there was a certain skepticism about Martin Luther King. For these civil rights workers, nonviolent resistance was understood to be a strategic tactic rather than a principled commitment. And there was a change in style. As sociologist Robert McAdam has noted, there was a feeling among these civil rights activists that they had to free themselves as much as the southern blacks they worked for. And that meant abandoning middle-class norms. Consequently, more rural dress (blue jeans and work shirt) became the mode. . . .

Another sign was the filthy speech movement at Berkeley. In the fall of 1964, the University of California at Berkeley was rocked by the free speech movement, an effort by students to retain their right to distribute political material on campus. Many of the leaders of the free speech movement had worked for SNCC in the South the summer before and a number of Freedom Summer tactics were adopted at Berkeley. Students used mass civil disobedience and sit-ins to pressure campus officials in November and December. They were generally successful. But the next spring, after the campus had quieted, a new twist came. A nonstudent who hung around in New York beat circles drifted to Berkeley to (in his words) "make the scene." On 3 March he stood on Bancroft and Telegraph and held up a sign that just said "FUCK." When asked to clarify his meaning, he added an exclamation point.

His arrest threw the campus into another controversy. Other "dirty speech" protests were held, with other students arrested for obscenity.

The counterculture of the 1960s can be traced back to the beats of the 1950s, earlier still to artistic modernism, and even before that to Rousseau's mid-eighteenth-century attack on politeness. But if there is a long subterranean history, a very visible counterculture began to surface in 1964. The first underground newspapers appeared; they were dominated by countercultural themes. By 1966 the counterculture was a mass media phenomenon. Perhaps its height of popularity were the years 1967 and 1968. And while no precise date marks its end, by the early 1970s it was fading fast at least in its most utopian projections.

From Rousseau through the 1960s, advocates of a counterculture valued authenticity over civility. The command to be polite (that is, to *be nice*) does not encourage personal expression. It suppresses impulsive behavior, relying on established social forms to guarantee comity. As Norbert Elias has put it, the civilizing process is about affect control. Counterculture advocates challenged these presumptions, arguing for the liberation of the self. In the name of personal freedom they attacked the restraints and compromises of civil society. In a phrase introduced to American life by sixties freaks, they were dedicated to "doing their own thing."

This translated into an extraordinarily colorful form of life. Shoulder-length hair on men, Victorian dresses on women, day-glo painted bodies, elaborate slang, and more open sexuality—it was all far removed from "straight" (that is, civil) society. Hippies looked different, acted different, were different. At its best, there was a glorious joy in the freedom of hippie life-styles. The "be-ins" of 1967 celebrated the love that would replace the stilted conformity of the established world. . . .

Drugs too were often defended as a liberating experience. (I myself did so ingenuously in the late sixties.) "It's like seeing the world again through a child's eye," one user noted in 1967. Drugs were "a transcendental glory." "When I first turned on," the owner of a San Francisco head shop reported in 1968, "it pulled the rug out from under me. Suddenly I saw all the bullshit in the whole educational and social system. . . . The problem with our schools is that they are turning out robots to keep the social system going." So "turning on, tuning in, and dropping out means to conduct a revolution against the system." . . .

To those with no respect for the counterculture, the alternative decorum was gross. There was just too much dirt. Hippies did not have the discipline to hold a job. The sex was too loose. The drugs were destructive. Some critics completely missed the claims to liberation and denounced hippies as simply negative. . . .

Yet while the distance from straight culture was deep, the counterculture might best be seen not so much an attack on politeness as an alternative politeness, one not based on the emotional self-restraint of traditional civility but on the expressive individualism of liberated human beings. It is no surprise that "love" was an important theme running throughout the counterculture. . . .

The counterculture, at its most utopian, tried to invent a new civility. It attacked the social roles of straight society and the implied social order contained within it. But it held firm to the other dimension of civility—that of being nice. But in the end, it could not be yoked together as easily as one thought. To some degree, the roles involved in civil etiquette are connected with the avoidance of discord. . . .

By 1965, as the counterculture was coming to national consciousness, there was another debate going on about the civil society. At least some radical activists had moved beyond the talking stage. Violent behavior became a considered option.

This happened first among black activists, later among whites. African American radicals like H. Rap Brown and Stokely Carmichael decisively split with the earlier civil rights movement. Carmichael's 1966 call to let the cities burn, the stream of urban riots after 1965, and the growing militancy in general frightened numerous Americans. . . .

Some white student and antiwar activists were making their own transition. The move from dissent to resistance was accompanied by a shift in rhetoric. "We're now in the business of wholesale disruption and widespread resistance and dislocation of the American society," Jerry Rubin reported in 1967. To be sure, not all white radicals accepted this, but some did, and the thought of disruption scared Middle America, whose more conservative press responded with almost breathless reports about imminent revolution. The heightened rhetoric, on both sides, contributed to the sense that the center might not hold. A string of burned buildings on university campuses as well as a handful of bombings over the next few years contributed as well.

Real violence, against property or person, however, was actually rare. Far more important was the *talk* about violence. The escalation of rhetoric, the easy use of hard words made more centrists very nervous. It reflected, in their eyes, a lack of faith in civil politics.

For these radicals, the hard words were part of their sense that polite society had its priorities backward. There was something grotesquely misguided about a middle-class decorum that masked the profound inequalities of America. The true obscenities, they argued, were the Vietnam War and racial hatred. In fact, some thought, the very idea of obscenity had to be rethought. "The dirtiest word in the English language is not 'fuck' or 'shit' in the mouth of a tragic shaman," one activist wrote, "but the word 'NIGGER' from the sneering lips of a Bull Conner." . . .

By the late sixties, then, countercultural politics might mesh with political radicalism. To be sure, the two movements never fit perfectly together. But there were connections. Even long hair could be a threatening statement laden with political overtones. One participant in the Columbia University uprising in 1968 welcomed the "bad vibrations" his long hair brought: "I say great. I want the cops to sneer and the old ladies swear and the businessmen worry. I want everyone to see me and say: 'There goes an enemy of the state,' because that's where I'm at, as we say in the Revolution game." . . .

The debate in the late sixties was clouded by the polarization of the times. Hippies and violent political radicals were tailor-made for the mass media. But despite the preoccupation with the more extravagant behavior, the nation's manners were changing in more subtle ways. There was a large move toward the informalization of American society.

Informalization is a term invented by sociologists to describe periodic efforts to relax formal etiquette. These periods of informality are then followed by a more conservative "etiquette-prone" reaction. While Americans in the sixties pressed toward more informal social relations, the phenomenon was by no means unique to that period. A significant relaxation of manners took place in Jacksonian America, tied to both egalitarian sentiment and the desire for authenticity. Still another important stage was the 1920s. And as Barbara Ehrenreich has pointed out, sexual mores were becoming less rigid inside mainstream society in the 1950s, a prelude for the next decade.

The counterculture of the mid-1960s was only picking up on debates already under way in mainstream America. Disputes about long hair surfaced not in 1966 with the counterculture but in 1963 when the Beatles first became known in the United States. The *New York Times* first reported on the issue in December 1964, four months after the Beatles began their first full-length tour in the United States. In those early years, the debate over long hair had a very different feel than it would beginning in 1966. The discussion was *not* about basic rottenness of a civilization. Rather, for the boys involved, it was about fun and girls. The look, as it evolved in the United States, was a surfer look. The "mop top," as it was called, was simply a bang swooped over the forehead. The sides were closely and neatly cropped. It was moderate hair by 1966 standards. . . .

Between 1963 and 1965, however, it was controversial. Adults who disliked the bangs claimed they blurred gender lines. Boys looked like girls, something both disquieting and disgusting. Nevertheless, the conservatives on this issue were like the "long hair" kids in not talking about the mop top as a frontal assault on civilization but in the more restricted terms of a threatening relaxation of order. It was only in 1966 that certain forms of male hair became associated with a wholesale attack on what was known as "the American way of life."

Something similar can be said about sexual mores. The urge to liberalize "official" sexual codes was certainly a prominent theme of the counterculture, but it was also a theme of Hugh Heffner's *Playboy,* first published in 1953. And a female variant, Helen Gurley Brown's *Sex and the Single Girl,* was a huge best-seller as early as 1962. By the mid-1960s there were a host of middle-class advocates for a more liberal sexuality, a trend culminating in the early 1970s in books like Alex Comfort's *The Joy of Sex.* The counterculture contributed, but it was neither the beginning nor the end of the change.

The same was true of obscenity. While counterculturalists by 1965 were fighting over "dirty words" at Berkeley, there was a corresponding effort in the mainstream to relax norms. Liberal judges had softened obscenity laws in the 1950s and 1960s. The pornography industry was growing throughout the sixties, with, to take one example, magazines catering to sadists making their appearance early in the decade. . . .

In countless ways you could see the mainstream's mores changing. . . . In August 1971 *Penthouse* magazine first contained pictures of female genitalia. *Playboy* followed five months later. The *New York Times* reported in the fall of 1967 that even doctors and stockbrokers, "traditional squares" the paper called them, were starting to let their hair grow longer. The miniskirt, which first appeared in the mid-1960s, was by no means only worn by girls and women hopelessly alienated from the culture. For its creator, the mini was explicitly tied to sexual liberation. . . .

The changes touched all sorts of mainstream venues. To trace *Cosmopolitan* magazine between 1964 and 1970 is to chart one variation of the move. In 1964 it ran rather staid articles such as "Catholics and Birth Control" and "Young Americans Facing Life with Dignity and Purpose." By 1969, however, *Cosmo* was reporting on

"The Ostentatious Orgasm" and "Pleasures of a Temporary Affair." A piece lauding "hippie capitalists" noted how "loose" and "free form" the new entrepreneur was, not tied to confining restraints of Wall Street. "Nobody, *but nobody,*" it observed, "calls the boss by anything except his first name." . . .

Parallel changes might be found in other magazines with no commitment to the counterculture, as *Esquire,* with its growing respect for sideburns, or *Ebony,* with its increasing tolerance for moderate Afros. This widespread informalization at the center was often missed during the sixties. It lacked the flair of the counterculture or the drama of the Left. . . .

For writers like Doris Grumbach and Lois Gould, a main point of attack was the older male/female etiquette. If there was one place where the new principle of "nonintervention" was set to the side, it was here. Calling grown women "girls," having men invariably take the lead in dancing, and presuming that men asked women out on dates were mentioned as suspect behavior. These authors introduced to mainstream audiences feminist arguments about the part that male "chivalry" played in female subordination. "If there is to be a new etiquette," Lois Gould wrote in the *New York Times Magazine,* "it ought to be based on honest mutual respect, and responsiveness to each other's real needs." . . .

This shift at the center of American culture did not take place without opposition. There were plaints for the older norms. Nor did the changes take place independent of the law. In fact, they were sanctioned and encouraged through new attitudes toward decorum promulgated by the federal courts, principally the U.S. Supreme Court. A number of decisions, most coming between 1966 and 1973, changed the relationship of the "civilizing process" to the rule of law. This was the legal version of informalization.

In a number of instances, the Court refused to use arguments of bad taste or decorum to uphold a law. In one celebrated case, a young man opposed to the Vietnam War had been arrested in the corridor of the Los Angeles County Courthouse for wearing a jacket with the words "Fuck the Draft" prominently inscribed on it. The Court overturned the conviction noting that there was no sign of imminent violence at the courthouse and that while the phrase was crude and vulgar to many, the open debate the First Amendment guaranteed necessitated its protection. In a far-reaching departure from earlier decisions, the Court also raised doubts about the possibility of any evaluation of taste: "For, while the particular four-letter word being litigated here is perhaps more distasteful than others of its genre, it is nevertheless true that one man's vulgarity is another's lyric." Since government officials "cannot make principled decisions in this area," it was important to leave "matters of taste and style largely to the individual."

This was a far cry from *Chaplinsky v. New Hampshire* (1942), in which the Court simply asserted that some utterances were of "such slight social value" that the First Amendment did not protect them. In the Chaplinsky case, the defendant was convicted for calling someone a "damned racketeer" and a "damned Fascist." In the next few years, the Court would protect the use of "motherfucker" in public debate. . . .

If the Court moved to open up public space to certain sorts of incivil behavior, there were limits. At no time did it accept the legitimacy of violence. The Supreme Court held fast to the notion that the state had a monopoly on the legitimate use of force. What the Court was doing was rewriting the line between behavior and violence, allowing far more space for aggressive words. Earlier laws had defended civil demeanor precisely because "incivil" behavior was thought to *lead* to discord. Now there was to be a toleration of more insulting behavior although it still had to stop short of violence.

At the same time that this whole string of cases opened up room for more "incivil" action in public, there was a parallel set of cases arguing that decorum had to be maintained. These cases all had to do with the functioning of institutions. In courts, schools, even the workplace, the Court upheld the need for civil decorum and left authorities broad discretion in setting standards.

One case, which had to do with a defendant whose "vile and abusive language" disrupted his criminal trial, prompted the Court to argue that "dignity, order, and decorum" must be "the hallmarks of all court proceedings." The "flagrant disregard of elementary standards of proper conduct . . . cannot be tolerated."

In cases like this, the Court explicitly called attention to the decorum of the protest. As it said in *Grayned v. Rockford* (1971), a case on picketing outside a school: "The crucial question is whether the manner of expression is basically incompatible with the normal activity of a particular place at a particular time."

When protest inside an institution was upheld, it was because it was not disruptive. No doubt the most important case of this kind was *Tinker v. Des Moines,* decided in 1969. A handful of students were suspended from a Des Moines high school in 1965 for wearing black arm bands to protest the escalation of the Vietnam War. Prior to this, the school board had voted to forbid the activity. The Court four years later vindicated the students, but precisely because of the civility of their action. The Court noted how the case did not relate "to regulation of the length of skirts or type of clothing, to hair style or deportment." Nor did it concern "aggressive, disruptive action." There was no evidence "that any of the armbands 'disrupted' the school." The Court, however, added that activity that *did* disrupt a school was *not* protected by the First Amendment.

Debate over institutional decorum also extended to discussion of hair and clothing. In 1975 the Court took up the case of a policeman who had broken the department's dress code by wearing his hair modestly over the collar. While he argued that the code infringed upon his civil rights, the Court's majority disagreed, arguing that the department's need for "discipline, esprit de corps, and uniformity" was sufficient reason for a dress code. Only Justice William O. Douglas dissented, asserting that the policeman should have the right to wear his hair "according to his own taste." . . .

All regimes wind up taking a stand on where decorum can be broken and where it has to be enforced. It is only where there is an abstract commitment to universal equal rights that decorum becomes legally problematic. But, to again repeat, there are different ways that such regimes can handle the issue. In the late 1960s there was a shift in American practice and law. The Supreme Court opened up all sorts of behavior in private life and in public. The Court would do nothing about people yelling "motherfucker" at school board meetings or in street protests. It declared unconstitutionally broad ordinances that outlawed incivil behavior because it "tended" to lead to a breach of the peace. . . . At the same time, however, the Court also carefully maintained the authority of institutions. The running of a school, a courtroom, or a workplace (for example, a police department) all demanded decorum. Here civil behavior, as defined by authorities, could be enforced by law.

Earlier thought had stressed the continuity between everyday life, public drama, and the avoidance of violence. To keep violence from erupting, the first two had to remain "polite." The new thinking cut that relationship. If one thinks about civil behavior as "affect control," the hiding of emotions, some of these new norms were not civil. . . .

. . . As the liberal historian C. Vann Woodward put it in 1975, "freedom of expression is a paramount value, more important than civility or rationality."

By 1990 this would be a controversial position within Left and liberal circles. In the late 1980s the notion of "offensiveness" reentered progressive political thought, at this point connected with arguments about the debilitating effect of rude insults and slurs on historically subjugated peoples. Speech codes adopted by a few campuses explicitly used "offensiveness" as a criterion to forbid some forms of expression. Some law professors indicated qualified respect for *Chaplinsky v. New Hampshire*. For them, it was no longer a matter of principle that the intolerant must be tolerated. The other side on this debate continued to argue that the concern for verbal niceties undermined free speech. In 1989 and 1991, cases reviewing campus codes outlawing offensive speech reached the federal courts. In both, the codes were declared unconstitutional. By the early 1990s, these debates not only divided progressives from conservatives but also split the Left-liberal community itself into those defending the "1970 position" and those adhering to arguments developed in the late 1980s. To some, at least, C. Vann Woodward's attitudes about free speech no longer sounded particularly progressive.

Institutional decorum coupled with a relatively unregulated civic forum is one historic way liberal politics has handled the issue of order and freedom. This was the path chosen by U.S. courts in the late 1960s, a legal version of the informalization going on in American society at large. And for the time being, at least, it has remained the law of the land.

George Wallace, Richard Nixon, and the Triumph of the Right

DAN T. CARTER

After his hairbreadth loss to John Kennedy in 1960, Richard Nixon had played the role of the magnanimous loser, congratulating Kennedy and discouraging supporters who wanted to challenge questionable election returns from precincts in Mayor Daley's Chicago. Two years later, faced with another heartbreaking loss to California governor Pat Brown, his mask of control slipped; exhausted, hung over, and trembling with rage, he had stalked into the press room of his campaign headquarters and lashed out at assembled newsmen in rambling remarks so incoherent that reporters—who are not noted for their empathy for wounded politicians—sat in silent embarrassment. For ten minutes (though it seemed like hours to his staff) the former vice president alternated between mawkish self-pity and bitter attacks on the press, which

From Dan T. Carter, *The Politics of Rage: George Wallace, the Origins of the New Conservatism, and the Transformation of American Politics* (Baton Rouge: Louisiana State University Press, revised edition, 2000), pp. 324–334, 337–338, 345, 347–349, 362–367, and 465–468. Reprinted by permission of the author.

he blamed for his defeat. He closed with the line memorable for its unintended irony: "Well, you won't have Nixon to kick around anymore, because, gentlemen, this is my last press conference. . . ." As stunned aids Herbert Klein and H. R. Haldeman pulled him from the room, the defeated candidate was unrepentant. "I finally told those bastards off, and every Goddamned thing I said was true."

By December 1967, memories of his losses had faded. With the determination that had led his Duke Law School classmates to dub him Richard the Grind, Nixon fought his way back to political center stage. . . .

If there was a turning point in the political recovery of Richard Nixon, it had come in 1964. Faced with the likelihood that his party would nominate conservative standard-bearer Barry Goldwater (and the certainty he would suffer a smashing defeat), the former vice president introduced the Arizona senator at the convention and then dutifully delivered more than one hundred and fifty speeches for Republican candidates in thirty-six states, always emphasizing his support for Goldwater even as he distanced himself from the nominee's more extreme positions. By the time the votes were counted in the Johnson landslide, Nixon had compiled a staggering number of chits from conservative and moderate Republicans. When he embarked on an equally aggressive speaking schedule for party candidates in the 1966 off-year elections, he became the odds-on favorite for the GOP nomination in 1968. And the long-coveted prize—the presidency—appeared within reach as the Democratic Party seemed to implode.

When Lyndon Johnson committed United States airpower and troops to support the tottering South Vietnamese government in 1964 and 1965, only a small minority of intellectuals and students challenged him. As the number of ground troops rose from fifty thousand in 1964 to nearly half a million in January of 1967, as casualties mounted, as the cost of the war doubled, tripled, then quadrupled, members of the antiwar movement, frustrated and impotent, escalated their tactics, from teach-ins to rallies to raucous street demonstrations. The war in Vietnam and the explosion of the antiwar movement, coupled with summer after summer of civil disorder, left the incumbent Democratic administration discredited and the nation deeply divided.

. . . Richard Nixon skillfully positioned himself to take advantage of the frustrations of middle-class and working-class Americans by holding out the chimerical promise that he could win the war by relying upon airpower rather than increasing the number of American ground troops.

But first he had to win the Republican nomination. And in that process, the South played a critical role.

To most political reporters, Richard Nixon's "Southern Strategy" was simply a continuation of Barry Goldwater's efforts to woo disgruntled whites in the old Confederacy, but Nixon adamantly rejected the notion that he had picked up where Goldwater left off. . . .

The Arizonan's huge majorities in the Deep South had made possible the election of dozens of Republican officeholders for the first time since the post–Civil War Reconstruction era, but his identification with hard-line segregationists weakened his party's appeal to moderates in the border states and in the North. The GOP, argued Nixon, should reach out to the South's emerging middle-class suburban constituency, more in tune with traditional Republican economic conservatism than with old-style racism.

If Nixon's analysis showed a shrewd grasp of the long-term weaknesses of the 1964 GOP campaign, it was disingenuous to pretend that his own manipulation of the politics of race bore no resemblance to that of Barry Goldwater. The political demands of the hour required him to walk a precarious ideological tightrope—to distance himself from Goldwater's explicit appeal to southern white racism while reaping the benefits of such a strategy. . . .

Nixon realized he couldn't be *too* moderate. Most southern GOP leaders were considerably to the right of the national political mainstream on economic, social, and racial issues. The majority of their mid-level and lower-level cadres had entered the party on the wave of the Goldwater campaign, and—while they were chastened by the Johnson landslide of 1964—they were not about to abandon their conservative and ultra-conservative views. To gain their allegiance required a deft political hand.

In the two years after the 1964 election, Nixon traveled 127,000 miles, visited forty states, and spoke to four hundred groups, nearly half of them in the South. On his southern swings, he was conservative, but not too conservative; a defender of civil rights, but always solicitous of white southerners' "concerns." He often prefaced his remarks with a reminder that he had supported the Supreme Court's decision in 1954 as well as the Civil Rights Acts of 1964 and the Voting Rights Act of 1965. His bona fides established, he would then launch into a stern lecture on the problem of "riots, violence in the streets and mob rule," or he would take a few swings at the "unconscionable boondoggles" in Johnson's poverty program or at the federal courts' excessive concern for the rights of criminals. The real culprits in the nation's racial conflicts were the "extremists of both races," he kept saying. . . .

During one of those southern forays in the spring of 1966, Nixon traveled to Columbia, South Carolina, for a fund-raising dinner for the South Carolina GOP. Senator Strom Thurmond had easily assumed command of the state's fledgling Republican Party when he officially switched to the GOP during the Goldwater campaign. In the years after his 1948 presidential run, he modulated his rhetoric and shifted the focus of his grim maledictions to the "eternal menace of godless, atheistic Communism." He had even learned (when pressed) to pronounce the word "Negro" without eliciting grimaces from his northern fellow Republicans. But race remained his subtext; he continued to Red-bait every spokesman for civil rights from Whitney Young of the Urban League to Stokely Carmichael of the Black Panthers. For the traditional southern campaign chorus of "Nigger-nigger-nigger," he substituted the Cold War battle cry: "Commie-Commie-Commie." On the eve of Nixon's visit, Thurmond was still attacking the civil rights movement, still accusing the Supreme Court of fostering "crime in the streets" and of promoting "a free rein for communism, riots, agitation, collectivism and the breakdown of moral codes."

The senator assigned Harry Dent to act as the vice president's host. Despite Nixon's reputation as wooden and aloof, he charmed Thurmond's aide by bluntly acknowledging his presidential aspirations and soliciting advice. He had no illusions about the difficulties of getting the nomination and defeating Lyndon Johnson, he told Dent. But the man he feared most was George Wallace.

In his public statements, Nixon always professed to be unconcerned about the Alabama governor. As a third-party candidate, Wallace might hurt the GOP in the

South, argued Nixon, but he would draw an equal number of votes from normally Democratic blue-collar voters in the North. "I don't think he'll get four million votes," said Nixon, who pointed to the dismal past experience of third-party candidates. Four million votes would translate into less than six percent of the expected turnout.

He was considerably more frank in his conversation with Dent. . . . If Wallace should "take most of the South," Nixon told Dent, as the Republican candidate he might be "unable to win enough votes in the rest of the country to gain a clear majority." Once the election went to the Democratic-controlled House of Representatives, the game was over.

Dent argued that Thurmond was the key to gaining the support of southern Republicans. Conservatives might privately deride the South Carolina senator as an egotistical fanatic, but his very estrangement from the traditional political process—his refusal to cooperate or compromise with fellow senators—made him the ideological measuring stick for southern GOP leaders baptized in the ideologically pure waters of Goldwater Republicanism.

At an afternoon press conference, Richard Nixon went out of his way to praise the former Dixiecrat. "Strom is no racist," he told reporters; "Strom is a man of courage and integrity." To Thurmond, laboring under the burden of his past as the "Dr. No" of American race relations, it was like being granted absolution from purgatory by the pope of American politics. Almost pathetically grateful, the senator seldom wavered in his support for Nixon in the years that followed.

Nixon's careful cultivation of southern white sensibilities and of power brokers like Thurmond paid off at the 1968 Republican convention. . . .

Flanked by his impassioned sidekick, Strom Thurmond, Nixon summoned the southern delegations to his suite at the Hilton Plaza for a virtuoso performance. (The meeting was captured on tape by an enterprising *Miami Herald* reporter who persuaded a Florida delegate to carry a concealed recorder into Nixon's suite.) Nixon first reaffirmed his commitment to economic conservatism and a foreign policy resting upon equal parts of anticommunism and military jingoism. Still, the issue of race preoccupied the group. Once again, Nixon showed that he was the master of the wink, the nudge, the implied commitment. Without ever explicitly renouncing his own past support for desegregation, he managed to convey to his listeners the sense that, as President, he would do the absolute minimum required to carry out the mandates of the federal courts. In a Nixon administration, there would be no rush to "satisfy some professional civil-rights group, or something like that."

Although some members of his audience believed that George Wallace had the right solution ("take those bearded bureaucrats and throw them in the Potomac") or that the golden-tongued Reagan was the more authentic conservative, the bitter memories of the Goldwater debacle made them pause and listen to Thurmond. "We have no choice, if we want to win, except to vote for Nixon," he insisted. "We must quit using our hearts and start using our heads." Believe me, he said, "I love Reagan, but Nixon's the one."

After the convention, Texas Republican senator John Tower described Nixon's southern brigade as the "thin gray line which never broke." A more appropriate analogy might be found in Margaret Mitchell's *Gone With the Wind.* Like so many

Scarlett O'Haras, Nixon's Dixie delegates reluctantly turned their backs on the dashing blockade-runner and resigned themselves to a marriage of convenience with the stodgy dry-goods merchant.

They received their first reward with Nixon's announcement that Spiro Agnew would be his running mate.

A few weeks before the convention, the candidate had accompanied his old law partner, John Mitchell, to an Annapolis restaurant to meet Maryland's governor. Afterward, Nixon told an aide: "That guy Agnew is really an impressive fellow. He's got guts. He's got a good attitude." Although he concealed his decision to the last to gain maximum leverage, it was a done deal. . . .

The former Maryland governor seemed perfectly suited for the job. . . .

. . . He had earned a reputation as a moderate in the Maryland gubernatorial contest when his opponent, a vociferous segregationist, promised to turn the clock back on civil rights. With his typical "on the one hand and on the other hand" rhetoric, Nixon insisted that he chose Agnew because he was a "progressive" border-state Republican who took a "forward-looking stance on civil rights, but . . . had firmly opposed those who had resorted to violence in promoting their cause."

What really sold Nixon, however, was the Maryland governor's performance during the five-day Baltimore race riot that followed Martin Luther King's assassination in April 1968. As the city returned to some degree of normality, Agnew summoned one hundred mainstream black city leaders—respected community organizers, middle-class preachers, lawyers, businessmen, and politicians—to a conference in Annapolis. Instead of holding a joint discussion, the governor lashed out at his audience's failure to condemn the "circuit-riding Hanoi-visiting . . . caterwauling, riot-inciting, burn-American-down type of leader[s]" who, he said, had caused the rioting in the city. Pointing his finger for emphasis, he accused the moderates of "breaking and running" when faced with the taunts of "Uncle Tom" from black radicals like Stokely Carmichael and H. Rap Brown. Three fourths of his audience—many still exhausted from long days and nights on the street trying to calm the rioters—angrily walked out of the meeting. These were the "very people who were trying to end the riots," pointed out the executive director of the city's Community Relations Commission, but Baltimore's television stations reported a flood of telephone calls supporting the governor. . . .

By the end of August, George Wallace held a commanding lead in the Deep South and trailed Nixon narrowly in much of the remainder of the region. In the long run, Nixon believed, Dixie's heartland—Mississippi, Alabama, Louisiana, and Georgia—would come home to the Republican Party because the national Democrats, sensitive to their black constituency, could not appeal to the region's racially conservative white voters. In the meantime, the GOP nominee abandoned his original goal of a southern sweep and adopted a modified Southern Strategy. Thurmond would give him South Carolina; he would work to carry the border South. His main weapon would be Spiro Agnew, who soon began sounding like a rather dignified clone of George Wallace. . . .

A Chattanooga Baptist preacher heralded Wallace's reemergence on the campaign trail with an apocalyptic invocation: "Outside the visible return of Jesus Christ," shouted the Reverend John S. Lanham, "the only salvation of the country is the election of George Wallace." In the city's ramshackle municipal auditorium six thousand

Tennessee farmers, factory employees and white-collar workers, small businessmen and retirees gave the Alabamian eleven standing ovations as he laid out his lambasted back-alley muggers, urban rioters, HEW bureaucrats, federal judges, and—most of all—the "out-of-touch politicians" who led the Democratic and Republican parties. "You could put them all in an Alabama cotton picker's sack, shake them up and dump them out; take the first one to slide out and put him right back into power and there would be no change." . . .

More than eighty percent of the nine million dollars raised by the [Wallace] campaign came from small contributions of less than fifty dollars, solicited by the increasingly slick direct-mail fund-raising techniques of televangelists and, more important, by fund-raisers where Wallace was present to press the flesh. Instead of the discreet private "occasions" favored by leading Democratic and Republican candidates, at which donors were asked to contribute from five thousand dollars on up, the Wallace staff emphasized smaller contributions. . . .

Wallace was not the first American political candidate to attract small donors through direct mailings and television appeals, but he broke new ground in the effectiveness of his campaign. In the early spring of 1968, an Alabama-based advertising agency, Luckey and Forney, threw together a half-hour television film, *The Wallace Story.* Little more than a crudely edited summary of the candidate's best applause lines delivered at rallies across America, the narrative was interrupted repeatedly with pleas for viewers to send in their dollars so that George Wallace could "stand up for America." When the agency marketed the film on small television stations in the South and in relatively inexpensive media markets in the Midwest and the Rocky Mountain states, even the Wallace people were stunned at the response. "The money is just coming in by the sackfuls," said an awed Jack House in April 1968. Most of it, he confided, was in small contributions from a dollar to a hundred dollars. "It's a gold mine." . . .

At least a dozen articles that appeared during the 1968 campaign compared Wallace to Louisiana's "Kingfish," Huey Long. Both were authoritarian, but the Kingfish rejected the politics of race. In speech after speech Wallace knit together the strands of racism with those of a deeply rooted xenophobic "plain folk" cultural outlook which equated social change with moral corruption. The creators of public policy— the elite—were out of touch with hardworking taxpayers who footed the bill for their visionary social engineering at home and weak-minded defense of American interests abroad. The apocalyptic rhetoric of anticommunism allowed Wallace to bridge the gap between theocratic and "moral" concerns and the secular issues of government economic policy, civil rights, and foreign policy. . . .

The trick, for candidates who hoped to benefit from the "Wallace factor," was to exploit the grievances he had unleashed while disentangling themselves from the more tawdry trappings of his message. The Republican number-crunchers knew the figures by heart: eighty percent of southern Wallace voters preferred Nixon to [Democratic presidential candidate Hubert] Humphrey; by a much narrower margin, northern Wallace voters preferred Humphrey to Nixon. How could they drive the southern Wallace voters into the GOP without disturbing those in the North? That balancing act was proving more difficult than Nixon had imagined, particularly since he wanted to run a nondivisive campaign.

The counterattack against the Wallace threat to the Southern Strategy was executed by Strom Thurmond's assistant Harry Dent. . . .

Dent repeatedly insisted that neither the Southern Strategy nor Nixon's generally conservative emphasis in 1968 was racist. And, in fact, he (like other members of the Nixon team) scrupulously avoided explicit references to race. The problem with the liberalism of the Democrats, Dent charged, was not that it was too problack, but that it had created an America in which the streets were "filled with radical dissenters, cities were literally burning down, crime seemed uncontrollable," and the vast social programs of the Democrats were creating an army of the permanently dependent even as they bankrupted the middle class. The rising tide of economic and social conservatism clearly complemented opposition to federal activism, north and south.

But the political driving force of Nixon's policies toward the South was *not* an abstract notion about the "preservation of individual freedom"; almost every aspect of the 1968 campaign was tightly interwoven with issues of race. . . .

In much the same way, racial fears were linked to concerns over social disorder in American streets. The threat of crime was real; every index of criminality showed an increase in the number of crimes against property and in crimes of violence. Americans were still more likely to be maimed or killed by their friends and relatives than by strangers, but the growth of random, brutal urban violence—an escalation of black-on-white violence attracted the most attention—made law and order an inevitable issue in the 1960s.

And Wallace simply erased the line between antiwar and civil rights protests, between heckling protesters and street muggers. By the fall, Nixon and even Humphrey were attempting to play catch-up with the crime issue, although both went to great lengths to insist that the issue was nonracial. (As the former vice president pointed out on several occasions, blacks were far more likely to be the victims of crime than whites were.) Occasionally, the façade slipped. Early in the campaign Nixon had taped a television commercial attacking the decline of "law and order" in American cities. As he reviewed it with his staff, he became expansive. That "hits it right on the nose," he said enthusiastically. "It's all about law and order and the damn Negro–Puerto Rican groups out there." Nixon did not have to make the racial connection any more than would Ronald Reagan when he began one of his famous discourses on welfare queens using food stamps to buy porterhouse steaks. His audience was already primed to make that connection.

For nearly a hundred years after the Civil War, politicians had manipulated the racial phobias of whites below the Mason-Dixon line to maintain a solidly Democratic South. To Nixon it seemed only poetic justice that the tables should be turned. The challenge lay in appealing to the fears of angry whites without appearing to become an extremist and driving away moderates. . . .

. . . Ultimately, an enormous gender gap emerged: women—particularly nonsouthern women—proved far less willing than men to vote for the Alabama politician. In the eleven states of the old Confederacy, half of the men and forty percent of the women were ready to vote for Wallace in late September, at the high-water mark of his campaign. In the North, one-fifth of white males claimed he had their vote, but less than half that number of women supported him.

Cultural and regional differences undoubtedly played a role, but the reason women most often volunteered for opposing Wallace was that he was "dangerous."

In his public performances—the speeches and rallies—Wallace often teetered along a razor's edge of violence. Where Nixon and Humphrey hated the hecklers and demonstrators, particularly the antiwar demonstrators, who appeared on the campaign trail, Wallace welcomed them, and had become a master at manipulating them. . . .

. . . And in one rally after another, Wallace's angry rhetoric ignited fist-swinging, chair-throwing confrontations between these hardcore followers and antiwar and civil rights demonstrators, who on occasion pelted the candidate with various objects. Wallace was hit by rocks, eggs, tomatoes, pennies, a peace medallion, Tootsie Rolls, a sandal, and a miniature whiskey bottle. By October, television crews always set up two cameras: one to focus on the stage, the other to capture the mêlées and bloodied demonstrators in the audience.

Wallace's troubles gave Nixon the opening he needed. . . .

During the last two weeks of the campaign, Nixon took to the air himself in advertisements specifically tailored to white southern voters: "There's been a lot of double-talk about the role of the South"—by which he meant the white people of the South—"in the campaign of nineteen sixty-eight, and I think it's time for some straight talk," he told his listeners. Without mentioning Wallace by name, Nixon warned that a "divided vote" would play into the hands of the Humphrey Democrats. "And so I say, don't play their game. Don't divide your vote. Vote for . . . the only team that can provide the new leadership that America needs, the Nixon-Agnew team. And I pledge to you we will restore law and order in this country. . . ." . . .

October 24, 1968, was overcast and drizzly, but unseasonably warm for New York City. More than a thousand police—a hundred of them on horseback—lined up on Seventh Avenue between West Thirty-first and West Thirty-third streets as the crowds began to pour into Madison Square Garden. Twenty thousand of the faithful packed the arena by eight P.M. for the largest political rally held in New York City since Franklin Roosevelt had denounced the forces of "organized money" from the same stage in 1936. At eight-twenty, George Wallace stepped out into the lights and the audience erupted. Although the campaign had another week to run, for Wallace, the evening was the emotional climax of his race for the presidency.

Across the street an astonishing collection of fringe groups gathered: a caravan of Ku Klux Klansmen from Louisiana who had driven all the way to New York; a delegation of followers of the "Minutemen of America," paramilitary ultra-rightists with neatly printed signs and armloads of brochures; a dozen jackbooted members of the American Nazi Party sporting swastika armbands and "I like Eich" buttons worn in memory of Adolf Eichmann, who had been sentenced to death by an Israeli court for his role in supervising the murder of millions of Jews during the Holocaust. New York police maintained an uneasy peace between the far-right contingent and the more than two hundred members of the Trotskyite Workers' World Party and several hundred members of the radical Students for a Democratic Society, bearing the black flag of Anarchy. Altogether, two thousand protesters—most in their early twenties—waved their picket signs and screamed their battle cries. Radical demonstrators mocked: *"Sieg heil! Sieg heil!"* The right wing countered: "Commie faggots! Commie faggots!"

Inside the Garden, while a brass band played a medley of patriotic songs, Wallace strode back and forth across the stage, saluting the crowd, which roared his name again and again in a chant that could be heard by the demonstrators half a block away. Soon he was joined by Curtis LeMay and his wife, Helen.

After more than fifteen minutes, Wallace finally brought his followers to order by having a country singer perform "God Bless America." Apparently overwhelmed by the fervor of the crowd, he began his speech awkwardly. In the southwest balcony of the Garden, a squarely built black man stood and held up a poster proclaiming "Law and Order—Wallace Style." Underneath the slogan was the outline of a Ku Klux Klansman holding a noose. Another demonstrator at his side suddenly turned on a portable bullhorn and began shouting: "Wallace talks about law and order! Ask him what state has the highest murder rate! The most rapes! The most armed robberies." The overwhelmingly pro-Wallace crowd exploded in rage, and police hurried to rescue three suddenly silent black demonstrators who were surrounded by a dozen Wallace followers shouting "Kill 'em, kill 'em, kill 'em."

The heckling seemed to ignite the Alabama governor: "Why do the leaders of the two national parties kowtow to these anarchists?" he demanded, gesturing toward the protesters in the balcony. "One of 'em laid down in front of President Johnson's limousine last year," said Wallace with a snarl. "I tell you when November comes, the first time they lie down in front of my limousine it'll be the last one they'll ever lay down in front of; their day is *over!*"

The crowd was on its feet for the first of more than a dozen standing ovations.

"We don't have a sick society, we have a sick Supreme Court," he continued, as he scornfully described "perverted" decisions that disallowed prayer in the classrooms even as they defended the right to distribute "obscene pornography."

Fifteen minutes into his talk, he shed his jacket as he weaved and bobbed across the stage, his right fist clenched, his left jabbing out and down as if he were in the midst of one of his youthful bantamweight Golden Gloves bouts. "We don't have riots in Alabama," shouted Wallace. "They start a riot down there, first one of 'em to pick up a brick gets a bullet in the brain, that's all. And then you walk over to the next one and say, 'All right, pick up a brick. We just want to see you pick up one of them bricks, now!'" . . .

Richard Nixon always saw the Alabama governor as the key to understanding the reshaping of American politics. Nearly twenty years after the former President left office in disgrace, historian Herbert Parmet interviewed him for a biography, *Richard Nixon and His America.* At the end of his fourth and last question-and-answer session, Parmet methodically outlined the conservative shifts Nixon had made after 1970 to placate the Wallace constituency.

"Your point is that we had to move to the right in order to cut Wallace off at the pass?" asked Nixon.

"Absolutely," replied Parmet.

"Foreign policy was my major concern. You start with that," said Nixon. "To the extent that we thought of it [the Wallace movement] at all—maybe subconsciously—anything that might weaken my base because of domestic policy reasons had to give way to the foreign policy priorities." There was "no question that all these things must have been there. . . . I think," he added, "it's a pretty clear-headed analysis." It was as close as the proud Nixon would ever come to admitting that, when George Wallace had played his fiddle, the President of the United States had danced Jim Crow.

In the decorous landscape of upscale malls, suburban neighborhoods, and prosperous megachurches that has become the heartland of the new conservatism, Ronald Reagan, not George Wallace, is the spiritual godfather of the nineties. During such moments of racial crisis as the spectre of cross-district busing, surburbanites occasionally turned to George Wallace in the 1960s and early 1970s to voice their protest, but he was always too unsettling, too vulgar, too overtly southern. With the exception of a few hard-line right-wingers like Patrick Buchanan, the former Alabama governor has been a prophet without honor, remembered (if at all) for his late-life renunciation of racism. . . .

But two decades after his disappearance from national politics, the Alabama governor seems vindicated by history. If he did not create the conservative groundswell that transformed American politics in the 1980s, he anticipated most of its themes. It was Wallace who sensed and gave voice to a growing national white backlash in the mid-1960s; it was Wallace who warned of the danger to the American soul posed by the "intellectual snobs who don't know the difference between smut and great literature"; it was Wallace who railed against federal bureaucrats who not only wasted the tax dollars of hardworking Americans, but lacked the common sense to "park their bicycles straight." Not surprisingly, his rise to national prominence coincided with a growing loss of faith in the federal government. In 1964, nearly 80 percent of the American people told George Gallup's pollsters that they could trust Washington to "do what is right all or most of the time." Thirty years later, that number had declined to less than 20 percent.

If George Wallace did not create this mode of national skepticism, he anticipated and exploited the political transformation it precipitated. His attacks on the federal government have become the gospel of modern conservatism; his angry rhetoric, the foundation for the new ground rules of political warfare. In 1984, a young Republican Congressman from Georgia explained the facts of life to a group of young conservative activists. "The number one fact about the news media," said Newt Gingrich, "is they love fights. You have to give them confrontations." And they had to be confrontations in a bipolar political system of good and evil, right and wrong. The greatest hope for political victory was to replace the traditional give-and-take of American politics with a "battleground" between godly Republicans and the "secular anti-religious view of the left" embodied in the Democratic Party.

The notion of politics as a struggle between good and evil is as old as the Republic; that moral critique of American society lay at the very core of populism in the late nineteenth century. But angry reformers of an earlier generation had usually railed against the rich and powerful; Wallace turned the process on its head. He may have singled out "elitist" bureaucrats as symbols of some malevolent abstraction called "Washington," but everyone knew that his real enemies were the constituencies those federal officials represented: the marginal beneficiaries of the welfare state. . . .

Much has changed in southern and American politics in the years since 1958 when George Wallace promised his friends that he would "never be out-niggered again." Middle- and upper-income suburbanites have fled the unruly public spaces of decaying central cities and created (or tried to create) a secure and controlled environment. Isolated from the expensive and frustrating demands of the growing urban underclass, suburbanites could control their own local government; they could buy good schools and safe streets—or at least better schools and safer streets than the inner city. "Big" government—the federal government—they complained, spent *their* hard-earned taxes for programs that were wasteful and inefficient and did nothing to help them. . . .

George Wallace had recognized the political capital to be made in a society shaken by social upheaval and economic uncertainty. As the conservative revolution reached high tide, it was no accident that the groups singled out for relentless abuse and condemnation were welfare mothers and aliens, groups that are both powerless and, by virtue of color and nationality, outsiders. The politics of rage that George Wallace made his own had moved from the fringes of our society to center stage.

He was the most influential loser in twentieth-century American politics.

FURTHER READING

John Andrew III, *The Other Side of the Sixties* (1997).
Mary Brennan, *Turning Right in the Sixties: The Conservative Capture of the GOP* (1995).
Robert Cantrell, *When We Were Good: The Folk Revival* (1996).
Richard Goodwin, *Remembering America: A Voice from the Sixties* (1988).
Elizabeth Cobbs Hoffman, *All You Need Is Love: The Peace Corps and the Spirit of the 1960s* (1998).
James Miller, *Democracy Is in the Streets* (1994).
Doug Rossinow, *The Politics of Authenticity: Liberalism, Christianity, and the New Left in America* (1998).
Tom Wolfe, *The Electric Kool-Aid Acid Test* (1968).

CHAPTER
14

Vietnam and the Downfall
of Presidents

The term Cold War *is a misnomer. Although borders were frozen in Europe, the war burned brightly—indeed raged out of control—for the United States in Vietnam. In Vietnam, the United States experienced what some consider its greatest failure as a nation, as well as the most obvious conflict between its historic "Spirit of 1776" ideal of self-determination and its military practice as a superpower.*

The United States became involved in Vietnam when President Truman decided to back France's attempt to retain its mutinous colony in 1946, following World War II. The American president ignored letters from independence leader Ho Chi Minh, who sought to free his nation from colonialism. Ho asked for U.S. support, but Truman decided to back his European Cold War ally instead. With U.S. financial support, the French fought the Vietminh (independence fighters under Ho Chi Minh) for four bloody years. By the time France acknowledged defeat in 1954, U.S. leaders had become convinced that it was necessary to divide the small nation permanently to ensure that the popular but communist Ho Chi Minh did not end up ruling the whole country. Flouting the peace treaty signed at Geneva, which temporarily partitioned the country at the 17th parallel in anticipation of elections two years later, the United States opposed a vote that would reunify the nation democratically. What followed was a twenty-year military commitment to the Republic of South Vietnam, a government wracked by civil war, corruption, and the suppression of domestic critics, including the Buddhist clergy. Why the United States decided to pursue the war— despite doubts within the government, the objections of our allies, and eventually the opposition of a majority of the American people—remains a subject for debate and national soul-searching.

The war boomeranged on the United States in a number of ways. It fueled a virulent protest movement, weakened the American economy, heightened racial and class conflicts, and brought home a generation of young men who were deeply disillusioned and in many respects damaged by the conflict. More than 58,000 Americans lost their lives, along with an estimated 3.8 million Vietnamese. The war also contributed to the downfall of two American presidents. Lyndon Johnson was the first to be accused of a "credibility gap," because of his insistence that the United States was not entering into a full-fledged war, even though it was. When it became clear that his Vietnam policy had cost him the confidence of the American

*people, Johnson announced that he would not run for reelection in 1968. Public
mistrust deepened considerably under Richard M. Nixon, who formed a "plumbers'
unit" to stop news leaks related to the war and to punish domestic political opponents. The Nixon administration eventually brought itself down when it attempted
to cover up its "bugging" of the offices of the Democratic National Committee at the
posh Watergate Hotel in Washington. Impeachment hearings in Congress, coupled
with the conviction of Vice President Spiro Agnew for fraud (a charge unrelated to
Watergate) and the conviction of other administration officials for perjury, led Nixon
to resign in disgrace on August 9, 1974. The president avoided criminal charges only
because his successor Gerald Ford (who had not been elected to either the presidency
or the vice presidency) issued him a blanket pardon one month later. The leadership
of America was deeply compromised; the nation's people were sorely divided.*

Q U E S T I O N S   T O   T H I N K   A B O U T

Was the Vietnam War necessary? Was it a tragic blunder, a noble cause, or an unfortunate but unavoidable outcome of the Cold War? How did it affect the American people
and the American presidency?

D O C U M E N T S

The documents in this chapter reflect different views on the Vietnam War. Document 1
sets out the initiating problem for the United States: did it want to support self-
determination or colonialism? In this letter to President Harry Truman, Vietnamese
independence leader Ho Chi Minh asks for the help of the United States, pointing to
Roosevelt's "Four Freedoms" and the recent grant of independence to the Philippines.
In Document 2, President Eisenhower articulates the influential "domino" theory: if
one country (like Vietnam) falls to communism, so will all the others. In Document 3,
President Lyndon Johnson claims that the United States is fighting to defend a vulnerable nation from aggressors sponsored by the Communist Chinese. The United States
seeks to defend the highest principles, Johnson claims, including peace, justice, and self-
determination. In Document 4, a defense analyst assigns percentage weights to U.S. war
aims in Vietnam for Secretary of Defense Robert McNamara. The preponderant reason
(70 percent) is to "avoid a humiliating U.S. defeat." The least important reason (10 percent) is to help the South Vietnamese enjoy a "freer way of life." Presidential adviser
George Ball advises Johnson in Document 5 to compromise with the North Vietnamese. Foreign white troops will not be able to defeat guerrillas who are supported
by the local population, Ball asserted in 1965, just before the full escalation of U.S.
forces. In Document 6, a young Marine relates his early idealism and subsequent disillusionment. The next two documents testify to growing opposition within the United
States. In Document 7, the Students for a Democratic Society urge Johnson to end U.S.
involvement, pointing to the contradiction between the Peace Corps, domestic reform,
and the war in Southeast Asia. In 1967 Martin Luther King, Jr., rejected the advice of
more cautious civil rights advocates and broke with Johnson over the war. In Document
8 he cites his higher responsibility as a minister to petition for peace. Document 9 shows
the paranoia and vindictiveness of the Nixon administration toward its critics, especially
those active in the antiwar opposition. In the last reading (Document 10), Senator Sam
Ervin, head of the Watergate investigation for the Senate, lists the crimes of the corrupt
administration. By 1974, the Vietnam War was finished, and so was Richard M. Nixon.
Public confidence in the American presidency had never sunk so low.

1. Independence Leader Ho Chi Minh Pleads with Harry Truman for Support, 1946

I avail myself of this opportunity to thank you and the people of United States for the interest shown by your representatives at the United Nations Organization in favour of the dependent peoples.

Our VIETNAM people, as early as 1941, stood by the Allies' side and fought against the Japanese and their associates, the French colonialists.

From 1941 to 1945 we fought bitterly, sustained by the patriotism of our fellow-countrymen and by the promises made by the Allies at YALTA, SAN FRANCISCO AND POTSDAM.

When the Japanese were defeated in August 1945, the whole Vietnam territory was united under a Provisional Republican Government which immediately set out to work. In five months, peace and order were restored, a democratic republic was established on legal bases, and adequate help was given to the Allies in the carrying out of their disarmament mission.

But the French colonialists, who had betrayed in war-time both the Allies and the Vietnamese, have come back and are waging on us a murderous and pitiless war in order to reestablish their domination. Their invasion has extended to South Vietnam and is menacing us in North Vietnam. It would take volumes to give even an abbreviated report of the crimes and assassinations they are committing every day in the fighting area.

This aggression is contrary to all principles of international law and to the pledges made by the Allies during the World War. It is a challenge to the noble attitude shown before, during and after the war by the United States Government and People. . . .

. . . [W]e request of the United States as guardians and champions of World Justice to take a decisive step in support of our independence.

What we ask has been graciously granted to the Philippines. Like the Philippines our goal is full independence and full cooperation with the UNITED STATES.

2. President Dwight Eisenhower Warns of Falling Dominoes, 1954

Q. Robert Richards, Copley Press: Mr. President, would you mind commenting on the strategic importance of Indochina to the free world? I think there has been, across the country, some lack of understanding on just what it means to us.

The President: You have, of course, both the specific and the general when you talk about such things.

First of all, you have the specific value of a locality in its production of materials that the world needs.

Ho Chi Minh to Harry Truman, February 16, 1946, reprinted in *Vietnam: The Definitive Documentation of Human Decisions,* ed. Gareth Porter (Stanfordville, N.Y.: Earl M. Corleman Enterprises, 1979), vol. 1, p. 95.

Public Papers of the Presidents of the United States: Dwight D. Eisenhower, 1954 (Washington, D.C.: U.S. Government Printing Office, 1958), 381–390.

Then you have the possibility that many human beings pass under a dictatorship that is inimical to the free world.

Finally, you have broader considerations that might follow what you would call the "falling domino" principle. You have a row of dominoes set up, you knock over the first one, and what will happen to the last one is the certainty that it will go over very quickly. So you could have a beginning of a disintegration that would have the most profound influences.

Now, with respect to the first one, two of the items from this particular area that the world uses are tin and tungsten. They are very important. There are others, of course, the rubber plantations and so on.

Then with respect to more people passing under this domination, Asia, after all, has already lost some 450 million of its peoples to the Communist dictatorship, and we simply can't afford greater losses.

But when we come to the possible sequence of events, the loss of Indochina, of Burma, of Thailand, of the Peninsula, and Indonesia following, now you begin to talk about areas that not only multiply the disadvantages that you would suffer through loss of materials, sources of materials, but now you are talking about millions and millions and millions of people.

Finally, the geographical position achieved thereby does many things. It turns the so-called island defensive chain of Japan, Formosa, of the Philippines and to the southward; it moves in to threaten Australia and New Zealand.

It takes away, in its economic aspects, that region that Japan must have as a trading area or Japan, in turn, will have only one place in the world to go—that is, toward the Communist areas in order to live.

So, the possible consequences of the loss are just incalculable to the free world.

3. Lyndon B. Johnson Explains Why America Must Fight, 1965

Why must this nation hazard its ease, its interest, and its power for the sake of a people so far away?

We fight because we must fight if we are to live in a world where every country can shape its own destiny, and only in such a world will our own freedom be finally secure.

This kind of world will never be built by bombs or bullets. Yet the infirmities of man are such that force must often precede reason and the waste of war, the works of peace.

We wish that this were not so. But we must deal with the world as it is, if it is ever to be as we wish.

The world as it is in Asia is not a serene or peaceful place.

The first reality is that North Viet-Nam has attacked the independent nation of South Viet-Nam. Its object is total conquest.

Of course, some of the people of South Viet-Nam are participating in attack on their own government. But trained men and supplies, orders and arms, flow in a constant stream from North to South.

Public Papers of the Presidents of the United States: Lyndon B. Johnson, 1965 (Washington, D.C.: U.S. Government Printing Office, 1967), 394–399.

This support is the heartbeat of the war.

And it is a war of unparalleled brutality. Simple farmers are the targets of assassination and kidnapping. Women and children are strangled in the night because their men are loyal to their government. And helpless villages are ravaged by sneak attacks. Large-scale raids are conducted on towns, and terror strikes in the heart of cities.

The confused nature of this conflict cannot mask the fact that it is the new face of an old enemy.

Over this war—and all Asia—is another reality: the deepening shadow of Communist China. The rulers in Hanoi are urged on by Peking. This is a regime which has destroyed freedom in Tibet, which has attacked India and has been condemned by the United Nations for aggression in Korea. It is a nation which is helping the forces of violence in almost every continent. The contest in Viet-Nam is part of a wider pattern of aggressive purposes.

Why are these realities our concern? Why are we in South Viet-Nam?

We are there because we have a promise to keep. Since 1954 every American President has offered support to the people of South Viet-Nam. We have helped to build, and we have helped to defend. Thus, over many years, we have made a national pledge to help South Viet-Nam defend its independence.

And I intend to keep that promise.

To dishonor that pledge, to abandon this small and brave nation to its enemies, and to the terror that must follow, would be an unforgivable wrong.

4. Defense Analyst John McNaughton Advises Robert McNamara on War Aims, 1965

1. U.S. aims:

70%—To avoid a humiliating U.S. defeat (to our reputation as a guarantor).

20%—To keep SVN [South Vietnam] (and the adjacent) territory from Chinese hands.

10%—To permit the people of SVN to enjoy a better, freer way of life.

ALSO—To emerge from crisis without unacceptable taint from methods used.

NOT—to "help a friend," although it would be hard to stay in if asked out.

5. Undersecretary of State George Ball Advocates Compromise with Hanoi, 1965

(1) A Losing War: The South Vietnamese are losing the war to the Viet Cong. No one can assure you that we can beat the Viet Cong or even force them to the conference table on our terms, no matter how many hundred thousand *white, foreign* (U.S.) troops we deploy.

"Annex—Plan for Action for South Vietnam," memorandum from John T. McNaughton, Assistant Secretary of Defense for International Security Affairs, for Secretary of Defense Robert S. McNamara, March 24, 1965; reprinted in *The Pentagon Papers: As Published by the New York Times* (New York: New York Times Co.,1971), 442.

"A Compromise Solution in South Vietnam," memorandum from Undersecretary of State George W. Ball for President Johnson, July 1, 1965; reprinted in *The Pentagon Papers: As Published by the New York Times* (New York: New York Times Co., 1971), 459–461, 464.

No one has demonstrated that a white ground force of whatever size can win a guerrilla war—which is at the same time a civil war between Asians—in jungle terrain in the midst of a population that refuses cooperation to the white forces (and the South Vietnamese) and thus provides a great intelligence advantage to the other side. Three recent incidents vividly illustrate this point: (a) the sneak attack on the Da Nang Air Base which involved penetration of a defense perimeter guarded by 9,000 Marines. This raid was possible only because of the cooperation of the local inhabitants; (b) the B52 raid that failed to hit the Viet Cong who had obviously been tipped off; (c) the search and destroy mission of the 173rd Air Borne Brigade which spent three days looking for the Viet Cong, suffered 23 casualties, and never made contact with the enemy who had obviously gotten advance word of their assignment.

(2) The Question to Decide: Should we limit our liabilities in South Vietnam and try to find a way out with minimal long-term costs?

The alternative—no matter what we may wish it to be—is almost certainly a protracted war involving an open-ended commitment of U.S. forces, mounting U.S. casualties, no assurance of a satisfactory solution, and a serious danger of escalation at the end of the road.

(3) Need for a Decision Now: So long as our forces are restricted to advising and assisting the South Vietnamese, the struggle will remain a civil war between Asian peoples. Once we deploy substantial numbers of troops in combat it will become a war between the U.S. and a large part of the population of South Vietnam, organized and directed from North Vietnam and backed by the resources of both Moscow and Peiping.

The decision you face now, therefore, is crucial. Once large numbers of U.S. troops are committed to direct combat, they will begin to take heavy casualties in a war they are ill-equipped to fight in a non-cooperative if not downright hostile countryside.

Once we suffer large casualties, we will have started a well-nigh irreversible process. Our involvement will be so great that we cannot—without national humiliation—stop short of achieving our complete objectives. *Of the two possibilities I think humiliation would be more likely than the achievement of our objectives— even after we have paid terrible costs.*

(4) Compromise Solution: Should we commit U.S. manpower and prestige to a terrain so unfavorable as to give a very large advantage to the enemy—or should we seek a compromise settlement which achieves less than our stated objectives and thus cut our losses while we still have the freedom to maneuver to do so.

(5) Costs of a Compromise Solution: The answer involves a judgment as to the cost to the U.S. of such a compromise settlement in terms of our relations with the countries in the area of South Vietnam, the credibility of our commitments, and our prestige around the world. In my judgment, if we act before we commit substantial U.S. troops to combat in South Vietnam we can, by accepting some short-term costs, avoid what may well be a long-term catastrophe. I believe we tended grossly to exaggerate the costs involved in a compromise settlement. . . .

. . . On balance, I believe we would more seriously undermine the effectiveness of our world leadership by continuing the war and deepening our involvement than by pursuing a carefully plotted course toward a compromise solution. In spite of the number of powers that have—in response to our pleading—given verbal support from feeling of loyalty and dependence, we cannot ignore the fact that the war is vastly unpopular and that our role in it is perceptively eroding the respect and confidence with which other nations regard us. We have not persuaded either our friends or allies that our further involvement is essential to the defense of freedom in the cold war.

6. A Marine Remembers His Idealism (1965), 1977

On March 8, 1965, as a young infantry officer, I landed at Danang with a battalion of the 9th Marine Expeditionary Brigade, the first U.S. combat unit sent to Indochina.

For Americans who did not come of age in the early sixties, it may be hard to grasp what those years were like—the pride and overpowering self-assurance that prevailed. Most of the thirty-five hundred men in our brigade, born during or immediately after World War II, were shaped by that era, the age of Kennedy's Camelot. We went overseas full of illusions, for which the intoxicating atmosphere of those years was as much to blame as our youth.

War is always attractive to young men who know nothing about it, but we had also been seduced into uniform by Kennedy's challenge to "ask what you can do for your country" and by the missionary idealism he had awakened in us. America seemed omnipotent then: the country could still claim it had never lost a war, and we believed we were ordained to play cop to the Communists' robber and spread our own political faith around the world. Like the French soldiers of the late eighteenth century, we saw ourselves as the champions of "a cause that was destined to triumph." So, when we marched into the rice paddies on that damp March afternoon, we carried, along with our packs and rifles, the implicit convictions that the Viet Cong would be quickly beaten and that we were doing something altogether noble and good. We kept the packs and rifles; the convictions, we lost.

The discovery that the men we had scorned as peasant guerrillas were, in fact, a lethal, determined enemy and the casualty lists that lengthened each week with nothing to show for the blood being spilled broke our early confidence. By autumn, what had begun as an adventurous expedition had turned into an exhausting, indecisive war of attrition in which we fought for no cause other than our own survival.

7. Students for a Democratic Society Opposes the War, 1965

Students for a Democratic Society wishes to reiterate emphatically its intention to pursue its opposition to the war in Vietnam, undeterred by the diversionary tactics of the administration.

We feel that the war is immoral at its root, that it is fought alongside a regime with no claim to represent its people, and that *it is foreclosing the hope of making America a decent and truly democratic society.*

The commitment of SDS, and of the whole generation we represent, is clear: we are anxious to build villages; we refuse to burn them. We are anxious to help and to

From *A Rumor of War* by Philip Caputo, pp. xii–xx. Copyright © 1977, 1997 by Philip Caputo. Reprinted by permission of Henry Holt and Company, LLC.

Kirkpatrick Sale, *SDS* (New York: Random House, 1973), 242–244.

change our country; we refuse to destroy someone else's country. We are anxious to advance the cause of democracy; we do not believe that cause can be advanced by torture and terror.

We are fully prepared to volunteer for service to our country and to democracy. We volunteer to go into Watts to work with the people of Watts to rebuild that neighborhood to be the kind of place that the people of Watts want it to be—and when we say "rebuild," we mean socially as well as physically. We volunteer to help the Peace Corps learn, as we have been learning in the slums and in Mississippi, how to energize the hungry and desperate and defeated of the world to make the big decisions. We volunteer to serve in hospitals and schools in the slums, in the Job Corps and VISTA, in the new Teachers Corps—and to do so in such a way as to strengthen democracy at its grass-roots. And in order to make our volunteering possible, we propose to the President that all those Americans who seek so vigorously to build instead of burn be given their chance to do so. We propose that he test the young people of America: if they had a free choice, would they want to burn and torture in Vietnam or to build a democracy at home and overseas? There is only one way to make the choice real: let us see what happens if service to democracy is made grounds for exemption from the military draft. I predict that almost every member of my generation would choose to build, not to burn; to teach, not to torture; to help, not to kill. And I am sure that the overwhelming majority of our brothers and cousins in the army in Vietnam, would make the same choice if they could—to serve and build, not kill and destroy. . . .

Until the President agrees to our proposal, we have only one choice: we do in conscience object, utterly and wholeheartedly, to this war; and we will encourage every member of our generation to object, and to file his objection through the Form 150 provided by the law for conscientious objection.

8. Martin Luther King, Jr., Takes a Stand, 1967

There is at the outset a very obvious and almost facile connection between the war in Vietnam and the struggle I, and others, have been waging in America. A few years ago there was a shining moment in that struggle. It seemed as if there was a real promise of hope for the poor—both black and white—through the Poverty Program. Then came the build-up in Vietnam, and I watched the program broken and eviscerated as if it were some idle political plaything of a society gone mad on war, and I knew that America would never invest the necessary funds or energies in rehabilitation of its poor so long as Vietnam continued to draw men and skills and money like some demonic, destructive suction tube. So I was increasingly compelled to see the war as an enemy of the poor and to attack it as such.

Perhaps the more tragic recognition of reality took place when it became clear to me that the war was doing far more than devastating the hopes of the poor at home. It was sending their sons and their brothers and their husbands to fight and to die in

Excerpt from speech delivered by Martin Luther King, Jr., "Declaration of Independence from the War in Vietnam." Authorized version of this speech reprinted in *Ramparts* (May 1967), 33–37. Reprinted by arrangement with the Estate of Martin Luther King, Jr., c/o Writers House as agent for the proprietor. Copyright Martin Luther King, Jr., copyright renewed 1991 Coretta Scott King.

extraordinarily high proportions relative to the rest of the population. We were taking the young black men who had been crippled by our society and sending them 8000 miles away to guarantee liberties in Southeast Asia which they had not found in Southwest Georgia and East Harlem. So we have been repeatedly faced with the cruel irony of watching Negro and white boys on TV screens as they kill and die together for a nation that has been unable to seat them together in the same schools. So we watch them in brutal solidarity burning the huts of a poor village, but we realize that they would never live on the same block in Detroit. I could not be silent in the face of such cruel manipulation of the poor. . . .

For those who ask the question, "Aren't you a Civil Rights leader?" and thereby mean to exclude me from the movement for peace, I have this further answer. In 1957 when a group of us formed the Southern Christian Leadership Conference, we chose as our motto: "To save the soul of America." We were convinced that we could not limit our vision to certain rights for black people, but instead affirmed the conviction that America would never be free or saved from itself unless the descendants of its slaves were loosed from the shackles they still wear.

Now, it should be incandescently clear that no one who has any concern for the integrity and life of America today can ignore the present war. If America's soul becomes totally poisoned, part of the autopsy must read "Vietnam." It can never be saved so long as it destroys the deepest hopes of men the world over.

As if the weight of such a commitment to the life and health of America were not enough, another burden of responsibility was placed upon me in 1964; and I cannot forget that the Nobel Prize for Peace was also a commission—a commission to work harder than I had ever worked before for the "brotherhood of man." This is a calling that takes me beyond national allegiances, but even if it were not present I would yet have to live with the meaning of my commitment to the ministry of Jesus Christ. To me the relationship of this ministry to the making of peace is so obvious that I sometimes marvel at those who ask me why I am speaking against the war.

9. White House Counsel John W. Dean III Presents the "Enemies List," 1971

[John W. Dean III to John D. Ehrlichman]   August 16, 1971

CONFIDENTIAL

MEMORANDUM

SUBJECT: *Dealing with our Political Enemies*

This memorandum addresses the matter of how we can maximize the fact of our incumbency in dealing with persons known to be active in their opposition to our Administration. Stated a bit more bluntly—how we can use the available federal machinery to screw our political enemies.

Senate Select Committee on Presidential Campaign Activities, *Hearings* (Washington, D.C.: U.S. Government Printing Office, 1973), vol. 4, pp. 1689–1690.

After reviewing this matter with a number of persons possessed of expertise in the field, I have concluded that we *do not* need an elaborate mechanism or game plan, rather we need a good project coordinator and full support for the project. In brief, the system would work as follows:

* Key members of the staff (e.g., [Charles] Colson, Dent Flanigan, [Patrick] Buchanan) should be requested to inform us as to who they feel we should be giving a hard time.
* The project coordinator should then determine what sorts of dealings these individuals have with the federal government and how we can best screw them (e.g., grant availability, federal contracts, litigation, prosecution, etc.).
* The project coordinator then should have access to and the full support of the top officials of the agency or department in proceeding to deal with the individual.

I have learned that there have been many efforts in the past to take such actions, but they have ultimately failed—in most cases—because of lack of support at the top. Of all those I have discussed this matter with, Lyn Nofziger appears the most knowledgeable and most interested. If Lyn had support he would enjoy undertaking this activity as the project coordinator. You are aware of some of Lyn's successes in the field, but he feels that he can only employ limited efforts because there is a lack of support.

As a next step, I would recommend that we develop a small list of names—not more than ten—as our targets for concentration. Request that Lyn "do a job" on them and if he finds he is getting cut off by a department or agency, that he inform us and we evaluate what is necessary to proceed. I feel it is important that we keep our targets limited for several reasons: (1) a low visibility of the project is imperative; (2) it will be easier to accomplish something real if we don't over expand our efforts; and (3) we can learn more about how to operate such an activity if we start small and build.

10. Senator Sam J. Ervin Explains the Watergate Crimes, 1974

Watergate was a conglomerate of various illegal and unethical activities in which various officers and employees of the Nixon reelection committees and various White House aides of President Nixon participated in varying ways and degrees to accomplish these successive objectives:

1. To destroy, insofar as the Presidential election of 1972 was concerned, the integrity of the process by which the President of the United States is nominated and elected.
2. To hide from law enforcement officers, prosecutors, grand jurors, courts, the news media, and the American people the identities and wrongdoing of those officers and employees of the Nixon reelection committees, and those White House aides who had undertaken to destroy the integrity of the process by which the President of the United States is nominated and elected.

Senate Select Committee on Presidential Campaign Activities, *Final Report* (Washington, D.C.: U.S. Government Printing Office, 1974), 1098–1101.

To accomplish the first of these objectives, the participating officers and employees of the reelection committees and the participating White House aides of President Nixon engaged in one or more of these things:

1. They exacted enormous contributions—usually in cash—from corporate executives by impliedly implanting in their minds the impressions that the making of the contributions was necessary to insure that the corporations would receive governmental favors, or avoid governmental disfavors, while President Nixon remained in the White House. A substantial portion of the contributions were made out of corporate funds in violation of a law enacted by Congress a generation ago.

2. They hid substantial parts of these contributions in cash in safes and secret deposits to conceal their sources and the identities of those who had made them.

3. They disbursed substantial portions of these hidden contributions in a surreptitious manner to finance the bugging and the burglary of the offices of the Democratic National Committee in the Watergate complex in Washington for the purpose of obtaining political intelligence; and to sabotage by dirty tricks, espionage, and scurrilous and false libels and slanders the campaigns and the reputations of honorable men, whose only offenses were that they sought the nomination of the Democratic Party for President and the opportunity to run against President Nixon for that office in the Presidential election of 1972.

4. They deemed the departments and agencies of the Federal Government to be the political playthings of the Nixon administration rather than impartial instruments for serving the people, and undertook to induce them to channel Federal contracts, grants, and loans to areas, groups, or individuals so as to promote the reelection of the President rather than to further the welfare of the people.

5. They branded as enemies of the President individuals and members of the news media who dissented from the President's policies and opposed his reelection, and conspired to urge the Department of Justice, the Federal Bureau of Investigation, the Internal Revenue Service, and the Federal Communications Commission to pervert the use of their legal powers to harass them for so doing.

6. They borrowed from the Central Intelligence Agency disguises which E. Howard Hunt used in political espionage operations, and photographic equipment which White House employees known as the "Plumbers" and their hired confederates used in connection with burglarizing the office of a psychiatrist which they believed contained information concerning Daniel Ellsberg which the White House was anxious to secure.

7. They assigned to E. Howard Hunt, who was at the time a White House consultant occupying an office in the Executive Office Building, the gruesome task of falsifying State Department documents which they contemplated using in their altered state to discredit the Democratic Party by defaming the memory of former President John Fitzgerald Kennedy, who as the hapless victim of an assassin's bullet had been sleeping in the tongueless silence of the dreamless dust for 9 years.

8. They used campaign funds to hire saboteurs to forge and disseminate false and scurrilous libels of honorable men running for the Democratic Presidential nomination in Democratic Party primaries. . . .

One shudders to think that the Watergate conspiracies might have been effectively concealed and their most dramatic episode might have been dismissed as a "third-rate" burglary conceived and committed solely by the seven original Watergate defendants had it not been for the courage and penetrating understanding of Judge Sirica, the thoroughness of the investigative reporting of Carl Bernstein, Bob Woodward, and other representatives of a free press, the labors of the Senate Select Committee and its excellent staff, and the dedication and diligence of Special Prosecutors Archibald Cox and Leon Jaworski and their associates.

⬛ E S S A Y S

The Vietnam War remains a political issue in modern America. Concerned about public cynicism toward government following Vietnam and Watergate, former Defense Secretary Robert McNamara admitted publicly in 1995 that "we were wrong, terribly wrong." In return, he received a firestorm of criticism, attesting to the continuing depth of feeling on this subject. After all, many of the military leaders, foot soldiers, widows, orphans, and witnesses are still alive. One of the most contentious issues is the necessity of the conflict. Americans still debate whether Vietnam was an important battle in winning the Cold War or a catastrophic detour from the pursuit of the nation's best interests. The first essay is taken from a book by Robert McNamara and historians James Blight of Brown University and Robert Brigham of Vassar College, with the assistance of professors Thomas Biersteker and Herbert Schandler. The book is based partly on the transcripts of meetings between 1995 and 1998 that brought together former enemies from Washington and Hanoi. The authors argue that the war resulted from a series of misunderstandings and was a tragedy for both sides. Because the book was written cooperatively, we have indicated in brackets the authors of the different sections. In the second essay, Michael Lind of the New America Foundation argues that the war was both moral and necessary. He asserts that U.S. involvement bolstered America's credibility as world leader and ultimately contributed to winning the Cold War.

Cold War Blinders and the Tragedy of Vietnam

ROBERT MCNAMARA, JAMES BLIGHT, AND ROBERT BRIGHAM

[*Blight and Brigham:*] According to an agreement worked out in Hanoi three weeks before the June 1997 conference, the first session would be taken up with presentations on the mindsets of the U.S. and Vietnamese sides.

The initial presentation was by Robert McNamara. It had been circulated in advance and was already familiar to the participants at the table. . . . McNamara admitted that he and his colleagues may well have misjudged Hanoi's motives and intentions due to the obsessive focus in Washington on the fear of falling dominoes. He concluded by inquiring as to whether Hanoi's estimate of Washington's intentions might have been similarly mistaken and thus connected to possible missed opportunities.

Former Foreign Minister Nguyen Co Thach gave the first Vietnamese presentation. He gave no ground whatsoever. The war was caused, he said, by the U.S. desire

From Robert S. McNamara, *Argument Without End: In Search of Answers to the Vietnam Tragedy* (Public Affairs, 1999), excerpts from pp. 38–42, 50–51, 62–72, 75–76. Copyright © 1999 by McNamara, Blight, Brigham, Biersteker and Schandler. Reprinted by permission of Public Affairs, a member of Perseus Books, L.L.C.

to become "master of the world." Because the United States backed the brutal and incompetent Diem, he added, it was forced to fight a war against the NLF and Hanoi. Thach agreed with McNamara that the U.S. mindset focused on dominoes as such was wrong. But Hanoi, he concluded, had the correct mindset—that the Americans were the "new imperialists." Nguyen Co Thach delivered this broadside with considerable emotion, and the audience in the large conference hall was utterly silent when he concluded. One wondered: Is it not possible, some four decades after events have transpired, to break into a genuine dialogue about mindsets— about the basic assumptions each side held about the other? The answer: yes—but not quite yet.

The second Vietnamese presentation was by former First Deputy Foreign Minister Tran Quang Co. He began by making a point that was to have considerable impact on the U.S. participants, one that would be made by all the Vietnamese participants: In order to understand the war, one must go back to 1945, not just to January 1961, when Kennedy came to office. He then listed the principal mistakes, as he saw them, in the U.S. mindset toward Vietnam leading to the war. . . .

Following are lengthy excerpts from what participants referred to as the "pre-dialogue" that started off our talks. Robert McNamara begins:

Robert McNamara: My thesis is that we must not permit the twenty-first century to repeat the slaughter of the twentieth; underlying any attempt to reduce the risk of future conflict, will be a better understanding of how past conflicts originated, and what steps might have been taken to avoid them or shorten them.

A retrospective study of the Cuban missile crisis made very clear that the decisions of the Soviet Union, the U.S. and Cuba, before and during the crisis, had been distorted by misinformation, miscalculation, and misjudgment.

Did similar forces shape the decisions of the United States, North Vietnam, and South Vietnam—and hence the course of the Vietnam War—during the 1960s? I now believe so. . . .

Now a major factor, of course, shaping the course of the war was the "mindset" that underlay the decisions of each of the participants. This is the subject of our first session this morning.

Before discussing the U.S. mindset, I want to state, and I want to state it quite frankly, that if I had been a Vietnamese communist in January 1961, when the Kennedy administration came to office, I might well have believed, as I judge they did, that the United States's goal in Southeast Asia was to destroy the Hanoi government and its ally the NLF—that the U.S. was an implacable enemy whose goal, in some fashion, was victory over their country.

Now why might I have believed that? Because the U.S. had:

- Rejected or ignored friendly overtures to President Truman from Ho Chi Minh in the summer and fall of 1945, following the defeat of the Japanese.
- Supported post–World War II French claims to its former colonies in Southeast Asia and had, in addition, throughout the early 1950s financed much of the French war against the Vietminh insurgents, led by Ho Chi Minh.
- Refused to sign the Geneva Accords of 1954, which thus thwarted the planned Vietnamese elections for 1956 that were mandated by the Geneva Agreement.

However, if I had been a Vietnamese communist and had held those views, I would have been totally mistaken. We in the Kennedy administration had no such view; we had no such aims with respect to Vietnam. On the contrary, we believed our interests were being attacked all over the world by a highly organized, unified communist movement, led by Moscow and Beijing, of which we believed, and I now think incorrectly, that the government of Ho Chi Minh was a pawn.

So put very simply, our mindset was indeed one of the fear of "falling dominoes."

Throughout the Kennedy and Johnson administrations, we operated on the premise that the loss of South Vietnam to North Vietnam would result in all of Southeast Asia being overrun by communism and that this would threaten the security of both the United States and the entire noncommunist world. Our thinking about Southeast Asia in 1961 differed little from that of many of the Americans of my generation who, after fighting during World War II to help turn back German and Japanese aggression, had witnessed the Soviet takeover of Eastern Europe following the war and the attempted move into Western Europe. We accepted the idea that had been advanced first by George Kennan in that famous 1947 "X" article anonymously published in *Foreign Affairs*: the view that the West, led by the United States, must guard against communist expansion through a policy of containment. That was the foundation of our decisions about national security and the application of Western military force for the next quarter-century.

Like most Americans, we saw communism as monolithic. We believed that the Soviets and the Chinese were cooperating and trying to extend their hegemony. In hindsight, of course, it's clear that they had no such unified strategy after the late 1950s. . . . At the time, communism still seemed on the march. Don't forget that Mao Zedong had aligned China to fight with Korea against the West in 1953. In 1961 Nikita Khrushchev had predicted communist victory through "wars of national liberation" in the Third World. Earlier he had told the West: "We will bury you." And that threat had gained credibility when in 1957 the USSR launched Sputnik, demonstrating its lead in space technology. . . .

So it seemed obvious to us that the communist movement in Vietnam was closely related to the guerrilla insurgencies being carried on in the 1950s in Burma, Malaya, and the Philippines. We viewed those conflicts not as nationalistic movements—as I think they were, with hindsight—we viewed them as signs of a unified communist drive for hegemony in Asia. . . .

We also knew that the Eisenhower administration had accepted the Truman administration's view that Indochina's fall to communism would threaten U.S. security. Therefore the Eisenhower administration had sounded the warning of the Chinese threat clearly and often. In 1954, it was President Eisenhower who coined that term "falling dominoes"; he said that if Indochina fell, the rest of Southeast Asia would indeed fall like a "row of dominoes." And he had added that "the possible consequences of that loss are just incalculable to the free world." . . .

Eisenhower wasn't alone in those thoughts. During his years in the Senate, John F. Kennedy had echoed Eisenhower's assessment of Southeast Asia. He had said—and I quote Kennedy's words in a speech he made in 1956: "Vietnam represents the cornerstone of the Free World in southeast Asia. It's our offspring. We can't abandon it, we can't ignore its needs." So we felt beset. We felt at risk. And that fear underlay the Kennedy administration's involvement in Vietnam. . . .

[*Blight and Brigham:*] It is hardly surprising that those who fought a brutal war against each other—whose everyday reality during the war seemed to confirm their assumptions regarding the enemy—that these former officials would only with difficulty, and over time, begin to probe the veracity of their decades-old mindsets.

This especially applies to the Vietnamese. To them, the U.S. was what may be called a "first order" aggressor or enemy. Americans came to their country and killed their people. As they saw it, this was without provocation on their part. As Tran Quang Co said, the Vietnamese did not ask for the war; it was brought to them by the American imperialists. Evidence of U.S. "imperialism," according to this view, is still everywhere to be seen in the unrepaired damage in Vietnamese cities and the countryside.

To the Americans, the Hanoi government was a "second order" aggressor or enemy that had invaded a U.S. ally. It did no direct damage to the United States as such. The damage the war did to the United States was real and is certainly still present, but it is less tangible than that to which the Vietnamese bear witness. Still, even to the participating former U.S. officials, there was a difficulty in facing, for the first time in most cases, in Hanoi, senior representatives of that ostensible "domino" that they had tried unsuccessfully to subdue.

The surprise was that real dialogue began soon after the break following the formal presentations. After some back-and-forth about the fallacy of falling dominoes, and several more attempts by some Vietnamese participants to establish the U.S. imperialist-colonialist "credentials," suddenly the ice was broken.

Chester Cooper, frustrated by the repetition of "imperialist" epithets, turns to the Vietnamese side—to anyone who cared to respond—and asks whether it is possible that they misread the United States. Luu Doan Huynh responds by saying that Hanoi did not want to fight a war with the United States—that they hoped to set up a coalition government in Saigon acceptable to all parties. He does not say Hanoi failed to do so, but that is what he meant, as he later clarified. Robert Brigham then asks the Vietnamese side whether they did not miss an opportunity to explain this to the United States. Nguyen Khac Huynh responds that they tried but that they lacked the sophistication and experience to know how to inform the United States without appearing to be weak.

From that moment, the discussion of missed opportunities, and of mistaken mindsets, became more reciprocal, a joint exploration by colleagues, rather than a latter-day confrontation of wary former enemies.

Luu Doan Huynh: . . . Between the early 1950s and the beginning of the Kennedy administration, the U.S. mindset toward Vietnam was influenced by some sort of irrational apprehension or nightmare. You know, there is something that they call the "blindness of history" that can be applied here. Everything, it seems, was perceived through the lens of Cold War politics. It was because of this that you gentlemen could not understand the rise of nationalist movements throughout the Third World, movements that became powerful in the 1950s and 1960s. These nationalist movements would eventually change the face of international relations. . . .

[*McNamara:*] As our discussions with Vietnamese officials and scholars evolved, I became keenly aware of how ignorant we had been. This first became apparent during our initial visit to Hanoi, in November 1995. At that time I conceived the period to be covered by the project would be the same as *In Retrospect*—that is, it should begin in January 1961, when the Kennedy administration came to office. That was what interested me. My tenure as secretary of defense was a period of escalation of the war. It was this period that I wanted to try to understand, and I went to Vietnam to propose that they join our group in the effort.

On November 8, 1995, I gave a preliminary presentation of our ideas at Hanoi's Institute for International Relations. In attendance was a group of about fifty Vietnamese, including current and former cabinet ministers, high-ranking military officers, and their top scholars of the war. Following my presentation, the floor was given to Nguyen Co Thach, former longtime foreign minister of postwar Vietnam and a key official during the war. He said that he supported the project, except for one flaw, which if not corrected would prevent it from being successful. "The flaw," said Thach, in a refrain we were to hear throughout all our subsequent discussions in Hanoi, "is that the most important missed opportunities happened before January 1961."

In particular, he mentioned two episodes that Vice Pres. Madame Nguyen Thi Binh would also bring up later in our visit: (1) Ho Chi Minh's unanswered appeals for support to Pres. Harry Truman in 1945 and 1946; and especially (2) the failure to implement the Geneva Accords of 1954—specifically, the failure to hold all-Vietnam elections in July 1956, which, he believed, would have permitted the reunification of Vietnam at that point. Thach's remarks were followed by those of Tran Quang Co, then the first deputy foreign minister, who supported Thach and who himself emphasized the singular significance of Geneva. "Without understanding Geneva, and the way we felt about it," Co said, "you will never understand our side of the Vietnam war."

Another member of our U.S. group intervened to say that, with all due respect, the former officials we were proposing to bring to a conference in Vietnam had no relevant experience during the earlier Truman and Eisenhower periods. In any case, he said, most of the relevant participants are dead. At this point Thach, who had been speaking in Vietnamese, intervened in English. Turning to Vietnamese scholar Luu Doan Huynh, seated next to him, Thach said: "Excuse me Huynh, are you dead? You're not dead, are you?" When Huynh reassured Thach on this point, Thach turned to me and said: "You see, he is not dead. And I am not dead either. Many of us on this side of the table are not dead. We would be happy to discuss the significance of the Geneva Conference with anyone you send to Hanoi who is not dead."

Of course, once his remarks were translated, the entire room fell into a fit of laughter, which helped to stimulate discussion following my presentation. But it also made a point that has remained vividly in my mind ever since: The Vietnamese see our conflict within a much longer span of time than we tend to in the United States. Our cabinet-level officials enter and leave government every four or eight years at most. The majority don't last that long. But many of the Vietnamese who would ultimately participate in our project had spent the better part of their long lives engaged in the singular task of fighting for Vietnamese unification and independence: against the French colonialists during the 1930s, the Japanese during the early 1940s, the French again during the 1950s, and later the Americans during the 1960s and 1970s. They thus had long memories and saw connections we needed to know more about if we were to understand their mindset during the 1960s, when the war escalated to an American war. . . .

I recalled the point made by Nguyen Co Thach and Tran Quang Co somewhat later, after we had agreed to include "Geneva, 1954" in our joint agenda. Instinctively, I opened *In Retrospect* to the index and looked up "Geneva," just to see what I had said about it in my memoir. But I discovered that "Geneva" is not an entry in the index. It now seems ironic to me that I had begun the second chapter of that book, "The Early Years," with an epigraph from Montaigne: "We must be clear-sighted in beginnings, for, as in their budding we discern not the danger, so in their full growth we perceive not the remedy." We begin . . . with the same epigraph, to emphasize the necessity of understanding how conflict begins as viewed by both sides. Why both sides? Because I had been equally struck on that first visit to Hanoi by the relative lack of knowledge—and even lack of interest—of the Vietnamese leaders in U.S. thinking during the 1950s and 1960s.

The View from Washington

[*Blight and Brigham:*] World War II ended in August 1945 when Japan surrendered unconditionally following the atomic bombings of Hiroshima and Nagasaki. Almost immediately, the number-one task in U.S. foreign policy became the rebuilding of Western Europe, including Germany, under what became the Marshall Plan. An important part of this effort involved finding ways to bolster the French in Europe and elsewhere, in return for French participation on the side of the West in the emerging confrontation with the Soviet Union, which was proving impossible to dislodge from the Central European countries it occupied after Germany surrendered on May 8, 1945. France, which had capitulated in 1940 and was occupied throughout the war by Germany, was in political turmoil. To policymakers in Washington, including President Truman and the man who would become his secretary of state in 1949, Dean Acheson, even liberated France might be at some risk of a communist takeover, by electoral or other means. Fear of this scenario led the United States to initiate a series of proposals that would, on April 4, 1949, lead to the formation of the North Atlantic Treaty Organization (NATO), with the United States and France among the signatories.

An important French quid pro quo for agreeing to participate in NATO and related collective security arrangements in Europe was U.S. assistance to France in reclaiming colonies in Indochina, including Vietnam. Incrementally, the United States acquiesced, despite its anticolonial past and inclinations. Dean Acheson later recalled:

> The U.S. came to the aid of the French in Indochina not because we approved of what they were doing, but because we needed their support for our policies in regard to NATO and Germany. The French blackmailed us. At every meeting when we asked them for greater effort in Europe they brought up Indochina. . . . They asked for our aid for Indochina but refused to tell me what they hoped to accomplish or how. Perhaps they didn't know.

In this way, with almost no thought given to the fate of Vietnam itself, Truman, Acheson, and their colleagues in Washington struck a Faustian bargain, by which the United States would eventually become the guarantor and underwriter of the unsuccessful French effort to reclaim its prewar colonies in Indochina. This was how U.S. involvement with Vietnam began: absent-mindedly, almost as a kind of "throwaway" in a grand bargain for the heart of Europe, to appease its defeated, temperamental, and proud French ally.

As seen in Washington, the stakes in Vietnam had risen dramatically by 1949. That year, the Soviets successfully tested their first atomic bomb, and the communists under Mao Zedong had simultaneously triumphed in China, raising the specter of a Soviet-Chinese effort to subvert U.S. interests in Asia, as well as Europe. The situation was deemed so dire that Acheson felt compelled to personally resolve a debate then in progress within the U.S. government about the true nature of Ho Chi Minh and his followers. In a May 1949 cable, he declared: "Question whether Ho as much nationalist or commie is irrelevant. All Stalinists in colonial areas are nationalists." Vietnam was about to become a pawn on the great global chessboard of the nascent East-West Cold War.

In mid-January 1950, "Red" China, as it quickly became known, recognized the Vietminh resistance in Vietnam, led by Ho Chi Minh. Ho's government became known as the Democratic Republic of Vietnam (DRV), even though the French still controlled the major Vietnamese cities of Hanoi, Saigon, and Haiphong. A few days after their formal recognition by Beijing, Ho Chi Minh and his colleagues reciprocated, recognizing the communist government in China. This led Acheson to proclaim in response that recognition of the DRV by the Soviet bloc (including Red China) "should remove any illusion as to the nationalist character of Ho Chi Minh's aims and reveals Ho in his true colors as the mortal enemy of native independence in Vietnam." In a countermove on February 7, the United States recognized the government in Saigon of the dissolute and ineffectual former emperor, Bao Dai, brought back by the French from Hong Kong in an attempt to provide a degree of legitimacy for their presence in Vietnam. So rather than recognizing French suzerainty over Vietnam, the United States chose to recognize the French puppet government. . . .

As Dwight Eisenhower, Truman's successor, would soon discover, underwriting the French effort in Indochina was a "dead-end alley." The French capitulation to Vietminh forces at the pivotal battle of Dien Bien Phu in May 1954 left Eisenhower administration officials unsure as to how they should proceed. . . .

The "containment" problem in Southeast Asia would be dealt with first in Geneva, at an international conference cochaired by the British and the Soviets. At first, the United States, Dulles in particular, wanted no part of an international conference cochaired by the Soviets that included communist Chinese participation on an equal footing with the other big powers. When it was clear, however, that the conference would unavoidably be the venue for deciding the Indochina question in the wake of the French defeat, the United States agreed to participate, as an "observer."

Whereas jockeying among the big powers consumed Dulles, the more mundane task of researching the Vietminh fell to Chester Cooper, a young CIA specialist on Southeast Asia. His first task, he later recalled, was to answer this question authoritatively: "Was there really a Ho Chi Minh—or more precisely, was the original Ho Chi Minh still alive?" Such was the level of Washington's knowledge of, and interest in, the Vietminh.

Dulles himself stayed only briefly in Geneva, conducting himself, as one of his biographers put it, like a "puritan in a house of ill repute," around the likes of the old Bolshevik, Vyacheslav Molotov, and "Long March" veteran Zhou Enlai, to say nothing of the representatives of the Vietminh guerrillas who were still at war with the U.S. French ally in Indochina. Dulles was heard to remark that the only way he would ever meet Zhou, who led the Chinese delegation, was if their cars collided. . . .

The Geneva Conference was driven by a deadline: If an agreement satisfactory to the principal participants was not reached by July 20, the new and fragile French government of Pierre Mendes-France would resign. This, it was generally believed, would completely destabilize the situation not only in France but also in Indochina, where the military and political situation was obviously far from resolved. . . .

From Washington's point of view, then, the result of the Geneva Conference was precisely the sort of disaster that had been feared. Among the provisions worked out at the last minute under the pressure of the July 20 deadline, the two most disturbing to the U.S. delegation were these: First, Vietnam would be partitioned at the 17th parallel, north of which the Vietminh would establish a "regroupment area" centered in Hanoi, and south of which France and the United States would organize a "regroupment area" centered in Saigon; and second, all-Vietnam elections would be held two years hence, on July 20, 1956, and based on the results, Vietnam would be reunified and a government established based on the results of the elections. In Washington, this could mean only one thing: A significant part of Vietnam was now "lost" to communism. On July 23, Dulles spoke about "the loss in Northern Vietnam." Walter Bedell Smith, head of the U.S. delegation, refused to sign the Geneva Accords, agreeing only to "take note" of these odious provisions. Smith felt compelled in the aftermath to deny publicly that Geneva was another Munich. But the analogy to the British attempt to appease the Nazis seemed all too apt in Washington.

Washington responded in two ways to this "loss" of part of a Free World "asset" in Indochina. First, the United States would establish the Southeast Asia Treaty Organization, on the model of NATO, for collective security from communist subversion in the area. But the more important and fateful move was to bring back to Vietnam Ngo Dinh Diem, a Roman Catholic Vietnamese expatriate who had been residing in the United States, to establish a government in Saigon that would provide a "democratic" alternative to the communist DRV. Arriving in early July 1954, Diem, financially underwritten by the United States, moved quickly to consolidate his control of the chaotic situation in South Vietnam—this new entity formally created in Geneva.

With money pouring in from Washington, with the South Vietnamese security forces being advised by the U.S. Military Assistance and Advisory Group in Saigon, and with a tough determination to prevail, Diem at first seemed to be the great foreign policy success Washington had been looking for ever since the Soviet bloc had begun taking assets after World War II. He was hailed as an "Asian liberator" who had succeeded in stopping the spread of communism in Indochina.

However, Diem would prove to be something of a Frankenstein's monster for Washington. The brutality of his regime increased, led by Diem's brother, Ngo Dinh Nhu, who directed internal security in South Vietnam. Predictably, such brutality backfired, and by the late 1950s a communist-led guerilla movement, with close ties to the Hanoi government, was already in control of parts of the South Vietnamese countryside. Moreover, Diem proved to be remarkably impervious to advise and counsel, even if it came from Washington. A mandarin, he believed he ruled with "the mandate of heaven," an attitude that infuriated his American underwriters and estranged his fellow Vietnamese. And so a vicious cycle was created. Diem used ever more brutal and arbitrary means to eliminate suspected communists, which in turn led to increased guerrilla activity. . . .

The View from Hanoi

In March 1945, the Japanese unilaterally ended French rule in Indochina and established a fictitious "independent" Vietnam under the emperor, Bao Dai. Meanwhile, the Vietminh, led by Ho Chi Minh, continued to gain strength, especially in the North and its major city, Hanoi. Following Japan's unconditional surrender on August 15, 1945, the Vietminh moved quickly in the chaos that followed to take the reins of government. During August 18–28, Vietminh-led insurrections occurred throughout Vietnam. Bao Dai abdicated on August 30. With the speed and efficiency of a blitzkrieg, the Vietminh movement had accomplished what would come to be known as the August Revolution. In less than a month, they had triumphed over the French colonialists, the Japanese invaders, and the imperial pretender.

On Sunday, September 2, after consulting with an American official in Hanoi about the wording of some phrases he wished to use from Jefferson's Declaration of Independence, Ho Chi Minh addressed a euphoric crowd of Vietnamese in Hanoi. He began and ended his remarks as follows:

> "All men are created equal. They are endowed by their Creator with certain inalienable rights; among these are Life, Liberty, and the pursuit of Happiness."
>
> This immortal statement was made in the Declaration of Independence of the United States of America in 1776. In a broader sense, this means: All the peoples on the earth are equal from birth, all the peoples have a right to live, to be happy and free. . . .
>
> We, members of the Provisional Government of the Democratic Republic of Vietnam, solemnly declare to the world that Vietnam has the right to be a free and independent country—and in fact is so already. The entire Vietnamese people are determined to mobilize all their physical and mental strength, to sacrifice their lives and property in order to safeguard their independence and liberty.

This was neither the first nor last time that Ho Chi Minh would reach out to Washington for support in the Vietminh's anticolonial struggle against the French. Ho was encouraged by what he saw as a common cause with the United States— both historically, as former colonies, and during World War II, in their joint fight against the Japanese. But Ho was unmindful of the postwar priorities in Washington, and for this reason his efforts to obtain U.S. support would come to nothing. Ho wrote at least eight poignant cables and letters to President Truman between October 1945 and February 1946, making the case for Vietnamese independence. But to no avail. None of the letters received a reply. At this stage, and for some years to come, Washington regarded France as the principal actor in the unfolding drama in Indochina. The indigenous Vietminh movement was perceived, if at all, as a "native" bit player.

By early 1950, the war against the French had settled into a grinding stalemate, with the Vietminh controlling much of the countryside, the French forces still holding the three major cities of Saigon, Hanoi, and Haiphong. Although the absence of U.S. support for the August Revolution was disappointing, and even though it was known that the United States was providing some support for the French effort in

Indochina, Ho Chi Minh and his followers at this point still seem to have regarded the French, and only the French, as their enemy. . . .

The mutual diplomatic recognition in January 1950 (that is, between the government led by Ho Chi Minh and the triumphant forces of Mao Zedong in Beijing) was an interesting and encouraging development. But a millennium of animosity and suspicion between China and Vietnam was scarcely to be overcome by an exchange of letters and diplomats. When criticized for negotiating a five-year term for continued French military presence in Vietnam in March 1946, Ho defended his position by implying that the alternative was to accept Chinese Kuomintang occupation forces of Chiang Kai-chek. He explained: "You fools. . . . The last time the Chinese came they stayed one thousand years. . . . As for me, I prefer to smell French shit for five years, rather than Chinese shit for the rest of my life."

Whatever illusions Ho Chi Minh may have had regarding assistance, or at least benign neglect, from Washington were exploded on May 8, 1950, when U.S. Secretary of State Dean Acheson announced that the United States would hereafter contribute to financing the French in Indochina. . . .

From this point forward—roughly from mid-1950—the Vietminh seem to have regarded Washington as a kind of deus ex machina of the French war effort. There would be no more citations of Jefferson and no more plaintive telegrams to the U.S. president. First, they must deal with the French.

But as Ho Chi Minh would soon discover, the interests of his Vietminh resistance were no safer with his fraternal Soviet and Chinese "allies" than they were with the French "number-one enemy" or the U.S. "interventionists." For in March 1954, when Vietminh forces under Gen. Vo Nguyen Giap were still dug in at the siege of Dien Bien Phu, discussions had already begun—discussions about which the Vietminh leadership knew little or nothing—among the French, British, Soviets, and Chinese regarding the terms under which the war in Indochina might be settled. They had agreed that the venue would be Geneva and had tacitly agreed that the best outcome—best for the big powers, that is—would involve a partition of Vietnam. . . .

Just as the French were surrendering at Dien Bien Phu (May 7, 1954), the Vietminh sent a delegation to Geneva headed by the acting minister of foreign affairs, Pham Van Dong. He was sent, as it were, to claim the spoils of military victory: a unified Vietnam, from which French troops would be withdrawn according to a fixed schedule. . . .

Such proposals were anathema to the Western delegations. The French were being asked to quietly fall on their sword, and their allies were being asked to assist the French in doing so. Of course, to the hardened guerrilla fighters representing the Vietminh in Geneva, the logic of their proposal must have been self-evident. They had won the war and now came to Geneva to take back their country. In theory, if they failed to get their way in Geneva, they could open a final offensive and physically drive the French out. However, the question such a possibility would pose was this: What will Washington do in response?

That question—would the Americans intervene?—may have provided the Soviets and the Chinese with all the leverage they needed with their nascent Vietnamese ally, as they repeatedly pressed Pham Van Dong and his team to agree to compromise after compromise. . . . Zhou and Ho Chi Minh met July 3–5 in Liou-Chow, on the Vietnam-China border, to discuss the Geneva talks, reportedly so Zhou could press Ho personally on the necessity for the Vietminh to accept a temporary partition of Vietnam and thereby avoid a U.S. military intervention.

Finally, they agreed. It must have been a doubly bitter pill to swallow for Ho and his compatriots, since the settlement was virtually identical to the one they had struck with the French in March 1946, with the temporary partition then being at the 16th parallel. Never again, one imagines, would the Vietnamese communists trust their big friends to look out for their interests. In fact, at the Paris Peace Conference, which settled the U.S. war in 1973, there were neither Soviets nor Chinese. They were not invited.

Ho Chi Minh claimed a partial victory on July 15 at a meeting of the Party's Central Committee. He said he understood that the burden of the Geneva settlement would fall hardest on his southern compatriots. He called on them, nevertheless, to "place national interests above local interests and permanent interests above temporary interests" over the following two years, until the elections leading to reunification would be held.

In spite of exuding what must have been forced optimism to buoy his southern comrades, Ho could not avoid expressing his deep concern that the United States was "becoming our main and direct enemy." His fear was prescient. As noted, there would be no elections. The Diem regime would turn out to be more efficient than expected at crippling the resistance movement in the South. As it happened, the situation in the South would become so desperate that Hanoi would be forced to abandon its line of pure political struggle and agree to direct support of an armed revolt south of the 17th parallel.

This shift happened in stages. First, with the passing of the deadline for the elections called for by the Geneva Accords, Le Duan, the Party's chief in the Nam Bo district in southern Vietnam (and destined to be named Party secretary in Hanoi in 1960), in 1956 had published an influential pamphlet called "The Path of Revolution in the South." Although not specifically endorsing armed struggle as the only path in the South, he implied strongly that the conditions there might soon warrant it. . . . Later, returning to Hanoi from a clandestine tour of the South in 1958, Le Duan reported to the Hanoi leadership that many Party organizations had been nearly destroyed by Diem's security forces.

In January 1959, the Party held its Fifteenth Plenum in Hanoi and passed what came to be known as Resolution 15. Declaring "the basic path of development of the revolution in the South is to use violence," Resolution 15 essentially permitted southerners to protect themselves and to fight back when necessary. In May 1959, Group 559 was formed, responsible for establishing the Truong Son Route, or Ho Chi Minh Trail, by which the North would resupply the resistance in the South. The momentum pulling Hanoi into the middle of an increasingly violent situation in the South culminated on December 20, 1960, with the formation of the NLF at a meeting in a secure area of Nam Bo (in the South). The formation and platform of the NLF was announced in an English-language broadcast over Radio Hanoi on January 29, 1961.

Hanoi officials had also apparently learned the lesson of Geneva. Hanoi's official history of the period indicates that in May 1960 the Chinese had exerted pressure on Hanoi to dampen enthusiasm in the South for armed revolt. The entry concludes defiantly: "Masters of their own destiny, the people of Vietnam strongly advanced the revolutionary war in the South." China, however, was only a big bully of an ally. The United States was now the big enemy, as indicated in Article 1 of the NLF Platform: "Overthrow the camouflaged colonial regime of the American imperialists and the dictatorial power of Ngo Dinh Diem, servant of the Americans, and institute a government of national democratic union." . . .

Nguyen Khac Huynh: First, about the Geneva Accords. I would have to say that we on the Vietnamese side regard the failure to implement the Geneva Agreement as the *biggest*—as the greatest and most important—missed opportunity to avoid the war. In retrospect, we can see that the Geneva Accords had wide support. The agreement responded to the hopes of the Vietnamese people and also corresponded, we believe, with the general international trend at that time. All participating countries approved of the agreement. Even the United States did not formally object, although the U.S. did not sign the document.

The implementation of the elections of 1956, as stipulated in the Geneva Accords, would, we believe, have been the best solution of all. Why do we say this? Because: First, the conflict would have been resolved in a free and open manner by all the people of Vietnam; and second, the elections would have been consistent with international law. If this had happened, then the so-called "Vietnam problem" for the U.S. would never have arisen again. Never again. Vietnam would have been unified and free, and thus no conflict among the different sides would have taken place. Mr. McNamara speaks in his book of the "tragedy" of the Vietnam war. The failure to implement the Geneva Accords is, we believe, the origin and main cause of the tragedy. . . .

. . . Historians must begin at the beginning, and the beginning—or at least where we believe it is fruitful to begin—is with the failure to implement the Geneva Accords. To do otherwise, we believe, would be doing an injustice to history.

Vietnam: A Necessary War

MICHAEL LIND

In the winter of 1950, Moscow was as cold as hell. On the evening of February 14, 1950, in a banquet hall in the Kremlin, three men whose plans would subject Indochina to a half century of warfare, tyranny, and economic stagnation, and inspire political turmoil in the United States and Europe, stood side by side: Joseph Stalin, Mao Zedong, and Ho Chi Minh.

In the 1960s, when the United States committed its own troops to battle in an effort to prevent clients of the Soviet Union and China from conquering Indochina, many opponents of the American intervention claimed that the North Vietnamese leader Ho Chi Minh's communism was superficial, compared to his nationalism. In reality, there *was* an international communist conspiracy, and Ho Chi Minh was a charter member of it. Beginning in the 1920s, Ho, a founding member of the French Communist party, had been an agent of the Communist International (Comintern),

Michael Lind, *Vietnam: The Necessary War* (New York: Free Press, 1999), 1, 4–5, 31–35, 38–41, 52, 54, 60–62, 64–65, 254, 256–257. Reprinted and edited with permission of The Free Press, a Division of Simon & Schuster, Inc. Copyright 1999 by Michael Lind.

a global network of agents and spies controlled with iron discipline by the Soviet dictatorship. In the 1930s, Ho had lived in the USSR, slavishly approving every twist and turn of Stalin's policy; in the 1940s, he had been a member of the Chinese Communist party, then subordinated to Moscow. Ho Chin Minh owed not merely his prominence but his life to his career in the communist network outside of his homeland. Because he had been out of the country for so many years, he had survived when many other Vietnamese nationalists, noncommunist and communist alike, had been imprisoned or executed by the French or by the Japanese during World War II. . . .

The Cold War was the third world war of the twentieth century. It was a contest for global military and diplomatic primacy between the United States and the Soviet Union, which had emerged as the two strongest military powers after World War II. Because the threat of nuclear escalation prevented all-out conventional war between the two superpowers, the Soviet-American contest was fought in the form of arms races, covert action, ideological campaigns, economic embargoes, and proxy wars in peripheral areas. In three of these—Korea, Indochina, and Afghanistan—one of the two superpowers sent hundreds of thousands of its own troops into battle against clients of the other side.

In the third world war, Indochina was the most fought over territory on earth. The region owed this undesirable honor not to its intrinsic importance but to the fact that in other places where the two superpowers confronted one another they were frozen in a stalemate that could not be broken without the risk of general war. The Soviet Union and the United States fought proxy wars in Indochina because they dared not engage in major tests of strength in Central Europe or Northeast Asia (after 1953) or even the Middle East. Indochina was strategic *because* it was peripheral.

Throughout the Cold War, the bloody military struggles in the Indochina theater were shaped indirectly by the tense but bloodless diplomatic struggles in the European theater. By going to war in Korea and simultaneously extending an American military protectorate over Taiwan and French Indochina, the Truman administration signaled its resolve to defend its European allies. American officials swallowed their misgivings about French colonialism and paid for France's effort in its on-going war in Indochina from 1950 until 1954, in the hope of winning French support for the rearmament of Germany. Khrushchev's humiliation of the United States in the Berlin crisis of 1961 persuaded the Kennedy administration that a show of American resolve on the Indochina front was all the more important. In 1968, concern by members of the U.S. foreign policy elite that further escalation in Indochina would endanger America's other commitments, particularly in the European theater, was one of the factors that led the Johnson administration to begin the process of disengagement from the Vietnam War. The Eastern European revolutions of 1989, which led to the collapse of the Soviet Union itself in 1991, deprived communist Vietnam of its superpower protector and ideological model. . . .

The Vietnam War, like the Korean War, the Afghan War, the Greek Civil War, the Taiwan crises, and a number of other conflicts, was at one and the same time a civil war and proxy battle in the Cold War. During the Cold War, Indochina mattered—and it mattered to the Soviet Union and China as well as to the United States.

Examining the Vietnam War in its Cold War context does not necessarily justify it. Indeed, some argue that while it was necessary for the United States to wage the

Cold War, success in the Cold War did not require the United States to establish or defend a protectorate over most of Indochina. This is the claim that was made by a number of American "realists" at the time of the Vietnam conflict and in the succeeding decades. Realism, or realpolitik, is the theory of international relations that emphasizes the primacy and legitimacy of power struggles in world politics. Several of the most prominent American realist thinkers—diplomat George Kennan, journalist Walter Lippmann, and scholar Hans Morgenthau, among others—criticized the Vietnam War in particular, and in some cases the Cold War as a whole, as an unnecessary or disproportionate response to the threats posed by Soviet expansionism and communist Chinese revolutionary radicalism. Within the U.S. government in the 1960s, Senator William Fulbright, chairman of the Senate Foreign Relations Committee, and Undersecretary of State George Ball, one of the Democratic party's most influential foreign policy experts, also used the language of realism to criticize what they considered to be an overly ambitious U.S. grand strategy.

The realist critique of the Vietnam War remains very popular today. It permits aging veterans of the sixties left, embarrassed by their former support for Ho Chi Minh's vicious dictatorship and their denunciations of American presidents as war criminals or their avoidance of the draft, to claim that they were right to oppose the war, even if their rationale was mistaken. . . . Finally, the fact that some of the policymakers who played a role in the war, like former Secretary of State Robert McNamara, have claimed that it was a mistake from the beginning has appeared to strengthen the realist critique (even though other policymakers, such as former national security adviser Walt Rostow, continue to argue that the war made sense in terms of U.S. strategy).

In light of all this, it is important to recall that there was, and is, a realist case in favor of the Vietnam War, as well as one against it. If some American realists such as Lippmann, Kennan, and Morgenthau doubted the importance of America's commitment to denying Indochina to the communist bloc, others, such as Walt and Eugene Rostow, Samuel P. Huntington, and John P. Roche, were convinced of the significance of that commitment. The fact that the United States was defeated in Vietnam does not necessarily discredit the strategic logic that inspired the U.S. commitment to South Vietnam, Laos, and Cambodia and their Southeast Asian neighbors. The failure of American policy in Indochina may have resulted from inappropriate military tactics, or the characteristics of the North Vietnamese and South Vietnamese societies and governments, or the support provided Hanoi by the Soviet Union and China, or the peculiarities of American political culture—or some combinations of all of these factors. The case that Indochina was worth a limited American war of some kind, particularly in the circumstances of the Cold War in the 1960s, is compelling in light of what we now know about the pattern and result of the Cold War as a whole.

Contemporary critics of the Johnson administration spoke of its "credibility gap" in connection with the Vietnam War. In addition to having exaggerated the progress of the United States and its South Vietnamese allies in the war, Johnson and his aides were accused of a failure to clearly explain the goal of the war to the American public and the world. Typical of this line of criticism is a comment in 1968 by William R. Corson, a former marine colonel in Vietnam, in his critique of the war, *The Betrayal:* "The emergence of the credibility gap came from the ill-fated attempts of Secretary [of State Dean] Rusk to justify the war successively as, first, a defense of Vietnamese freedom, then a defense of our national interest, and finally the defense of the world from the yellow peril."

Indeed, Johnson and officials of his administration provided several rationales for the escalation of the U.S. effort in Vietnam. Johnson cited "the deepening shadow of China. The rulers in Hanoi are urged on by Peking." On another occasion he stressed the need to thwart guerrilla warfare as an instrument of communist expansion: "Our strength imposes on us an obligation to assure that this type of aggression does not succeed." Secretary of State Dean Rusk stressed the potential effects of a defeat of U.S. policy in Southeast Asia on America's global alliance system, including "our guarantees to Berlin."

From today's perspective, the Johnson administration does not appear to have been more inconsistent or disingenuous in describing the aims of U.S. foreign policy than other U.S. wartime administrations. During World War II, the Roosevelt administration sometimes justified the U.S. effort in terms of the security of the United States and at other times claimed that the defeat of the Axis powers would help promote a utopian world characterized by the "Four Freedoms." In the run-up to the Gulf War, the Bush administration provided a number of rationales, including the atrocities committed by Saddam Hussein's regime (some of which were exaggerated) and the importance of Middle Eastern oil for American jobs. President Clinton and members of his administration explained the U.S.-led NATO war against Serbia in terms of a number of different rationales: the moral imperative of preventing or reversing the ethnic cleansing of Albanians in Kosovo by the Serbs, the need to demonstrate the military credibility of NATO and the United States, the economic importance of a stable Europe, and the danger that the conflict would expand and draw in Greece and Turkey. Government officials addressing different audiences on different occasions for different purposes may emphasize different goals of foreign policy. The apparent inconsistencies that result are not necessarily evidence of official duplicity or official confusion. Nor does the fact that some official goals were misguided or overemphasized mean that others were not sound.

What is more, the notion of the "credibility gap" ignores the possibility that in escalating the Vietnam War the Johnson administration had several purposes, not just one. By successfully defending South Vietnam against subversion from North Vietnam, a client of the Soviet Union and China, the United States could deter the Soviets, reassure its allies, discourage the adoption of the Chinese and Vietnamese model of revolutionary "people's war" by antiwestern insurgents in developing countries, and encourage the economic development and liberalization of South Vietnam as well as of South Korea and Taiwan, all at the same time.

While the U.S. intervention in Vietnam served a number of complementary purposes, there was a hierarchy among U.S. goals. The administrations of Kennedy, Johnson, and Nixon may not have made the hierarchy as clear as intellectuals would like. Nevertheless, in hindsight it is possible to identify the place assigned to different goals in the hierarchy of purposes by these three presidents and their aides. The chief purpose of the United States in Vietnam was to demonstrate America's credibility as a military power and a reliable ally to its enemies and its allies around the world. The danger was that if the United States were perceived to be lacking in military capacity, political resolve, or both, the Soviet Union and/or China and their

proxies would act more aggressively, while U.S. allies, including important industrial democracies such as West Germany and Japan, would be inclined to appease the
communist great powers. It was in this global geopolitical context that preventing
"falling dominoes"—whether in Southeast Asia proper, or in Third World countries
far from Vietnam—was important. Least important of all the U.S. purposes in intervening in Vietnam was promoting liberty, democracy, and prosperity in South Vietnam itself. The defeat of the attempted takeover of South Vietnam by North Vietnam
was a necessary, but not sufficient, condition for the evolution of the authoritarian
government of South Vietnam toward liberalism and democracy. But America's
political goals in South Vietnam were appropriately incidental and subordinate to
America's goals in Southeast Asian power politics, which, in turn, were incidental
and subordinate to America's global strategy in the third world war. . . .

Credibility, in power politics, is a country's reputation for military capability
combined with the political resolve to use it in order to promote its goals. The concern of statesmen with the reputation of their states for military ability and resolve is
as old as interstate politics. . . .

The natural concern of U.S. leaders with credibility was heightened into something like an obsession by the peculiar dynamics of the Cold War—a world war
fought by means of sieges and duels. Unlike World Wars I and II, the third global
conflict of the twentieth century took the form of a half-century siege on the European front and duels or proxy wars in a number of other theaters. The forward de-
ployment of U.S. troops in Central Europe, Japan, and South Korea following the
Korean War, together with U.S. efforts to maintain conventional and nuclear superiority, made up the siege aspect of the Cold War. In the long run, the superior military-
industrial capability of the United States and its affluent allies was bound to wear
down the military-industrial base of the Soviet empire, as long as two conditions
were met. The first condition for western success in the Cold War was alliance unity;
the alliance of the United States, West Germany, Japan, Britain, France, and the other
major democracies could not be split by a Soviet diplomatic strategy of divide-
and-rule. Meeting this condition required periodic reaffirmations of alliance unity,
like the development of the Euromissiles by NATO in the early 1980s in response
to Soviet intimidation. In addition, the American bloc was required to match and
surpass the Soviet imperium in the arms race. Because the goal was to spend the
Soviet Union into bankruptcy, not merely to defend the western allies against an
implausible threat of invasion, the American bloc could not accumulate a sufficiency
of nuclear missiles and other weapons and then quit. The arms race was an auction
that had to be continued until one side dropped out.

The military-industrial siege of the Soviet empire took far longer than early
Cold War leaders such as Truman and Eisenhower and their advisers had expected.
In the 1950s, Eisenhower hoped that U.S. troops might be withdrawn from Europe in
the next decade. Instead, the siege lasted almost half a century. While manning the
siegeworks in Europe and northeast Asia, the United States also had to demonstrate
its determination by threatening war, or, if the threat failed, by waging limited war,
with the Soviet Union and/or China and their proxies in regions on the periphery of
the main theaters of Cold War competition. Sometimes the United States had to fight
where it was challenged by its enemies, not where it would have preferred to fight.
Because perceived power is power (except in times of war, when actual power is

tested), the danger that a strategic retreat will be misinterpreted as evidence of a loss of will or capability is quite real. To refuse to duel is to lose the duel.

Thus defined, credibility became the central strategic concern of the United States in the Cold War. Henry Kissinger described the American interest in Indochina in terms of U.S. credibility in global power politics: "With respect to Indo-China, we are not equating the intrinsic importance of each part of the world, and we are not saying that every part of the world is strategically as important to the United States as any other part of the world. . . . [The question of aid to allies in Indochina] is a fundamental question of how we are viewed by all other people." John Foster Dulles made a similar point in calling on the United States to protect the anticommunist remnant of the Chinese Nationalist regime on Taiwan in spring 1950: "If we do not act, it will be everywhere interpreted that we are making another retreat because we dare not risk war."

Who was the intended audience for American displays of credibility? Makers and defenders of U.S. Cold War strategy reasoned that the United States had to deter its enemies and reassure its allies at the same time. In a speech at Johns Hopkins University on April 7, 1965, President Johnson invoked these two reasons for demonstrations of credibility in the context of the war in Indochina. First, he cited the need to reassure America's allies: "Around the globe, from Berlin to Thailand, are people whose well-being rests, in part, on the belief that they can count on us if they are attacked. To leave Vietnam to its fate would shake the confidence of all these people in the value of America's commitment, the value of America's word." Second, President Johnson sought to discourage America's enemies: "The central lesson of our time is that the appetite of aggression is never satisfied. To withdraw from one battlefield means only to prepare for the next. We must say in Southeast Asia, as we did in Europe, in the words of the Bible: 'Hitherto shalt thou come, but no further.'"

Using less orotund language, Johnson adviser John McNaughton, in a memo of March 25, 1965, emphasized American credibility in listing the aims of U.S. policy in Indochina:

70%:—To avoid a humiliating defeat (to our reputation as a guarantor)

20%:—To keep South Vietnam (and the adjacent territory) from Chinese hands

10%:—To permit the people of South Vietnam to enjoy a better, freer way of life. . . .

In the mind of the western public, the idea of defeat in the Cold War was associated with nuclear armaggedon. But the defeat of the United States in the global struggle might have resulted from America's backing down in confrontations involving Berlin, or Korea, or Taiwan, or Indochina, or Cuba, or similar contested areas charged with significance by the superpower rivalry. After the first major defeat or retreat, or perhaps the second or third or fourth in a row, confidence in America's military capability, or its determination to use it, would have collapsed. At that point, something akin to a panic in the stock market would have ensued. In a remarkably short period of time—a few years, perhaps even a few months—the worldwide American alliance system would have unraveled, as European, Asian, Middle Eastern, African, and Latin American states hurriedly made deals with Moscow. Thanks to runaway bandwagoning, the United States would have found itself marginalized in a world now aligned around the Soviet Union (there having been no other military power with global reach and global ambitions at the time). The Soviets might not have had to fire a shot in anger. There need not have been any additional communist revolutions. The same elites might even have remained in power in the same capitals around the world. Indeed, America's alliances such as NATO and the U.S.-Japan alliance might have lasted formally for a few more years, though moribund. But Moscow would have displaced Washington at the apex of the global military hierarchy, and everybody would have known it.

The bandwagon effect is the reason why it was a mistake to argue that the Soviet empire was bound to collapse of overextension. Power in the international arena is relative, not absolute. If the Soviet Union had managed, by means of military intimidation, to divide the alliance of the United States, Western Europe, and Japan, or to frighten the United States into isolationism and appeasement, then it might have achieved and maintained a position as the world's leading military power in relative terms even while it reduced its expenditures on the military. In the same way, the abatement of the Soviet challenge permitted the United States to become relatively more powerful in world politics in the 1990s, even as it slashed its defense spending and overseas troop deployments. . . .

The Cold War, then, was most likely to end with a rapid and more or less bloodless global diplomatic realignment in favor of the superpower that was perceived to be the most militarily powerful and the most politically determined. We know that this is how the Cold War would have ended if the United States had lost, because this is how the Cold War ended when the Soviet Union lost. . . .

It is possible to argue that even if the Soviet Union and China considered the fate of Indochina to be important, the United States could have ceded the region to one or both of the communist great powers with little or no damage to its foreign policy. During the Cold War, minimal realists such as George Ball, George Kennan, and Walter Lippmann advocated a strategy of finite containment limited to the North Atlantic and North Pacific as an alternative to the policy of global containment that the United States actually pursued. Ball wrote that U.S. strategy should focus on "the principal Atlantic nations." The only area of the non-European world of any importance, apart from Japan, was the Middle East, because of its oil reserves. The Vietnam War (and presumably the Korean War) was based on the mistaken equation of a commitment "in the jungles and rice paddies of a small country on the edge of nowhere with our most important treaty commitments to defend our Western allies in the heart of Europe—the center of world power and hence the center of danger." Like other minimal realists, Ball saw little reason for the United States to oppose Soviet imperial gains anywhere outside of an imaginary border that encircled North America, Western Europe, and the Middle East. Even the nearby nations of the Caribbean and Central America should be "free to create their own versions of chaos." . . .

. . . It might be argued that the "three fronts" of Korea, Taiwan, and Indochina were not as important in Cold War power politics as American presidents from Truman to Nixon believed. The question of whether a given country or region is strategic or not can be approached by means of a simple question: Do the great powers of a given era consider it worth fighting for? . . .

... [B]etween 1946 and 1989, every major military power of the Cold War era—the United States, China, France, the Soviet Union, and the British Commonwealth—sent at least some troops into combat in Indochina or nearby countries in Southeast Asia. If Indochina was a peripheral region of no strategic importance in world politics, it is curious that this fact escaped the attention of policymakers in Washington, Moscow, Beijing, Paris, and London.

If Indochina *was* a key strategic region during the Cold War for which the two superpowers were willing to fight, directly or indirectly, why was it of strategic importance? The answer has less to do with sea-lanes than with symbolism. The symbolic significance of Indochina in the global rivalry for world primacy between the American bloc and the communist bloc, and in the simultaneous competition within the communist bloc between the Soviet Union and China, arose from the fact that the Cold War was an ideological war as well as a power struggle. . . .

Even the relatively moderate Soviet leader Nikita Khrushchev emphasized that Moscow's support for communist revolutionaries in Asia was inspired not by the "national interest" of "Russia" but by the Soviet regime's ideology: "No real Communist would have tried to dissuade Kim Il-Sung from his compelling desire to liberate South Korea from Syngman Rhee and from reactionary American influence. To have done so would have contradicted the Communist view of the world." The Soviet Union was not only a superpower but the headquarters of the global religion of Marxism-Leninism, with zealous adherents in dozens of countries who looked to Moscow not only for military and economic support but for ideological guidance. Mao and his colleagues also viewed support for foreign communists as a test of their commitment to Marxism-Leninism. Zhou Enlai told North Vietnamese leaders in 1971, "Not to support the revolution of the Vietnamese people is like betraying the revolution." This viewpoint can be compared instructively with a recent description of Shiite Iran's foreign policy: "Because Iran sometimes portrays itself as a guardian of Shiites worldwide, experts in the region said today that it may feel under pressure to respond with military force if it can be proven that the Shiites [in Afghanistan] were attacked for reasons of religious faith."

The global alliance that the United States led in the Cold War was far more diverse than the communist bloc; it included liberal democracies, military dictatorships, and Muslim theocracies that shared little more than a common fear of Soviet power and influence. To the disappointment of Americans who wanted the United States to crusade for a "global democratic revolution," U.S. policymakers properly limited the goal of American grand strategy to the negative one of preventing hostile great powers from winning military hegemony over Europe, Asia, or the Eurasian supercontinent as a whole. The democratic wave of the 1990s was a byproduct of America's Cold War victory, not the goal of America's Cold War strategy. U.S. foreign policy had to be narrowly anticommunist because a pro-democratic foreign policy would have prevented the United States from having many allies outside of Western Europe, where most of the world's outnumbered democracies were found during the Cold War. . . .

What conclusions are to be drawn about the morality of the methods used by the United States in the Vietnam War? Johnson administration adviser John McNaughton, in a 1964 memo about U.S. Vietnam policy, stressed how important it was that the United States "emerge from the crisis without unacceptable taint from methods used."

A compelling case can be made that the United States was wrong for moral as well as for practical reasons to rely heavily on a strategy of attrition in South Vietnam between 1965 and 1968, when the war was a mixture of an insurgency and a conventional war. The attrition strategy was more defensible during the predominantly conventional stage of the Vietnam conflict from 1969–75.

The moral alternative to waging the Vietnam War by indiscriminate and disproportionate means, however, was waging it by more discriminate and proportionate means—not abandoning Indochina to Stalinism, to the detriment of both the peoples of Indochina and the U.S.-led alliance system. One can condemn many of the tactics used by the United States in Vietnam without condemning the war as a whole, just as one can condemn the terror bombing of civilians in Germany and Japan during World War II without arguing that the war against the Axis powers was unjust. . . .

Once the Vietnam War is viewed in the context of the Cold War, it looks less like a tragic error than like a battle that could hardly be avoided. The Cold War was fought as a siege in Europe and as a series of duels elsewhere in the world—chiefly, in Korea and Indochina. Both the siege and the duels were necessary. Power in world politics is perceived power, and perceived power is a vector that results from perceived military capability and perceived political will. The U.S. forces stationed in West Germany and Japan demonstrated the capability of the United States to defend its most important allies. U.S. efforts on behalf of minor allies in peripheral regions such as South Korea and South Vietnam and Laos proved that the United States possessed the will to be a reliable ally. Had the United States repeatedly refused to take part in proxy-war duels with the Soviet Union, and with China during its anti-American phase, it seems likely that there would have been a dramatic pro-Soviet realignment in world politics, no matter how many missiles rusted in their silos in the American West and no matter how many U.S. troops remained stationed in West Germany.

FURTHER READING

Stephen Ambrose, *Nixon* (3 volumes, 1987–1989).
Christian Appy, *Working-Class War: American Combat Soldiers and Vietnam* (1993).
Doris Kearns Goodwin, *Lyndon Johnson and the American Dream* (1977).
George Herring, *America's Longest War* (1986).
Mary Hershberger, *Traveling to Vietnam: American Peace Activists and the War* (1998).
Joan Hoff, *Nixon Reconsidered* (1994).
Frederik Logevall, *Choosing War: The Lost Chance for Peace and the Escalation of War in Vietnam* (1999).
Jonathan Shay, *Achilles in Vietnam: Combat Trauma and the Undoing of Character* (1994).
Marilyn Young, *The Vietnam Wars, 1945–1990* (1991).

CHAPTER
15

Ronald Reagan and the Conservative Resurgence

In the 1970s, Americans felt something that most of them had not experienced for a long time: economic fear. After two decades of steady expansion and rising incomes, the U.S. economy faltered badly. The combined effect of the Vietnam War and steady government spending on new social programs (guns and butter, economists fretted) sent the country into a recession. President Nixon took the U.S. dollar off the gold standard—devaluating the currency—and in 1973 the Organization of Petroleum Exporting Countries (OPEC) sharply reduced supplies of oil, forcing a steep increase in the price. Cheap gas was history. Under President Jimmy Carter, conditions worsened. Inflation and interest rates rose to record highs, and the plague of unemployment affected millions. Economic woes, along with the still-fresh loss of the Vietnam War, caused many Americans to wonder if the nation had begun to decline irrevocably. Carter articulated this crisis of confidence, but it didn't make anyone feel better to have the problem spelled out.

Ronald Reagan had played a hero on horseback in many a Hollywood film, and he promised that America would stand tall again. Reagan had no use for hand-wringing. As president, he brought to Washington the easy confidence of a movie star, and simply proclaimed that America was the greatest country on earth, entitled and needed to lead the Free World. Conservatives gloried in the moment. At last they had a president who could win the support of the country without compromising with liberals. Reagan promised to fight the Cold War against the "evil empire" to the finish, release the economy from intervention by government, lower taxes, and restore traditional family values. In office, Reagan presided over a wave of deregulation that dismantled structures that had been in place for decades and announced his sympathy for free enterprise by siding against unions. He also increased military budgets dramatically to restore confidence in American leadership and fight the Cold War. However, contrary to what most conservatives had expected, he did little to reduce government spending. Reagan cut back on welfare, but he refused to touch the most expensive entitlement programs, such as Social Security and Medicare. Because Reagan pursued his spending programs while cutting taxes, especially for the wealthy, the government budget deficit soared. The United States borrowed money from foreign lenders to make ends meet. By 1985, for the first time since 1914, America was a debtor nation. Supporters and critics alike called it the "Reagan Revolution," but they differed sharply on whether or not the changes were for the better.

As is always true in history, many of the problems and challenges that Reagan faced were beyond the control of any politician. For example, new technologies permitted a level of global integration never before possible. The "dot.com" revolution had its beginnings in the Reagan years, when the explosion in personal computers, networking, and satellite transmissions exposed Americans to an exhilarating and frightening world of economic interdependence. With a smaller and smaller government safety net, it seemed that individuals could fly higher and fall farther than before. In 1992 Arkansas governor Bill Clinton campaigned successfully against incumbent President George Bush (former vice president to Reagan) on a platform of fiscal prudence, economic reinvestment, reductions in defense, and job training for the poor. At the same time, Clinton supported welfare reform and positioned himself as a "New Democrat," neither liberal nor conservative as typically defined. The country entered a period of economic boom, and by the end of the century the U.S. government actually had an enormous budget surplus. The Reagan Revolution had shifted the nation to the right, but where it would go from there—and how it would maintain its position relative to other nations—was a matter for the future.

▶ Q U E S T I O N S   T O   T H I N K   A B O U T

What was the Reagan Revolution, if there really was such a thing? Did the president restore faith in America, as he intended, or did he split the nation between rich and poor? How did social values change during the Reagan era?

▶ D O C U M E N T S

The documents in this chapter look at the Reagan era from a variety of perspectives. In Document 1, President Jimmy Carter describes the disillusionment of Americans on the eve of the 1980 election. Apparently Americans did not trust Carter (who was soundly defeated by Reagan) to restore their confidence. Document 2 is President Ronald Reagan's second inaugural address, in which he cites renewed public faith in America as one accomplishment of his administration. Document 3 reveals Reagan's militant, implacable hostility toward the Soviet Union. In an address to a convention of evangelical Christians, he calls Communist Russia an evil empire. Document 4 outlines the goals of social conservatives who heartily supported Ronald Reagan and hoped that he would diminish the government's role in private life. Document 5 similarly expresses the sentiment of social conservatives who, like the president, opposed the Equal Rights Amendment, a proposed constitutional amendment that would guarantee women equal rights under the law. In this selection, Reverend Jerry Falwell articulates his hostility to feminism. As the founder of the Moral Majority, a political network of "born again" Christians, Falwell helped to lead the successful campaign against the constitutional amendment, which expired in 1982 when it failed to achieve ratification by the necessary three-fourths of the states. Document 6 reveals the economic woes that continued to plague the nation, some of which may have been worsened by Reagan's policies. The graphs given in this document show that the Reagan program did mean greater hardship for some Americans. Income inequality rose and real earnings fell through the mid-1980s. Document 7 illuminates some of the external causes of economic instability: new technologies and the global economy. In Document 8, Secretary of Labor Ann McLaughlin criticizes unions for resisting these trends. McLaughlin advocates deregulation of the workplace, alleging that union protectionism prevents people in the high-tech age from what is now called "laptop commuting." Document 9, however, reveals the darker side of deregulation and "home work"—a new kind of sweatshop employment for the poor, especially women and immigrants. In the last selection (Document 10), a journalist predicts that in the 1992 election, Americans will vote their purses. As a sign at Clinton's campaign headquarters instructed staff and volunteers: "It's the economy, stupid."

1. President Jimmy Carter Laments the Crisis of Confidence, 1979

It's clear that the true problems of our Nation are much deeper—deeper than gasoline lines or energy shortages, deeper even than inflation or recession. And I realize more than ever that as President I need your help. So, I decided to reach out and listen to the voices of America.

I invited to Camp David people from almost every segment of our society—business and labor, teachers and preachers, Governors, mayors, and private citizens. And then I left Camp David to listen to other Americans, men and women like you. . . .

These 10 days confirmed my belief in the decency and the strength and the wisdom of the American people, but it also bore out some of my long-standing concerns about our Nation's underlying problems.

I know, of course, being President, that government actions and legislation can be very important. That's why I've worked hard to put my campaign promises into law—and I have to admit, with just mixed success. But after listening to the American people I have been reminded again that all the legislation in the world can't fix what's wrong with America. So, I want to speak to you first tonight about a subject even more serious than energy or inflation. I want to talk to you right now about a fundamental threat to American democracy.

I do not mean our political and civil liberties. They will endure. And I do not refer to the outward strength of America, a nation that is at peace tonight everywhere in the world, with unmatched economic power and military might.

The threat is nearly invisible in ordinary ways. It is a crisis of confidence. It is a crisis that strikes at the very heart and soul and spirit of our national will. We can see this crisis in the growing doubt about the meaning of our own lives and in the loss of a unity of purpose for our Nation.

The erosion of our confidence in the future is threatening to destroy the social and the political fabric of America. . . .

The symptoms of this crisis of the American spirit are all around us. For the first time in the history of our country a majority of our people believe that the next

Jimmy Carter, "Address to the Nation," *Weekly Compilation of Presidential Documents,* July 20, 1979, pp. 1235–1241.

5 years will be worse than the past 5 years. Two-thirds of our people do not even vote. The productivity of American workers is actually dropping, and the willingness of Americans to save for the future has fallen below that of all other people in the Western world.

As you know, there is a growing disrespect for government and for churches and for schools, the news media, and other institutions. This is not a message of happiness or reassurance, but it is the truth and it is a warning.

These changes did not happen overnight. They've come upon us gradually over the last generation, years that were filled with shocks and tragedy.

We were sure that ours was a nation of the ballot, not the bullet, until the murders of John Kennedy and Robert Kennedy and Martin Luther King, Jr. We were taught that our armies were always invincible and our causes were always just, only to suffer the agony of Vietnam. We respected the Presidency as a place of honor until the shock of Watergate.

We remember when the phrase "sound as a dollar" was an expression of absolute dependability, until 10 years of inflation began to shrink our dollar and our savings. We believed that our Nation's resources were limitless until 1973 when we had to face a growing dependence on foreign oil.

These wounds are still very deep. They have never been healed. . . .

What you see too often in Washington and elsewhere around the country is a system of government that seems incapable of action. You see a Congress twisted and pulled in every direction by hundreds of well-financed and powerful special interests.

You see every extreme position defended to the last vote, almost to the last breath by one unyielding group or another. You often see a balanced and a fair approach that demands sacrifice, a little sacrifice from everyone, abandoned like an orphan without support and without friends.

Often you see paralysis and stagnation and drift. You don't like it, and neither do I. What can we do?

First of all, we must face the truth, and then we can change our course. We simply must have faith in each other, faith in our ability to govern ourselves, and faith in the future of this Nation. Restoring that faith and that confidence to America is now the most important task we face. It is a true challenge of this generation of Americans.

2. President Ronald Reagan Sees a Stronger America, 1985

There are no words adequate to express my thanks for the great honor that you've bestowed on me. I'll do my utmost to be deserving of your trust.

This is, as Senator Mathias told us, the 50th time we the people have celebrated this historic occasion. When the first President—George Washington—placed his hand upon the Bible, he stood less than a single day's journey by horseback from

Public Papers of the Presidents of the United States: Ronald Reagan, 1985 (Washington, D.C.: U.S. Government Printing Office, 1988), vol. 1, pp. 55–58.

raw, untamed wilderness. There were 4 million Americans in a union of 13 States. Today, we are 60 times as many in a union of 50 States. We've lighted the world with our inventions, gone to the aid of mankind wherever in the world there was a cry for help, journeyed to the Moon and safely returned.

So much has changed. And yet, we stand together as we did two centuries ago. When I took this oath 4 years ago, I did so in a time of economic stress. Voices were raised saying that we had to look to our past for the greatness and glory. But we, the present-day Americans, are not given to looking backward. In this blessed land, there is always a better tomorrow.

Four years ago, I spoke to you of a new beginning, and we have accomplished that. But in another sense, our new beginning is a continuation of that beginning created two centuries ago, when, for the first time in history, government, the people said, was not our master, it is our servant; its only power that which we the people allow it to have.

That system has never failed us. But, for a time, we failed the system. We asked things of government that government was not equipped to give. We yielded authority to the national government that properly belonged to States or to local governments or to the people themselves. We allowed taxes and inflation to rob us of our earnings and savings and watched the great industrial machine that had made us the most productive people on Earth slow down and the number of unemployed increase.

By 1980 we knew it was time to renew our faith; to strive with all our strength toward the ultimate in individual freedom, consistent with an orderly society. . . .

At the heart of our efforts is one idea vindicated by 25 straight months of economic growth: Freedom and incentives unleash the drive and entrepreneurial genius that are a core of human progress. We have begun to increase the rewards for work, savings, and investment, reduce the increase in the cost and size of government and its interference in people's lives. . . .

The time has come for a new American emancipation—a great national drive to tear down economic barriers and liberate the spirit of enterprise in the most distressed areas of our country. My friends, together we can do this, and do it we must, so help me God.

From new freedom will spring new opportunities for growth; a more productive, fulfilled, and united people; and a stronger America—an America that will lead the technological revolution and also open its mind and heart and soul to the treasuries of literature, music, and poetry and the values of faith, courage, and love.

A dynamic economy, with more citizens working and paying taxes, will be our strongest tool to bring down budget deficits. But an almost unbroken 50 years of deficit spending has finally brought us to a time of reckoning. . . .

We must act now to protect future generations from government's desire to spend its citizens' money and tax them into servitude, when the bills come due. Let us make it unconstitutional for the Federal Government to spend more than the Federal Government takes in. . . .

History is a ribbon, always unfurling; history is a journey. And as we continue our journey, we think of those who traveled before us. . . .

A general falls to his knees in the hard snow of Valley Forge; a lonely President paces the darkened halls and ponders his struggle to preserve the union; the men of the Alamo call out encouragement to each other; a settler pushes west and sings a song, and the song echoes out forever and fills the unknowing air.

It is the American sound. It is hopeful, big-hearted, idealistic, daring, decent, and fair. That's our heritage, that's our song. We sing it still. For all our problems, our differences, we are together as of old. We raise our voices to the God who is the Author of this most tender music. And may He continue to hold us close as we fill the world with our sound—in unity, affection, and love. One people under God, dedicated to the dream of freedom that He has placed in the human heart, called upon now to pass that dream on to a waiting and a hopeful world. God bless you, and may God bless America.

3. Reagan Calls for a Fight Against Sin, Evil, and Communism, 1983

The other day in the East Room of the White House at a meeting there, someone asked me whether I was aware of all the people out there who were praying for the President. And I had to say, "Yes, I am. I've felt it. I believe in intercessionary prayer." But I couldn't help but say to that questioner after he'd asked the question that—or at least say to them that if sometimes when he was praying he got a busy signal, it was just me in there ahead of him. I think I understand how Abraham Lincoln felt when he said, "I have been driven many times to my knees by the overwhelming conviction that I had nowhere else to go." . . .

There are a great many God-fearing, dedicated, noble men and women in public life, present company included. And, yes, we need your help to keep us ever mindful of the ideas and the principles that brought us into the public arena in the first place. The basis of those ideals and principles is a commitment to freedom and personal liberty that, itself, is grounded in the much deeper realization that freedom prospers only where the blessings of God are avidly sought and humbly accepted. . . .

I think the items that we've discussed here today [abortion and school prayer] must be a key part of the nation's political agenda. For the first time the Congress is openly and seriously debating and dealing with the prayer and abortion issues—and that's enormous progress right there. I repeat: America is in the midst of a spiritual awakening and a moral renewal. . . .

Now, obviously, much of this new political and social consensus I've talked about is based on a positive view of American history, one that takes pride in our country's accomplishments and record. But we must never forget that no government schemes are going to perfect man. We know that living in this world means dealing with what philosophers would call the phenomenology of evil or, as theologians would put it, the doctrine of sin.

There is sin and evil in the world, and we're enjoined by Scripture and the Lord Jesus to oppose it with all our might. Our nation, too, has a legacy of evil with which

Public Papers of the Presidents of the United States: Ronald Reagan, 1983 (Washington, D.C.: U.S. Government Printing Office, 1984), vol. 1, pp. 359–364.

it must deal. The glory of this land has been its capacity for transcending the moral evils of our past. For example, the long struggle of minority citizens for equal rights, once a source of disunity and civil war, is now a point of pride for all Americans. We must never go back. There is no room for racism, anti-Semitism, or other forms of ethnic and racial hatred in this country. . . .

And this brings me to my final point today. During my first press conference as President, in answer to a direct question, I pointed out that, as good Marxist-Leninists, the Soviet leaders have openly and publicly declared that the only morality they recognize is that which will further their cause, which is world revolution. I think I should point out I was only quoting Lenin, their guiding spirit, who said in 1920 that they repudiate all morality that proceeds from supernatural ideas—that's their name for religion—or ideas that are outside class conceptions. Morality is entirely subordinate to the interests of class war. And everything is moral that is necessary for the annihilation of the old, exploiting social order and for uniting the proletariat. . . .

Yes, let us pray for the salvation of all of those who live in that totalitarian darkness—pray they will discover the joy of knowing God. But until they do, let us be aware that while they preach the supremacy of the state, declare its omnipotence over individual man, and predict its eventual domination of all peoples on the Earth, they are the focus of evil in the modern world. . . .

Because [communist leaders] sometimes speak in soothing tones of brotherhood and peace, because, like other dictators before them, they're always making "their final territorial demand," some would have us accept them at their word and accommodate ourselves to their aggressive impulses. But if history teaches anything, it teaches that simple-minded appeasement or wishful thinking about our adversaries is folly. It means the betrayal of our past, the squandering of our freedom.

So, I urge you to speak out against those who would place the United States in a position of military and moral inferiority. . . . In your discussions of the nuclear freeze proposals, I urge you to beware the temptation of pride—the temptation of blithely declaring yourselves above it all and label both sides equally at fault, to ignore the facts of history and the aggressive impulses of an evil empire, to simply call the arms race a giant misunderstanding and thereby remove yourself from the struggle between right and wrong and good and evil. . . .

While America's military strength is important, let me add here that I've always maintained that the struggle now going on for the world will never be decided by bombs or rockets, by armies or military might. The real crisis we face today is a spiritual one; at root, it is a test of moral will and faith. . . .

I believe we shall rise to the challenge. I believe that communism is another sad, bizarre chapter in human history whose last pages even now are being written. I believe this because the source of our strength in the quest for human freedom is not material, but spiritual. And because it knows no limitation, it must terrify and ultimately triumph over those who would enslave their fellow man. For in the words of Isaiah: "He giveth power to the faint; and to them that have no might He increased strength. . . . But they that wait upon the Lord shall renew their strength; they shall mount up with wings as eagles; they shall run, and not be weary. . . ."

Yes, change your world. One of our Founding Fathers, Thomas Paine, said, "We have it within our power to begin the world over again." We can do it, doing together what no one church could do by itself.

God bless you, and thank you very much.

4. *National Review* Explains Social Conservatism, 1988

By now everyone knows that pro-family conservatives are a powerful political force. . . . What follows are the presumptions of the moral traditionalists.

The family is the fundamental institution of society; in the traditional society, it was your main source of comfort and strength. When you were a child, your father geared his life to providing shelter for your mother and you. As you grew, your family imparted the skills of survival, and gave you your religion and your politics. In your old age, someone with a blood connection would offer you a bed and a seat by the fire.

Today, these functions have atrophied. Your existence needn't cause your father to change his lifestyle, and in many circles it changes your mother's as little as she can possibly arrange. It is no reason for your father to stay with your mother; in the modern myth, she may even be more "fulfilled" without him around. If they do stay together, they play an increasingly small role in your up-bringing: the public-education system, backed by the courts, positively puts obstacles in the path of parents wishing to exercise control over what their children read and study, while government-sponsored clinics are permitted to dispense contraceptives and perform abortions on teenagers without their parents' even being told. In your old age, Medicare will pay the costs of your medical treatment if you are put into an institution, but not if your relatives care for you at home. It's likely that your children and their spouses will all have careers anyhow, which means they can hire someone to look after you but can't spend time with you themselves.

In one area after another, functions once performed by the family are now provided by the government or government-style agencies and institutions. The goal of the pro-family movement is not to destroy these institutions but to restore to the family its proper functions, and to restore to the institutions an understanding of the proper proportion of their role. . . .

It all comes down to values. Traditional values work because they are the guidelines most consistent with human nature for producing happiness and achievement. Children who are not trained to traditional values are deprived of the best opportunity to understand their own nature and achieve that happiness. Children who *are* trained to these values are nonetheless free, upon maturity, to reject them: that is why, contrary to what the relativists insist, instilling them is not oppressive. But if these values are at least transmitted to all members of society, the possibility for a fundamental consensus on behavior exists.

Ronald Reagan got elected and reelected in large part because enough people agreed that the policies of the welfare state had failed, and enough wanted to hear more about traditional values. The public wanted government to shrink its role in their lives. That basic impulse has been developed for eight years now. In the meantime, we still have a welfare state that shows no signs of curing a single social ill, let alone withering away—it is, of course, intrinsically incapable of doing either. . . . This system perpetuates itself and the problems it pretends to solve; and yet we cannot follow the vision on which Ronald Reagan was elected until the way society organizes its approach to problems is changed—until people are again in charge of their own affairs, and those of their local community.

5. Baptist Minister Jerry Falwell Condemns Feminism and the Equal Rights Amendment, 1980

I believe that at the foundation of the women's liberation movement there is a minority core of women who were once bored with life, whose real problems are spiritual problems. Many women have never accepted their God-given roles. They live in disobedience to God's laws and have promoted their godless philosophy throughout our society. God Almighty created men and women biologically different and with differing needs and roles. He made men and women to complement each other and to love each other. Not all the women involved in the feminist movement are radicals. Some are misinformed, and some are lonely women who like being housewives and helpmeets and mothers, but whose husbands spend little time at home and who take no interest in their wives and children. Sometimes the full load of rearing a family becomes a great burden to a woman who is not supported by a man. Women who work should be respected and accorded dignity and equal rewards for equal work. But this is not what the present feminist movement and equal rights movement are all about. . . .

The Equal Rights Amendment strikes at the foundation of our entire social structure. If passed, this amendment would accomplish exactly the opposite of its outward claims. By mandating an absolute equality under the law, it will actually take away many of the special rights women now enjoy. ERA is not merely a political issue, but a moral issue as well. A definite violation of holy Scripture, ERA defies the mandate that "the husband is the head of the wife, even as Christ is the head of the church" (Ep. 5:23). In 1 Peter 3:7 we read that husbands are to give their wives honor as unto the weaker vessel, that they are both heirs together of the grace of life. Because a woman is weaker does not mean that she is less important.

---

6. Facts and Figures: Graphs on Earnings, Inequality, and Imports, 1986

Real Average Weekly Earnings, 1947–1986 (in 1986 dollars)

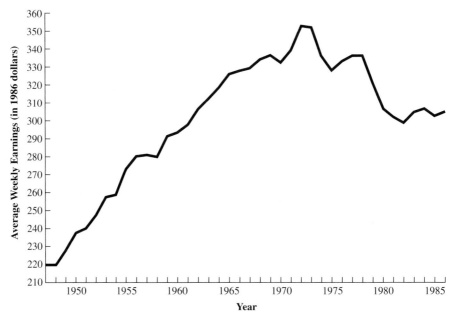

Source: Council of Economic Advisers, *Economic Report of the President, 1987* (Washington, D.C.: Government Printing Office, 1987).

The Import Surge into the United States

	Total Imports as a Percentage of GNP	Imported Merchandise as a Percentage of GNP Originating in the U.S. Manufacturing Sector
1929	5.7	—
1939	3.7	—
1949	3.8	9.5
1959	4.7	10.8
1969	5.7	13.9
1979	10.9	37.8
1986	11.4	44.7

Sources: Council of Economic Advisers, *Economic Report of the President, 1986* (Washington, D.C.: Government Printing Office, 1986); Council of Economic Advisers, "Economic Indicators" (September 1986); and U.S. Department of Commerce, Bureau of Economic Analysis, *Survey of Current Business* 67, no. 4 (April 1987).

Bennett Harrison and Barry Bluestone, *The Great U-Turn: Corporate Restructuring and the Polarizing of America* (New York: Basic Books, 1988).

Family Income Inequality, 1947–1986 (GINI Index)

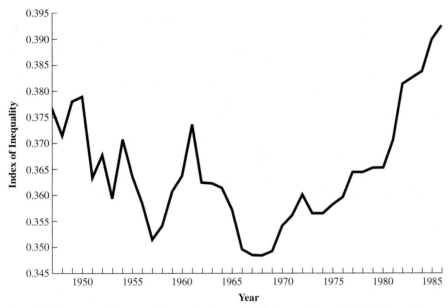

Source: U.S. Department of Commerce, Bureau of the Census, "Money Income of Households, Families, and Persons in the United States: 1984" (Washington, D.C.: Government Printing Office, 1986) and unpublished tabulations provided by the U.S. Census Bureau.

7. A Unionist Blasts the Export of Jobs, 1987

For the past 15 years, we have been occupied with the very real problem of jobs leaving this country. In most cases, these are jobs like the making of a wrench, or making apparel, steel, autos. We have tried to deal with this problem through legislation as well as in collective bargaining. However, with the advent of new technology, such as satellite communication and computers, it is easier than ever for employers to move new technology and capital across borders.

One example of this is American Airlines, which historically used keypunch operators earning between $8 and $10 an hour to process the previous day's used tickets and handle the billing and record-keeping. This is now done in Barbados for $2 an hour!

Each day an American Airlines aircraft flies to Barbados and deposits the tickets which are keypunched at one-fourth or one-fifth the U.S. wage level, and then transmitted back to the United States via satellite in finished form.

Trammel Crow Company, the nation's largest real estate company, has established a series of data bases in the People's Republic of China. They train university students in the English language, not in reading and writing, but in the recognition of

Speech in possession of Eileen Boris. This document can be found in Eileen Boris and Nelson Lichtenstein, *Major Problems in the History of American Workers* (Boston: Houghton Mifflin, 1991), pp. 646–647.

letters so they can keypunch them into the data base. Then, upon graduation, they are hired at a wage of a dollar a day!

When questioned, Trammel Crow said that it did not go to China for the dollar a day wage, but that the Chinese workers are more efficient because they cannot read and understand the English language, so they don't become engrossed in what they are punching.

Pier 1 Imports became the first American company to store its inventory records in China. Several hospitals followed, and now American hospitals are storing medical records in China.

The scope of this is endless.

Anyone who has a business where record-keeping is a vital part can store data anywhere in the globe through satellite transmission and a relatively simple computer with a printer. And it can retrieve it at will. . . .

What makes all of this technology frightening as well as exciting is that it was supposed to create a new type of service job that was going to somehow supplement, if not totally offset, the blue collar jobs that have been lost.

But the lesson it teaches us is that notwithstanding our particular occupations or job titles, that job, if not now, in the very near future, is going to be totally done in another country where wages are cheaper.

Therefore, it is important that we face these problems today and take charge of our own destiny, because no one else is going to do it.

8. The Secretary of Labor Applauds Deregulation of Home Work, 1988

One axiom of public life is that great battles are often fought over small issues: case in point, industrial home work.

In November, the Department of Labor lifted a 45-year-old ban on industrial home work in five industries—jewelry, buttons and buckles, embroideries, handkerchiefs and gloves and mittens.

The prohibitions had had some ridiculous consequences. It was illegal, for example, to make women's underwear at home, but boxer shorts you could have sewn to your heart's content.

Nevertheless, given the history of this issue, we expected that the end of the ban would generate controversy and perhaps legal obstructions (courtesy of organized labor), and we were right. Attacks from a number of sources began immediately. . . . In truth, the issue of industrial home work has relatively little to do with whether a mother with young children can supplement her family's income by making knitted hats or belt buckles at home. It has everything to do with whether millions in the work force, using new technology such as personal computers and fax machines, will be able to do so. It is the latter that organized labor opposes—it wants to prevent business technology from leaving the traditional work place. As early as 1983, the

Excerpt from "The Small Issue, The Big Picture," by Ann McLaughlin, *The Washington Post,* Dec. 31, 1988. Copyright © 1988 by *The Washington Post.* Reprinted with permission.

Service Employees International Union, which represents 780,000 clerical and health workers, forbade its members to work at home. . . .

Suppose, as organized labor claims, industrial home work does have the potential for worker exploitation. The fact is, the Department of Labor is serious about enforcing laws that prevent abuse.

The unions' approach to preventing labor abuse is to prevent labor. They are willing to see workers go idle, including older workers and those in economically depressed areas.

By contrast, our approach is to build an enforcement mechanism, and then allow people to work. If providing job opportunities for America's workers isn't the mission of the Department of Labor, I don't know what is.

So there it is. A small issue with some big symbols attached. As the rhetoric heats up in January, remember what the real debate is about—freedom of choice.

9. Immigrants Do "Home Work" in Modern Sweatshops, 1988

A building that looks like it never saw better days is home to a cramped belt factory on Eighth Avenue.

Here, in the heart of Manhattan's Garment District, are about 20 workers— packed into a windowless room with only one door, partially blocked by stacks of boxes.

Welcome to the sweatshop of the 1980s.

Cats dart across the factory, ignoring the incessant whir of high-speed sewing machines and the clatter of presses stamping holes in the belts. The machines and their operators compete for space.

There is not much room for error. An errant bump or nudge could mean a lost finger or arm.

Against the wall is a broken clock with dusty time cards. But that doesn't matter. Chances are, the employees are being paid "off the books" anyway, at salaries below the minimum wage.

Joe Halik wants to change all that.

"We're looking for victims of opportunity," he said.

Halik is one of the supervisors of the state Labor Department's Apparel Industry Task Force, whose job it is to crack down on the undesirables in the garment industry.

The state Labor Department estimates there are an estimated 4,000 such shops in the metropolitan area, employing about 50,000 workers. The European immigrants who toiled in these shops at the turn of the century have been replaced by poor women and illegal aliens, most of them Hispanic and Chinese.

"They're bypassing California and coming straight here," Halik said.

The 20 investigators on the task force are looking for violations of laws governing the minimum wage, industrial homework and child labor. They also check

Excerpt from Heidl Hartmann in Lourdes Benerla and Catherine R. Stimpson, eds., *Women, Households, and the Economy,* 1987, pp. 33–36, 41–49, 54–59, with some abridgements, no footnotes. Reprinted by permission of Rutgers University Press.

whether a business is paying for unemployment and disability insurance, as well as making contributions to the workers' compensation fund.

The task force has been able to keep better tabs and more vigorously enforce those laws since January, when makers of women's and children's wear had to register with the state to prove those payments are being made.

During two days spent with task force investigators in Manhattan, Rockland, and Westchester, it became clear that registration has been slow to catch on in an industry leery of outsiders. Perhaps with good reason.

"What they're doing is perpetuating the system to keep everyone low," said another task force supervisor, Charles DeSiervo, who estimated that 70 percent of the apparel makers are not registered.

Eight task force members start their work on a recent day on Eighth Avenue, watching other people go to work.

A slight Hispanic woman walks toward a building on 38th Street carrying a large shopping bag. She soon has company. Two investigators have trailed her to the top floor of a building housing dozens of clothing firms.

They hit paydirt when they arrive at a business and discover that the bag contains hundreds of pieces of lace that will go on gowns and dresses. By all appearances, it is a violation of rules governing doing industrial work at home.

The practice is banned because it usually means the employee is not getting overtime for work done after a full day in the factory. Payment is usually by the piece and is invariably done "under the table."

DeSiervo believes that curbing home work is one of the keys to cleaning up the industry.

"Home work was rampant; it was all through the streets," DeSiervo said. "They're starting to notice us. What it takes is strict enforcement."

While investigator San Bargas quizzes, in Spanish, the woman with the shopping bag, the surprised owner of the shop insists it is the first time this has ever happened. Halik looks mildly amused.

"It's always the first time," he said.

10. Bill Clinton's 1992 Campaign: "It's the Economy, Stupid"

At the Clinton campaign headquarters in Little Rock, Arkansas, a simple slogan is taped to the wall for staff members to ponder. In large letters, it reads: "The Economy, Stupid." That is what will win their man the election. All else is mere distraction.

In poll after poll, interview after interview, the message is confirmed. A recent New York Times survey showed 77 per cent of voters disapproving of George Bush's handling of the economy, with only 17 per cent giving him the benefit of

Excerpt from David Usborne, "The US Presidential Elections: American Voters Give Priority to Their Purses," first published in *The Independent* (London), October 5, 1992. Reprinted by permission.

the doubt. And every poll shows that issues such as Bill Clinton's avoidance of the Vietnam draft or the Republican emphasis on family values matter little to voters besides their purses.

For Governor Clinton, President Bush's economic record offers a veritable pick'n'mix of campaign attack lines. As he takes to the stump every day, he recites an unemployment rate that is more than 2 per cent higher than when Mr Bush took office, an economic growth record worse than any during a presidential term since the Second World War and income figures showing most working Americans worse off than they were four years ago. . . .

. . . Meanwhile, retail sales struggle, new house sales fell 6.1 per cent in August and all measures of consumer and business confidence continue to be depressed.

In his favour, the President can point to an inflation rate that has been squeezed down to around 3 per cent and interest rates lower than they have been for 30 years. But both, though welcome, are functions largely of the weakness of the economy and the efforts being made to revive it.

Joseph Duncan, president of the National Association of Business Economists, said last week: "Basically, the recovery is about four quarters away—and we've been saying that for four years."

Critics say Mr Bush could have avoided his economic hole had he not depended so completely for salvation on the Federal Reserve and low interest rates.

. . . He is also haunted by his acquiescence in 1990 to tax increases that betrayed his 1988, read-my-lips pledge.

The President's only option, then, was to divert attention away from his record to the future. On 10 September, belatedly perhaps, he presented a coherent economic programme, "Agenda for American Renewal." It contains little surprising, but is an expression of his faith in keeping taxation and government spending low as the best path to recovery, with additional incentives such as capital gains tax credits. . . .

. . . Governor Clinton is offering a $200 [billion] investment programme over five years to generate new employment with government projects such as road and bridge building coupled with increased job training. He says he will pay for it with tax increases on the top 2 per cent of American earners and increased taxes for foreign companies. That, with greater cuts in defence spending than Mr Bush is contemplating, will also leave enough to cut the federal deficit in half by 1996.

. . . Republicans are attempting to imply that Mr Clinton will only be able to finance his investment programme by extending tax increases to middle-income Americans—exactly the people to whom the Governor has promised some kind of tax alleviation. Mr Bush, meanwhile, is promising again, "never, ever" to allow another tax increase. . . .

So far, Mr Clinton's promise of some renewed government intervention—after 12 years of "hands-off" Republican stewardship—to kick life back into the economy is what the voters seem most keen to hear. Above all, it would represent a change and hope of something better. . . .

When asked who is most likely to bring back the good times, most Americans today are answering Bill Clinton—by 52 per cent to 36 per cent in a recent Gallup Poll. That is what may, and probably will, win him the White House.

The Reagan administration brought economists to the forefront of national debate. The following essays show two sides of the argument about whether the Reagan Revolution liberated the economy or damaged it for generations to come. The debate is still with us, because the debt created during the 1980s is also still with us. Economist Martin Anderson, one of Reagan's chief advisers, argues that the president restored the health of the nation and created a new capitalism. Harvard professor Benjamin Friedman, on the other hand, bitterly rues the spending spree undertaken by the conservative president. He argues that the nation will be digging itself out of an economic hole for the foreseeable future.

The Reagan Revolution and the New Capitalism

MARTIN ANDERSON

It came like a rising tide—silently, inexorably, gently lapping forward. Only the political waves were noticeable, and these rushed in, then receded, only to rush in again and again—each time higher, stronger.

First came Barry Goldwater in 1964. The United States had not seen his like before. In his black, owl-like glasses, he burst upon the American political scene and seemed to speak for millions of Americans unsatisfied with the United States as it was. They wanted more individual liberty, less government, more national defense. And they wanted it now. The middle-of-the-road establishment sniffed and raised its eyebrows. The left was appalled.

Goldwater was attacked and vilified, first by the Left and then even by members of his own party as his political power grew. He won the Republican nomination for president in 1964 and pulled down almost 40 percent of the vote in the general election against Lyndon Baines Johnson. Goldwater was labeled an extremist and a radical, and his loss to the liberal Democrat Johnson was offered as proof that his presidential campaign was an aberration. Some even speculated that Goldwater's loss marked the end of the Republican party in the United States, that it locked in for good the political philosophy of liberalism. Goldwater was seen as a lonely phenomenon, a likeable, friendly man from the Southwest who somehow temporarily bewitched a surprisingly large number of Americans.

By the mid-1960s there was a general consensus that the Goldwater legions had passed from the political stage and the American establishment was secure and serene.

Then came Richard Nixon in 1968. Shy, brilliant, a man cursed with a five-o'clock-shadow beard, Nixon plotted his comeback from political exile with great cunning and skill. Defeated in his attempt to become governor of California in 1962, he returned, persuasively presenting the case for virtually all of Goldwater's policies and programs. And he was elected president in 1968 on the basis of those policies, very narrowly to be sure, with just a hair under 50 percent of the popular vote. It was

Martin Anderson, *Revolution* (New York: Harcourt Brace Jovanovich, 1988), xv–xix, 7–8, 175–180, 438, 456. Reprinted with permission of Harcourt, Inc.

the Goldwater campaign in 1964 and Nixon's victory in 1968 that established the political base of conservatism. Without Goldwater and Nixon there probably would have been no Reagan.

The Goldwater wave had been small and tentative. The Nixon wave was much stronger and more powerful. The policies that Nixon pursued, many of them the same policies that labeled Goldwater an extremist just four years earlier, proved so popular and effective that Richard Nixon was reelected in 1972 by one of the largest vote margins in U.S. history. The establishment was shocked. The Left was frightened. How could this man Nixon acquire so much political power? He was not a mesmerizing speaker. He looked dark and foreboding on television. He was not an affable personality like Barry Goldwater. Why? . . .

Then came 1980 and Ronald Reagan. A famous movie star who had twice been governor of the largest state in the United States, Reagan combined the personal appeal of Goldwater and the political skill of Nixon. And he believed in the same policies—more individual liberty, less government, and a stronger national defense. The Reagan wave that crashed down on the American political beach was much stronger and more powerful than those of Goldwater or Nixon. Once again the establishment was shocked. Even the corporate leaders of America did not support Reagan until they knew he was going to win, first supporting John Connally in the presidential primaries and then, after Reagan defeated Connally, switching to George Bush until he, too, lost to Reagan. . . .

The more you look, the more you are forced to conclude that these three men did not cause the events in America during the last few decades. No, they were caused by them. The rising tide of a new capitalism, a powerful intellectual movement that is still rising created the political momentum that swept these men to political prominence and power. Neither Goldwater nor Nixon nor Reagan caused or created the revolutionary movement that often carries their name, especially Reagan's. It was the other way around. They were part of the movement, they contributed mightily to the movement, but the movement gave them political life, not the reverse.

. . . The fundamental changes in national policy still occurring in the United States and in virtually every country of the world are the inevitable result of intellectual changes that have already occurred. This political movement—the new capitalism—transcends personality, transcends political party. . . .

That movement was no accident, but rather the logical outgrowth of policy ideas and political forces set in motion during the 1950s and 1960s, ideas and forces that gathered strength and speed during the 1970s, then achieved political power in the 1980s, and promise to dominate national policy in the United States for the remainder of the twentieth century. There have been many contributors to this movement: the traditional Republicans and the old conservatives who formed its core; the libertarians who gave it consistency and sharply defined goals, at the same time widening the boundaries of intellectual debate; the neoconservatives whose desertion from the Left seemed to confirm the validity of the movement and who infused that movement with new intellectual vigor; the New Right with their political enthusiasm and persistence; and the Moral Majority with their large numbers and moral certitude. They were all necessary, though none by itself sufficient, to have achieved the kind of intellectual and political change that occurred in so short a time.

By 1980, liberalism, the dominant political philosophy of the United States, was intellectually bankrupt. A new American political philosophy, not yet fully formed, but built on the framework of conservative and libertarian ideas of the last several decades, was beginning to dominate and control the national policy agenda. The ideas of statism and collectivism were crumbling before the ideas of individualism and liberty.

American liberalism is but a pale cousin of real socialism, and a very distant relation to the real thing, communism. And throughout the world the philosophy of socialism and communism [has] been discredited, as country after country watches the glittering dream of socialist theory turn to ash.

The major policy changes recently realized in the United States did not happen by accident. They were undertaken purposely. . . .

It was the greatest economic expansion in history. Wealth poured from the factories of the United States, and Americans got richer and richer. During the five years between November 1982 and November 1987 more wealth and services were produced than in any like period in history.

There were 60 straight months of uninterrupted economic growth, the longest string of steady peacetime growth in national production since we first began to keep such statistics in 1854.

Close to fifteen million new jobs were created. It was the greatest five-year employment growth in U.S. history. At the end of 1982 the number of Americans working was 100,697,000. Five years later 115,494,000 were working.

The production of wealth in the United States was stupendous. Reagan's run from the end of 1982 to the end of 1987 produced just a hair under $20 trillion dollars of goods and services, measured in actual dollars, unadjusted for inflation or changes in the quality of goods and services. The sum is so large that the value of the treasure is perhaps beyond comprehension. A million dollars is a lot of money. There are a thousand millions in every billion, and a thousand billions in every trillion, so basically a trillion is a million squared. Twenty of them is a lot.

By the end of 1987 the United States was producing about seven and one-half times more every year than it produced the last year John F. Kennedy was president. By then we were producing 65 percent a year more than when Jimmy Carter left office in January 1981. The U.S. economy is now an economic colossus of such size and scope that we have no effective way to describe its power and reach.

The numbers are stunning.

Yet one thing should be made clear. The Reagan economic expansion of the 1980s was not a perfect expansion; we shall never have one. In particular, the federal deficits we ran were too high, too many federal regulations lay unreformed, the trade deficit is worrisome, and there are dozens of details of the economy that urgently need attention, as any economist will tell you.

In fact, the Reagan economic expansion may not even have been the best economic expansion in history. Every economic expansion must be judged by many criteria: by the number of jobs created, the wealth produced, the steadiness of the production, the distribution of the benefits, the effect on tax rates, on inflation, on interest rates, on government regulation, and the impact on personal liberty. But if we use the word great in the literal sense of being large in size then, by the primary criteria we have used in the past to judge the size of an economic expansion—jobs created, wealth produced, constancy of increasing production—then the five-year economic run that produces 14.8 million new jobs, $20 trillion of new wealth, and does so steadily over a period of 60 months is, by that definition, the greatest economic expansion in history.

The results of the Reagan expansion were felt everywhere. Although personal income tax rates fell dramatically (the highest marginal tax rate fell from 70 percent to 28 percent, the largest percentage reduction in tax rates in U.S. history) federal tax revenue soared. As more people went to work and kept more of what they made, the amount they produced leapt upward. The total receipts of the federal government were $618 billion in 1982. Five years later, in 1987, those receipts totaled $1,016 billion, an increase of $398 billion. That's almost a billion dollars a year extra to spend for every single congressman.

The first to feel the economic transfusion was the military. Fulfilling his presidential campaign pledge of defense first, President Reagan invested heavily in military manpower and defense weapons. In 1980, the year before he became president, the United States spent $134 billion on national defense. In 1987, the seventh year of Reagan's presidency, the United States spent $282 billion. That was an additional $148 billion, making the annual total more than twice as much as we were spending for national security before Reagan took office.

During the first seven years that Reagan was president of the United States he spent over $1.5 trillion on national defense, a staggering amount by anyone's standards, but an impossible one if it was not for the spectacular performance of the economy. The economy pays the bills.

There were other major reorderings of public spending priorities under Reagan. The best way to cut through the fog of explanation that involves some of the most exquisite political combat in the world is to simply look at the dollar outlay numbers for different years and compare them. How much did the federal government spend for certain public services before Reagan became president? How much is being spent for them after Reagan has worked his will, to the extent he could, for seven full years?

It is commonly believed that federal spending on social welfare programs was slashed during the presidency of Ronald Reagan. It is not true. Spending on social welfare programs increased surely and steadily, perhaps more than Reagan would have liked, but nonetheless it did increase. And this fact dramatizes a little-appreciated fact in American political life. The real power of the purse, the power to spend or not to spend, lies with Congress.

A president may be able to influence spending up in some areas and down in others, but ultimately he must get congressional approval for every nickel. On the other hand, he can somewhat restrain the spending impulses of Congress by the judicious use of the veto power. But the veto power can be used only sparingly. Often its effect is muted by the huge catch-all spending bills sent to the president for signature, which force him to veto the good programs along with the bad if he wishes to veto at all. In the final analysis, Congress can always, with a two-thirds vote, cheerfully override any presidential veto.

So while President Reagan cannot and should not be given full credit for all the spending that did take place, he also should not be blamed for cutting federal spending that was not cut.

The biggest percentage change in spending priorities came in the agricultural sector. As they have proved in country after country around the world, farmers are the champion lobbyists of all time, getting a large share of the public purse. In 1980 the federal government paid U.S. farmers and ranchers $8.8 billion. After seven years of having a president who prides himself on being a rancher, the United States was doling out over $31 billion a year—a 252 percent increase, far higher than the rate of increase of military spending.

But high as the percentage increase in public spending was for agriculture, the really big money went into social welfare programs. Reaganomics turned the economy into a money-making machine that allowed him to preside over the largest increases in social welfare spending of any country in history. In 1980 the United States spent just under $174 billion a year for the large social welfare programs— social security, medicare, and health—and by 1987, annual spending on these programs had increased by $145 billion a year to a total of over $319 billion a year, an 84 percent increase.

The Reagan administration gets a lot of credit for increasing national defense spending but, somehow, what happened in the huge area of spending for social security, medicare and health seems to have been neglected, benignly. In 1980 we spent $40 billion a year more on these programs than on national defense. After seven years of Reagan, after the largest military spending streak of any country in history, the United States is still spending $37 billion a year more on social security, medicare and health programs than it is on national defense.

The program receiving the next biggest spending increase under Reagan was welfare. Spending for the poor was just over $86 billion a year in 1980. By 1987 President Reagan had largely done on a national level what he did as governor of California—tried hard to get people off the welfare rolls who could take care of themselves, and then supported substantial increases in welfare spending. In 1987 federal spending for the poor was up by over $38 billion a year to a total of almost $125 billion a year—a 44 percent increase under Reagan.

Not everything went up. Federal spending on natural resources and the environment was maintained at the same dollar level it was during President Carter's last year in office—almost $14 billion a year. And federal spending on some programs went down. Cutting back programs he thought were ineffective or wasteful, President Reagan reduced spending in a few program areas—education, training, employment and social services, community and regional development, commerce and housing credit, and energy. Spending for all these programs totaled almost $63 billion in 1980. By 1987 Reagan trimmed them back some 22 percent, to just over $49 billion a year.

But on the whole, President Reagan set spending records right and left. Holding to his many pledges over the years to strengthen social security, the health care system, and welfare, and to build up our national defenses, he directed massive increases in social welfare and welfare spending and for national defense. That's where most of the money went.

There were other things that happened during this unprecedented economic expansion. Thrashing the conventional wisdom of economics, inflation plummeted as the economy rolled on. From high double digits in 1980, inflation dropped to low single digits and stayed there. Interest rates dropped. And the stock market boomed, setting new historical highs nearly every week, it seemed, in the optimistic summer of 1987.

But past expansions don't guarantee future ones. The almost unbelievable economic surge of the earlier 1980s may or may not continue in the late 1980s and early 1990s. The stock market may rise or it may fall. Nobody ever really knows.

Most of what we accomplished in this decade was possible because of economic growth, the main fuel for the spending engine, but we also had a little help from others. From 1980 through the end of 1987, President Reagan borrowed $1 for every $5 he spent, so that the national debt increased by $1.2 trillion dollars. The United States was one of the best credit risks in the world, people pressed money on us, and we obliged, borrowing easily, quickly and almost guiltlessly. But credit carries with it danger and risk. Borrowing the trillion plus dollars may have been the smartest thing we ever did, but we will soon have to cut back our lust for borrowing. . . .

Whether we can maintain the economic miracle that continues to unfold in front of us will perhaps depend largely on three things: (1) whether we can hang onto the economic policy reforms we have won so far, keeping tax rates low, government regulations sparse, and continuing to move in the direction of freer trade; (2) whether we can control the growth of federal spending, likely only with the passage of a balanced-budget amendment to the Constitution; and (3) whether we can move steadily in the direction of sounder money, toward a greater role for gold. . . .

What Reagan and his comrades have done is to shape America's policy agenda well into the twenty-first century. The prospects are nil for sharply progressive tax rates and big, new social welfare programs, some of the former mainstays of the Democrats' domestic policy agenda. Everyone is for a strong national defense, differing only in the degree and quality of it. Massive funding for nuclear missile defense efforts and the turning from arms control to arms reduction will remain high on our foreign policy agenda. By and large the United States has reached a consensus on the big policy items—national defense and the economy—that always dominate the political process. . . .

The political legacy they helped create is sweeping.

Anyone who is born an American is very lucky. Americans have more individual liberty than any other people in the world. Their country is the wealthiest in the world. And they are defended by the most powerful military force in the world.

All this did not happen by accident.

It did not happen because Americans are superior people. We are not stronger or smarter than other people in the world. The natural resources and the climate of the United States are good, but they are not unmatched. It did not happen because of culture or heritage. Many other countries have had sophisticated civilizations for thousands of years. In terms of culture the United States is just reaching full strength. It has not yet begun to stretch its muscles, to test the limits of its power.

What gave birth to this young, growing giant was the invention of a new political philosophy—just over 200 years ago—a political philosophy that has grown, and changed, and matured over those years.

In its current form it is United States capitalism, very different from most people's idea of the old capitalism. It is a new blend of extraordinary personal freedom, great economic wealth, and overwhelming military power.

As we move relentlessly toward the beginning of the twenty-first century, we enter the age of a new capitalism. That new capitalism is most fully formed in the United States, but elements of it are now spreading rapidly in other countries throughout the world. A new, restless, surging capitalism is on the move.

Mortgaging the Future and Bankrupting the Nation

BENJAMIN FRIEDMAN

What can you say to a man on a binge who asks why it matters? Flush with cash from liquidating his modest investment portfolio and from taking out a second mortgage on the inflated value of his house, he can spend seemingly without limit. The vacation cruise his family has dreamed about for years, the foreign sports car he has always wanted, new designer clothes for his wife and even his children, meals in all the most expensive restaurants—life is wonderful. What difference does it make if he has to pay some interest? If necessary, next year he can sell his house for enough to pay off both mortgages and have enough left over to buy an even faster car. What difference does it make whether he owns a house at all? For the price of the extra sports car, he can afford the first year's rent in the fanciest apartment building in town. Why worry?

Americans have traditionally confronted such questions in the context of certain values, values that arise from the obligation that one generation owes to the next. Generations of Americans have opened up frontiers, fought in wars at home and abroad, and made countless personal economic sacrifices because they knew that the world did not end with themselves and because they cared about what came afterward. The American experiment, from the very beginning, has been forward looking—economically as well as politically and socially. The earliest Americans saw this experiment as an explicit break with the past and devoted their energies to constructing the kind of future they valued both individually and collectively. The generations that followed accepted their debt to the past by attempting to repay it to the future.

. . . [T]he radical course upon which United States economic policy was launched in the 1980s violated the basic moral principle that had bound each generation of Americans to the next since the founding of the republic: that men and women should work and eat, earn and spend, both privately and collectively, so that their children and their children's children would inherit a better world. Since 1980 we have broken with that tradition by pursuing a policy that amounts to living not just in, but for, the present. We are living well by running up our debt and selling off our assets. America has thrown itself a party and billed the tab to the future. The costs, which are only beginning to come due, will include a lower standard of living for individual Americans and reduced American influence and importance in world affairs.

For many Americans, the sudden collapse of stock prices in October 1987 punctured the complacency with which they had accepted a national policy based on systematic overconsumption. After all, the resulting economic environment had looked pretty appealing to the average citizen. Jobs were plentiful in most areas, inflation and interest rates were both down from the frightening levels that had marked the beginning of the decade, and taxes were lower. Plenty of foreign-made goods were still available at cheap prices despite the falling dollar. Most companies' profits were high and going higher. The business recovery that began at the end of 1982 had already become the longest sustained economic expansion in American peacetime history, and there was no recession in sight. The phenomenal stock market rally, with the average share price almost tripling in just five years, seemed both to reflect this prosperity and to foretell its permanence.

By now it is clear that this sense of economic well-being was an illusion, an illusion based on borrowed time and borrowed money. Jobs are plentiful and profits are high because we are spending amply, but more than ever before what we are spending for is consumption. Prices have remained stable in part because business was depressed at the beginning of the decade, and also because until recently the overpriced dollar delivered foreign-made cars and clothes and computers more cheaply than the cost of producing them in America. Our after-tax incomes are rising because we are continuing to receive the usual variety of services and benefits from our government, but we are not paying the taxes to cover the cost.

In short, our prosperity was a false prosperity, built on borrowing from the future. The trouble with an economic policy that artificially boosts consumption at the expense of investment, dissipates assets, and runs up debt is simply that each of these outcomes violates the essential trust that has always linked each generation to those that follow. We have enjoyed what appears to be a higher and more stable standard of living by selling our and our children's economic birthright. With no common agreement or even much public discussion, we are determining as a nation that today should be the high point of American economic advancement compared not just to the past but to the future as well.

The decision to mortgage America's economic future has not been a matter of individual choice but of legislated public policy. Popular talk of the "me generation" to the contrary, most individual Americans are working just as hard, and saving nearly as much, as their parents and grandparents did. What is different is economic policy. The tax and spending policies that the U.S. government has pursued throughout Ronald Reagan's presidency have rendered every citizen a borrower and every industry a liquidator of assets. The reason that the average American has enjoyed such a high standard of living lately is that since January 1981 our government has simply borrowed more than $20,000 on behalf of each family of four.

Worse still, we owe nearly half of this debt to foreign lenders. At the beginning of the 1980s, foreigners owed Americans far more than we owed foreigners. The balance in our favor, amounting to some $2,500 per family, made the United States the world's leading creditor country, enjoying the advantages of international influence and power that have always accompanied such a position. Today, after a half dozen years in which our government has borrowed record sums on our behalf, we owe foreigners far more than they owe us. The balance against us, already amounting to more than $7,000 per family, now makes the United States the world's largest debtor.

Foreigners have already begun to settle these debts by taking possession of office buildings in American cities, houses in American suburbs, farm land in the heartland, and even whole companies. We are selling off America, and living on the proceeds.

Our unprecedented splurge of consumption financed by borrowing has broken faith with the future in two ways, each of which carries profound implications not just for our standard of living but for the character of our society more generally. Whether we continue or reverse our current economic policy will determine how Americans in the future will think of themselves and their society, whether the free ideals and democratic institutions at the core of the American experiment will continue to prosper, and whether America as a nation will be in a position to advance these ideals and institutions beyond our own borders.

The cost of the economic policy we have pursued in the 1980s is no more than what any society pays for eating its seed corn rather than planting it. With the federal deficit averaging 4.2 percent of our total income since the beginning of the decade, compared to a net private saving rate of just 5.7 percent, our rate of investment in business plant and equipment has fallen beneath that of any previous sustained period since World War II. So has our investment in roads, bridges, airports, harbors, and other kinds of government-owned infrastructure. Our investment in education has also shrunk compared to our total income despite the urgent need to train a work force whose opportunities will arise more than ever before from industries oriented to technologically advanced production and the processing of information. . . .

. . . [T]his policy has broken faith with future generations . . . by sacrificing a part of America's sovereignty. It is no accident that the great sums we have borrowed to finance our overconsumption have included large amounts borrowed from abroad. As we shall see, the link connecting the government's fiscal deficit—the difference between federal spending and federal revenues—and our international trade deficit—the difference between what we import and what we export—is real enough. With government borrowing absorbing nearly three fourths of our private saving, heightened competition among business and individual borrowers for the remainder has raised our interest rates, in relation to inflation, to record levels—and, importantly, to levels well above what investors could get in other countries. For half a decade, therefore, the dollar became ever more expensive in terms of other countries' currencies, as foreign investors competed among themselves to acquire dollars with which to buy high-interest debt instruments in America. As the dollar rose, the ability of our industries to compete with foreign producers all but collapsed not only in world markets but even here in America.

With the dollar so overvalued, we increased what we consumed faster than what we produced not only because the deficit absorbed our potential investment capital but because we increasingly imported more than we exported. As we paid for our growing excess of imports our exports, we sent ever more dollars abroad for foreigners to invest in our financial markets. Indeed, because so little of what we save is left over after the government has financed its deficit, this reinvestment of our own dollars by foreign lenders now finances most of what little investment we are able to do. . . .

One worrisome implication of America's becoming a debtor nation is simply our loss of control over our own economic policies. Losing control over one's affairs is, after all, what being in debt is all about—no less for a nation than for an individual or a business. The era when other countries surrendered autonomy over their monetary policies in order to peg their currencies to the dollar is already giving way to an era in which we contemplate sacrificing the independence of our monetary policy in order to fix the dollar's value in marks or in yen. . . .

World power and influence have historically accrued to creditor countries. It is not coincidental that America emerged as a world power simultaneously with our transition from a debtor nation dependent on foreign capital for our initial industrialization, to a creditor supplying investment capital to the rest of the world. But we are now a debtor again, and our future role in world affairs is in question. People simply do not regard their workers, their tenants, and their debtors in the same light as their employers, their landlords, and their creditors. Over time the respect, and even deference, that America had earned as world banker will gradually shift to the new creditor countries that are able to supply resources where we cannot, and America's influence over nations and events will ebb. . . .

The challenge to American economic policymaking is twofold. We must first set a new fiscal policy that commits most if not all our saving to investment in productive capital rather than to funding the government deficit. That means paying more taxes or cutting back on government spending or both. Second, we must adjust our economic policy in the broadest sense to confront the debt left by the Reagan era. Even a complete reversal of our current fiscal policy beginning immediately will not magically wipe away the legacy of almost a decade of overconsumption and excessive borrowing. But it will be a start, and the sooner we start the smaller the sacrifices we shall eventually be forced to make.

Neither of these tasks will be accomplished simply. The agonizing bipartisan negotiations that finally delivered a $30 billion grab bag of small tax hikes, small spending cuts, and assorted accounting gimmicks in the wake of the October 1987 stock market crash showed once again that there are no easy solutions to our current problem. But then why should there be? Nobody enjoys consuming less. Nobody likes doing without the services or the benefit payments that our government provides. And nobody wants to pay more taxes. Our new fiscal policy abandoned the long-standing American commitment to paying our government's way, and the excess consumption that resulted sacrificed our future prospects, but few Americans found the experience unpleasant along the way. To correct course will now require a retrenchment from the combined levels of private consumption and government services to which we have become accustomed.

Moreover, we missed the opportunity to begin this retrenchment when our economy was vigorous and resilient. By 1984 business was solidly recovering from the unusually severe 1981–82 downturn. Unemployment had already dropped from 11 percent of the labor force to 7 percent, and business activity overall had grown by an average 5.6 percent per annum, after inflation, since the recession's end. The economy no longer needed the continued stimulus provided by government spending far in excess of revenues. But instead of acting then to bring spending and taxes into line, we mindlessly continued a policy that raised the deficit to yet a new record level the next year and again the year after that. . . .

The place to begin to understand what happened is to remember that Americans chose the fiscal policy their nation has followed in the 1980s, at least in part because its architects had assured them that it would lead to a better future, not mortgage that future or squander it. It is safe to say that few Americans who welcomed Ronald Reagan's election victory over Jimmy Carter in 1980 or applauded his string of legislative victories in 1981 foresaw fully what his fiscal policy would bring. The persistent argument used to sell this policy to the public—and at the same time to market the candidates who proposed it—was that it would revive America's economy and provide what Reagan billed as a "New Beginning for the Economy" after the harsh experience of the mid- and late seventies.

No one asked Americans to vote for doubling our national debt or diverting our saving away from productive investment or making our industry uncompetitive or turning our country into the world's largest debtor, all within less than a decade. Yet the policy that Americans were asked to endorse and that they did endorse has had just that effect.

Above all, Reagan was explicit and emphatic, both as a candidate and then as President, that his policy would deliver a balanced budget. Throughout the campaign he held forth the prospect of balancing the budget by 1983. This was a central objective that his fiscal policy, in contrast to Carter's, would achieve. In the very first minute of his first televised address to the nation after taking office in January 1981, he pointed to that year's "runaway deficit of nearly $80 billion" as evidence that "the federal budget is out of control." And two weeks later in his first address to Congress, he echoed the same warning in a different way. "Can we, who man the ship of state, deny that it is somewhat out of control?" he asked. "Our national debt is approaching one trillion dollars."

As Reagan's presidency ends, it is difficult to recapture the sense of alarm that these numbers aroused so few years ago. The $79 billion budget deficit that Reagan took over from Carter in 1981 was the last he would ever be able to express in two digits. Over the next six years the deficits ranged from a low of $128 billion in 1982 to a high of $221 billion in 1986. The average for the six years 1982–87 was $184 billion. By 1988 the idea that the U.S. government might complete a year having spent only $80 billion more than its revenues has come to represent almost hopeless optimism. When Reagan leaves office, the national debt he leaves to his successor will not be the $914 billion he inherited from Carter but $2.6 *trillion.* . . .

The essence of the "supply-side" argument that Reagan advanced in 1980 (and to which he has resolutely clung ever since) is that the incentive effects of across-the-board cuts in personal tax rates would so stimulate individuals' work efforts and business initiatives that lower tax *rates* would deliver higher tax *revenues.* Lower tax rates, according to this notion, would help balance the federal budget, despite sharp increases in military spending, without requiring cuts in the nondefense programs that people genuinely valued. Americans could therefore enjoy both continued government spending and lower tax rates too. There was no need to worry about what deficits meant for the nation's future, because under this policy the government would run no deficits. . . .

But is it realistic to suppose that American voters really believed this fairy tale just because Ronald Reagan asked them to? Did the 323 congressmen and the 67 senators who voted for the Kemp-Roth tax cut in the summer of 1981 actually believe that lowering tax rates would increase tax revenues? No one who examined the available evidence in 1980 would have made or accepted such a claim, and there was surely no lack of opponents—including George Bush, who proclaimed it "voodoo economics"—who bluntly said that it made no sense. Further, once record deficits began to emerge, as they were bound to under this bizarre policy, no one who examined the Kemp-Roth experiment in progress would have expected that the economy could simply grow its way out of the deficits that that policy had created. . . .

The most favorable construction to place on this extraordinary abdication of our long-standing commitment to the future is that the architects of the new fiscal policy genuinely believed the claims they made for it, and that the level of economic frustration on the part of voters was sufficient to induce them if not entirely to believe, then at least to suspend their disbelief. Reagan's startling question in 1980—"Are you better off than you were four years ago?"—tapped a frustration that had been building for more than a decade. Failure in Vietnam during the sixties and more recently the drawn-out hostage crisis in Iran had harshly demonstrated the limits of American military power. Inflation, high oil prices, flagging productivity growth, and repeated business recessions had likewise emphasized the limits of American economic power. But the very idea of limits, and especially a limit to economic progress, was foreign to a nation whose traditions and self-perceptions had arisen from the experience of pushing back the frontier at home and then extending America's reach abroad. Reagan's supply-side economics, with its promise of unbounded growth if only individual incentives and entrepreneurial efforts could be freed from the shackles of high taxes and oppressive regulation, was in many ways a direct response to the "limits of growth" ideas that reflected in part the repeated economic failures that had marked the seventies. In their frustration, Americans seem to have gambled on hope rather than analysis, on a willing suspension of disbelief. . . .

It has been too easy to rationalize continued allegiance to a failed policy by pointing the other way, by citing the fact of higher consumption while ignoring lower investment, and by hailing the illusion of fatter incomes and profits while forgetting about the swollen debts and the assets surrendered to foreigners. Even as the true shape of our false prosperity has become unmistakable, it has then been too easy to complain that there is no conclusive evidence, no proof beyond the shadow of doubt, that the spreading disorder has anything to do with fiscal policy in the first place.

These attitudes work well for professional sports and the criminal justice system, but they are disastrous for economic policy. Boosterism that systematically sees only the bright spots makes for fine home-team loyalty. Maintaining that the accused is innocent until proven guilty beyond any doubt ensures careful trials and cautious punishments. But few families run their personal economic affairs by clinging indefinitely to ill-based hopes as they become ever more patently out of touch with reality, and few owners or executives manage their businesses by refusing to cut their losses until the failure of a new venture is proven with absolute certainty. For our government to persist in the kind of attitudes that people would immediately shun in their own affairs is irresponsible. When the burden of such irresponsibility falls mostly on our children, it is immoral.

As we shall see, fixing the problem will mean making genuine sacrifices, not just gestures. Because of the accumulated damage that our binge of overconsumption has already done, those sacrifices must now be greater than they need have been if we had corrected course by the middle of the decade. What is economically necessary will therefore be politically possible only if Americans fully comprehend what is at stake.

FURTHER READING

Sidney Blumenthal and Thomas Byrne Edsall, *The Reagan Legacy* (1988).
Paul Boyer, ed., *Reagan as President* (1990).
Robert Dallek, *Ronald Reagan and the Politics of Symbolism* (1984).
Barbara Ehrenreich, *The Worst Years of Our Lives* (1990).
Bennett Harrison and Barry Bluestone, *The Great U-Turn* (1988).
Michael Hogan, ed., *The End of the Cold War: Its Meaning and Implications* (1992).
Joseph Nye, *Bound to Lead: The Changing Nature of American Power* (1990).
Susan Tolchin and Martin Tolchin, *Dismantling America: The Rush to Deregulate* (1983).